THE HOLY EUCHARIST
THE WORLD'S SALVATION

Quoties hujus hostiae commemoratio celebratur, opus nostrae redemptionis exercetur

(Roman Liturgy)

Gracewing Publishing wishes to thank
Fr François-Marie Lethel OCD,
Prelate Secretary of the Pontifical Academy of Theology,
Professor of Dogmatic Theology and Spirituality at the
Pontifical Theological Faculty Teresianum,
Consultor for the Cause of Pope St John Paul II,
for his kind assistance in the preparation of this text.

THE HOLY EUCHARIST
THE WORLD'S SALVATION

STUDIES ON THE HOLY SACRIFICE OF THE MASS,
ITS CELEBRATION AND ITS CONCELEBRATION

FR JOSEPH DE SAINTE-MARIE, OCD

GRACEWING

First published in French as
L'Eucharistie, salut du monde
by
Editions DMM,
42 rue Jean Jaurès,
BP 263,
86000 Poitiers,
France
© 1982 Editions DMM

English edition first published in 2015
by
Gracewing
2, Southern Avenue
Leominster
Herefordshire
HR6 0QF
www.gracewing.co.uk

ISBN 978 085244 310 1

Imprimi potest: R. P. R. Moretti, OCD—15 June 1981

                R. P. Ph. Boyce, OCD—15 June 1981

Imprimatur: R. P. Ph. Sainz de Baranda, Praep. Gen. OCD—18 June 1981

The *Imprimi potest* and *Imprimatur* are declarations that a book or pamphlet is free from doctrinal or moral error. No implication is contained therein that those who have granted the *Imprimi potest* or *Imprimatur* agree with the contents, opinions or statements expressed.

CONTENTS

ABBREVIATIONS

AAS	*Acta Apostolicae Sedis*
CNPL	Centre National de Pastorale Liturgique
DS	H. Denzinger—A. Schönmetzer, *Enchiridion symbolorum, Definitionum et Declarationum de rebus fidei et morum*
La Doc. Cath.	*La Documentation Catholique*
LMD	*La Maison Dieu*
LPC	*La Pensée Catholique*
PG	*Patrologia Graeca,* ed. J. P. Migne
PL	*Patrologia Latina,* ed. J. P. Migne
PLS	*Patrologia Latina Supplementum*
PNMR	*De la Cène de Jésus au sacrament de l'Eglise,* in *L'Eucharistie, pain nouveau pour un monde rompu*
S.T.	*Summa Theologiae,* St Thomas Aquinas
In Sent.	*Scriptum super Libros Sententiarum Petri Lombardi,* St Thomas Aquinas

INTRODUCTION

H OW MANY PEOPLE ever question the number of Masses offered to God in a concelebrated Eucharist? Very few, no doubt, can be found among both the faithful and the clergy; for, for them, the response is quite evident: the concelebrated Mass is 'one Mass,' and therefore *only one,* whatever be the number of concelebrants. Among those who ever do pose the question and know its importance the responses vary, and the reasons given are often unclear.

We ourselves have given the question some reflection, having had several opportunities to discuss it. On one occasion, after having presented our views and arguments, our listener, a dear priest friend of ours, asked us, 'Could you write a short text on this question?' That text, which had been quickly put together, he later wanted to publish. Such is the origin of the present book, the first chapter of which it forms. The initial text needed to be followed up by one or two articles dealing with the Church's teaching on the Sacrifice of the Mass and on the value of the multiplication of Masses.

Our 'reflections,' however, would later stir up reflections from others. And though the majority of them were in agreement with us, such was not the case with all. Joseph Kleiner critiques our views in his *Esprit et Vie—L'Ami du Clergé.* We owe him a response (Ch. II). If we once seemed disturbed at the manner in which our respect for the Church's Magisterium had been called into question, we are now grateful for such an accusation regardless of its author; for, without it we would never have been motivated to study the root of the problem at hand. It was while trying to show what the true teaching of the Second Vatican Council was that we discovered the real request to which we were unknowingly in the process of responding, one which would find an echo in the initial problem we had set out to study.

This request was none other than the one formulated on the eve of the Council by the Sacred Congregation of Rites, as it was then called. During the pre-preparatory phase it asked, in effect, 'that in the Council's preparation a new and careful investigation be raised, both historical and dogmatic, on the origin, nature and extension of properly sacramental concelebration' (Ch. VI, footnote 344).

This obviously important request never received a response before, during or after the Council. Consequently, and because of various other factors, erroneous ideas imposed themselves, both on the historical and doctrinal levels, which have contributed greatly to the distortion of understanding. In addition, the very manner in which the problem had been presented was also incorrect. It is most admirable to see (we shall show it in our study of the history of concelebration at the Council) how the bishops were able, during Vatican II, to recall certain fundamental principles on the practice of concelebration. In spite of this, the absence of the investigation requested by the Sacred Congregation of Rites on the eve of the Council was apparent. And still today, the incertitude that reigns over the whole of the question continues to demonstrate this deepening of our understanding of the issue would have been.

Therefore, it is to this request, formulated by the Sacred Congregation of Rites in the framework of the preparation for the Council, that the collection of studies presented here—modest as it is—seeks to respond. Morever, it is this which inspired us to follow the order that we did, after having raised the key question concerning the number of Masses in a concelebrated Eucharist: the research needed to be both historical and dogmatic. Our work is divided into three parts. In the first, *A Disputed Question,* we establish that only one Mass is offered to God in a concelebrated Eucharist, and we show the insufficiency of the reasons advanced in favour of the contrary thesis. Our task here, in truth, was rather easy, so clear is the agreement of theologians and the Magisterium on this point. The only difficulties encountered came from a certain text of Pius XII, which is quite frequently interpreted out of its context and consequently beyond its intention. This misinterpretation gives rise to an argument which, seeing only the subjective aspect of concelebration, lends primacy to the persons of the concelebrants over the act which they accomplish as a whole.

The second part is dedicated to *The Historical Investigation*. We needed to begin by a critical study of our immediate sources, that is, the contemporary studies on the question; this is what we entitled, *History of a History*. We then retraced the stages of *The History of Concelebration* by going directly to the sources. We were led to discover, much to our surprise, that, under its full and sacramental form, concelebration had not appeared in the Church until the eighth century, and then around the Pope, in Rome, and very rarely. We also discovered that the majority, so it seems, of the Eastern Rites always refused concelebration, and that where they did adopt it, this was in no way through fidelity to origins of which they were ignorant, but rather under the influence of the West. Finally, we needed to show that there was an *iter* (a certain path taken) of concelebration at the Council, discovering as we did what had and had not taken place, and what still needed to be clarified on this vital liturgical question.

Finally, in the third part, we dealt with *The Theological Investigation.* Actually, the theological investigation begins already in the first part, but here we go to the heart of the problem. We first recalled the Tridentine dogma, an irreplaceable foundation of the entire theological study of the Eucharist. Then, we compared it to different contemporary theories. In such a way we were led to take up again and develop the theology of the sacrament by reflecting on symbolism, which sheds much light on the sacramental fulfillment of 'the Mystery of Christ' in the Church, in the eschatological continuation of the salvific *kairos,* where its history unfurls. Finally, after an examination of the different current conceptions of the 'fundamental structure' of the Mass, meal, 'blessing' and assembly, we show how this structure can be found only in the reality of the Sacrifice of the New and Eternal

Covenant. From here we rediscover necessarily both the value of private Masses and the value of their multiplication in and for the Church.

More than anyone, we ourselves are conscious of the limits and imperfections of these pages, written—may we be permitted to confess it and to beg the indulgence of the reader—in oftentimes difficult conditions. If we are taking the risk of publishing them, it is because we have seen no other in-depth study of the problem of the Eucharistic Celebration in the essential perspective which we present here—namely the multiplication of grace and of the action of graces which follow upon the multiplication of the sacramental offering of the redemptive Sacrifice. And at the same time, we see the urgent need of such a multiplication today, and therefore the urgent need as well of clarifying and dismissing the factors that oppose it. For if it is true that, 'each time that we celebrate the memorial of the Sacrifice of Christ, the work of our redemption is accomplished' (*Roman Liturgy;* cited by the Council's Constitution on the liturgy, n° 2), if it is true, as St Ambrose affirmed, that 'each time that His Blood is poured out, it is poured out for the remission of sins' (*De Sacramentis* IV, 28), if it is true, as one of the great Eastern commentators on the liturgy, Nicholas Cabasilas, maintains, that 'the descent of the Holy Spirit ... always takes place after the Sacrifice is accomplished,' namely in the celebration of the Eucharist (*Explanation of the Rites of the Divine Liturgy,* n° 11), then it is also true that each new celebration of the Mass procures these divine blessings for the Church and for humanity, rendering at the same time thanksgiving and glory to God. From there we can measure the loss that 'the work of redemption' suffers in the Church each time that a Mass that could have been and ought to have been celebrated is not.

That some particular aspect of our work might call for a minor modification or complement we willingly admit, and we thank in advance those who point out such needs. But the fundamental truths that we present are too firmly rooted in Tradition (in the homogenous development of Eucharistic doctrine and liturgy) for us to be able to doubt their validity.

It is, therefore, with an appeal that we bring our work to a close: We entrust it to Christ the High Priest and to the Blessed Virgin Mary, the Mother of priests, that they might make it known to our fellow priests in the presbyterate. For it is to them primarily, and to each one personally, that this book is addressed; to them, who have received from God and the Church the incredible power to bring down upon the world, through the celebration of the Holy Sacrifice of the Mass, the redemptive Blood of Christ.

Joseph de Sainte-Marie, OCD
Professor on the Theology Faculty of the Discalced Carmelites, Rome

N.B. The text that we present is one that originally appeared in different articles. The majority of the modifications made have been in the form. We note, nevertheless, some adjustments and, above all, some updated additions, especially in Chapters XI and XII.

The main *bibliography* is found at the end of Chapter IV for studies on concelebration, and at the beginning of Chapter VI for the texts and documents of the Second Vatican Council.

FOREWORD

Concelebration Today, Yesterday and Tomorrow

Concelebration Today

'I AM NEVER GOING to do that again!' The outrage and anger of the young priest who uttered these words were palpable. He had just returned from World Youth Day 2003. His dream since his ordination but a year before had been to concelebrate Holy Mass with the Pope, but it turned into a nightmare.

The nightmare involved being amidst brother priests whose attire, attitude and behaviour was far from what one would expect of a priest offering the Holy Sacrifice of the Mass. It meant standing at such a distance from the altar that the elements being consecrated could barely if at all be seen, and even included a dispensation from the reception of the Precious Blood for those concelebrants too far away from the altar for this to be 'practical.'

This young priest was no crypto-traditionalist rejecting any change or development beyond some fetishized date in history. One of the 'John-Paul II generation' of vocations, he belonged to a new apostolic community full of faith and zeal, which celebrated the new liturgy in the vernacular, faithfully. And it was from this faithfulness and zeal for all that is holy and of God that his outrage and anger erupted. His participation as a priest-concelebrant in the papal Mass at World Youth Day had truly and profoundly scandalised him.

It is a sad and ongoing reality of modern liturgical life that large-scale concelebrations often manifest some concelebrants' (mis)understanding of precisely what they are about: I speak of the phenomenon of priests and bishops vested (more or less) to celebrate Holy Mass but nevertheless occupying themselves with the taking of souvenir photographs. Such abuse—and let it be said clearly: any sacred minister in sacred vestments who is taking photographs during the Sacred Liturgy is committing a grave abuse and is giving profound scandal, no matter what the occasion or how many or few other sacred ministers are similarly vested—indicates clearly that the perpetrators have simply 'lost the plot' in terms of what the putting on of vestments means and of what the sacramental concelebration of the Holy Mass in fact is.

Unfortunately, one need not travel to World Youth Days or to other Masses involving concelebration on an immense scale to be scandalised at what one finds. The near universal practice of daily concelebration by priests and bishops at almost every conceivable opportunity over recent decades may have somewhat desensitized us, but it is necessary to recall abuses which are alive and well today. These include:

> Concelebrants whose vesture is so minimal as to be a parody of the Holy Sacrifice they are offering. In some circumstances insufficient vestments are available, certainly,[1] but this does not excuse priests who habitually 'throw on a stole' over ordinary clothes, an ill-fitting alb or even just a habit (a particularly common feature in some communities of religious priests),[2]

---

[1] Paragraph 209 of the *General Instruction of the Roman Missal* permits concelebrants to omit the chasuble for a "just cause", for example "a more considerable number of concelebrants or a lack of vestments". The 25 March 2004 Instruction of the Congregation for Divine Worship and Discipline of the Sacraments, *Redemptionis Sacramentum*, clarifies this, stating: "Where a need of this kind can be foreseen, however, provision should be made for it insofar as possible" (n. 124).

[2] Some communities possess an indult or other forms of permission to do this. But one must ask why such a permission was ever sought or granted in the first place? Is not the offering of the Holy Sacrifice of the Mass sufficiently important to take the necessary time and effort to vest? St John Paul II, gives a theological foundation to "the source of the duty to carry out rigorously the liturgical rules

where complete Mass vestments are available or which, with a modicum of organisation, could be provided.

Concelebrants whose posture and gestures, or even chatter with other concelebrants throughout Mass, indicate a level of non-engagement with if not boredom at the rite which they are concelebrating.

Concelebrants who arrive late 'joining in' in spite of the explicit prohibition of this abuse,[3] often involving the unedifying sight of a priest scrambling into vestments on the sidelines. Here one should add the utterly incredible phenomenon of a priest vesting and commencing Mass as a concelebrant and then *leaving the concelebration early* because of another (foreseen) engagement—an absurdity sometimes seen at ordination or funeral Masses where one wants to be present even if this is only possible for part of the rite. Apart from showing scant regard for the office of a concelebrant of Holy Mass, such behaviour suggests that the priest concerned knows of no other way to be liturgically present at a Mass without concelebrating and betrays a seriously defective liturgical formation.[4]

Concelebrants who are concelebrating even though they have already offered or shall be offering other Masses on that day on occasions not foreseen by the law. Perhaps there now exists a

---

and everything that is a manifestation of community worship offered to God himself, all the more so because in this sacramental sign he entrusts himself to us with limitless trust, as if not taking into consideration our human weakness, our unworthiness, the force of habit, routine, or even the possibility of insult," in his first encyclical, *Redemptor Hominis,* 4 March 1979, n. 20.

[3] *General Instruction of the Roman Missal,* paragraph 206: "No one is ever to join a concelebration or to be admitted as a concelebrant once the Mass has already begun."

[4] Assisting at Mass in choir dress is not the sole preserve of the pre-conciliar rites; indeed, paragraph 114 of the *General Instruction of the Roman Missal* mandates choir dress for priests assisting at Mass who are not concelebrants. See further: Thomas Kocik, "Preaching through the Choir: the Merits of Assisting at Mass *In choro*" in: *Antiphon* vol. 10 (2006), pp. 204–11.

generation or two of priests who, as well as being unable to conceive of attending Mass other than as a concelebrant, have little or no formation in or regard for the liturgical and canonical law regulating how many times on a given day a priest may offer Holy Mass.[5] Or perhaps, somewhat indicatively, some priests would retort: "What's the problem? I'm *only* concelebrating."

Priests concelebrating a Mass who cannot speak the language in which the Mass is being offered, contrary to the explicit prohibition of this in liturgical law.[6]

Bishops who 'step down' to the ranks of priest concelebrants so as to allow a priest to perform the role of principal celebrant. Apart from displaying a false humility and an appalling lack of respect for the theological and liturgical nature of the episcopal office and ministry, this abuse, which has been proscribed by the Holy See,[7] betrays a worrying lack of liturgical formation in how bishops can and should be present at Mass if there is a reason that they (or another bishop) are not the principal celebrant.[8]

Concelebrations in which even the limited rites to be performed by concelebrants (such as processing, kissing the altar,

---

[5] See, for example, the faculties stated in the *General Instruction of the Roman Missal* paragraphs 114 and 204 and canon 905 of the *Code of Canon Law*.

[6] "Where it happens that some of the Priests who are present do not know the language of the celebration and therefore are not capable of pronouncing the parts of the Eucharistic Prayer proper to them, they should not concelebrate, but instead should attend the celebration in choral dress in accordance with the norms (see: *General Instruction of the Roman Missal* para. 114);" Congregation for Divine Worship and Discipline of the Sacraments, Instruction: *Redemptionis Sacramentum*, 25 March 2004, n. 113.

[7] "Responsa ad dubia proposita" in: *Notitiae* vol. 46 (2009) p. 170.

[8] See: *The Ceremonial of Bishops* (Liturgical Press, Collegeville 1989) chapter 3. It is significant that the 2009 response published in *Notitiae* (referred to above) draws on numbers 175 and 186 of this chapter in giving its reasons why a bishop may not act as a concelebrant to a priest; it is clear that other modes of attendance and participation are normative in the post-conciliar liturgy in such circumstances.

etc.) are habitually omitted. There is a given rite for concele-bration,[9] yet in many religious houses, seminaries, etc., priest concelebrants will 'don a stole' and take their seat privately, omitting the prescribed rites. Too frequently, also, the minis-terial functions concelebrants should assume in the absence of a deacon, etc., are performed by the principal celebrant.

Concelebrations in which there are different 'classes' of con-celebrants. Certainly large concelebrations require organisa-tion, but this is possible without sacrificing the dignity of what in fact concelebrants are doing. Where distinctions are made between concelebrants who may wear chasubles, walk in the entrance procession, kiss the altar, approach the altar for the Eucharistic Prayer and Holy Communion, etc., a 'second class' concelebrant is created.

Concelebration become 'the way of priestly life,' where a priest very rarely celebrates Mass other than as a concelebrant. This is often the case with priests who live in religious or other communities either permanently or throughout the academic year, etc. In such cases priests can go months on end without themselves being the celebrant of a Mass and may never do so on greater feasts if it falls to the superior, abbot, etc., to celebrate on such occasions. This cannot but impact adversely on the spiritual life and identity of a priest.

What we might call 'Rambo' concelebrations—where episco-pal or 'fraternal' pressure is such that priests must 'concele-brate or die,' as the film character would put it. That in some dioceses, religious houses, seminaries or colleges it is incon-ceivable for a priest present at a Mass not to concelebrate for fear of being accused of being somehow not in communion with that diocese or community is a parody of the theological reality of being in communion with Christ and His Church. Whilst sacramental concelebration can certainly be a liturgical manifestation of that communion and of the unity of the

---

[9]   See paragraphs 210–51 of the *General Instruction of the Roman Missal.*

priesthood, it is not an essential prerequisite for communion with Christ, His Church or the diocesan bishop. Bishops who bully clergy into concelebrating exceed their mandate as the moderators (and not the proprietors) of the Sacred Liturgy in their dioceses—even more so those who seek a promise to concelebrate before a deacon is ordained priest or a priest is permitted to work in a diocese.[10]

Conversely, there is what might be called the 'concelebrate or bust' mentality, whereby a priest who does not have a public Mass to celebrate himself will not celebrate Mass on that day unless he can concelebrate at one. Whilst a priest may not be compelled to offer Mass privately, the Church earnestly recommends it.[11] His not doing so because he has not been formed in either why or how he should do so deprives the Church and the priest himself of the pastoral, spiritual and theological good that comes the offering of the Holy Sacrifice of the Mass, 'even' privately. The loss to the Church and to the world from this approach is immense.

This list of all-too-frequent abuses of concelebration, in which one can identify strands of liturgical sloth, theological ignorance and spiritual impoverishment, does not take away from those places where the practice of sacramental concelebration is carefully prepared and observed in a dignified manner utterly worthy of the wondrous sacrifice being offered. But the fact is that such places are rarer than they should be and that the widespread experience of concelebration today, even

---

[10] It is very difficult to see how, morally, any priest can be compelled to concelebrate on any occasion given that his concelebrating is not necessary so as to provide the Mass for the pastoral good of the faithful. It is also difficult to see how promises exacted by authority acting beyond its competence can be held to be binding.

[11] "Remembering always that in the mystery of the Eucharistic sacrifice the work of redemption is exercised continually, priests are to celebrate frequently; indeed, daily celebration is recommended earnestly since, even if the faithful cannot be present, it is the act of Christ and the Church in which priests fulfil their principal function;" canon 904 of the *Code of Canon Law*.

when grave abuses are absent, is less edifying (literally, does not build up the Church and the life of faith) than it should be, and is in fact a very long way indeed from the practice envisaged by the Fathers of the Second Vatican Council when they called for its extension.

The liturgical issues are apparent. If we follow the teaching of the Second Vatican Council's Constitution on the Sacred Liturgy, that the liturgy is "the font from which all [the Church's] power flows" (n. 10), they are most certainly not without their importance, above all when these issues touch the celebration of the Holy Sacrifice of the Mass. For if, somehow, the font from which the Church's power flows is not as it should be, how can the Church draw from it all that she needs for her daily life and mission in the world? This is not a tangential question of 'mere' liturgical ceremonial; no, it is a question of profound theological and pastoral import: Does concelebration as it is practiced in the Western Church today serve the Church's mission in the world well, or not?

Father Joseph de Sainte-Marie, OCD, perceived the importance of this issue a little more than a decade following the Council's conclusion. The result was *The Holy Eucharist—The World's Salvation*. It is worth noting that his work does not focus primarily on liturgical issues (when or how to concelebrate) but on theological ones (what effect concelebration as it has come to be practiced has on the salvation of the world).

Two questions are fundamental to his extensive and thorough scholastic investigation: "How many Masses are offered at a concelebration: as many Masses as there are concelebrants, or one?" and "How many Masses are offered when a number of priests offer Mass individually?" An examination of these presupposes a clear theology of the Mass and of its fruits—of the good that each celebration of the Mass brings about for the priest himself, for the Church and for the world—something this volume provides more than adequately.

Nevertheless, particularly given the confusion that abounds, it seems apposite to cite the author's conclusion to the first of these questions. At a concelebrated Mass, he asserts:

> ...*one sole Mass is offered to God.* This assertion, dictated by good sense and by language ('concelebrate' means to celebrate together one act of worship), is established by theological reason... It is also based on the declarations of the Magisterium, especially the *Decree* of the Sacred Congregation of the Rites, '*Ecclesiae semper*' (7 March 1965) and the *Decree* of the Second Vatican Council, 'On the Ministry and Life of the Priests' (*Presbyterorum ordinis,* no. 8).[12]

In the light of this Father de Sainte-Marie's second question takes on considerable importance; so too does his clear exposition of the probity of concelebrating priests accepting individual stipends for the one Mass. Theologically this is a demanding study, certainly, but one with which professors of sacramental theology and Sacred Liturgy must reckon and from which students can draw a great deal.

In addition to providing a sound theological investigation, *The Holy Eucharist—The World's Salvation* engages in historical inquiry. There is a great deal indeed to learn from this, and it is to that we shall now turn. As this book was published in French in 1982 and Father de Sainte-Marie died in 1985, its bibliography, particularly in respect of the liturgical reform following the Council, requires some augmentation. It is a pleasure to have the opportunity to do so here at least partially.

Concelebration Yesterday

In the first place we must draw some important distinctions between:

> Concelebration in the wide sense, that is, in every public Mass in which the faithful offer the Sacrifice of Christ with the priest: by him and with him.

---

[12]   See p. 552 below. Emphasis original.

Concelebration in a ceremonial sense, where the clergy share
in the same liturgy to enhance its solemnity, without the priests
consecrating with the celebrant.

Concelebration in the strict sense, with all the priests present
truly consecrating.[13]

It should be clear that here the first of these types of concelebration
is not at issue (unless it be viewed in a Protestant manner to deny the
specific ministry of the priest). However the distinction between
ceremonial concelebration and *sacramental concelebration* is crucial
when asking what, precisely, is the history of concelebration in the
Eastern and Western Churches?

It is also important to note that in the 1950s a dispute about the
essential requirements for sacramental concelebration broke out
amongst liturgists keen to promote its restoration. One group argued
that the pronunciation of the words of consecration was essential for
each concelebrant truly to offer Mass. The other group held that
silent, intentional, concelebration was valid.[14] Pope Pius XII settled
this dispute in his 22 September 1956 address to the International
Congress of Pastoral Liturgy by stating that "The concelebrants
themselves must say over the bread and the wine 'This is my body,'
'This is my blood,' otherwise their concelebration is merely 'ceremonial.'"[15] This judgement was underlined by a ruling of the Holy Office
of 23 May 1957 which declared the pronunciation of the words of
consecration necessary for validity "ex institutione Christi."[16]

---

[13]   Claude Richard, "La Concélebration" in: *Collecteana Cisterciensa* vol. 26
      (1964) pp. 100–36 (p. 124), cited in: Archdale A. King, *Concelebration in the
      Christian Church* (Mowbray, London 1966) pp. 7–8.

[14]   See: Alcuin Reid, *The Organic Development of the Liturgy*, 2nd edn (Ignatius
      Press, San Francisco 2005), pp. 202–03.

[15]   *The Assisi Papers: Proceedings of the First International Congress of Pastoral
      Liturgy—Assisi-Rome, September 18–22 1956* (Liturgical Press, Collegeville
      1956) p. 230.

[16]   *AAS*, vol. 49 (1957), p. 370.

"Ex institutione Christi" means, of course, that this requirement has always been the case and is not a new condition created and imposed by Pius XII. Following this ruling many instances of concelebration in Western history must be regarded as ceremonial, not sacramental. Works such as Archdale King's 1966 *Concelebration in the Christian Church* point to many witnesses of the celebration of Mass by the bishop with the assistance of his priests and deacons in the early Church, and indeed of the offering of Eucharistic hospitality from one bishop to another at times, but it is quite difficult to establish historically,[17] and even more so theologically in the light of the 1957 ruling, that on the whole, with few exceptions,[18] these were anything more than the solemn celebrations of the Mass by the local Church including the ceremonial concelebration of the priests as much as the deacons and other ministers—literally a 'celebration together' rather than a simultaneous exercise of the priestly office in respect of bringing about the Eucharistic sacrifice. That is to say, all were present ceremonially but only the presiding bishop was, in fact, effecting the consecration of the elements of bread and wine. Certainly, liturgists seem to be in broad agreement that "in the first centuries only the principal celebrant said the Eucharistic prayer."[19] Similarly it is utterly clear that "concelebration among priests without the bishop," is not found in history and indeed is contrary to "the earliest custom of the

---

[17] See: King, *Concelebration in the Christian Church*, pp. 22–23.

[18] Nicola Giampietro, *La concelebrazione eucharistia e la communione sotto due specie nella storia della Liturgia* (Fede & Cultura, Verona 2011) chapter 1 explores possible instances of sacramental concelebration in the early Church and gives extensive bibliographical references.

[19] Adrien Nocent, OSB, "Questions about Specific Points" in: A. Chupungco, ed., *Handbook for Liturgical Studies III: The Eucharist* (Liturgical Press, Collegeville 1999) pp. 295–320 (p. 297). Nocent goes on to argue that in respect of the 1957 ruling we may not "project our modern way of seeing into the past or even the future, since the Church has the power to determine the conditions under which a sacrament is performed, and since these can be modified..." ibid. See also p. 295.

Roman Church which knew only the concelebration of the priests with their bishop."[20]

Full sacramental concelebration is, however, unquestionably present in the papal Mass described in both *Ordo Romanus* III and IV from the end of the eighth century, where cardinal priests join the pope at the altar to recite the Roman Canon with him on major feasts.[21] In major sees the ceremonial assistance of priests, deacons and subdeacons on greater feasts and major occasions vested in chasubles, dalmatics and tunicles was and continued to be a feature of many solemn liturgies. The papal practice of sacramental concelebration, however, would seem to have been a rare exception. It is attested up until the twelfth century (*Ordo Romanus* XI), but had become obsolete by the fourteenth.[22] Apart, then, from the rites of the ordination of priests and the consecration of bishops, and small local instances such as the six priests who concelebrated the Holy Thursday pontifical Mass in Lyon,[23] sacramental concelebration is not found in the West from the late middle ages onward.[24]

---

[20] Nocent, "Questions about Specific Points" p. 296.

[21] See: Giampietro, *La concelebrazione eucharistia e la communione sotto due specie nella storia della Liturgia*, pp. 20–21.

[22] See: King, *Concelebration in the Christian Church*, pp. 37–38.

[23] See: Archdale A. King, *Liturgies of the Primatial Sees* (Longmans, Green & Co., London, New York & Toronto 1957) pp. 55, 75–76. It is interesting to note that the *ceremonial* concelebration of priests with another priest is found in the Lyon rite on greater feasts; see: Denys Buenner, OSB, *L'Ancienne Liturgie Romaine: Le Rite Lyonnais* (Emmanuel Vitte, Lyon & Paris, 1934) pp. 268–71.

[24] Both rites involve the newly ordained or consecrated reciting the Canon with the ordaining bishop, however in the ordination of priests the newly-ordained communicate only with the Sacred Host after which they drink a purification of unconsecrated wine, leaving the question of true sacramental concelebration somewhat unclear; see the rubrics in the *Pontificale Romanum* (Rome, Apud Iacobum Lunam; Impensis Leonardi Parasoli & Sociorum 1595[/6]) pp. 70, 110. In the blessing of abbots a rubric explicitly states that the newly blessed abbot reads all of the Mass "exceptis verbis consecrationis," precluding sacramental concelebration in this case; ibid., p. 158. These rubrics remain up until and including the 1962 *Editio typica* of the *Pontificale Romanum* (3

No doubt the development from at least the seventh century of
the practice of priests offering Mass privately on occasion, and the
increasing understanding of this individual offering of the Mass as an
act of priestly ministry of supreme value for the priest himself, for the
Church and for the salvation of the world,[25] is a significant factor when
considering the history of concelebration. In the first Christian
centuries priests who were not presiding at the celebration of the
Eucharist (which was by no means celebrated daily), would nevertheless be present and, on solemn occasions, assist the bishop ceremonially. As the Church increasingly appreciated the great treasure of the
Eucharistic Sacrifice the value of it being celebrated for particular
intentions underpinned the more frequent offering of Holy Mass.
This did not detract from participation in the bishop's Mass on great
feasts, but gave individual priests a greater ministry of intercession
and oblation in the life of the Church.

We know, of course, that in some—indeed too many—cases,
practices related to the offering of private Mass became abusive and
required correction, most notably by the Council of Trent. Nevertheless such abuses and the ensuing dogmatic errors of Protestant
reformers led the Council's 22nd session (17 September 1562) to
formulate a positive and binding declaration of the value of priests
offering Mass individually:

> [The Council] approves and commends [Masses in which only
> the priest communicates sacramentally] for they too should be
> considered truly communal Masses, partly because the people
> communicate spiritually in them and partly because they are
> celebrated by a public minister of the Church, not for his own
> good alone, but for the faithful who belong to the body of Christ.[26]

___

vols, Typis Polyglottis Vaticanis, Vatican City 1962).

[25] See: Joseph A. Jungmann, SJ, *The Mass of the Roman Rite: Its Origins and Development* (Four Courts Press, Dublin 1986) vol. I, pp. 212ff.

[26] Heinrich Denzinger; Peter Hünermann, Robert Fastiggi & Anne Nash, eds., *Enchiridion symbolorum definitionem et declarationem de rebus fidei et morum*, 43rd edn, Latin-English (Ignatius Press, San Francisco 2012) n. 1747, p. 419. See also canon 8 of the same session: "If anyone says that Masses in which the

The celebration of individual Masses was opposed by the Synod of Pistoia in 1786, which decreed numerous liturgical reforms in keeping with the principles promoted by "the Enlightenment liturgists."[27] Specifically, in the one (amalgamated) monastery that was henceforth to be allowed in any city, it ordered that "not more than one or at most two Masses be celebrated each day and that it should be satisfactory to the other priests to celebrate in common together with the community [*una cum communitate concelebrare*]."[28] Whether this concelebration was intended to be sacramental, ceremonial or simply assisting at the communal Mass is not clear; but the intention to end the celebration of individual Masses by priests is. Pope Pius VI explicitly condemned this as an error in his Apostolic Constitution *Auctorem fidei* of 28 August 1794.[29]

In the Christian East, the history of concelebration is far simpler. J.A. Jungmann, SJ, relates:

> In the Orient (ceremonial) concelebration was customary and common from time immemorial, but it is only in the Uniate groups that the joint pronouncing of the words [of consecration] was added, apparently not till the start of the 18th century and then under the influence of Rome... It is only in the Byzantine rite even outside the Uniate groups...[30]

In other words, sacramental concelebration is a late Western imposition on the venerable Eastern custom of ceremonial concelebration.

It is from this historical background that some twentieth century liturgists promoted the idea of the "reintroduction" of sacramental concelebration in the Roman rite. However the history of concelebra-

---

priest alone communicates sacramentally are illicit and therefore should be abolished, let him be anathema;" ibid., n. 1758, p. 421.

[27] See: Reid, *The Organic Development of the Liturgy*, pp. 51–54.

[28] Denzinger; Hünermann, Fastiggi & Nash, *Enchiridion symbolorum definitionem et declarationem de rebus fidei et morum*, n. 2692, p. 554.

[29] *Ibid.*, nn. 2600–2700, pp. 527–56.

[30] Jungmann, *The Mass of the Roman Rite*, vol. I, p. 196.

tion makes clear that, in fact, it had never been a widespread or universal practice. At most it was only ever an exceptional practice employed on most solemn occasions around the bishop. And in the East sacramental concelebration was unknown until it was imposed on Uniate Churches by Rome. It would seem, therefore, that what was being proposed was not a reintroduction, or even an extension of the very limited survivals, but an innovation.

At this point it is necessary to examine the reforms proposed to and approved by the Second Vatican Council. Certainly one cannot exclude *a priori* the possibility of the Council deciding upon even a new discipline in respect of sacramental concelebration; however an examination of the Council's work is instructive.

Here one must emphasise that chapter six of *The Holy Eucharist—The World's Salvation* is an exemplary study of the preparation and redaction of the Council's text. Students of *Sacrosanctum Concilium* would do well to imitate Father de Sainte-Marie's methodology, although since he wrote more material has become available.

For example, to the study of the redaction of article 44 of the *Schema Constitutionis,* which would become article 57 of the Constitution, it is now possible to study the genesis of the *Schema* itself back to at least October 1960.[31] So too, a single volume has been published which provides a synopsis of the development of the text of the *Schema* from the end of 1961 until the definitive text approved by the Council, including the interventions of the Council Fathers and the clarificatory *Declarationes* provided by the Conciliar Liturgical Commission.[32]

---

[31] See: Angelo Lameri, ed., *La « Pontificia Commisio de sacra liturgia praeparatoria Concilii Vaticani II » Documenti, Testi, Verbali* (Centro Liturigco Vincenziano, Rome 2013).

[32] See: Francisco Gil Hellín, *Concilii Vaticani II Synopsis: Constitutio de Sacra Liturgia Sacrosanctum Concilium* (Liberia Editrice Vaticana, Vatican City 2003). This material had previously been published, however by collecting disparate material into one volume Gil Hellín has provided a reasearch tool second to none. One should be aware, however, that some interventions of the Council Fathers not included in this volume may be of value to researchers.

Studies of the liturgical reform also shed light on the preparation for, Conciliar discussion and the implementation of the new discipline on concelebration. Don Nicola Giampietro's study of the role of Ferdinando Cardinal Antonelli, OFM, makes available not only details of the discussions of the Conciliar Commission's revision of the text in the light of the Council Fathers' debate,[33] but also details of the 1952 discussion of the possible introduction of ceremonial concelebration during work on the reform of Holy Week promulgated in 1955.[34] His observations as a member of the post-conciliar *Consilium* are similarly not without import.[35] Giampietro's later work also contains pertinent material prior to the Council,[36] though its most significant contribution must be the extensive consideration it gives to the Conciliar debate on concelebration and its implementation after the Council.[37]

Archbishop Bugnini's autobiographical history of the liturgical reform is clearly an essential source, particularly for the implementation *Sacrosanctum Concilium*. It also yields one interesting fact in respect of the Conciliar period itself: "Even before the Constitution on the Sacred Liturgy was promulgated in November 1963, Father Cipriano Vagaggini had been studying an earlier draft of a rite of concelebration."[38]

One of the great services Father de Sainte-Marie's study of the redaction of the text of the Constitution renders is his identification of both the limitations of the Council's own discussion of concelebration ("the very method of the debates, the number of participants,

---

[33] See: Nicola Giampietro, *The Development of the Liturgical Reform: As Seen by Cardinal Ferdinando Antonelli from 1948–1970* (Roman Catholic Books, Fort Collins 2009), pp. 93–94, 117, 123.

[34] See: *ibid.*, pp. 247–48.

[35] See: *ibid.*, p. 167.

[36] See: Giampietro, *La concelebrazione eucharistia e la communione sotto due specie nella storia della Liturgia*, chapter 2.

[37] See: *ibid.*, chapter 3.

[38] Annibale Bugnini, CM, *The Reform of the Liturgy 1948–1970* (Liturgical Press, Collegeville 1990), p. 123.

and the multiplication of the questions treated as a whole did not always allow one to stop at the essential points or to go to the heart of the matter at hand"),[39] and of the work of revision that took place at the level of the Conciliar Commission:

> It belonged to the Commission ... to discern among th[e] mass of *modi* those which truly represented the majority tendency of the conciliar assembly, by keeping close watch not to replace it by the tendency which was the strongest on its own level. Was this even possible? Given the conditions under which the Commission worked, the question is a reasonable one.[40]

So too of importance is his identification of the profound historical error on the origins and practice of sacramental concelebration that was contained in the materials and draft texts presented to the Fathers of the Council, "making the Fathers believe that what they were being asked to vote on, namely sacramental concelebration, was the rite of Tradition, whereas Tradition knew only ceremonial concelebration." "One can see the weight that this false argument from Tradition had in the hearts of the Fathers," Father de Sainte-Marie asserts.[41]

Students of the liturgical reform following the Second Vatican Council sometimes encounter a form of 'Vatican II fundamentalism,' as historically uncritical as it is theologically deficient, which dismisses such considerations and holds conciliar texts to be virtually irreformable regardless of their nature or content, and labelling any criticism of them akin to heresy. In the light of this it is appropriate to underline Father de Sainte-Marie's 1982 justification of his own critical study:

> Our calling into question of practices and opinions which are today so widespread can appear to some as an attack on the Magisterium of the Council. The weight of habit moves them to identify to such a degree a certain 'spirit of the Council' with the Council itself, that every critique and even simply every

---

[39] See p. 240 below.

[40] See p. 243 below.

[41] See p. 230 below.

questioning of that 'spirit' appears to them to be a grave rejection of the Magisterium itself. And yet, if one considers the matter closely, they are the ones who scorn the Council and who do not respect the authentic Magisterium.

For our part, far from calling into question the conciliar institution in its work at Vatican II, we are showing its greatness, but its limits as well. Both aspects need to be recognized; for, if the Holy Spirit assists the Church gathered in a council, it does so by supporting the activity of men, and not by substituting it. Hence the possibility of resisting His action, not to the point of an error in what concerns the Faith, certainly; but at least enough to create a partial obstacle to the divine work.[42]

It is, therefore, with an historical and theological sobriety that one must assess disciplinary reforms ordered by a Council of the Church. In respect of concelebration the text promulgated by the Council on 4 December 1963 reads:

57. § 1. Concelebration, whereby the unity of the priesthood is appropriately manifested, has remained in use to this day in the Church both in the East and in the West. For this reason it has seemed good to the Council to extend permission for concelebration to the following cases:

(i). a) on the Thursday of the Lord's Supper, not only at the Mass of the Chrism, but also at the evening Mass.

b) at Masses during councils, bishops' conferences, and synods;

c) at the Mass for the blessing of an abbot.

(ii). Also, with permission of the ordinary, to whom it belongs to decide whether concelebration is opportune:

a) at conventual Mass, and at the principal Mass in churches when the needs of the faithful do not require that all priests available should celebrate individually;

---

[42] See p. 279 below.

b) at Masses celebrated at any kind of priests' meetings, whether the priests be secular clergy or religious.

§ 2. (i). The regulation, however, of the discipline of concelebration in the diocese pertains to the bishop.

(ii). Nevertheless, each priest shall always retain his right to celebrate Mass individually, though not at the same time in the same church as a concelebrated Mass, nor on Thursday of the Lord's Supper.

58. A new rite for concelebration is to be drawn up and inserted into the Pontifical and into the Roman Missal.

Given that the background and context make clear that the Council is speaking of *sacramental* concelebration, the historical error in respect of both Eastern and Western liturgical history contained in article 57 § 1, which forms part of the premise for the reform authorised, is an embarrassment of the first order (as Father de Sainte-Marie makes perfectly clear). It was, nevertheless, an error that was widely accepted and promoted. Indeed, prefacing *Concelebration in the Christian Church*, Dom Aelred Silem wrote:

> Although the ceremonial obscured used the fact, concelebration [in the sense of truly celebrating Mass] has never died out in the Latin Church since, at the consecration of bishops and the ordination of priests, those who receive the order subsequently concelebrate with the presiding bishop. Apart from these two cases, concelebration was forbidden in the Latin rite ... although in one form or another it has always been used in the Eastern Churches ... [43]

One contemporary commentator was nearer the mark: "In widening the use of concelebration, the Constitution is following theological, pastoral and practical reasons, rather than historical and traditional ones. Concelebration as introduced by the Constitution must be called a real innovation..."[44] Certainly its provision for priests to

---

[43]   King, *Concelebration in the Christian Church*, p. v.

concelebrate with another priest, and not the bishop, is a most radical innovation indeed.

Another commentator indicates something of the spirit of the reform when he states that the extension of concelebration:

> Renders more functional the celebration of the Eucharist in cases where several priests are called to celebrate Mass in the same place and at about the same time: instead of isolating themselves in chapels or at side altars, they place themselves together around the altar and associate themselves with their presiding priest in a common celebration of the Eucharist.[45]

Yet another commentary regards the "avoidance of the inconveniences in multiple celebration by several or many priests," as a "secondary" motivation for the reform, and the appropriate manifestation of the unity of the priesthood and the stimulation "of the piety of priests" as its primary goals.[46]

---

[44] Adalbert Franquesa, OSB, "Concelebration" in: Annibale Bugnini, CM, & Carlo Braga, CM, (eds), *The Commentary and the Instruction on the Sacred Liturgy* (Benzinger Brothers, New York 1965), pp. 144–54 (p. 147). The author goes on to assert that this is a development in line with *Sacrosanctum Concilium* article 23. It is difficult to see how this assertion can be justified in respect of elements of the new discipline of concelebration, most particularly the concelebration of priests with priests and not the bishop. *Sacrosanctum Concilium* article 23 cannot be regarded as a 'blank cheque' for liturgical innovation; see: Alcuin Reid, "*Sacrosanctum Concilium* and the Organic Development of the Liturgy" in: Uwe Michael Lang, ed., *The Genius of the Roman Rite: Historical , Theological, and Pastoral Perspectives on Catholic Liturgy*, Hillenbrand Books, Chicago 2010, pp. 198–215.

[45] Francois Vandenbrouke, OSB, "Communion under Both Species and Concelebration" in: William Baraúna (ed.), *The Liturgy of Vatican II*, vol. II (Franciscan Herald Press, Chicago 1966), pp. 108–18 (p. 116).

[46] Frederick R. McManus, *Sacramental Liturgy* (Herder & Herder, New York 1967), pp. 102–03. McManus goes on to argue for the "gradual suppression" of priests accepting Mass stipends, deprecating "the whole related development of scholastic speculation upon the 'fruits' of the Mass" which "has certainly hindered rather than helped a sound understanding of the Eucharistic celebration as the action of the Christian community in union with its head;" pp. 107–08.

It is clear from the conciliar text that the Council intended the practice of concelebration to be occasional, to take place "only with permission of the Ordinary" apart for those instances "established by common law" (Holy Thursday, the Mass of the Chrism, etc.), and that concelebration "is never of obligation" except in the instances where it is mandated in the pontifical (newly ordained priests at the Mass of their ordination, etc.).[47] Nevertheless, the likelihood that "the revision of the Roman rite may of course involve the extension of concelebration, as a regular thing, to occasions other than those mentioned" was foreseen by some liturgists at the time.[48]

It is in this context that one must study and assess the implementation of the Conciliar reform. A study of the rite called for in article 58 of the Constitution and promulgated in 1965, bears out the modest if not restrained use of concelebration intended by the Council.[49] But, as Archbishop Bugnini made clear, the Council's permission for concelebration "at conventual Mass, and at the principal Mass in churches when the needs of the faithful do not require that all priests available should celebrate individually," a permission naturally contained in the 1965 ritual, "left the door open to use of this rite on many occasions and contributed, in fact, to the growth of the view that concelebration is the proper and preferred form of celebration for the priestly community."[50]

Five decades later concelebration is not simply preferred but is often assumed if not imposed, as noted above. Father de Sainte-Marie deprecates "the rapid extension of concelebration during the years

---

[47]   See: Franquesa, "Concelebration" p. 152.

[48]   See: McManus, *Sacramental Liturgy*, p. 103.

[49]   See: *Ritus Servandus in Concelebratione Missae et Ritus Communionis sub Utraque Specie*, Editio Typica (Typis Polyglottis Vaticanis, Vatican City 1965). Bugnini gives a summary of the rite in *The Reform of the Liturgy*, pp. 129–32. Significantly, Bugnini reports the rite as saying "1. Concelebration is allowed *only* in the following cases…" (emphasis original), p. 130. However the ritual itself does not contain any such restrictive adverb (see: *Ritus Servandus*, p. 13).

[50]   Bugnini, ibid., p. 130.

following the Council, and even the existence of official documents encouraging this practice," and concludes:

> With such an innovation being imposed in the name 'of the Council,' we are faced with two questions, the responses to which will give us our conclusion: 1) Is it truly the Council which prescribed this practice?; 2) Or at the very least, can the post-conciliar evolution legitimately be presented as the homogenous development of the letter and the spirit of Vatican II? [51]

His answer is clear: "The current practice of concelebration, *insofar as it is general and systematic,* and even at times tyrannical, is not in any way the work of the Council, nor can it find support in its letter or its spirit."[52]

Concelebration Tomorrow

Father de Sainte-Marie's principal concern is the theological and pastoral impoverishment of the life of priests and of the Church through the reduction of the number of Masses offered as a direct result of the unforeseen spread of concelebration. *"Which manner of celebrating the Holy Sacrifice of the Mass can be the source for the greatest glory of God and for the greatest treasury of redeeming graces for the Church?"* he asks, insisting that *"the need for the latter in today's world explains the urgency of this question."*[53]

His questions, surely, remain pertinent. So too, his exegesis of the conciliar reform and text is sound. Father de Saint Marie is not *opposed* to the Council's permission for concelebration on more occasions, indeed he himself made appropriate use of it in his priestly life. What concerns him profoundly is the radical reduction in the number of Masses being offered. For:

---

[51] See p. 262 below.
[52] See p. 268 below. Emphasis original.
[53] See p. 4 below.

Each Mass, being the very sacrifice of Christ, the one redemptive sacrifice of Calvary, *has an infinite value.* Each Mass is an act of the entire Church; for, she is present there both in Christ, Who offers Himself for her as her Head, and in the priest, who represents her, and prays for her and in her name ... It is this which establishes the *value of Masses said 'privately,'* that is, those celebrated by a priest in the absence of any assistants: *each Mass pours the redemptive Blood of Christ upon the Church and the whole world.*

While each Mass has in itself an infinite value, the dispositions of men for receiving its fruits are always imperfect and in this sense limited. For this reason the number of *celebrations of the Mass is so important for multiplying the fruits of salvation.*[54]

If he is right—both historically and theologically—it is high time that we look again at the practice of concelebration as it has become today. Before it is asserted that 'universal concelebration' is now customary, let us remember Saint Cyprian of Carthage's adage, *consuetudo sine veritate vetustas erroris est* (custom without truth is simply error grown old).[55] Before this error grows too old, it is necessary to revisit it with theological, historical and liturgical truth.

This *The Holy Eucharist—The World's Salvation* most certainly does. Since its original publication there has been much talk of a "reform of the liturgical reform,"[56] and of a "new liturgical movement."[57] That the practice of concelebration be reviewed in the light of the abuses to which it has given rise and which the Fathers of the Second Vatican Council most certainly could not have imagined they were authorising—most especially large-scale concelebrations which

---

[54] See p. 553 below. Emphasis original.

[55] Letter to Pompeius, 73/9.

[56] See: Thomas M. Kocik, *The Reform of the Reform? A Liturgical Debate: Reform or Return* (Ignatius Press, San Francisco 2003).

[57] See: Joseph Cardinal Ratzinger, *The Spirit of the Liturgy* (Ignatius Press, San Francisco 2000), especially pp. 8–9; Alcuin Reid, "The New Liturgical Movement after the Pontificate of Benedict XVI" in: *Sacred Music* vol. 141 (2014), pp. 10–26.

situate priests at great distances from the altar, and the indignity and indecorous behaviours in priests which such events often bring forth—is surely an important element of such liturgical renewal.[58]

In such a review competent authority may wish to consider the implications of the erroneous historical assumptions in article 57 § 1 of *Sacrosanctum Concilium*. Experience of concelebration since the Council, and theological arguments such as those of Father de Sainte-Marie, might even suggest a prudent restriction of its practice in the future. Formation "in the spirit and power of the liturgy" itself (see: *Sacrosanctum Concilium*, 14),[59] and specifically on why and how priests can and should offer Mass privately and on how they can assist at Mass when not concelebrating, would seem urgently to be necessary in many places. It may even be appropriate for the competent authority to modify the rite of the ordination of priests and the blessing of abbots in the *Pontificale* of the *usus antiquior* of the Roman rite to ensure sacramental concelebration on those occasions.

Let concelebration in the Roman rite tomorrow be what the Council truly intended: an occasional, edifying and dignified rite by modest or at least manageable numbers of priests. And let the Church of today and tomorrow continue to benefit from more and more devout and, where necessary, individual celebrations of Holy Mass —something the Second Vatican Council never intended to abolish—for the Holy Eucharist is indeed the world's salvation.

Dom Alcuin Reid
Epiphanytide 2015

---

[58] Pope Benedict XVI highlighted the problem of large-scale concelebrations in his Apostolic Exhortation *Sacramentum Caritatis* (22 February 2007), n. 61.

[59] See: Alcuin Reid, "Thoroughly imbued with the spirit and power of the Liturgy—*Sacrosanctum Concilium* and Liturgical Formation" in: *Sacred Liturgy* (Ignatius Press, San Francisco 2014) pp. 213–36.

Part One

A 'Disputed Question'

1 REFLECTIONS AND QUESTIONS ON THE SUBJECT OF CONCELEBRATION

THE TEXT WE now present was first submitted to a certain number of friends, the majority of whom agreed with our conclusions.[1] Others, on the contrary, had some difficulties with it; their arguments, however, did not truly respond to ours. They were, in fact, appeals to the authority of the Church's use, which is perfectly valid for justifying the possibility of concelebration (this is the key argument of St Thomas himself); but they did not treat the question of the appropriateness of frequent concelebration, and less still the question of knowing whether in concelebration one or several Masses are offered to God. The recourse to antiquity was not able to be a determining factor; for, according to the Catholic teaching of the 'homogenous development' of dogma—and of the Liturgy—the Church, throughout the ages, has deepened her knowledge of the treasure which Christ has left to her in the Sacrament of the Eucharist. The development of the worship of the Real Presence is one example of this, the awareness of the value of the multiplication of Masses is, in our opinion, another. Moreover, we shall see what actually is the true testimony of antiquity.

In publishing the following reflections we would like to clarify as much as possible the two following points. First, it is of prime importance to distinguish between the question of the unicity of the renewal of Christ's sacrifice in concelebration and the appropriateness of frequent concelebration.

With regards to the first question, it seems that it should not be difficult to establish agreement in favour of the unicity, for reasons both magisterial and theological, which we shall present.

---

[1]   It appeared in *La Pensée Catholique*, no. 180 (May–June 1979), pp. 21–36.

With respect to the second question—and it is the second one we shall limit ourselves to—the response which we offer seems to flow so logically from the one given to the first question, that we believe we have proven it.

It goes without saying, however, that in this matter it belongs to the Magisterium to give the definitive response. In presenting what seems to be the truth, we submit to the Magisterium's future decisions; and as we wait for them, we fully respect the position of those who are not convinced by our argument. We would even be happy if they would present—with clarity and precision—the reasons which they think they can advance in favour of their position. It is difficult, however, for us to see how a contrary thesis could be advanced in the face of the truths which we here defend, and which simply re-present the traditional teaching and practice of the Church. The only raison d'être of this task of clarification, as the reader will understand, is to know which manner of celebrating the Holy Sacrifice of the Mass can be the source for the greatest glory of God and for the greatest treasury of redeeming graces for the Church. The need for the latter in today's world explains the urgency of this question.

That the practice of concelebration today has spread far and wide throughout the Church is an indisputable fact. This fact, nevertheless, is not universally known; it ought to be. Reservations are being expressed and questions posed which not only leave an impact upon the personal piety of the priest, but also relate to dogmatic theology and affect the common good of the Church. Among these questions, two merit our special attention: that of the unicity or the plurality of the Sacrifice of the Mass in the case of concelebration; and, following upon the response given to the first question, that of the appropriateness of frequent concelebration for the common good of the Church.

The first question is stated concretely in the following manner: When several priests concelebrate, is there one Mass, one sacramental sacrifice, or on the contrary are there as many sacrifices as there are priests concelebrating? If we state this as a question, it is because, in fact, it is still today a question in the minds of many priests, even those of a solid theological formation. One of the arguments which they advance in favour of the plurality of Masses is the fact that the Church permits each concelebrating priest to receive a Mass stipend, which presupposes, they say, that each one celebrates one Mass; and therefore, they conclude that there are as many Masses as there are concelebrating priests. This argument is based also on one particular phrase of Pius XII, which we shall examine later on, and which is based on the principle according to which, 'the multiplicity of agents calls forth a multiplicity of actions.'

Against this position others will justly remark that the very word 'concelebration' signifies the unity of the accomplished liturgical act, and therefore the unicity of the sacrifice that is offered 'in the sacrament,' '*in sacramento*,' as St Thomas, after St Augustine, expressed it. And in fact, both the Magisterium and theology confirm that this latter position is the corret one, and they indicate how to resolve the difficulties which are advanced against it.

I. The Magisterium

To the best of our knowledge, it is under Pope Pius XII, at least in the contemporary period, that the question began to be raised. This can be considered a good thing for the simple fact that, treating it for the first time, Pius XII himself did not base his teaching on any previous magisterial document, which he certainly would have done had one existed. To this we can add that his own teaching seems to have encountered a certain hesitation before arriving at its definitive formulation, which would be taken up again after the Council.

We must, however, point out, from the Middle Ages, the text of Innocent III (1198–1216), cited by St Thomas Aquinas in his treatment of concelebration.[2] He is concerned here with a work titled *De Sacro Altaris Mysterio*.[3] This text does not directly treat our question;

---

2   *S.T. III*, q. 82, a. 2; cf. *In IV Sent.* d. 13, q. 1, a. 3, sol. 2

however, it clearly leans in the direction of the unicity of the sacrifice, not to mention the fact (as one could) that it formally implies it. Let us examine, however, the texts of Pius XII, who, progressively and compelled by the movement of ideas, came to treat concelebration explicitly.

A) Pius XII

The two principal texts of Pius XII on the question are the great discourses of 1954 and 1956. Nevertheless it will be interesting to recall how the theme of concelebration appeared since 1947.

1) The Encyclical *Mediator Dei*[4] did not treat concelebration in the strict sense, even if it made use of the word. What it refutes is the opinion, already put forth at that time by some, according to which there is, without any distinction, only one priesthood in the Church, and that consequently, the priest is simply the delegate of the community. The Mass then is one 'concelebration' in the proper sense of the whole congregation. Whence one logically concludes, that in order to get the most out of this action of the congregation, it is better that, when several priests are together, they 'concelebrate' with all the people, by assisting with them in the one Mass celebrated by the one among many, than celebrate each one in private.[5] The possibility of concelebration, such as it is practiced today, was not even envisioned then, at least publicly. However, with regards to the effacement of the priesthood by a false exaltation of the congregation, we see that the present errors have already been in existence for a long time.

2) By a careful reading we see that the *Allocution* of 2 November 1954[6] also does not treat the theme of concelebration in the strict sense. Pius XII begins by recalling that only the priest can offer the sacrifice of the Mass (we saw that this was necessary already at that time) and that when he acts, 'he puts on the person of Christ and is

---

[3]   L. IV, ch. 25 (*PL* 217, 873).

[4]   20 November 1947. *AAS* 39, 1947.

[5]   *Ibid.* p. 553.

[6]   *AAS* 46, 1954, p. 668.

the only one [the priest insofar as he is the minister] who sacrifices.'[7] Next, the Pope denounces again the error already condemned in *Mediator Dei,* that of a priest's 'concelebration' with the people (without any distinction other than a simple one between the respective functions). Finally, he rejects the new error which has since become manifest and which claims 'that the concelebration of one sole Mass at which one hundred priests piously assist is the same thing as one hundred Masses celebrated by one hundred priests.' It is absolutely not so, affirms the Pope. In that which concerns the oblation of the Eucharistic sacrifice, there are as many actions of Christ the High Priest as there are celebrating priests, and not as there are priests piously listening to the Mass of a bishop or of another celebrating priest.'[8]

Such then is the phrase on which some believe to be able to base their position, that in a concelebration there are as many Eucharistic sacrifices as there are celebrating priests: ... *tot sunt actiones Christi ... quot sunt sacerdotes celebrantes* ... One must admit that if Pius XII had said nothing else on this subject, the argument could seem very strong. Nevertheless it would not be decisive; for if one pays attention to the principal question to which the Pope wishes to respond—that of the conditions according to which a priest celebrates—one sees what it is that he wishes to affirm first and foremost, namely that the priest does not celebrate the Mass unless he himself accomplishes the liturgical acts, and that he does not do so by assisting at a Mass celebrated by another. And yet, one might object, the Pope does affirm that there are as many actions of Christ as there are priests celebrating. However, this is not conclusive; and we will better see this further on when we examine the relations which exist between Christ the sole High Priest and His ministers. We must now point out that the alternative envisaged in this text and in its context is not between one Mass concelebrated by one hundred priests and one

---

[7]   *Ibid.*

[8]   *Ibid.,* p. 669.

hundred Masses celebrated separately, but between one Mass cele-brated by one among many, at which the many assist, and one hundred Masses which the many would celebrate separately. This modifies at the very least the significance of the final affirmation, showing as it does that the text does not aim to respond to the problem which we are examining in this book. Furthermore, as we are going to see, Pius XII himself recognized the necessity of clarifying his thought, even in the context or problem posed to him.

3) He did so two years later, on the occasion of the *International Congress of Pastoral Liturgy,* held at Assisi in 1956, in a very important discourse which he preached at the closing of the Congress, in Rome, on 22 September. It is here that he deals for the first time with the problem of priestly concelebration in the strict sense. Taking up his discourse of 22 November 1954, he denounced again 'the error regarding the equivalence between the celebration of one hundred Masses by one hundred priests and that of one Mass at which one hundred priests piously assist.'[9] Then he added: 'Some recent events give Us the occasion of clarifying certain points regarding this.' Here then are the clarifications. Having just recalled that 'the central element of the Eucharistic sacrifice is that where Christ intervenes as *se ipsum offerens,* to use the words of the Council of Trent,'[10] and therefore that 'the consecration ... is the central point of the *actio Christi cuius personam gerit sacerdos celebrans*—or the *sacerdotes celebrantes* in the case of true concelebration'—Pius XII adds, in order to clarify his thought: 'When the consecration of bread and wine is validly achieved, the entire action of Christ Himself is accomplished.'

From this essential action he then carefully distinguishes the *oblatio hostiae super altare positae,* which, he says, 'can be made and is made by the priest celebrant, by the Church, by the other priests, by each of the faithful.' But he says this in order to clarify that this offering is not the action of Christ Himself acting sacramentally through the

---

9   *AAS* 48, 1956, p. 717; the original text is in French.
10 Session XXII, Ch. 2.

priest, who takes His place in virtue of his ministerial powers. And it is here, on the basis of the principles thus recalled, that we find the main part of the pronounced 'clarification,' and with it the decisive affirmation of that which concerns our problem:

> In reality the action of the consecrating priest is the very one of Christ, Who acts through His minister. In the case of a concelebration in the proper sense of the word, Christ, in place of acting through one minister, acts through many.[11]

As we see (and the rest of the text shows it even more), the two questions which the Pope planned to treat were the following: 1) the difference between 'true concelebration' and 'purely ceremonial concelebration'—a question which is today completely outdated, as even those who floated it at the time acknowledge;[12] 2) the conditions required for a 'true concelebration.' The response to the first question is founded on the essential difference, and not only one of degree, that exists between the ministerial priesthood of priests, conferred by Holy Orders, and the common priesthood of the faithful, received at Baptism, even if these terms are not employed here.[13] The principle used to resolve the second question is that it is Christ Himself Who acts through the priest at the essential moment of the celebration of the Mass; wherefore it follows that, for a true concelebration, all priest concelebrants 'must themselves perform the actions and pronounce the essential words.'[14] A little further on Pius XII would again recall this principle: 'the decisive question [for the concelebration as for the Mass of one priest] is not knowing what is the fruit which the soul draws from it, but what is the nature of the act performed: the priest, as minister of Christ, performs or does not perform *actio Christi se ipsum sacrificantis et offerentis.*'[15] Now this action being accomplished

---

[11]   *Ibid.*

[12]   Cf. A. M. Roguet, *op. cit.*, p. 377.

[13]   Cf. Vatican Council II, *Lumen Gentium*, 10; *Presbyterorum Ordinis*, 2.

[14]   *AAS* 48, 1956, p. 718; declaration confirmed by a response from the Holy Office, 8 March [23 May] 1957: *AAS* 49, 1957, p. 370; cf. DS 3928.

in the liturgy by the sacramental rite, the priest achieves it 'if, with the necessary interior intention ... [he] accomplishes the exterior action and above all pronounces the words which constitute the *actio Christi* ...'[16] We see the twofold danger against which the Pope took up opposition by referring his listeners to the objective sacramental order: namely, the dangers of blurring the understanding of the sacramental mystery and of sliding into subjectivism.

However, by putting in these terms the principle which allows one to determine the conditions required for a true concelebration, Pius XII clearly indicated the sense in which must be resolved—and in which, in fact, it would be officially resolved later—the question of the unicity of the sacrifice of the Mass in the case of concelebration. Moreover, in the decisive affirmation which we quote above, it seems to us that it can be said that he already did resolve the question. His response, in fact, is clearly inspired by St Thomas Aquinas, whose words he repeated almost verbatim. We shall see this further on when we study the text of St Thomas. The content of the text is this: that which matters is *the action that Christ Himself accomplishes.* The fact that He accomplishes it through one priest or through many priests, as in the case of concelebration, does not change a thing with respect to the action itself; for, 'in place of acting through one priest, Christ acts through many.' This conclusion imposes itself from the moment that one returns to the foreground the action of Christ in the liturgical celebration of the sacrament, and from the moment that one considers precisely the sacramental nature of that action, and therefore, the essentially ministerial function of the priest through whom Christ accomplishes the action.

By beginning there, in fact, one sees how, in order for a priest to concelebrate, it is necessary and sufficient that he accomplish with the right intention the liturgical rite of the sacrament: this is the question directly resolved by Pius XII. However, as soon as the priest

---

15   *Ibid.*
16   *Ibid.*

accomplishes the rite with the other concelebrants, he participates, by becoming a minister, in the one sacramental action of Christ, which, consequently, is not multiplied by the number of concelebrants: such is the question directly resolved by the same text, this conclusion flowing immediately and necessarily from the principles which were posited.

The context in which this discourse was pronounced sufficiently explains the reason why the Pope did not explicitly cite St Thomas: namely, this 'authority' had more of a risk of indisposing the listeners than it had a chance of convincing them. Moreover, the reference to the Thomistic text was obvious to theologians. This is why one is equally permitted to think that it is to the Common Doctor that they would have recourse who would draw Pius XII's attention to the problem resolved by the affirmation of 1954: *tot actiones ... quot celebrantes.*

For all that, this 'clarification' is not a retraction, for we can easily see how the two declarations (that of 1954 and of 1956) are reconciled; and in this way we also see how to preserve the truth contained in the first declaration. When we affirm that there are as many actions of Christ the High Priest as there are celebrating priests, we consider the matter *from the point of view of the minister* and the conditions that he must meet in order that Christ might act in him, namely, in order that he himself might accomplish the *sacramental action.* What is meant then is that Christ the High Priest acts only in the priest who actually celebrates the Mass (and the question to which the discourse attempts to respond allows us to understand it clearly). On the other hand, when we affirm, as did the discourse of 1956, that in a concelebration Christ acts by several ministers instead of acting by one alone (but always for the sake of accomplishing one action), the point of view immediately adopted is really *that of Christ,* Who acts, that is to say, Who accomplishes Himself the *sacramental action* through His minister or *ministers.* Certainly the question to be resolved is always that of the condition to be fulfilled by the priest in order to celebrate or concelebrate truly. However, in the second case the response that was given is based more directly on the personal action of Christ. It is this which permits us to define better the relation between the priest, who is Christ's minister, and Christ as the principal agent of the sacrifice. To conclude: where the sacramental rite is placed, there is accomplished the action of Christ; and that action is one, as is the rite by which it is realized, whatever be the number of ministers or 'instruments' which Christ uses in order to accomplish it. Such (as well as a clearer perception of the evolution of the liturgical movement) are no doubt the fundamental principles and theological perspectives that moved Pius XII to return to his 1954 discourse, as he did in 1956, explicitly declaring his desire to 'clarify' the matter. At the same time, however, we can see what truth there is in the first discourse.

4) Finally, we recall the *Decree of the Holy Office* of 8 March 1957, approved by the Holy Father on 23 May, which reaffirmed the necessity for concelebrants to pronounce the essential words: 'For, by divine institution, he alone celebrates who pronounces the words of consecration.'[17]

5) We can add to these texts of the Magisterium of Pius XII the *Instruction on Sacred Music and the Liturgy, from* the Sacred Congregation of Rites, 3 September 1958.[18] Here it was recalled 'that sacramental concelebration in the Latin Church is limited by law to particular cases.'[19] The following number adds: 'Nevertheless, Masses said 'synchronized' are forbidden. These are Masses celebrated in a particular manner: two or more priests say Mass simultaneously at one or more altars in such a way that all their actions and words happen at the same moment.'[20]

---

[17]   *AAS* 48, 1957, p. 370; DS 3928.
[18]   *AAS* 50, 1958, pp. 630–63.
[19]   *Ibid.,* no. 38.
[20]   *Ibid.,* no. 39.

The direction, therefore, clearly went towards the sense of maintaining a limit to concelebration, to the point of dismissing even what could seem to come near to and prepare its adoption.

B) The Second Vatican Council. The Council introduced into the Church a wider use of concelebration

1) Sacrosanctum Concilium[21]

This extension happened primarily by the *Constitution on the Sacred Liturgy,* promulgated at the end of the second session. It said nothing on that occasion regarding the unicity or plurality of the Masses offered to God by the concelebrants. It is all the more regrettable that one can clearly see in that document a twofold tendency regarding the subject of concelebration. One tendency seeks to maintain the principle of limitation, while adding some new cases to those which had already been provided for by law. It is this which is expressed in paragraph 1 of Article 57 of the Constitution:

§1. Concelebration, by which the unity of the priesthood is fittingly manifested, has remained in use in the Church until now in both the East and the West.[22] Therefore the Council is pleased to extend the faculty of concelebrating to the following cases:

1. a) Holy Thursday, for both the Chrism Mass and the Mass in the evening;

b) Masses at Councils, Episcopal Conferences and Synods;

c) Mass for the Blessing of an Abbot

The other tendency, that of widening the use, is manifested in number two of the same paragraph; but it is found in the first as well:

2. Furthermore, with the permission of the Ordinary, to whom it belongs to judge concerning the fittingness of concelebration:

---

[21] 4 December 1963.

[22] Contrary to what this declaration allows one to think (*without affirming it however*), concelebration in no way goes back to the first years of the Church.

a) At a Conventual Mass and the principal Mass of churches, when the good of the Christian faithful does not require the individual celebration of all priests present;[23]

b) At Masses at any sort of gatherings of priests, whether secular or religious.

The first tendency is present in the prudent clause that concelebration must always be regulated by the Ordinary; the second tendency, in the list of cases where it may be permitted, and in the absence of criteria which would fix the conditions where this permission would be able to be considered 'unfitting.' Leading to its conclusion according to its own logic, this second tendency opens the way to an unlimited use of concelebration. At the same time, however, it annuls the restrictive value and the very sense of the intention explicitly taken by the first tendency and inscribed in the conciliar text. This is why it must be considered as contrary to the logic of the text.

Yet the text adds a crucial intention, not only in order to safeguard the right of priests but also because it implicitly recognizes the value of so-called 'private' Masses, that is the value of the Mass itself, independent of the number of participants:

§2. ... 2. Nevertheless, every priest always has the faculty to celebrate Mass individually, but not in the same church at the same time, and not on Holy Thursday.

However, there again we have the right to regret the clause which says: 'but not in the same church at the same time.' Moreover, it suffices to go to Lourdes—despite the scarcity of private Masses that systematic concelebration has now brought about—or to any other

---

[23] By that statement alone we see a disposition that reveals the decrease in the sense of the value of the so-called 'private' Mass, and therefore of the Mass insofar as it is a sacrifice of Christ. On the historical origins of this theology, see below, Ch. 2 and Ch. 5. On the other hand, paragraph 2 of the same article, by recognizing the right of priests to say their own Mass on every occasion, implicitly reaffirms the value of these 'private' Masses. We have here a new sign of the internal tension and lack of coherence in this article.

great sanctuary in order to notice that, the mentioned clause being inapplicable in these cases, it is not applied. It does not make sense except for chapels or very small churches. Unfortunately, outside of these cases, it is still very often invoked in order to prevent priests from saying their Mass.

It is all the more legitimate to note the weaknesses of these 'pastoral' positions since their 'doctrinal' basis has in no way been presented and since they represent a definite break with the ancient tradition of the Latin Church. The only thing said in favour of concelebration is that it 'manifests' the union of priests with their bishop and among each other.[24] This is not enough to establish the innovation represented by the generalized extension of this usage. It is even less so in the face of what each new Mass offers to God of praise and reparation on the part of the Church, and of the graces of redemption to the Church on the part of God. For here we see, from the point of view of the common good of the Church, the problem that has arisen from the frequent practice of concelebration: the more one multiplies concelebration, the more one diminishes the number of Masses.

2) *Presbyterorum Ordinis*[25]

While the Constitution on the Liturgy said nothing of the unicity of the sacrifice offered to God in concelebration, a passage from the *Decree on the Ministry and Life of the Priests,* on the contrary, clearly affirms it:

> Each member of this Presbyterate is joined to the other members by special bonds of apostolic charity, ministry and fraternity: which is signified liturgically from ancient times when the Priests are invited to lay hands on the newly elect with the ordaining bishop, *and when they concelebrate the Holy Eucharist with one heart.*[26]

---

[24] Vatican II, *Presbyterorum Ordinis* nos. 7 and 8.

[25] 7 December 1965.

[26] Number 8.

This rarely mentioned text—the content and force of which we ourselves discovered during our later investigations—had been added *in extremis.*[27] Its value has thereby in no way been diminished; it was voted on and approved by the Fathers as the other texts. It considers two cases where priests express their unity in apostolic charity: that of the ordination of a new priest, and that of Eucharistic concelebration. We can already observe that in these two cases the liturgical action accomplished and the sacrament celebrated are one: there is one sole priestly ordination, and there is also one sole offering of the Eucharist.

Most importantly, however, to say that the priests 'concelebrate the Holy Eucharist with one heart,' is to take up again what had been explicitly affirmed some months earlier by the Decree *Ecclesiam semper,* which we shall present below, namely that the priests who concelebrate, 'act by one intention and one voice ... and [that] they offer to God one sole sacrifice.'

We have here, then, an incontestable affirmation by the Council itself of the fact that one sole Mass is offered to God in concelebration.

C) The Magisterium after the Council (and before it ended, but outside of its work)

The doctrinal limits and internal tensions of the Council manifested themselves in broad daylight and produced their effects in the period which followed, revealing at the same time the contradictions and explosive forces of which they were the bearers. For, while on the one hand, the official encouragements for the widening of concelebration were not lacking, without however having ever been made the object of a document of major juridical importance; on the other hand, three perfectly clear texts have been given us—the first of which is in reality prior to the last session of the Council—which take up again and reaffirm the definitive teaching of Pius XII on the subject of the unicity of the Eucharistic Sacrifice offered to God in concelebration. The

---

[27]   See below, Ch. 6, section 5.

contradiction is flagrant; for, what such a doctrine calls for is obviously the maintaining of the fundamental principle of limiting concelebrations—at least if we consider at the same time that other doctrinal principle, according to which each Mass has in itself an infinite value and represents for the Church and for humanity a new outpouring of graces from the redemptive Blood.

The three documents discussed here are all issused by the Sacred Congregation of Rites, which became the Congregation for Divine Worship between the writing of the second and third documents. It is always the responsibility of this Congregation to determine the rites of worship.

1) The General Decree Ecclesiae semper[28]

This Decree affirmed three times that there is only one sole sacrifice:

> Therefore [namely, by reason of the unity of the priesthood just mentioned], when individual priests offer the Sacrifice, all act nevertheless in virtue of the same priesthood and all act in the person (*in persona*) of the High Priest, Who can equally consecrate the sacrament of His Body and Blood by one priest or by many gathered together.

Here, a note at the bottom of the page makes reference to a text of St Thomas which we indicated above and which we shall examine later.[29] A little further on we read:

> In this manner of celebrating Mass [concelebration], several priests, in virtue of the same priesthood and by acting in the person of the High Priest, *act together* with one intention and one voice, and *they confect and offer by one sacramental act one unique sacrifice,* and they participate in it together.—… *simul una vol-*

---

[28]   7 March 1965 (*AAS* 57, 1965, pp. 410–12).

[29]   A note for the reader who consults the original text: We point out something that is extremely rare, namely the misprint that slipped into the text of the *AAS*: it is 'a. 2' and not 'a. 3' which one must read. The correction becomes self–evident when one refers to the text of St Thomas.

untate et una voce agunt, atque unicum Sacrificium unico actu sacramentali simul conficiunt et offerunt, idemque simul participant.

The text continues, giving us the third affirmation of the unicity of the sacrifice:

> This is why in the celebration of the Sacrifice ... there is truly the principal manifestation of the Church in the unity of the Sacrifice and of the Priesthood, *in one unique act of thanksgiving,* around one sole altar with ministers and the holy people.–
> ... *in unica gratiarum actione, circa unicum altare cum ministris et populo sancto.*[30]

The teaching, therefore, is clearly and definitively formulated. And if we look attentively at the text, and especially at the vocabulary used, we have a strong impression that it was inspired by the 1956 discourse of Pius XII, even if no reference to it is made (which is sufficiently explained, once again, by the circumstances). Moreover, seeing that the reform which limited the tenure in offices of the Curia to five years, had not yet taken place, the consultors of the Holy Office of 1965—clearly questioned on the matter—were still for the most part those who had studied the question under Pius XII. This is why they were able to give immediately and without hesitation the response asked of them.

2) The Instruction de Cultu Mysterii eucharistici[31]

This text affirms:

> 47. *Concelebration.* By Eucharistic concelebration, *the unity of the sacrifice and that of the priesthood* is fittingly *manifested;* and each time that the faithful actively participate, *the unity of the people of God appears* in a singular manner, especially if it is the bishop who presides (italics are ours).

As one can see, this text is much less clear than the preceding one, placing on the same level, apropos of concelebration, the unity of the priesthood (which is a received order and a power) and the unity of

---

[30] In these two citations the emphasis is ours.
[31] 25 May 1967 (*AAS* 59, 1967, pp. 539–73).

the sacrifice (which is here an accomplished act). Furthermore, in the confusion thus introduced and from one point of view—which seems to be the only one 'manifested' and the only one which 'appeared'— the people of God are associated with that unity of the priesthood and the sacrifice under the possible 'presidency' of the bishop. Let us avoid all equivocation: it is not this manifestation of the Church's unity that is being called into question, but rather the confusion in which it is here conceived and presented. We clearly see reappearing the dangers which were already manifest under Pius XII: the predominance of the subjectivist point of view, the disappearance of the sense of the sacramental mystery in what concerns the sacrifice and the priesthood, the false exaltation of the congregation.

Nevertheless, in what concerns the unicity of the sacrificial act accomplished in concelebration, a look again at the note in the Decree *Ecclesiae semper* will tell us in what sense we ought to understand the expression 'the unicity of the sacrifice' as it is used here. It is, therefore, the same doctrine which is reaffirmed.

3) The Declaratio de concelebratione[32]

This document affirms it again:

> The fraternal concelebration of priests signifies and reinforces the bonds which unite them to each other and to the community, because in this manner of celebrating the sacrifice, in which all participate consciously, actively and in a manner proper to each person, there appears more clearly the action of the entire community and there is realized a very special manifestation of the Church *in the unity of the sacrifice* and of the priesthood, *in the one unique action around one sole altar* [italics are ours].

We see that the text reveals the same tendencies as those noted in the preceding text. The congregation is openly in the foreground, and in a manner insufficiently expressed: the phrase, 'in a manner proper to

---

[32]   7 August 1972 (*AAS* 64, 1972, pp. 561–3).

each person,' was added to safeguard the specificity of the ministerial priesthood. And yet, not only is this specificity not reaffirmed, but the priority given to the action of 'all,' making 'appear' more clearly the action of 'the community,' gives the opposite meaning, absorbing to some degree the action of the priest into that of the congregation. Therefore, the sense towards which this text moves is diametrically opposed to the teaching of the Council of Trent. The former does not deny the latter, rather it silently passes over it and pushes the mind (and the liturgical practice even more so) into an opposite *sense*. Such a manner of acting is in reality more effective, and therefore even graver, than an open negation; for, the latter would immediately be countered by an intervention of the Magisterium.

On the other hand, with regards to our problem (which is of only secondary importance in the above text), the affirmation of 'the unity of the sacrifice … in a unique action around one sole altar,' and the reference in a footnote to the *Decree* of 1965 and to the *Instruction* of 1967 which we just cited, show clearly the confirmation and the continuity of the doctrine of unicity, which would henceforth be fixed.[33] However, in seeing the tendencies which manifest themselves and which are affirmed more and more clearly in these two latter texts, those of 1967 and 1972, we understand all the more the extreme importance of the *Decree* of 1965; for it is this text, by making a connection with the Magisterium before the Council, which assured the continuity and stability of the doctrine concerning this point. In conclusion, we can say that to the question regarding the Church's teaching on the number of Masses in a concelebration, since the discourse of Pius XII to the Liturgical Congress of Assisi in 1956, the response of the Magisterium is clear and constant: irrespective of the number of priests, there is always only one Mass in a concelebration.

*   *   *

We shall not return here to the question regarding the relationship of each Mass to the one sacrifice of the Cross. It has already been decided

---

[33]   It is reaffirmed in *Notitiae* 8, 1972, no. 77, p. 327 f.

by the Council of Trent;[34] and we have already studied it on another occasion.[35] It will suffice to recall that the Mass is not simply a symbolic representation and spiritual offering of the sacrifice formerly accomplished by Christ on Calvary—which is the thesis of Calvin, taken up again today by, among others, Max Thurian.[36] It is, rather, in virtue of the mystery and power of the 'sacrament' instituted by Christ, an efficacious and real representation, and better still, it is a unique type of re-actualization (of the sacramental order) of the one sacrifice of the Cross. It is thus that this one act, while impossible to renew according to its own proper mode under which it was realized in history, can nevertheless be infinitely renewed in the sacramental order. The mission of the Church, thanks to the ministerial priesthood, is precisely to assure this sacramental renewal in order to assume and preserve history—something which will continue to be done until the end of time. It is, therefore, in this mystery of the sacramental order that (as Dom Vonier admirably shows, following St Augustine and St Thomas) is found 'the key to the doctrine of the Eucharist,' and very particularly that of the relation between the unique historical sacrifice of Golgotha and the innumerable sacramental Eucharistic sacrifices of the Church.[37]

* * *

II. The theological argument

---

34 Session XXII, Ch. I

35 The author is alluding to an article titled *Sacrificium Missae* (*La Pensée Catholique*, no. 153, November–December 1974), and reproduced below, Ch. 9.

36 See his book *L'eucharistie, Mémorial du Seigneur, sacrifice d'action de grâce et d'intercession*, Neuchâtel, Delachaux et Niestlé, 1963, especially pages 170–4 and 223–57.

37 St Augustine, *Epistle* 98, 23 (*PL* 33, 363), taken up by St Thomas in *S.T. III*, q. 83, a. *1 sed contra*.; Dom Anscar Vonier, *A Key to the Doctrine of the Eucharist* (1925).

The theological argument was given in substance by the Magisterium itself, and we were able to discern its principal elements, especially by analyzing the two discourses of 1954 and 1956. Nevertheless, it will not be superfluous to revisit them and give them shape with the help of the texts of St Thomas, whose doctrine was decisive in this case. We shall also examine the problem of Mass stipends, which, in our opinion, causes no special difficulty.

In the *Summa Theologiae* the question examined is not directly that of the number of Masses, but rather that the possibility of concelebration. The principal objection which St Thomas raises (against the thesis which he will defend) is 'whether it is superfluous to do by several priests that which can be done by one priest.' Here is how he responds:

If each of the priests acted by his own power, one alone sufficing for the celebration, the other celebrants would be too many. But because the priest consecrates only by acting in the person and name of Christ (*in persona Christi*), and because many are 'one in Christ' (Gal 3:28), it matters little whether this sacrament be consecrated by one or by many. What is necessary is that the rite of the Church be observed.[38]

In analyzing this text we can distinguish three things: 1) the central affirmation, that which responds to the formulated objection: for the celebration of '*this* sacrament,' therefore of one sacrifice only, it matters little whether there be one or several priests; more than the expression 'this sacrament,' it is the very tenor of the objection that demands that the case under consideration be that of one sole sacrifice, of one sole consecration, for it is precisely on this fact that the objection supports itself—namely, that one *unique* consecration cannot be made by *several* priests at the same time; 2) the principal reason put forward both to answer this objection, and in order to uphold at the same time that several priests can together confect one consecration: namely, that the ministerial character of the priesthood

---

[38]   *S.T.* III, q. 82, a. 2, ad. 2.

with which the priest is endowed and in virtue of which he acts allows one to say truly that it is not by his own power that the priest acts but by the power of Christ, Whose minister he is; in other words, the priest is a consecrated instrument; 3) the third and final element that can be gathered from the above text is the condition required for 'this sacrament' to be consecrated: namely, the respect and completion of the liturgical rite of the Church.

In reality this condition is added as a second fundamental reason to first the one, which was advanced in order to establish the proposed solution. The body of the article insists more on the importance of the sacramental act accomplished by the concelebrating priests and its unity: 'the intention of all must be directed towards the same moment of consecration.'

This teaching was already found in the *Sentences*. The objection there was formulated thus: 'If several consecrate, there are several consecrations for the same host, which is injurious to the sacrament.' The response: 'Since the intention is required for the realization of the sacrament, when all have one and the same intention of consecrating, there is one consecration only.' It can also be translated (which amounts to the same thing): 'When all have the intention of bringing about one (only one and the same) consecration, there is one sole consecration.'[39]

Again, in a hypothetical case—reproved by St Thomas—concelebration of Baptism by two priests: 'Each one, insofar as it depends on him (*quantum est in se*), would baptize. However, they would not confect two different sacraments (*aliud et aliud sacramentum*), but Christ, Who alone baptizes interiorly, would by each confer one sacrament only' (*unum sacramentum per utrumque conferret*).[40]

There are undoubtedly many other things to be noted in these texts, but by gathering together the different arguments already put

---

[39]   *In IV Sent.*, d. 13, q. 1, a. 2, sol. 2, ad. 1.

[40]   *S.T.* III, q. 67, a. 6.

forward, we shall restrict ourselves to the following conclusions regarding our subject:

1) The Holy Sacrifice of the Mass is accomplished by Christ Himself working through His minister in the sacramental liturgical act. The mystery of 'the sacramental order,' proper to the New Covenant, with the specific reality which is its own, is at the heart of the question. Let us not forget that this bears essentially on the action of Christ Himself in the Mass. And as Christ accomplishes it through the priest in the liturgical act, it is therefore necessary to consider it from the side of the priest, the minister of Christ's action, and from the side of the liturgical act, essentially the consecration.

2) The priest is, at the altar more than anywhere else, the minister, that is to say the conscious and free instrument of Christ. He acts, according to a very strong Latin expression, *in persona Christi,* that is, in the very person of Christ, Who is present and acts through the priest. This is the argument put forward by St Thomas in order to explain that Christ can act equally through one or several priests. In reality, the manner in which the question is posed is noticeably different than ours. For St Thomas as for his objectors, the unicity of the sacrifice in concelebration is a given from the very start, admitted without discussion by reason of the practice of 'certain Churches.'[41] The question which must be resolved is how: How is it possible that several priests by concelebrating confect and offer one sacrifice only? And the response that is given is based first of all on the ministerial aspect of the priesthood and its action.

3) For a completely well-founded response, nevertheless, it is necessary to recall the sacramental character of this ministerial action. It is this to which St Thomas implicitly refers at the end of his response, when he explains 'that it is necessary that the rite of the Church be observed.' To speak of the rite in this context is in fact to speak of the liturgy; and to speak of the liturgy of the Church is to say that a sacrament has been celebrated.

---

[41]   *In IV Sent.*, d. 13, q. 1, a. 2, quaest. 2, *sed contra.*

4) Such are the three fundamental doctrinal truths which allow us to resolve the question of concelebration. One can even say that there is but one fundamental truth, the *sacramental nature of the action* accomplished in the Mass; for, it is there that one must begin. However, at the same time we can consider this primary truth in two immediate corollaries: a) *the ministerial character of the priest* of the Church, through whom Christ acts, and b) *the liturgical character and ritual* of the accomplished act. We consider also the ordering and subordination of the *ministers* to the *liturgical and sacramental ritual* which they accomplish, and in which they themselves are fulfilled— hence the primacy of the sacramental act over the person of the ministers when considering the number of Masses in a concelebration.

Based on this foundation, both unique and threefold, we can understand why the number of ministers through whom Christ the High Priest acts, matters little, or more precisely why it matters not at all (*non refert*), as St Thomas says, for the concelebration of a Mass. And, consequently, the only way of multiplying the number of Eucharistic sacrifices is not by multiplying the number of ministers of concelebration, which produces the opposite effect, but rather to multiply the liturgical celebrations of the sacramental rite of the Mass.

A final question still remains to be examined, and it is this: How can the Church permit each of several concelebrating priests, who bring about one and the same sacrifice, to offer the Mass for a particular intention and to receive the responding stipends? Here is the response in essence.

In the explanation of the efficacy of the sacrifice of the Mass, 'theologians are unanimous in distinguishing, in relation to the subject to whom the sacrifice is applied, a threefold fruit of the Mass: a general fruit for the whole Church; a special or middle fruit (what certain theologians call ministerial) for certain persons for whom the Eucharistic sacrifice is especially offered; and finally, the most special fruit for the celebrant himself.'[42] In addition, each Mass having an infinite

---

[42]   A. Michel, article *Messe*, in *Dic. Théol. Cath.*, vol. X, col. 1294.

value, and 'each of the concelebrants accomplishing for his part the entire act of the sacrifice, this act produces the same fruit as if each priest celebrated the Mass by himself,' affirms A. Michel apropos of the 'special fruit'—that for which an offering (the stipend) is made by the faithful.[43] Does it produce exactly the same fruit? This is a legitimate question. Yet we can respond in the affirmative for the most part, that is insofar as the Mass is the act of Christ Himself offering His very Self in sacrifice to His Father, through His minister and in the sacramental rite. And this suffices to justify the current practice of accepting Mass stipends; the infinite value of the sacrifice which all offer together permits each concelebrant to apply it to a particular intention entrusted to him.

*   *   *

Commenting in the 1967 edition of the *Revue des Jeunes* on the article of the *Summa Theologiae* which treats this question, Fr Roguet wrote: 'The theology of concelebration is still to be formed.' Let us note that this judgment, formulated two years after the closing of the Council, is still valid today. Unfortunately, what the author added was not likely to advance the reflection, especially where he pleaded in favour of concelebration of Baptism. Nevertheless, from this theology of concelebration one point at least is acquired (which we just examined), namely that in a concelebration, whatever be the number of priests, there is always but one Mass, one sacramental renewal of the unique redemptive sacrifice of Calvary.

This response, however, only poses the crucial question in a more intense manner: Does not the systematic (and today very widespread) practice of concelebration, which brings with it a proportionate decrease in the number of Masses celebrated and offered to God by the Church—does it not result in a very serious decrease in graces for the Church, which the sacrifice of the altar brings down upon her? The reasons which we have presented oblige us to respond in the affirmative, and we do not see how one could say the opposite.

---

[43]   *Ibid.,* col. 1295.

Concelebration, it is said, signifies and reinforces the union of priests among themselves. One cannot deny that this argument has a real albeit limited value. But do these (somewhat external despite everything else) factors of signification and of reinforcement (the latter being obtained above all by the kindled communitarian fervour) have value, when compared to that which represents, in adoration rendered to God and in redemption for the Church, the very act of Christ renewing sacramentally in each Mass the immolation and offering of His sacrifice to the Father? One must at least recognized that the question has in no way been treated, at least at the level of official documents. And while it is a very serious question, it is not the only one. All the other aspects already called to mind have to be considered: the decrease in the sense of sacramental mystery, the practical obliteration of the ministerial priesthood for the sake of the congregation, the decrease in priestly piety, the privation of Masses for the faithful, etc. It is not a question of passing judgment on another's conscience, but simply of recognizing a movement of ideas and a practice, the reality of which forces itself on every attentive observer.

This is why an authorized clarification from competent bodies seems to us greatly desirable. While waiting for it we are, in conscience, permitted to rely on the faculty expressly recognized by the Council for every priest to celebrate his Mass in private and to make use of this faculty in every possible measure. This manner of acting is not only inspired by a personal preference, which is entirely respectable. It is also based on the reality of the Eucharistic Mystery and on the doctrinal truth according to which each new celebration of the Mass realizes sacramentally a new outpouring of the redemptive Blood of Christ on His Church and the world.

2 A CRITICAL NOTE ON A 'THEOLOGY OF CONCELEBRATION'

WE HAD HARDLY finished compiling a certain number of *Témoignages et Documents*[1] on the subject of concelebration when we received Joseph Kleiner's *Théologie de la Concélébration. Réponse à quelques objections.*[2] Looking back a little later over the publication of those testimonies and other sympathetic responses evoked by our previous work, we wanted to present and analyze first the article from *Esprit et Vie;* for the 'objections' to which it wishes to respond are ours, those which we raised in our work of May 1979: *Réflexions et questions au sujet de la Concélébration.*[3] Furthermore, we had great joy in seeing this new reaction, above all because of the journal in which it had been published. That proved to us once again the urgency of the problem which we had raised. Unfortunately, the reading of that text disappointed us somewhat (abstracting from all questions regarding the person involved); for, in order to respond to objections, it is necessary first of all to begin by presenting them, and in their entirety—which in fact had not been done, the inevitable result being that there is an inexact idea of the thought refuted. That is exactly what happened. But while, having not exposed the thought, he also did not refute our 'thesis,' Joseph Kleiner, on the contrary, presented us his own, diametrically opposed to ours. This is what interests us above all else; and it is because of this that his work merits attention.

---

[1] 'Testimonies and Documents'.

[2] 'Theology of Concelebration–A Response to Some Objections'. In *Esprit et Vie*, 89, 1979 (no. 51; 20 December), pp. 671–80. We will reproduce the main points of these testimonies in the following chapter. The first part of the present chapter reproduces an article which appeared in *La Pensée Catholique* (henceforth cited as: *LPC*), no. 184 (January–February 1980), pp. 17–41.

[3] In *LPC*, no. 180 (May–June 1979), pp. 21–36 (*see above*, Ch. 1).

We shall examine therefore his thesis by faithfully presenting its content and its essential argument; and we shall show where its error lies. It is this which caused us to return to our own position in order to recall what had not been explained and, it seems, not even known by Joseph Kleiner, namely the theological argument on which it rests and which establishes its perfect conformity with both the teaching of the Common Doctor, St Thomas Aquinas, and the teaching of the Church's Magisterium.

In order to begin, let us be permitted to bring order once again to the matter and to pose the 'question' as we had posed it and think it ought necessarily to be posed. We shall justify this point of methodology in a moment by recalling especially the true place of the 'praxis' in sacramental theology. The question was twofold: doctrinal and practical. On the level of doctrine we asked: 'In a concelebrated Mass is there one or several Masses?' According to the response given to this first question it can already be said how the second question would be oriented, that of the practical order: 'Is it fitting *to multiply*—we emphasize this word—the practice of concelebration?' In fact, if in a concelebration the number of Masses were equal to that of the priest concelebrants, it would be indifferent for the common good of the Church whether these Masses be offered by way of concelebration or by way of private celebration. On the other hand, if in a concelebration there is only one Mass, we see the *dimunition* of the number of Eucharistic sacrifices brought about by the *multiplication* of concelebration. Still to be proven is the value of the multiplication of Masses for the Church, which constitutes the third question. Here we have, however, a theological teaching commonly admitted, about which our adversary agrees with us (indeed, his whole demonstration presupposes it). This is the precise point on which we propose to enter in a subsequent study in order to attempt a theological development.

The key question therefore which presently occupies our attention regards the number of Masses offered to God for the Church in a concelebrated Eucharist. This is of the doctrinal order. It is here where one must begin; for, in order for pastoral directives to be rightly ordered, they must be founded on doctrine. Joseph Kleiner is so convinced of this, giving so much space to the 'praxis' of the Church in a matter of liturgical and sacramental theology, that he devotes the greatest part of his study to explaining and justifying theologically his own thesis.[4] This thesis is summed up in the following statement: in

---

4   This is why we do not understand very well the logic of his discourse, where he excuses himself from not being able to 'follow' us when we ask our readers 'to tell us—but with clarity and precision—the reasons they think can be raised in favour of the thesis opposed to ours' (p. 21 of our article from May–June 1979; cited here p. 673, col. 1). First of all, we did not ask that one 'follow' us, but that one respond to us and even possibly that one oppose us. Our contradictor remembers the rest, in speaking immediately afterwards, as in the title of his article, of 'a response'. He did it, however, in a rather strange manner, since he writes: 'We do not think that his "reflections and questions" can receive a satisfactory response in an "anti–thesis"' (*ibid.*). This is, however, exactly what he proceeds to do. He himself recognizes this towards the end of his report, when having presented (as we had asked) the reasons that he thought could be advanced in favour of his thesis, which is opposed to ours, he writes concerning it: 'The "thesis" of the author surprises by its novelty and its lack of support in magisterial and theological tradition' (p. 679, col. 2). Why does he begin by pretending not to want to oppose one thesis with another, when that is exactly what he is going to do? We confess that we do not understand him. On the other hand, we formally protest against the procedure, which consists in exposing the thesis of an author as lacking magisterial and traditional theological support without even having taken care to present faithfully that same thesis. For, the reader of *Esprit et Vie*, after what is said to him, is incapable of knowing what it is we wrote. What is presented to that reader is even a gross distortion of our true thought, such as it was explicitly formulated in the article to which a response is supposedly given, and such as the reader can find in our present 'Note'. We account for Joseph Kleiner's attitude by the haste with which he wished to present and defend his own thesis; and we will show some proofs of his hastiness, notably in the way in which he pulls to his defense the Magisterium and St Thomas. We are counting on his intellectual honesty in order to establish the truth before the readers of *Esprit et Vie*, of which *La Pensée Catholique* reaches unfortunately but a small part. At least it will reach the most eminent part, notably the level

a concelebration there are as many Masses as there are concelebrating priests. And here is the theological foundation: it is that in this case, 'Christ brings about one consecration, but the ministers bring about many consecrations.'[5] And again: 'Christ confects one Sacrament, but the ministers perform many sacramental acts.'[6] This is the heart of the question; and page 675, col. 2, seems to convey the essential

---

of Episcopal authorities, and above all the Roman authorities, who regularly receive it, or who will receive this issue especially (no. 184, January–February 1980).

[5]   *Art. cit.,* p. 675, col. 2.

[6]   *Ibid.* As unacceptable as the preceding statement, this one seems to us even more inexplicable, since immediately beforehand the author wrote: 'Again, since the sacrament is accomplished in the consecration of the matter (*perficitur in ipsa consecratione materiae, S.T.* III, q. 83, a. 1, ad 3), Christ confects one Sacrament, but the ministers perform several sacramental acts.' Clearly he knows neither the sense nor the decisive impact of the text of St Thomas. We already have a clue in the shift which takes place between the 'Sacrament' (with a capital 'S', the signification of which we wonder at) which Christ works and which is unique, and the 'sacramental acts' which the ministers perform and which are as numerous as they are. The following citation (which we reproduce in our text) brings out this shift, since we see the thought passing from the *unique sacrifice* offered by Christ in concelebra- tion, to the *multiple ministerial offerings* of this unique sacrifice made by the concelebrants. We have here, to the letter (in the second part of this phrase), full Calvinism, since, as we know, for the church of the reform, at 'the Supper' there is a Eucharistic sacrifice in this sense: namely, there is offered to God the sacrifice of Christ formerly accomplished on Calvary (cf. ref. *in LPC,* no. 180, p. 31). The first part of the phrase and the citation from St Thomas shows that the author rejects this heresy and firmly holds by faith to the Catholic doctrine. However, there results a singular contradiction in his thought, at least such as he presents it to us here. We shall have the occasion of recalling the profound reason during our long analysis, but we can discern it now in the double shift which we just noted and even more still in this disassociation between what Christ does—which is unique, 'one consecration', 'one Sacra- ment', 'His unique sacrifice'—and what the ministers do—which is multiple, the 'ministerial offerings'. The reason for this contradiction is that *the instru- mental causality of the 'sacramental act'* has not been perceived, and only *the instrumental causality of the 'ministerial agent'* has been retained.

thought of the author. We read: ' … the consecration … Christ offers His unique Sacrifice, but each minister offers instrumentally this same sacrifice, such that there are *several ministerial offerings* of the unique sacrifice' (the italics are in the text). And to conclude, St Thomas is invoked in order to support this thesis:

> To sum up, for St Thomas, concelebration necessarily includes: a unique principal agent, Christ, the power of Whom is unique; multiple instruments; *multiple instrumental actions;* a unique end caused by the power of the principal agent acting *through the multiple agents* [here the italics are ours].

Such then is the thesis of the author and such are his arguments. Their mere reading leaves a strange impression, not to mention a contradiction. It can be asked, in fact, since priests do not act except insofar as they are ministers of Christ, how can they confect 'several consecrations' where He Whose ministers they are confects only one; and again, how can there be at the same time and in one liturgical act one sole sacrifice on the part of Christ and '*several ministerial offerings*' on the part of His ministers? How can this be, since precisely at the consecration Christ offers Himself through His ministers? Incidentally, that this contradiction has not been perceived by the author is not surprising, now that we know what it is that represents both the strength and the flaw of his argument.

He considers, in fact, only one thing: the fact that the priest acts as minister of Christ, and therefore that Christ acts only through His ministers. And he completely passes over in silence another fact—at least in practice and at the level of his theological implications; for he does mentions it here and there, particularly when he studies the question of the effect or fruits of the Mass: namely, the fact that the priest exercises his ministry in the accomplishment of the sacramental rite, and that Christ therefore accomplishes His work only by means of that ritual and sacramental gesture. Yet the cause of the sacrament, at the level of the ecclesial mediation, is neither solely in the *ministerial action* of the priest, nor solely in the *sacramental gesture,* but in both at the same time and inseparably. Such was the foundation of our own argument, in full conformity with the teaching of St Thomas Aquinas and the Magisterium of the Church. This is without a doubt the gravest point, but not the only one, on which Joseph Kleiner twists our thought by giving it only a partial presentation. Moreover, before ours it is the very thought of St Thomas that he deforms by mutilation. Clearly he did not understand its meaning. Furthermore, we have here a proof of that frequent ignorance of the essentially sacramental nature of the Eucharistic sacrifice which we ourselves denounce.[7] The author no doubt speaks well of the sacrament and the sacramental acts. However, in order to prove that in concelebration there are as many offerings of the sacrifice of Christ as there are concelebrating priests, he speaks of the '*ministerial offerings* of the unique sacrifice,' and not the *sacramental offerings;* and he himself emphasizes the expression which he uses in order to show that for him the crux of the question is here.

We shall reproduce in its entirety the central paragraph of the passage which we are analyzing (p. 675, col. 2); for it is here that he justifies the expression 'ministerial offering' and shows the decisive value that can be attributed to it. Here also appears the fundamental lacuna of this entire argument, as well as the ambiguity and theological errors which flow from it. Kleiner states:

> This multiplicity, at the level of the ministers, is not of the subjective order, for it is founded on that objective reality, of the spiritual order, which is the priestly character. According to the Common Doctor, the priestly character is especially ordered to that act of worship which is the offering of the sacrifice (qu. 63, a. 6). To deny the real multiplicity of the ministerial acts is to deny the real instrumental causality of the priests; and this is to call into question the theology of the

---

7   *LPC,* no. 180, p. 32. See also our work in *LPC,* no. 153 (November–December 1974); see below, Ch. 9.

minister as elaborated by St Thomas, followed by the Council
of Trent and Vatican II.

In itself this paragraph is perfect (at least in the doctrine which is
recalled, if not in the manner in which it is presented). And he adds
what we ourselves present in our own thesis. However, by the silence
concerning the *sacramental act,* the notion of the *ministerial act* which
emanates from it becomes charged with ambiguity, an ambiguity
which redounds to the entire argument and ends up completely
draining it of all force as well as the definitive character which one
believed to be able to give it. If the aspect of the ministerial offering
were the only one to be considered, this argument would in fact be
decisive, and we would have to grant that the number of ministers
suffices to multiply the number of Masses in one and the same
concelebration. But if, on the contrary, in addition to this ministerial
aspect and *at the same time as it,* one must consider as well the aspect
of the sacramental offering—which the author does not do—then
his reasoning does not hold; for, in this case what is decisive for the
question of the number of Masses is the fact that the sacrifice that is
offered happens only by and in the rite, and therefore by and in the
sacramental act that is celebrated. Such was the substance of our
thesis, following St. Thomas and the Magisterium, as we have shown
and shall repeat again later on: since it is only by and in the sacramental act that the sacrifice of the Mass is offered, where one sole
sacramental act is performed, whatever be the number of concelebrants, one sole Mass, one Eucharistic sacrifice is immolated and
offered to God.

How so? Excuse us for repeating it once more; but we shall present
it now by adding a new explanation, which, while it also is a reminder,
will help our opponent to understand that *it is impossible to reduce as
he does the entire instrumental causality to only the ministerial causality
of the priest.* For it is definitely there that the error is found. The
reminder of which we are thinking is the distinction (which is also
fundamentally thomistic) between an immanent act and a transitive

act: *actus immanens* and *actus transiens*.[8] The first act is called immanent because its term remains within the subject that performs it, as
for example, the act of thinking or imagining. On the other hand, the
act whose term is found outside the subject that performs it is called
transitive (*transiens*), because there is a passage, a 'transition' from
the interior to the exterior of the subject that acts. Thus, for example,
to conceive or to imagine a house is an immanent act; for, to accomplish this act it suffices to make use of the faculty of interior representation and to exercise it. But to build the house of one's dreams is a
transitive act; for it is not accomplished except by using a certain
number of instruments and materials, exterior to the builder (trowel,
bricks, cement, etc.), and by the performance of a certain number of
operations and acts equally exterior, in view of assembling harmoniously these materials by means of these instruments.

We see immediately how this doctrine, as profound as it is simple,
shines light on our problem, especially if we recall also that the
transitive act, in order for it to be fully human—to be an *actus
humanus* and not just simply an *actus hominis*—always presupposes
a previous immanent act of which it is the execution. Thus, in the
concelebration of the Mass, the intention to celebrate and the implementation of the knowledge of the rites to be accomplished are the
immanent acts previous to the celebration itself and presupposed by
it. But the celebration of the rite itself is a transitive act: it is accomplished in essence when the priest pronounces the words of consecration over the matter to be consecrated. This very act is *ministerial*
insofar as it is accomplished by the priest; for he does it only insofar
as he is the minister of Christ. It is *sacramental* insofar as it is accomplished by the pronouncing of Christ's words over the bread and wine,
the matter of the sacrament, that is by the execution of the liturgical

---

8   *S.T. I*, q. 54, a. 2. This distinction is not to be confused, despite the closeness,
     with that which moral theology makes between the 'interior act' (*elicitus a
     voluntate*) and the 'exterior act' (*imperatus a voluntate*); I–II, q. 18, a. 6; q. 19;
     q. 20. See below, note 42.

rite instituted by Christ and later ordered by the Church; for, it is in this rite that the sacrament is confected. Joseph Kleiner was completely right in proclaiming strongly the realism of the instrumental causality of the priest, and in calling it a 'ministerial causality,' since the priest acts here insofar as he is the minister. However, in order to know in their totality both the Eucharistic mystery and, in a general way, the instrumental causality which is at work in its celebration, it is necessary to affirm *at the same time as* this instrumental ministerial causality—and not in place of it—the realism of the instrumental causality of the liturgical rite, which we call 'sacramental instrumental causality' by reason of the rite's sacramental character. We insist on the simultaneity of these two aspects. They are so inseparable that one is astonished to see them disassociated from each other. This is the very reason, we confess, why it did not seem to us possible to support a thesis opposed to that of St Thomas. However, we included it without the surrounding nominalism. Yet what we present in detail is elementary. How, in fact, in a 'transitive action,' does one consider *the subject that acts* without considering at the same time *the act* which it accomplishes? Can the effect be accomplished by only the interiority of the subject without the performance of the exterior acts? This is obviously impossible. That is why the author himself was moved to speak of that exterior act, but without recognizing its proper instrumental causality. And yet, what then is the *ministerial action* apart from *the sacramental act* which it performs and in which the minister exercises his ministry and actualizes the sacrifice of Christ?

* * *

All of the weakness of our author's argument comes then from the fact that he has in reality held onto only the ministerial aspect. This was, in fact, the only means of establishing his thesis; and yet we have seen how it affects his demonstration. In addition, he does not manage to sustain the thesis except at the price of a certain amount of silence and deformed interpretations: silence concerning our own very explicit texts, which, even if they had been lacking in authority, would nevertheless needed to be reproduced, since it was to them that he wanted to respond first of all; silence concerning the key passage of a central text of St Thomas, which, consequently, is interpreted in the opposite sense; and the distorting as well as contradictory interpretation of the Magisterium's principal text concerning our problem. We shall prove this.

Here, first of all, is our own text, which ought to have been at the very least cited or summarized. Synthesizing our own explanation, we said:

> Such are the three fundamental doctrinal truths which allow us to resolve the question of concelebration. One can even say that there is but one fundamental truth, the *sacramental nature of the action* accomplished in the Mass; for, it is there that one must begin. However, at the same time we can consider this primary truth in two immediate corollaries: a) *the ministerial character of the priest* of the Church, through whom Christ acts, and b) *the liturgical character and ritual* of the accomplished act. We consider also the ordering and subordination of the *ministers* to the *liturgical and sacramental ritual* which they accomplish, and in which they themselves are fulfilled—hence the primacy of the sacramental act over the person of the ministers when considering the number of Masses in a concelebration. Based on this foundation, both unique and threefold, we can understand why the number of ministers through whom Christ the High Priest acts, matters little, or more precisely why it matters not at all (*non refert*), as St Thomas says, for the concelebration of a Mass. And, consequently, the only way of multiplying the number of Eucharistic sacrifices is not by multiplying the number of ministers of concelebration, which produces the opposite effect, but rather to multiply the liturgical celebrations of the sacramental rite of the Mass.[9]

---

9   *LPC*, no. 180, p. 34; and above, pp. 20–1, where one will note the paragraph which we subsequently added.

Instead of taking up this text and discussing it, as he would have had to do in order to give a 'response' (which is what he declared he would do), the author passes over it in silence and gives us his thesis right away, the sense and argumentation of which we have already related. It is only in this manner, however, that is by beginning with an explanation of the opposing point of view before critiquing it, that the reader is placed in a position to compare the two theses and to form his personal opinion.

There is the same silence regarding the most important passage of the text of St Thomas. Here is the text itself:

> But because the priest consecrates only by acting in the person and name of Christ (*in persona Christi*), and because many are 'one in Christ' (Gal 3:28), it matters little whether this sacrament be consecrated by one or by many. What is necessary is that the rite of the Church be observed.[10]

We find here the three fundamental truths on which we rest our thesis: the sacramental character of the sacrifice of the Mass, the liturgical and ritual aspect of the act in which the sacrament is celebrated, and the ministerial function of the priest. Here, in opposition to our thesis, is the commentary of Joseph Kleiner:

> But since the priests consecrate by the power of Christ, all are one in Christ, and it matters little if the sacrament is consecrated by one or by several. *This unique effect* which is the consecration, considered in relation to the principal agent Christ, results from the unique power of Christ; but considered in relation to the multiple instruments which are the

---

[10] '*Quia sacerdos non consecrat nisi in persona Christi, multi autem sunt unum in Christo (Gal 3;28), ideo non refert utrum per unum vel per multos hoc sacramentum consecratur: nisi quod oportet ritum Ecclesiae servari*' (*S.T. III*, q. 82, a. 2, 3.). When he speaks about the role of the ministers, St Thomas emphasizes the unity realized in concelebration. The last part of the phrase was cited on p. 672, col. 1, but only under the aspect of the 'practice of the Church' which this rite represents.

priests, acting *in persona Christi* by the fact of their priestly character, there result multiple acts.[11]

One can see that not a word is said about what is for St Thomas the essential condition: the performing of the essential sacramental gesture, the consecration, in deference to the rite of the Church. Certainly it is not denied. One might even say that it is presupposed. But one only needs to look at the analyses of the author's texts which we made above and which tell us whether this instrumental causality of the sacramental gesture accomplished in the liturgical rite is truly presupposed. Evidently, the opposite is the case, as is necessary for the author's thesis. Only one of the following is possible: either the instrumental causality is entirely from the side of the minister, and it then becomes possible to hold that the number of concelebrants multiplies by itself the number of Masses ('possible' but not yet proven; for the conditions would still need to be examined for this); or the *instrumental* causality is simultaneously exercised both by the *minister* and by the *sacramental liturgical* gesture, and then one is forced, with St Thomas, to admit that where one sole sacramental and liturgical act is performed, only one Mass is offered, whatever be the number of co-ministers who accomplish this act.

With St Thomas, and with the Magisterium; the author does not pass over the latter in silence. Knowing its importance, he gives it a very long and grammatical analysis. Let us recall first the text itself, the *General Decree, Ecclesiae semper* (7 March 1965). Therein is written, concerning concelebration:

> In this manner of celebrating Mass [concelebration], several priests, in virtue of the same priesthood and by acting in the person of the High Priest, act together with one intention and

---

[11] *Art. cit.,* p. 675, cols. 1–2. We note—for it is extremely significant—that it is insufficient to call the consecration an 'effect'. The consecration is first of all the sacramental act which the priests bring about. Its effects are transubstantiation, which effectively causes one consecration of the 'matter', and that which accompanies it.

one voice (*simul una voluntate et una voce agunt*), and they
confect and offer by one sacramental act one unique sacrifice
(*atque unicum Sacrificium unico actu sacramentali simul conficiunt et offerunt*), and they participate in it together.[12]

The doctrine of St Thomas is clearly found here, cited moreover in
the paragraph immediately preceding this one. There is also found,
however, both in the interpretation and especially in the author's
translation, the deviations noted above. In fact, playing on the fact
that the Latin language does not have a definite article, he translates
'*unicum sacrificium*' as 'the unique Sacrifice,' by explaining that the
end of the action of the concelebrants is 'the Sacrifice of Christ
[which] is one,' the Sacrifice of the Cross. Yet the manifest intention
of the text is to oppose 'this manner of celebrating,' where 'by one
unique sacramental act one unique Eucharistic sacrifice' is offered, to
the other manner of celebrating, that of private celebrations, where
by multiple sacramental acts multiple Eucharistic celebrations are
offered. With respect to the 'complement of the agent'—which
indicates precisely the instrumental sacramental cause that he passed
over in silence, author explains: 'the complement of the agent (*unico
actu sacramentali*) is singular because the *virtus* of the principal agent
is one.'[13] Here the author places himself in contradiction not only
with the text of the Magisterium, but also with himself; for if he
rereads his words, he will see that he ends up denying that which he
affirmed so strongly above, namely the ministerial instrumental
causality. In fact, he considers the act of consecration as being
produced immediately by the principal cause, Christ. But what is even
more unacceptable for a disciple of St Thomas is the manner in which
the *act* is reduced to the *power,* the '*virtus.*' Nothing in fact prevents

---

[12]   *AAS* 57, 1965, pp. 410–12. See our commentary in *LPC*, no. 180, p. 29. We
do not wish to give to this text a weight greater than it has. Nevertheless, solidly
founded in tradition and theology, referred to twice by the Magisterium itself
(cf. *LPC*, no. 180, pp. 30–1), it enjoys a level of incontestable authority.

[13]   *Art. cit.*, p. 677, col. 2.

one single power from producing several acts. As we saw above, this is precisely the thesis of the author, since for him where Christ works only one consecration the ministers work several! He does not escape a series of contradictions to which his silence about the instrumental causality of the rite (that is the sacramental act) necessarily leads. What needs to be said here, as the text explicitly does, is that 'the sacramental act' is unique because the liturgical rite accomplished is one: '*unico actu sacramentali*' [*quia*] '*simul una voluntate et una voce agunt.*' This is why, in concelebration, there is only one Mass: one sole sacrifice, '*unicum sacrificium,*' is offered to God for the common good of the Church.

We see how, from there, ambiguities arise concerning the principal texts, which we cited above. We repeat simply the last one, the analysis of which also allows us to rectify the others: 'In summation,' he says, 'concelebration necessarily includes ... *multiple instrumental actions*' between the beginning, Christ, Who is one, and the end, which is also one, that is the sacrifice of Christ. We see better now how this manner of presenting the mystery telescopes the sacramental action. Where he speaks of *multiple instrumental actions,* we say yes, in a strict sense, if it is a question of *ministerial* actions; for it is exactly true that the unique liturgical action is produced by multiple ministerial concelebrants. But we say no, if it is a question of the sacramental action itself; for this is one, as is the liturgical rite by which and in which it is accomplished. By referring to the schema-summation of the author, we see then, that among his 'multiple *sacramental* actions,' presented as exclusively *ministerial,* and the 'end,' the sacrifice of Christ, there is lacking the essential, namely the *sacramental* act, by which alone the sacrifice of Christ is 're-acted' on the altar.

The practical ignorance regarding this central aspect of the sacramental mystery appeared even more obviously (if that is possible) where the author treats the fruits of the sacrifice of the Mass. In fact, in recalling the doctrine of the Council of Trent and the teaching of Pius XII, he mentions explicitly and twice 'the sacramental and sacrificial act of the priest': 'the fruits of the Mass,' he says, 'are caused principally by the bloody sacrifice of Calvary, but instrumentally by the sacramental and sacrificial act of the priest.' They 'derive from the nature of the sacramental and sacrificial act performed by the priest.'[14] This is exactly right; and we find there not only our own thesis but the traditional teaching of theology and the Magisterium. In the following paragraph, however, this entire teaching is effaced; for again, he retains only the instrumental causality of the action of the priest: 'All these fruits of the Mass, without distinction, derive therefore from the *ministerial act* of the priest as the effect from *its* instrumental cause. When *the cause* takes place, the effect follows.'[15] It is clear: the totality of the instrumental causality is placed in 'the ministerial act' of the priest, with all the ambiguity with which this expression is here charged. What follows confirms it, showing at the same time why the author is drawn to this aspect alone and in what sense he intends it. He will even write, not without radically falsifying the sense of the text of Pius XII on which he pretends to base himself: 'The spiritual fruits of the Sacrifice *are caused ministerially* by the intention which the exterior act of each priest follows; the fruits are multiplied with the intentions and corresponding acts.'[16] Here the emphasis is the

---

[14]   *Ibid.*, p. 679, col. 1.

[15]   Emphasis ours.

[16]   Immediately before, the author had written that Pius XII, in his discourse of 1954, 'does not distinguish in any way between the fruits of one hundred Masses celebrated individually and the fruits of one hundred Masses concelebrated by those same priests, because the nature of the act is identical, so are the fruits of the Mass'. The first part of the sentence is correct, but the explanation of it, which is given in the second part, is entirely without any motive or foundation. The truth is that Pius XII in no way distinguished between the fruits of one hundred Masses celebrated individually and the fruits of one Mass celebrated by the concelebration of one hundred priests, because he was not concerned with this problem in this discourse. The only question he was examining at that time was the difference between one Mass celebrated by one sole priest, the other priests assisting, and the one hundred Masses that they would have celebrated individually. We showed this in our *Réflexions et questions au sujet de la Concélébration* (*LPC*, no. 180, p. 24). We showed there also how it is only in the 1956 discourse that Pius XII developed the question of concelebration, with the

author's own. We are not therefore misrepresenting his view when we affirm that Kleiner in fact retains only the ministerial causality without recognizing in the sacramental liturgical act its proper instrumental causality. For him, the multiplicity of 'intentions' seems sufficient to realize the multiplicity of 'exterior acts.' Without mentioning the unacceptable latent idealism which such a proposition conceals, it denies the fact that, in concelebration, all the priests act *'simul una voluntate et una voce.'* It is not, therefore, simply the exterior act of concelebration which is one, but also the will, and therefore the intention, which animates and unites those who accomplish it. Certainly, each priest has personally the intention of celebrating, and in this sense there are as many intentions as priests. But all those intentions are united in that 'one will,' as all those voices unite in that 'one voice,' in order to accomplish the 'one sacrifice' offered to God in the one concelebration. On the other hand, the author makes the multiplicity of fruits flow from the multiplicity of intentions, and thus they are as numerous as the ministers offering the sacrifice; and he does this because from that multiplicity of intentions he makes flow first of all the 'corresponding acts ... ,' that is, not the consecration or sacrifices which they sacramentally bring about, but the *'ministerial*

---

declared explicit intention of 'clarifying certain points regarding it.' It is there that he recalls, without citing him, the teaching of St Thomas on this question: 'In the case of a concelebration in the proper sense of the word, Christ, in place of acting through one minister acts through many.' 'The decisive question', he added, is that of the accomplished act; 'Does the priest or not, as minister of Christ, perform the *actio Christi se ipsum sacrificantis et offerentis?'* And he does it only 'if, with the necessary interior intention ... [he] accomplishes the exterior action and especially pronounces the words which constitute the *actio Christi* ....' From this we see that 'the interior intention' is not sufficient to make the exterior act. It is required, certainly; but what takes place at the same time is the accomplishment of the exterior rites, gests and words. This is so evident that no one would dream of denying it; but the theological consequences are not equally perceived by all. What concerns us here, and what Pius XII in fact teaches by his implicit reference to St Thomas, is that where the exterior rite is one, as in concelebration, 'Christ, in place of acting by one sole minister, acts by several,' in order to offer one sole sacrifice. Whence it follows that, with regards to the *actio Christi, the fruits* are those of one sole Mass.

offerings of the one sacrifice ... ' Once again, this is to retain only one point of view; or more precisely, it is to consider the exterior act—for it is mentioned—as immediately and necessarily produced by the interior act, the intention, without considering it in itself, in its proper reality and in the realism of its specific instrumental causality: the sacramental causality of the liturgical rite. This, then, is to go backwards in what is required in healthy sacramental theology; and in every way, it is to go directly against the most explicit teaching of the Magisterium and the Common Doctor.

In reality the true inspirer of Kleiner's theology is not St Thomas Aquinas, even if the author presents himself as his 'disciple,'[17] but Suarez. The long, the very long text of his that he reserved for the end as his strongest argument from theological authority merits examination. We find there the radical defect which we were able to observe in the course of the preceding analyses, namely the polarization of attention to the acting subject to the detriment of the exterior act which that subject accomplishes, and consequently the reduction of instrumental causality to the ministerial aspect alone, the sacramental and ritual aspect of this same causality being practically effaced, indeed even doubted. Did not Suarez go so far as to consider as 'probable, but not certain,' that in concelebration transubstantiation is made by one sole act?[18] It is logical to begin at the moment that he says that: 'although the *result* is one, there are *as many actions* as there are instruments regardless of who makes it happen' [i.e. the sacrament]—*tot actiones ... quot instrumenta totalia.* From here there is but a step—which he immediately takes—to the 1954 text of Pius XII. We immediately point out, however, the two essential differences which exist between the two texts. The first is that Pius XII does not explicitly treat of concelebration in this discourse of 2 November 1954, even if he mentions it; but rather, he is thinking about a very particular question: he compares the concelebration of one sole Mass

---

[17] *Art. cit.,* p. 672, col. 2.

[18] *Ibid.,* p. 680, col. 1.

by one sole priest with 99 other priests present and assisting, with the celebration of one hundred private Masses by the same one hundred priests. It is in this context that his words must be understood: there are 'as many actions as there are priests celebrating'—'*tot actiones quot sacerdotes celebrantes.*' One must not, then, make the text say what in fact it does not.[19] The second difference is that Pius XII speaks of '*sacerdotes celebrantes,*' not of '*instrumenta totalia,*' an ambiguous expression which he never used.

Now if it is correct that the concelebrating priests are as many instruments 'regardless of who makes the sacrament happen,' insofar as each one is fully the co-minister of the sacrament, it is necessary to add that the instruments that they are, are not in themselves the complete and total cause of the sacrament; or, if you will, they are not the complete and total cause of the 'one result' which their action produces. In order to be complete, this cause, in its own order—that of instrumentality—must equally include the sacramental liturgical act which the ministers con-celebrate together; and since this act is one, we have a concelebration, and one sole Mass is offered. This is what Suarez, being too exclusively attached to one point of view, did not see. His error is easily explained when one thinks of the intellectual climate in which his theology was conceived. Nominalism had left its traces, and young humanism was already making its effects felt. The subject would later outweigh everything, and the thinking *ego* would become the center of the world, its first principle and its ultimate end. It certainly was not yet there during the sixteenth century; but if we compare this theology to that of St Thomas, we see that the way was already being paved.

For the theologian of the sixteenth century, the fact 'that the thing offered is one,' that the 'matter' ('the sacramental species of bread and wine') is one also, and that transubstantiation takes place by one sole act—specifically the sacramental act accomplished in the liturgical rite—matters nothing at all.[20] What matters most for him is the

---

[19]   See our analysis in *LPC*, no. 180, p. 24.

number of ministers and the interior acts which they make. For St Thomas, on the other hand, this number does not matter, *non refert*; what matters first and foremost is that the liturgical rite be accomplished, for it is principally in this, that is, in the action which is realized, that the sacramental instrumental causality resides. The opposition between the two positions is radical and the change of orientation highly significant. From the incontestable fact that each priest in a concelebration 'acts as an integral minister,' one passes to the assertion which makes of each of them the *instrumentum totale* of the sacrifice, with all the ambiguity which this expression carries: it is correct if we speak of a total instrument insofar as the minister exercises the fullness of his priesthood—at least with respect to the essential act of the Mass, the consecration; but it is false if we speak of a total instrument insofar as he causes and confects the sacrament by himself. We believe we have sufficiently shown why.

With respect to the conclusion which follows that long citation and which claims to emphasize the agreement of Suarez, St Thomas and Pius XII, we see as well why it is without foundation. Yes, Pius XII is in full accord with the Common Doctor, certainly; but they both teach a doctrine which is the radical negation of Suarez's theses.

There is no difficulty with regard to the fact that many persons acting together can accomplish only one action; for, as we are appropriately reminded by Joseph Kleiner, in good Thomistic doctrine, 'it is no way contradictory that a reality be one under one relation and multiple under another.'[21] The reality under consideration here is the concelebration of the sacrament of the Eucharist: all that happens by the ministers is the multiplicity aspect; but they celebrate only by the accomplishment of the liturgical and sacramental rite, which is the unity aspect. This is what the word 'concelebration' very fittingly and precisely expresses: several priests con-celebrating, that is, celebrating together one sole Eucharist, offering together one sole sacrifice of the

---

[20] *Art. cit.*, pp. 679, cols. 2–680, col. 1.

[21] *Ibid.*, p. 675, col. 2.

Mass. To deny this is to empty concelebration of that which is most substantial and most significant in it.

In order to help us understand how several persons acting together can accomplish only one sole act, we shall take two examples, one from below, the other from above concelebration. The example from below is taken from the case of building a house: there are several persons who build, several builders, and nevertheless by the fact that they work together for the same project, there is one sole construction which takes place and one sole house which is built. One would not speak of *constructions*, but of *the construction* taking place, and consequently of the construction realized by the builders. The example from above is that of the 'procession' of the Holy Spirit in the Trinity: nothing 'distinguishes' the Father from the Son in the 'spiration' of the Third Person of the Trinity; and nevertheless both really 'spirate,' since the Holy Spirit proceeds from the Father and Son. There is in the Trinity two Persons Who spirate, but one sole spiration. St Thomas affirms that there is even only one Principal Spirator: '*duo spirantes,*' but '*unus spirator*' and '*una spiratio.*'[22] All proportions being respected, it is the same in concelebration, where there are several '*celebrantes,*' the 'concelebrants,' but one sole '*celebratio,*' the concelebration.

Simple analogies, the close examination of which takes us very far and is quite enlightening, but which suffice to allow us to understand where, in a eucharistic concelebration, is the multiplicity—that is, of the ministers—and where is the unity—namely in the accomplished liturgical act, and therefore in the celebrated sacrament and the sacrifice offered. This unity of the sacramental act is so strong that it pulls along with it, in a sense, the action of the ministers themselves. This is what is emphasized by the text of the Decree *Ecclesiae semper,* when it affirms that the concelebrants 'act together by one sole will and one sole voice.' The unity is realized, therefore, already on the side of the ministers themselves insofar as they act together, accomplishing in common one and the same exterior action.

---

[22] *S.T. I,* q. 36, a. 4, 7.

This is why, in the perspective where the author is situated, more than of 'the multiple ministerial *actions*,' he wants to speak of multiple ministerial *agents*, the personal and ministerial action of these multiple agents finding a certain unity in concelebration precisely insofar as it is ministerial. This is what we shall be thinking about later on when we will concede only with reservations that one can speak of 'multiple (ministerial) instrumental actions': yes, that is what we said 'strictly speaking'; for, if one considers the ministers in their own personalities, it is undeniable that each of them poses a personal act. In this sense there are as many acts as concelebrants. However, if we consider them precisely insofar as they concelebrate, we see that in this action they make but one in the priesthood of Christ. It is this which the several cited documents emphasize. In this sense we must therefore say that there is but one sole *ministerial action;* while there are always as many *ministerial agents,* or priests acting ministerially, as there are concelebrants. It is a question, as Joseph Kleiner justly said, of a 'collective unity.'[23] It is there that concelebration manifests the unity of the

---

[23] *Art. cit.,* p. 677, col. 2: 'In a word, it is a question of a collective unity, that of the *Ordo sacerdotum* .... ' However, what follows shows us once more how, speaking 'materially' of the sacramental act, the author 'formally' passes over in silence its efficacy, at least concerning concelebration: '... a collective unity, that of the *Ordo sacerdotum,* in which each priest and each of the sacramental acts of the priest has an irreducible and unconfused efficacy, from the fact of the infinite power of the principal agent: that which happens by one happens also by several, but in every case, whether the instrument be one or multiple, the nature and value of the instrumental act are the same' (pp. 677, cols. 2–678, col. 1). Very well, but the conclusion which clears it up is that, where 'the instrumental act', the sacramental act, is one, there is only one sacrifice. Moreover, this is the impression which one has in reading that page, where the author is constrained to admit: 'the documents of the Magisterium, after the Council, insisted more, it must be admitted, on the unity in concelebration than on the multiplicity'. They have, in fact, explicitly taught that whatever be the number of concelebrants, the concelebration produces one sacrifice only. And yet the author did not abandon his thesis, which he reaffirms on the following page: that of 'the multiplicity of the sacrifices offered' in concelebration (p. 679, col.1). The lack of clear logic which can be observed here comes

priesthood of Christ, and the unity of the priests in this one priesthood of which they are ministers.

For, that which is 'ministerial' in the proper sense is the agent who accomplishes the sacramental act, the priest who acts insofar as he is the minister of Christ. And that which is 'sacramental,' in the strict use of the term, is the act which he accomplishes, with the rites, words and matter of which it is composed: it is in this that the sacrament consists; it is in this that the sacrament is celebrated and administered. Certainly, this act can be called 'ministerial' insofar as it is accomplished by the authorized minister. Just as this minister can be called 'sacramental' insofar as he is consecrated by a sacrament and in order to celebrate the sacraments. But in the proper and immediate sense, *primo et per se,* the adjective 'ministerial' pertains to the agent who celebrates the sacrament, and that of 'sacramental' to the act in which the sacrament is celebrated. This is why, in the case of the Eucharist, where this act is one, one also is the sacrifice of the Mass offered to God.

Unity of sacramental action, plurality of ministerial agents: this formula could summarize our explanation, but on the condition that it is not too inflexible. In reality, it is already at the level of the ministers, as we have seen, that without denying their plurality, the unity begins to be realized. This is what was indicated by the formula we employed above: 'one sole ministerial action'; we now see in what sense it is to be understood. And it is necessary that it be so; because in order for the *sacramental action* to be one, it does not suffice that the *liturgical act* be one. It is necessary also that a certain unity be realized, through the plurality of agents, on the side of the *ministerial cause* itself. Joseph Kleiner speaks, in a general way, only of a *collective*

---

entirely, in our opinion, from the constant ambiguity in which the thought moves, and from the reduction of the fact (at the moment of drawing the conclusions) of the instrumental causality to the ministerial causality alone; to the point that 'the sacramental act' itself is not formally seen, with regards to its efficacy as well as to the fact that it is ministerial. This is really the only way of maintaining that the number of ministers suffices for multiplying the number of sacrifices offered.

unity, an expression inspired by Fr de la Taille. But de la Taille spoke at first of a collegial unity: *'unius collegii una actio collectiva.'*[24] And, as we see here, the unity of the college acting as such brought about the unity of action, which it accomplished collegially.

More precise still, St Thomas tells us exactly how to understand this unity. While in the *Summa* he is content with recalling briefly the initial foundation: the priests 'are one in Christ,' that is to say in His priesthood, for He remains the true 'Principal Celebrant';[25] in the *Sentences,* St Thomas shows in what this unity consists and how it is realized, namely in the act accomplished by all the priests together, and precisely by their intention to accomplish it together. Responding to the objection that is based on the principle according to which a plurality of agents brings about a plurality of actions, he responds: 'the intention is required for the accomplishment of the sacraments. Consequently, by the fact that all [the concelebrating priests] have the intention of performing one [sole] consecration, there is there only one sole consecration': *Quia intentio requiritur ad perfectionem sacramentorum, ideo, cum omnes habeant intentionem unam consecrationem faciendi, non est ibi nisi una consecratio tantum.*[26]

One cannot oppose to this reasoning the fact that each priest offers the Mass according to the particular intention which is confided to him: whence the plurality of intentions, one would say. For, we immediately see the equivocation on which this objection rests: the intention of confecting the sacrament, about which St Thomas speaks, is not the same as the intention by which the fruits are applied, that on which the objection attempts to base itself. Or more precisely, perhaps, the particular intentions to which the Mass is applied are always registered within and dependent upon the primary and general intention for which the Eucharistic sacrifice is primarily offered. This intention is directed towards the whole of the Church, the Mystical

---

[24] *Mysterium fidei,* Paris, Beauchesne, 1931, p. 328, note 1.

[25] *S.T. III,* q. 82, a. 2, 2.

[26] *In IV Sent.,* d. 13, q. 1, a. 2, qla. 2, 1.

Body of Christ. It is one with the intention of 'confecting the sacrament' of which St Thomas speaks, and it is in it that the particular secondary intentions of the different concelebrants are registered. It is, then, in this primary intention, that of confecting the sacrament and offering the sacrifice for the whole Church, that the concelebrants unite in order to form but *one sole ministerial cause* of the *one unique sacramental action,* which they accomplish together.

Thus it is—it seems to us—that, in concelebration the unity and the plurality meet on the level of the ministerial cause itself. It is important to emphasize that this unity is realized in act only in the accomplishment of the sacramental action. The latter, therefore, is one, both because one also is the liturgical ritual action in which it is accomplished and because one, formally, is its instrumental ministerial cause, despite its material plurality: the concelebrating priests are united to the point of becoming one through their intention of consecrating together one and the very same host, in one and the very same ritual action. The doctrine of St Thomas and of the Decree *Ecclesiae semper* seem to impose this theological explanation.

Such then is 'our' thesis. We say 'our' thesis; or rather, it is attributed to us as 'our' thesis, because we presented it by demonstrating its theological foundations. However, we also brought forward magisterial documents, which oblige the reader to recognize that there is here more a doctrine taught by the authority of the Church than a particular theological thesis. This is all the more reason why it is not possible to attribute to us a doubtful opinion. We have also seen that the opposing thesis does not stand up to analysis, and that it is unable be defended except at the price of an amputation and a seriously deformed interpretation of magisterial texts, not to mention its opposition to the teaching of the Common Doctor. It also goes against what the best informed liturgical sense moves us to think, as proven by the statement below, from one of the principal representatives of the liturgical movement after the war, whose authority is widely recognized in the matter by the promoters of this movement:

Dom Bernard Botte, OSB. Comparing the concelebrated Eucharist to an Episcopal consecration, which is done by several consecrating bishops, he writes:

> From both sides we are faced with a collective sacramental act, which consists in an action the sense of which is given by the prayer of the presider. Just as the bishops have the intention of communicating the Holy Spirit and manifesting it through their common action, so the priests who stand around the bishop have the intention of offering the Eucharistic oblation with the bishop; and they manifest this intention at the same time by their presence around him and by the action which they perform with him. However, we must also say that *this oblation is one.* Just as there are not several synchronized episcopal consecrations, but one only, made by the whole episcopal body present, so *there is only one sole Eucharistic consecration accomplished by the whole priestly body, and not several synchronized Masses.*[27]

On the basis of these most certain doctrinal and liturgical facts we will be ready to pass directly to the following question—one of the practical order—by asking the reader to distinguish what we said from what we did not say: we rejoice with the whole Church over the widened use of Eucharistic concelebration brought about by Vatican II; but we ask ourselves whether the extension, the generalization, the systematic multiplication of concelebration is appropriate, that is whether it is in conformity with the common good of the Church. We said, on the basis of the response to the preliminary doctrinal question, in which sense there is a need for a response to this second question; but we added that we were expressing there an opinion and personal request, one which we submit in advance to the decisions of the Magisterium.[28]

---

[27] *Note historique sur la concélébration dans l'Eglise ancienne*, in *La Maison Dieu*, no. 35 (3rd trim. 1953), p. 13. The italics are ours.

[28] *LPC*, no. 180, p. 21.

Nevertheless, before pursuing our reflection on this point—at the same time with respect for the Magisterium and in the just exercise of the liberty of development which the latter grants to the theologian—the article of Joseph Kleiner obliges us to halt here in order to pose one or two other questions. We had left them aside, for the most part, we confess, because of their extreme seriousness (at least as regards the second question), but also out of concern for the method, that is we did not want to deal with all the problems at the same time. These two questions regard the following: 1) the nature and place of the 'practice of the Church' in matters of liturgical and sacramental theology; 2) the Magisterium in some of its post-conciliar manifestations.

*   *   *

Concerned with establishing his path theologically, Joseph Kleiner describes his method in these words: 'Theology, considered as such, is a science subordinated to the science of Christ; it draws its principles from divine revelation received by faith. The theology of the sacraments, in particular, proceeds from principles furnished by that expression of the faith, which is the *practice* of the Church.'[29] Here it is necessary to note that the line which binds these two sentences is not immediately evident. We hold, in good logic, that the theology of the sacraments, as all theology, 'draws its principles from divine revelation,' given in the Gospel and Tradition,[30] and that it finds them 'in particular' in that privileged part of Tradition, which is the liturgical practice of the Church. Such is the sense in which this declaration can and must be understood.

Neverthelesss, because of its imprecision, the declaration can be taken in another sense. There is, in fact, a sort of break between the two sentences of which it is composed (and we can understand this, as the grammatical logic of the text even invites it) like this: in what

---

[29]   *Art. cit.*, p. 671, col. 2.

[30]   'Sacra Traditio et Sacra Scriptura unum verbi Dei sacrum depositum constituunt Ecclesiae commissum.' (Vatican II, *Const. Dogm. De Divina Revelatione*, 10; cf. Vatican I, *Const. Dogm. De Fide Catholica*, cap. III: DS 3011).

concerns the 'particular' case of the theology of the sacraments, the point of departure is found completely in 'that expression of the faith—[by which divine revelation is received]—which is the *practice* of the Church.' Now what follows shows that this in fact is the sense which was retained by the author. He even ends up writing: 'The theology of the sacraments therefore is legitimately founded only on usage, and the current usage of the Church.' It is this which we feared when we read in the initial declaration: the absolute point of departure of sacramental theology is in the practice, that is, in the usage of the Church. What is more, its ultimate norm is its 'current usage.'

We can immediately see the double inversion which has been employed. According to this theological methodology, a recent innovation would be placed above the traditional practice—one which is ancient; and this same practice would be considered to have more value for founding sacramental theology than the theological principles drawn from divine revelation and which are found primarily in Sacred Scripture and in magisterial texts, as well as in the Fathers of the Church. Such methodological principles are liable to lead one far off, indeed ... Strangely—for, this meeting clearly places us at the antipodes of the author's intentions—these principles remind one of those condemned by Pope St Pius X, which concern certain notions of the formulation of dogma: from lived evangelical formulas the Christian community would gradually become conscious of its experiences and would then formulate these experiences into dogma.[31] Certainly, 'life normally precedes the science of life,'[32] when it

---

[31] Cf. Encyclical *Pascendi* (8 September, 1907; DS 3488. For a fuller exposition of the text of the Encyclical, see earlier editions of Denzinger, 2088–9). In fact by taking the second sentence literally, which makes possible the imprecision of the line attaching it to the first, our author has sacramental theology 'begin' not from the institution of Christ, such as the Gospel relates it to us, but from an 'expression' of the Church's faith. Such is obviously not his thought. However, the lack of clarity which manifests itself here, thanks to a certain priority given to the subject, will turn up again all throughout his work, as we have been able to show.

is a question of natural life; but they go together in the Founder of the Church, Who is the 'Word of Life' (1 Jn 1:1); and Christ left to His Church science and life at the same time. We must even say that He taught the 'science' before giving the 'life': He taught for three years before giving us the life in sacrificing Himself, in rising from the dead and sending the Holy Spirit (cf. Jn 10:17–18). Science and life have always been given from the very beginning of the Church's life, at least in their substance; and they are at the same time subordinate to the law of believing through time. This is why there is a homogenous development of the liturgy, as there is a homogenous development of dogma (we are happy to see that the author picked up this idea proclaimed in our earlier work,[33] even if the manner in which he applied it seems strange). However, in order to be homogenous, the development of the liturgy must first of all be regulated by dogma, and therefore life by science, and not only on the practical plane. This is why the hierarchical Authority, which has charge of regulating the liturgical and sacramental practice, cannot do it except by taking as a first and absolute principle not 'life,' such as it is manifested in the different liturgical practices of its Tradition, but 'science,' that is the absolute theological principles on which this practice is founded. They are revealed partially in 'the life,' certainly; but again, they are given primarily by the Gospel and by the whole body of Tradition, especially the patristic Tradition, as well as by the totality of the

---

[32]   *Art. cit.*, p. 672, col. 2. This primacy attributed to life in the area of the revealed and dogmatic deposit for establishing theology is not without surprise, even when dealing with sacramental theology. It causes one to recall the atmosphere spoken of in the preceding footnote.

[33]   *Art. cit.*, p. 673, col. 2. We wrote: 'The recourse to antiquity was not able to be a determining factor; for, according to the Catholic teaching of the "homogenous development" of dogma—and of the liturgy—the Church, throughout the ages, has deepened her knowledge of the treasure which Christ has left to her in the Sacrament of the Eucharist. The development of the worship of the Real Presence is one example of this. That of the sense of the value of the multiplication of Masses is, in our opinion, another.' (*LPC*, no. 180, p. 21).

teaching of the Magisterium of past ages. Therefore, it is primarily on this doctrinal data that the Magisterium must regulate itself, and in fact does. It is enlightened by traditional practice, where dogma is found in some sense at the lived and incarnate level: *lex orandi, lex credendi;* but it is first by dogma that it enlightens the practice itself.

For, in the immense material handed down by the liturgical Tradition of the Church there is practice and there is practice; and this remark is of extreme importance. In fact, one would not be able to attribute the same doctrinal authority or the same exemplar value to this or that practice of a local Church or a particular rite, and to the hundreds of years old, or even more ancient still, practice of the Roman Church. Yet it is a fact that, even if the Holy See has always respected the practice of concelebration, be it occasional as in the Latin Rite, or habitual as in this or that Oriental Rite, it has always throughout the ages given preference in its own rite to celebration by one sole priest, in public as in private; and it has encouraged the practice more and more explicitly.

At least it did so up until a certain document published after the Council—*not from the Council itself*—which we shall soon discuss. Conforming as it does to his own methodological principles, this document will have a definitive authority for the author of the thesis of the plurality of Masses in concelebration—and all the more so, since for him a single text of the Magisterium suffices to institute a 'practice of the Church.'[34] Therefore, it will come to enjoy a twofold authority:

---

[34] *Art. cit.,* p. 672, col. 2. That the authority of the Magisterium has the power to institute a liturgical 'practice' is beyond question. But beginning with the moment the practice (especially if it is a new practice) is introduced by the Magisterium, and therefore by way of authority, cannot be invoked as being, by that fact, the reflection of the life of the Church's custom. The same confusion is found concerning the notion of 'practice' among that which comes from Authority and that which is the fact of custom, and a custom by ancient and long established definition—for it is from there that it draws its proper 'authority' by establishing sacramental theology—where the author speaks of the *Institutio generalis* of the *Novus Ordo Missae.* That the Magiste-

that of the Magisterium and of practice. Moreover, this authority is the
greatest possible when it concerns a recent document; for, there one
finds (always on the level of the document itself, according to our
author) 'the actual practice of the Church" that is to say, 'the life
[which] precedes the science of life,' such as it is lived by the people of
God. We have, therefore, the following process: the decree of Authority
by itself institutes the practice, and then the doctrine issues forth from
here. This is the radical inversion of the path followed by the Church,
according to which the authority does not regulate the practice except
by first being enlightened by the doctrine.

*   *   *

We come now to the question of the Magisterium; and we begin with
the document to which we have just alluded. We will limit ourselves
to the sentence which interests us here. It is, for Joseph Kleiner, the
argument from authority which resolves all problems, while for us it
is the very thing which raises the gravest problems. We are not
concealing it: we do not wish to deal with it directly; we prefer instead
first to study the theological problem according to the most certain

---

rium itself is 'the most authoritative witness of the Church's practice' (p. 674,
col. 1) is most certain, if it is a question of instituting a practice: *de usu
instituendo*. However, this does not necessarily imply, and in no way does it
imply, that, when it is a question of introducing a new manner of acting, that
document is the most authoritative witness of the practice in use: *de usu jam
instituto*, that is of a custom—*de consuetudine*. Yet, it is on this latter that
theology is based (cf. *S.T.* III, q. 82, a. 2, *sed contra*). One cannot claim at one
and the same time for a document of this genre both the authority of the
Magisterium, which prescribes, and that which the established custom
theologically grants. We even see the exact opposite, and according to the
principles professed by the author himself: we see how the established custom
will be one of the criteria—and for him, one of the principal criteria—which
will permit one to judge the fittingness of the new practice that one wishes to
introduce. This here is precisely our point. And it is in this sense that it seems
to us that one can and must say that the frequent and systematic practice of
concelebration represents in the Latin Church a new practice without foundation in tradition.

texts of the Magisterium and those most in conformity with Tradition. We even think that it was fitting to confront the problem posed by the 'Instruction' of 1967 (for it is only a simple 'Instruction') first in a private manner by posing the question directly to the Authority itself. However, since the questioning which was made to us publicly constrains us, here is the sentence in question:

> This is why the competent superiors will facilitate, or even favour, concelebration whenever a pastoral necessity or another reasonable cause does not demand otherwise.[35]

Here is why it poses a grave problem: what this 'Instruction' recommends, without being based on any satisfying theological justification, is a 'practice' which already had been encouraged, and moreover had been formally prescribed at the end of the eighteenth century by the famous Synod of Pistoia; and it had been explicitly condemned in a most solemn and most formal manner by Pius VI in the Apostolic Constitution, *Auctorem fidei*. Here is the passage concerning concelebration in the religious communities as condemned by Pius VI:

> ... that no more than one sole Mass, two at the most, be celebrated each day, and that it suffices for the other priests to concelebrate with the community.[36]

The reason invoked by the schismatic Synod of Pistoia for adopting this measure is, that it is necessary to avoid differentiating between

---

[35] Instruction *Eucharisticum mysterium* (*AAS* 59, 1967, p. 566; in *Art. cit.*, p. 674, col. 1). It is of this instruction especially that we were thinking when we spoke of 'the official (granted) encouragements for the widening of concelebration' (*see above*, Ch. 1).

[36] ' ... *ut non plus quam una aut ad summum duae in diem Missae celebrentur, satisque ceteris sacerdotibus esse debeat una cum communitate concelebrare.*' (Proposition 84, Art. VIII of the Synod of Pistoia, condemned by Pius VI in the Constitution *Auctorem fidei* of 28 August 1794. DS 2691). It is clear that the doctrinal authority of this 'Constitution' is incomparably superior to that of the simple 'Instruction' of 1967; the distance between dates here has less importance than the fact that it is the very errors condemned at the Synod of Pistoia which reappeared in our day.

religious priests and religious who are not priests. But this is only a pretext, and a poor one at that. It is, moreover, very interesting; for it reveals that what was attacked, along with the priesthood and the Eucharist, was the religious life itself. We have here an ample confirmation of it by studying the acts of that particular Council of unhappy memory and of principally jansenist inspiration. A reading of these acts shines much light on that period of history.

The opposition therefore between the Apostolic Constitution of Pius VI and the simple 'Instruction' of 1967 is obvious—the latter encourages what the former condemned. The author asks: 'Have we ever seen an intervention of the Magisterium contradicting a Declaration of the Magisterium?'[37] And in his mind the response to be given to this question is clearly in the negative: in the name of the infallibility of the Magisterium. This infallibility, certainly, means that the Church cannot contradict herself, but under one condition, which our author forgets, namely that the Church engages in her act the fullness of her infallibility. Or better, when it is a question of the ordinary Magisterium, the authority of which we must take great care not to minimize, it is a necessary condition that it conform itself to what the infallible Magisterium teaches, whether it be in solemn acts or in its continual teaching. If these conditions are not respected, it is not impossible for an 'intervention' of the Magisterium to contradict another. The faith is not troubled by this, for infallibility is not on trial; but the sense of the faithful has the right to be scandalized, for such happenings reveal a profound disorder in the work of the Magisterium. To deny the existence of these facts in the name of an erroneous understanding of the Church's infallibility, and to deny it *a priori* is in conformity neither with the exigencies of theology, nor those of history, nor those of the most elementary good sense.

For the facts are there, and they cannot be denied. We have given one example of them, and others can be given. Let it suffice to recall, in that tempestuous period after the Council (and always in the area

---

[37]   *Art. cit.*, p. 674, col. 2.

of the liturgy), that first redaction of the *Institutio generalis* presenting the *Novus Ordo Missae,* notably its famous 'Article 7.' The dogmas of the Eucharist and the priesthood were presented there in terms so ambiguous and so obviously oriented towards Protestantism, to put it mildly, that it was necessary to correct them.[38] And nevertheless

---

[38]   Permit us to recall the text: '7. The Lord's Supper, otherwise called the Mass, is a sacred synax that is the assembly of the people of God, under the presidency of the priest, for the sake of celebrating the memorial of the Lord. This is why the local congregation of the Holy Church realizes in an eminent manner the promise of Christ, "Where two or three are gathered in My Name, there am I, in their midst" (Mt 18:20).' This 'description' (if you will), where the role of the priest was presented as being a simple presidency, where the Real Presence, the fruit of transubstantiation, was replaced with a simple spiritual presence, and where the sacrament was reduced to a simple memorial, the general economy of the sentence depriving that expression of the force it has in Catholic tradition—such a 'description', we say, was all the more shocking in that it was preceded in the presentation of the *Missale Romanum* by the text of the Apostolic Constitution of the same name (*Missale Romanum,* 3 April 1969), and was thus covered up, in a sense, by its own authority.

It was not astonishing, then, to see the new *Ordo Missae* presented to French Catholics by the Protestant pastor of Taizé, Max Thurian. He presents it in *Le Journal La Croix* (30 May 1969) by declaring: 'One of the fruits (of this New Order of the Mass) will be, perhaps, that some non–Catholic communities will be able to celebrate the Last Supper with the same prayers as the Catholic Church. Theologically this is possible.' The logic of these facts, so confusing for the faithful, appeared in broad daylight when it became clear that six 'non–Catholic observers', led by Max Thurian, had participated in the composing of the new *Ordo Missae* (see *La Doc. Cath.,* no. 1562, 3 May 1970, pp. 416–17 and the cover photo). It becomes even clearer when we see the numerous resemblances that there are between this *Ordo* and that which was in use at Taizé in 1959 (See 'Eucharistie à Taizé', *Les Presses de Taizé,* 1959; a comparative study of the two will have to be made).We recall these facts, so troubling and grave, only so as not to forget what was the historical context in which the frequent and systematic practice of concelebration spread and was imposed, in a sense going well beyond the limit set by the Council itself (see on this point our reflections in *LPC,* no. 180, p. 28; *see above,* p. 19. See also below, chapter XI, p. 368, the statements of L. M. Chauvet, of CNPL, regarding that Article 7.). At the end of 1980, in view of the *Congrès Eucharis-*

this *Institutio* was an 'intervention of the Magisterium.' Must it be accepted for this simple reason, while it clearly goes in a direction opposed to the Council of Trent, where the Church's infallibility had been engaged? Yes, if you follow the attitude advocated by Joseph Kleiner and so many others. And it would be necessary at the same time to adopt his own contradiction by denying that there is a contradiction, which is clearly contradictory; it represents an authentic abdication of the intelligence, and surrenders without defense to a principle of authority which no exigency of truth can come to rule. Such an attitude is not in conformity with what the Magisterium itself asks of the faithful. It belongs typically to that form of fideism justly denounced by S. Harent:

> One arrives at fideism by another way: *by the exaggeration of the principle of authority.* One has a fear of not submitting the individual enough to God or the Church; of giving too much control and autonomy to individual reason; and finally, of reducing faith by making it depend on a fallible reason.[39]

Now faith demands the submission of the intellect before the Mystery which surpasses it, not its resignation before the exigencies of intellectual coherence of which it is competent to judge, insofar as it is a power of the intellect. This is why, when a contradiction is obvious, as in the two cases just cited, the duty of the believer, and even more so of the theologian, is to direct oneself to the Magisterium in order to ask it for clarification. This is what was done by those whose protestations obtained from the Magisterium the correction of the *Institutio generalis.* This is what we are doing now regarding the passage cited from the Instruction *Eucharisticum Mysterium.* The response, by definition, cannot be given by way of a disciplinary

---

tique International at Lourdes (July 1981), Chauvet recalled this text and presented it as a 'definition' and the very point of departure for his reflection. When one knows the decisive part that the CNPL had in the liturgical reform, one cannot but admire his constancy.

[39]   In the article '*Foi*' in *Dic. de Théol. Cathol.*, vol. VI/1, col. 180.

decree. Such a path, on the part of the theologian, in no way signifies a lack of respect for the authority of the Magisterium; on the contrary, it is a most certain mark of the submission which he has towards it, since it is to that same Magisterium that he directs himself in order to receive from it the response which it alone can give. Moreover, this manifests the service which he is called to render.[40]

---

[40]   On many occasions we have had the opportunity to note the singular usage which our contradictor made of the magisterial texts, notably in the manner in which he interprets them, in order to support his thesis. In reading them in this distorted manner, he causes us a certain number of grievances to which it is not difficult to respond. We proved it during this study. And here again are some examples.

He sees 'a calling into question of "the authority" of the Church' where we simply note certain 'doctrinal insufficiencies and internal tensions of the Council'; and by openly distorting our text, he even goes so far as to reproach us for speaking of 'contradictions' in the Council itself (Art. cit., p. 672, col. 2). Yet he began his own study by recognizing the 'lacuna' which we currently suffer in the theology of concelebration (p. 671, col. 1.). In this way he recognized that there is a doctrinal insufficiency which the Council has not rectified. Certainly, such was not the intention of Vatican II, which wished to be essentially pastoral. For those who forgot the internal tensions that manifested themselves all throughout its development, it would suffice to read the newspapers from that epoch in order to be convinced of their reality and their depth.

Joseph Kleiner also contests the 'tendency' which we observed in the *Declaratio de concelebratione* of 1972, namely placing the congregation on the primary level. He finds support for this in the two passages of that document, where, he says, 'the specificity of the ministerial priesthood is clearly recalled' (p. 677, col. 2; cf. *LPC*, no. 180, pp. 30–1). However, did we deny that this specificity was recalled? And most of all, do two citations suffice to prevent the whole of a text and its profound orientation from going into a direction contrary to what they themselves recall? We know, by sad experiences, that this is nothing. It is thus that, in his work, Joseph Kleiner speaks on several occasions of the 'sacramental act' accomplished at Mass. This does not prevent him, as we have seen, from retaining in fact (when be draws his conclusions) only 'the ministerial actions' in his reasoning.

Once again he reproaches us for lacking 'filial reverence towards Our Mother the Holy Church' by not citing the *Institutio generalis* of the new *Missale*

Romanum of Paul VI. Yet we did not revert to this 'Institution' simply because it does not contain any text dealing with the problem we are studying, namely the number of Masses offered in a concelebration. Our contradictor refers to it because he believes he can find in it an argument from authority in favour of his thesis. Let us see what it is. Noting that Chapter IV treats 'of diverse manners of celebrating Mass', *De diversis formis missam celebrandi*, he emphasizes that: 'In this chapter the three successive paragraphs are titled: 1. *De missa cum populo.*— 2. *De missis concelebratis.*— 3. *De missa sine populo* (p. 674, col. 1). And he comments: 'One can at least ask oneself the question whether this plural '*de missis*' was used intentionally when speaking of concelebration, while the singular '*de missa*' was reserved for the Mass celebrated individually.' One can, in fact, pose the question, for (and we agree here) language reveals things and the manner in which they are conceived. However, in order to respond to this question, it is necessary to read the text from these paragraphs and not simply their titles. Moreover, even at that level, one can remark that these three subtitles are found under the general title of the chapter, which treats of 'the Mass' in the singular: ' ... *missam celebrandi*'. But most especially, let us read the text itself: everywhere it is a question only of 'the unity of the priesthood and the sacrifice' which concelebration manifests (no. 153), and 'the Mass' in the singular (no. 153, 1) a.b.c.; 2) a.b.; 156; 157; etc.). We cite here some particularly clear texts: 'The concelebrated Mass is organized, whatever form it takes, according to the rules of the Mass celebrated by one priest ...' (no. 159); 'If, at a concelebrated Mass, neither a deacon nor other ministers assist ...' (no. 160). And to conclude, in the next to the last number of this paragraph: 'The principal celebrant, according to his office, does all the rest as he is accustomed, for the rest of the Mass ... ' (no. 207). The principle invoked by the author, when he stops at the title of this paragraph, turns against him. But then, we would ask, why the plural in the title, *De missis concelebratis*? We see that it is without rationale; for, one ought to have placed the three subtitles equally in the singular or the plural. We have here a proof of the many anomalies of these documents, which includes many others far graver, as mentioned in our preceding note.

We take no pleasure in entering into all these details; we have no interest in them as such. However, we think we have the right, before the gravity of the accusations leveled at us, to ask the reader to honestly consider them. For, they reveal once again the excessive haste with which our contradictor desired to defend at all cost his thesis and the weakness (and oftentimes inconsistency) of the arguments on which he bases it, not to mention the criticism he made of our own thesis.

Therefore, it is with complete confidence that we await the response we requested, both on the doctrinal level as well as on the practical level; for, having posed our question in the name of the truth and the common good of the Church, this response cannot be given to us by the Magisterium except in a sense which satisfies these two exigencies. The truth always ends by manifesting itself: this is our absolute hope. *Veritas liberabit vos* (Jn 8:32). That being the case, the theological discussion remains useful and even necessary. It prepares the decisions of the Magisterium by allowing one both to develop the questions and bring to light their different aspects. In this sense we rejoice in Joseph Kleiner's article. Without a doubt he defends a thesis which we think is impossible to hold. However, in examining it, and by beginning with presenting it such as it had been presented by the author himself, we were able to convince ourselves even more so both of its impossibility and the soundness of our own thesis, the latter being in full conformity with the teaching of the Common Doctor, St Thomas Aquinas, and the Magisterium of the Church.

*   *   *

On another article by Joseph Kleiner

Contuining his reflection, Joseph Kleiner just published a new study on the *Théologie de la concélébration*.[41] We do not know who this theologian (or more probably this liturgist) actually is, whose name is unknown. We wonder, the author's name not being known, whether it is not in fact a pseudonym. However, what we would like to clarify in order to undeceive certain readers and the less warned, is that the author of these articles has absolutely nothing to do with the venerable Rev Fr Dom Sighard Kleiner, Abbot General of the Order of Citeaux. With respect to the article itself, we find there the same gratuitous affirmations, the same confusion, and the same silence as in the preceding article. We must respond to it however; for, the

---

[41] *Esprit et Vie* 90, 1980 (no. 41; 9 October), pp. 548–54. The pages which follow are reproduced from no. 189 of *LPC* (November–December 1980), pp. 30–7.

simple dismissal we made of his critique in our preceding work risks appearing to the author as a confession of our inability to refute it. We must also provide a response, because on one point he proposes a new argument in order to justify his position.

1. We find it in no. 7 of his article. Having recognized (conclusion of no. 2), apropos of the number of Masses, that 'this question ... is at the center of the theology of concelebration,' he tries to defend the thesis that he makes his own: according to which, the number of concelebrants multiplies by itself alone the number of Eucharistic sacrifices. Regarding this, after a complete series of considerations more or less *ad rem* (nos. 1–6), about which we shall speak in a moment, he takes up our own analysis of concelebration by insisting on the difference, which we mentioned, between the interior act and exterior act of the acting subject. He very rightly emphasizes the unity of these two elements in the human act, namely the interiory formulated intention (the aspect which is immanent to the subject) and the exteriorly performed act (the transitive aspect). However, this doctrine is applied in a very different manner—analogically—in the case of the singular act performed by one sole person, and in that of the collective act accomplished by several persons acting together. In this latter case, in fact, if it is true that each of the participants really accomplishes an immanent act, that is, if he interiorly formulates the intention to accomplish the collective act (which he does), then he intends to accomplish this act with the others, such that his intention is united to theirs in order to form morally only one sole and unique common intention. It is precisely by this that their act is fully, 'humanly,' a collective act, and not simply exteriorly, 'materially.'[42]

---

[42]   The paragraph which we just read reproduces without any modification the text of our study from *LPC*, no. 189, pp. 30–1. Here is the beginning of Joseph Kleiner's, the passage which we are analyzing: 'This total human act, at once immanent and transitive, is one, indivisible and irreducible. In fact, it cannot be reduced to the immanent act, for in the sacramental order it is necessary that the intention be signified ... ; on the other hand, it cannot be reduced to the transitive act, for it would no longer then be a question of a human act, but of

that which St Thomas calls an "act of man", a reflex act without consciousness and without finality' (*loc. cit.*, p. 550, col. 1). Our contradictor clearly takes up here the data of our analysis: but he does it by confusing two perspectives which we ourselves juxtaposed without perhaps distinguishing sufficiently (*see above* note 7, which was not in our study from January–February 1980). The obstruction which he thus creates shows us the necessity of better distinguishing these two perspectives.

We say in note 7 that there are two different perspectives: the first concerns the distinction between immanent action and transitive action, the second concerns the distinction between the interior and the exterior act. The first distinction is made in relation to the effect produced, and the action (for we are speaking there of action) will be called immanent or transitive according to its effect being either interior or exterior to the subject. Example: to imagine the pleasure which I am going to give my friend, or the evil which I am going to do to my enemy, is one immanent action. On the other hand, to actually do this pleasant thing or this evil, will be a transitive action. It is in this perspective that we put ourselves when we recalled that the *intention*, considered in itself and independently of the acts which follow it, is an immanent action, while the *celebration* is a transitive action.

However, when we add that, in order to be fully human the transitive action presupposes an action, or better an immanent action, we pass over to the second perspective, which moves us to distinguish the interior act from the exterior act. We have taken care to clarify this, for we had not clearly perceived it at that moment. In taking up our analyses Joseph Kleiner completely obstructed the two points of view. It is necessary therefore to see that this second distinction is made in a perspective different than the first; the point of reference is not the effect produced by the action, but on the contrary, the place of departure: the act of the will.

This distinction, in fact, appeared in the psychological analysis of the human act insofar as it is moral, that is, insofar as it is morally good or bad (references *above*, note 51). The good or the evil comes principally from the act of the will (*I–II*, q. 20, a. 1 and 2); hence one is moved to distinguish the free, conscious and voluntary 'human act', the act emitted—'elicited'—directly by the will, that is the very act of the will, for example: to desire to please my friend; from the act accomplished under this motion of the will, the act 'commanded' by it, for example: the concrete gesture by which I effectively do something pleasant for my friend. The first act is *interior*, for it takes place totally within the will: it is the act by which the will desires and commands (*imperat*)—*actus voluntatis imperantis*; the second act is called *exterior*, always with relation to the will: this is the act commanded by the will—*actus a voluntate imperatus*. Together (as form and matter) they form the one 'human act'—*actus humanus*—freely willed and accomplished.

There is a great temptation to identify the two distinctions with each other by saying: the interior act is the immanent act and the exterior is the transitive act; and yet, it is not exactly thus. If it undeniable that *the interior act,* insofar as it is completed in the subject, presents an aspect of immanence; on the other hand, insofar as it commands an exterior action, it becomes transitive. In this sense the intention considered in itself, independently of its effect, is more an immanent act; but accompanied by a command (*imperium*) it produces the execution and thus becomes in some sort a transitive act.

In addition, *the exterior act* can be an immanent action. It is thus, for example, when I want (interior act) to imagine the good or evil I could do (an act exterior to the commanding will, but remaining immanent to the subject which is completed in this imagination).

It follows that the transitive aspect of the interior act, that of the will which desires and commands the execution of the exterior act, can be realized on two levels, according to which the desired and commanded act will be simply exterior to the will while remaining interior to the subject, and therefore immanent; or according to which it will be equally exterior to the subject, and therefore transitive, consisting in an effect produced in the world of men and things. Here is an example of the interior transitive act of the first degree: I will to dream of a good (or evil) which I will do under such and such a condition. A transitive act of the second degree: I will and I effectively do this good (or this evil). In both cases the produced exterior act, which consists in an immanent action or in a transitive action, is a complete 'human act'. In these two cases, in fact, it is equally composed of an interior act—willing—and an exterior act (exterior to the will which 'commands')—executing what was willed.

We can see that this is not just a question of vain subtleties by considering the importance that these analyses bear on the judgment of the human act in moral theology. In what concerns concelebration, the first thing to be said, is that it is in itself and for each concelebrant a transitive act. It is also an exterior act requiring from each a previous interior act, or better requiring that each one makes at one and the same time an interior act, namely willing (this is the commanding intention), and an exterior act, namely the accomplishment of the ritual gestures of concelebration (this is the execution).

The *transitive* aspect of the commanding intention is as important as that of the *interiority*. They are inseparable, and it is these which establish at the same time the unity, for each concelebrant, of the action which he accomplishes and the

Such is the explicit teaching of St Thomas Aquinas and the
Magisterium regarding concelebration. Let us recall the essential part

---

communitarian (or collective) unity of the action itself insofar as it is accomplished by all the concelebrants willing and acting together. Each concelebrant
accomplishes a 'human act' which forms a whole, being the result of his interior
intention and his exterior gestures and words. This is why he truly celebrates
the Mass. However, this celebration is a concelebration, for it is accomplished
in a unique communitarian action, which is the unique result of the intentions
(interior) and the gestures (exterior) of all the concelebrants. For, as St Thomas
explains it, in order to show how it is possible to have one consecration by this
rite of concelebration, all bears on their intention to accomplish one and the
same exterior gesture (cf. *see above*, note 24; see also notes 20 and 11). This is
why (and it is very important that one sees it) the unity of the exterior action
has its principle in that of the interior act—that common intention of realizing
together one unique exterior action.

How is that possible? That is, how is it possible that each concelebrant realizes
personally an authentic celebration of the Mass (accomplishing for his benefit
a complete 'human act'), and nevertheless realizing with the other concelebrants
only one sole celebration of the Mass—to speak precisely, one concelebration
(all accomplishing together one unique 'communitarian act')? We repeat: what
makes it possible on the psychological level is the double distinction which we
analyzed, and more precisely the distinction between the interior and exterior
acts, but by extricating the aspect which is both immanent and transitive from
the first of these, the two aspects being inseparable. Insofar as it is immanent
and therefore proper to each subject, the interior act establishes *more directly*
the fact that each concelebrant accomplishes a complete 'human act', and
therefore truly celebrates the Mass. Insofar as it is transitive (in the second
degree), the same interior act establishes *more directly* the unity of the communitarian act; for it is in the intention to celebrate together, that is to concelebrate,
one unique oblation, that all the concelebrants are already and fundamentally
united.Leaving aside the technical analyses and the terminology, let us speak
more simply: insofar as it proceeds from the will of each, the intention makes
each concelebrant an authentic *celebrant*, an offerer and sacrificer of the Victim
offered and immolated at the Mass; insofar as all these personal intentions are
united in order to bear together upon the accomplishment of one liturgical
action, they are based in one unique communitarian intention, producing one
sacramental gesture, and they make all the celebrating priests the *concelebrants*
of this one Mass.

of these texts, since their decisive importance has visibly escaped Joseph Kleiner. St Thomas: 'As all have the intention of bringing about one consecration, there is only one consecration.' The *Summa Theologiae,* from another point of view, mentions again this unity of the intention which establishes the unity of the consecration: despite the multiplicity of concelebrants, 'the consecration over the same host is not repeated (*nec per hoc iteratur*) ... for the intention of all must bear upon the same instant of the consecration,'[43] which is one, as stated by the very title of the question and the problem raised at that time by the adversaries of that rite.[44] The Magisterium states: 'the concelebrants act together *by one intention* and one voice, and [this is why] they perform and offer one sole sacrifice by one sole sacramental act.'[45] It is on the basis of this reason, explicitly or implicitly held, that all the authors cited by us, from Msgr Martimort to Cardinal Journet, equally affirm that one sole sacrifice is offered to God in the Eucharistic concelebration.[46] However, Joseph Kleiner passes these over in silence as well. This is understandable from the point of view of his own thesis; but we are still astonished at the method—from which method the criticisms that he opposes to our argument fall (without even presenting it correctly; see his note 15).

It is the proper character of the collective action which clearly escapes him. We recall, in order to illustrate in a simpler manner, the example he himself gives (at the beginning of no. 7), that of the conductor of an orchestra. He affirms that its unity is better developed the greater the number of performers, which demands some explanation; 'just as,' he continues, 'the unity of the High Priest and His sacrifice is more manifested, the greater the number of priests there are who do together what He said to do.' Let us pass over the notable

---

[43] *S.T. III*, q. 82, a. 2 c.

[44] Cf. *LPS*, no. 180, pp. 22–32; *see above*, Ch. I.

[45] General Decree *Ecclesiae semper* of 7 March 1965; *AAS* 57, 1965, pp. 410–12; cf. *LPC*, no. 180, p. 29; see above, Ch. I.

[46] We read above the judgement of Dom Botte. The texts of the authors to which we refer here can be found in the following chapter.

differences that there are between the two cases and emphasize especially the fact that the author adds here a new term, which is not in the first part of the comparison. In the first part he spoke only of the unity of the principal musician, the conductor. And now, in the case of concelebration, he mentions not only the unity of the 'principal agent, Christ,' but also that of the action accomplished collectively and sacramentally, His sacrifice. Hence he goes against his own main thesis. One can see it by completing his comparison: just as the multiplicity of performers makes only one sole performance—there is only one concert, one performance of the Fifth Symphony, so the multiplicity of the concelebrants makes only one sole Eucharistic liturgy, one sole sacramental act collectively accomplished—there is only one sole Mass. We add still another example, which resembles the sacrifice more, and which moreover is of the same mode. If a prisoner of war, in order not to betray his country, refuses to reveal a secret and is therefore condemned to death by the enemy; and if he is executed by a firing squad of twelve men, there will certainly be twelve executors of the sentence, and twelve murderers, twelve men responsible for a murder. But there will be only one execution, and therefore only one murder, one sole assassination accomplished by this collective action. And for the hero who is the victim, there will be only one sole death, one sole sacrifice of his life for his country.

These examples and explanations teach us how to understand the statement of St Thomas, when he declares that the number of concelebrants does not matter. It is true that he says this by basing his position on the fact that the priests act only by the power of Christ, the true Principal Celebrant. We see clearly by the explanation given in the body of the article what he wishes to show by this—where he basis himself on the unity of the intention formulated in common by all, that is the unity of the act which they accomplish together. As we saw, this argument is equal to that which he uses in his commentary on the *Sentences*. The two approaches are complementary. It is evident, therefore, that one sole Mass is offered to God in the

Eucharistic sacramental concelebration. In what concerns this question. This is the absolutely certain basis on which to construct a theology of concelebration

2. By holding—and in order to hold—the contrary thesis, Joseph Kleiner finds himself constrained to multiply not only the silences on the arguments from reason and from authority which oppose him, but also the gratuitous, erroneous or unrelated assertions, the incoherencies and even the contradictions. It is not necessary and it would be of no interest to consider all of them. We single out only some with the intention of showing at the same time that this position is untenable and that it is completely lacking in foundation for the accusations against us (especially in the preceding article, but more implicitly in this one, since the author not only does not withdraw them, but attempts to show the justice of his thesis and the falsity—according to him—of the doctrine which we present, which is his right, but without even responding to the criticisms and arguments which we opposed to him, which is not correct.)

The first six numbers are all practically unrelated, except in the manner (for the first two) that they introduce the question: the emotional mentioning of concelebration with the Holy Father—and we ourselves have also concelebrated with him, and with joy—but that has nothing to do with our problem, which is the daily concelebration of priestly and religious communities; and yet, Kleiner places them on the same level (no. 1), which is an obvious misinterpretation (rectified belatedly and insufficiently in the Conclusion); the considerations on unity and multiplicity in the case of the priesthood of Christ and the priesthood of His ministers (no. 3), in the case of the sacrifice of the Cross and the Eucharistic sacrifices (no. 4), in the case of the Real Presence (no. 5) and the Mystical Body of Christ (no. 6). Why are these problems not related? Because the problem of concelebration, which, on the philosophical plane, is primarily that of the unity and multiplicity in the collective action, is either not posed in the preceding cases, or it is not posed where it could have been posed (nos. 4 and 6: the action of the Church, the Mystical Body of Christ).

With respect to the erroneous affirmations, incoherencies, etc., we shall limit ourselves to speak about the most obvious ones concerning the texts of the Magisterium, as well as the statement of the author regarding the actual practice of concelebration.

3. The manner in which Joseph Kleiner uses the texts of the Magisterium (we already observed it in his preceding work) is at once very selective and fairly personal. In addition to the silences already pointed out, we note three or four more examples.

- He holds the misinterpretation committed by many[47] on the subject of the famous phrase of Pius XII: '*tot sunt actiones Christi quot sunt sacerdotes celebrantes*' (no. 7 and note 13 of Kleiner's text), pronounced, as we remember, in 1954 regarding the problem of synchronized Masses, not concelebration. And he completely passes over in silence the proof that we furnished regarding this misinterpretation.[48] To this is added an equally false assertion (note 13) regarding the discourse of Pius XII to the Liturgical Congress of Assisi in 1956. For, if it is correct that the Holy Father cites there his phrase of 1954, he only does it, in a certain sense, 'materially,' by simply citing it; and this was in order to declare immediately his intention of 'clarifying some points regarding this problem.' Hence his clarifications, the urgency of which was made known to him by 'recent events,' result in clarifying the problem of concelebration in the strict sense (not treated in 1954), and in affirming that in this case one sole 'action of Christ Himself' was accomplished, and therefore one sole Mass was said.[49]

---

[47] Cf. *LPC*, no. 188, p. 22; *see below*, Ch. VI.

[48] *LPC*, no. 180, pp. 23–7; *see above*, Ch. I; no. 184, pp. 27–9.

[49] Cf. *LPC*, *loc. cit. see above.*

- Regarding the condemnation of the Synod of Pistoia by Pius VI,[50] Joseph Kleiner thinks he is able to deny the opposition that exists between this condemnation of daily concelebration, which that particular Synod wished to impose on religious, and the recent encouragements given to act in this manner.[51] Basing himself on the employed formula, he holds that what Pistoia prescribed and Pius VI condemned was only ceremonial concelebration, where the 'principal celebrant' alone pronounces the words of consecration and offers sacramentally the sacrifice; while that which is approved today is sacramental concelebration, where the concelebrants, by pronouncing the words of consecration together, all immolate and offer the Eucharistic sacrifice. Hence, according to him, in sacramental concelebration, the number of these sacrifices is multiplied by the number of concelebrants. There would be, then, no true opposition between the solemn act of Pius VI and the current encouragements to concelebratate. The argument is clever, but dangerous for him who employs it. For, by resorting to it, one would need to recognize that in the case where sacramental concelebration does not multiply the Masses, there would in fact be opposition. Yet it was demonstrated that one sole Mass is offered to God in this type of concelebration, as well as in ceremonial concelebration. There is, therefore, between these different magisterial acts, the opposition we noted: the first maintaining the principle and practice of the multiplication of Masses; the others leading in fact to the decrease in number of Masses, and in considerable proportions. With respect to the interpretation of the Synod of Pistoia which Joseph Kleiner proposes, it does not seem to hold up to analysis. His only argument is the formula, *'una cum communitate concelebrare,'* which is a good rendering of Pistoia's: *'gli altri sacerdoti dovranno*

---

[50]   Apostolic Constitution *Auctorem fidei,* of 28 August 1794; DS 2691.

[51]   See his note 22 and our study of the question in *LPC,* no. 184, pp. 37 ff.; see above pp. 41 ff.; no. 188, p. 61; *see below,* Ch. VI.

essere contenti di concelebrare colla communità.'[52] Taken literally, moreover, it would mean rather that the religious priests ought to 'concelebrate with the community' in the very large sense of that word, that is by participating at Mass with and as the rest of the community,[53] not by concelebrating 'ceremonially.' But such an interpretation goes against that decree, the intention of which was to give those religious priests the possibility of exercising their priesthood even then, despite the general principles which tended at once towards the suppression of the priesthood of religious and towards the decrease of the number of Masses. In addition, for such an interpretation to be admissible, the distinction between sacramental concelebration and ceremonial concelebration would have had to be familiar to the Fathers of the Synod of Pistoia. Now, we have taken the trouble of assuring ourselves that there was in fact no allusion made to it—not once—in the acts of the Council. And the argument from silence is alone sufficient in a question which requires such a delicate reflection.

- Regarding Vatican II, it would suffice to compare what Kleiner said (in no. 1) with our preceding work[54] in order to see that he did not know the teaching of the Council on concelebration. Particularly devoid of foundation is his allusion to 'the theology of the Church whose synthesis the Council presented,' since, on the contrary, we showed that, despite the requests of the Central Preparatory Commission, disciplinary decisions had been made without the prerequisite doctrinal questions having been clarified first. As with all fideism (for that is what this is[55]), faith in the infallibility of the Magisterium, when this latter has obviously not

---

[52]   Mansi, *Amplissima Collectio Conciliorum* ... , vol. 38, col. 1099.

[53]   Cf. DS 3850.

[54]   Cf. *LPC*, no. 188 (*see below*, Ch. VI), published in October 1980, and therefore prior to this note which was published in December of the same year.

[55]   Cf. *LPC*, no. 184, p. 39.

made use of such infallibility, is always a presupposed danger in theology and even more so in history.

- It is in virtue of the same fideistic faith that Joseph Kleiner believes that he is also able to deduce from statements of the hierarchy after the Council (no. 2) that there is a plurality of Masses in concelebration. On one hand, he observes, the hierarchy encourages priests to daily Eucharistic celebration by insisting on 'the value of each Eucharistic sacrifice'; on the other hand, it favours concelebration. His conclusion: there are in concelebration as many sacrifices as there are priests. We must recognize that the reasoning is correct. Unfortunately for Kleiner there is one thing against his position, namely that it is precisely in the decree cited by him (in note 7), *Ecclesiae semper,* that the hierarchy explicitly affirms that one sole Mass is offered to God in concelebration.

The conclusion that this novel element imposes, but which blind faith in an absolute and unlimited infallibility of the Magisterium— namely in every act of the hierarchy—always prevents one from recognizing, is that a real and profound disorder was introduced after the Council, and (in this case) even more so in the exercise of the disciplinary power (*potestas regendi*) than in that of the Magisterium in the strict sense (*potestas docendi*), and most especially in the Sacred Congregation of Divine Worship. The fact is so obvious that there are very many who recognize it and speak of it in private; but few would dare to say it openly. We are more than grateful to those persons (unfortunately all too rare) who have the courage to declare it publicly. Cardinal Ratzinger—to cite only him—is of this number, as we shall see in a moment.

4. After the area of the Magisterium the second point we wish to note is the assertion of Joseph Kleiner, according to which, following a 'homogenous development,' the actual practice of concelebration would henceforth be 'a well-founded rite,' which would be the proof of its right and its excellence (no. 1 and note 5)

Is it the fruit of a 'homogenous development,' this daily and systematic practice of concelebration (for it is only this which is being considered here)? Reread our preceding work,[56] as well as those which we dedicated to the history of concelebration in the twentieth century,[57] and one will see that this assertion is contrary to all that history teaches us.

'A well-founded rite'? In no way; and we have shown why.[58] Moreover, what ought we to say of the argument which would desire—in the rupture with an older than thousand year-practice, namely the multiplication of Masses, especially in religious communities—that a profoundly 'new' practice of 'seventeen years' ('new' except for a few very particular cases which had existed at one time) should confer the status of 'a well-founded' and even 'traditional rite' (note 5)? This is, to say the least, a strange conception of Tradition. It is astonishing for a liturgist; but it reveals the extent of this rupture with Tradition in very large sections of the contemporary Catholic mentality.

In order to show that this new practice (and with it several other aspects of the current liturgical reform) is far from being 'well founded,' many things still need to be said. We shall cite only the following words of Cardinal Ratzinger on the reform of the Missal, and especially the *Ordo missae* of 1969:

> Despite all its qualities, the new Missal was edited as if it were a work reviewed and corrected by some professors, and not one of the phases of a continuous evolution. Never has anything like it been produced; this is opposed to the very essence of the evolution of the liturgy, and it is this fact alone which gives rise to the absurd idea that the Council of Trent and Pius V would themselves have drafted such a missal four hundred years ago. The Catholic liturgy was thus lowered to the level of products coming from the beginning of the modern era,

---

[56]   See no. 180 of *LPC*, reproduced further on in Ch. VI of this book.

[57]   Cf. *LPC*, no. 185; 186–87; *see below*, Ch. III and IV.

[58]   Cf. *LPC*, no. 188, pp. 58 ff; *see below*, Ch. VI.

with the result being that a disturbing change of perspective
was provoked. Although few persons resent this malaise and
clearly weigh these facts, everyone instinctively knows that the
liturgy cannot be the product of an ecclesial decree or learned
study, but rather that the liturgy is what it is because it is the
fruit of the living Church.[59]

Mutatis mutandis, these words can equally be applied to concelebration.
We can discuss the number of persons who 'resent this malaise.' We
ourselves think, especially with regards to the Mass, that it is a higher
number than the cardinal seems to believe, and we base our position
on the massive disaffection of the faithful as regards the parish liturgy.
But the estimation of Cardinal Ratzinger only makes his reasoning all
the more interesting; and we fully agree: whatever be the number of
people who resent it, confusedly or clearly, the malaise provoked by
the liturgical reform and the disorder which it is causing is certainly
there. And we must get to the root of the problem to address it.

5. We come now to Joseph Kleiner's conclusion, which he states
in number 9 of his work, where he studies 'the fruits of the Mass.' We
admit that that we cannot understand his logic, or rather that we can
demonstrate the illogicalities and obscurities of his exposition (notably those key passages, p. 553, c. 1, the paragraph beginning with the
words: 'The Eucharistic sacrifice'). At least he recalls the fundamental
principle which must rule the problem of concelebration, which we
are now studying: 'Every time there is a sacramental action, there is a
real offering of the infinite power of the sacrifice of Christ to His
Father and its fruits for the Church.' We add: because there is a real
offering and immolation of that very same sacrifice. Yet, Kleiner
continues, in concelebration there are as many of these sacramental
actions as there are concelebrating priests. Concelebration causes no
decrease, but on the contrary, it assures the multiplication in the
Church of the fruits of Christ's Eucharistic sacrifice.

---

[59]   *Communio* II, 1977 (no. 6), p. 43.

And yet, teaching with one accord and rigorously demonstrating their position, the Magisterium of the Church, the Common Doctor and the best theologians and liturgists of our day[60] teach that concelebration is one sole sacramental act, which realizes only one sole Eucharistic sacrifice. Therefore, the only way of multiplying the fruits of this sacrifice is to multiply the sacramental celebrations. At the same time, by diminishing the number of them, the daily concelebration of priestly communities also diminishes in the Church the fruits of the Eucharistic sacrifice.

Such, once again, is the fundamental truth on which one must base the entire theology and disciplinary regulation regarding concelebration. Other aspects are yet to be considered, which Kleiner justly evokes, like the manifestation of the unity of the priesthood, or the eschatological aspect of this rite. However, these questions must be ordered, and they ought to be studied separately, in an analytical manner, before making a synthesis of them. It is this analysis of questions not yet studied and this synthesis of them which we shall propose in our next articles.[61]

---

[60] Cf. *see above*, note 46.

[61] Our discussions with Joseph Kleiner ended with this critique of his *Théologie de la concelebration*. It appeared in *LPC*, no. 189 (November–December 1980), pp. 30–7, and it remains without a response.

3 CONCELEBRATION: *SENSUS FIDEI* AND THEOLOGY

W E BELIEVE WE have sufficiently established in our previous studies the fact that one Mass only is offered to God in a concelebrated Eucharist, showing as we did at the same time the foundations of this doctrine in the Magisterium and the most certain theological tradition.[1] The research on this subject, which we were able to undertake since then, showed us -and more than we expected—to what degree this position had always been the Church's own. However, one might remember from our first study that we clearly distinguished from this first question the question regarding the fruits that redound to the Church from the multiplication of the sacrifice of the Mass. If, despite this distinction, we clearly showed at that time in what sense there seemed to be a need to go to the second question's response (without even having developed it), namely that a decrease in the number of Masses brings along with it a decrease in the fruits of the Eucharist for the Church, it is because we naïvely stopped at the elementary principle formulated by St Thomas in the following words: *multiplicata causa, multiplicatur effectus.* Which can be translated: 'In multiplying the cause, one multiplies the effects.' Whence he concludes regarding the fruits of the Mass: 'In several Masses the oblation of the sacrifice is multiplied. And consequently the effect of the sacrifice and the sacrament is multiplied.'[2] We went no further than that because this principle—almost universally admitted thirty years ago, and even more so fifty years ago—found its confirmation in the ecclesial practice of multiplying offerings of

---

[1]   It seems to us that, in refuting the arguments of Joseph Kleiner, we also showed the impossibility of holding to the thesis which is opposed to this doctrine. The present chapter first appeared in *LPC*, no. 185 (March–April 1980), pp. 13–41.

[2]   *S.T. III, q.* 79, a. 7.

the Mass for a given intention: triduums of Masses, novenas of Masses, thirty Masses, Gregorian Masses, etc.

We forgot a bit, we admit, the subtleties by which a certain theology has sought in our day to take issue with such practices and the principle on which they are founded. We are alluding especially, of course, to the works of Karl Rahner, SJ.[3] But we are thinking also of the arguments which he and others were able to take from the positions on concelebration of certain other famous theologians, such as Suarez, for example, or, before the First World War, de la Taille, whose position is, in reality, more nuanced than it first appeared.[4]

This rediscovery of a trend of thought—which, as its authors themselves admitted, fell into almost general oblivion[5]—has moved

---

[3]   One recalls the impact felt by his article at the time: *Die vielen Messen und das eine Opfer. Eine Untersuchung über die rechte Norm der Messhaüfigkeit*, published first in the journal *Zeitschrift für Katholische Theologie* (71, 1949, pp. 257–317), and as a small separate work in 1951 (Freiburg, Herder).

[4]   With regards to Suarez, see the explanation and refutation which we made in our earlier work (*LPC*, no. 184, p. 28). Regarding de la Taille, it is incontestable that the principles which he posits lead one to think that the fruits of the Eucharist depend principally on the number of concelebrants, and not on the number of Masses. He even ends up expressly affirming this (*Mysterium fidei*, 3rd edition, Paris, Beauchesne, 1931, pp. 355–6). However, at the beginning of his reflection on this question he is much less formal in his assertion (*ibid*, p. 328). And in the conclusion he returns nevertheless to the practice of the Church regarding the multiplication of Masses: '*Quare, omnibus perpensis, servet unusquisque bonas consuetudines Ecclesiae probatas ...* ' (*ibid*, p. 352, note 1). It is interesting to note the continuity which exists among these three Jesuit theologians. For, just as de la Taille was inspired by Suarez (*ibid*, pp. 327–8), so Rahner was inspired by de la Taille.

[5]   It is the French translators of Rahner's work who made this confession: after 1955, they said, ' ... there was silence' (K. Rahner, A. Häussling, *Le sacrifice unique et la fréquence des messes* (Coll. 'Quaestiones Disputatae'—31), Paris, DDBr., 1972, p. 9). Why this silence? This introduction to the translation of the famous work of Rahner, taken up after the Council by his disciple Häussling, does not tell the reader. But we know the reason: the discourse of Pius XII to the Liturgy Congress in Assisi, in 1956, explicitly treated the question of concelebration, by clarifying what it had not in 1954 (cf. *LPC*, no.

us to examine this second question. And since in order to resolve it adequately, the entire theology of the Eucharistic mystery must be considered, one cannot, even clinging to the essentials, examine it in one sole article—especially if one wishes to consider (as it seems must be done) both the history of the celebration of the Eucharist in the Church, and the studies made on these questions during the last years.

What we shall see in the present study is the bringing forth of some convergent testimonies, showing the agreement which definitely seems to emanate from among the 'sensus fidei,' theologians and liturgists on the question of the unicity of the sacrifice offered to God in concelebration, and on the necessity of multiplying the celebrations of the Mass, for the fruits of the Eucharist to be multiplied in the Church.

I. Testimonies Belonging to the Sensus Fidei

Our *Réflexions et questions au sujet de la concélébration,* which appeared in June 1979, have produced for us, apart from the article in *Esprit et Vie* to which we responded, a certain number of responses, both written and oral, which confirmed for us at once the validity of the 'reflections' which we proposed and the urgency of the 'questions' which we raised. This is why we believe it useful to reproduce some

---

180, p. 24) which made it difficult to hold to Rahner's theses. Furthermore, the decree of the Holy Office, 23 May 1957 (DS 3928), which is directed explicitly at certain key points of those theses, renders them impossible to defend. This did not prevent them from reappearing at the Eucharistic Congress in Munich, in 1960, on the eve of the Council. However, in 1955, Rahner was still able to defend his ideas openly; for, although he noted it in an article when he did, the discourse of Pius XII of 1954 did not treat 'concelebration expressly or immediately' (*Dogmatische Bemerkungen über die Frage der Konzelebration,* in *Münchener Theologische Zeitschrift* 6, 1955 (2), pp. 81–106; cf. pp. 81 and 82). On this point at least, one cannot but agree with the celebrated German Jesuit, against the interpretation of Joseph Kleiner (*Esprit et Vie* 89, 1979 (no. 51), p, 676). This last article of Rahner has been translated and published in *QLP* (= *Questions Liturgiques et Paroissiales*) 36, 1955, pp. 119–35.

of the more significant reactions which have come to us. We are encouraged also by what the recent Dutch Synod said regarding the 'sensus fidei'; for it is to it that these responses belong, and it is its contents which they reveal. In the final document of that now historic Synod, the Pope and the bishops of Holland said regarding this subject:

> The bishops note their consensus on the fact that there exists, among the believing faithful of all times, a *sensus fidei* to which theologians ought to always pay attention, and which it is necessary to take advantage of as an element of interpretation of Tradition.[6]

Certainly, the text immediately clarifies the limits of this *sensus fidei*, by recalling that 'it is not constitutive of revelation' and that it cannot have the same force as the Magisterium itself. But it does not affirm any less its existence and its value, referring back to the Council's Constitution on revelation, where it is a question of the slow work of the entire Church, through which 'the perception of Tradition increases.'[7] Therefore, it is in this perspective that we shall cite some of these witnesses.

We shall mention four of them: one from a priest, and three others from particularly qualified members of the laity. We shall reproduce these essential passages by allotting them a number, which will allow the reader to refer back to them when we offer our concluding synthesis.

1. Rev X wrote:

a) Instinctively I always realized that concelebration cannot multiply the sacrifice of the Mass, since all consecrate the same species.

b) Passing then to the point of view of priestly piety and of what we call today 'identity,' our correspondent tells us

---

[6]   *Le Document contenant les conclusions des travaux du Synode*, no. 7 (*L'Osservatore Romano*, February 1, 1980). Cf. Vatican II, *Lumen Gentium*, 2: 'Universitas fidelium ... in credendo falli nequit, atque hanc suam peculiarem proprietatem mediante supernaturali sensu fidei manifestat ....'

[7]   *Ibid.*, reference to *Dei Verbum*, 7.

what he experienced on the occasion of a concelebration in which he had participated:

> The impression of becoming a devalued priest, especially on the days when it is possible to say Mass of one's choice in harmony with the intention [which is entrusted to the priest]. It seems obvious to me that the personal prayer of the priest undergoes a harsh shock, and that the priest who finds himself at ease in this multitude cannot live long with any profundity. Indeed, let every man have his own accent, his rhythm, his breathing, his impact.

Indeed, one cannot imagine a Curé of Ars, a Charles de Foucauld or a Padre Pio habitually concelebrating.

   c) 'There is a temptation … towards less effort.'
   d) 'I knew a group of three priests in charge of some ten parishes. Weekly, except for funerals or marriages, in place of each one celebrating in the parishes, these priests concelebrated.'

2. Here now are the reflections of Mr. François Saint-Pierre, well known in the Parisian region for his tireless dedication to the housing service.[8] He formulated them in his book, *Que renaisse ton bel olivier,*[9] which he had the kindness of sending us in response to our preceding article. Let us reread the page which he dedicated to the question of concelebration. He begins by noting quite correctly that: 'The study of the problems posed by concelebrated Masses has hardly begun.' And he allows himself to propose to the reader 'some personal remarks':

---

[8] A writer, Francois Saint–Pierre is also Secretary General of the Mouvement d'Aide au Logement, Administrator of the Caisse d'Allocations Familiales of the Parisian Region, of the OPAC of Val–de–Marne, and of the Office of HLM. In addition, he is a member of the Directing Committee and Secretary General of the Association of Catholic Writers.

[9] Published as 'Supplément au no. 154 de l'Aide au Logement', 14, rue Violet, 75015 Paris, 1978. The passages which we cite here are found on pages 93–4.

a) There is the problem of concelebrated Masses in themselves—it is the Church who will decide—and that which
is posed to those who assist or participate.

b) They are causes of a reduction of the number of Masses,
and this is not without its importance. I remember that
Charles de Foucald decided to be a priest by thinking,
particularly, that the number of Masses would thus be
increased. Dom Delatte[10] thought about the possible existence of a relation between the number of Masses and the
number of souls finally saved.[11]

I believe in the importance of each Mass. If the number of
Masses celebrated did not have importance, would we not need
to approach a priest to ask him to say a Mass but once a year,
for example?

c) Passing then from this point of view, which is that of the
common good of the Church and the value of each Mass
for the entire Mystical Body, to that of the good of the

---

[10]   Abbot of Solesmes.

[11]   Here is the text of Dom Delatte: 'Have we ever imagined the number of
Masses? It is the eternal sacrifice. With the difference of the hours and thanks
to the continuity of its circular motion, the earth, ever since Calvary, will
always offer before our sight this spectacle, which it will henceforth be
impossible to pass by. Is one permitted to think that there is some sort of
relation between the number of the elect and the number of these sacrifices:
each elect has his Mass, and consequently his Calvary, the Lord being able to
say to each one of these souls redeemed by His Blood, "I offered Myself for
you"?' (*Contempler l'Invisible* (Coll. 'Sources de spiritualité', 13), Paris, Alsatia,
1964, p. 50.) We would like to point out the interrogative form under which
the Abbot of Solesmes presents his idea. He wished to underline by it the
hypothetical character which he gives to his idea. However, to be equally noted
is the difference between that which is just a hypothesis: the idea according
to which each elect has 'his Mass'; and that which is certitude: namely a global
correspondence between the number of Masses and the application by the
Church of the fruits of redemption, accomplished by the sacrifice on Calvary
and the Paschal Resurrection, for the salvation of souls.

faithful in particular, that is the different groups of faithful who directly assist at a given Mass, Mr Saint-Pierre adds:

Even if the number of Masses celebrated did not have importance, could we nonetheless ask whether the reduction of their number is appropriate? I am not speaking of certain convents where the number of Masses concelebrated is not sufficient for the number of those assisting; but today numerous faithful are deprived of the celebration of the Eucharistic sacrifice in a given village, a given quarter, at a given hour of the day; and at the same time that they cannot assist at Mass because of the lack of priests in the village or the quarter at a given hour, several priests are celebrating one sole Mass.

3. Another personality, from the Centre d'Etudes et d'Entreprises, wrote us at length in order to share with us reflections which are no less correct. Willingly leaving aside the theological aspect, this correspondent limits himself to present 'the view of the faithful, the perhaps very commonplace view, but which many no doubt suffer as it goes unrecognized in so many parishes.'

a) For one of the results of the habit of concelebration is that there are no longer Masses in order to respond to the needs of the faithful, and I am thinking especially of the weekdays.

b) Having had the occasion to travel, I happened to knock at the doors of 10 successive churches, between the hours of 6:30 AM and 8:30 AM, in order to hear that only one sole Mass was scheduled, often at 9:00 AM or 10:00 AM, or 6:00 PM: 'the workers' have been abandoned. This one Mass, in the parishes of the large cities which still have many pastors, is concelebrated.

A few years ago it was easy to find in your average city one or more Masses before the working hours; today this is becoming increasingly rarer ...

c) Even in places of pilgrimage the situation is becoming similar.

At Lourdes, a hospice worker, who needed 'to offer his services' for the sick before 7:00 AM, was certain to find (taking advantage of a little free time), either before or in the course of the morning, several possibilities for Mass in one or another of the sanctuaries. Today, I know many cases where those who work and do not have a sufficient flexibility in their schedule are obliged to go without Mass.

d) In another place of pilgrimage, run by a community pf priests, a group of 30 pilgrims, arriving at 10:00 AM, plans to show a film rather than celebrate Mass; for Mass is concelebrated in the evening ...

e) No doubt the participation of the poor laity adds hardly anything to the efficacy of a Mass; however, for us it is not the same thing ...

Certainly, it is not the same thing; for, it is precisely for the faithful that the Mass is said, since it is for all those whom He came to redeem that Christ offered His sacrifice. This is why, contrary to the modest expression of our correspondent, his reflections are not 'commonplace,' but rather touch an essential aspect of the general problem posed by the actual practice of concelebration: that of the good of the faithful and groups of faithful for whose service priests had been assigned. And how many oral testimonies do we have to add on this point to what has been given here in writing!

4. Finally, to conclude, we cite here some extracts of the account of Louis Salleron, in *L'Aurore,* 19 June 1979. He begins by reporting the following fact, which he received from a priest:

a) In a large urban parish, a woman who lost a member of her family asked her parish priest for thirty Masses ... Since the priest was able to begin them the next day, the woman went to the Mass—which was concelebrated by ten priests, among whom was her priest. She was a bit astonished, but did not dare ask for an explanation. The following day, there was concelebration again; the third day, concelebration;

the fourth day, no one. She went to see the parish priest, who explained to her that the thirty Masses had been said, since on each of the three days ten priests concelebrated, making a total of thirty Masses. The poor woman did not return. In addition, she asked herself who received the stipends which she had given to her parish priest when she had requested the Masses.

b) The distinguished chronicler 'admitted that he had difficulty believing in the authenticity of the anecdote, too beautiful, he said, to be true. However, he continued, if it is false, it does indeed reflect a situation to which attention must be given. The faithful are asking for less and less Masses for their dead. The reasons for this are numerous. Concelebration is one of them.

c) The fundamental question which concelebration poses is this: Does concelebration constitute one sole Mass, or are there as many Masses as there are concelebrating priests?

After several very correct reflections, Louis Salleron declares in favour of the first response and refers his readers to our earlier work in *La Pensée Catholique* (no. 180; *see above*, Ch. I). He then recalls the teaching of the Council on the practice of concelebration, especially that which concerns its facultative character and the strict right recognized for every priest to celebrate Mass individually.[12]

Finally, he asks the question:

d) What do the innovators of concelebration hope for? They are hoping to be able to persuade the 'people of God' that it is they who really concelebrate, because in the Church what matters is the 'congregation'; the priest counts only as the 'presider' of that congregation. He himself becomes the 'congregation' with the other priests when there are some present. It is important that the laity understand that they are themselves priests, the priesthood being common

---

[12] *Sacrosanctum Concilium*, 57.

to both laity and priests alike, and the latter being only the
delegates of the congregation ...

e) The crisis of the priesthood and the crisis of the Mass go
together.

f) The innovators, on the other hand, no longer believe in
purgatory, not even in eternal life, which in turn excludes
Masses for the dead. There is a crisis of faith in general, then,
which goes hand in hand with the crisis of the intellect. Such
is the dark cloud in which is inscribed the mode of concelebration.

We cannot but agree with these reflections.

While we try now to gather together and classify the ideas contained in these different responses, we will notice that they are ordered
around four major headings of the chapter. The first two are the most
easily distinguishable. They concern respectively the good of the
priest (1 *b*; 4 *d*) and that of the faithful who wish to assist directly at
Mass (1 *d*; 2 *c*; 3 *a*).

With regards to the priest, if participation in a solemn concelebration can be for him the occasion of feeling strengthened in his
membership in the priestly body, as well as one of an intense prayer
and great spiritual joy (in writing these lines, I am thinking most
particularly of what I myself experienced in concelebrating with the
Holy Father, Pope John Paul II, at St Peter's in Rome, on Holy
Thursday, 1979), daily concelebration, on the contrary, especially in
those dilapidated and eccentric liturgies, where the borders between
the group of priests and the faithful fade away more and more, where
the differences among the functions of the two are less and less
perceptible, such a practice of concelebration can only contribute to
the dimunition of the priests' consciousness of their own priesthood
and their life of properly priestly prayer. But it reinforces, one might
object, the fraternal sentiment which unites the priests to each other,
which is precious especially in a monastic or religious community.
This is well understood. And yet! What ought we to think of such a

'sentiment'? Does it not risk, especially with the very familiar style of the new liturgy, coming close to a natural 'unanimity' rather than a supernatural communion? Moreover, it can be asked whether it truly promotes the sense which each of the members of the celebrating community has of his priesthood. It can be asked yet again when one sees the manner in which the laity, when they are there, are associated with the celebration. They are often entrusted with the functions that belong properly to the priests, while the latter sit, doing nothing. It can be asked especially when such concelebrations take place—and we have seen that this is often the case—to the detriment of the needs of the faithful.

In what concerns the faithful, therefore, it is necessary to note before all else, that they are the first victims of the harm which the priests permit. The pseudo-promotion which one offers them by means of a deformed exaltation of 'congregation' turns against them by depriving them of priests and Masses, without which there are neither Church nor Christians. There are only sects, each one dependent on its own leader. This is what is being prepared by the famous ADAP: Assemblées Dominicales En l'Absence de Prêtres[13] (whose acronym does not lack an assonance with the word agape, which evokes the Eucharistic banquet, and which leaves one to understand that, in any case, it is always a question of nothing but a simple meal). For the Catholic faithful the most obvious harm of the actual practice of concelebration, as the correspondents rightly note, is being deprived of their most precious good, the Mass. Without raising the pitch, but only in order to call things by their name and thus preserve in ourselves the sense of good and evil, true and false, it must be said frankly: this is a true scandal.

These two first headings of the chapter bring us to the third, which seems to correspond to the central and proper question of concelebration, that of the number of Masses celebrated (1 *a*; 2 *b*; 3, in the beginning of the letter, not transcribed; 4 *c*). This is the question

---

[13]   'Sunday Assemblies in the Absence of Priests'.

which we treated in our preceding studies, and it is interesting to see that our correspondents have also raised it themselves, resolving it spontaneously in the sense which we indicated. If the two preceding questions are related to the proper good of the priest celebrating the Mass and to that of the faithful who attend it, the latter touches directly on the common good of the entire Church. Each Mass, in fact, is as a beat of the Heart of Christ in His Body which is the Church, a new injection, as it were, of His divine-human blood into all His members, and yet another aspiration of these latter towards their Center. This is why the number of Masses matters, and why it is even of the greatest importance for the life of the Church and the salvation of the world. We shall seek to show this in our next studies by recalling and trying to develop the fundamental truths of the theology of the Eucharistic sacrament and sacrifice.

Such must be the next step in our study; for the fundamental question which all the earlier ones raise, the fourth of those which our correspondents express or come close to expressing (1 *c*; 2; 3 *c*; 4 *d, f*), is the nature of the Mass and its central place at the heart of Christian dogma and the life of the Church. As Louis Salleron said so correctly: 'The crisis of the priesthood and the crisis of the Mass go together.' And they are at the center of the current crisis of the Church. It is a vicious circle; for, if the decrease of faith is the cause of the crisis in the liturgy, reciprocally, this degradation of the sense of the Mass and the priesthood is among the principal causes of the decrease of and current deviations from the faith. Deviations, we say, for every religious awakening is not automatically beneficial to the Church and therefore for the salvation of men. History teaches this, and the reflection ought to be meditated upon in our day. It could even be said that every religious awakening in a period of crisis is inevitably menaced with deviation. It would be easy to multiply examples in proof of this.

Thus, this is indeed to yield to 'the temptation towards less effort' and towards the ease of concelebrating automatically (1 *c*). But more profoundly, such a 'trend,' in the strict sense of the word (which is imposed upon us tyrannically by its use in a given age), comes from the lack of belief in the mystery of the Mass; as proof of this we bring forward the third witness which we cited above (3 c). And it is always necessary to remember that this 'trend' had been launched before the theology of concelebration was ever elaborated, which still remains to be done, said Fr Roguet in 1967.[14] And F. Sainte-Pierre could also correctly write in 1978 that 'the study of the problems posed by concelebrated Masses is barely even formed' (2). We are still at the same point today.

When song and word—the word of God as well as the human commentary on it—take precedence over the Mystery and the sacramental sacrifice, when the ministry of the priest disappears behind the technique and art of 'the animator,' when the search for an emotional unanimity, a unanimity desired at any price, immediately and without respect for the secrecy of persons—when all this replaces the long and delicate development which leads to true communion, when the cult of fervour of the senses really begins to supplant the cult of God, in short, when the assembly becomes its own proper end (in ignorance of that towards which it is directed)—and who would deny that concelebration, *such as it is more and more frequently practiced,* favours all these deviations?—when this is the case, there is something very grave taking place.

It is said that the Church makes the Mass and the Mass makes the Church: the Church celebrates the sacrament, offers the sacrifice of the Eucharist and it is by this first and foremost that she is built. However, in order for this to be true, we must add that this Mystery is accomplished only by the ministry of the priest, the consecrated representative and Vicar of Christ the High Priest. The priest is

---

[14] In the volume 'L'Eucharistie' (French translation of the *Summa Theologiae,* from the 'Revue des jeunes'): there is a note on concelebration in the commentary on question 82, article 2 (vol. II, p. 374). He simply states here a fact which Rahner and Häussling also mention (*see below,* note 17).

ministerial in the celebration of this sacrament and the offering of this sacrifice in a very particular way. This is why it is no less true to say, by analogy with the adage mentioned above, that the priest makes the Mass and the Mass makes the priest. It is he who especially and essentially celebrates the Mass *in persona Christi;* and it is in the Mass before all else that he realizes his vocation as priest, that is as 'mediator between God and man' (cf. Heb 5:1). This is why all that undermines the Mass undermines the priest, and vice versa. All that attacks them both, and one through the other, attacks the Church, which is the Mystical Body of Christ, in its totality; for, it is for her that they have been instituted.

Wherefore there is a certain urgency in clarifying all those questions concerning concelebration in order to address the abuses and deviations of the current practice. In this sense the few witnesses we cited here are to be considered as revealers of the 'sensus fidei' of the instructed Church. Obviously, it will be easy for them to oppose the others who go in the contrary direction, especially by addressing themselves to the milieu of the regularly retrained laity. But what organism would be prepared to lead an investigation, having the rigor and the impartiality sufficient to permit one to see not so much from what side come the majority of votes today, but rather in what sense Catholics spontaneously respond? Two other witnesses, or series of witnesses, will allow us nevertheless to see that this sense is the one which indicates the reactions which we collected. We personally posed the question to numerous persons in a sort of lighthearted manner, so as not to influence their response: 'In your opinion, in a concelebration, are there one or many Masses?' The response was invariable: one only. And it was often accompanied by a reflection of this sort: 'I admit that I could not imagine that one would even pose such a question!'

The second witness is that of Rahner and Häussling. They acknowledge from the beginning of their work that 'throughout the centuries the Church of the West considered without great difficulty the frequent celebration of Mass as normal, and this, it seems, in virtue of the historical development of the liturgy';[15] and that, in relation to this centuries-old tradition, the position which they represent, one which pleads in favour of a reduction of the frequency of the Mass, is 'new.'[16] Although a number of their assertions are eminently contestable, especially some of their interpretations of the Council, one cannot but be in agreement with them on these facts; as is necessary when they bring up again 'the isolation in which the dogmatic reflection on the frequency of the Mass is found.'[17] From the very confession of those who contest its validity, we see then—and we shall see it even better later on—that the several testimonies which we reported correspond well to the profound thought and practice of the Church 'for centuries': in fact, practically forever in what concerns the unicity of the sacrifice offered in concelebration, and ever since the Middle Ages in what concerns the appropriateness of the frequent celebration of the Mass.

Nevertheless, could it be said, perhaps, that these two questions have been resolved sometimes in different manners by modern theologians, and that the Church seems to have recognized that the decrease of the number of Masses caused by concelebration was without importance? What exactly is the case? In order to know the answer, here again we shall try to bring forward some testimonies. However, this time we shall ask liturgists and theologians.

II. Testimonies from Liturgists and Theologians

It would be vain to pose our questions to the Church Fathers; for, they were absolutely foreign to them, at least in the terms that we ask them. For the Fathers, as has often been mentioned, the chief principle was the unity of the Eucharist around the bishop, representing

---

[15] *Op. cit.*, p. 15.

[16] *Ibid.*, pp. 18 ff.

[17] *Ibid.*, p. 21.

Christ the High Priest. The texts of St Ignatius of Antioch on this subject are well known.[18]

The theologians of the Middle Ages, on the contrary, inquired at length and with passion about the possibility of concelebration. We saw how St Thomas Aquinas proved it. However, the opposition which it would encounter would be great and would contribute not a little to the disappearance of this rite. At least the principal objection, the trace of which is found in St Thomas' *Summa,* is interesting for us: these theologians did not see how several priests could pronounce the words of consecration—the 'form' of the sacrament—in such a way as to consecrate only one host.[19] It was obvious for them from the beginning that concelebration constituted one Mass only, one sole consecration took place. We see here how their thought was in continuity with the High Middle Ages and the first centuries of the Church.

In the sixteenth century we saw that Suarez considered it as something 'probable,' but no longer as something 'certain.'[20] We have here the sign of a rupture more profound than it first appeared. The attention of Suarez is concentrated principally on the question of the fruits of a concelebrated Mass. It is necessary to mention his name, for, especially by means of another theologian, de la Taille, he seems to have exercised a huge influence on the contemporary discussions. Well known is the success in his own time of the monumental work of this celebrated professor of the Gregorian University, *Mysterium fidei.*[21] Despite certain poignant reservations which it encountered,[22]

---

[18]   Especially the following: 'Take care to practice one sole Eucharist, for there is only one flesh of our Lord Jesus Christ; and one sole cup to unite us to His blood, just as there is only one bishop with the priesthood and the deacons, my companions in service' (*Letter to the Philadelphians,* 4, 10).

[19]   St Thomas, *S.T. III,* q. 82, a. 2.; cf. B. Botte, *La concélébration,* in *LMD* (= *La Maison Dieu*), no. 7 (1946/3), pp. 8–10; A. M. Roguet, *Pour une théologie de la concélébration,* in *LMD,* no. 88 (1966/4), pp. 117 ff.

[20]   *De Eucharistia,* disp. 79, sect. 12 (cited at length in *Esprit et Vie* 89, 1979, pp. 679–80; see our critique in our earlier work (*LPC,* no. 184, pp. 28–30).

[21]   Published for the first time in 1915. We cite it here according to the third and

the work became authoritative for decades in large sectors of ecclesial life; and this also must be noted. We shall understand why later on, when we take up the question of the fruits of the Eucharistic sacrifice.

1. ONE SOLE EUCHARISTIC SACRIFICE IS OFFERED TO GOD IN CONCELEBRATION

In what concerns the unicity of the concelebrated Mass, Fr de la Taille states clearly (and more firmly than his teacher Suarez), and for the very same reason which we mentioned, that 'concelebrants constitute only one sacramental sign, and consequently [they pronounce] only one consecrating form ... And thus all consecrate, and the consecration is one.'[23] He adds an interesting footnote which calls to mind the opinion, in order to oppose it, the opinion of those who say that, in concelebration, 'the consecration is one and the oblation multiple.' 'It is more exact,' the response goes, 'to say that the oblation is formally one, insofar as it is the collective action of a unique college, whether it be virtually or equivalently multiple.'[24] Among the theologians to whom allusion is made, we must mention J.-M. Hervé, author of a manual (otherwise excellent) which was widely read before and after the war. It is to be noted, moreover, that this statement disappeared from the last edition of that work, revised by Fr Larnicol, CSSp.[25]

---

latest edition (Paris, Beauchesne, 1931).

[22] The chief reservation, in our opinion, is that which concerns the manner in which de la Taille conceives the relation between the oblation and the immolation. His contradictor, Fr Swaby, OP, certainly seems to be right. The response which he gives the eminent Jesuit does not convince him (*Mysterium fidei* (3rd edition), pp. 654 ff.). And the teaching of Pius XII in the Encyclical *Mediator Dei* gives weight to the Dominican's argument, when the latter speaks of an oblation that is made in the immolation itself (to compare the positions of Swaby as reported by de la Taille, see *op. cit.*, p. 654; p. 656, note 1; and those of Pius XII in *Mediator Dei*: DS 3848; 3851). See also the critiques of A. Michel in the *Dic. de Théol. Cath.*, vol. X/1 (1928), cols. 1244 ff.

[23] *Op. cit.*, p. 355.

[24] *Ibid.*, p. 328, note 1.

[25] The following passage, found in the first edition of the *Manuale Theologiae*

In the meantime the question progressed considerably, and this thanks to the liturgists. The journal, *La Maison Dieu,* the organ of what was then the Centre de Pastorale Liturgique or CPL (now the Centre National de Pastorale Liturgique or CNPL), allows one to follow the initial stages of this evolution. Wishing to reestablish concelebration, and even more, to institute the innovation of an unlimited practice of that rite, and knowing well moreover that one of the principal obstacles which would have to be surmounted would be the universal conviction regarding the importance of the multiplication of Masses, the authors of this journal made use of various means in surmounting the obstacle. A first attempt was made in 1946. It was then only a first try. Use was made of testimonies about the way in which Mass had been sometimes concelebrated in concentration camps. And here is a remark made in passing regarding this:

> We learn nothing at all by recalling that, in concelebration, each priest personally offers the Eucharistic sacrifice. There are as many sacrifices as concelebrants.[26]

This was obviously the simplest way to resolve the question of the multiplication of Masses, as well as Mass stipends (always a delicate topic). Without a doubt the author of this footnote made an implicit

---

Dogmaticae, was pointed out to us, though we were not able to verify it: '*Multiplicatis enim concelebrantis et coofferantibus, multiplicantur et oblationes sacrificales*' (Paris, 1936 (16th edition), vol. IV, p. 151). In its place, in the edition revised and published by P Larnicol on the eve of the Council, we find an unambiguous assertion of the unique consecration and unique sacrifice: '*formulae omnes unicam constituent causam efficientem transsubstantiationis, vel, si mavis, unum constituent signum sacramentale et sacrificium ac ideo unam consecrationis formam*' (*ibid*, Paris, Berche et Pagis, 1962, vol. IV, p. 135, no. 138). It is just, however, to note that some expressions such as these from this manual (first edition) are in the logic of distinctions posed by de la Taille. And it is to the thought which they express that the author himself will return when he tries to determine the fruits of the concelebrated Mass.

[26]   *LMD,* no. 5 (1946/1), p. 132, note 1.

reference to theologians such as Hervé (first edition) or de la Taille, not, moreover, without forcing or even falsifying their true thought.

Unfortunately for him, and fortunately for the truth, the author's assertion immediately clashed with the categorical opposition of two eminent liturgists. The first was A. G. Martimort, who wrote in the next number of the same journal, the 2nd trimester of 1946:

> It must not be said, as in a footnote of the preceding *Maison Dieu*, which needs to be rectified, that there are 'as many sacrifices as celebrants.' This formula would have made St Paul and the Fathers of the Church justifiably jump: there is but one altar, one sole Eucharist, one sole sacrifice of Christ—this can never be said forcefully enough.[27]

That intervention was decisive. Henceforth this point of doctrine would no longer be discussed, all the more so since it was confirmed in the following number (the 3rd trimester of the same year) by a brief but substantial study by one of the great liturgists of our age, Dom Lambert Beauduin. It merits a lengthy citation:

> In order to know the entire impact of concelebration, let us reconstruct the first setting of the Christian congregations. In its first sense, to concelebrate is to associate oneself with the liturgical act of the principal celebrant. There exists in the Catholic Church a sacred hierarchy the members of which, according to different degrees, are destined to the sacred ministry of the altar. In the primitive Church, the Eucharistic celebration brought about the participation of the entire Christian community under the presidency of the hierarchical head, the bishop. Each occupied his place and participated according to his order: the pontiff at the center of the altar, surrounded by his presbyterate: the priests of second rank, invested also with the power of offering, but subordinately; then the deacons, entrusted with service and helped in these functions by a whole lower hierarchy. And in the nave, all the

---

[27] *LMD*, no. 6 (1946/2), p. 116.

brethren, associating themselves ritually through the offering and communion in the great sacrifice, and concelebrating with its hierarchical head. This is *concelebration* in the truest and most comprehensive sense.[28]

Although this study leaves in suspense certain historical and theological questions, the author's thought on the matter which concerns us is without ambiguity; and this is so—it is interesting to note—for a theological reason different from and complementary to that which we have been invoking thus far, and which we found in de la Taille. This reason is the same as that of the Fathers, which was mentioned above, namely 'that principle of episcopal unity':

> Such is the raison d'être of concelebration: the ancient rite which gathered the diocesan community around the bishop, the sole depositary of the priestly fullness of the Eternal High Priest (*tôn agiôn leitourgos*).[29]

Dom Beauduin states here a fundamental principle, one which it is important not to lose sight of when establishing the correct norm before regulating the practice of concelebration. Some years later, in 1949, there appeared in Germany some key studies on the question. The noted historian of liturgy, J. A. Jungmann, and the Jesuit Karl Rahner reaffirmed the same principle: the former, for the same reason as Beauduin;[30] the latter was moved and greatly inspired by the argument which had already convinced de la Taille.[31] This shows at

---

[28]   Dom L. Beauduin, OSB, *La Concélébration*, in *LMD*, no. 7 (1946/3), pp. 7–26; cf. pp. 11–12.

[29]   *Ibid.*, p. 13.

[30]   'The role played by the clerics, and especially by the priests, in this collective ceremony is expressed by the principle of *concelebration*. This principle signifies only that the interested parties participated in the common celebration according to their degree in Orders; but it does not necessarily mean that the priests present cooperated in the consecration.' J. A. Jungmann, *Missarum Solemnia* (Coll. 'Théologie'—19), Paris, Aubier, 1956, vol. I, p. 244.

[31]   Cf. *see above*, note 3. Rahner did not even discuss this question; but his personal position is brought out by both his title and the very intention of his

the same time in what sense the effort of theologians would henceforth be directed: recognizing that concelebration, by the fact that it is one sole Eucharistic sacrifice, diminishes the number of Masses, they would strive to show that the Church loses nothing from this decrease in Masses. That same year, in France, Fr Dalmais, OP, brought up this same problem; but he evaded it more than he solved it.[32]

Before approaching it, let us collect some more particularly signif-icant testimonies which show the agreement of liturgists and theolo-gians on the fact that a concelebration is the celebration of one sole Mass. Fr Gy, OP, reaffirms it the following year from the patristic perspective.[33] He would repeat it more explicitly again in 1953, in number 35 of *La Maison Dieu,* dedicated to the problem of concele-bration, which, he said, 'is not a simple juxtaposition of individual Masses.'[34] He was inspired by the following remark of Dom Botte, who reveals in passing how this question on the number of Masses presents itself as the principal obstacle to the recovery and extension of concelebration:

> Concelebration appeared in the Middle Ages as a means of reconciling a celebration more expressive in the communitar-ian character of the Mass and unity of the Church with the multiplicity of Masses. Concelebration was conceived at that time as a synchronization of several Masses. Is that what the Fathers of the fourth century thought?[35]

His work would end up responding in the negative to this question; but he began with the following remark: 'To thus modernize the terms

---

work.

[32] Art. *'Concélébration'* in *Catholicisme* (vol. IV (1949), cols. 1435–38; cf. col. 1436). Imprecise from the historical point of view and too summarized from the theological point of view, this brief article shows well what was the position on concelebration in 1949.

[33] *Les rites de la communion eucharistique,* in *LMD,* no. 24 (1950/4), p. 154.

[34] *LMD,* no. 35 (1953/3), p. 3.

[35] B. Botte, *Note historique sur la concélébration dans l'Eglise ancienne, ibid,* pp. 9–23; cf. p. 9.

of the problem, one risks falsifying the facts and reducing the texts to nothing but arguments for or against the thesis.'[36] This frequently cited number of *La Maison Dieu* exerted a huge influence within the liturgical movement, especially by that authoritative study of Dom Botte and that of P. A. Raes, SJ, on the Oriental Rites.[37]

Over and above this journal and the CPL, the principle of the unicity of the concelebrated Mass was affirmed no less clearly. The discourse of Pius XII, November 2, 1954, does not mention it for the good reason that he was not treating the problem of concelebration. His famous affirmation, 'as many actions of Christ the High Priest as celebrating priests,' was understood at that time in the sense given it by the context, that of 'communitarian Masses,' and what was recalled by the following phrase: 'and not as many priests *listening* piously to Mass.'[38] In 1955, it was Canon E. Catta, Professor at the Institut Catholique of Angers, who, in an article in all points remarkable, reaffirmed, among other things, the principle which we recall here.[39] In that same year Rahner revived the topic of concelebration, one which, he had seen, Pius XII did not treat explicitly in his discourse of November. His position did not change.[40] Dom Frénaud, in

---

[36]   *Ibid.*, pp. 9–10.

[37]   A. Raes, SJ, *La concélébration eucharistique dans les rites orientaux, ibid*, pp. 24–47.

[38]   *AAS* 49, 1954, p. 669 (emphasis ours). See our commentary in *LPC* no. 180, p. 24. See also the reflections of K Rahner in his article from 1955 (*see above* note 109), and those of P. B. Schultze, SJ, *Das theologische Problem der Konzelebration* (*Gregorianum* 36, 1955, pp. 212–71; cf. p. 271, note 147), which agree with our studies on this point. On the other hand, two years later Pius XII condemned the position of these two authors on the question of silent concelebration, so–called 'ceremonial', by declaring that it would not be a valid consecration (*Discourse* of 22 November 1956, and the *Decree* of the Holy Office of 23 May 1957); with the official commentary by Fr Hürter, SJ (consultor of the Holy Office) in *Periodica de Re morali* ... 46, 1957, pp. 243–48.

[39]   E. Catta, *La concélébration hiérarchique de la messe*, in *Revue Grégorienne* 34, 1955, pp, 137–53.

response to Rahner, and A. Michel, in *L'Ami du Clergé*, reaffirmed the unicity of the concelebrated Mass.[41] We see appearing as well the two new questions which occupied minds at the time: that of the sacramental value of 'silent concelebrations,' where only the principal celebrant pronounces the formula of consecration, and that of the value of concelebrated Masses from the point of view of the fruits of grace which they bring to the Church. It is on the first question that Dom Frénaud opposes K. Rahner, while another Jesuit, P. B. Schultze, supports it in the journal of the Gregorian University.[42] On the second question, Dom Frénaud finds himself in agreement with A. Michel in order to take up again the thesis of de la Taille, whose influence is particularly shown on the author of the *L'Ami du Clergé*. Without a doubt they had been influenced by a hasty and distorted reading of the text of Pius XII cited above. It is known how, by his 1956 discourse in Assisi, and by the Decree of the Holy Office of 8 March 1957, the same Pope needed to clarify these questions.[43] However, we shall return to this later.

Such was the case, it seems, on the eve of the Council. During and after the Council the question, and indeed all of the questions, were raised again. And we see that they continue to be raised on the level of principal doctrines—which is not surprising, since the Council itself did not treat them. However, with regards to the number of Masses offered in a concelebration, despite certain occasional hesitations the principle established before the Council was hardly questioned. As early as 1964 Fr Le Guillou, OP, mentioned it again very clearly in a journal, *Parole et Pain*,[44] which was founded for the sake

---

[40] Art. cit., see above, note 5.

[41] Dom G. Frénaud, OSB, *Remarques doctrinales au sujet de la concélébration eucharistique*, in *QLP* 37, 1956, pp. 114–28; A. Michel, *Valeur de la messe et de la concélébration* (*L'Ami du Clergé* 66, 1956, pp. 583 ff.); *Réflexions sur la concélébration* (*ibid* 67, 1957, pp. 156–9).

[42] Art. cit., see above, note 38.

[43] AAS 48, 1956, pp. 717; 49, 1957, p. 370 (cf. DS. 3928); cf. *LPC*, no. 180, pp. 4 ff.

of maintaining the new orientation that it wished to give to the liturgical movement. Fr Tihon, SJ, echoed this in the *Nouvelle Revue Théologique*.[45] We recalled elsewhere the very clear response from Rome on this question in 1965;[46] and a group as progressive as that which met at the Abbey Saint-André-les-Bruges expressed the same view on this point.[47] We could recall as well the judgment of Fr Bouyer, theologian and liturgist, which is of equal weight. He also does not conceive concelebration except as a communtarian act, which makes sense only in its total unity.[48]

However, it would be fastidious and without interest to multiply citations and references. What we have already given seems to us to

---

[44] M. J. Le Guillou, *La concélébration, manifestation de Mystère*, in *Parole et Pain* (a journal directed by the Fathers of the Blessed Sacrament, Paris–Brussels–Geneva), no. 1 (March–April 1964), pp. 18–25; cf. p. 25.

[45] P. Tihon, SJ, *De la concélébration eucharistique*, in NRT (=*Nouvelle Revue Théologique*) 86, 1964, pp. 579–607; cf. p. 598.

[46] We alluded to the Decree *Ecclesiae semper* of 7 March 1965 (*AAS* 57, 1965, pp. 410–12), where the following statement is explicitly found: 'They bring about and offer, by one unique sacramental act, one unique sacrifice.' This document is cited again in the Instruction on the Cult of the Eucharistic Mystery of 25 May 1967 (no. 47) and in the *Declaration on Concelebration* of 7 August 1972 (see references and commentaries in *LPC*, no. 180, pp. 30 ff.). This doctrine is reaffirmed in a commentary of *Notitiae*, no. 10 (October 1975), p. 287.

[47] *Liturgie et Monastère. Etudes 3. Eucharistie et vie conventuelle* (Bruges, Publication de Saint-André, 1968), *passim* (see, for example, pp. 40, 66, etc.).

[48] L. Bouyer, *Le métier de théologien. Entretiens avec Georges Daix* (Paris, France–Empire, 1979), p. 241. On the other hand, the scornful manner in which the author speaks of 'little Low Masses', whose multiplication he criticises by attributing them only to 'the individualist devotion of the celebrants and not to the needs of the Church' (*ibid*), calls forth the strictest reservations. Fr Bouyer was then among the most influential inspirers of the CPL, which he vehemently criticises today and from which he has since separated himself. However, everything had not the same luck, far from it: the ideas which he then floated and the decisive influence which they had, as he himself notes (see his letter to Fr Duployé of 8 October 1943 (pp. 234–242), which is an historical document).

suffice greatly for establishing the first point we wish to illustrate. They are all the more convincing because they come from personalities who belong to extremely different milieus of thought and leanings, sometime even opposite. Permit us, in conclusion, to add one more testimony, that of Cardinal Journet. Here is what he wrote on this subject in 1971:

> A word about *concelebration*. Let us imagine several persons coming together to baptize simultaneously a little child. There would be several baptizers but only one baptismal action, *plures baptizantes, una baptizatio*. In concelebration, one also finds several 'consecrators,' *plures ex aequo consecrantes*, but only one consecrating action, *una consecratio*.[49]

2. THE VALUE OF CONCELEBRATED MASSES

Having established that a concelebration is one sole Mass, the big question which poses itself is that of the value of this Mass in relation to all those, whether private or not, which would have been offered to God by the priests had they not concelebrated. Rahner understood this when, in 1949, he tried to respond to the question. The Spanish theologian, Miguel Nicolau, SJ, said it again with the same insight during the Council: this is 'the principal problem of Eucharistic concelebration.' And he repeated it immediately after the promulgation of the Council's Constitution on the liturgy.[50]

This problem, as we know, had already been resolved by thomistic theology on the one hand, and on the other hand by the liturgy itself and the practice of the Church, the authority of the pastors approving the spontaneous movement of the '*sensus fidei.*' We cited at the

---

[49]   Charles Journet, *La sacrifice de la Messe*, in *Nova et Vetera* (Fribourg) 46, 1971, pp. 241–50; cf. p. 248.

[50]   M. Nicolau, SJ, *La Concelebración eucaristica*, in *Salmanticensis* 8, 1961, pp. 269–94; *Problemas del Concilio Vaticano. Vision teologica* (Madrid, 1963, cf. pp. 151–7); *La Misa en la Constitucion liturgica de Vaticano II (nos. 47–8)*, in *Salmanticensis* 11, 1964, pp. 267–82. The phrase which we cite is found in *Problemas ...* , p. 133, and in *La Misa ...* , p. 280.

beginning of this chapter the fundamental principle of St Thomas. We shall study later the response of the Church, who, since the High Middle Ages and at a time when concelebration was in use, has never ceased to encourage the multiplication of Masses.

Let us recall also that, without being formally contained in the Tridentine dogmas, this principle of the value of the multiplication of Masses for the glory of God, for the life of the Church and the salvation of man, flows immediately from what the Council teaches on the application of the salvific power of the sacrifice of the Cross by the sacrifice of the altar, especially 'for the remission of sins which we commit every day.'[51] The Liturgy itself has for a long time now formulated this principle thus: 'As often as the memorial of this Sacrifice is celebrated, the work of our redemption is accomplished.'[52] This very beautiful formula, taken up by the Second Vatican Council at the beginning of its *Constitution on the Liturgy*,[53] demonstrates well the thought of the Church.

Moreoever, we are compelled to state that this question had been posed anew, and even in an extremely muddled manner, by certain theologians after the war. Without undertaking here a complete history of these debates, we shall at least try to clarify the principal positions and the reasons upon which they are founded. We mentioned those of the Church and those of theology which adhere most closely to the Magisterium. Let us now look at those which are opposed to them. We note first of all that this question regarding the supernatural fruits from concelebrated Masses is approached in two different perspectives: first and in an imperative manner, in relation to the particular intentions which have been entrusted to the priests

---

[51] Session XXII, cap. 1, cf. *LPC*, no. 153, p. 9 (*see below*, ch. IX) for a translation and the analysis which we propose of this dogmatic text.

[52] Secret from the Ninth Sunday After Pentecost (in the Novus Ordo it is found on the Second Sunday '*per annum*'): *Quoties huius commemoratio celebratur, opus nostrae redemptionis exercetur.*

[53] ... *in divino Eucharistiae Sacrificio*, '*opus nostrae Redemptionis exercetur*'... (S.C., 2).

and to the corresponding stipends; then, in relation to the fruits of redemption which each Mass brings to the Church, as well as to the glory which it renders to God. If we add a third aspect, by no means insignificant, namely the fruit which each priest draws from the Mass he celebrates, we would recognize the three fruits that are usually distinguished in the Mass: the special, the general and the very special. This distinction obviously does not have the weight of dogma, but it does represent an approach to the mystery to which no serious objection can be made. We mention it especially for the following reason: despite several common points, the question which we are studying here is posed in a very different manner, insofar as it is viewed under one or another of these three points of view. The first posed no serious difficulty, and the third is subordinate to the second, which is the principal: Does concelebration, yes or no, bring with it a loss in the effusion of the graces of Redemption by the fact that it diminishes the number of Masses celebrated in the Church? (It is most obvious that our question is to be understood in relation to systematic and daily concelebration, and not in relation to solemn and occasional concelebration, as it was desired and reinstituted by the Council.) Let us consider, nevertheless, each of the three points of view. This is necessary for the history of the ideas, and also in order to have a complete vision of the problem.

a) The question of particular intentions and stipends

Is it possible for each concelebrating priest to apply the Mass to a particular intention, and therefore to receive a 'stipendium,' that is, a stipend? Certainly, for the value of each Mass being infinite (since it is the very sacrifice of Christ that is immolated and offered), there is no opposition to the multiplication of particular intentions for which the Mass is applied. This was the solution which we proposed.[54] It is also that around which a liturgist as qualified as Msgr Martimort,[55] and so many others with him, spontaneously rallies.

---

[54] Cf. *LPC*, no. 180, p. 34.
[55] *Art. cit.*, p. 116.

Fr de la Taille proposes another solution, founded upon the way in which he distinguishes (sometimes to the point of separating) the oblation from the immolation, and therefore from the consecration. He seems to have been inspired by Suarez.[56] 'The Mass,' he says, 'is nothing other than our current oblation of the ancient immolation accomplished in the Passion [of Christ].'[57] It thus renews the Last Supper, in which the Lord offered the immolation which he would make of Himself on the Cross (Eluc. III). It is a 'symbolic immolation,' 'the imitation of a real immolation, and not the thing itself of which it is the image.'[58] Furthermore, in this theory, the priest is seen essentially as he who, having '[consecrated] insofar as he is an instrument of God, offers insofar as he is a representative of the Church.'[59] It is always this aspect of the offering or oblation which is retained before all else;[60] it is this which moves one to place the action of man on the primary level. No doubt, it is considered insofar as it is the Church's, but it is the relation of the Church to Christ which does not always appear clearly. Consequently, we see that the author ends up, at first, thinking that the number of concelebrants 'virtually' multiplies the number of oblations,[61] and finally, concluding that 'although there is one sole sacrifice of all the concelebrants, nevertheless, this sacrifice, as it has been said, equals many.' This is why each concelebrant can receive a stipend, each one making the offering for his own particular intention.[62] This did not prevent de la Taille from

---

[56] Cf. *op. cit.*, p. 327.

[57] 'Missam non esse nisi nostram oblationem recentem antiquae immolationis in passione actae' (*ibid*, p. 103, note 1). This terse formula, in which the author sums up his conception of the Mass, leaves one a bit perplexed.

[58] *Ibid.*, p. 327, text and note 2, where Fr de la Taille defends himself against the accusations that his theses have no value.

[59] 'Ut instrumentum Dei consecrat, offert autem ut procurator Ecclesiae' (*ibid*, p. 328).

[60] *Ibid.*, pp. 355 ff.

[61] *Ibid.*, p. 328, note 1 (cf. *see above*, note 24).

[62] *Ibid.*, p. 357.

recommending even so the multiplication of Masses, but only on account of the great devotion which it procures for the priests and faithful.[63] However, at the end of his work, he recalls the fundamental truths of the dogma on the application of the merits of the Cross by each Mass,[64] but without drawing the practical consequences.

In order to know at what point this theology is questionable it suffices to return to its beginning. It is astonishing, in looking back, to see how it was able to have the influence it did. The prestige enjoyed then by the Gregorian University, where the well-known Jesuit taught, and the support which he had from the Society, were certainly a great help. The fact remains that it is this which, at the beginning of his reflection, always inspired K. Rahner, taking it up as he did into the framework of the great *'anthropologische Wende'*—the great 'anthropological,' that is anthropocentric, 'shift'—which was at the heart of his thought. It is more astonishing to see how some theologians, such as Dom Frénaud or A. Michel (the more critical of the two[65]), had been able to adopt without difficulty these explana-

---

63   *Ibid.,* p. 352, note 1 (cf. *see above,* note 4).

64   *'In sacrificio enim missae, activa quaedam appropriatio peragitur litationis salutiferae Christi, et efficaciae propitiatoriae, quam infinitam habuit in remissionem peccatorum'* (*ibid,* p. 617). This declaration, as can be seen, is in full conformity with Thomistic theology and Tridentine dogma; and it moves one to think that, if its author had needed to confront the problem of the multiplication of Masses from the perspective of frequent concelebration, he would have given a solution other than that which he retained in his work. At least the logic of the doctrine recalled here would have required it.

65   Cf. *see above,* notes 41 and 22. In order to illustrate the influence which these two authors had in their day, it would suffice, for A. Michel, to think of the influence and authority of *L'Ami du Clergé,* as well as the great merits which this theologian acquired by his numerous works. For Dom Frénaud, we note the following small but revealing fact: In a work of collaboration, which had a certain impact, *Teologia e practica della concelebrazione* (French translation: *Théologie et pratique de la concélébration,* Tours, Mame, 1967), Vittorino Joanes quickly evokes the question which occupies us. He resolves it by reproducing verbatim the response of Dom Frénaud (*QLP* 37, 1956, p. 115), but without naming him and referring in a footnote ... to the works of C.

tions on the value of concelebrated Masses, and especially how they reapplied such explanations to a problem which was not the same one to which they had been applied by their author. For, it is necessary to render this justice to de la Taille, who did not study the problem which occupies us here from the perspective of the common good of the Church, but only from the point of view of particular intentions.

b) The value of the multiplication of Masses for the common good of the Church

We saw how this topic began to be examined after the war, when the liturgical movement undertook to reestablish concelebration and to widen its use as much as possible. On this point Rahner, who was the first (to our knowledge) to approach the question, brought in a new element. He insisted on the fact that Christ posits no new act in the offering of the Mass;[66] this needs to be nuanced, for such a summary assertion does not exactly take notice of the mystery; and he maintains that the sole factor capable of enriching the Church by the Mass is the great devotion which the latter can arouse; such a statement is not without its ambiguity. Essentially what is being said here is, that it will be necessary to search for a principle which would allow us to find 'the just norm which regulates the frequency of Masses' in the Church.[67] These theses, such as they are presented here, place us in full sacramental nominalism.

However, there is absolutely no need to follow Rahner in all the subtleties of his discourse to show how profoundly injurious it is, however correct some of his reflections can be when taken in isolation. His fundamental flaw is in a theology of the sacramental sign, which is not only insufficient, but false. Having deliberately and explicitly concealed from the beginning the necessity of clarifying in what sense the Church asserts that the sacrifice of the Mass is the 'representation' of the sacrifice of the Cross,[68] he asserts that: 'regarding the act of

Vagaggini ...

[66]   *Die vielen Messen* (1951), pp. 20–6.
[67]   *Ibid.*, pp. 76 ff.

sacrifice (*Opferakt*), renewed and reiterated each time it takes place in the sacrifice of the Mass (*im Messopfer*), it is the sacrifice of the Church.'[69] Without a doubt, he immediately asserts that this act is completely related to that of Christ, but without clarifying the nature of this relation; and this is precisely due to a lack of adequate theology of the sacramental sign and mystery. In reading these texts one cannot escape the impression that a true break is produced between the act of the Church—which is the only one to accomplish the 'visible' gestures of the liturgical cultus—and the act of Christ.[70] The dogma is thus denied at the very moment when the words that recall it are pronounced.

The 1966 edition noticed this lacuna. It added a paragraph here to explain this notion of the 'constitutive sign' used by the author, that is to say the sacramental sign;[71] but it was in vain, and without any more clarity besides. This is why we are not astonished to see the same edition, published by a disciple of Rahner, push to their extreme consequences the errors contained in the principles posited in 1949. The few pages added to the beginning of the chapter, where the norms for regulating the frequency and therefore the number of Masses in the Church are proposed, bring them into bold relief. '*The sacrifice of the Mass,* assert the authors, *is only a sign* representing that salvific action [the sacrifice of the Cross]; it cannot be that action itself.'[72] If such is the case, one can in fact hold that, 'the fact that the Mass re-presents the sacrifice of Calvary ... does not imply in itself a norm regulating the frequency of this renewal.' We understand this to mean: it does not imply that the multiplied renewal of the Mass is a source of graces for the Church—which is what he needed to demonstrate.

---

68   *Ibid.,* p. 19.

69   *Ibid.,* p. 23.

70   *Ibid.,* 24.

71   Rahner–Häussling, *op. cit.,* pp. 42–5.

72   *Ibid.,* p. 99, italics in the original text.

But if, on the other hand, the sacrifice of the Mass *is,* in the mystery of the sacramental sign instituted by Christ, the same sacrifice of Calvary, then each time that it is renewed, the blood of Christ is poured out on the Church. Now, such is the faith of the Church, defined at the Council of Trent, recalled by Pius XII in *Mediator Dei* and by the Second Vatican Council. This is why the Church, growing more and more with the passing of time in her understanding of the richness of this Mystery, has increasingly encouraged the multiplication of her celebrations. We shall see this in our next study.[73]

Without adopting Rahner's errors, and certainly not always perceiving them, the few rare authors who, both before and after the Council, studied the importance of the number of Masses were left no less affected by these conclusions; all the more so since these conclusions practically agree with those of de la Taille. Particularly representative of this are the works of Fr M. Nicolau, which we cited above; for, the convergent influence of these two authors is shown in him.

We are speaking here, obviously, of the authors who were able to read the articles in the principal theological and liturgical journals. No doubt an inquiry more exhaustive than our own would allow one to discover other voices being expressed in an opposite direction, such as that of Fr Garrigou-Lagrange, for example[74] (We should be happy if someone would give us the names of these other authors in order to complete our own investigation.). However, what audience would still agree with these voices? One cannot deny, nevertheless, from the

---

[73] Cf. *see below,* Ch. VIII.

[74] R. Garrigou–Lagrange, OP, *La valeur infinie du sacrifice de la messe et la célébration quotidienne des messes pour la pacification du monde,* in *XXXV Congresso Eucaristico Internacional—1952—La Eucaristica y la paz* (Barcelona (n.d.), pp. 37–44). This text was first published in *LPC* no. 23 (1952), pp. 7–17. It would be interesting to read the responses of this International Eucharistic Congress reported in that number. The comparison that is made with the recent Congress at Lourdes (July 1981) allows one to measure the current collapse of Catholicism.

historical point of view, the fact of these current oppositions, nor underestimate their importance.

We must mention again the very brief essay of Fr Roguet, because of the role he played in the liturgical movement after the war. The Assembly of Cardinals and Archbishops of France (ACA), having firmly recalled in 1953, in the face of various attempts at 'communitarian Masses' (at which the priests contented themselves with assisting instead of celebrating), the Assembly, having firmly recalled the importance of the multiplication of Masses for the life of the Church, Fr Roguet responded in *La Maison Dieu* by openly contesting this traditional doctrine. His response hardly surpasses the arguments of de la Taille and Rahner; and one is astonished at the poverty of his references to St Thomas, despite the length of his one and only citation made. We note in particular his silence on the text which we recalled at the beginning of this chapter, one which is certainly fundamental in this matter. Later, seeing that a note, complementary to the one from the ACA, applied to this problem the theory which was conceived for the sake of resolving another by de la Taille, Roguet ceased trying to develop it further.[75]

---

[75] This 'Note' of the ACA (1953), on *La pratique des messes dites 'communautaires'*, has an obscure history, and a content that poses some questions. The first part, which contains the three first paragraphs, had been published in *La Doc. Cath.*, no. 1447, 17 May 1953, cc. 585–7, which took it from the *Semaine religieuse* of Bordeaux (c. 585, note 1). The second part, which contains paragraph IV, appeared only fifteen days later, in no. 1148, 31 May, cc. 701–702. Now, it is stated that the three first paragraphs recall, in precise and strong terms, the traditional doctrine of the Church: ' ... it appeared, on the contrary, opportune to reinforce the sentiments of the faithful regarding the infinite value of the Holy Sacrifice, and to multiply the number of Masses rather than voluntarily diminish them.' It is this reminder which provoked Roguet's reaction (*LMD*, no. 34 (1953/2), pp. 151 ff.). However, the second part, while offering a *Note on the value of private Masses according to the Encyclical 'Mediator Dei'*, practically annulled the effect of these reminders by asserting, according to a theology of Rahnerian inspiration, that the objections made to the practice of 'communitarian Masses', among which we note the

With respect to this argument, according to which the greater devotion stirred up by the number of concelebrants would compensate for the loss brought about by the decrease in the number of Masses—with respect to this argument, it seems that it has hardly been retained. And for this reason: as intense as that devotion might be, what weight does it have in relation to the very act of Christ, Who offers Himself at each Mass through the ministry of His priest?

c) The good of the priests

In relation to the two preceding questions, and especially to the second, this third question may appear of lesser importance. However, if it is true that only the holy priest makes the people faithful, then one would admit that the question is not without interest. Regarding his celebration of the Eucharist, then, in what way does a priest sanctify himself best: in celebrating alone at the altar, or by concelebrating? If one wanted to respond to this question by referring only to the testimonies received from priests, one would go on discussing it *ad infinitum* without ever obtaining a result. On the other hand, what cannot be denied is that, if concelebration indisputably reinforces, at that very moment, the sentiment of belonging to a community, it no less deprives the priest of a quantity of gestures and

---

decrease in the number of Masses which it causes, have no weight 'against true concelebration'. This was to affirm that the latter does not diminish the number of Masses, over which Roguet immediately rejoiced (*ibid*, p. 154). For those who will be tempted to reproach us for making a selection in an episcopal document in order to retain only what is favourable to 'our thesis', we will have them observe that the distinction which we make is, in fact, not arbitrary. It, on the contrary, was imposed upon us by the fact that what we retain is what is in conformity with the Church's Magisterium, while what we reject is what deviates from it, and which, clearly, had only been added afterwards. By which route and by whose hands? This is for the historians to answer. In regard to what concerns us, we shall only apply the principle which says that the teachings of the episcopal Magisterium be received only in proportion to their conformity with the supreme and ordinary Magisterium of the Church.

words, which come down to him as his right or priority: to say the prayers of the Church, to read the Word of God, to offer the oblations placed on the altar, to give thanks after Communion in the name of the people, to bless, etc. In place of this, when he concelebrates, he responds to the prayers of the principal celebrant, like all the other people assisting; he listens to the readings (often done by a layman); he frequently presents the oblations, called 'gifts,' to the same principal celebrant (whereas this is a gesture proper to the laity); he receives Communion, the final blessing, etc. For, as K. Rahner and his disciple Häussling said: 'His cooperation in the liturgical action scarcely goes beyond the joint pronunciation of a few words.'[76]

Is all this truly of such a nature to favour the priestly conscience and piety? Who could seriously maintain this? And when we see how very frequently in communities it is the entire congregation standing cramped around the altar (blurring as much as possible the distinctions which could be made between priests and non-priests), how can one not admit that such a practice places not only the spiritual life of the priests in crisis, but even the consciousness of their priestly identity?

d) Vatican II

Sometimes number 27 of the *Constitution on the Liturgy* is invoked in order to say that 'the Council' itself encouraged frequent and even daily concelebration;[77] whereas, on the contrary, the sense of the dispositions which it took was to reestablish it by limiting its usage. The most certain sign of this intention is that, outside of planned cases, it is prescribed that the authorization of the bishop be required for concelebration.[78] With regards to no. 27, it is clear that, when it

---

[76] *Op. cit.,* p. 115.

[77] *Ibid.,* p. 19.

[78] *Constitution on the Liturgy,* 57, no. 2: ' ... with the permission of the Ordinary, to whom it belongs to judge the appropriateness of concelebration.' This permission loses all of its meaning, and with it the rules given in this number, if it is not understood as being occasional or limited, and if concelebration

speaks of preferring the common celebration of the sacraments whenever possible, it is referring only (as it explicitly states) to the presence of the people, not to the concelebration of many ministers: 'one common celebration with the attendance and active participation of the faithful.'[79]

Regarding the doctrinal questions which we are examining here, the Council, at least in the promulgated texts, did not treat these. This can be explained for two reasons: first, because it wished to be 'pastoral,' and not 'doctrinal'; second, because it envisioned only a limited revival of concelebration—something which practically eliminated, or at least rendered less urgent, the problem of the number of Masses. We can regret this silence of the Council; for, in recommencing the history of the preceding liturgical movement and in considering the real intentions of those who continued to animate it in the different countries, it was bound to happened that, from the limited opening made by the *Constitution of the Liturgy,* it rapidly burst forth into an unlimited extension of concelebration. And this, in fact, is what happened.

However, the doctrinal questions, which needed to be resolved in order to justify theologically such an extension, remained without a response—at least for those who approached them in the perspectives begun by K. Rahner and by the use which he made (and others along with him) of the theories of de la Taille. Yet the response which the secular practice of the Church brought forth, the 'sensus fidei' of

---

becomes the habitual norm.

[79] Here is what the Council states: 'Each time that the rites, according to the proper nature of each one, include a common celebration, *with the attendance and active participation of the faithful,* this latter, insofar as it is possible, ought to be preferred to the individual and quasi–private celebration. This pertains especially to the celebration of Mass, the public and social nature of each Mass always being safeguarded, and to the administration of the sacraments.' (*SC* 27). The italics are obviously ours. They indicate what the text intends by 'common celebration', namely a celebration with the attendance and active participation of the faithful, and not a concelebration.

Catholics, both priests and laity, the theology of St Thomas Aquinas, in line with the dogmatic texts of the Council of Trent—this response was always present: 'In many Masses the oblation of the sacrifice is multiplied. Consequently, the effect of the sacrifice and sacrament is equally multiplied.' And this is too profoundly tied to the very faith of the Church (notably in what concerns the reality of the sacramental order) and to its entire life, to be validly called into question. This is why we think we can state that the unlimited extension of concelebration is a post-conciliar work, not a conciliar work in the proper sense, and that it represents a rupture and not a homogenous evolution of the liturgy.

*   *   *

Some conclusions follow from this inquiry and these analyses. We shall try to formulate them briefly.

1) The doctrine according to which, in concelebration, one sole Eucharistic sacrifice is offered to God, cannot be seriously called into question. It is regrettable that the Council did not reaffirm this.

2) The question regarding the value of a concelebrated Mass in relation to multiple Masses, which could be said in its place by the concelebrating priests, is of the utmost importance, most especially from the point of view of the common good of the Church. Karl Rahner had definitely seen this in 1949, as did Miguel Nicolau afterwards.

3) To this question there was a response, which can be taken from the practice of the Church and the 'sensus fidei' of the 'People of God.' It is expressed in perfect clarity in him whom the Church calls the 'Common Doctor' of her theologians, and it flows directly from the Tridentine dogmas: of its very nature, the multiplication of Masses is a source of the greatest effusion of Christ's redeeming grace.

4) Yet this question seemed new; and this was due, to a certain extent, to the manner in which it had been posed by the

innovators after the war and by the obscuring of the traditional doctrine and practice which, by their doing, had been produced in the minds of many.

5) This question of the value of the concelebrated Mass, especially for the common good of the Church, was not explicitly treated by the Council. The practical norms which it established are not formally binding; they do not make a clarification on this subject any less desired. We shall see, moreover, that Vatican II in fact required the multiplication of Masses. Nevertheless, the ideas of the pre-Council continued to make their way into publications of all kinds and into the minds of many.

6) It is in this context that this same question is posed again after the Council, and this time in an urgent and truly new manner, when systematic concelebration had been adopted without any disciplinary or theological justification.

7) If we consider attentively the tradition of the Latin Church and the very teaching of Vatican II on the one hand, and on the other hand, the resistance of a significant number of priests, theologians and faithful, systematic concelebration can be considered an homogenous evolution of the liturgy only with difficulty. Furthermore, those very persons who were the principal ones responsible, from the doctrinal point of view, were conscious of creating a rupture, indeed even a revolution.[80]

8) The entirety of these questions had never been adequately treated; and the 'astonishment,' which our few very brief and modest reflections on this subject were able to arouse, is a sign of the confusion that continually surrounds this topic.[81]

---

[80] See, for example, Rahner–Häussling, *Op. cit.*, pp. 15–22; or also the oppositions of C(N)PL to the French episcopate, at the same time the support that had already been found in it (*see above*, note 75).

[81] Cf. *Esprit et Vie* 89, 1979 (no. 51, 20 December), pp. 43–79, under the name

9) Furthermore, it is not a matter of calling into question the practice of solemn or occasional concelebration such as the Council desired and reestablished it. The true question, then, is to find criteria that will allow us to establish the relation which must regulate the practice of concelebration, where the hierarchical unity of the Church is expressed, and that of particular celebration, which allows the multiplication of sacramental offerings and immolations of the one redemptive Sacrifice of Christ.

10) The ultimate criterion is always the glory of God, the salvation of souls and the building-up of the Church in truth, charity and unity. However, in order to know what concelebration and the multiplication of Masses means concretely in the life of the Church, we must develop the teaching that comes down to us from history and the theology of the Eucharistic Mystery, that is the Mystery of Christ insofar as it is accomplished by the Eucharist.

This is what we shall try to do in the next chapters. Those of the second part will be dedicated to the historical questions; those of the third will take up again, develop and complete the examination of the theological problems.

---

of 'Joseph Kleiner'. Note this declaration, the value of which one can now better appreciate: 'Neither in St Thomas, nor in any magisterial document is there the least allusion to a reduction of the fruits of the Sacrifice in the case of concelebration. This is an *a posteriori* proof of the multiplicity of sacrifices offered by the ministers of Christ and the Church [in concelebration, obviously]. The "thesis" of the author surprises one by its novelty and its lack of support in magisterial and theological tradition' (p. 679). Not only do we not doubt, but we are convinced of the sincerity of him who wrote these lines. It is precisely this which is so revealing of the prevailing confusion, and even the inversion, which is produced in people's minds: A doctrine so well founded in theology and tradition ends up appearing as a particular 'thesis' and 'novelty' which is totally contrary to them.

Part Two

Historical Inquiry

4 CONCELEBRATION: THE HISTORY OF A HISTORY

TWO QUESTIONS, ESSENTIALLY, have kept our attention until now: the number of Masses offered to God in concelebration, and the value of the concelebrated Mass. In fact, having shown that concelebration is always the celebration of only one Mass, it remains for us to ask whether this one Mass represents an act as rich in graces for the salvation of souls and the glory of God as all the sacramental and sacrificial acts which those concelebrating priests would have accomplish if they had each celebrated one Mass. We saw how the *sensus fidei* and the surest theology agree in affirming, with St Thomas Aquinas, that only the multiplication of the sacrificial offering of the Mass obtains for the Church a multiplication of Christ's grace.[1]

However, these two responses, important as they might be, do not suffice to found a theology of concelebration. They are rather something presupposed, indicating the erroneous paths which such a theology ought to avoid. We still need to show positively what concelebration means and what it brings to the Church, in order to establish the practical norm regulating its use. We recalled how, in fact, this norm had been established, at least in its principle, by the Council, provided that it is correctly understood.[2] However, the fact remains that Vatican II developed neither the dogmatic nor the historical questions which alone would allow us to understand and apply correctly its practical norms, for which reason there is a lack of precision. It is necessary, therefore, to revisit it and pursue the study of it, inasmuch as a certain amount of confusion has been introduced

---

[1] *S.T.* III, q. 79, a. 7, ad 3. See our earlier work, *La Concélébration: Sensus fidei ... in LPC*, no. 185 (March–April, 1980), pp 13, 37; *see above*, Ch. III. The present chapter is taken from *LPC*, no. 186–7 (May–August, 1980), pp. 62–96.

[2] See above, Ch. I; and also our study, *L'Eglise demande la multiplication des messes, see below*, Ch. VIII.

into these dogmas and historical questions, even among specialists. We have already seen this;[3] and we will have the opportunity to look at it again later. We ought, in fact, to show the contemporary research and ideas which have been scattered over the subject of the history of concelebration; this preliminary task will prove to be indispensable today for re-doing such history.

This history 'has thus far not yet been written,' Fr Schultze said in 1955;[4] and such a statement is still true today. A certain number of certitudes can nevertheless be acquired, as the same author recognizes, which suffices to clear up the theological and liturgical problem of concelebration. Unfortunately, as we shall see, they have not always been used as they ought. To recall them and bring them out into the light will be the principal goal of this study. In order to accomplish this better, we shall begin by positing a state of the question, which consists of what may be called a history of the history of concelebration in the twentieth century. Having thus presented and 'critiqued' our immediate sources, we shall state what will be the object of our next chapter, the principal milestones of the history of concelebration such as they can be pinpointed and fixed in the current state of the investigation. We shall limit ourselves to aspects and points about which a certain light has already allowed us to have an historical certitude. It is principally from here that we shall draw the elements that will allow us to develop our theology of concelebration. The abundance of material received and still to be received obliges us to carry it over to a later study.

The history of the investigations from the contemporary period on the problem of concelebration in general, and most especially on what concerns its proper history, may be divided into three periods: before the end of WWII; from the end of WWII until Vatican II; since

---

3   *See above*, Ch. III.

4   Schultze (1955), p. 216. See the bibliography listed in chronological order, which is found at the end of this chapter. The indication of the year after the name of the author allows one to find easily the cited work.

Vatican II—and more precisely, since the announcement of its convocation by John XXIII, 25 January 1959; for it is from this date that a turning point is clearly perceptible.

A general look at the bibliography of the principal works will allow one to get an idea of these different periods. If we wished to sum-up each of them, we could say the following: the first period was that of the fundamental studies; the second, that of discussions and developments; the third, that of commentaries and applications. To this it is necessary to add immediately that, if the first furnished the essential documentation, at least for the Church of the West, and brought out the principal historical problems, then the second was marked by an increasing tension among the supporters of the liturgical movement and the Magisterium. This led sometimes to a certain obfuscation of historical, liturgical and theological facts. The Magisterium itself had been disturbed by this, not only during this period, but also and more so during the following period. The analysis of the principal documents allows one to see this quickly.

I. The First Period: Until the End of the Second World War

Three important works mark the first period: those of Dom de Puniet (1914), Dom Lambert Beauduin (1922) and Fr Hanssens (between 1927 and 1932). The first and last provided the essential pieces of the historical dossier; the second, from the historical point of view, has rather a character of great disclosure. Its author, whose role and merits in the liturgical movement between the two wars are well known, takes up the data furnished by Dom de Puniet, and accompanies them with liturgical commentaries, which account for the true value of his work. Unfortunately he does not, or does not sufficiently, pay attention to certain nuances clearly noted in the article of the *Dictionnaire d'Archéologie Chrétienne et de Liturgie;* whence certain deceptive simplifications in the historical vision which he presents. It would be the great merit of Fr Hanssens, SJ, to take up the inquiry in its totality and bring forth all the desired clarity on certain points which still had remained a bit confused in the work of de Puniet, at least on the level of principles and in what concerns the Western liturgy.

What is this inquiry about? First of all, it is about knowing when Eucharistic concelebration had begun to be practiced, when its use disappeared in the West, the forms which it took and its expansion into different regions of the Church; it is also about clarifying the reasons which established its usage, as well as those which brought about its disappearance in the Latin Church, with some very rare exceptions, from the beginning of the twelfth century. One can see the importance of these questions for the theology of concelebration, especially the first question, that of knowing if this rite extends back to the first centuries of the Church, and still more, under what form it is encountered there. This would be, in fact, a very weighty argument in its favour.

'One will be tempted to believe *a priori* that true Eucharistic concelebration had been universally practiced during the first centuries,' writes Puniet at the beginning of his work; and by 'true concelebration,' he means that where all the concelebrants pronounce the words of consecration, and by this fact confect the sacrament and offer the sacrifice. However, he immediately adds: 'the conclusion will be extreme; for, there could have been exceptions; it is even certain that there had been, and formal testimonies prove it.'[5] He cites in this sense the Letter to the Smyrnians of St Ignatius (Chapter VIII), and then passes immediately on, with a leap, to the *Ordines Romani* of the eighth and ninth centuries. Finding support in Msgr Duchesne (*Les origins du culte Chrétien*, Paris 1903, 3rd edition), he claims to be able to go from there, back to the liturgy of fifth century Rome, and even earlier. It should be noted, moreover, that in the passage of the *Liber pontificalis* which he cites, the bishop alone celebrates the Mass.[6] He passes from there, without noting the essential difference which

---

5   De Puniet (1914), col. 2472.

6   *Ibid.*, col. 2473. He cites the edition of Duchesne, Paris, 1886, p. 139.

there is between one rite and the other, to the *Ordo Romanus I,* which dates form the eighth century, and where it is expressly stated that 'the cardinal priests ... say the canon with the Pope.'[7]

Before presenting these different testimonies, and others still, Dom de Puniet stated the principle that would have allowed him to distinguish them better. His research caused him, in fact, to observe on one hand 'a concelebration in the strict sense,' 'true concelebration,' where the priests together consecrate one and the same host, because they recite the entire canon; and on the other hand, apart from all co-consecration, 'the participation of many in the sacred functions, which, in itself, is a sort of concelebration in a wider sense of the term.' In both cases, he adds, 'it is always the same idea which [the word concelebration] transmits, that of the unity of the Church'[8]—hierarchical unity, it should be added. And this is why: 'The one officiating was always, in principle at least, the bishop, the sole depositary of the fullness of the priesthood, who represents Christ and is the celebrant par excellence, *tôn agiôn leitourgos.*'[9] Unfortunately, this capital distinction somewhat fades away in the rest of the article, where many historical inaccuracies appear again (We can assert this today on the basis of articles published since then.). In such a way the reader gets the impression that, apart from a few exceptions, concelebration was the ordinary practice of the early Church. This is correct if the word is taken in its wide sense; it is not correct if it is taken in its strict sense, which is its modern sense. Yet it is this modern sense which Dom de Puniet applies to concelebration in the early Church, and without any historical proof. For which reason there is an equivocation, to say the least, on which his work ultimately rests.

The imprecision which is at the foundation of this equivocation partly explains, perhaps, why Dom Lambert Beauduin, in 1922, paused at this vision of things and thought he could conclude at the

---

7   *Ibid.,* citing *PL* 78, 958.

8   *Ibid.,* col. 2471.

9   *Hebrews:* 8:2: '*Sanctorum minister*' (Vulgate).

end of a quick exposé which was often incorrect from the historical point of view: 'We believe that we have established the existence for twelve centuries of the rite of concelebration in the Latin liturgy, and the very great significance which the Church attached to it.'[10] This historical error is all the more regrettable since its author actually brings to light in a remarkable manner the signification of concelebration: 'The profound notion which inspired the rite of concelebration is the hierarchical unity of the Church.'[11]

The authority which the eminent Belgian Benedictine had acquired by his activity, zeal and liturgical competence, contributed to the accreditation and spread of this historical view both before and after WWII. For, it is this view which is essential in the opinion of many and which, it seems, is still the most widespread today: up until the twelfth century the Church of the West would have 'concelebrated'; then, especially due to the scholastics, she would have to renounce this ancient practice, which we must therefore revive; which in fact has been finally done, since the Council.

And yet, a large-scale study, pursued by Fr Hanssens from 1927 to 1932, had established in a definitive manner how little this simplistic view corresponded with historical reality. His conclusions are essential to the best specialists, even if some of them discovered these conclusions very late. However, as we shall see, they did not always perceive the significance of this study, due, it seems, to a lack of sufficiently enlightened theological sense; such that these conclusions could not block the contrary ideas, which had always been adopted and propagated by the chief persons responsible for the liturgical movement.

The great merit of Hanssens was to have clearly posited at the beginning of his study the distinction made by Puniet between what he calls concelebration '*plena vel minus plena,*' according to which the concelebrants either pronounce or do not pronounce the words of

---

10   Beauduin (1922), p. 285.
11   *Ibid.,* p. 277.

consecration.[12] From the very beginning he calls the first type 'sacramental,' and the second 'ceremonial'; however, he does not yet speak
about the specifically consecratory value of this latter. He insists with
force on this point of method and on its doctrinal weight, telling us
at the same time how the question had been debated at that time:
'The question of Eucharistic concelebration … is not about knowing
whether it existed or not, but rather *what* it was, sacramental or only
ceremonial.' And he states that documents continue to be collected
which prove the existence of this practice in the first centuries, which,
he says, is to light a candle at high noon, without paying attention to
the question regarding the nature of this early concelebration—which
is precisely the question which needs to be resolved.[13] It is, in fact,
only after having responded to this question, that one would be able
affirm that the practice of concelebration, such as he wished to
reestablish it and such as it has been restored for the last 15 years or
so, really represented a return to the liturgy of Christian origins.

Fr Hanssens, whose study is to this day the most complete and
most exhaustive that has been made (not only in our opinion, but also
according to the judgment of a specialist as qualified as Fr Schmidt),
considers successively the case of concelebration at the Ordination
of priests or the consecration of bishops; concelebration outside of
Ordinations; and he ends by posing the question regarding the nature
of the ceremonial concelebration of the first centuries. We shall take
up again in the next chapter the essential points of his conclusions;
but for the sake of understanding what is to follow, we now list the
principal points:

    1) Sacramental concelebration, the only one which is surely
       sacrificial, did not appear in a certain manner until the
       eighth century, in Rome: it is that of the Pope with the
       cardinal priests, described by the *Ordo romanus I*, which
       Puniet already mentioned;

---

[12] Hanssens (1927), pp. 143 ff.
[13] *Ibid.*, (1928), p. 106.

2) It disappeared during the twelfth century. With some very
    rare exceptions, it was no longer found except at the Masses
    of Ordinations;

3) It does not appear in the Oriental Rites,[14] except much later,
    not before the eighteenth century among the Catholics, and
    only by the authority of Pope Benedict XIV;[15] it still meets
    with the liveliest opposition among the Greek Orthodox;[16]

4) Finally, he concludes by showing why sacramental concel-
    ebration was practically inconceivable in the first centuries:
    the absence of a fixed text for the Eucharistic prayer.

Curiously, after this last section of Hanssens' work, in 1932, there is
silence. Apart from the brief monograph of Fr Daout on the Maronite
Rite in 1940, this silence would last some ten years. In 1942, H. von
Meurers would take up the question once again; however, unless we
are mistaken, he brings forth nothing new, borrowing chiefly the
results of earlier works.[17]

II. Second Period: From the End of the War to the Council

It is not until after the war that the question of concelebration is raised
again. It seems to have been considered in a rather radical manner

---

14 'I will take the liberty to recall the rules, so often forgotten or poorly understood,
    of the French usage, according to which *rite* was used to designate the liturgical
    families (the Roman *Rite*, the Oriental *Rites*), as well as the ceremonies themselves
    (the *rites* of the Church, the *rites* of Baptism, the *rite* of blessing of clocks)' (Dom
    A. Wilmart, OSB, *Annotations sur 'Le génie du rit romain', de E. Bishop*, Paris, Art.
    Catholique, p. 70: cited by Charles Journet, *La Messe*, Paris DDBr., 1958, p. 295).

15 *Consti. Apost., Demandatam*, 24 December 1743, no. 9; and *Lit. Apost., Allatae
    sunt*, 27 July 1755, no. 38; cf. Hanssens (1958), p. 260; (1932), p. 215; etc.

16 Cf. Hanssens, *ibid*; see the texts which we cite below.

17 Cf. J. A. Jungmann, *Missarum Solemnia* (Théologie—19), Paris, Aubier, 1956,
    p. 244, note 6. In this second (German) edition of this massive work, the
    renowned liturgist introduces a brief note on concelebration. It is based
    entirely on the works of Hanssens and von Meurers, the latter being inspired
    by the former.

right from the very beginning, since in 1947, the supreme Magisterium would see itself obliged to condemn certain errors as glaring as those which, denying all fundamental distinction between the ministerial priesthood and the common priesthood of the faithful, affirmed: that Christ had directly addressed to all the Church the commandment of doing what He Himself had done at the Last Supper; that the priest acted at the Mass only as a delegate of the community, and that, 'consequently, the Eucharistic Sacrifice [was] a concelebration in the strict sense of the term,' and 'that it is better that the priests 'concelebrate' with the people than offer the Sacrifice in private, in the absence of the people.' For, such were the errors denounced—already—by the Encyclical *Mediator Dei* (20 November 1947).[18]

These ideas belonged at that time to only a very few; and it could seem that they are only very remotely related to the problems which we are treating here. We shall see later that this relation was not as remote as it would seem at first glance. The ideas have their own logic; and this logic is the virtual bearer of a formidable dynamism, when it is implemented by groups determined to achieve their own ends. These groups, as we see, were at work in this period. We shall soon see it even better; as we also will be able to observe that, after numerous detours, their ideas are triumphant today under their radical form.

If in 1947 there were few who shared the prophetic lucidity of the Pontiff, the most competent among the liturgists nevertheless refused to analyze these extreme theses and others similar to them, which their contemporaries had been seeking to spread. Thus in 1946, while certain persons, in order to revive the movement of concelebration, wished to assert that in that rite there are as many Masses as concelebrants, there were others, like Martimort and Dom Beauduin, who would immediately rectify the error. We already noted it, and we shall render them this homage again: they have the merit of understanding and asserting with clarity that a concelebration is one unique liturgical act, and that,

---

[18]   *AAS* 39, 1947, p. 553; cf. DS 3850.

consequently, in a concelebration one sole Mass is offered to God. The intervention of A. G. Martimort was decisive on this point.[19] Unfortunately, their insights were not always as good on other theological problems, and therefore on questions of history as well.

Resuming in 1946 his studies begun before the war, but in the context of a liturgical movement of which he was the inspiration, Dom Lambert Beauduin revived the idea according to which concelebration—such as he tried to restore it—had been the habitual practice of the Church ever since its beginning, and up until 'the thirteenth century.'[20] At the same time Martimort showed that such was also his conviction, although he fixed the eighth century as the date when concelebration had begun to disappear in the West.[21] These variations in dates, despite the complete harmony when it comes to the origins, are notable errors of interpretation on the subject of Oriental Rites among the most renowned specialists, which show well what confusion then existed. Yet it is in this context that the movement of the revival of concelebration was initiated. While this certainly does not condemn it from the start, it does show, however, at the very least, how some adjustments were still needed for it to have certain and well-founded results.

In 1948, M. Andrieu published the second volume of his *Ordines Romani,* thus offering a precious instrument to historians: critically established texts and dates on the subject of fundamental documents for the history of the liturgy.

The research, however, did not progress much. This can be seen by reading the brief article, *Concélébration,* which Fr Dalmais, OP published in 1949 in the encyclopedia *Catholicisme.* This text, which cannot be considered acceptable, is a revealing witness not of histor-

---

19   *LMD* no. 6 (1946/2), pp. 115 ff.; cf. our preceding work, *La concélébration: 'Sensus fidei'...* , *LPC,* no. 185, p. 25; *see above,* Ch. III.

20   Beauduin (1946), p. 19.

21   Cf. *see above,* note 19.

ical research of that period—that would in fact be saying too much—
bbut of the ideas liturgical experts had at that time on this question.

That same year, K. Rahner, SJ published his well-known work on
The One Sacrifice of Christ and the Number of Masses. It is extremely
significant that the historical aspect in itself is totally absent. It is a
purely speculative reflection (and not the best scholasticism), the
presuppositions and weaknesses of which we already demonstrated.[22]
Its influence was nevertheless immense, which is easily explained by
two reasons: it went in the direction of the liturgical movement; and
it is incontestable that it enjoyed the phenomenon of a theological
trend—Rahner was already at that time the author to be read and
cited. Nevertheless he must be credited with this much: he had
understood that the central theological question to be resolved in
order to be able to establish frequent concelebration was that of the
fruits of the Mass: Did this manner of celebrating bring about for the
Church a diminution in these fruits? No, he responded. However, we
believe we have shown why his response cannot be accepted, opposed
as it is to St Thomas Aquinas and the homogenous development
which led the Church to multiply Masses.

The following years, from 1951 to 1954, would see the multiplication
of works on concelebration. The question of the fruits of the Mass, the
vital importance of which had been seen by many, was taken up again in
1951. The year 1953 was marked by two events: first, the conflict which
arose between the journal *La Maison Dieu,* the organ of the *Centre
Pastoral (Française) de Liturgie,* and the *Assemblée des Cardinaux et
Archevêques de France* (ACA) regarding the fruits of 'communtarian'
Masses; second, the publication of number 35 of *La Maison Dieu,*
dedicated almost entirely to concelebration, in response to the 'Note' of
the ACA. It merits, therefore, a close look; for, frequently cited as it is, it
played a huge role in the recent history of this liturgical rite.

The two in-depth historical studies it is based on are that of Dom
Botte—which retraces the history of concelebration in the Church

---

[22] Cf. *La concélébration: 'Sensus fidei'…* in *LPC,* no. 185, p. 33; *see above,* Ch. III.

of the West from its beginning to the Middle Ages; and that of Fr Raes, SJ—which treats the Church of the East. This latter work, made firsthand, brings forth the complement which Hanssens' research was waiting on, especially the origins of sacramental concelebration among the Russian Orthodox. In addition, it confirms his conclusions, which were partially those of Dom Puniet; for, what stands out from the article where he presents a certain number of historical documents, is this: 'The Greek tradition is ... in agreement with the ancient Oriental practice in that it attributes the celebration of the mysteries to one single celebrant ... The earlier documents allow us to find these same characteristics up until the tenth century.'[23] And: 'The more one goes back in time, the more the role played by the concelebrants fades away.'[24] In the same vein, Puniet already noted that since the fourteenth century, 'the Greeks notably accentuated the part of the concelebrants,' but always reserving to one sole principal celebrant 'the words of institution of consecration (to which, moreover, they refuse the character of consecrating words); this concelebration is common at solemn feasts and funerals.'[25]

Whatever be the theology of the Greeks on the value of the words of consecration—the reason which moves them to reserve it to one alone, usually the bishop—the recitation of these words is obvious, and it is long developed by their entire tradition since its beginning: it is, that he who pronounces the words of institution represents Christ, the One Mediator, and he alone offers Christ's one unique sacrifice. Raes analyzes a very beautiful passage from Symeon of Thessalonica (15th c.), exalting this role of the bishop, the sole

---

[23]   Raes (1953), p. 33.

[24]   *Ibid.*, p. 36.

[25]   Puniet (1914), col. 2479. We say 'since the fourteenth century', because in the paragraph which precedes the one we cited there is an obvious misprint: 'The *ordo* of the patriarchal Mass of Constantinople, drafted in the fourth century by the proto–notary Demetrius Gemiste, etc ... ' This *ordo* is, in fact, of the fourteenth century, and not the fourth—it would have been unthinkable in this earlier age.

representative of Christ.[26] He also shows that it was under the Latin influence that the Russians, from the seventeenth century only, adopted a liturgy where the concelebrants really pronounce the words of consecration.[27]

'Let us note,' Raes adds, 'that in every case there is concelebration only on feast days, in order to give the liturgy more lustre.'[28] Significant is the manner in which he several times calls 'the new concelebration'[29] that form which Hanssens called 'sacramental,' and which Dom Puniet called 'the true concelebration.' If, in fact, a conclusion is drawn from these convergent studies, it is that the adoption of this form of concelebration in no way represents for the East a return to ancient practices; on the contrary, concelebration is an innovation counter to all of its tradition, and one which came from the West.

Finally, Raes presents 'a final evolution in the practice of concelebration … among Catholics of the Byzantine Rite.' For reasons of suitability, and at the same time in order to satisfy a desire (one of Western origins) to 'celebrate Mass frequently, every day,' in religious communities and seminaries, a concelebration *in forma simplici* was established, even for daily Mass. This, the author notes, gave birth to a movement in opposition to the entire Oriental tradition, where concelebration is a means to solemnizing the Mystery of the Eucharist on great feast days.[30]

It is no less true that, under the influence of the West, a certain number of Eastern Rites adopted sacramental concelebration. Raes mentions them;[31] and it is this which is generally retained from his work, without mentioning the recent date and innovative character of these practices in the East. For there are other rites, those which have reserved the heart of the Eucharistic liturgy for the principal

---

[26]   Raes (1953), p. 31.

[27]   *Ibid.*, pp. 36–41.

[28]   *Ibid.*, p. 45.

[29]   Apropos of the Maronite (*ibid*, p. 45) and Coptic (p. 46) *rites.*

[30]   *Ibid.*, p. 47.

[31]   We shall give a list of them in the following chapter where we retrace the history of concelebration.

celebrant alone (normally the bishop), which reflect the state of a very ancient liturgy.[32] Hence the words of Raes: 'Eucharistic concelebration, as it is said to have existed in the East.'[33] This is because he perceived the importance of the distinction between sacramental and ceremonial concelebration: the study of the Eastern liturgies profoundly convinced him. He therefore notices every equivocation with which are marked the majority of dissertations made on 'the concelebration of the Eastern Churches.' One believes it to be 'sacramental,' or one recognizes it as 'ceremonial,' but without acknowledging the importance of these differences. The truth is that it is indeed 'ceremonial,' but the difference between this rite and that of 'sacramental' concelebration is essential: it is that which there is between a solemn pontifical Mass with the active participation of the clergy and a Eucharistic concelebration in the strict sense. For such is the conclusion at which one arrives when reading this work of Raes, after those of Hanssens and Dom de Puniet: 'Concelebration, as it is said to have existed in the East'; and therefore, this concelebration, from its very beginning and as long as it was continued, is in the final analysis nothing but a pontifical Mass in which the role of the presbyterium is placed in bold relief, but without ever going so far as co-consecration. In concelebration in the proper sense of the word, on the contrary, there is a communion among all the priests gathered around the bishop in the accomplishment of the sacramental act, by which the sacrifice is offered. From the point of view of *sacramental theology,* the analogy can never justify the use of the same word 'concelebration' in both cases without more precision: it is used in the proper sense in one, and the equivocal sense in the other. The same equivocation is found from the *liturgical* point of view; for the essence of the Eucharistic liturgy is in the sacramental act of consecration, where the very sacrifice of Christ is offered. Whence the essential difference, and not only a difference of degree, that exists between these two forms of

---

[32]   *Ibid.,* p. 24.
[33]   *Ibid.*

'concelebration'; whence also, we repeat, the abuse in speaking in an imprecise manner of 'concelebration' in both cases.

It is this which Dom Vandenbroucke, whose article immediately follows that of Raes, failed to see. He asserts without any historical or theological justification (and for very good reason) that, 'The traditional concelebration is a 'sacramental' concelebration, where all the priests who take part truly celebrate the sacrifice of the Mass.'[34] This is true, if you like, but only in the general sense, where all who 'take part' in the celebration of the Mass participate in the sacramental offering of the sacrifice in virtue of the common priesthood of the baptized. For, in what is called 'ceremonial concelebration,' the priests do not exercise the proper act of their ministerial priesthood. Such language is therefore equivocal to say the least. The context of that period explains it: there was a desire to hasten the passing from 'communitarian Masses,' at which priests assisted and communicated in place of celebrating each one his own Mass, to concelebration in the strict sense. The use of 'communitarian' Masses, in fact, had been recently, if not condemned, at least restricted to narrow limits by the French episcopal hierarchy. We are reminded of the manner in which the CPL had been opposed to its decisions, defending and encouraging the practice which the bishops did not want to see spread. It is in no. 34 (2nd trimester, 1953), that *La Maison Dieu* was obliged to publish the 'Note' from the ACA. It brought about a very severe critique, owing to Fr Roguet, whose theological insufficiency we already noted.[35] On the other hand, in a paragraph added to the end, the 'Note' of the ACA offered an opening to the possibility of concelebration. It was in order to seize immediately the occasion which had been thus presented to it and to whose creation it[36] perhaps had contributed, that the CPL dedicated no. 35 of its journal to this subject. The 'communitarian Masses,' because they contained both

---

34   Vandenbroucke (1953), p. 50.
35   Cf. *La concélébration: 'Sensus fidei'* ... , in *LPC* 185, p. 35; *see above*, Ch. III.
36   *Ibid.*, note 70.

the legitimate—the desire for praying together—and the unsatisfactory—the fact that participating priests did not celebrate the Mass—all these allowed the idea of concelebration to pass. It was now necessary to show its foundations in Tradition and theology.

It was extremely important to establish that this manner of celebrating Mass was rooted in the earliest tradition, and therefore it was necessary to dissolve every difference between 'sacramental concelebration' and 'ceremonial concelebration.'

We believe that it belongs to our historical study to demonstrate these facts and to underline these factors. For, by showing the somewhat tense climate in which historical and theological research was carried out at that time, we will be aided in understanding how it could happen that even the specialists had not seen that which, with the passing of time, appeared to us so clearly. What is certain is that the truths, however so clearly drawn out by Puniet and especially by Hanssens and Raes, escaped at that time the majority of authors of the liturgical movement.

This was also the case with Dom Botte; for, we must now return to his work. Although he works directly with texts, he goes in the same direction as Vandenbroucke and the entire no. 35 of *La Maison Dieu*, with the same ignorance of Hanssens' work and the same theological confusion between the two profoundly different forms of concelebration. Nevertheless, Dom Botte does admit the historical fact of the passing, at a certain date, from the recitation of the canon by one priest to its recitation by all the concelebrants. And he does not avoid the decisive question of 'the import of this change': 'Is there a rupture ... or a development?'[37] Certainly one can always speak of development in a certain sense. But the dilemma in the midst of which the word is used shows the sense given to it: Does the passing from one form of Eucharistic celebration to another represent a simple 'development,' that is, a secondary change, without major liturgical or theological impact, and homogenous in every way, or is it a mutation so profound that one ought to speak of a 'rupture'? We saw the thoughts of Raes

---

[37]   Botte (1953), p. 19.

on this point: for him, 'the new concelebration,' as he calls it, has no foundation in ancient Tradition; in comparison to the latter, it represents a major change, a 'rupture' and not a simple 'development.' Hence the resistance with which it is opposed by the Greeks, as well as a certain number of Eastern Rites (the majority it seems).

For Dom Botte there is, on the contrary, no break of continuity: 'With what right,' he asks, 'does one assert that the first is less, non-sacramental, and that the second introduced a radical change?'[38] Pius XII in 1956, and the Holy Office in 1957, respond to him: the theological reason—the 'right'—which establishes this affirmation of a radical difference, is that the celebration of a sacrament requires, by divine institution, that the minister pronounce the words which confect the sacrament. That it had been necessary to recall such an elementary truth, and that all the theological and liturgical implications were not better seen, is revelatory of the confusion which then reigned in the minds of many.

There is another, more subtle indication, it is true, in this remark made by Dom Botte at the beginning of his article. Recalling the existence of these two forms of 'concelebration,' ceremonial and sacramental, he writes: 'There is here a modern distinction, which appeared to me stripped of all meaning in antiquity.'[39] We see here great confusion between the command (or sacramental act itself such as it had been instituted by Christ) and the theological idea that one can have of it. This, in fact, would have made no sense, as Hanssens noted very well in 1932. Moreover, it is a flagrant anachronism to ask whether the priest 'concelebrants' of the first centuries *had thought* about 'consecrating' the host without pronouncing the words of Christ over the bread and wine; for, this is to pose the question under a form that the later doctrinal development alone rendered possible.[40] In fact, it is not an anachronism to think that they were aware of

---

[38]   *Ibid.*, p. 20.

[39]   *Ibid.*, p. 12.

[40]   Hanssens (1932), p. 219.

participating directly in an act which the bishop alone accomplished in its fullness, insofar as he alone represented in a complete manner Christ the High Priest. But to ask whether, in itself, the 'concelebration' of the first centuries *was* sacramental or simply ceremonial, because the concelebrants did not pronounce the words of consecration, is in no way anachronistic. This question, in fact, deals with the being of things, with the reality itself, and not with the idea one can have of it at one or another period. That is why the response to be given does not depend (except perhaps for its precision and clarity) on the degree of development of the Eucharistic doctrine at one or another period of the Church's history, but rather on the very nature of the sacrament of the Eucharist such as Christ instituted it.

We can see, with these few reflections, to what degree certain judgments of the historical order depend on theological and historical principles. It cannot be otherwise when the matter of that history is the liturgy itself. This is easily seen with respect to the implications which the passing from one mode of concelebration to another has for the priest and the Church. For the priest, it represents an essential difference, since only in the second case he really celebrates the Mass and offers the sacrifice *in persona Christi.* For the ecclesial community, the two principal differences concern the manner in which the hierarchical unity is represented, and the abundance of grace which the Eucharist makes descend upon the world. This second aspect can only be perceived if one recalls (and it must be recalled) the development by which the Church, by always becoming more conscious of the mystery of the Eucharist, had been moved to multiply the celebrations of the Mass. It is impossible to pose correctly the problem of concelebration if one does not consider this essential aspect.

However, these delicate questions can be correctly posed only with difficulty, and still less can they be clarified, when, in order to obtain a return to concelebration, one wishes before anything else to show that it would represent only 'a return to the ancient practice' and that it 'would not be a regression in Eucharistic piety'[41] and when one does not hesitate to multiply historical, liturgical and theological confusion in order to obtain one's ends. The remarkable article of Raes clashes with the entire number 35 of *La Maison Dieu*. To a superficial and partial glance it could seem to go in the same direction as the others and, by this fact, support their theses. Denis-Boulet, for example, committed this error when he cited it in order to assert, *without distinctions,* that concelebration, in the modern sense of the word, is practiced 'by a certain number of Eastern Churches.'[42] This assertion is irrefutable to the letter; for the fact is exact, and Raes brings it to light. However, by the silence concerning the other cases and the fundamental movement of the Eastern tradition, it becomes an untruth; for, it gives the impression that concelebration is a fact proper to the Churches of the East, all the more so that the following phrase underlines the limits which this rite encounters in the 'Latin Church.' We have here a typical example of the way in which the supporters of the liturgical movement contributed to the spreading of erroneous ideas by clinging to only a part of the historical facts, by falsifying them at times, and by interpreting them in an inexact theological manner. Nevertheless, regarding the work of Raes, it furnished the attentive reader of good faith with all the elements necessary for seeing what was the true Tradition of the early Church and the Church of the East in the area of concelebration. In this respect, we say, it clashed with the collection of other articles in the midst of which it had been published.

The following year (1954) would not see appear any detailed work on the history of concelebration. The use of the 'communitarian Masses' continued to spread and to increase confusion by false ideas, by means of which some were trying to justify these Masses. This ended up provoking the intervention of the supreme Magisterium: the Allocution of Pius XII on 2 November, which would constitute, from the point of view of the history of the liturgical movement, the notable

---

[41]   Botte (1953), p. 22.
[42]   Denis–Boulet(1961), p. 320.

event of the year. Regarding the Eucharist, the Pope recalled that only the priest has the power to offer the sacrifice, and that, consequently, one must reject as erroneous the idea of a concelebration of the entire community without the essential distinction between the function of the priest and that of the faithful. Then, presenting it as a new error, he denounces the theory by which one seeks to defend the 'communitarian Masses,' and according to which 'the celebration of one single Mass, at which one hundred priests piously assist, is the same as one hundred Masses celebrated by one hundred priests. It is not so. Regarding the oblation of the Eucharistic sacrifice, there are as many actions of Christ the High Priest as there are celebrating priests, and not priests piously listening to the Mass of a bishop or a priest.'[43]

We already showed the misinterpretation commonly made regarding this statement of Pius XII. It was believed that it was necessary to apply it to concelebration, when in fact Pius XII compares only the case 'of one single Mass at which one hundred priests piously assist,' to that of 'one hundred Masses celebrated by one hundred priests.' This misinterpretation is explained for the most part by the equivocation resulting from the historical context in which the Pope spoke. That context, in fact, was, on the level of the liturgical movement of the time, that of the propaganda for the use of 'communitarian Masses'; it is of this alone which Pius XII is thinking in the comparison that he makes, when he proclaims that, 'there are as many actions of Christ the High Priest as there are celebrating priests,' and not 'concelebrants.'[44] However, on the level of the doctrinal discussion, the theoreticians of the liturgical movement were already examining the true question at stake, that of concelebration in the strict sense. While there was no lack of minds perceptive enough to know the profound difference that exists between the two things—that is, the 'communitarian Mass' and concelebration—we are compelled to

---

[43]   *AAS* 46, 1954, p. 669.

[44]   That is to say, each one celebrating a Mass, and not concelebrating one single Mass. See our analysis of this text in *LPC*, no. 180, pp. 23 ff; *see above*, Ch. I.

state that, for a long time, the words of Pius XII were understood by many as being applied to the case of concelebration as well. It indeed seems that this ignorance contributed not a little to the promotion of that rite at the moment of the Council. We shall see this later.

A good number of specialists, on the other hand, and Rahner first of all, understood well that there was no question of concelebration in the November 2nd discourse. Moreover, the correct interpretation of the words of Pius XII goes in the direction which these specialists had desired. For, while the words had been opposed to the use of the 'communitarian Masses,' they could be considered as leaving the door open to what concerns concelebration. Perhaps this is why their studies multiplied during the year 1955. Rahner takes up again his theses from 1949. His new article gives birth to new discussions, both for and against him. But in general, they barely advance any historical research or theological reflection. Still, we must note a few fortunate exceptions: like the remarkable synthesis of Canon Catta, a sign that a profound maturation was taking place; or the little work of V. Raffa, which recalls the Catholic doctrine on the value of each Mass as an action of Christ, and therefore the efficacy which it has independently not of the celebrant's *intention,* but of his *devotion.* It is aimed directly at the anthropomorphic assertions of Rahner, which Schultze moderately supports in his lengthy article in the *Gregorianum.* This last article is interesting; for it also bears witness to the profound maturation which we just mentioned—especially by the brief historical synthesis and presentation it gives of the theses of Afanasieff, professor at the Institut Saint-Serge in Paris. Basing himself on the earliest and most widespread Eastern Tradition, and agreeing to a certain degree with the conclusions of Raes, Afanasieff strongly opposed the idea of daily concelebration.

For the year 1956, mention must be made of the study of Dom Franquesa, a monk of Monserrat. It has the merit of having been carried out directly from the texts. It agrees completely with the theses of Hanssens, but moves back the beginning of sacramental concelebration to the fifth and sixth centuries. These conclusions are not convincing; for, as was noted, the author is not sufficiently attentive to the meaning of the expression '*nobiscum celebrare*' and other similar phrases, where he tends always to see the expression of a sacramental concelebration. The most indisputable texts show that it is the contrary which is most often true[45]: '*concelebrare*' often has a very general meaning.

Nevertheless, as in 1954, the notable event of 1956 was again a discourse of Pius XII to the members of the International Congress of Pastoral Liturgy in Assisi. The Pope reaffirmed this time his teaching from the preceding discourse, denouncing again 'the error regarding the equivalence between the celebration of one hundred Masses by one hundred priests and that of one Mass at which one hundred priests piously assist.'[46] This time the terms used formally excluded the possibility of applying them to the case of concelebration; but it does not seem that this clarification has always been sufficiently observed, something which the rest of the text rendered even clearer.

Yet the new element of this discourse was when the Pope taught that, in order to concelebrate truly, that is sacramentally, all the priests 'must themselves say over the bread and wine, "This is My Body," "This is My Blood"; if not, their concelebration is purely ceremonial.' This was the ratification by the supreme authority of the distinction between 'sacramental concelebration' and 'ceremonial concelebration.' It was at the same time the explicit condemnation of the theses held for years by Rahner and by the group from *La Maison Dieu*, and by all those who followed them.

The great silence that followed this magisterial declaration therefore comes as no surprise. Though of a strictly theological order, it nevertheless had an immediate importance on the historical level, as we showed above (when analyzing no. 35 of *La Maison Dieu*). It

---

[45]   See the review of Franquesa's book in *Les Questions de Liturgie Paroissiales* 37, 1956, p. 145.

[46]   *AAS* 48, 1956, pp. 716–18. See our analysis of this text in *LPC*, no. 180, pp. 24–7; *see above*, Ch. I.

pointed out, in fact, that the passing from 'ceremonial concelebration' to 'sacramental' was not simply the transition from one liturgical rite to another without doctrinal and practical impact; but rather, it represented a profound transformation, the importance of which, it is true, could appear only by the light of a sufficiently developed theology of the sacrifice of the Mass and the ministerial priesthood. More particularly, it is the doctrine and practice of the Latin Church regarding the private Mass, its value and multiplication, which allows one to understand the true impact of the change from one form of 'concelebration' to another.

At the beginning of the following year, on 8 March 1957, in a 'response' to a '*dubium*' (the 'response' was approved by the Holy Father on 23 May), the Holy Office reaffirmed the declarations of Pius XII: 'by the institution of Christ, he alone validly consecrates who pronounces the words of consecration.' We noted above how the need for a reaffirmation by authority of such an elementary truth reveals the confusion in the hearts of many at that time. From the point of view of the history of ideas, we must now note that the necessity of this new intervention by the Magisterium some months after that of November 1956 is no less revealing of the climate of opposition to the hierarchical authority of the time. And Fr Hürth, SJ, Consultor for the Holy Office, confirmed in an article of official character the impact of that 'response' from the historical point of view: treating the very reality of things, he said, and not the mere idea which one had of them at different epochs of history, this doctrinal assertion had value retrospectively for the first centuries of the Church.[47]

The thesis, therefore, which wished to see in the restoration of 'sacramental concelebration' a simple return to the early Tradition became impossible to sustain. And yet ... it is that which ended up

---

[47] Hürth (1957), pp. 254 ff. The analysis of this article shows that Fr Hürth bases himself principally on the historical works of Hanssens and Raes, and that the Response of the Holy Office is concerned principally with the theses of Rahner (1955), defended as well by Schultze (1955), and those of the authors of *La Maison Dieu* (no. 35).

being triumphant in the opinion of many—but at the price of how much sustained silence and confusion! (Something we shall return to later.) At the least, the promoters of the liturgical movement would not return to this question for some time. On the other hand, encouraged probably by the Holy See, Fr Hanssens took up again the publication of the fruit of his labors. He synthesized and updated them in two extremely precious works (despite the hesitancy which is found there on the question of the number of Masses in concelebration, a hesitancy found in many studies of that period): one constitutes the chapter of a voluminous collaborative work on the Eucharist, published in 1957 under the direction of Msgr A. Piolanti; the other appeared the following year in the newly founded journal of the Pontifical Roman Academy of Theology, *Divinitas*.

The rupture into two opposing currents must become always more pronounced. We say two currents, and not two camps, because we would never finish if we wished to trace the frontiers of their terrain. We must note, moreover, that the more time passed, the less the question was one of knowing whether one must opt for or against concelebration; for the idea of a certain revival of this rite was going increasingly imposing itself. The question was one of fixing the form and the frequency of its usage. It is regarding this question most of all that it seems correct to speak of two currents: that which turned towards an unlimited use of concelebration, even if initially it only asked for an occasional use; and that which insisted from the beginning that the conditions and limitations of concelebration be clearly fixed. In general, it can be said that the name of Dom Beauduin is definitely found at the head of the first current, which was that of the 'liturgical movement' (especially in France, Belgium and Germany); while Hanssens' name represents the other current, followed in general in the Roman circles. Such was also, on the eve of the Council, the position of Rev Fr Dom Gut, the Abbot General of the Benedictines.[48]

---

[48] *Acta et Documenta Concilio Oecumenico Vaticano II Apparendo*, Series I (*Antepreparatoria*), Vol. II, Pars VIII (*Consilia et vota. Superiores Generales*

III. Third Period: Since the Announcement of the Convocation of the Council

Times had changed. On 25 January 1959, John XXIII announced his intention to convoke an ecumenical council. His objective was chiefly pastoral: he wanted to adapt the Church to the needs of the age. This was the programme of '*aggiornamento.*' The liturgy was in a favourable position, and it is within this context that the problem of concelebration would be placed.

While from the theological point of view several fundamental questions still awaited clarification on the level of the Magisterium and the common opinion of theologians—questions such as the number of Masses offered in a concelebration, or that of the value of concelebrated Masses—while they still awaited clarification from a theological point of view, from the historical point of view it can be said that the principal pieces of the dossier had already been assembled (To a certain degree, moreover, it can be said as much for theological questions.). All would depend, therefore, on the manner in which they would be utilized, both among the specialists and the pastors who have to adhere to the decisions, as well as the general public. For these pieces and these arguments were not in fact known except by a very small number of persons, even among the specialists, who themselves were divided into historians, liturgists and theologians. Not all were equally qualified in these different domains; hence the persistent confusion which impacted the interpretation of historical facts.

Nevertheless, one advancement was made, thanks especially to the works of Puniet, Hanssens and Raes, and confirmed by the 1956 and 1957 interventions of the Magisterium, namely the distinction between

---

Religiosorum), (Typ. Poligl. Vatic., 1961), p. 15: '*S. Concilium indicet, quando et sub quibus conditionibus, etiam in Ecclesia Occidentali Concelebratio permitti possit.*' Diverging on this point from the line indicated by their abbot general, the abbots of the Benedictines of France and Belgium asked for daily concelebration (*ibid*, pp. 25; 42)—something which was far from reflecting the thought of all Benedictines, even in these two countries alone.

the two forms of 'concelebration': one purely ceremonial, the other sacramental and sacrificial. Jungmann takes this up again in his brief notice in the *Lexikon für Theologie und Kirche,* in 1961. The preceding year, Fr Schmidt, SJ, professor at the Gregorian University, insisted on it, naming two rites respectively: *concelebratio participationis* and *concelebratio confectionis* (from the Latin expression *conficere sacramentum*). Basing himself principally on the studies of Hanssens and Raes, which he qualifies as 'foundational,' he reaffirms that the traditional and primitive form of 'concelebration,' both in the East and the West, is the first of the two, the 'ceremonial'; this henceforth represents another indisputably acquired point of history.[49] He and others along with him noted as well that sacramental concelebration, having appeared in Rome around the eighth century, had always preserved a solemn and exceptional character, being reserved as it was to the Pope and cardinal priests; and that it was adopted by certain Eastern Rites only under Latin influence and only at a very recent period. It did not develop into a daily practice except until recently and only among certain communities, and to the great scandal of the Greek Orthodox.[50]

However, hardly anyone would listen to such voices, no matter how firmly established they were both historically and theologically. They would end up being concealed for a long time by those of the 'liturgical movement.' In the very important lecture which was delivered in Munich in 1960, and which was published in 1963 in the *Ephemerides Liturgicae,* at a decisive moment for the conciliar debates in progress, Msgr A. G. Martimort, while declaring that he was not concerned with questions of history, approached them nevertheless and resolved them in the same way as Dom Beauduin did in 1922. He even cited Raes, from whom he borrowed conclusions on the level of historical facts: before 'the end of the sixteenth century or the beginning of the seventeenth,' in the 'concelebration' of the Byzantine

---

[49]   Schmidt (1960), p. 411.

[50]   Cf. Raes (1953), p. 30; Afanasieff (1952), cited by Schultze (1955), p. 222 and by Franquesa (1956), p. 90, etc.

Rite, only the principal celebrant said the anaphora. 'However,' he adds, 'the innovation brought forward at that time consisted only in the fact that all celebrants were obliged to say the anaphora.' The word 'only' is revealing. It is the bearer of a theological interpretation which goes a long way, and which is explained immediately after: before this 'innovation,' 'ceremonial' concelebration 'was developed and fixed throughout the ages according to an uninterrupted tradition, such that the change—so important in the eyes of modern theology—which consists in allowing all priests to say the text of the anaphora, was but the final stage in a homogenous evolution.'[51]

Let us, then, consider again the theses from no. 35 of *La Maison Dieu*. The intervention of Msgr Martimort has done much to persuade opinions regarding these theses, especially that of the Council Fathers; and even more was done by Msgr Bugnini, 'an Italian Lazarist from the staff of *Ephemerides Liturigicae*,' who was at work once again to circulate the theses. We know the decisive role which this religious played before, during and after the Council. Fr Gy himself, from whom we borrowed this information, recalled that Bugnini had been 'secretary of the commission of the reform instituted by Pius XII,' then named secretary of the pre-conciliar commission of the liturgy by John XXIII—an 'excellent choice' according to Fr Gy.[52] Nevertheless, on the eve of the Council, when on 22 February 1962, Cardinal Larraona succeeded Cardinal Cicognani as head of the Sacred Congregation of Rites, Fr Bugnini (he had not yet been made bishop) 'lost his chair at the Lateran and did not become the secretary of the conciliar commission.'[53] John XXIII had distanced him from both positions. Why? He was no less actively present in Rome. It was he who asked Msgr Martimort for the text of the latter's Munich lecture in order to publish it in the *Ephemerides Liturigicae* in 1963.[54] What

---

[51] Martimort (1963), p. 151.

[52] Gy (1967), p. 114.

[53] *Ibid.*, p. 118.

[54] On 5 March 1964, the *L'Osservatore Romano* announced the creation of a

we see now is the close collaboration of the 'staff of the *Ephemerides Liturgicae,*' led by Bugnini, and that of the *La Maison Dieu,* for the sake of convincing the conciliar Fathers that the concelebration which they were being asked to restore was but a return to the practice of the early Church and a traditional liturgical form. And as we shall see later, they were successful in their endeavor.

Nevertheless, we showed above (though it is not superfluous to say again) that this thesis was not historically or theologically tenable. For, to affirm that the passing from 'ceremonial concelebration' to 'sacramental concelebration' represents an 'homogenous evolution' of the liturgy does not conform to facts either for the East or the West; and such an assertion rests on a theology of the Eucharist that is manifestly insufficient. The difference between these two forms of 'concelebration' is, in fact, important not only 'in the eyes of modern theology,' but for the liturgy of the Mass itself; for, it calls into question the very reality of the Eucharistic Mystery, and regarding such a reality the faith and doctrine of the Church cannot have changed. Great already for the priest himself, this difference is greater still from the Church's point of view. For the priest, it is not the same thing to associate himself with the celebration of the Eucharist by simply participating, even under a special hierarchical rank, and associating himself by the properly priestly consecration and offering which the principal celebrant alone makes, or those co-consecrating and therefore sacramentally co-offering the sacrifice with him. It is, nevertheless, from this point of view that one would be able to speak

---

'Council for the application of the Constitution on the Sacred Liturgy', the secretary of which was Fr Bugnini (cf. Ralph M. Wiltgen, SVD, *The Rhine Flows into the Tiber (New York: Hawthorne, 1967).* An indispensable work for the history of Vatican II). Fr Bugnini, now Msgr Bugnini, then became the Secretary of the Sacred Congregation for Divine Worship, up until the day when, just like John XXIII, Paul VI relieved him of his duties; that was the spring of 1975. At the beginning of January 1976, (cf. *L'Oss. Rom.,* 5–6 January) he was sent to Iran as pro–nuncio, finding himself now definitively removed from liturgical matters.

most reasonably of a homogenous development; the manner of sacramental concelebration, introduced in Rome in order to honor the cardinal priests, could be seen in this sense.

But from the point of view of the Church: when one considers the movement from becoming more and more conscious of the value of the Mass and of multiplying its celebration—a movement whose history we shall later examine (Ch. VIII)—then it is no longer possible to speak simply of a homogenous evolution, especially when one ends up, in the name of this same evolution, systematically replacing for priests the personal celebration of the Mass with its collective celebration. We must always return to the important principle stated by St Thomas Aquinas: the multiplication of Masses causes a multiplication of grace. Whence it follows that the decrease in the number of Masses brings about, all things being equal, a decrease in grace. The number is not everything, this is true; and we will have to return to this question later in order to develop it. But it is not nothing either. To forget this is to fall into an idealism absolutely contrary to the realism proper to the sacramental order and to the economy of redemption.

This aspect is not the only one that prevents us from speaking purely and simply of an 'homogenous evolution.' There is also the role of the principal celebrant in the celebration of the liturgy, to which the East seems to be particularly sensitive, as well as the manner of showing the hierarchical unity of the priesthood and the ecclesial community. And nevertheless, the authority of names such as Dom Beauduin and Msgr Martimort, the silence regarding the most certain conclusions of specialists as competent as Raes and Hanssens, and regarding the declarations of the Magisterium (the Decree of 1957), the tireless work of groups such as those of the *Ephemerides Liturgicae* and *La Maison Dieu*—all these factors were successful in bringing to the Council this thesis of 'the homogenous evolution,' which paradoxically allowed one to sustain the thesis of a return to the origins.

* * *

We now move to the Council itself; and the issue of historical research has become immediately practical. At this point we must analyze the Council. Given its importance, we have dedicated a separate chapter to it; but for now we can consider our principal conclusions. To our great surprise, and despite a certain number of remarkable interventions, neither the historical questions nor some of the most important theological questions had truly been discussed at the Council, at least on the level of the works of the Central Commission and in the Council aula.[55] Whence the difficulty of interpreting correctly the doctrinal value (that is, clarifying the meaning) and disciplinary impact of the promulgated texts. One thing at least seems certain: that the Council Fathers, even if they mention them in passing, did not have the intention of treating the historical questions. One cannot, in fact, pretend to form a judgment on a question which had not been studied. Yet these questions had not at any time been submitted to the Council Fathers for discussion. We must see then in what they say, not so much a definitive judgment following a debated question, but rather a mere echo of the prevailing opinion. And we saw of what conflicts this opinion had been the object, and how the indisputable historical facts had been passed over in silence in order that this opinion might triumph. We shall see it better still when we study later the acts of the Council themselves.

*   *   *

It is not surprising, therefore, that in the works published after the approval of the Council's Constitution on the Sacred Liturgy, at the end of the second session (4 December 1963), numerous questions—almost all of them in fact—were posed once again. To tell the truth, they had hardly been developed at this time, but they appeared here and there. While for certain official representatives of the liturgical movement, such as Fr Gy, OP, in 1967, concelebration was one of those question which 'had already been ripe ten years before

---

[55]   These can now be studied thanks to the publication of the *Acts of the Council* (cf. *see above*, note 233). This will be the goal of our next chapter.

the solution was given,'[56] for others, on the contrary, such was not the case. The preceding year, Fr Roguet, OP, wrote: 'The theology of concelebration is yet to be made.'[57] These two judgments are clearly contradictory, and it is the second which is true, if one considers the problem at its roots. However, from their authors' points of view, they are equally true; they even complement each other. The first establishes that the decisions of the Council—not the decisions in themselves, but such as the reform movement would interpret them—were the fruit of a work whose practical conclusions had been deduced ten years before. The second opened the doors to the still far-off evolution: Roguet in fact proposed the concelebration of all the sacraments, at least all those which, according to him, lend themselves to it; and he gave as a prime example of this the sacrament of Baptism.

In the same sense, but with more seriousness and sobriety, Fr Tihon equally recognized this in 1964, when he declared that, in the history of concelebration, 'many points still remain obscure.' He limited himself to mentioning discreetly in a footnote, apropos of the origins of concelebration: 'The Council itself was content with asserting that concelebration "remained in use even until now," without wishing to fix a *terminus a quo*: cfr. *Const. De Sacra Lit.*, no. 57, § 1.'[58] Beyond this, his long study shows well that, in addition to the historical questions and their interpretation, numerous other points remained to be clarified.

The tragedy is that the works that appeared during the following years only contributed to obscuring these questions instead of clarifying them. Two factors in particular contributed to this, which Roguet's article just cited brought out. First of all, the radical innovation of the practice injected into the facts, and this by means of an interpretation

---

[56] Gy (1967), p. 114.

[57] Roguet (1966), p. 116.

[58] Tihon (1964), p. 580, note 4. In its brevity, this footnote shows that Fr Tihon had definitely seen that the problem regarding the origins of concelebration existed, and that the Council had not resolved it.

of conciliar decrees so stretched that it ends up contradicting them. In fact, Roguet himself recognized this: 'Neither the antiquity of the West nor the East has known or does know these daily concelebrations which include, in some communities, up to forty priests; some of these, in more exceptional cases but frequent enough, include more than one hundred priests.'[59] Is this *radical innovation, with no basis in Tradition,* what the Council Fathers had approved? Of course not.

The second factor is a no less radical calling into question of all the aspects of the mystery of Eucharistic concelebration, including those which had already been clarified before the Council: 'It certainly seems,' adds Roguet, 'that the speculations which had multiplied before the Council, the distinctions sketched out between sacramental, ceremonial, silent, etc. concelebrations, are totally obsolete.'[60] If one looks back at what we wrote above concerning that fundamental distinction—a distinction not simply 'sketched out' but firmly established historically and theologically, not purely an object of vague 'speculations' but sanctioned by two formal interventions of the Magisterium (1956 and 1957)—if one looks back at this, one will know how to appraise such language. One will also better understand retrospectively why the Decree of the Holy Office had been necessary some months after the Pope's discourse in 1956: Fr Roguet belonged to the group of theologians it was addressed to. In 1966 he thought he could speak freely; and in fact he was able, for no one prevented him. But the levity with which he treated the Magisterium, and the systematic silence he had regarding its acts as well as the very accurate work of historians, contributed to the increase of confusion.

This calling into question of the most certain truths would be frequently repeated later on,[61] to the point of grave deviations from

---

[59]   Roguet (1966), p. 116.

[60]   *Ibid.*

[61]   See, as an example of this, the sections published by the Abbey Saint–André–les Bruges and titled *Liturgie et monastère* (in our bibliography, see Rouillard (1968); but there are especially the other articles which proceed with this radical calling into question). See also Vogüë (1967), etc.

and even open negations of the faith, which are deplored today, especially in what concerns the priesthood, transubstantiation and the sacrifice of the Mass.[62] Among these errors, which simultaneously attacked the priesthood and the Eucharist, there is one which relates most directly to concelebration. It is the one that consists in making the congregation as such the proper subject of the liturgical action, without any other distinction than that of some interchangeable 'ministers.' We shall return to this later.

According to Fr Gy, it is this communitarian aspect of the Eucharist that had been the sole reason retained by the Council for taking up again the practice of concelebration.[63] Moreover, understood correctly, this principle would have been perfect, as well as the application which would have been drawn from it. But it was inscribed within a 'movement' that had falsified the understanding of it, and that would do so even more after the Council. This latter takes up again in its texts only the traditional teaching. However, the absolute primacy, which the 'liturgical movement' gave to the notion of the congregation, was at one and the same time the strength and the weakness of all its work; for, it prevented the proper placing of the other, no less essential aspects—aspects which alone would have allowed one to understand exactly the true nature and different functions of the congregation itself. One may think, for example, of aspects such as mystery, sacredness, sacrifice, redemption, etc. Finally, by the absolutizing that was done, this communitarian aspect lead to anthropocentrism, the congregation celebrating itself—a conclusion which followed logically from the principles posited.

It is not within our present plan to retrace the stages of this rapid degradation, which is not one of the less important aspects of the 'self-destruction' of the Church, deplored by Paul VI. We mention only some names as points of reference. The article of Manders, in *Concilium* (February 1965), gives us a valuable echo of Dutch

---

62 Cf. *see below*, note 72 and following.
63 Gy (1964), p. 129.

thought. He presents 'the hierarchical community insofar as it is the subject of concelebration'; and he affirms that 'the entire community celebrates the *Mysterium Passionis Domini.*'[64] Manders adds, that each one participates in it according to his rank, seeming to explain by this the sense which he gives to the word 'hierarchical'; but rather, it is in order to define immediately the priests as 'the college of those whose mission is to serve the Church.'[65] This is the passing—explicitly taught today—from the 'ministerial priesthood' to the 'priestly ministry' The inversion of the substantive and adjective in these two expressions is full of meaning. What it signifies is that the point of departure for the ecclesial hierarchy is no longer the priesthood of Christ, but a simple ministry, that is to say a service, and one which is not defined and can be attributed indifferently to all, because it is founded on membership in the ecclesial community. This latter is the true point of departure for the Church. In the ambiguity of the formulas employed, some reflections, such as that of Fr Manders, and others which multiplied during that period, were gravely corrosive instruments for the liturgy and for the faith itself.

It is in this movement that we would see, in 1967, Dom Adalbert de Vogüé, OSB, suggesting that the conventual Mass could no longer be celebrated daily—a Mass he could hardly conceive of as anything other than concelebrated. The argument he uses: it was not celebrated daily in the early days of monasticism.[66]

---

[64] Manders (1965), p. 126.

[65] *Ibid.*

[66] Vogüé (1967), pp. 161 ff. Dom de Vogüé is openly opposed to Dom Paul Delatte, whose *Commentaire sur la Règle de Saint Benoît* (Paris, 1913) he cites. Dom de Vogüe holds that the monastic life has its center in the Divine Office, and *not* in the Mass; that the daily solemnization of this latter is the fruit of the clericalization of monasticism (which the study of Eastern monasticism discredits); that 'the Mass is poorly introduced into the monastic day. It is juxtaposed and added to a liturgical *cursus* already complete and onerous enough' (p. 166); etc. In conclusion, he asks for the suppression of at least the obligatory character of the daily conventual Mass.

The collection of studies published in 1968 by the Abbey Saint-André-les-Bruges, under the title *Liturgie et Monastère,* is no less destructive. Ph. Rouillard retraces here the history of concelebration, balancing well the aspect of sacrifice and that of the assembly; but his vision remains deformed because of its failure to recognize how significant the difference is between ceremonial and sacramental 'concelebrations.'[67] He does emphasize, however, the great innovation, in relation to Tradition, which is represented by the fact that concelebration, after the Council, was habitually performed in absence of the bishop.[68] However, the greater part of the other studies tends to exalt the congregation in an abusive manner, reducing as much as possible the role of the priest, especially the studies by Gerard Dubois and Eloi Dekkers.[69]

---

[67] Rouillard (1968), pp. 50-3, 54.

[68] *Ibid.,* p. 54.

[69] The work of Gerard Dubois, *L'Eucharistie au Coeur de la vie conventuelle,* is interesting by the fact that it speaks of *the conventual Mass.* It uncovers the inconveniencies, especially those which come from the fact that it brings about a 'regrouping of the latter (the priests of the monastery) to a special place', which, especially if these priests are numerous, 'accentuates the division of the community into two categories, more than it favours the unity of the community.' (p. 39). We know the solution given to this difficulty in a number of religious communities: all the members are grouped around the altar, priests and non–priests without distinction. Eloi Dekkers (Abbot of Steenbrugge) made analogous remarks, observing that in certain monastic concelebrations which he had seen: 'In the choir remains only the *pusillus grex* of the formerly brother confreres.' And that: 'Just recently pushed completely aside, the monks see the monk–priests now regrouped immediately into a new cast. What injuries have not come from this! Concelebration manifests the unity of the priesthood; we recognize this. But is it necessary that it be detrimental to the unity of the Christian people?' (*Limites de la concélébration; ibid,* p. 79). Of course not. And this is why Eloi Dekkers pleaded for silent or ceremonial concelebration, which, according to him, is 'the authentic concelebration' (p. 83), 'by avoiding emphasizing unduly the words of consecration' (*ibid*). Thus, concelebration will truly be the work of the whole congregation, without distinction between priests and non–priests. In 1968 such ideas still belonged

In order to have a clear view of the situation, it is necessary to remember that the current which we point out here represents only one aspect, that it is difficult to appraise the size of it, and that the true Tradition followed its course amidst these stirrings. However, it cannot be denied that a desire for a profound transformation animated those who inspired the liturgical reform, in whose surroundings the new practice of concelebration was instituted little by little. Fr Gy openly testified to this when he wrote in 1967: 'The liturgical reform of Vatican II, unlike that of the Council of Trent, asked priests and faithful to change their liturgical behavior, to transform their piety as well as the very image that they had of the celebration.'[70] This is far from the thesis of the 'homogenous evolution' maintained during the Council. And Gy explains in what especially consists the difference between this 'reform impacting the very spirit of the liturgy' and that of Trent, which changed nothing in relation to what was done in the Middle Ages. It is that, after Vatican II, 'the different elements of active participation, enlightened by the ecclesiology of *Lumen Gentium* and by ten or fifteen years of practice, re-combined from the idea, explained by Y. Congar, of "the Ecclesia or Christian community as the integral subject of the liturgical action".'[71] These texts are enlightening from a more profound aspect. They put an end to all the equivocations that weighed upon the most current and, in themselves, best ideas: for example, that of 'active participation.' To tell the truth, in order that the equivocation completely come to an end, it is necessary to say again that, much more than 'the ecclesiology of *Lumen Gentium*' used in an abusive manner, it was especially the 'ten or fifteen years of practice' which preceded, and the ten more than the fifteen, which allows one to understand what must be meant here

---

to only some 'progressive' groups. Today, and since 1974, they are the object of official directives of the CNPL (cf. *see below*, notes 73–78).

[70]   P. M. Gy, OP, *La réforme liturgique de Trente et celle de Vatican II*, in *LMD*, no. 128 (1967/4), pp. 61–75; cf. p. 70.

[71]   *Ibid*, citing the title of Fr Congar's contribution, in Jossua–Congar(1967), pp. 241–82.

by the expression 'Christian community as the integral subject of the liturgy': what it introduced was the idea of the concelebration of the Eucharist by the entire congregation under the presidency of a 'minister,' named and delegated by the congregation. The ministerial priesthood and the common priesthood are founded on one and the same thing: the communitarian priesthood.

No less interesting from the historical point of view is this other reminder of Fr Gy: 'In the wake of the conciliar Constitution, the French Episcopal Commission saw indeed that a "change in mentality" was required.'[72] 'The historical analysis,' he continues, 'confirms such an assessment.' This latter was in fact a declaration of intention, and a very old intention; for the Commission which expressed itself thus had played a decisive role at the Council, and it intended to continue playing a no less important role in its application.

It did indeed play that role; and it continued to do so, as the three following texts bear witness. They come from official organs: the first two were published by the CNPL, or under its direction; the third was published by the Centre de Pastorale Sacramentelle et Liturgique of the Diocese of Paris.

1974

To the question, 'Who must celebrate?' the journal *Notes de Pastorale Liturgique* responds: 'The congregation that is there ("your family," "your people"), that small group of believers who represent the entire Church of God … It has within its midst an "ordained" priest, who says certain words and makes certain gestures in order that his Eucharist might be the action of the whole Church and of Christ in it. But it is truly the congregation that recalls, that offers ("we offer"), that pro-

---

72 *Ibid*, p. 72, referring to the *Pastoral Letter on the Sacred Liturgy* (14 January 1964): 'What is being asked of all … is a vigorous change in mentality, a true new education on our liturgical life' (*La Documentation Catholique* 61, 1964, col. 258) (*ibid*, note 21). One can see the insistence of the authors of this *Letter* on the depth of the changes and innovations which they had proclaimed.

claims the wonders of God, that sings, that prays, that partakes of the meal.'[73] The quotation marks which surround the word 'ordained' before the word priest are significant: it is, for the author, a conventional term to be overcome, or at least reinterpreted. The priest is only one minister among others. The priesthood is only one ministry among others within 'the community,' and this latter can choose and name whomever they want to exercise that ministry. The 'ordination' does not create an essential difference between this ministry and the others.

1975

In the second series of *Fiches de Formation pour Animateurs de Célébration* (FAC), a sheet on 'The Eucharistic Prayer' explains: 'The consecration is not a magical action accomplished by the priest. It is an act of the Spirit Who animates the Church ... ,' that is to say the congregation, whose role is exalted here in an abusive and false manner.[74] Another sheet, titled, '*Presiding Over the Assumbly,*' explained in what consists this key function, filled indifferently by a priest or layman.[75] If all is gathering and congregation, then the fundamental ministry is that of the community; and *within the community,* the principal particular ministry will be the presidency or animator. They are sometimes distinct, sometimes confused.

In the third series of these FAC sheets, one titled 'Doctrine' is explicitly devoted to 'The Congregation.' Here we read: 'One alone presides,

---

[73] *Notes de Pastorale Liturgique,* no. 112 (October 1974), titled: *La prière eucharis-tique,* p. 21 (see also, p. 47). On the inside front cover we read: 'A journal published under the direction of Centre National de Pastorale Liturgique ... Redaction: 4, avenue Vavin, Paris, 6e. Administration: Editions du Cerf ... '

[74] *FAC Doctrine 2/Série* 2, p. 3. The pamphlet instroducing these cardboard sheets we read on page 1: *Les fiches Formation pour Animateurs de Célébration,* and on page 4: 'Centre National de Pastorale Liturgique–4, avenue Vavin –75006 Paris.' Pages 2 and 3 contain the list of three series of 24 sheets published in 1975, 1976 and 1977. The diffusion of these sheets has become the object of an intense labor on the part of the CNPL.

[75] *FAC Animation 2/Série* 2.

signifying the head of the Ecclesial Body: Christ. But all are servants of each other. It is not the ministers but the congregation that celebrates.'[76] Here we have something which removes all ambiguity, but destroys at its roots the constitution of the Church, hierarchical and communitarian.

1979

In a brochure from the Centre Jean-Bart on *The Sunday, Today and Tomorrow,* the relation between the theses on concelebration, condemned in 1947, appeared in broad daylight: 'It is a question of returning to an ancient tradition, which Fr Liégé recently recalled in the symposium on the Eucharist: *in the Eucharistic assembly, each member of the faithful concelebrates with all the other faithful;* the priest does not consecrate alone, but the whole congregation consecrates with him—a common ministry where each officiates with all the others.'[77] This time the word is loosened: there is only this *common ministry,* of which all partake without distinction.

---

[76] *FAC Doctrine 3/Série* 3, p. 3. The opposition, 'not … but,' makes this formula unacceptable. It expresses clearly the doctrine contained in all these sheets.

[77] Centre Jean–Bart. René Dufay, *Le dimanche hier et aujourd'hui* (mimeographed leaflet of 65 pages, presented, on the back cover, in the following manner: 'Publication périodique du Centre Jean–Bart (Reproduction interdite), 8 rue de la Ville–l'Evêque, 75008 Paris … 790301,' that is the first quarter of March 1979), p. 63; cf. p. 47, etc. Every section is a radical attack on 'Sunday, the Lord's Day'. The *Ordo Administratif* 1980' from the dioceses of Paris, Créteil, Nanterre, Saint–Denis, indicates that 8 rue de la Ville–l'Evêque is not only the seat of the Archbishop of Paris, but also that of the Secretariat of the Province and the Central Zone, the Ecclesiastical Province of Paris, comprising, in addition to those dioceses already mentioned, those of Corbeil, Meaux, Pontoise, Versailles and the Vicariate for the Army (p. 7). It is, therefore, all these dioceses of France, and beginning with Paris as the center, which have been touched by this 'pastorale'. René Dufay is 'responsible for the Diocese of Paris', in the department of Catechism and Penitence of the Centre Jean–Bart, which is the Centre of 'Pastorale Sacramentelle et Liturgique' (*Ordo* … , p. 25). We see then that it is no exaggeration to say that the 'self–destruction' of the Church, as Paul VI called it, is, in France, the work of the official organs of the Episcopate.

The examples could be multiplied,[78] but these will suffice. The continuity which they reveal is noteworthy: the errors condemned in the Encyclical *Mediator Dei* in 1947 are now taught by the official organs of France's Pastoral Liturgy. We can thus understand what the French Episcopal Commission means when, in the wake of the Council, it becomes involved, in the name of the Council, in 'a change of mentality': it was a radical change of Catholic doctrine and dogma that was under way. The practice had to follow; and it did follow to a great degree.

It is not a question for us of putting persons on trial. Moreover, more than one of the members of the CPL of 1946 was rejected by the movement itself in the course of time; and some of these today firmly oppose the group's destructive action. We are thinking of persons such as Msgr Martimort or Fr Louis Bouyer.[79] What we are noting is the existence of a current of ideas and the groups that are being used to promote those ideas in theory and practice. These facts do not take us away from our subject; for, they bring to us the context in which the history of concelebration had been studied and, above all, presented by the members of the CNPL since 1946. They also show us, when considered in their current outcome, what was the true issue of all those specialized works and debates.

We also add that, when one considers the whole ensemble of facts, and more particularly the manner in which certain questions have been muddled again after the Council, while they had already been resolved by the Magisterium itself, when one notices the silence made concerning certain points of history or the deformed interpretation given to them—when one considers all these facts, it becomes

---

[78]   Especially by looking at the bibliography which René Dufay (see preceding note) gives at the end of this work. One can see there, among other things, the most recent numbers of *LMD* (124; 129; 130). We can add today no. 137, *Problématique de l'eucharistie* (Colloquium from the section of Theological and Religious Sciences of the Institut Catholique of Paris, 24–26 January 1979) (1979/1). Etc.

[79]   We have already noted this latter's recent book, *Le métier de théologien. Entretiens avec Georges Daix* (Paris, France Empire, 1979).

impossible to consider the practice after the Council as the confirmation of the authentic interpretation of the Council. The interpretation
which was confirmed was that which the supporters of the liturgical
movement imposed, along with the practice; it happened not without
a begging of the question. This amounts to saying: 'here is what
happened; therefore, this is what the Council wanted.'

For the very same reason it is equally impossible (and here we are
diametrically opposed to Fr Gy) to consider as 'irreversible'[80] the
profound 'change of mentality' and the liturgical practice itself which
the same liturgical movement realized, to a great extent by means of
'its own' conciliar texts and the interpretation it made of them.[81]

---

80   Art. cit. (*see above*, note 70), p. 72.

81   We became aware only lately of the article by E. Dekkers, OSB, *La concélébration tradition ou nouveauté?* (in *Mélanges liturgiques offerts au R.P. Dom Bernard
Botte OSB de l'Abbaye du Mont César—A l'occasion du cinquantième anniversaire de son ordination sacerdotale (4 juin 1972)*, Louvain, Abbey of Mont
César, 1972, pp. 99–120). It is worth noting for the abundant documentation
which it presents, as well as for its reflections and conclusions. They fully
confirm all that we said. The essentials can be summed up as follows:

1) Eucharistic concelebration was the current practice of the ancient Church:
'Concelebration is the normal Mass, the Mass simply, *each time there were
several priests in assistance*' (p. 109). One will notice the last words of the
sentence, italicized by us.

2) Nevertheless the concelebrating priests remained silent; only the principal
celebrant [the bishop] pronounced the words of the canon (pp. 110–12). The
author does not try to clarify the date when the concelebrants began to say
the prayers with the bishop.

3) The question is, in fact, secondary for him; for, he asserts that these silent
'*comministri*' consecrated with the bishop. The only argument that he brings
forward in support of his assertion is, that to hold to the contrary 'would be
to interpret the ancient sources with the help of categories borrowed from
modern theology' (p. 112). Yet it is not a question of interpreting 'ancient
sources', but of judging theologically the sacramental value of a liturgical act.
This is something which belongs to a doctrine unchangeable in itself, whatever
be the time of maturation necessary for it to come to full light. We see again
here both the importance of theology for the study of liturgical history, as well
as the consequences of a dogmatic evolution which, failing to be 'homoge-

nous', leads to an historio–doctrinal relativism.

4) Regarding the Eastern Rites, E. Dekkers expresses himself even more forcefully than we. What he writes deserves mentioning. Stating that: 'The East ignored spoken [and therefore sacramental] concelebration for centuries,' (p. 113), he presents it, when it is finally introduced, as an 'innovation' (p. 115). And he continues: 'When question occurred, in our day, of reintroducing concelebration into the Latin Church, it was believed that concelebration with the collective recitation of the principal parts of the Eucharistic anaphora was the traditional and habitual form of the Eastern Rites. Consideration was not given to the fact that an innovation was introduced into the Latin Church by Pierre Moghila, and that it was inspired neither by the living liturgy of the Orthodox Church nor by an ancient tradition, but by the manuals of theology, discussing *in vitro* the exigencies of a rite [*sic*] practically nonexistent (except in the case of ordinations; but here it raises the difficulties which are known to us from its introduction in the twelfth century)' (pp. 115–16). In its negative part, this conclusion fully coincides with our own: concelebration in is modern form, spoken and sacramental, is unknown to ancient tradition; it represents, especially for the Eastern Church, an innovation in no way inspired by its 'living liturgy', having been introduced under the influence of the Latin Church. This convergence between the conclusions of Fr Dekkers and our own is not surprising, since he draws from the same sources as we do (see our bibliography), and bases himself, consequently, on the same facts. On the other hand, what he asserts regarding the origins and causes of sacramental concelebration is more debatable. Furthermore, one will note the imprecision of his thought in general. He attributes it to the exigencies of the manuals (which did not exist at that time), he gives the impression of placing the origins in the twelfth century (which is the very period in which it disappears), and he considers only in last place what he calls 'the desire to keep as much as possible a private Mass in the common celebration' (p. 116). This last phrase, where one can sense a certain depreciation of the private Mass, very much diminishes the theology of the Eucharist and the priesthood to the point that it unjustly overestimates the motives for introducing the common recitation of the canon. This latter took place, as we saw, in the eighth century; and the interpretation which is given here for such motivations is made—it cannot be denied—'by the help of the categories of a modern theology'.

The rest of the article presents a certain number of valuable details, especially regarding the communitarian aspect of concelebration. Its conclusion is both interesting and disappointing: 'In ritualizing concelebration and in reserving it for feast days, it has been solemnized. The ceremonies pass to a deeper level and

Therefore, it is this collection of questions which must be revisited and clarified in order to understand precisely the problems at their root and to give *a correct interpretation of the Council's texts*. For, such is the fundamental question, it seems, which still awaits our response. It is out of a desire to help find this response which, after having examined the question of the number of Masses offered to God in a concelebration, and having shown that this one celebration, by the decrease of the number of Masses that it entails, also causes a decrease in the grace of the Eucharist in the Church—it is out of desire to help that we wish show now what was the true history of concelebration. However, given the importance of this question, we have left a close examination of it for another chapter.

In order to introduce it, and at the same to conclude this chapter, we present for the meditation of the reader this thought from St Jerome:

Multi labuntur errore propter ignorantiam historiae.[82]

---

risk concealing the essentials' (p. 120). The author seems to forget that, during the first centuries of the Church, the Mass was not celebrated except on Sundays and feast days. The limited frequency of concelebration is therefore not the fruit of a restrictive evolution, but an original fact. What does result from a development, both liturgical and dogmatic, is its increasing ritualization and solemnization; but these things are progress, not impoverishments.

The conclusion which is drawn from this study, in addition to those produced by its author, is that the normal form of sacramental concelebration is precisely this solemn form, taking place especially on Sundays and feast days. This practice alone is founded on tradition: the community gathered around its pastor, and in the first place are the priests. They celebrate the liturgy according to the function which their priesthood gives them, insofar as it is possible in these conditions, that is to say by celebrating sacramentally with their superior, at the head of their ecclesial community, which they aid him in governing, teaching and sanctifying in this supreme thanksgiving and praise rendered to God.

[82] *In Matth.*, I, 2; CCL 77, 15.

Foundational Bibliography for the History of Concelebration

Although we are adhering primarily to the historical aspect, we shall also note some principal studies of the theological or liturgical order, which have influenced historical research. These three areas are in fact closely tied together and shed light on each other.

One could compare our bibliography to that of Schmidt (1960), by which we have been helped. We thank him for this. We have been helped by other bibliographies as well, especially those presented by authors such as Denis-Boulet (1961), Tihon (1964), Manders (1965), Joannes (1967), Rouillard (1968), in order to ensure that no foundational work has escaped us.

We found it useful to mention the principal interventions of the Magisterium, which have punctuated this history of the history (and theology) of concelebration in the twentieth century. In order to aid the reader in finding them more easily, we pointed them out with an asterisk (nos. 9*; 17*; 19*; 28*; 37*; 39*; 42*; 50*; 56*; 65*).

The chronological order which we have adopted allows one to distinguish between the three major periods outlined: I.—Until the end of WWII; II.—Until the announcement of the convocation of Vatican II; III.—From this announcement until the present day.

I. Before the End of the Second World War

1914

1.   de Puniet, OSB, *Concélébration liturgique,* in *Dictionnaire d'Archéologie Chrétienne et de Liturgie* (*DACL* or *DAL*) III (1914), col. 2470–88. (One of the foundational works still worth consulting today). One will find therein (cols. 2488) a bibliography of the most important works that appeared earlier, the earliest going back as far as the seventeenth century.).

1922

2.   L. Beauduin, OSB, *Concélébration eucharistique,* in *Les Questions Liturgiques et Paroissiales* (*QLP*) 7, 1922, pp. 275–85; 8, 1923, pp.

23–4. (Dom Beauduin would disseminate his ideas at the Eucharistic Congress of Amsterdam in 1924.).

1923

3. Pl. de Meester, OSB, *De concelebratione in Ecclesia Orientali, prae-sertim secundum ritum byzantinum,* in *Ephemerides Liturgicae (EL)* 37, 1923, pp. 101–10; pp. 145–54; pp. 196–201.

1928

4. J. M. Hanssens, SJ, *De concelebratione eucharistica,* in *Periodica de Re Morali, Canonica, Liturgica* (Rome, Gregorian University) 16, 1927, pp. 143–154; 17, 1928, pp. 93–127; 21, 1932, pp. 193–219. (This is, even until today, the fundamental study on the question.).

1930

5. J. M Hanssens, SJ, *Institutiones liturgicae de ritibus orientalibus,* 2 vols., Rome, Gregorian University. (The course of Fr Hanssens, from which were edited the articles cited in the preceding entry.).

1940

6. Daout, *Note sur les origines de la concélébration dans le rite maronite,* in *Orientalia Christiana Periodica* 6, 1940, pp. 11–27.

1942

7. H. von Meurers, *Die eucharistische Konzelebration,* in *Pastor Bonus* (Trier) 53, 1942, pp. 56–77; pp. 97–105.

II. From the End of the War to the Announcement of the Council (25 January 1959)

1946

8. L. Beauduin, OSB, *La Concélébration,* in *La Maison Dieu,* no. 7 (1946/3), pp. 7–26. (The idea of concelebration had been revived in the previous numbers of the same journal: no. 5 (1946/1), pp. 131 ff.; no. 6 (1946/2), pp. 115–19: the article by A. G. Martimort and the letter of a Dominican prior.).

1947

9*.   Pius XII, Encyclical *Mediator Dei et hominum,* in *AAS* 39, 1947, pp. 528 ff. (The passage which concerns concelebration made by the congregation is found on p. 533; and in DS 3850.).

1948

10.   M. Aandrieu, *Les Ordines Romani du haut Moyen Age* (Spicilegium Sacrum Lovaniense), Louvain, vol. II, in 1948. (Volume I appeared in 1931. With tome II begins the publication of text and their critically established dates; it ends with volume III in 1951.).

We mention the same author's: *Pontifical Romain au Moyen Age,* 4 vols. (Studi e Testi, pp. 86–9), Vatican City, 1938–1941.

1949

11.   I. H. Dalmais, OP, *Concélébratio,* in *Catholicisme* IV (1949), 1435–38.

12.   K. Rahner, SJ, *Die vielen Messen und das eine Opfer. Eine Untersuchung über die rechte Norm der Messhäufigkeit,* in *Zeitschrift für Katholische Theologie* 71, 1949, pp. 257–317.—Later augmented and published in a book under the same title in 1951 (Freiburg, Herder).

1950

13.   A. A. King, *The Rites of Eastern Christendom* (2 vols.), London, Burns and Oates, 1950. (Although not dedicated especially to concelebration, this work must be mentioned here by reason of its foundational character. Unfortunately, we ourselves have not been able to consult it; but we base our evaluation on what Dalmais has drawn from it (cf. *see below,* no. 78; with regards to concelebration, we think that it adds nothing substantial to the works of Hanssens and Raes.).

1951

14.   M. Schmaus, *Das Kommen des Herrn und die Feier der Eucharistie,* in *Vom christlichen Mysterium. Festgabe O. Casel,* Dusseldorf, Patmos-verlag, 1951, pp. 22–43. (It treats the question of the fruits of the Mass. Several other articles on the same subject from the same period are in response to Rahner (1949), who published his article in a book the same year. See some other titles of works published this year on the question of the fruits of the Mass in Schmidt (1960).).

1952

15.   J. A. Jungmann, SJ, *Fermentum. Ein Symbol kirchlicher Einheit und sein Nachleben im Mittelatter*, in *Colligere Framenta*, Beuron, Beuroner Kunstverlag, 1952, pp. 185–90.

16.   N. Afanasieff (or Afanas'ev), *Trapeza Gospodnja* (*La cène du Seigneur*), Paris, 1952 (It seems that some have erroneously dated this work from 1951.). (The Orthodox author was professor at the Institut Saint-Serge of Paris (Botte, 1953, p. 11). Whence the interest of his book, which raised reactions from specialists: see also the review by Schultze in *Orientalia Christiana Periodica* 19, 1953, p. 441; pp. 443–49; and his article from 1955, which we cite below.).

1953

17*. L'Assemblée Des Cardinaux et Archevêques de France (ACA) approves and communicates to the bishops a *Note de la Commission épiscopale de Pastorale et de Liturgie* on *La pratique des messes dites 'Communautaire'* (Text in *LMD*), no. 34 (1953/2), pp. 145–7; and in *La Doc. Cath.*, no. 1447 (11 May 1953), pp. 585–7).

18.   A. M. Roguet, OP, *Commentaire* (on the preceding 'Note' from the ACA) in *LMD*, no. 34 (1943/2), pp. 148–56. (On this 'Note' and on this 'Commentary' which radically contests it, see our remarks in our two earlier articles: *La Concélébration: 'Sensus Fidei'*... (Ch. III), and *L'Eglise demande* ... (Ch. VIII), in *LPC*, no. 185 (March-April 1980).

19*. ACA New *Note* in response to the *Commentaire* of P. Roguet, in *LMD*, no. 36 (1953/4), p. 8.

20.   D. Alarcia, *Misas comunitarias*, in *Liturgia* (Silos) 8, 1953, pp. 284–6. (An example of the numerous studies which appeared on these questions during this time.).

21.   *La Maison Dieu*, no. 35 (1953/3): *Qu'est-ce que la concélébration?*, special number dedicated to this problem, with articles by:

22.—B. Botte, OSB, *Note historique sur la concélébration dans l'Eglise ancienne* (pp. 9–23);

23.—A. Raes, SJ, *La concélébration eucharistique dans les rites orientaux* (pp. 24–47) (A fundamental study on the question);

24.—F. Vandenbroucke, OSB, *La concélébration, acte liturgique communautaire* (pp. 48–57);

25.—P. Martin, *Une survivance de la concélébration dans l'Eglise occidentale: la messe pontificale lyonnaise du jeudi saint* (pp. 72–3); etc.

1954

26.   G. Frénaud, OSB, *Concélébration et messes communautaires,* in *Facultés Catholiques de l'Ouest. Bull. Trim.,* no. 3 (April 1954), pp. 43–58; (July 1954), pp. 29–38. (refutes Rahner (1949)).

27.   J. Colson, *La concélébration avec l'évêque,* in *Prêtres Diocésains* (1954), pp. 117–23.

28*.   Pius XII, Allocution of 2 November 1954, in AAS 46, 1954, pp. 668–70. (Pius XII discusses 'communitarian Masses.' His text has often been wrongly interpreted. See our analysis of it in LPC, no. 180 (May-June 1979), pp. 23–4; see above, Ch. I.).

1955

29.   E. Catta, *La celebration hiérarchique de la messe,* in *Revue Grégorienne* 34, 1955, pp. 137–53. (An excellent outline of the theology of concelebration.).

30.   A. Franquesa, OSB, *La concélébration, rite de l'hospitalité ecclésiastique,* in *Paroisse et Liturgie* 37, 1955, pp. 169–76.

31.   K. Rahner, SJ, *Dogmatische Bemerkungen über die Frage der Konzelebration,* in *Münchener Theologische Zeitschrift* 6, 1955, pp. 81–106.

——*Dogmatique de la concélébration* (translation of preceding work) in *Questions Liturgiques et Paroissales* 36, 1955, pp. 119–35.

32.   K. Rahner, SJ, *Die vielen Messen als die vielen Opfer Christi,* in *Zeitschrift für Katholische Theologie* 77, 1955, pp. 94–101. (This study, like the preceding one, is a defense of his theses of 1949.).

33.   V. Raffa, *Sul criterio circa il numero delle Messe,* in *Rivista Liturgica* 42, 1955, pp. 106–9. (He insists on the value of each Mass as an action of Christ.).

34.   B. Schultze, SJ, *Das theologische Problem der Konzelebration,* in *Gregorianum* 36, 1955, pp. 212–71. (He studies Afanasieff (1951) and moderately supports Rahner (1955).).

1956

35. A. Franquesa, OSB, *La concelebraciòn. Nuevos Testimonios?* in *Liturgica-1 Cardinali I.-A. Schuster in Memoriam*, Montserrat, 1956, pp. 67–90.

36. G. Frénaud, OSB, *Remarques doctrinales au sujet de la concélébration*, in *Questions Liturgiques et Paroissiales* 37, 1956, pp. 114–28. (A good refutation of Rahner (1956); but the typical example of the misinterpretation which we noted regarding the text of Pius XII from November 2 1954.).

37*. Pius XII, *Discourse of 22 September 1956*, in *AAS* 48, 1956, pp. 716–18. (The Pope develops here the doctrine of the 'actio Christi' in the Mass; and he resolves by answering in the affirmative the question of whether it is necessary for the concelebrants to pronounce the words of consecration in order to celebrate truly.).

1957

38. J. M. Hanssens, SJ, *La concelebrazione sacrificale*, in *Eucharistia. Il Mistero dell'altare nel pensiero e nella vita della Chiesa* (A. Piolanti, Rome-Tournai, Desclée et Cie, 1957), pp. 809–26.

39*. *Decree of the Holy Office, 8 March (23 May) 1957*, in *AAS* 49, 1957, p. 370 (cf. DS 3928.) (It reaffirms that, 'by the institution of Christ, he alone celebrates validly who pronounces the words of consecration.').

40. F. Hürth, SJ, *Adnotationes super dubio 'de valida concelebratione,'* in *Periodica de Re Morali, Canonica, Liturgica* 46, 1957, pp. 243–8. (The official commentary on the preceding decree. A foundational work.).

1958

41. J. M. Hanssens, SJ, *La concelebrazione sacrificale della messa*, in *Divinitas* 2, 1958, pp. 242–67.

42*. *Instruction 'De Musica Sacra' of the Sacred Congregation of Rites* (9 March 1958), in *AAS* 50, 1958, pp. 644–5. (It authorizes, under certain conditions, 'communitarian Masses'; it forbids 'synchronized Masses.').

III. Since the Announcement of the Convocation of the Council (25 January 1959)

1960

43. H. Schmidt, SJ, *Introductio in Liturgiam Occidentalem*, Rome Freiburg, Herder, 1960, cf. pp. 401–13. (A good bibliography up until 1958.).

1961

44. K. Rahner, SJ, and J. A. Jungmann, SJ, *'Konzelebration,'* in *Lexikon für Theologie und Kirche* (2nd edition), VI (1961), pp. 524–5. (Two brief articles where the authors consider the recent decisions of the Magisterium.).

45. A. G. Martimort, *L'Eglise en prière. Introduction à la Liturgie* (A collaborative work.), Paris-Tournai, Desclée et Cie, 1961 (See the index under the word concelebration.).

46.—N. M. Denis-Boulet, *La concélébration eucharistique*, in Martimort, *L'Eglise en prière* (1961), pp. 319–22.

47. M. Nicolau, *La concelebraciòn eucaristica*, in *Salmanticensis* 8, 1961, pp. 269–94.

1963

48. M. Nicolau, *Problemas del Concilio Vaticano. Vision teologica*, Madrid, 1963. (On concelebration, see pp. 132–72; especially pp. 151–7.).

49. A. G. Martimort, *Le ritual de la concélébration eucharistique*, in *Ephemerides Liturgicae* (Rome), 77, 1963, pp. 47–168 (This is a text of a lecture given at liturgical congress in Munich, in August 1960; cf. *see above*, Ch. IV).

50*. Constitutio de Sacra Liturgia, *Sacrosanctum Concilium*, Vatican Council II, approved on 4 December 1963 (On concelebration: nos. 57–8).

1964

51. M. Nicolau, *La Misa en la Constituciòn liturgica del Vaticano II*, in *Salmanticensis* 11, 1964, pp. 267–87 (On concelebration: pp. 277–82).

52. P. Tihon, SJ, *De la concélébration eucharistique,* in *Nouvelle Revue Théologique* 86, 1964, pp. 579–607. (One of the principal studies on the subject appearing after the promulgation of the conciliar Constitution.).

53. *La Maison Dieu,* no. 77 (1964/1), *Commentaire complet de la Constitution conciliare sur la Liturgie.* Fr Gy comments on numbers 57 and 58, which discuss concelebration (pp. 128–231).

1965

54. H. Manders, CSSR, *Concélébration,* in *Concilium* 1965 (no. 2), pp. 120–32. (This article is interesting because it is richly documented, and it reflects the thought of Dutch theology.).

55. *Teologia e pratica della concelebrazione* (Written by a group of Italian authors; translated into French in 1967; see below.).

56*. *General Decree 'Ecclesiae semper,'* from the Sacred Congretation of Rites, 7 March 1965, in *AAS* 57, 1965, pp. 410–12. (This explicitly affirms that one sole Mass is offered in concelebration, thus resolving the doubts raised by many through an erroneous interpretation of Pope Pius XII's text of 1954. Cf. *LPC,* no. 180 (May-June 1979), pp. 29–31; *above,* Ch. I.

1966

57. P. Jounel, *La Concélébration. Textes français et Commentaires,* Paris-Tournai, Desclée, 1966 (Historical: pp. 11–24).

58. A. M. Roguet, OP, *Pour une théologie de la concélébration,* in *LMD,* no. 88 (1966/4), pp. 116–25.

1967

59. *Théologie et pratique de la concélébration.* Translated from the Italian by M. Bombieri. Preface by P. Roguet, Paris-Tours, Mame, 1967. Especially noteworthy are the studies by:

60.—V. Joannes, *Aspects théologiques de la concélébration* (which ends with a rather thorough bibliography, the majority of which is borrowed from Schmidt (1960): pp. 158–62);

61.—B. Neunheeuser, *La concélébration dans la tradition de l'Eglise occidentale* (pp. 13–20).

62. A. de Vogüe, OSB, *Problèmes de la messe conventuelle dans les monastères,* in *Parole et Pain,* no. 20 (1967), pp. 161–72. (Basing himself on the fact that, at the beginning of monasticism there was no daily Mass, he suggests that it not be celebrated daily.).

63. J. P. Jossua, OP, and Y. Congar, OP, *La Liturgie après Vatican II* (*Unam Sanctam—6*), Paris, Cerf, 1967. (A presentation of the conciliar Constitution and some commentaries. Few things on concelebration; see below: Gy.).

64.—P. M. Gy, OP, *Situation historique de la Constitution,* in *La Liturgie après Vatican II* (1967), pp. 11–126.

65*. *Instruction 'Eucharisticum mysterium'* from the Sacred Congregation of Rites, in *AAS* 59, 1967, p. 566. (This encourages frequent concelebration. We showed the opposition between this text and the Apostolic Constitution of Pius VI, *Auctorem fidei,* 28 August 1794, condemning the errors of the Synod of Pistoia: DS 2691. See our analysis of these texts in *LPC,* no. 184 (January-February 1980), pp. 37–8; *above,* Ch. II).

1968

66. Ph. Rouillard, OSB, *Les diverses formes de la concélébration eucharistique au course des siècles,* in *Liturgie et Monastère, Etudes—3: Eucharistie et Vie conventuelle,* Bruges, Publication de Saint-André, 1968, p. 43–55. (This collection includes several other studies which often transgress the acceptable boundaries. See the contributions of Gerard Dubois, Romain Swales, Eloi Dekkers, etc.).

1972

66bis. E. Dekkers, *La concélébration tradition ou nouveauté?,* in *Mélanges liturgiques offerts au R.P. Dom Bernard Botte OSB de l'Abbaye du Mont César—A l'occasion du cinquantième anniversaire de son ordination sacerdotale,* Louvain, Abbey of Mount Cesar, 1972, pp. 99–120.

1979

67. Joseph de Sainte-Marie, OCD, *Réflexions et questions au sujet de la concélébration,* in *LPC,* no. 180 (May-June 1979), pp. 21–36. (This shows, on the basis of magisterial texts, that a concelebration is the celebration of one single Mass.) (This has been reproduced in the

present work, Ch. I, under the title: *Reflection and Questions on the Subject of Concelebration*).

68. J. Kleiner, *Théologie de la concélébration. Réponse à quelques objections,* in *Esprit et Vie (L'Ami du Clergé)* 89, 1979 (no. 51), pp. 671–80. (Apropos of the preceding article, the author puts forth his own thesis, namely that of the plurality of Masses, founded principally on the theology of Suarez.).

1980

69. Joseph de Sainte-Marie, OCD, *Note sur une 'Théologie de la concélébration,'* in *LPC*, no. 184 (January-February 1980), pp. 16–51. (A refutation of the preceding article by Kleiner.). (This has been reproduced in the present work, Ch. I, under the title: *A Critical Note on a 'Theology of Concelebration'*)

70.——, *La concélébration: 'sensus fidei' et théologie,* in *LPC*, no. 186–7 (March-April 1980), pp. 13–41. (This studies the value of the concelebrated Mass from the point of view of grace.). (This has been reproduced in the present work, *Ch. III, under the title: Concelebration: 'Sensus Fidei' and Theology*)

71.——, *L'Eglise demande la multiplication des messes, ibid,* pp. 42–58. (A study of the historical development of the multiplication of Masses in the Church.). (This has been reproduced in the present work, *Ch. VIII, under the title: The Church Asks for the Multiplication of Masses*)

72.——, *La concélébration: histoire d'une histoire,* in *LPC*, no. 186–7 (May-August 1980), 62–96 (A critical study of the principal historical studies on concelebration since the beginning of the twentieth century.). (This has been reproduced in the present work, *Ch.IV, under the title: Concelebration: The History of a History*)

73.——, *La concélébration eucharistique dans le magistère du Concile Vatican II,* in *LPC*, no. 188 (September-October 1980), pp. 18–65. (An analysis of the texts of Vatican II, their preparation, and the principal interventions of the Council Fathers on this question.). (This has been reproduced in the present work, Ch. VI, under the title: *Eucharistic Concelebration in the Magisterium of the Second Vatican Council).*

74. J. Kleiner, *Théologie de la concélébration,* in *Esprit et Vie (L'Ami du Clergé)* 90, 1980 (no. 41), pp. 548–54. (The author resumes his own

theses with the same misunderstanding of magisterial texts and the opinion of theologians. We refute him in *LPC,* no. 189, pp. 30–7; reproduced in the present work, in Ch. II, second part.).

75.   Joseph de Sainte-Marie, OCD, *Esquisse d'une histoire de la concélébra-tion,* in *LPC,* no. 189 (November-December 1980), pp. 14–37. (Logically follows the study mentioned in no. 70 above; it is founded on the critical analysis of the sources.).

76.——, *Messes inutiles et superflues, ibid,* pp, 38–53. (An analysis of Article XXIV of the Augsburg Confession: 'On the Mass.').

77.   J.–Ch. Didier, *Petite histoire de la concélébration,* in *Esprit et Vie* (*L'Ami du Clergé*) 90, 1980 (no. 48), pp. 641–7. (This work follows, on the historical plane, those of Joseph Kleiner (*see above,* nos. 68; 74), but with this difference: Canon Didier recognizes and affirms that concelebration brings about only one Mass. On the other hand, on the historical plane, his study suffers from numerous lacunae. We mention these in *LPC,* no. 191, p. 10, note 2; reproduced in the present work at the beginning of Ch. V, note 269.).

78.   I. H. Dalmais, *Liturgies d'Orient,* Coll. 'Rites et Symboles,' Paris, Cerf, 1980. (New edition. We mention this work for the very brief note that it contains on concelebration (p. 92, note 2). See our critique of it, *below,* Ch. V, note 324).

1981

79.   P. C. Landucci, *La concelebrazione, un problema teologico fondamentale,* in *Palestra del Clero* 60, 1981 (no. 3; February), pp. 136–43. (A typical example of the erroneous interpretation of Pius XII's phrase from 1954 (*tot … quot*), with the contradictions which flow from this. Despite this, the author, who enjoys great authority in Italy, stands firmly against the current abuse of concelebration.).

80.   Joseph de Sainte-Marie, *La liturgie, mystère, symbole et sacrament,* in *LPC,* no. 191 (March–April 1981), pp. 10–57. (In view of a develop-ment of the sacramental reality, this work studies the notions of mystery and symbol by considering the current principal research on the question.).

81.——, *Le Saint-Sacrifice de la messe et sa célébration,* in *LPC,* no. 193 (July-August 1981), pp. 11–41. (This has been reproduced in the present work, Ch. XI, under the title: *The Mass, Meal, Benediction, Congregation or Sacrifice.*).

82.——, *Le sacrifice de la messe dans sa célébration et dans sa multiplication,* in *LPC,* no. 194 (September-October 1981), pp. 28–56 (A conclusion of all the preceding studies, showing the meaning of concelebration and the value which each sacrifice of the Mass has for the salvation of the world.).

83.   R. M. Schmitz, *Zur Theologie der Konzelebration,* in *Theologisches,* Nr. 139 (November 1981), 4323–4334. (Takes up again and presents, in full accord with us, the substance of our articles from *LPC.*).

5 CONCELEBRATION: AN HISTORICAL SUMMARY

AFTER HAVING SHOWN in our preceding chapter what had been the study of concelebration's history in the twentieth century, we are ready to propose now a quick summary of this same history.[1] Our preceding investigation allowed us to evaluate critically the principal works of contemporary historians and liturgists on the question. It has also aided us in learning what the real issue was: namely, whether the current usage of this liturgical rite is or is not founded on Tradition, whether it is or is not in line with its homogenous development. This work, as we have seen, has already been done by certain liturgists, especially since the Council. Like us, they depend on historians, while they themselves are not. But both liturgists and historians equally depend on the data of theology and dogma whenever it is a question of the interpretation of data, and even sometimes from their reconstruction phase. It is at this level, as we have shown, that a certain clarity has often been lacking. Therefore, it is that light of theology which we seek to project onto the facts. However, the primary difference between our investigation and that of the others is the fact that ours is the only one preceded by a critical analysis of the works of contemporary historians of the liturgy and their use by the liturgists themselves.[2] It is here, we think, that one

---

[1] The present chapter appeared in *LPC*, no. 189 (November–December 1980), 14–37, under the title: *Esquisse d'une histoire de la concélébration*. It could be clarified and completed by what will be said later in Chapter VIII.

[2] This critical analysis of historical studies is lacking in the article by J.–Ch Didier, *Petite histoire de la concélébration* (*Esprit et Vie* (*l'Ami du Clergé*) 90, 1980 (no. 48; 27 November), 641–7). It was published, however, after the study reproduced in the preceding chapter. It followed the reflections of Joseph Kleiner, by offering an historical study which Kleiner proclaimed in his preceding article (*ibid*, no. 41 (9 October), p. 548, note 1).

The work of Canon Didier calls for numerous remarks. We shall limit

ourselves to three points: 1) The author poses as an historian (641/1: p. 641, col. 1) and pretends to assemble a dossier, that is to say a collection of 'facts' of history, which he presents by concluding with the reflection of a theologian (647/2). He mentions also the importance of not projecting our new views into the past (641/1; 646/1). But what is an 'historical fact'? And such a pretentiousness of making the history of the Church, and especially the history of her liturgy, an abstraction from theology—is such a thing tenable? It is not, neither theoretically (think of the debates on the nature of the 'fact' in the human sciences), nor practically; the enterprise of the Author proves it once again. In fact, in order to elaborate his 'history', he is lead to resolve some theological questions, such as the distinction between ceremonial and sacramental concelebration, a distinction which he rejects (646/1); and consequently, he deals with the question of the sacrificial character for the so-called secondary concelebrants of the ceremonial concelebration, a character which he affirms—contrary to the judgment declared by the Church (Decree of the Holy Office of 23 May 1957; an article by Fr Hürth in the same year, in the *Periodica de re morali* (see the references in *LPC*, no. 186–7 (May–August 1980) 78). 2) The second error is one of method. The author attempts to draw some general conclusions about concelebration. Yet he practically makes no statement about two of the principal authors in the matter, Fr Hanssens (cited late, note 44, in order to be rejected without examination, but not utilized for the historical investigation: it does not appear in note 4, where the foundational bibliography is given), and Fr Raes, deliberately dismissed (644/2, note 28). Yet it is the works of these two historians, following Puniet, which throw the most light on the history of concelebration, as was recognized before the Council by J. A. Jungmann, who follows them (*La Liturgie dans les premiers siècles* (Lex Orandi, 33), Paris, Cerf, 1959, p. 333), and as was proven by the 1957 *Decree* of the Holy Office, with its official commentary by Fr Hürth. By this selection produced on the level of the sources, the interpretation proposed by that *Petite histoire de la concélébration*, however abundant be the material collected (but not critically evaluated), the interpretation is itself deprived of a solid foundation which alone would have been able to give it some value. 3) On the other hand, J. Ch. Didier clearly affirms, as he already did in 1968 (*Esprit et Vie*, no. 2 (11 January) 30–1), that one sole Mass is offered to God in concelebration (647/1). Here he is in disagreement with J. K., but in full accord with the Magisterium and all theologians and liturgists who have recognized this truth (cf. *LPC*, no. 189, 31; *see above*, Ch. II). We are happy to end on this positive note, and to be able, on this occasion, to render homage to the valuable journal *Espirt et Vie*, for its openness with which can bring forth some new elements to the history of concelebration. We are conscious of its limits; but in consulting the works of synthesis which appeared before and after the Council, we think that no essential aspect of the problem was absent, even if certain names did not appear in our work.

In a general way concelebration appeared in two cases: on the occasion of priestly ordinations, episcopal consecrations or abbatial blessings; and outside of these ordinations, consecrations or blessings. We shall study most especially the second type, which is by far the more important: concelebrations of the Pope with the bishops or priests, the bishop with his priests, the bishop among the priests, or the priests among priests. It will be necessary to study them according to regions and rites, after having assembled and examined closely the principal testimonies, which allow one to retrace the history. Basing our study on the analyses which we mentioned in the preceding chapter, we shall present our historical synthesis according to the following schema: 1) antiquity; 2) the appearance of sacramental concelebration in the West; 3) its expansion and its vestiges in the East before the post-VC II period; 4) the reasons for reducing concelebration in the West to the single case of priestly ordinations; 5) concelebration in the Churches of the East.

This schema, as can be seen, is founded upon the distinction between ceremonial and sacramental concelebration; but the latter has no need of being vindicated after the stand taken by the Magisterium in 1956 and 1957. On the other hand, what still needs to be done is to learn its historical and theological impact. This is something which many have not yet done. Therefore, we think that it is here that an important restatement of the question imposes itself. We began, in our preceding work, to propose some elements of reflection in order to help in this regard, especially by analyzing the articles of Fr Raes (1953), Dom Botte (1953) and Msgr Martimort (1963).[3] The

---

it can welcome into its columns authors freely expressing their opinions, even when the latter are not always in complete agreement.

historical vision which we are going to propose now will allow one to understand better still the aspects of the problem. However, it is only by the theological reflection which we shall add that we can put forth the solution, such as it appears to us; and we will thereby bring to light the profound difference that exists between these two forms of concelebration. Such is the way required by sacramental theology, which, beginning with the revealed data, goes from history to theology and from theology to history.

I. Antiquity

The first testimony that we have on the liturgy of the early Church show us the Christian community, hierarchically gathered around its bishop for the offering of the sacrifice. Pope St Clement and St Ignatius of Antioch demonstrated this in some celebrated texts. We cite at least the latter, which is one of the most explicit:

> Take care to partake of one sole Eucharist; for there is only one Flesh of Our Lord Jesus Christ and only one cup to unite us to His Blood; and only one altar, just as there is only one bishop assisted by the presbytery and deacons.[4]

In this sense one can say then that, from the beginning, the form of the Eucharistic liturgy had been 'concelebration.'

But it is a question of what we now call 'ceremonial concelebration'; for, one sole person, the bishop, pronounces the Eucharistic prayer and consecrates the host. This is clearly seen especially in the rite which St Irenaeus left us, and what was passed on to us by

---

[3]   For references in the present chapter please refer to the bibliography given at the end of the preceding chapter.

[4]   St Ignatius of Antioch, *Epistle to the Philadelphians*, 4. This text and the others are cited in the principal studies on the history of concelebration: St Clement, *Epistle to the Corinthians*, 40, 1–5, in *PG* 1, 287–90; cited in Beauduin (1946), p. 12; St Ignatius, *Epistle to the Magnesians*, VII; *Epistle to the Smyrnaeans*, VIII (Edit. Funk (1887), vol. I, pp. 194–7; 240–1), cited in Puniet (1914), col. 2472; etc.

Eusebius: welcoming at Rome the Bishop of Smyrna, St Polycarp, Pope St Anicetus 'cedes the Eucharist,' which means, as Dom Botte explains, that he left him the honor of celebrating the Eucharist.[5] Such a gesture, which was obviously meant to be a mark of honor and even more so of communion, is a proof that the use of sacramental concelebration, that is a consecration made by two or more priests together, did not exist in Rome at that time, in the middle of the second century. Fr Hanssens, who correctly mentioned this, adds that 'there is no case found in the history of the first two centuries of the Church of a bishop concelebrating sacrificially with another bishop in a public synaxe.'[6]

The *Apostolic Tradition* of St Hippolytus of Rome, at the beginning of the third century, equally bears witness to this idea. For, the imposition of the priests' hands over the oblation of which it speaks is but the simple rite of offertory; and the interpretation which wishes to give it a consecratory value is not only without foundation, but it is contrary to the most certain aspects of Catholic doctrine on the sacraments.[7]

The *Didache of the Apostles*, towards the middle of the third century, in Syria, shows us a type of Eucharistic concelebration practiced in the name of hospitality, and one which is totally particular. The bishop in residence (the one who welcomes) and the bishop who is passing through participate in the consecration in the following manner: one of the two consecrates the bread, the other consecrates the wine. However, Botte himself adds: 'This division of the anamnesis can represent only a very limited local usage.'[8] Therefore, there is no time for dwelling on this any more, except to note that such a rite

---

5   Eusebius, *Hist. Eccl.,* V, 24, 17; cf. Botte (1953), pp. 14 ff.

6   Hanssens (1958), p. 247; cf. (1928), p. 193. This remark cannot be annulled by the completely particular case which is mentioned in the *Didache of the Apostles* (see below).

7   This is shown by Hanssens (1927), pp. 191–193; (1928), p. 117; (1958), pp. 248–249; against Botte (1953), pp. 10–12.

8   On this point, Dom Botte (1953), p. 13, is certainly correct.

poses some theological problems, and that it clearly indicates a deviation rather than a development in the liturgical sense.

Moreover, several reasons rendered concelebration in the proper sense impossible and always render it unthinkable in the first centuries of the Church's history. The first is the very notion of a hierarchical unity, which requires that the role of the bishop appear unique, according to the image of Christ. The second is that we do not see the reasons that could have caused a change in that law or custom which reserves the celebration of a sacrament to one single minister. Why perform by many a rite which can already be celebrated by one alone, the bishop? On the other hand, we shall see the particular and very precise reasons which caused, in the unique case of the Pontifical Roman liturgy, certain priests to be associated very closely to the Pope in the offering of the Eucharistic offering. The third reason, which is not the lowest on the practical level, is that there was not at that time a fixed form of the canon.[9] However, from the theological and liturgical point of view, the strongest reason is the first; and we saw in the preceding chapter that it remains decisive still today for the majority of the Eastern Rites.

The other testimonies which some believe can be brought forward in favour of sacramental and frequent concelebration, especially in Rome, are not convincing: neither that of Pope Hilarius at the beginning of the fifth century (contrary to what Duchesne[10] thought), nor the famous letter, so frequently cited, of Pope Innocent I (410–417) to the Bishop of Gubbio. The interpretation that has been given it by Dom de Puniet and Dom Botte is not tenable.[11] On the other hand, what the letter tells us of the *fermentum,* that particle of the Eucharist consecrated by the Bishop of Rome and carried to the priests of different 'parishes' of 'The City,' is of the greatest interest.

---

9   Hanssens (1932), pp. 217–18. The few pages which complete this series of studies would be worth citing as a whole. The third reason was often cited. (for example, by Schultze (1955), p. 216).

10 Hanssens (1928), p. 115.

11 Puniet (1914), col. 2474; Beauduin (1946), pp. 13 ff.

On this point we willingly agree with the very accurate reflections of Dom Beauduin: this use is an eminent witness of the concern which there was for maintaining the liturgical unity of the Church around the bishop, particularly in the Sunday Eucharistic celebration.

One cannot speak of concelebration in the sacrificial sense under St Gregory the Great,[12] nor even in the last years of the seventh century, at the time of the Third Council of Constantinople (680), especially by beginning with a witness such as Fortunius, Bishop of Carthage. While passing through Constantinople he was invited to concelebrate with the Greeks. Yet, Dom Botte very accurately observes: 'One cannot even imagine a moment when an African bishop would know enough Greek to recite the anaphora of St John Chrysostom. Therefore, it is always the same form of concelebration which we are dealing with, that which we find among St Cyril and Pseudo-Dionysius,' namely purely ceremonial 'concelebration.'[13]

This conclusion imposes itself with all the more force since this form of 'concelebration,' of great liturgical value, was the only one known in the East at that time; testimonies that come down to us from these Churches oblige one to affirm this. There is first of all the argument from silence, which is of great weight: none of the descriptions of the liturgy which have come down to us speak of concelebrants pronouncing the words of institution with the bishop. Moreover (all the authors recognize this), it is necessary to be very attentive to the sense of the words *'sunleitourgein'* and others like it;

---

[12] St Gregory, *Epistle* L, VIII, 34, *PL* 77, 892; *'missarum solemnia mecum celebrare feci'*. Cited by Puniet (1914), col. 2475; and by Hanssens (1932), p. 194. St Gregory said this of the legates of Constantinople, whom he received in Rome. A concelebration in the strict sense is therefore unthinkable: the date of this encounter and the tradition of the guests received absolutely exclude the possibility.

[13] Dom Botte (1953), p. 17. He recognizes (p. 19) that this concelebration was silent; therefore, it was only ceremonial.

for they do not necessarily imply sacramental concelebration.[14] Finally, silent concelebration is the practice since the beginning.[15]

Where contemporary historians and liturgists differ is in the interpretation they give to these facts: one wants all these forms of 'concelebration' to have been both sacramental and sacrificial; the other recognizes that a 'silent concelebration' cannot be sacramental. We limit ourselves to mentioning the names of some of the principal Eastern theologians who were most firmly opposed to the very principle of sacramental concelebration. The most well known are Narsai de Nisibi, in the sixth century, and Pseudo-Dionysius the Areopagite.[16] 'It will be easy to multiply examples,' asserts Dom de Puniet. 'The prescription of celebrating by one single celebrant is found as a constant not only in the liturgical books ... but also in the commentaries on the liturgy.' And he cites the names of Theodore of Amida, St Germain of Constantinople, St Maximus the Confessor and Simeon of Thessalonica.[17] It is necessary to recognize that we have here a collection of rather impressive texts.

Two key ideas come from Pseudo-Dionysius, whose immense authority was known in the Middle Ages, as it still is today, albeit to a lesser degree:

1) The Hierarch (our 'principal celebrant') celebrates 'in imitation of Christ; he sensibly represents Christ';[18]

2) The celebration is confected by the high priest alone, surrounded by the clergy hierarchically assembled:

---

[14]   *Ibid.,* p. 16; cf. Puniet (1914), col. 2471; Hanssens (1932), p. 211; 215; etc.

[15]   Puniet (1914), col. 2478; Raes (1953), *passim*; Botte (1953), p. 19; Hanssens (1958), p. 259; etc.

[16]   Puniet (1914), col. 2478; Hanssens (1932); p. 210. On the other hand, Dom Botte (1953) and others of the liturgical movment do not mention these witnesses, essential though they are for the history and theology of concelebration.

[17]   Puniet (1914), cols. 2478; 2479, note 4. Raes (1953), *passim*.

[18]   Pseudo–Denys, *De Ecclesiastica hierarchica,* cap. III, in *PG* 3, 444.

> The Hierarch takes his place at the center of the altar of the divine sacrifices and some *Leitourgoi* alone stand around him with the most worthy priests. Then, having praised the holy works of God, the Hierarch accomplishes in a holy manner the divine mysteries.[19]

The testimony of Symeon of Thessalonica, in the fifteenth century, shows us how these two main complementary points are maintained in the Byzantine tradition. And we can see how 'ceremonial concelebration' allowed them to harmonize.

II. The appearance of sacramental concelebration in the West

It is with the *Ordo Romanus III*, at the end of the eighth century, that sacramental concelebration appeared for the first time in a certain manner.[20] And it is at Rome that this event takes place. There is unanimity today on this point of history, or at least on the very fact that it is during this period that, for the first time, all the concelebrants are seen pronouncing together the words of consecration.[21] For as

---

[19]   *Ibid.*, col, 425; the '*Leitourgoi*' are the ministers of an inferior rank, beginning with the deacons. See also col. 445, where he speaks of 'the order (or organization) of priests hierarchically assembled.' However, it is the whole Chapter III which shows at once that the Hierarch alone, or the high priest (*hierarchès*), celebrates, consecrates: accomplishes 'the divine mysteries', and that he does this surrounded by the clergy, or more exactly by a part of the clergy, 'the most worthy priests' and some '*Leitourgoi*' who represent the others.

[20]   Andrieu (1948), p. 122 (cf. 127), situates this *Ordo* in 'the last years of the eighth century'. In order to avoid confusion we note that, along with Andrieu who enjoys authority in the matter, we call the *Ordo Romanus III* that which before him had been called the *Ordo Romanus I*, by showing that sometimes it was only a question of an appendix of this *Ordo* (Puniet (1914), col. 2473; Hanssens (1928), pp. 107 ff.; Botte (1953), p. 18, note 22). The text is found, according to Mabillon, in *PL* 78, 958–9, and in the critical edition of Andrieu (*loc. cit.*, pp. 131–3).

[21]   Already admitted by Puniet (1914), col. 2472; by Beauduin (1922), p. 284; by Botte (1953), p. 18; also admitted by Denis–Boulet(1961), p. 321; Martimort (1963), p. 156; by Tihon (1964), p. 583; ...

we saw, when it is a question of recognizing the complete importance of the passing from one form of concelebration to another, all do not agree, even after the declarations of the Magisterium and the authorized commentary of Fr Hürth in 1957.[22] And yet this passing, when we consider it, is nothing but that of a Pontifical Mass, where the role of the clergy is particularly developed to the point of a concelebration in the strict sense.

What is revealed in the *Ordo Romanus III* is, that 'on the feasts of Easter, Pentecost, St Peter (June 29) and Christmas,' (therefore, on four very solemn occasions), the cardinal priests of the city of Rome gather together to concelebrate with their bishop, the Pope. And that: 'when the latter reaches the altar, they come around him, from the right and from the left, and speak the canon with him while holding the oblations in their hands, and not on the altar, and in such a manner that the voice of the Pope dominates their own. Together they consecrate the Body and Blood of the Lord.'[23] The cardinal priests were at that time those who served the principal parishes in the city under a stable and permanent title.

This chief testimony is confirmed by several others, both contemporary with it and after it, such as the *Ordo Romanus IV*,[24] or that of Amalaire of Metz.[25] In the twelfth century, between 1140 and 1143, the *Liber politicus* of Benedict, canon of St Peter's, does not mention a concelebrated Mass by cardinal priests with the Pope, except at the

---

[22] Discourse of Pius XII in 1956; Decree of the Holy Office in 1957; cf. Hürth (1957).

[23] *In diebus festis, id est Paschae, Pentecostes, sancti Petri, Nativitatis Domini, per has quatuor solemnitates habent colligendas presbyteri cardinales, unusquisque tenens corporalem in manu sua ... Et accedente Pontifice ad altare, dextra levaque circumdant altare et simul cum illo canonem dicunt, tenentes oblatas in manibus, non super altare, ut vox pontificis valentius audiatur, et simul consecrant corpus et sanguinem domini, sed tantum pontifex facit super altare crucem dextra levaque'* (cf. *see above*, note 20).

[24] Andrieu (1948), p. 163.

[25] *PL* 105, 1016; cited in Puniet (1914), col. 2474; Hanssens (1928), p. 106; etc.

third Mass of Christmas, at the church of St Mary Major.[26] At the end of the same century, in 1192, Cardinal Cencio de' Sabelli, the future Honorius III (1216–1227) does not mention it. 'At this time,' concludes Fr Hanssens (from whom we borrowed this information), 'that form of concelebration had probably fallen out of use.'[27] In fact, when an allusion is finally made to it later on, it is spoken of as something passé and no longer practiced. Such is the case of Innocent III (1198–1216), in his great work, *De sacro altaris mysterio,* which St Thomas Aquinas would later cite in the middle of the thirteenth century, when he treats this question.[28]

Contrary to the opinion of Dom Botte, the letter of Pope John VII to Photius, towards the end of the ninth century, does not speak of a true sacramental concelebration.[29] Moreover, apart from this text, there is nothing that would permit one to affirm the presence of that rite in the East at this time.

We arrive then, along with Msgr Martimort, at the following conclusion: 'Since the *Ordo III,* from the Carolingian period until the *Liber politicus* of Canon Benedict in the middle of the twelfth century, there is an undeniable continuity.'[30] Moroever, this, we must add, takes place exclusively in the West, indeed only in the City of Rome. It is between these two points, in fact, that the period of sacrificial concelebration of the Pope with the cardinal priests extends. How and why did it begin? This is not clear. We can think of the growing awareness of the Mass' value, and therefore the desire on the part of those cardinal priests (obliged to 'assist' at the Pope's Mass) not to be deprived of the grace of celebrating themselves. This reason

---

[26]   *Le Liber censuum de l'Eglise Romaine,* Ed. Fabre–Duchesne, vol. II, p. 146; cited by Hanssens (1958), p. 256.

[27]   Hanssens (1958), p. 256.

[28]   Innocent III, *De sacro altaris mysterio,* L. IV, cap. 25 (*PL* 217, 873); St Thomas, *In IV Sent.,* d. 13, q. 1, a. 2, qu. 1a 2; *S.T.* III, q. 82, a. 2.

[29]   *PL* 126, 871 (Latin text); Mansi 17, 413 (Greek text): Botte (1953), p. 18; cf. Hanssens (1928), pp. 111–12; 194; (1957), p. 819; ...

[30]   Martimort (1963), p. 156.

appears to us very probable in the liturgical context of the period, marked as it was by a much accentuated movement towards the multiplication of Masses and the development of the private Mass.[31]

Why did this form of concelebration come to an end? We can study the reasons. But before doing so, we shall first see how from Rome, where it all began, sacramental and sacrificial concelebration spread into the other churches where it was encountered.

III. The spread of concelebration and its vestiges in the West before the post-Vatican II period

We must first note with Hanssens that there is no trace of concelebration in the documents of the Gallican (ancient), Mozarbic or Ambrosian Rites.[32] It is only in the Roman Rites which spread '*extra Urbem*' that we find them; and it is primarily at episcopal consecrations or priestly ordinations. It seems that Fr Tihon sums up the question well when he writes: 'While the Roman practice ceased to be in use at Rome itself ... we see appearing, between the ninth and middle of the twelfth century, the two sole forms commonly considered as concelebration in the Church of the West: the Mass of a bishop's consecration; and then a little later, the Mass of priestly ordination. This latter served as a basis for the reflection of Medieval theologians, being the only practice of their time. Moreover, for St Thomas it was a question only of a custom a little widespread; and certain pontificals seem to have allowed it only with reluctance. It did not become obligatory except much later, with the publication of the Roman Pontifical of Clement VIII in 1596—therefore, only at the end of the sixteenth century, in the great movement of the unification of the liturgy, beginning with the Roman model which followed the Council of Trent.[33]

---

[31] See our article, *L'Eglise demande la multiplication des messes*, in *LPC*, no. 185 (March–April 1980), pp. 42–58, reproduced below, Ch. VIII.

[32] Hanssens (1932), p. 195.

[33] Tihon (1964), p. 584. On the preceding page Fr Tihon asserts that, under the Roman influence, sacramental concelebration began to spread into the West

In reality, it is only with the thirteenth century that we begin to see evidence of concelebration at an episcopal consecration;[34] and St Thomas is the first, in 1254, to mention the concelebrated Mass for priestly ordinations.[35] With respect to a concelebrated Mass for the blessing of an abbot (which could not have preceded that of an episcopal consecration), it seems that we cannot be certain when exactly it changed from the sacramental concelebration it had become, back to purely ceremonial concelebration. We know that this happened somewhere around the middle of the sixteenth century.[36]

We must note the particular case of concelebration in the blessing of the oil of the sick, which began to be fixed for Holy Thursday around the beginning of the sixth century.[37] Amalaire of Metz, in outlining this rite during the ninth century,[38] believed that the priests concelebrated the Mass as well. Yet this does not seem to have been the case, for, 'all the Roman documents show that this Mass was never

---

in the ninth century, and survived only at the Lyonnaise Mass of Holy Thursday 'until its reestablishment by Vatican II'. This presentation of the matter is not exact. The author demonstrates this when he says (as he does in the passage which we just cited) that, in the Middle Ages, 'the two sole forms commonly considered as concelebration in the Church of the West were: the Mass of a bishop's consecration; and then a little later, the Mass of priestly ordination'; and that, 'This latter served as a basis for the reflection of Medieval theologians, *being the only practice of their time.*' These two assertions cannot be reconciled except if one takes the expressions 'Middle Ages' and 'Medieval' as two distinct periods: the one being the ninth century onwards, the other being the twelfth century onwards. What is said about the first period is too general. We shall see this later on insofar as it concerns concelebration around the bishop in certain Churches of the West.

34 *Pontifical d'Appamée*, in Andrieu, *Le Pontifical Romain au Moyen Age* (Cited from the Vatican, 1938–1941), vol. II, p. 365; cited in Martimort (1961), p. 511.

35 Cf. *see above*, note 28.

36 Hanssens (1928), p. 107.

37 Martimort (1961), p. 584.

38 *De Eccl. Offic.* I, 12 in *PL* 105, 1016; cited in Puniet (1914), col. 2480; and in Hanssens (1928), p. 109.

celebrated in Rome.'[39] It is to this period as well that one can trace back the use of concelebration at the Chrism Mass of Holy Thursday in certain French cities, such as Lyon.[40]

In addition to these different cases, but especially the two principal cases of episcopal consecrations and priestly ordinations, what was concelebration in the Latin churches outside of Rome? After having shown that a certain number of testimonies, which had been cited at times in its favour, that is in favour of its sacramental form, were in no way conclusive, Fr Hanssens concludes that the Churches of the Latin Rite outside of Rome did not know any other cases of concelebration than those of 'priestly and episcopal ordinations.'[41] He rightly insists on the argument from silence, which can be taken from the authors who do not speak about concelebration except at ordinations, where it would have been normal for them to do so. We have the names of those three chief witnesses: Innocent III (*De sacro altaris mysterio*: 1216); St Thomas Aquinas (in his Commentary on the *Liber Sententiarum* of Peter Lomabard, L. IV: 1254), Durandus of Saint-Pourçain (1571). All three know of no other concelebrations, in the strong sense which that word had already taken on at that time, except those of ordination where, at Rome, it was the Pope surrounded by the cardinals (St Thomas does not even speak of this.). Another testimony, that of Jacobus of Vitry, clearly shows that outside of cases of ordination, concelebration was unanimously considered in the West as a rite reserved exclusively to the Pope and his cardinal priests. In his *Historia orientalis et occidentalis,* he writes: 'The priest cardinals had the custom of assisting the Supreme Pontiff in the sacrament of the altar and of celebrating with him.'[42] This was written in 1241 by

---

[39]   Hanssens (1958), p. 257, note 36.

[40]   Martin (1953); cf. Hanssens (1932), p. 209; 1958, p. 257, note 36.

[41]   Hanssens (1932), p. 205; see the study of the texts in the preceding pages, pp. 195–204.

[42]   Jacobus Vitriacensis, *Historia orientalis et occidentalis,* L. III, cap. 38: '*Consueverunt presbyteri cardinales summo pontifici in sacramento altaris assistere et cum eo pariter celebrare*' (cited in Hanssens (1932), p. 201).

an historian who was also a great traveler. Perhaps—and one can see this—he does not give to the word 'celebrare' the precise sense given to it by theologians, and instead uses a wider sense, one still frequently used at that time. Moreover, we know that at the time of his writing concelebration by the Pope and cardinals was no longer in use in Rome. His testimony therefore retains all its value; for it produces the same conclusion which many studies have produced: at Rome there had been the custom of concelebration with the Pope and cardinals, and this concelebration, as we know, was sacramental.

Other than Rome and the ceremonies of ordination there is nothing but silence regarding concelebration. It must be added that from St Albert the Great, the teacher of St Thomas Aquinas, up until Cajetan, St Thomas' best-known student in the sixteenth century, and even further still, a very large theological current is completely opposed to concelebration.[43] It seems that then, even as today, the ideas about the history of this rite were not always accurate; but this imprecision, while much less serious than the present errors, when in the opposite direction, that is it was used to reject concelebration absolutely. St Thomas, one will remember, does not take it so far. But that extremely large and powerful current of opposition would not have been possible if concelebration truly existed in a great number of Churches outside of Rome. Therefore, it is a certain indicator of both its extinction in the Roman pontifical liturgy, and of its reduction to a very small number of cases outside of Rome. St Thomas speaks of it only as the use of 'certain churches,' of churches totally unknown to him.

There are, nevertheless, all the cases which turned up at the beginning of the eighteenth century in the *Voyages liturgiques* of 'the Sir from Moleon': Vienna, Angers, Sens, Orleans, Chartres, etc.[44] However, for some of these it is in no way proven that there was sacramental concelebration; and for the others it is positively

---

[43] Cf. Hanssens (1932), p. 203; and the list of references given p. 202, note 180.

[44] Martimort (1961), p. 247; 321; cf. Puniet (1914), col. 2476; Hanssens (1932), p. 205.

excluded.[45] The result is that these testimonies, apart from the case of Lyon,[46] do not constitute reliable documents in favour of the existence of sacramental concelebration outside of Rome. In fact, it is barely supported by them.[47]

It must be concluded, then, that if sacramental and sacrificial concelebration spread forth from Rome into the West in the ninth century (or even later), it was barely encountered there, with some very rare exceptions, except in cases of priestly or episcopal ordinations. Such that Canon 803 of the 1917 Code, in reserving this rite to these cases alone, can be considered a faithful reflection of the liturgical Tradition of the Church of the West.

IV. The reasons which brought about the extinction or extreme reduction of concelebration in the West

They seem to be summed up in the following three points:

1) With respect to the Church of Rome, 'most likely the coup de grâce had been given to the concelebration of cardinal priests by the absence of the Pope,' obliged as he was to reside more and more frequently outside of Rome, on account of troubles and wars at that time;[48]

2) the Roman example had its influence beyond Rome; but more importantly still seems to have been, beginning with the thirteenth century, the opposition of the very strong theological current, which we mentioned above;

3) added to these factors is the movement which tended towards the multiplication of Masses, something which was particularly strong at the end of the High Middle Ages.

---

[45]   Puniet (1914), col. 2475; Hanssens (1932), pp. 205–9.

[46]   Cf. *see above*, note 40.

[47]   The silence of an author such as Denis–Boulet(1961) is significant in this regard.

[48]   Hanssens (1958), p. 256.

It is no doubt the influence of this last movement which one finds in the attitude of Bishop Theoldule of Orleans in the ninth century. It seems that, in order to try to reconcile the advantages of 'concelebration' and the desire of priests to celebrate their own Mass, priests were authorized to say Mass secretly very early in the morning; but they were required to participate at the bishop's Mass with all the faithful.[49] The raison d'être of this requirement was the traditional principle of one Sunday Mass with the bishop; and it seems that at Orleans in the ninth century, as in the majority of the Eastern Rites till this day, the exigencies of this principle are considered sufficiently satisfied by the practice of ceremonial 'concelebration.' For, it is to a concelebration of this genre which the priests are invited.

With respect to the theological reasons opposed to concelebration, they answer to an excessively formalist sacramental theology. More than to a traditional and Eastern principle of the unicity of the altar and priesthood of Christ, the reasons put forward are actually linked to the mystery of consecration: 'Several priests *cannot* and must not consecrate one (one and the same) host together,' asserts St Albert the Great.[50] For, if one alone suffices to consecrate, the others do nothing, especially if they do not pronounce the words exactly at the same time as the principal celebrant; therefore, their action is useless, even injurious for the sacrament. St Thomas takes up this objection in the *Summa Theologiae,* and his admirable way of responding to this is well-known: 'the priest does not do it 'by his own power,' but *in persona Christi;* hence, several priests do but one thing in Christ. This is why it does not matter that the sacrament is confected by one or several.'[51] Let us understand this well: it does not matter, and precisely from the point of view which St Thomas considers it here: that of the

---

[49] *Capitulare, PL* 105, 206, 209; cf. Hanssens (1932), p. 202; Tihon (1964), p. 583.

[50] *De eucharistia distinctiones VI,* tract. IV, c. 2, no. 15–16 (Edit. Paris, 1899, vol. 38, pp. 428–30), cited and analyzed by Hanssens (1932), p. 203.

[51] *S.T.* III, q. 82, a. 2.

possibility of consecrating the host by several priests; all the other problems of concelebration remain unresolved. St Thomas responded to the objection raised during his time, but his voice remains isolated, and it was the other current which won the day. At the same time that it witnesses to the extreme scarcity of concelebration in the thirteenth century, this current contributes to reinforcing the state of things.

To that third factor which we mentioned, the movement toward the multiplication of Masses, it is necessary to add an increasing awareness of the dignity of the priesthood. One could also speak of a decrease in the sense of the community and incipient individualism, especially with the beginning of the Renaissance. However, these factors will come into play only when the practice of concelebration will have been totally reduced.

V. Concelebration in the Church of the East

The multiplicity of the Oriental Rites and the drama of the separation of a great number of these Churches from Rome render the history of concelebration extremely difficult. According to the studies of the best authors we will classify these rites, Catholic or not, into two groups: those which have always refused sacramental concelebration, and those which have adopted it. We shall retrace the history of these latter. We shall also recall that, during the first eight centuries of the Church, in the East as in the West, 'concelebration' was known only under the 'ceremonial' form. The East, as we saw above, insists even more than the West on the theological and liturgical principle that desires that, after the image of Christ, the principal celebrant be the only one at the altar, or at least the only one to accomplish the central act of Eucharistic celebration. It is this reason, it seems, along with a profound concern for fidelity to Tradition, which moved a good number of Eastern Churches never to adopt Eucharistic concelebration and to reserve jealously to one principal celebrant only the honor of representing Christ in the offering of His sacrifice. Let us note in passing that, for these Churches as for the Catholic Magisterium, the difference between the two forms of 'concelebration' is in no way a secondary question or of little importance. It is doubtful that they could be made to acknowledge the passing from one form to another as the fruit of a 'homogenous development.'

It is to Fr Raes that we shall go for the essential information.[52] Among the rites or Churches that have maintained the practice of offering the Eucharistic sacrifice by one sole priest, and therefore 'concelebration' under its 'ceremonial' form (often very richly adorned exteriorly), he cites:

a) the Chaldean Rites (Catholic) (p. 25);
b) the dissident Coptics (p. 28);
c) the Ethiopians (*ibid*);
d) the Syrians (p. 30);
e) the Armenians (*ibid*);
f) the Greek Orthodox, as the *Hieraticon* of Constantinople (1825) attests, cited verbatim by that of Athens (1951) (p. 30).

It is in this great Byzantine Tradition that one finds the most fervent defenders of the principle and practice of one celebrant offering the sacrifice.

Among the rites or Churches that adopted sacramental and sacrificial concelebration throughout their history, Fr Raes, in showing what Fr Hanssens has for the most part already shown, namely that this evolution happened under Western influence, cites the following:

a) The Russian Orthodox, which adopted 'the new concelebration' (as Fr Raes calls it) only in the seventeenth century. In reporting this fact, Raes brings out how this practice and the idea which inspired it are foreign to the 'Greek Orthodox' or to the 'other dissident rites' (p. 37);

---

[52] Raes (1953). See also P. Jounel, *La célébration et la concélébration de la messe*, in *LMD*, no. 83 (3rd trim. 1965), 168–82; especially p. 175: 'The Practice of the East'.

b) The Greek Catholics, where it is evident that concelebration came from the Latins, and not without a certain
number of historical errors regarding the practice of this
rite in the East in the preceding centuries (p. 43–4);

c) The Melkites (p. 44);

d) The Maronites (p. 45);

e) The Coptic Catholics (p. 46).

It must be noted that, in all these rites, concelebration is not scheduled
except for feast days, in order to give more luster to the liturgy; and
that the Coptics, like the Maronites, adopted it because they incor-
rectly believed that it had been an ancient custom of their Church (p.
46). With regard to the other Eastern Rite Catholics, they did not
practice sacramental concelebration.

Fr Raes then mentions a final evolution, more recent than the last,
which is encountered among the Catholics of the Byzantine Rite.
Wishing to unite the Latin principle of frequent concelebration and
the ancient practice kept in the East of one sole altar and one sole
Mass, but at the same time sacrificing for this the practice of one sole
(consecrating) celebrant, they obtained for religious communities
and seminaries the permission of concelebrating even daily (p. 47).
However, it is here, Raes strongly insists, that we have a practice which
goes contrary to the traditional sense of the Eastern liturgy; for, it ends
up simplifying the rite of concelebration, while the very reason for
this latter is precisely the solemnization of the Eucharist.

*   *   *

From these points which our study has allowed us to assemble, some
conclusions follow, the importance of which will immediately appear
to anyone who understands all the theological and liturgical impact
of the distinction between 'ceremonial concelebration' and 'sacramental concelebration.' Let us very briefly recall its history. Outlined
by Dom de Puniet in 1914, it was developed by Fr Hanssens between
1917 and 1932; and it found its ecclesial confirmation in the interventions of the Magisterium between 1956 and 1957, whose correct sense

and historical and theological implications were shown by Fr Hürth.[53] By the light of this distinction and the certitudes already acquired by historical research, the following can be said:

a) that 'concelebration' from its beginnings was only ceremonial;

b) that it was maintained under this form in the majority of Eastern Rites, especially among the Byzantines;

c) that sacramental concelebration did not appear for sure until the eighth century, and that it was first of all a privilege which the Pope granted and reserved to the cardinal priests of Rome; it existed under this form and in this precise context from the eighth to the twelfth century;

d) that apart from this case, it spread in the West in a sporadic manner first, and then in a more general way, until the end of the sixteenth century, for Masses of Ordination, especially priestly Ordinations;

e) that the Latin Middle Ages considered it above all, even exclusively, as a custom proper to the Church of Rome, and as a privilege reserved to the Pope and the cardinal priests; and that a certain time was needed in order to admit a generalization in the case of Ordinations;

f) that, most likely, all the other cases of 'concelebration' which are found in the West, save for that of the Holy Thursday Mass in the Church of Lyon, are cases of ceremonial 'concelebration'—this is to say, such concelebrations are pontifical Masses celebrated by the bishop of a place, at which the clergy 'assist' by fulfilling certain functions and receiving certain particular marks of honor;[54]

g) that in the Eastern Churches where it is found, far from being faithful to an ancient tradition, sacramental concele-

---

[53] Cf. Hürth (1957).

[54] At the very least it must be asserted that the case of the Church of Lyon is the only one where concelebration appeared in a sacramental manner.

bration appeared, on the contrary, as an innovation in opposition to that tradition and under the weight of Latin influence;

h) that apart from the last type mentioned by Fr Raes, one which represents an absolute innovation for the East, concelebration had always been reserved, in both East and West, for feast days, having for its principal purpose the solemnization of the Eucharistic liturgy.

We see then how inaccurate is the assertion of Dom Lambert Beauduin, and how distant he himself was from reality when he said in 1922: 'We believe we have established that the rite of concelebration had existed in the Latin liturgy for twelve centuries, and that the Church had attached great significance to it.'[55] What is regrettable is that (just as we showed in the preceding chapter), a good number of authors, moved as they were more by a concern for the triumph of a thesis than by a concern for researching the historical truth, failing also to perceive clearly the liturgical, theological and historical significance and impact of the difference between the two forms of 'concelebration,' ceremonial and sacramental—these authors, belonging primarily to the liturgical movement, did not correctly utilize the results already acquired by the works of the most competent historians.

This is how some have brought about the triumph of the thesis, which states that concelebration in the modern sense of the word, that is sacramental and sacrificial concelebration, is a survival of the ancient liturgy. Yet the works of Puniet himself, but especially those of Hanssens and Raes, have established in a definitive manner that such an interpretation of history—for it is a question of interpretation—is no longer possible; and it is not possible to find support in the Council in order to defend such an interpretation.[56]

---

[55]   Beauduin (1922), p. 285.

[56]   See our preceding article. *La concélébration: histoire d'une histoire* (LPC, no. 186–7, p. 84, note 60; *see above*, Ch. IV, note 58; cf. no. 188, pp. 23 ff.; cf. *see below*, Ch. VI).

It must be said, on the other hand, that sacramental concelebration, when and where it had been adopted, always appeared as *an innovation,* and that it was only accepted, up until most recent times, on the basis of the two following principles: 1)that the function of the principal celebrant be reserved to the bishop (or his replacement, or a religious superior), and that this function be brought out in such a manner as to manifest clearly the hierarchical unity of the Church gathered around its bishop as around Christ; 2)that this liturgy be reserved for feast days, indeed big feasts, for the sake of solemnizing them by continuing to develop ceremonial 'concelebration,' which was the Sunday form of celebration in the early Church.

We can now propose a theology of concelebration, beginning with the elements received from this and the preceding study, and developing them somewhat. One can already see the outline according to which such a theology must be developed. Nevertheless, it is first absolutely necessary to gather more data still, namely the teaching of the texts, and especially the *Acts,* of the Second Vatican Council. Such then will be the object of our next chapter: to see the basis of the historical, liturgical and theological arguments, and to show under what conditions and within what limits the Fathers of the Council wished to introduced the practice of concelebration into the Church and into the Latin Rites.[57]

---

[57] We had completed the redaction of this study when a journal by Dom G. Oury (in *Esprit et Vie—L'ami du Clergé,* July 18, 1980, no. 29, p. 215) made known to us the recent reedition of I. H. Dalmais' book, *Liturgies d'Orient* (Coll. 'Rites et Symboles', Paris, Cerf, 1980). Recognizing that 'a certain impoverishment of the Roman liturgy had been the involuntary consequence of the liturgical reform inaugurated by Vatican II,' and that, in order to face up to it, (among other reactions) certain persons turned toward the Oriental liturgies, which are poorly known—recognizing all this, 'this little book is most welcome,' affirms Dom Oury. But perhaps he risks not reaching the goal he proposes; for, revealing a prolonged contact with the world of Oriental liturgies, the work seems to be both too much for a simple initiation and insufficiently established for an already well–informed audience. The absence of references throughout the work reduces their value and usefulness for a great number of these explanations. This

is to be regretted, for they are often very interesting. But the reader would have appreciated being directed to the sources in a way other than by very general bibliographical indications.

Regarding the problem which concerns us, ones finds only this simple note (the author writes in French 'rite' where, according to the French practice one would usually write 'rit'; cf. *see above*, Ch. IV, note 199): 'It is known that the Byzantine Rite has maintained in all its fullness the ancient rite of concelebration. Even in the absence of a bishop, several priests concelebrate by dividing up the priestly prayers. Among the Catholics all chant together the words of consecration. The Orthodox preserved the practice of having only the first celebrant chant these words; the others are united to him in a low voice, or even by pointing to the Holy Gifts by a single gesture of the hand. Among the Syrian Catholics each celebrant has his own altar and offerings, but the first celebrant pronounces in a loud voice the priestly formulas. Among the Maronites, and especially the Copts, the use of concelebration is more limited. Among the Chaldeans the ancient practice was that a priest was designated each time to present the oblation in the name of the bishop and the priestly college' (p. 92, note 2).It's a bit brief and even imprecise and ambiguous, not to say equivocal (let us not forget that it is only a simple initiation). At least we find there, under the pen of a specialist, a new and totally recent confirmation of our analysis, notably on the following two points: 1) ancient concelebration maintained in the Church of the East, which often wants nothing else, is purely ceremonial concelebration, where only the 'first celebrant', normally the bishop, confects and offers sacramentally the Eucharist; 2) the fact that the decisive importance, from a liturgical and theological point of view, of the difference between ceremonial and sacramental concelebrations had not been perceived by liturgists.

We note in the bibliography, in addition to the works of Hanssens and Raes of which we made much use, the fundamental work of A. A. King, *The Rites of Eastern Christendom* (2 vols., London, Burns and Oates, 1950). These three authors are, even still today, the principal references for these questions.

6 EUCHARISTIC CONCELEBRATION IN THE MAGISTERIUM OF THE SECOND VATICAN COUNCIL

THE HISTORY OF the Second Vatican Council is still to be written. 1. A few valuable chronicles have already been written, such as those of Laurentin or Wiltgen.[1] Access is now available to the collection of official acts of the Council. However, its history (in the proper sense of the word) has not yet been made, and there is no doubt a certain amount of time needed before it is, simply because of the amount of documentation which must be consulted in the process. We are thinking in particular of the work of all the commissions and sub-commissions. Such a history will nevertheless be very useful. It will shed great light on what John Paul II considers to be 'the fundamental question' which the Church must resolve today, namely that of 'the authentic interpretation of the Council.'[2] It is 'necessary,' the Holy Father said, 'to concentrate all forces on the correct, that is the authentic, interpretation of the conciliar Magisterium.' The study which we are presenting here on the subject of concelebration is a very modest contribution to the effort asked for by the Pope. The appeal which he made has been for us a great encouragement, for it signifies unambiguously that there is still much to be done in order to arrive at the correct interpretation of the Council. The rest of that same discourse by the Pope shows no less

---

[1] R. Laurentin, *L'enjeu du Concile*, Paris, Seuil, 1962; *L'enjeu du Concile—II. Bilan de la Première Session* (1963); *L'enjeu du Concile—III. Bilan de la Deuxième Session* (1964); (*Henceforth cited ass: L'enjeu; Bilan I; Bilan II*).—R. Wiltgen, *The Rhine Flows Into the Tiber* (1973). The present chapter appeared in *LPC*, no. 188 (September–October 1980), 18–65. We have numbered the paragraphs for convenience of the analysis and the internal cross references which we make.

[2] Discourse to the Bishops of France, in Issy–les–Moulineaux, 2 June 1980.

clearly that, on some points, a certain amount of rectification will even be necessary. Such is, we think, the case of concelebration; and it is this which we shall try to show here, by submitting in advance our reflections to the Magisterium itself. For, it alone has the authority to declare which is the 'authentic' interpretation of the Council.

2. Our method will be simple. The essence of what concerns concelebration is found in the *Constitution On the Sacred Liturgy*; it is this text above all which we shall study. Moreover, the principal source of our documentation being the collection of the *Acta* from the Council, we shall examine this Constitution in the different phases of the preparation and unfolding of Vatican II. Here it will be a question of studying:

1) the ante-preparatory phase;

2) the preparatory phase;

3) the first 'period' of the Council—or 'session' as it is usually called—in the course of which the 'schema' of this Constitution was presented and discussed;

4) the second 'period,' where it was voted upon, and at the end of which the Constitution itself was finally approved by the conciliar Fathers.[3]

---

[3]   These *Acta*, edited by the Typis Polyglottis Vaticanis, represent an imposing mass of twelve volumes, about 88 to 1000 pages each. They are divided into three main parts: the preparation, the unfolding of the Council, the texts approved by the Council. The first part is divided into two 'series', corresponding to the ante–preparatory and preparatory phrases; the second is divided into four 'volumes', corresponding to the four 'periods' or sessions of the Council. Each of these 'series and each of the 'volumes' contain several tomes. Here are the complete titles, the principal divisions, and the acronyms under which we shall refer to them:

Acta et Documenta Concilio Oecumenico Vaticano II Apparendo—Series I (Antepreparatoria) (17.V.1959–14.IX.1960): *Vol. I* (Acts of the Pope); *Vol. II* ('Vota' of the bishops and religious: 8 tomes); *Vol. II—Appendices* (Classification and summary of the 'vota' from *Vol. II*: 2 tomes); *Vol. III* (Roman Curia); *Vol. IV* (Universities: 3 tomes).

Acta et Documenta Concilio Oecumenico Vaticano II Apparendo—Series II

We shall also examine the other texts which have to do with concelebration: the *Decree on Ecumenism,* and especially that on *The Ministry and Life of the Priests,* which is completely indispensable on this point as on many others. We shall also consult several other documents which do not make mention of concelebration, such as the *Decree On the Restoration and Adaptation of Religious Life* or the *Decree on Eastern Catholics.* Our conclusion will be to gather together the broad outlines of the conciliar Magisterium, which will in turn allow us to see how the post-conciliar evolution can or cannot claim an association with it.

(Preparatoria) (14.IX.1960–11.X.1962): *Vol. I* (Acts of the Pope); *Vol. II* (Acts of the Central Preparatory Commission: 4 tomes); *Vol. III* (Texts of schemas: 2 tomes).

Acta Synodalia Sacrosancti Concilii Vaticani II.

Volumen I—Periodus Prima (11.X–8.XII.1962–C. G. I–XXXVI): report in 4 '*Partes*' (4 tomes) the *Sessiones publicae* (solemn opening sessions, closing sessions, promulgation of decrees, etc.) and the *Congregationes generales* (ordinary work meetings) of the first session: *Pars I* (C. G. I–IX); *Pars II* (C. G. X–XVIII); *Pars III* (C. G. XIX–XXX); *Pars IV* (C. G. XXXI–XXXVI).

Volumen II—Periodus Secunda (29. IX–4.XII.1963–C. G. XXXVII–LXXIX): in 6 '*Partes*' (6 tomes): *Pars I* (C. G. XXXVII–XXXIX); *Pars II* (C. G. XL–XLIX); etc.

Volumen III—Periodus Tertia (14.IX–21.XI.1964–C. G. LXXX–CXXVII): in 8 '*Partes*' (8 tomes);

Volumen IV—Periodus Quarta (14.IX–8.XII.1965–C. G. CXXVIII–CLXVIII): in 7 '*Partes*' (7 tomes).

There had been a sum total of 168 *Congregationes Generales* and 10 *Sessiones Publicae.*

Acronyms: AD I–III, 532 refers to Acta et Documenta…, Series I, Vol. III, p. 532; AD I–II. App./2, 53–5 refers to Acta et Documenta … , Series I, Vol. II–Appendices, tome 2, pp. 53–55; *AD II–II/1, 125* refers to *Acta et Documenta …, Series II, Vol. II,* tome 1, p. 125; *AS III–II, 18* refers to *Acta Synodalia …, Vol. III, Pars II,* p. 18.*

For the conciliar documents we use the customary abbreviations of the Latin titles.

I. The Ante-preparatory Phase (17 May 1959 to 14 September 1960)

3. One will recall that this is the phase where there was established the list of questions to be treated by the Council. To this end a consultation was made throughout the entire world, organized and admirably conducted under the care of the Curia. The responses received were gathered together into three 'volumes.' The first contains the 'votes' (*vota*) of the bishops and religious; it consists of no less than eight tomes, about nine hundred pages each. The second volume contains the 'votes' of the Roman Curia (in one single tome). The third contains the *vota* of the universities (in three tomes). These are respectively the second, third and fourth 'volumes' of this 'Series,' volume I (one single tome) being given to the acts of the Holy Father. In an 'Appendix' (two tomes) to volume II are contained the 'votes' of the bishops and religious.

Regarding the liturgy of the Eucharist, there were only about forty requests concerning concelebration.[4] Even if we add the names of the two faculties of theology which asked for it, that of the Salesians in Rome and of Trier in Germany,[5] even then this group of requests represents only a very small minority: about 1.9% of 2,109 *vota* collected by that consultation.[6] The smallness of this percentage diminishes even more if one considers that, of these forty some voices, more than one raised the question of concelebration only in order to respond, or only in order to ask that there be a response, to the question posed by the true representatives of that minority, and not in order to ask for the introduction of this rite. Such is the case, among others, of the Sacred Congregation of Rites, which admitted the possibility of this reform more than it desired it.[7] It is also that of the

---

[4]   *AD I–II. App./2*, 53–5.

[5]   *AD I–IV/1*, p. 165; *I–IV/2*, pp. 761 ff.

[6]   R. Laurentin, *L'enjeu*, p. 117.

[7]   *AD I–III*, pp. 256–9.

Abbot General of the Benedictines, Dom B. Gut, who limits himself to asking that it be clarified 'when and under what conditions is concelebration permitted even in the Church of the West.'[8]

Hence we see the importance of checking the summaries of this 'Appendix' by going back to the cited sources. With regards to concelebration, we can read for example the following *votum* under column nine: 'That the use of concelebration be permitted in religious houses and ecclesiastical gatherings.'[9] A note on the bottom of the page presents this 'vote' as coming from three Benedictine Abbots: Dom Gut for the entire Order of St Benedict, Dom Prou for the French Congregation and Dom Dayez for the Belgian Congregation. Yet, while it is correct that Dom Prou and Dom Dayez expressed this question—which is, by the way, far from all the Benedictine abbeys of France and Belgium—nevertheless, regarding Dom Gut, we saw to what his *votum* can be reduced. And those abbots of the Benedictine liturgical centers of France and Belgium tell us the reason for Dom Gut's request: far from resting his authority on the movement which he saw taking shape among some of his sons in France and Belgium, he sought rather to channel it. Such was his position on the eve of the Council.

4. In examining the whole collection of these *vota* one sees that about a third of the questions envisage concelebration only on occasion. With respect to the others who desired it more frequently, even daily, they come from three or four clearly identifiable centers: the Benedictines of France and Belgium, the liturgical groups from Germany and Austria, namely from the University of Trier and the Bishopric of Linz.[10] Solesmes in particular seems to have exercised a consider-

---

8   *AD I–II/8*, p. 15: '*S. Concilium indicet, quando et sub quibus conditionibus, etiam in Ecclesia Occidentali Concelebratio permitti possit.*'

9   *AD I–II. App./2*, 54.

10 For the University of Trier, see above, note 4. For the Austrian group, Vienna (Card. König)–Linz (Msgr Zauner): *AD I–II. App./2*, 54 (Proposition 8, which in fact can be reduced to the König–Zauner group). But even this group asked for concelebration only for certain occasions: for 'priests gathered in

able role, thanks to the prestige which it still had from the work of Dom Gueranger. Yet its abbot asked that daily concelebration be permitted: 'In order to better signify unity, and to eradicate more easily the practice which consists in making collective participation at one single Mass celebrated by one sole priest follow the individual celebration by several priests.'[11] We find here the teaching of the Centre de Pastorale Liturgique of Paris, which expressed itself to some degree in this *votum*, but not that of the Encyclical *'Mediator Dei'* on the value of private Masses. In the same vein Dom Dayez asked for daily concelebration: 'in order that priests not be disunited in the celebration of the one sacrament of unity.'[12]

As we have seen (and in conformity with the dominating tendency of the liturgical movement of that time), these requests give supreme prominence to the congregation. Though they obviously do not deny the aspect of sacrifice—the immediate foundation for the Ecclesial value of Masses said privately—they in fact disregard it.

5. In opposition to this movement, numerically minute but extremely active and supported by prestigious names, such as those of the abbot of Solesmes or Cardinal König, Archbishop of Vienna, the *votum* of the Sacred Congregation of the Rites merits a close examination.[13] The Congregation in fact consecrates almost five pages to this one question of concelebration a long *status quaestionis* preceding their *vota*. What must be called today a theological error unfortunately injures an otherwise excellent presentation of things, and gives place to positions which would most likely have been different in a overall vision more conformed to the truth.

Positing from the very beginning, and rightly so, the fundamental distinction between sacramental and ceremonial concelebration, the

---

large numbers at spiritual retreats or congresses': *'Sacerdotibus magno concursu occasione exercitium spiritualium vel congressuum convenientibus'* (AD I–II/1, 78).

[11]   *AD I–II/8*, p. 25 ff.

[12]   *Ibid*, 42.

[13]   Cf. *see above*, note 7.

votum of the Sacred Congregation of Rites actually states something which is less fortunate, namely that, in the first case one sole Mass is said, while in the second there are 'as many sacrifices as concelebrating priests.'[14] The origin of this erroneous assertion, corrected on 7 March 1965 by the same Congregation,[15] is, according to all appearances, in the incorrect interpretation of the words pronounced by Pius XII in 1954 apropos not of concelebration, but of the practice of 'communitarian Masses': '*tot sunt actiones Christi ... quot sunt sacerdotes celebrantes.*' We believe we have sufficiently analyzed this text and shown its true sense such that there is no need to return to it now.[16] On the other hand, we must recognize that we ourselves were in error when we thought that the erroneous interpretation of this text belonged only to a small number of people. One can see that it was supported by many—and even those in high places.[17] However, it was not the position of all; and we can immediately observe this by seeing Cardinal Larraona[18] actually affirm that one sole Mass is offered to God in a concelebration. Such in fact is the official doctrine of the Church ever since the Decree *Ecclesiae semper* of 7 March 1965.

---

[14]   In 'Concelebratio rubricalis seu ceremonialis', 'agitur ergo de una Missa seu de uno Sacrificio tantum' (*Ibid.*, p. 256). On the other hand, according to this *votum*, in 'Concelebratio sacramentalis', 'agitur ergo de tot Missis seu Sacrificiis, quot sunt sacerdotes concelebrantes' (p. 257).

[15]   '*Unicum sacrificium unico actu sacramentali conficiunt et offerunt*' (General Decree *Ecclesiae semper* of 7 March 1965—*AAS* 57, 1965, p. 411).

[16]   Cf. *LPC*, no. 180, pp. 23–7; *see above* Ch. I; no. 184, pp. 27–9; *see above*, pp. Ch. II. cf. *AAS* 46, 1954, p. 669; and also 48, 1956, p. 717.

[17]   There is another proof in the intervention of Msgr Elchinger during the first session. He explicitly cited Pius XII (Allocution of 22 September 1956) in order to claim that one Mass concelebrated by ten priests has the same value as the ten Masses which those priests would have offered had they celebrated individually. Such, according to him, is the teaching of Pius XII (AS I–II, p. 82). Yet, as we have seen, this is an incorrect interpretation of the pontiff's words.

[18]   Named Prefect of the Sacred Congregation of Rites on 22 February 1962.

This reaffirmation of the truth is valuable for us today. Unfortunately the error committed on the eve of the Council would carry much weight in the decisions made later. If one considers the Church's doctrine on the value of each Mass offered to God, it is by this error alone that one can explain that the Sacred Congregation of Rites agreed, as it then did, to envisage the idea of daily concelebration 'in the large monasteries'[19]—an expression, we note in passing, which reveals the Benedictine influence in the writing of this *votum*.

We can also note that, by this premature stance, and due to the pressure which its writing reveals, this *votum* contradicts the very principles which itself posited. It in fact declared that: 'In the preparation of the Council [it was necessary] to engage in a new and careful investigation, both historical and dogmatic, on the origin, nature and extension of properly sacramental concelebration.'[20] Yet, by admitting from that moment on the idea of a daily concelebration 'in the large monasteries,' the direction which it gave rested on an assertion insufficiently and in even erroneously founded, from a theological standpoint. It was all the more serious since the same text quite correctly saw in the introduction to the rite of concelebration 'a notable change in the liturgical discipline of the Latin Church.'[21]

On the other hand, on the historical level the Sacred Congregation of Rites recalled and strongly underlined a certain number of points of the greatest importance. Here one finds the confirmation of the conclusions to which our own research has led us.

> It is most necessary to note that this practice [of sacramental concelebration] had not been transmitted by antiquity, but that it was introduced in the Middle Ages. Furthermore, even

---

[19]   *AD I–III*, 258.

[20]   *Ibid*: 'In praeparatione Concilii curetur nova et accurata indagatio sive historica sive dogmatica, in originem, naturam et extensionem concelebrationis vere sacramentalis.'

[21]   *Ibid*: 'Agitur vero de mutatione notabili disciplinae liturgicae Ecclesiae latinae quae magna cum circumspectione tractanda est.'

the sacramental concelebration currently in certain Eastern Rites is not ancient, but was introduced through these rites, coming from the Latin Church two or three centuries ago at the most. Sacramental concelebration was not known in Christian antiquity (at least according to the knowledge we currently have).[22]

And, as we saw, it was not able to be known, since it was contrary to the fundamental principle of the one sacrifice on the one altar around one bishop, who represents the one Mediator.[23] One wonders whether, if these truths had been recalled by the conciliar Fathers (for they were not able to be), the efforts they gave to limiting the practice of concelebration would have been stronger and therefore more efficacious.

6. The three major points which can be extracted from this *votum*, so fundamental in view of the authority from which it comes, are the following:

---

[22]   *Ibid*, p. 257.

[23]   See our earlier works and the authors to which we refer, especially A. Raes, SJ, *La concélébration eucharistique dans les rits orientaux*, in *LMD* no. 35 (1953/3), pp. 24–47. 'The Greek tradition,' writes Fr Raes, 'is therefore in agreement with the ancient Oriental practice in that it assigns the concelebration of the mysteries to one sole celebrant' (p. 33), namely the bishop, 'because he is, says Simeon of Thessalonica, the image, the type, of Him Who immolates Himself for us' (p. 31). With the same sense of respect for tradition and sacramental symbolism, the Sacred Congregation asks that for the Mass of Holy Thursday one priest does everything: 'in order to preserve the very ancient Tradition, not only of the Roman Church, but also of all the Churches and all the rites, and according to which on this day alone (whatever necessities having been done ahead of time to provide for the needs of the people), the Last Supper was represented in the Holy Liturgy in such a way that one sole priest celebrant accomplished the sacred rite (*'ita ut unice sacerdos celebrans Sacrum conficiat'*), and that all the other priests (and the other clerics as well as the faithful) participated by a simply ceremonial concelebration' (*loc. cit.*, pp. 258 ff.). By permitting sacramental concelebration on this day (*SC* 57, § 1,1) the Second Vatican Council adopted a measure which represents an innovation with respect to Tradition.

1) the need for a more developed dogmatic and historical study before every disciplinary decision;

2) a very pertinent historical reminder;

3) an erroneous theological assertion.

Unfortunately, as we shall see, if the third point seems to have been retained, it had not taken into account the previous two points. We shall also see how the absence of the requested development would lead to the introduction of a new error, this one on the historical level, added to the doctrinal error already committed.

Such then was the situation on the eve of the preparatory phase of the Council. A tiny minority, but very strong and organized, requested a concelebration of which almost no one would have dreamed, especially when one considers the practically unlimited extension that was claimed for it. And this minority found in opposition to itself a Curia conscience of the importance of the issue and yet insufficiently prepared theologically. The same can be said—without too great a risk of erring—about the rest of the Church.

II. The Preparatory Phase (14 September 1960 to 11 October 1962)

7. The preparatory phase of Vatican II was officially opened by John XXIII on 14 September 1960, on the Feast of the Exaltation of the Cross.[24] In reality, his work had begun the preceding 5 June, with the publication of his *Motu proprio* 'Superno Dei nutu,' by which the Supreme Pontiff organized and established the organs before immediately preparing the Council. Twelve commissions and secretariats had been created. Their members were nominated between 16 June and 30 November.[25] The Pope personally presided over the central Commission, which had Msgr P. Felici for its secretary. This Commission had for its task the coordinating of the work of the other

---

24 R. Laurentin, *L'enjeu*, p. 133.

25 *Ibid.*

commissions, as well as the examination and approving of their schemas. The commission in charge of the liturgy was presided over by Cardinal Gaetano Cicognani, who died on 5 February 1962. A few days before, 1 February, he had signed not without serious hesitations the schema drawn up by his commission. On 22 February Cardinal Larraona succeeded him. The secretary of the commission was Fr Hannibal Bugnini.[26]

The task of these commissions was to receive the results from the consultation given during the course of the preceding phase, and to establish 'not simple elements or suggestions (as was done during the preparatory phase), but texts capable of being promulgated by the Council.'[27] Their role was therefore of an extreme importance, for one knows the influence of the initial project over the text finally voted upon.

8. Below is the text (in what concerns concelebration) drawn up by the preparatory Commission on the Liturgy, as it was presented to the central Commission (we shall call it text A):

> II. Sacramental Concelebration.—44. [*That the practice be enlarged*].
>
> Concelebration has remained in use until now in both the Eastern as well as the Western Church. It is desired that it be

---

[26]   P. M. Gy, O P, *Situation historique de la Constitution*, in *La Liturgie après Vatican II* (*Unam Sanctam* 66), Paris, Cerf, 1967, p. 118. Fr Gy notes that, following the examination of the schema by the central Commission: 'Fr Bugnini, who was at the helm of the ship next to the deceased Cardinal Cicognani, lost his chair at the Lateran and did not become secretary of the conciliar commission [of the liturgy].' A few lines earlier he wrote: 'Before the profusion of the program of reform, the old president of the commission of the liturgy, Cardinal Gaetano Cicognani, hesitated one last time and waited a week. On 1 February he countersigned the text. He died on 5 February.' This allows one to see clearly that the driving role in the ante–preparatory commission had been played by Fr Bugnini, and that 'the old president' had been reticent about what was presented to him. The central Commission would have the same reaction. On the activity of Fr Bugnini during the Council, see *LPC*, no. 186–7, p. 81; *see above*, Ch. IV.

[27]   R. Laurentin, *L'enjeu*, pp. 133 ff.

extended to a greater number of cases than at present, and especially:

a) at the Chrism Mass of Holy Thursday;

b) at the conventual Mass and the principal Mass in churches when there are more priests than the needs of the faithful require, always respecting the freedom of each priest to celebrate individually, though not in the same church at the same time;

c) at gatherings of priest, such as spiritual exercises, sessions of study, pilgrimages, etc., especially when individual Masses cannot be celebrated without inconvenience;

d) at extraordinarily festive celebrations, for example on the occasion of a diocesan Synod, a pastoral visitation (concelebration of the bishop with clergy of the visited Parish).

45. [*The rite of concelebration*] ...

46. [*Appropriateness of concelebration and the number of concelebrants*]. It will belong to the local Ordinary to judge in each case the appropriateness of concelebration and the number of concelebrants...

47. [*Stipends*]. The disposition of Canon 824 of the Code of Canon Law, regarding Mass stipends, pertains to each concelebrant.[28]

---

[28] *AD II–II/3*, 107–9. The same text is reproduced verbatim in *AD II–III/2*, 33–6 (see our prefatory note on *AD II–III/1,7*): '4. [*Usus amplificetur*]. *Concelebratio tam in Ecclesia Orientali quam in Occidentali in usu hucusque remansit. In votis est ut ad plures casus extendatur quam in disciplina vigenti et praesertim: a) ad Missam chrismatis, feria V in Cena Domini; b) ad Missam conventualem et ad Missam principalem in ecclesiis, ubi plures sacerdotes adsunt quam utilitas fidelium requirit, salva semper cuiusque sacerdotis libertate individualiter celebrandi, non tamen in eadem ecclesia, eodem tempore; c) ad conventus sacerdotum, uti sunt exercitia spiritualia, cursus studiorum, peregrinationes, etc., praesertim ubi singulae Missae sine incommodo celebrari nequent; d) ad extraordinarias celebrationes festivas, exempli gratia occasione Synodi diocesanae, visitationis pastoralis (concelebratio Episcopi una cum clero illius paroeciae) ... 45. [Ritus concelebrationis] ... 46. [Opportunitas concelebrationis]. De opportunitate concelebrationis et de numero*

This text was preceded by an introduction (*Prooemium*) and a first chapter, which expounded 'The General Principles of the Liturgy.' The second chapter treated 'The Most Holy and Most Sacred Mystery of the Eucharist.' Its first section dealt with 'The Mass' (nos. 37 to 43); the second section treated concelebration. Each number was followed by an explanatory note (*Declaratio*), at least as important as the text itself, and supporting the tendency towards the greatest extension possible.

9. This all requires a long analysis. We shall limit ourselves to the following few considerations.

The first will be to note the internal contradiction of the text, revelatory of tensions which manifested themselves within the commission even from the very first stage. In fact, to request on the one hand concelebration for the conventual Mass (and under such conditions that make it immediately appear as a daily occurrence), and to request on the other hand that the bishop judge in each case regarding the appropriateness of concelebration and the number of concelebrants—to do this is to present two practically incompatible requests.

Moreover—and this is our second point—one can see that the Commission of the Liturgy was content with saying that an extension of concelebration was desired, '*in votis est ...*,' without giving any indication of the numerical and qualitative importance of the manifestations of such a desire. As the discussions on this question caused a certain uproar during the course of the preceding years by the simple fact of the specialized centers, the members of the central Commission had the impression that these 'votes' came from many, when in reality they represented only a very small minority, especially when it came to the topic of concelebration. Moreover, they went not only

---

concelebrantium, in singulis casibus, Ordinarii loci erit iudicare... 47 [Stipendium]. *Dispositio can. 824 Codicis Iuris Canonici, relate ad stipendium Missae, valet pro unoquoque concelebrante ... '*—The passages between the brackets are in the text. We leave out no. 45 and will not linger on no. 47; for, they have practically no impact on the question which occupies us here, namely that of the extension to be given to concelebration.

against the traditional practice and the desires of the overall majority, but they were in opposition to the Church's Magisterium, especially in what concerns the conventual Mass. And this happened in two ways: first, because such a practice led to ignoring the value of private Masses, as numerous Fathers noted; and second, because this was essentially a return to the Synod of Pistoia, solemnly and formally condemned by Pope Pius VI in the Apostolic Constitution 'Auctorem fidei' of 28 August 1794 (Proposition 84, Article VIII).[29]

This brings us to our third remark. In the *Declaratio* which follows no. 44, the Commission of the Liturgy gives the list of 'principal documents of the Church concerning concelebration.' Yet this list mentions neither the documents of Pius XII, which in one way or another touch on the question and which are pertinent here,[30] nor the fundamental text of Pius VI, which we just mentioned. As regrettable as it is that this latter was forgotten, it is understandable to a certain point; for, it is not found in the chapter on the Liturgy of the Constitution of Pius VI, but in the one dedicated to the reform of religious. Such a lacuna is nevertheless grave on the part of specialists, called as they are to place their competence at the service of the Magisterium. Less excusable is the omission of the texts of Pius XII, which no one can ignore. Yet the teaching of Pius VI and that of the 'Angelic Pastor' harmoniously complement each other, the latter giving the theological rational of the former. In fact, in developing the doctrine of the value of private Masses, Pius XII tells us why his predecessor had condemned the Jansenist Synod of Pistoia's pretense to impose daily concelebration for the conventual Mass in religious

---

[29] DS 2691. cf. *LPC*, no. 184, pp. 37 ff; *see above*, Ch. II. We shall reproduce this text again below (note p. 459).

[30] We are thinking especially of the following documents: the Encyclical *Mediator Dei* (20 November 1947); cf. *AAS* 39, 1947, p. 553); the *Allocution* of 2 November 1954 (cf. *AAS* 46, 1954, pp. 668–9); and above all the *Decree* of the Holy Office of 23 May 1957 (cf. *AAS* 49, 1957, p. 370). We reproduced and analyzed the essence of these documents in *LPC*, no. 180; pp. 23–7; *see above*, Ch. I.

houses. We see therefore the seriousness of the silence regarding these teachings in the Schema on concelebration. The omitted texts, which are perfectly inscribed in the homogenous development of dogma and liturgy, would have shed an essential light on the problem of concelebration, its meaning and its limits.

Our fourth remark is as follows. The same list of 'principal documents of the Church...' limits itself to mentioning the case and rites where concelebration had been permitted by the Church. It does not speak about all the Eastern Rites (at least as numerous if not more so) which have always refused sacramental concelebration.[31] Perhaps the objection can be raised that it was not necessary under the adopted rubric, which is not so evident. The fact remains that the error of historical perspective thus introduced gave the impression that concelebration was the normal and current practice of the Churches of the East, something which is far from the truth. The contrary assertion is much closer to reality. The East in general either refused concelebration, or, when it did adopt the practice, considered it only as an occasional and particularly solemn mode of celebrating the Eucharist. The case of the Byzantine Catholic Rite, which received permission for daily concelebration at the end of nineteenth century, is an exception. It would be difficult to find many others.

With respect to the reasons brought forward in favour of concelebration's extension (which is our fifth remark), they are far from being completely convincing: 1) the fact that 'the unity of the Church is better demonstrated in the unity of the priesthood'; 2) the priestly piety, which would be better fostered; 3) the practical advantages and conveniences of this manner of celebrating.[32] In fact, only this last reason is incontestable. For, the second is debatable; the contrary is

---

[31]   Cf. *see above*, note 23.

[32]   AD II–II/3, p. 108: '*Rationes cur optatur extensio: a) Unitas Ecclesiae in unitate sacerdotii melius demonstratur:* (citation from St Thomas, *Summa Theologiae,* III, qu. 82, 1.2, ad 2 and 3); *b) Pietas magis foveatur* ... ; *c) Vitantur difficultates practicae...* '

easily maintained, especially when one considers the lives of the saints. With respect to the first, it pretends to be based on a text of St Thomas the meaning of which it falsifies somewhat; and only aspects of unity and congregation are retained, considering them only from the point of view of their exterior manifestation. It is reflections of this type which moved the central Commission to reject this text of the preparatory Commission of the Liturgy.

The text of St Thomas cited in support of the first argument is that of the *Summa Theologiae,* Tertia Pars, question 82, article 2, response to objections 2 and 3.[33] Yet St Thomas is not speaking here of the *manifestation* of the unity of the priesthood and of the Church. Still less is he making an apologia for concelebration, a rite which practically disappeared and was very much contested at that time.[34] He limits himself to showing the theological possibility, his two arguments being 'the custom of certain churches' and the fact that the priest consecrates only *'in persona Christi,'* in which, according to St Paul, the multitude which we form is one (Gal. 3:28).[35] This is to

---

[33]   This is a parallel text to *IV Sent.,* d. 13, q. 1, a. 2, qla. 2, ad 1. We analyzed this in *LPC,* no. 180, pp. 32–5; *see above,* Ch. I; no. 185, pp. 40–1; *see above,* Ch. II.

[34]   Cf. J. M. Hanssens, SJ, *De concelebratione eucharistica,* in *Periodica de Re Morali, Canonica, Liturgica* (Rome, Pont. Univ. Greg.), 21, 1932, p. 203. He cites among those opposed to this rite names such as St Albert the Great (*De eucharistica distinctiones VI,* Tract IV,, c. 2, nos. 15–16).

[35]   Fr Roguet rightly notes the somewhat rapid character of this text of St Thomas (*LMD,* no. 34 (1953/2), 148–56), which does not weaken its strength, but shows the neeed for a further development of the question. Regarding the expression '*in persona Christi*', one could meditate on the admirable commentary, both theological and mystical, of John Paul II: '*Sanctissimum Sacrificium a sacerdote offertur "in persona Christi", quod plus sane significat quam "nomine Christi" vel etiam "Christi vicem". Offertur nempe "in persona": cum celebrans ratione peculiari et sacramentali idem prorsus sit ac "summus aeternusque sacerdos", qui Auctor est princepsque Actor huius proprii sui sacrificii, in quo nemo revera in eius locum substitui potest ... Conscientia autem huius rei aliquot modo illuminat significationem et indolem sacerdotis celebrantis qui, Sanctissimum immolans Sacrificium atque "in persona Christi" agens, inducitur inseriturque*

make the text of St Thomas say more, and even something other, than what he himself said—presenting it as if it supported the thesis which states that the advantage of concelebration is that 'the *manifestation* of unity in the Church is in the unity of the priesthood.' He does not support this, and he does not even speak of a *manifestation* of unity in this practice; his only intention there is to show the possibility of concelebration. Yet it is on the faith of this *Declaratio* of the prepara-tory Commission that several of the Fathers once again committed an error in their interpretation of St Thomas during the conciliar debates; and, no doubt, many were influenced by this 'authority.'

The sixth remark is this. Nowhere in these explanations is it a question of the Mass as a sacrifice, or of its finality of adoration, reparation, propitiation or intercession. Moreover, the manner of the text's expression shows that this aspect, which is primary, is not considered: the only reason the singular celebration of Mass is considered valuable is the 'utility of the faithful' (44, b). This means: the immediate needs of a determined group who desires to assist at Mass. To present the matter thus is not to consider what each Mass

---

modo sacramentali (simulque ineffabili) in hoc intimum "sacrum" ubi is vicissim spiritaliter omnes consociat eucharisticae congregationis participes' (*Epistula ad universos Ecclesiae Episcopos; de SS. Eucharistiae Mysterio et Cultu*, 9; AAS 72–1980, pp. 128 ff.).'The Most Holy Sacrifice is offered by the priest "*in persona Christi*", which certainly means more than "in the name of Christ", or even "in the place of Christ". To offer "*in persona*" means that the celebrant is absolutely identified in a particular and sacramental manner "with the Eternal High Priest", Who is the Author and the Principal Subject of His own sacrifice, in which no one truly can substitute in His place ... The knowledge of this truth illuminates in a certain way the significance and character of the priest celebrant who, *in offering the Most Holy Sacrifice and acting "in persona Christi"*, is introduced and inserted, in a sacramental (and at the same time ineffable) manner, into the very heart of this "*Sacrum*" [that is the Sacrifice offered in this sacred rite], in which, he in turn associates spiritually all those who participate in the Eucharistic assembly.' We see especially how such a text, while preserving its strength in the case of concelebration, nevertheless finds its full meaning in the case of the celebration where the priest is alone at the altar, as Christ is alone on the Cross.

does for the glory of God, for the life of the Church and the salvation of the world—a contribution which comes entirely from the fact that it is always the sacrifice of Christ and the Church. This obscuring of the value of private Masses would appear once again during the conciliar debates, and would be noted by more than one of the Fathers.

The seventh and last remark flows immediately from the two preceding ones: the exclusive insistence on the aspect of the manifestation of unity, and therefore on the congregation, on one hand; and on the other hand, the underestimation of the sacrificial, and therefore infinite value of each offering of the Eucharist for the Church. We find here the two major characteristics of the post-war liturgical movement. In fact, it is clearly that movement which is expressed in no. 44, as it is that which dominated the whole of the first schema on the liturgy.

In recalling the need for a regulation of the new practice, and in entrusting it to the local Ordinary, no. 46 tried to build a dam, as it were, not against the movement as a whole, but against its excesses. We shall see the difficulties which this request for a regulation would encounter in order to make itself heard at the Council; for, it did make itself heard, and it ended winning the cause, albeit somewhat imperfectly and inefficaciously. At least it saved its principles.

This text being such, with its numerous inaccuracies and lack of internal cohesion, it was nonetheless approved unanimously during the course of the plenary session of the preparatory Commission for the Liturgy, on 12 and 13 January, 1962.[36]

10. Such was not the case when, on 26 March of the same year, this schema was presented to the central Commission. In his presentation, Cardinal Larraona[37] was the first to make several adjustments, which were imposed; and he recalled the questions which were at stake. After having noted the difference between ceremonial and sacramen-

---

[36]   *AD II–II/3*, 109.

[37]   He had just succeeded G. Cicognani as head of the Sacred Congregation for Divine Worship as well as the preparatory Commission for the Liturgy.

tal concelebration, he requested the following 'in order to avoid confusion':

a) a declaration from the Holy Office on the value of the concelebrated Mass—whether one sole Mass concele-brated by ten priests has the same value as ten Masses celebrated by ten priests;

b) a declaration on the legitimacy, for each concelebrating priest, of collecting and requiring stipends.[38]

By these requests alone one can see the distance, to say the least, which separated the Commission for the Liturgy from its new president (who—it is morally certain—expressed here thoughts in complete conformity with those of his predecessor, perhaps even directly inspired by him). We note in particular that he considered the question on the value of the concelebrated Mass in no way resolved, and that this question was for him the first of those which needed to be clarified before any decision could be made on the level of discipline about the practice of concelebration. The question was posited without delay the moment it was recognized that one sole Eucharistic sacrifice was offered to God in concelebration—such a recognition came about because of the manner of speaking of 'a [i.e. singular] concelebrated Mass.' The question of Mass stipends did not cause major difficulties; but it too called for a declaration.[39]

The cardinal then indicated the cases to which sacramental concelebration ought to be limited (*contrahenda*) and those where the bishop can occasionally allow it. He introduced here a principle of distinction, which needed to be taken up by the Council. Unfortunately his two preceding requests would not be granted, especially the first one—something quite tragic. In any case the opposition

---

[38]　*AD II–I/3*, 115.

[39]　We indicated how, in the absence of that long–awaited official declaration, this question seemed to require some regulation (*LPC*, no. 180, pp. 34 ff; *see above*, pp. 28 ff; no. 185, pp. 31 ff; *see above*, Ch. III). The solution which we proposed agrees with that given by Msgr Martimort in 1946 (*LMD*, no. 6 (1942/2), p. 116; cf. *see above*, Ch. III).

between this report and the schema which it presented was obvious: the latter requested the largest possible extension of concelebration, while the former clearly allowed only a limited use.

11. The same opposition to the schema of the Commission for the Liturgy was manifested by a great number of members of the central Commission. Thus Cardinal Godfrey, Archbishop of Westminster, 'foresaw the difficulties and abuses which would occur if the occasions were not clearly established when concelebration would be allowed.'[40] Cardinal Ottaviani was no less perspicacious. His pastoral sense was joined in his reflection to his doctrinal concern. Without mentioning the knowledge which he had of the abusive tendencies of the liturgical movement, the cardinal accurately observed that, more than concelebration,

> the current needs seem rather to require the multiplication of Masses for the people, both morning and evening … Furthermore, that decree will be an encouragement to omit the celebration of private Mass, as in fact some liturgists have already unfortunately done.[41]

This prediction, like the preceding one, was correct. The most recent Instruction from the Sacred Congregation for Catholic Education shows it, recognizing that the aforementioned omission is widespread. Eighteen years after Cardinal Ottaviani, it was Cardinal Garrone's turn to recall,

> that the Church heartily recommends to priests the daily celebration of Holy Mass, as an act offered by Christ and by the Church, for the salvation of the whole world, even if they are not bound by pastoral obligations, or even if there are no faithful participating.[42]

---

[40] *AD II–II/3*, p. 122.

[41] *Ibid.*, p. 125.

[42] *Instruction for the Liturgical Formation in Seminaries*, no. 26 (we cite it according to the *L'Osservatore Romano* of 12 April 1980).

Dated 3 June 1979, this Instruction had not been made public until April 1980, which is surprising. Nevertheless we welcome it with joy as a fortunate 'sign of the times.'

And returning to the central preparatory Commission's meeting of 26 March 1962, we hear the same things expressed by Cardinals Browne, Tappouni, Guigan, Gilroy, Traglia, Santos, etc. as was expressed by the two speakers cited above. Other members of the Commission, such as Cardinals König, Döppfner, Alfrink, etc. expressed the opposite viewpoint. Inspired as they were by the then reigning theology of Karl Rahner, they approved the project, but not without falling again into the error of historical perspective which we mentioned above.[43] However, they were but a small minority.

12. Among all those interventions, one of the most remarkable, theologically speaking, was that of the Secretary of the Sacred Congregation for Religious, the Rev Fr (today Cardinal) Paul Philippe, OP It was also one of the most noted, having been approved especially by persons such as Cardinal Godfrey and the Most Reverend Father Janssens, General of the Jesuits.[44] Admitting the principle of occasional concelebration,

> because thus the union of all priests with the bishop in the one priesthood of Christ is manifested, which is sometimes good, [Philippe added:] this, however, does not seem to be a sufficient reason to extend concelebration to the daily conventual Mass ... In fact, the union of priests of the same diocese with their bishop, or that of the priests of the same religious house with their superior, is but the consequence of the union of each of them with Christ the Priest Himself, Whose place they take at the Mass ... Yet the action of Christ offering Himself and sacrificing Himself by means of the sacramental action is manifest in a much more expressive manner in the Mass celebrated by one sole priest than in a concelebrated Mass; and this not only for the celebrant himself, but also for the faithful, who see

---

[43]   For example: *AD II–II/3*, p. 127; ...

[44]   *Ibid.*, pp. 137; 141.

in this one priest 'the image of Christ' the Priest (Cf. St Thomas Aquinas, III, q. 83, a. 1, 3 m.).[45]

We find here the fundamental theological reason for which the early Church, up until the eighth century, as well as the majority of the Eastern Rites, especially the Greek Orthodox, up until today, did not know and always refused sacramental concelebration.[46]

From here flow, Fr Paul Philippe continued, the dangers of this practice for priestly piety. For, 'it is to be feared that priests will attach more importance to their union among themselves and with their bishop or religious superior, than to their personal union with Christ.' Leaving aside the concern for union with the superior or bishop, the facts have confirmed the soundness of this warning. The criteria according to which priests especially, but also the faithful along with them, very often judge the success of a concelebration is in the sentiment that they have experienced being together. What matters is this felt and flawless unanimity; the congregation is on the verge of becoming its own end. To this degree the inversion of the Eucharist is complete: from being theocentric it has become totally anthropocentric.

The third reason which that eminent religious brings forth rests on the doctrine of the Mass' fruits. He observes:

> For in this manner, one must consider not only the fruit produced by one fervent (*devota*) and fraternal celebration, but especially by the nature of the act which is accomplished, that is to say Christ's sacramental sacrifice. Yet the objective fruit of the Mass (that is the fruit of appeasement or reparation, and of impetration for the living and the dead) is the principal fruit; and it is not produced in an equal manner by one concelebrated Mass and by several Masses celebrated by several priests. Therefore, it is to be feared that, if the practice of frequent concelebration spreads, this correct doctrine will

---

[45]   'Sacerdos gerit imaginem Christi, in cuius persona et virtute verba pronuntiat ad consecrandum' (*loc. cit.*).

[46]   Cf. *see above*, note 23.

be obscured and the faithful will no longer concern themselves
with having Masses celebrated for the living and the dead.

Once again the prediction has come true. For, that is in fact what has
happened, with the immense loss of graces not only for the particular
intentions of the faithful, but also for the common good of the
Church, since each Mass is offered first of all for the entire ecclesial
community. We note as well that, for this Dominican theologian, a
faithful disciple of St Thomas, concelebration is the common celebration of one single Mass.

One can see here, then, that the three reasons put forward in favour
of a limitation on concelebration are well founded … and that they
are almost diametrically opposed to those presented by the preparatory Commission for the Liturgy in favour of its extension.

13. The result of this examination of the schema on the liturgy by the
central Commission was what was to be expected after all those
oppositions. Regarding concelebration especially, the schema was
rejected and submitted to a thorough revamping,[47] such that it was
another text ostensibly modified which had been presented to the
Council Fathers. As we shall see shortly, this did not prevent that
minority, which animated the liturgical movement, from having its
initial schema taken up again at the end of the first session. The
rejection of such a schema by the central Commission during the
preparatory phase is full of meaning, especially when one considers
first, that this Commission, appointed by John XXIII, was at the time
the organ empowered to express the sentiment of the Church's
Magisterium, and second, the theological and pastoral value of the
reasons on which its refusal was founded.

These reasons, we note, are the very same as those which we
explained in our preceding works, written before we were able to
consult the acts of the Council. To tell the truth, they reveal a good
elementary theological sense; but this authorized confirmation is

---

[47]   On the manner in which this was done, see the declarations made during the
first session in response to the questions of the Fathers: *AS I–II*, pp. 106–8.

valuable for us in the face of the darkening of these truths in the minds of a great number of priests today. Just as valuable is the recent declaration of Cardinal Garrone, which we related above; for, by its implications it agrees with the interventions of Cardinal Ottaviani and the Rev Fr Paul Philippe, and it pleads with them in favour for the multiplication of the offering of the Eucharistic sacrifice, and therefore for a limitation of concelebration.

This also allows us to state once again (experience having taught us that we can never say it enough): the precise point of the discussion is not the very principle of concelebration, which no one questions, but only the application of this principle, that is the indication of the circumstances in which it is possible to use this rite, which is to say the regulation of its frequency. As we shall see, because the Council has not clearly defined the matter, the question remains legitimately open. We are thinking most especially of the problem of the conventual Mass of religious communities, or the daily Mass of priestly communities.

We see then, that while this practice had been requested before the Council by some isolated groups (small in number, but active and determined), it would meet with a very strong opposition from the central preparatory Commission, and especially from the Secretary of the Sacred Congregation of Religious, the Dominican Paul Philippe, as well as the General of the Jesuits, the Most Reverend Fr Janssens. We mention only these representatives of two of the largest religious Orders, whose acts from the Council bear witness for us. The two tendencies which faced each other at the Council were therefore already made manifest. To tell the truth, they had been known for a long time. The first, that of the unlimited expansion, had been brought forward for the first time at the level of the preparatory Commission for the Liturgy; the second time, the central Commission supported the second tendency, that of a moderate opening. What would happen at the Council?

III. The Constitution on the Liturgy during the first session of the Council (11 October to 8 December 1962)

14. Once their work was complete, the preparatory Commissions had been dissolved. The first seven schemas, prepared by the specialized Commissions and approved by the central Commission, had been sent to the Fathers as early as 13 July 1962.[48] It was now necessary to establish the order in which the texts would be considered at the Council and the procedure by which they would be studied. It was also necessary (and no less crucial) to name the conciliar Commissions. This problem, according to Fr Laurentin, 'conditioned the future of Vatican II.'[49] This is not the place (and it would be difficult anyhow) to recall in detail the manner in which these Commissions were named. The public facts of 13 October 1962 are known. What is necessary to remember is, that following a devised intervention by Cardinals Lienart, Tisserant, Frings and several others,[50] the tendency which defined itself as the progressive wing of the Church would begin to take control of the majority of the Commissions—something they managed to do with great intensity and with incalculable conse-

---

[48] R. Wiltgen, *op. cit.*, p. 22.

[49] R. Laurentin, *Bilan* I, p. 17.

[50] On this question we have today the explicit testimony of Cardinal Tisserant himself. He is recorded by J. Guitton, of the Académie Française, in his book, *Paul VI secret* (Paris, D. D. Br., p. 123). The testimony of Cardinal Lienart, despite the denial which he puts forth, actually confirms it instead. One cannot clearly see on what precise point bears his denial of a preliminary dialogue from the moment that he recognized the following, as he did: [the recognition] that he spoke of this question with the French bishops; that he went to see Cardinal Tisserant in order to include him in on their reflections, which implies that he gave a report of this action to his colleagues; and that Cardinal Tisserant, at the moment of his intervention, while he had not given him the word, did not keep him from taking it either (*Vatican II par le Cardinal Liénart, ancien évêque de Lille*, in *Mélange de Sc. Relig.*, XXXIII Année. No. Supplémentaire, Lille, Fac. Cath., 1976, pp. 65–8). On the importance of this intervention of Cardinal Liénart, see R. Wiltgen, *op. cit.*, p. 17.

quences. One ought not be surprised at these conflicts; all the Councils had them. But it is important not to lose sight of them, if one wishes to understand the genesis of the conciliar documents; it is indispensable for correctly interpreting them. For, an angelic, irenic atmosphere would all of a sudden conceal the reality of history.

It is also by opposing itself to the function of the regular structures of the Council, and outside of Rome, that the other question of which we spoke was resolved (at least with respect to the first point): namely, the question on the order in which the different schemas were to be examined. This was, in fact, the work of the Dutch episcopate, helped by Fr Schillebeeckx;[51] and his point of view was accepted by the new Commissions and by the Council Presidency.

Thus, on 16 October, at the second general Congregation, the announcement of this order was made to the Fathers, and on 22 October, during the fourth general Congregation, the *Schema of the Constitution on the Sacred Liturgy* was presented to them.[52] In fact, it had been sent to them on the preceding July 23,[53] but it was in October that it was officially presented in the Council aula. We saw above that as a result of the numerous critiques made by the central preparatory Commission to the first project (text A), this text had been greatly modified. Here, then, in what concerns concelebration, is the new text, as it was presented to the Fathers during this fourth general Congregation (let us call it text B):

> II. Regarding Sacramental Concelebration. 44. [*That the practice might be expanded*].
>
> Concelebration has remained in use up until the present in both the Eastern and the Western Church
>
> (11). The Council is pleased to extend this faculty of concelebration to the following cases (12):

---

51 R. Wiltgen, *op. cit.*, p. 23.

52 Or at least its *Prooemium* and Chapters I and II: *AS I–I*, pp. 262–82.

53 *Ibid.*, p. 262.

c) at the Chrism Mass of Holy Thursday;

d) at gatherings of priests, if it is not possible to provide otherwise for individual celebrations, and at the judgment of the Ordinary.

45. [*Appropriateness of celebration and the number of concelebrants*]. It belongs to the Ordinary to judge in each case the appropriateness of concelebration and the number of concelebrants.

46. [*The rite of concelebration*] .... [54]

15. Even the least attentive reader of these two articles cannot let escape the extreme reduction imposed on the initial schema. In fact, what we have is an entirely new project; and the new text prepared by the designated Sub-Commission is no more satisfying than the previous one. Certainly, it did not reduce the number of cases, as the central Commission had asked, but perhaps it went beyond its intentions. One notes the inversion of numbers 45 and 46. Also notable, and even more important, is that, when speaking of the 'Local Ordinary,' the Sub-Commission withdrew from bishops' control of concelebration in religious communities. For these latter the 'Ordinary' is the major superior: the abbot, provincial, etc. This suppression, provoking as it did lively reactions from many of the Fathers, would give the Council an occasion to reaffirm both the principle of the bishop's authority over the liturgy within his own diocese, as well as the limitation of concele-

---

[54]   *Ibid.*, p. 280: II.—*De Concelebratione Sacramentali.*—4. [*Usus amplificetur*]. *Concelebratio tam in Ecclesia Orientali quam in Occidentali in usu hucusque remansit (11). Concilio facultatem concelebrandi ad sequentes casus extendere placet (12): a) ad Missam chrismatis, feria V in Cena Domini; b) ad conventus sacerdotum, si ad singulares celebrationes aliter provideri non possit et de judicio Ordinarii. 45 [Opportunitas concelebrationis et numerus concelebrantium]. De opportunitate concelebrationis et de numero concelebrantium, in singulis casibus, Ordinarii erit iudicare. 46. [Ritus concelebrationis]* ... The question of the 'stipendium' was not treated.

bration, the regulation of which belongs properly to the *Local* Ordinary. We shall see this when studying the second session.

What's more, the new text supported the historical error (which had already been denounced) on the origins of concelebration, making the Fathers believe that what they were being asked to vote on, namely sacramental concelebration, was the rite of Tradition, whereas Tradition knew only ceremonial concelebration. One can see the weight that this false argument from Tradition had in the hearts of the Fathers. In order to support it, and in order to obtain a reaction which would allow them to return to the original schema, the Sub-Commission, which had supplied the editing of this new schema, added to it in a footnote (especially notes 11 and 12) all the 'explanations' (*Declarationes*) by which the preparatory Commission for the Liturgy had sought to establish its requests. The fruit of a conciliatory agreement between 'the preparatory Commissions,' these 'notes ... which did not belong to the chapters of the schemas,'[55] and therefore which did not belong to the schemas themselves, would come to play a huge role (as we shall see) in obtaining a return to the original schema. They went completely in this direction and took up again the errors on which it had been based.

However, the Fathers did not have the time to undertake the studies which would have allowed them to see and demonstrate this. They found themselves in the presence of a hybrid and even contradictory text, as some of them did not hesitate to note.[56] The 'notes' which they needed to clarify were concerned with a tendency opposite

---

[55] *Ibid.*, p. 262, that is at the bottom of the first page of the schema, a note informing the Fathers: '*Notae, quae singulis schematum capitibus adiciuntur, schematum partem non habent: sed a Commissionibus Praeparatoriis ideo exaratae sunt, ut Patribus schemata pervestigantibus exstent subsidio.*' One cannot see very well what are these 'preparatory Commissions', since the redaction of this text had been entrusted to an *ad hoc* Sub–Commission. Therefore, the immediate origin of this note is not clear. Perhaps it is from the Liturgy Commission acting through the designated Sub–Commission.

[56] Thus, for example, Msgr J. Khoury: *AS I–II*, p. 83.

to that which it had for the most part inspired. The central Commission had put forth its point of view in the text itself, especially in number 44. The Commission for the Liturgy had reintroduced its own in the modification introduced in number 45 ('the Ordinary' in place of 'the Local Ordinary'), and more so in the notes. The liturgical movement was constantly present.

16. Cardinals Frings and Döpfner would proceed to revive this movement with that fourth general Commission by asking that the original schema of the preparatory Commission for the Liturgy be given back to the Fathers.[57] The intervention of Msgr Dante towards the end of the same meeting, which requested that concelebration take place only with the bishop and in cases established by the Holy See,[58] did not carry much weight in the face of the interventions of the powerful German cardinals.

The debates which followed bring us names already well-known, those of Cardinals Godfrey, Browne, Spellman, Rufficini, etc., who expressed their reservations regarding an excessive extension of concelebration.[59] In the opposite direction we have Cardinals Léger, Garcias, Bea, etc., who asked for a very large extension.[60]

However, what matters more than the names of the persons, what needs to be examined closely, are the reasons put forward for and against this general extension of concelebration. In analyzing them we discover a complex situation, which cannot be reduced to just two opposing camps. By way of simplification, one can say that between those who were for a practically unlimited extension of the rite and those who were against all or almost all extension, there is found a strong current, with a few nuances, of those who were for a certain extension, but one which would be limited and under the control of the bishop, and those who were against a generalized extension, but

---

[57]   *AS I–I*, pp. 309; 319.

[58]   *AS I–I*, p. 331.

[59]   *Ibid.*, pp. 374; 377; 599; 601; …

[60]   *Ibid.*, p. 602; I–II, 13; 23; …

would allow for a certain widening. Both of these placed in the Holy
See the care of establishing the limits, and in the Ordinaries the care of
making sure those limits were respected. It is in this tableau, much more
than in a simplistic and dialectic view, that is found the true image of
the Council, insofar as it was entirely composed by the bishops.
Certainly, the two tendencies which we noted above did exist: the one,
extreme in its desire for an opening up of concelebration; the other, in
favour of a moderate opening. A third tendency, extreme in its refusal
of concelebration and little supported, also showed itself. It would be
an error to want to identify it with the moderate tendency, or rather to
want to reduce the latter to the former. The truth is, that between these
two opposite poles the majority of the Fathers converged towards a
middle tendency, which can be qualified as a moderate opening, or, if
we can dare say, an open closure. The real debate, then, was between
this tendency, which, under the aspect of a moderate opening, belonged
to the central preparatory Commission, and the tendency towards an
extreme opening.

17. The principal reasons put forward for a generalized extension of
concelebration were the following:

1) a better manifestation of the unity of the priesthood,
   Church, and sacrifice;[61]

2) the piety of the priests;[62]

3) the return to the traditional liturgical practice;[63]

4) the practical advantages of this manner of celebrating.[64]

---

[61] *Ibid.*, I–I, pp. 602 (Léger); I–II, 23 (Bea); 48 (S. Kleiner); 49 (König); ...

[62] The same; and also: I–II, 73 (Devoto); 82 (Elchinger—but he admits that
one can see the matter otherwise); ...

[63] I–I, *Ibid.*, 626 (Gut); I–II, 23 (Bea); ...

[64] *Ibid.*, I–I, 626 (Gut, whose evolution is noteworthy, and whose assertion
astonishing. Speaking of the monks, who for ages assisted at the conventual
Mass and who celebrated their own private Mass, he writes: '*Haec duplicatio
quotidiana est onus nimis grave ratione temporis, pietatis, altarium et supellectilis.*'—
'This daily duplication is a very great burden with respect to time, piety, the
altars and the accoutrement.'); I–II, 23 (Bea); 48 (S. Kleiner: '*Taedium oriri*

The first two reasons are often presented together;[65] however, it is the first which is especially emphasized. One can see here the influence exercised by the addition of notes 11 and 12 'to the chapters of the schema.'[66] The third reason, of the historical and traditional order, is also frequently put forth. There is sometimes added to it an ecumenical motive: by adopting this rite we come closer to the Churches of the East![67] With respect to the practical reason, even if several of the Fathers favourable to the opening, thinking that it was not sufficient, insisted that one not attach too much importance to it[68]—it in fact played a huge role, oftentimes being the sole or principal reason invoked.[69]

18. The reasons put forth against a general extension and for a limited and controlled widening are the following:

1) due to the lack of priests, one would thus deprive the faithful of the Mass;[70]

---

potest ob duplicem ... '—'A disgust can arise on account of the duplication.'); 96 (Van Cauwlaert); 139 (Théas: for the sanctuary of Lourdes); ...

[65]   See notes 61 and 62.

[66]   They are moreover explicitly cited by several of the Fathers: *Ibid.,* I–II, p. 23 (Bea); 48 (S. Kleiner); p. 67 (Jubarny); p. 71 (Przyklenk); pp. 150 ff. (Zak); ...

[67]   *Ibid.,* I–I, 626 (Gut); I–II, 49 (S. Kleiner); 70 (Przyklenk); 83 (Khoury); 133 (Vincuña); 265 (Prou); ... Note the convergence of the interventions of monastic abbots, who had accepted the points of view from the liturgical centers (cf. I–I, pp. 627 ff.)

[68]   *Ibid.,* I–II, 23 (Bea); 88 (Edelby); ...

[69]   It is to this reason which the supporters of an open limitation sometimes cling, thus joining those who advocate a limited opening: *ibid,* I–II, 11 (Godfrey); 139 (Théas, Lourdes: who places the practical reason on the first level and develops it more than the reason which he calls 'spiritual'; his request is uniquely applied to the sanctuary at Lourdes); 208 (Bidawid, Chaldean Rite: '*propter practicas utilitates...*, *relinquendo Synodo patriarchali, ut determinet ea quae in nn. 45 et 46...* '); 234 (Hakim: supports the request of Msgr Théas, asking for the same thing for the sanctuaries of the Holy Land); 273 (Sfair, Maronite: against concelebration, but he admits it as 'necessary' for 'the large sanctuaries such as Lourdes', or the international Eucharistic congresses).

[70]   This reason returns frequently: *ibid,* I–I, 599 (Spellmann); I–II, 11 (Ottavi-

2) the danger that this would lead to a contempt for private Masses;[71]

3) the decrease in the glory rendered to God and the graces obtained for the Church;[72]

4) the danger that this would lead to the confusion denounced in the Encyclical *Mediator Dei* regarding the subject of concelebration, between the celebration of the priests and the participation of the faithful, that is to say between the ministerial priesthood and the common priesthood of the baptized;[73]

5) the obscuring of the priest's sacramental signification: alone at the altar, he better represents Christ, the one Mediator;[74]

6) priestly piety is fostered by personal celebration;[75]

7) the insufficiency of reasons advanced in favour of the general extension.[76]

---

ani); 44 (McQuaid, in the name of the Irish episcopate); 67 (Jubarny); 143 (Modrego y Casàus); 199 (Santos); 231 (Gonzales); ...

[71] Several of the Fathers already noted this danger apropos of no. 26 (which later became no. 27; cf. see below, no. 19, *b* in our work): *ibid*, I–I, 374 (Browne); 645 (P. Philippe, OP). Regarding no. 44: I–II, 19 (Ottaviani); ... , see also the following note.

[72] The same as in the preceding note. See most especially: *ibid*, 62 (Iglesias–Navarri); 67 (Jubarny: cites *Mediator Dei*); 265 (P. Philippe); ... One must note here the sometimes violent critiques against this doctrine of the value of the private Mass and the fruits of the Mass, especially those of Msgr Khoury (I–II, 83), or the incorrect opinions on this subject: I–II, 133 (Seitz); 82 (Elchinger); 266 (Prou); 273 (Sfair); ... While they might merit a veneration and even admiration, nevertheless some of these Fathers did not give their ideas a rectitude which they here lack; however, their stances simply prove that, despite their great merits, they did not totally escape the erroneous opinions of the times.

[73] *Ibid.*, I–II 145 (Modrego y Casàus).

[74] *Ibid.*, I–II, 264 (P. Philippe); ... And also, implicitly, Msgr Seitz, when he asks that: '*in omnibus ritibus Liturgicae nostrae, signa authentica Iesu adstantis inveniant velut mysterii pachalis in Ecclesia primarii actoris*' (*ibid*, 134).

[75] *Ibid.*, I–II, 265 (P. Philippe); ...

Of all these reasons, the most frequently put forth were the first and the second, which were often combined with the third. But the others, despite their not being advanced as frequently, have no less value. Our preceding studies have shown us in particular how justified were not only the fears of seeing the faithful deprived of the Mass, but also the fear of seeing the confusion introduced into the way one understands the participation of the congregation at the offering of the sacrifice, as well as the decrease or even complete loss of the sense of the Mass' value among the priests themselves.[77]

The question of Mass stipends was rarely brought up,[78] and it never constituted an objection, contrary to what the intervention of Msgr Zauner would have one believe—an intervention made at the moment that the Council president was going to close the discussion on concelebration. It is, by the way, the only objection to which he responds, and for a very good reason.[79]

19. Some reflections come spontaneously to mind for the reader of these debates, or rather of this chain of juxtaposed interventions and the reasons they put forward.

a) If one confronts these two series of arguments, one sees that the determining factor in favour of frequent concelebration, without speaking here of its suitability, is in the aspect of unity, seen from the point of view of its exterior manifestation, and therefore from the aspect of the congregation. While that which makes a stronger case for a limitation is the fact that the Mass is always and before all else the very sacrifice of Christ in, by and for the Church. We find ourselves, then, in exactly the same situation as during the work of

---

[76] *Ibid.,* I–II, 63 (Iglesias–Navarri); 67 (Jubarny); 145 (Modrego y Casàus); ...

[77] And this, not only on the level of certain 'regrettable excesses' or certain occasional abuses, but at the level of the official teaching of certain countries, for example France (cf. *LPC,* no. 186–7, pp. 88 ff.; cf. see above, pp. 137 ff.).

[78] AS I–II, 11 (Godfrey); p. 71 (Pryzklenk: the Church allows them for the Oriental Rites); p. 215 (Coudere: he raises the question and suggests a half–stipend); ...

[79] *Ibid.,* I–II, p. 153.

the preparatory phase. Nor could it be otherwise, the very same forces being involved, as well as the same reality in question. This obscuring of the sacrificial aspect of the Mass is certainly the major lacuna of the liturgical movement. It is manifested in a particular way in the numerous interventions of the supporters of frequent concelebration, some of them even going to the point of speaking of the multiplication of private Masses in contemptuous terms and contrary to the Church's Magisterium.[80]

b) That the aspect of the congregation is inherent in the liturgy there is evidence even for those who accept its classical definition of the 'Church's public worship.'[81] In this sense one can only adhere to the principle recalled by no. 27 of the Constitution on the Liturgy, which at that time was no. 26 of the schema of this Constitution:

> 26. [*That common celebration is to be preferred*]. Each time that the rites, according to the proper nature of each, include a celebration in common with the attendance and active partic- ipation of the faithful, it will be noted that, insofar as it is possible, the common celebration is to be preferred to an individual and quasi-private celebration.[82]

In the course of the debates a second paragraph had been joined to this latter (which remained unchanged), and this new paragraph would follow it in the conciliar text:

> This goes most especially for the celebration of Mass, respect- ing always the public and social nature of every Mass, and for the administration of the sacraments.

---

80 Cf. *see above*, notes 62 and 72.

81 '*integer cultus publicus*' (*SC*, 7; these last two paragraphs of no. 7 are among the most beautiful passages of the Council's Constitution on the Liturgy); cf. Pius XI, Enc. *Ad catholici sacerdotii* (1935; DS 3757): Pius XII, Enc. *Mediator Dei* (1947; *ibid*, 3840).

82 AS I–I, p. 273: '26. [*Celebratio communis praeferenda*]. *Quoties ritus, iuxta propriam cuiusque naturam, secum ferunt celebrationem communem cum frequentia et actuosa participatione fidelium, inculcetur, hanc, in quantum fieri potest, esse praeferendam celebrationi eorundem singulari et quasi privatae.*'

And yet, from its first revision, which did not at that time include this second paragraph, this article turned out to be profoundly ambiguous. This was seen by the Fathers as well, who energetically criticized it. They denounced in particular, and rightly so, the argument which could be drawn from it against the value of private Masses: 'One could conclude from this,' observed especially Cardinal Browne, 'that in itself, it would be better for a priest to assist and actively participate with the faithful at a Mass celebrated by another priest than celebrate his own Mass.'[83]

In reaffirming 'the public and social nature of every Mass,' the second paragraph responded to this objection. However, it did so only in an incomplete manner; for, it did not explicitly mention the infinite value of every Mass, and therefore of each private Mass. On the other hand, it did insist once again on applying to the case of the Mass the general principal posed in the preceding paragraph, one posed with an ambiguity we noted. Thus that number 26 served as an introduction to number 44 by saying in what sense it needed to be understood.

This is what Msgr Khoury noted in a very lively intervention (He was a fervent supporter of frequent concelebration and an equally resolute adversary of private Masses): There is a contradiction, he said, between this number (and that which follows it) and number 44. For, in the former there is posited as a principle the necessity of preferring common celebration; while in the latter, when it comes to the practical application, common celebration is to be granted only when it is not possible to do otherwise.[84] We must recognize that here he is right, even if we cannot follow him in his violent attack against private Masses (to which he devoted himself immediately afterwards) nor in his errors regarding the priesthood. Therefore, the internal logic, if not the very words of this number 26, goes against the sense of frequent concelebration.

---

[83] Cf. *see above*, note 72.

[84] *AS* I–II, p. 83.

Such as it was, and such as it still is now, this number, which became number 27, contributes to accenting the aspect of the congregation to the detriment of the sacrifice aspect. It is clearly in this sense that it was used after the Council. Rahner and Häussling, for example, did not hesitate to see it in 1966 as nothing other than a condemnation of the Catholic doctrine on the importance of the 'number of Masses,' or at least as an invitation to revise this doctrine, reduced for them to no more than the expression of 'ideas prevailing until now.'[85]

This interpretation was clearly an abuse. It was the same for number 27 of the Council's Constitution, the inspiration of which (as Msgr Khoury clearly saw), contradicted the norms of number 57 (and not only those of number 44 of the schema); and, in order for this number 27 to be understood, there was need of a complement. It will not be superfluous to note now what is found in number 13 of the *Decree on the Ministry and Life of Priests,* where it says:

> In the mystery of the Eucharistic sacrifice, where the priests exercise their principal function, it is the very work of our redemption which is continually accomplished (Secret of the Ninth Sunday after Pentecost). This is why it is strongly recommended to them to celebrate Mass every day; even if the faithful cannot be present, it is still an act of Christ and His Church.

And this act is essentially the sacrifice of the Cross. This reminder, inspired by a text of Paul VI and reappearing in a note to numbers 26 and 27 of the Constitution on the Liturgy, simply developed the aspects which the latter had presented in an all too rapid and sometimes equivocal manner. Therefore, it is only by keeping this in mind that one can understand the teaching of the Council. For, it must be admitted that the Constitution on the Liturgy does not speak sufficiently well of the Mass as sacrifice; and it is not only on this point that it is fortunately supplemented by the Decree of the Life of Priests.

---

[85]   K. Rahner, A. Häussling, *Le Sacrifice unique et la fréquence des messes* (*Quaestiones disputatae,* 10) (Fribourg, Herder, 1966), Paris, DDBr., 1972, pp. 19 ff.

c) Furthermore, regarding the very notion of congregation, there is an important lacuna to be pointed out. In fact, in the requests of the supporters of frequent celebration there is no mention of the preeminent place of the bishop in the Eucharistic celebration. The movement which thus developed would end up by not caring which priest presided at the concelebration—something which is an especially sensitive matter in religious and priestly communities. It is certainly possible theologically speaking, but here concelebration loses much of its meaning; and this is all totally new.

The principles recalled in chapter one of the schema would nevertheless need to make it known at what point this innovation was in opposition to Tradition. For this latter the Eucharist was not even conceivable except around the bishop. This is what was noted by number 32 of the first chapter (later to become number 42 of the Constitution), where it is asserted that 'the principal manifestation of the Church, that is the congregation, takes place in the liturgy:

> especially in the Eucharist itself, in one sole prayer, around one sole altar, at which the bishop presides, surrounded by his presbytery and his ministers.

A long note cites the Letter of St Ignatius of Antioch, which inspired this passage, and which was even more explicit: 'one altar and one bishop with the presbytery and the deacons, my fellow servants.'[86] We know, moreover, that the concelebration here was purely ceremonial, with the bishop accomplishing the sacramental action of the offering of the sacrifice. However, the precise point which we must underline here is the following: the congregation, and therefore the traditional concelebration, is essentially hierarchical, formed around the bishop; and it is by this alone that concelebration fully realizes its meaning and finality, which are to be manifested and, still more, which are to build the Church's unity. On the other hand, the notion of the congregation which is introduced with the new way of conceiving

---

[86] '*Unum altare et unus episcopus cum presbyterio et diaconis, conservis meis*' (St Ignatius of Antioch, *Letter to the Phillipians*, 4; *cited in note AS* I–IV, p. 325).

concelebration, without formally denying this essential hierarchical principle, tends to make it disappear. In fact, it is already its implicit negation.

d) We must also note the narrowness of the limits in which a true dialog was able to be developed at the level of the conciliar meeting. It can be seen that one given intervention was made to respond to another.[87] However, the very method of the debates, the number of participants, and the multiplication of the questions treated as a whole did not always allow one to stop at the essential points or to go to the heart of the matter at hand. Therefore, it was on this level of the commissions that this work took place. This decisive importance of the commissions is certainly one of the most remarkable traits of Vatican II.

e) Another significant fact also merits to be brought out. Whereas the supporters of a limited revival of concelebration themselves admitted and professed the principal argument in its favour, namely the manifestation of the unity of the priesthood and the Church, 'which is sometimes good,' according to Rev Father Paul Philippe, the supporters of an unlimited extension did not respond to the major objection which opposed them, namely the value of each Mass insofar as it is the sacrifice of Christ and the Church. In their quasi-totality they did not even consider it.

The last intervention of the Abbot of Solesmes, toward the end of the debates, reveals that they had even been moved to recognize that this was a major obstacle for them, which Rahner understood back in 1949.[88] However, the given response (whose internal coherence is difficult to see), is hardly satisfying.[89]

---

[87]   Thus, for example: *AS* I–II, p. 82 (Elchinger, responding to the objection taken from the loss of the sense of private Masses); p. 266 (Prou, the same question); or again: I–II, p. 21 (Ottaviani, responding to the argument taken from the practical advantages); 67 (Jubarny, the same question); etc.

[88]   K. Rahner. *Die vielen Messen und das eine Opfer. Eine untersuchung über die rechte Norm der Messhaüfigkeit*, in *Zeitschrift für Katholische Theologie* 71, 1949, pp. 257–317.

f) Moreover, we now know—and it can be known from this period, as is proven by the *votum* of the Sacred Congregation of Rites—the lack of foundation in the historical and traditional argument put forward. Despite the intervention of the Chaldean bishop, Msgr Bidawid, who recalled that concelebration was unknown in his rite[90] (it is true that his intervention was not read in the Council aula), the assembly of the Fathers were convinced that the practice of sacramental concelebration represented a return to the origins. This did not prevent them, during the course of the second session, of asking for a limitation by submitting it to the control of the bishop. Their

---

[89]   Believed to be supported by the teaching of Pius XII (quickly evoked), this response essentially asserts: '*Valor cultualis etenim ponderatur non ex actu I. C.* [=Jesus Christ] *causae principalis missae, qui actus unicus fuit, sed ex actibus sacerdotum qui causae instrumentalis gratia sacrificium offerunt*' (*AS* I–II, p. 266). This theology is in accord with that of our contradictor, Joseph Kleiner (cf. *LPC*, no. 184, pp. 17 ff; *see above*, Ch. II. See especially pp. 21 ff; *see above*, Ch. II). The sentence is not clear; it is even contradictory. By its construction, in fact, it denies that the 'cultic' value of the Mass comes from the act of Christ, and it attributes it entirely to the act of the priest: '*non ex actu I. C., qui unicus fuit* ... , *sed ex actibus sacerdotum*'; but by the terms which it employs, '*causa principalis*', '*causa instrumentalis*', it returns the act of the priest to the present dependence on that of Christ, according to Catholic dogma. Of these two interpretations, therefore, it is the second which complies with the mystery of the sacramental order, and it is by this that the number of Masses augments the fruits of grace: because each time Christ, the 'principal cause', acts in and by the 'instrumental cause', the priest and the liturgical rite. Nevertheless, it is the first interpretation which the response obliges one to retain, by considering the interior act of the priest more than his exterior liturgical action; for, it alone permits one to support the thesis which is being defended here, namely that the number of concelebrants, and not the number of Masses, multiplies the fruits of the Eucharist's grace. However, it is at the cost of a negation of the sacramental mystery and of theology, which is contrary to the thought of the author. This is why we say that that response, obviously hasty, is contradictory, and does not respond to the objection which it wishes to refute. (For the development of these question, see our articles from nos. 180 and 184 of *LPC*; *see above*, Ch. I and II.)

[90]   *AS* I–II, p. 208.

Catholic sense of the liturgy outweighed the incorrect interpretation of Tradition, which they had proposed. However, this latter was of no less considerable weight in what it succeeded in moving them to accept.

20. Therefore, this series of interventions on concelebration ends, *without any real conclusion,* with this grave historical error regarding the subject of the liturgical Tradition of the Church, and in this climate of a partial but noteworthy obscuring of Catholic doctrine on the sacrificial value of the Mass. The central question was that of the limits or extension to be given. On 6November, during the thirteenth General Congregation, after the fourth intervention on chapter II of the schema (where one finds no. 44, which treats concelebration), the Presidential Council interrupted the discussion in order to propose to the Fathers to vote on what was there, and to move on to an examination of chapter III. The need to move the work along moved them to approve the proposition immediately. Here is a significant fact: of the four last speakers who spoke that morning, the first two were Msgr Zak, Bishop of Sankt-Polten (Austria), and Msgr Zauner, Bishop of Linz (Austria). They belonged to the same group, both being among the most fervent supporters of a generalized concelebration. One ought to read especially the responses Msgr Zauner made to the objections to such an unlimited extension: in fact, he eludes them more than he responds to them.[91] The other speakers were not able to express themselves publicly.

On 14 November, during the nineteenth General Congregation, by a vote which approved almost unanimously 'the criteria of orientation,' the Fathers sent back the Prooemium and Chapters I and II of the schema to the Commission for the Liturgy. This latter had to 'examine and order the proposed amendments (*modi*)' in order to prepare a new text, which would have to be submitted to an examination by the assembly.[92]

---

[91] *Ibid.,* p. 153.

[92] *Ibid.,* I–III, p. 10.

21. In order to better understand the impact of this vote, one must read it in context. The question of concelebration was lost in the midst of a hundred others, several of which appeared, and sometimes really were, more important, such as the question on the revision of the *Ordo missae*. Furthermore, no decision had yet been taken by the Council. As Laurentin said: 'This was, without a doubt, the moment when one asked with the greatest incertitude if it was truly desired, if it would truly succeed.'[93] The chronicler himself recalls that, on the eve of this vote, 13 November, the Secretary of State had come 'to interrupt the conciliar discussion in order to announce the introduction of St Joseph among the saints mentioned before the consecration'—a move which broke the principle held as absolute until now, that the canon of the 'Roman Missal' was untouchable. On the other hand, the conciliar assembly always did nothing. Whence the state of mind in which it welcomed the proposition of 14 November: 'Finally [it] had been called to a vote on the guiding principle of the liturgical schema and its orientations: namely the principle of pastoral adaptation.' Such then was the fundamental 'criteria of orientation' and, along with it, the impatient desire to act and to move the work ahead, which brought about the unanimity of the vote: '2,162 in favour; 46 against = more than 97%.'[94] However, apart from these fundamental criteria of pastoral adaptation, which truly brought about unanimity, many of the questions returned to the Commission, such as concelebration, with its series of requests for very diverse and often opposed amendments. It belonged to the Commission then to discern among that mass of *modi* those which truly represented the majority tendency of the conciliar assembly, by keeping close watch not to replace it by the tendency which was the strongest on its own level. Was this even possible? Given the conditions under which the Commission worked, the question is a reasonable one.

---

[93]   R. Laurentin, *Bilan I*, p. 27.

[94]   *Ibid.*

IV. The Constitution on the Liturgy during the second session of the Council (29 September to 4 December 1963)

22. Thus it is that, at the beginning of the second session of the Council, during the forty-third General Congregation, 8 October 1963, when the second chapter of the *Schema on the Constitution of the Liturgy* was presented anew to the Fathers, we see the return of a text which had taken up again all the essential elements of the initial schema of the Preparatory Commission for the Liturgy. However, they were now being presented under a noticeably different form and order; the introduced changes, the happy fruits of the conciliar institution, were of great importance. Let us first of all attentively read the new text, noting that numbers 44 and 45 of the preceding text (B) have become one number, number 57 (we shall call it text C):

> 57. § 1. Concelebration, whereby the unity of the priesthood is appropriately manifested, has remained in use until now in both the Eastern and Western Church. This is why it has pleased the Council to extend the faculty to concelebrate to the following cases:
>
> 1° *a*) Holy Thursday, at both the Chrism Mass and the Evening Mass;
>
> *b*) At Masses celebrated at councils, episcopal assemblies and synods;
>
> *c*) At the Mass of the blessing of an abbot.
>
> 2° Furthermore, with the permission of the Ordinary, to whom it belongs to judge the appropriateness for concelebration and to regulate and direct (*moderari*) the practice:
>
> *a*) At the conventual Mass and the principal Mass of churches, when the needs of the faithful do not require that all the priests celebrate individually;
>
> *b*) At Masses at all types of assemblies of priests, both secular and religious.

§ 2. However, the faculty for each priest to celebrate individually shall always be respected, but not at the same moment in
the same Church, nor on Holy Thursday.[95]

As can be seen by consulting the promulgated text, it was already close
to the definitive edition. Nevertheless, there is still a difference
between the two, one which we shall see later, and which is of the
greatest importance for interpreting this number.

23. But let us first compare this text (C) with the two preceding ones.
The first impression which one has is that its difference with the latter,
presented during the first session (B), is great, and that its similarity
with the entire first schema (A) is no less. Whence the conclusion
that must be drawn: the tendency towards the greatest opening
possible, that of the Preparatory Commission for the Liturgy (text
A), brought it to the level of the conciliar Commission for the Liturgy

---

[95] AS II–III, p. 286: '57. § 1. Concelebratio, QUA UNITAS SACERDOTII
OPPORTUNE MANIFESTATUR, in Ecclesia tam Orientali quam Occidentali
usque adhuc in usu remansit (18). *Quare* facultatem concelebrandi ad sequentes
casus Concilio extendere *placuit* (19): 1° *a*) FERIA V IN CENA DOMINI,
TUM AD MISSAM CHRISMATIS, TUM AD MISSAM VESPERTINUM:
b) AD MISSAS IN CONCILIIS, CONVENTIBUS EPISCOPALIBUS ET
SYNODIS; *c*) AD MISSAM IN BENEDICTIONE ABBATIS.—2°
PRAETEREA, ACCEDENTE LICENTIA ORDINARII, CUIUS EST DE
OPPORTUNITATE CONCELEBRATIONIS IUDICARE EIUSQUE
DISCIPLINAM MODERARI: *a*) AD MISSAM CONVENTUALEM ET AD
MISSAM PRINCIPALEM IN ECCLESIIS, CUM UTILITAS
CHRISTIFIDELIUM SINGULAREM CELEBRATIONEM OMNIUM
SACERDOTUM TUM SAECULARIUM TUM RELIGIOSORUM. — § 2.
SALVA TAMEN SEMPER SIT CUIQUE SACERDOTI FACULTAS
MISSAM SINGULAREM CELEBRANDI, NON TAMEN EODEM
TEMPORE IN EADEM ECCLESIA, NEC FERIA V IN CENA DOMINI.'
—A note at the beginning of the schema (*ibid*, p. 283) points out that the
italicized letters indicate minor changes, and that the capitals signify changes of
the greatest importance. By this typographical detail one can see that we are
dealing with an entirely new text in relation to the one which immediately
preceded it (text B). One will note the *Quare* (which follows no. 18): it shows
the influence of the historical error contained in the preceding phrase.

(text C), and that it now seeks, by a new schema, to obtain the approval of the Council.

This conclusion is unfortunately not without a foundation. Nevertheless it must be balanced out by another consideration, which imposes itself when one attentively compares the text of 1963 (C) with that of the whole first schema (A). If it is true that we find the same elements in both places, that is to say the same cases where concelebration ought to or can be used, it must be noted that the order in which the cases are presented had been modified. The difference consists in this: while in the first schema all the cases were placed on the same level, in the second schema the mention of the Ordinary's authority came in second place, with the two categories carefully distinguished. Thus there are those for whom the Council would give the general faculty to concelebrate, and those for whom the use of this faculty would have to be submitted to the approval of the Ordinary. This amounts to granting to the Ordinary the faculty to permit concelebration in this second category of cases, in place of giving that permission directly to the priests themselves.

This fundamental distinction, already made by Cardinal Larraona during the preparatory phase,[96] was the fruit of resistances to the general extension, which had manifested themselves during the first session of the Council. It sheds light on the interpretation to be given to the text which was finally approved. It is interesting to note now that the reactions of the Assembly of Fathers performed in this case, with respect to the work of the Council's Commission for the Liturgy, in the same way that those of the central preparatory Commission did in relation to the work of the preparatory Commission for the Liturgy.

24. Another sign of opposition—in itself completely normal—between the two tendencies[97] is perceptible in what was said or not said

---

[96] See above, number 10 of our work.

[97] That is the tendency towards a total opening and the tendency towards a limited opening.

on the subject of the Ordinary's power. We note, in fact, the disappearance in the new text (C) of that which was number 45 in the preceding text (B), namely the passage which reaffirms the bishops' power of regulating concelebration. No doubt the power 'of the Ordinary' was maintained in the new schema (no. 57, § 1, at the beginning of subheading 2). However, the term used, 'the Ordinary,' can also be extended to major superiors of religious orders, such that the bishop now saw himself deprived of his power of regulating the liturgy in houses of religious within his own diocese.

A note added in an appendix to the new schema by the Commission for the Liturgy explained, apropos of the two cases (*a* and *b*) mentioned under '2°': 'For these two cases it must be noted: ... 3. 'That the judgment of the Ordinary is required. There had been a discussion as to whether we ought to say 'the Bishop' instead of "the Ordinary," in order to avoid conflicts which could very easily arise among religious. The expression "the Ordinary" prevailed.—4. To the same Ordinary is reserved not only the judgment regarding the appropriateness for concelebration, but also the vigilance over the mode and circumstances of concelebration.'[98] Satisfying the desires of the moderated tendency insofar as it clearly reaffirmed that, outside of cases foreseen by the general law (§ 1, 1°), concelebration cannot take place except by permission of 'the Ordinary,' this response favoured more still the supporters of the other tendency, especially in monastic circles, insofar as it removed them from the authority of the bishop with regards to the use of the new rite. Foreseeing the consequences which would result in their dioceses, these latter would later react strongly, as noted by Fr Gy at the beginning of 1964.[99]

---

[98] *AS* II–II, p. 306.

[99] In the commentary which he gave to this Article 57 of the Council's Constitution: 'The role of the bishop had not been mentioned in the early text. This mention having been omitted, numerous Council Fathers asked that it be reinserted during the general vote on Chapter 2, 14 October 1963; and they obtained their request' (*LMD*, no. 77 (1964/1), p. 131).

25. We note another detail, one not so important on the practical level, but significant on the doctrinal level and also with respect to the determining importance of the work done on the level of the Commission. While the first schema (A) spoke of the manifestation of 'the Church's unity,' the last schema (C) speaks of the unity 'of the priesthood.' This change had been made by the Commission in response to the request of certain Fathers, who desired to see explained a bit more thoroughly this manifestation 'of the Church's unity.'[100] In addition to not responding to their request, this response, in its shortsightedness, manifested rather the absence of the desired and requested development. As we saw, it had been requested by the *votum* of the Sacred Congregation of Rites and by the central preparatory Commission. The historical investigation had not been corrected, and the error regarding Tradition remained.

26. As such, that is to say with the reappearance of elements from the whole first edition, in whose indetermination had been left a certain number of doctrinal, historical and practical questions, and despite the corrections already brought forward, the new schema, like that by which it had been inspired, appeared to be charged with an internal tension, in which one could not yet see the tendency which would prevail. Two important factors would play in favour of the tendency towards the greatest opening, which was—let us not forget—that of the Commission, supported by the Presidency Coucil.

On one hand, the number of questions debated did not always, in fact did not usually, permit one to go back and examine the arguments put forward. In rereading the acts of the Council one is astonished at the unbelievable rhythm of the work imposed on the Fathers. The second session began with the discussion of the schema on the Church. We recall some of the principal questions which had been discussed: collegiality, the sacramentality of the episcopate, the deaconate, the status of religious, the inclusion or not of the schema

---

[100] *AS* II–II, p. 305: '*Commissio propositioni annuit, sed loco "Ecclesiae" scripsit "sacerdotii".*' Why this change? The Commission does not say.

on the Virgin Mary, etc. The schema on ecumenism had brought forth new earnest points, including that of 'religious liberty.' The passionate debates brought about by these questions are well known. The Fathers had to follow several at a time, often needing to reflect on or pronounce on two, three and four different schemas in the course of one morning. Therefore it was in this climate, between the two discussions on the Church and ecumenism, that the Fathers were called to pronounce on the amendments to the schema on the liturgy. On the simple material level it was not possible to take up the discussion again, a discussion which had taken place during the first session. The second session had had the voting. However, a good number of questions had required a more developed examination. As that did not take place, the Fathers were reduced to submitting it to the judgment of the experts, and therefore to the commissions.

The second factor which contributed to the impossibility of a discussion was the modality initially chosen for the voting. As had already happened during the first session for the Prooemium and First Chapter, the votes had simply to be *Placet* or *Non placet* ['Yes' or 'No']. A notification even clarified that votes given under the form of a *Placet iuxta modum* ['Yes, with qualifications'] would be considered null. This norm had been explicitly recalled on 8 October 1963, during the presentation of the new text of chapter II.[101] If one recalls the state in which the question had been left at the close of the discussion, during the first session, the procedure clearly appeared as an abuse. No doubt it was at that time preoccupied with not slowing down the pace of the work; but even so the questions of importance needed to be examined as was advisable, and needed to be proposed again for discussion. Such was the reaction of numerous Fathers, whose protestations would obtain a change in the procedure. Some days later, on 11 October, at the beginning of the forty-sixth General Congregation, the vote by *Placet iuxta modum* was reintroduced; however, the Fathers were still

---

[101] It even happened twice: at the beginning (*AS* II–II, p. 276) and end (p. 308) of the schema's presentation.

warned that it would be considered as a simple *Placet* if the 'modum' request was not given at the same time.[102]

It is no less thanks to this change that, during the forty-seventh General Congregation, 14 October 1963, during the voting on the whole of chapter II, this chapter did not obtain the majority required for approval. For this it needed 1,495 *Placet*; it obtained only 1,417. Therefore it was sent back to the Commission with 781 'modi' of the Fathers, who had exercised their right to vote *Placet iuxta modum*.[103] These requests for amendments, although they did not obtain satisfaction on all the points, nevertheless brought about a certain change, the significance of which is all the greater since it was laboriously obtained.
27. During that time the discussion continued on other schemas. It is to be noted that the discussion on ecumenism, the new edition of which had been presented in the aula on 18 October (at the sixty-ninth General Congregation), did not yet concern itself with concelebration,[104] perhaps out of deference for the Oriental Rites, which did not admit it. Let us not forget that this point of the liturgy had disappeared a bit before the important question which mobilized everyone's energy, that of religious liberty.

At the end of that same sixty-ninth General Congregation, the Secretary General announced that the booklet containing the amendments to chapter II of the schema on the liturgy would not be able to be distributed until the following day.[105] The next day then, during the seventieth General Congregation, the booklet was distributed to the Fathers. However, it had been announced to them beforehand that they would vote only by *Placet* or *Non Placet*,[106] which was admissible, and which was imposed just in time.

---

[102] *Ibid.*, p. 440.

[103] *Ibid.*, p. 520. The secretary general commented on the result of this vote in these terms: '*Cum igitur non sit habita maioritas requisita, pro nunc Cap. II non est approbatum.*'

[104] *Ibid.*, II–V, pp. 462 ff.

[105] *Ibid.*, p. 545.

[106] *Ibid.*, p. 549.

The acts of the seventy-first General Congregation, which was held the next day, Wednesday, 20 October allow us to see the amendments requested by the Fathers during their 14 October vote, or at least those which had been retained by the Commission for submission to the Council's approval. It is absolutely necessary to study them attentively, as well as the explanations of the Commission which accompany them, in order to understand the finally approved text. For, this text is the one which had been presented to the Fathers that day, and it is the fruit of those amendments. Here is the text; and we can see what distinguishes it from the preceding text (text C), and what was added to it (let us call it text D):

> (57, § 1) 2° Furthermore, with the permission of the Ordinary, to whom it belongs to judge the appropriateness of concele-bration: ....
>
> § 2. 1° It belongs to the bishop to direct and to regulate (*moderari*) the practice of concelebration in his own diocese.[107]

The difference introduced consisted in this: the power of 'moderating' the practice of concelebration now became the object of a special paragraph, and it was explicitly attributed to the bishop of the diocese,

---

[107] *Ibid.*, p. 575 (a new edition proposed for Article 57, following the requests of the Fathers): '*legatur—2° Praeterea, accedente licentia Ordinarii, cuius est de opportunitate concelebrationis iudicare (a): ... —§ 2. 1° Ad Episcopum vero pertinet concelebrationis disciplinam in diocese moderari (b). — 2° Salva tamen semper sit cuique sacerdoti, etc. (c).*' Cf. *see below*, note 433. The lettering *a, b, c* introduced here is ours. It is for the purpose of noting: *a*) that the passage which followed here in the preceding edition, '*eiusque disciplinam moderari*', was moved from that § 1, 2° to the new § 2, 1°, and thanks to the replacement of the word '*Ordinarii*' (§ 1, 2°) with the word '*Episcopum*' (§ 2, 1°), this regulation of the practice of concelebration was now explicitly attributed to the bishop, with no exception for houses of religious; *b*) that this § 2, 1° represents a new paragraph, whose normative importance needed to be great, according to law; in practice, after the Council, it was not taken into account; *c*) that this § 2, 2° takes up again without changing that which was before the only paragraph of § 2.

and no longer simply to 'the Ordinary' (which can be the major superior of religious), as in the preceding text (C), that of October 8. One will remember, however, that the Commission had examined this question, and that despite the requests made to use the term 'the bishop,' it had been decided to keep 'the Ordinary,' with the imprecision of this term and the practical consequences which would follow from it. It is in opposition to that imprecision and its easily foreseen consequences that 558 bishops[108] asked for the amendment we just saw. Here is the Commission's response to that request; it merits to be cited in its entirety:

> The Commission declared unanimously that it had never wished to take away what belongs by right (*iure*) to the bishop, according to the current law (*ius*), namely the regulating and directing (*moderari*) of the worship in his own diocese. However, in order to render the sense of this article more clear, the Commission proposes that the competence of the bishop in the direction and regulation of the practice of concelebration be preserved more explicitly by adding a new number to the second paragraph, with these words: 'It belongs to the bishop to regulate and to direct (*moderari*) the practice of concelebration in his own diocese.' The text, consequently, will be the following: (the note reproduces here text D). 'Consequently, the sense of the article is that it belongs to the bishop to direct and regulate concelebration, according to the norm of the law, even in the churches of exempt religious.'[109]

This response, which was hardly convincing when it sought to minimize the difference between the new edition and the preceding one, did satisfy the bishops. No doubt it only made explicit the obvious meaning of the text; but this explanation has the force of confirmation, given its official character. To this it must be added that

---

[108] *Ibid.*, p. 595, no. 80.

[109] *Ibid.*, pp. 595 ff., no. 85. We reproduce here the original from the last paragraph: '*Ideo sensus articuli est Episcopo competere concelebrationem in ecclesiis quoque religiosorum exemptorum ad normam iuris moderari.*'

the text and its official interpretation make sense only to the extent that the 'norm of law' does not render this recourse to the Ordinary's permission superfluous, and the power conferred on the bishop vain or pointless. This implies that, outside of cases foreseen by the general permission given by the Council (§ 1, 1), for the other cases (§ 1 2), concelebration was presented as something occasional and not general and systematic. These then are those dispositions of the Council's Constitution which constitute the fundamental 'norm of law' by which the other dispositions must be regulated, and not vice versa.

28. How ought this recourse to the bishop's authority be made? And how does the bishop understand and exercise his power? Two responses of the Commission to two complementary questions allow us to clarify this somewhat.

To one Father, who wished that the judgment of the Ordinary be requested each time, 'in singulis casibus,' the Commission responded that 'it would be too onerous a burden and sometimes even impossible.'[110]

However, to another Father who asked, in the opposite direction, 'that concelebration be permitted only by the episcopal conference,' there was the response: 'this certainly would be very impractical.'[111]

These two responses are complementary; for, while the first admits the idea that the permission of the Ordinary is not required case by case, the second implies that this recourse to authority is understood as something needed quite regularly. In fact, to declare that asking the permission of the episcopal conference 'would certainly be very impractical,' definitely signifies that this request cannot be made once for all. The response therefore dismisses the possibility of general permissions given by the episcopal conferences. The personal power of Ordinaries and bishops was firmly safeguarded and their responsibility fully invested. At the same time and yet once again, concelebration appeared

---

[110] *Ibid.,* p. 592, no. 69: *'Sed hoc esset nimis onerosum, immo aliquando impossibile.'*

[111] *Ibid.,* p. 591, no. 64: *'Quod certo esset valde incommodum'*; and p. 592, no. 74, to a similar request: *'Quod videtur nimis restrictivum.'*

for the cases foreseen (§ 1, 2) as something limited by diocesan regulation. No doubt the bishop himself could permit it with a certain frequency, to a greater or lesser degree, according to his liking. However, he could not, under pain of going against 'the norm of law' thus fixed, decree it in a general manner nor systematically impose it.

29. Nevertheless, there remains a large margin between the exclusion of a case-by-case recourse and that of a general permission; what is most striking in this text and these responses is their lack of precision. Thus it is that, after the Council, the tendency toward a maximal extension finally succeeded in being very widely imposed. Today, for a very great number of people, this seems to go without saying, insofar as it is true that habits are a second nature, and more still, that the consensus of fashions, intellectual or otherwise, hold the place of supreme authority. However, this would be to commit an anachronism—the question and responses that we just read prove this—projecting back onto the conciliar assembly a mentality which dominates today. On the other hand, and over and above the tension between the two tendencies which we noted, one sees that what goes without saying for the great majority of the Council Fathers, is beyond the cases foreseen by number 57, § 1, 1, where concelebration is envisaged only under the control of the bishop of the place, and therefore only in a limited manner.

The official responses and declarations of the Commission prove that it is in this spirit that Article 57 had been presented to the Fathers and voted upon and approved by them. Could it be said that the later evolution was in line with the same spirit, if not the very letter of this text? Such a contradiction would be cumbersome for the text itself; however, we shall examine this question later, at the end of this work.

On 4 December 1963, the *Constitution on the Sacred Liturgy* was approved by the Council. The teaching and the disciplinary dispositions, which we presented in the two last texts of the schema (C and D), are found in number 57. Number 58 requested moreover (but without going into detail) that there be composed 'a new rite of

concelebration, to be inserted into the Roman Pontifical and Missal.'
This work also would be entrusted to the post-conciliar commissions.

V. The third and fourth sessions (14 September to 21 November 1964; 14 September to 8 December 1965)

30. Before concluding we still have to consider the teaching of these last two sessions on concelebration. It is only an occasional matter; but the little that is said of it, and still more the silence surrounding it, is not without significance.

31. The two other Council documents where concelebration is mentioned are the *Decree on Ecumenism* and the *Decree on the Ministry and Life of Priests.*

   a) The schema for the former returned to the Council aula at the beginning of the third session, 23 September 1964. While formerly, as we have seen,[112] there was nothing concerning concelebration in it, it does get a mention in the new text, in no. 15:

> By the celebration of the Eucharist of the Lord in those particular Churches, the Church of God is built up and increases, and by concelebration their communion is manifested.[113]

This declaration, which would be kept (under the same number) in the final approved text, is in line with the Constitution on the Liturgy. It takes up again the aspect of 'manifestation' of communion and, in passing over in silence all the non-Catholic Oriental rites which refuse sacramental concelebration—the only type of concelebration treated in the Council texts—it renews the historical error. However, the declaration does not seem to have provoked a discussion, even if the term 'communion' used here posed some problems.

   It's the same with regards to the statement contained in the first part of the sentence, namely the one which speaks of Eucharistic concelebration as an act efficacious for the building up of the Church.

---

[112] Cf. *see above*, note 104.

[113] *AS* III–II, p. 315.

We cannot dwell on these discussions, which would take us beyond our present subject.[114] If we wish, nevertheless, to mention them, it is by reason of the interest which they present for the question of concelebration. They, in fact, recall that the Mass, by the mysterious power of the sacrament, is not only nor primarily a manifestation, but first and essentially a 'mysterious' building-up of communion and the ecclesial communities.

b) The other document that makes allusion to concelebration is the *Decree on the Ministry and Life of Priests.* It speaks of it twice, in no. 7 and no. 8; and yet the question was not treated in the text presented during the third session, on 13 October 1964 (Hundredth General Congregation). This silence is all the more remarkable in that, while attentively paging through the parts which relate the written observations of the Fathers on the schema,[115] one sees that oftentimes the matter of concern was the fraternal bonds which must unite the priests to each other and to their bishop; one also sees that many of the Fathers recalled the importance of the celebration of the sacrifice of the Mass for the sanctification of the priest. A group of fifty or so of them deplored that same 'total silence of the schema on the Eucharistic cult.'[116] However, unless we are mistaken, there never was any

---

[114] One might recall that, as a result of the separation of these Churches, the celebration of the Eucharist was not able to contribute in the same way to the building up of the one Church, the Mystical Body of Christ, according to which it had a place in those separated Churches or in the Catholic Church itself. The Commission rejected the objection by declaring that the difference came only from the exterior circumstances, of a canonical order, and not from the Eucharist itself insofar as it is a sacramental reality (*AS* III–VI, pp. 679 ff.). This was, at one and the same time, to underestimate and to falsify the nature of the separation of these Churches, reducing to accidental circumstances the profound reasons for the division, and to give to the *opus operatum* point of view an absolute value and exclusive consideration in little conformity with both the sacramental theology and pastoral aim of the Council.

[115] *AS* III–IV, pp. 537–666.

[116] *Ibid.,* pp. 541 ff.

allusion to concelebration; this shows how foreign concelebration was to the priestly mind at that time.

In fact, it is only at the very last moment, during the fourth session, that the passages mentioning concelebration were added: number 7 appeared in the text presented to the Fathers during the 159th General Congregation, 12 November 1965; number 8 was introduced into the last version of the schema submitted to a vote, and was not presented until the 166th General Congregation, 2 December, just a few days before the end of the Council. Below is the text of no. 7 (formerly no. 6); we cite the entire paragraph, for it is very beautiful—in its content if not in its construction—and clarifies the meaning of concelebration:

> 7. (Formerly no. 6) [*Relations between the bishops and presbyterate*]. All priests, *with the bishops*, participate in one and the same priesthood, in one and the same ministry of Christ, in such a way that the very unity of their *consecration* and mission requires their *hierarchical communion* with the Order of bishops (A); and joined to them, *sometimes even in liturgical concelebration*, they celebrate the Holy Eucharist (B).[117]

The passages which we italicized are in the text: they indicate what had been added to the earlier version. The letters in the parentheses refer to the explanatory notes which justify those additions. One will note the introduction of the idea of 'hierarchical communion.' Regarding concelebration, note (B) explains that it is mentioned 'in order to recall that it is the sign and summit of the unity of the presbyterate with the bishop.'[118] On the sacramental level this is perfectly correct; but the

---

[117] AS IV–VI, p. 356: '7. *(Olim n. 6). (Habitudo inter Episcopos et Presbyterium.) Presbyteri omnes, una cum Episcopis, unum idemque sacerdotium et ministerium Christi ita participant, ut ipsa unitas consecrationis missionisque requirat hierarchicam eorum communionem cum Ordine Episcoporum (A), cum quibus coniuncti, aliquando etiam in liturgia concelebratione (B), profitentur se Eucharisticam Synaxim celebrare.'* [Translator's note: Austin Flannery's English translation was consulted for this and the following two quotes.]

[118] *Ibid.*, p. 394: ' ... *ad commemorandum concelebrationem eucharisticam esse*

notion of 'sign,' and therefore of manifestation, is not in the schema. It would reappear in the final text, where the last phrase, beginning at letter (A) of the text cited above is thus written:

> ... the hierarchical communion with the Order of bishops, which they (the priests) sometimes manifest in an excellent manner in liturgical concelebration; and joined to them they celebrate the Holy Eucharist.[119]

While this last modification reintroduces the idea of 'manifestation,' it retains from the preceding text the following two fundamental ideas: concelebration is the act of the presbyterate united to its bishop in a hierarchical communion; it is occasional (*aliquando* means 'sometimes,' 'from time to time'). Moreover, these two ideas are a pair; for, if by its nature it must take place with the bishop, then concelebration can take place only occasionally; and it would clearly be an abuse and contradiction to practice it habitually in the absence of the bishop, around a priest who takes the latter's place.

On 2 December, a few days before the end of the Council's fourth session, a new allusion to concelebration was made, at the request of 17 Fathers,[120] in number 8 of the same document:

> Each one is joined to the rest of the members of this priestly body by special ties of apostolic charity of ministry and of brotherhood, which is signified liturgically from ancient times when the priests present at an ordination are invited to impose hands, along with the ordaining bishop, on the chosen candi-

---

> *signum et culmen unitatis Presbyterii cum Episcopo.'*

[119] *Ibid.,* ... *hierarchicam eorum communionem cum Ordine Epsicoporum, quam optime aliquando in liturgica concelebratione manifestant, et cum quibus coniuncti profitentur se Eucharisticam Synaxim celebrare.'* One will note the inversion undergone by the phrase in the construction of the last two propositions and the reappearance of the idea of manifestation.—The Centurion edition of the acts of the Council being the most widespread, we note the error in the translation: it translates '*aliquando*' by 'in the case of'. This is obviously incorrect.

[120] *AS* IV–VII, p. 165, no. 115.

> date, *and when they concelebrate the Holy Eucharist in a spirit of harmony.*[121]

The Commission welcomed the request for the insertion of this new passage (italicized in the text of the *Acta*), 'because concelebration is an eminent expression of priestly fraternity.'[122] The intention to reopen larger perspectives on the use of concelebration is manifested here, especially after what had been said in number 7. However, contrary to what the text suggests by its allusion to 'ancient times,' this opening, as we have seen, cannot recommend itself to Tradition. Another aspect under which this passage is valuable for us is, that it clearly affirms—and this precisely in the italicized words—that one sole Mass is offered to God in concelebration (as was shown in the preceding chapter of this book).

These two additions made at the last minute were not discussed; there was no time. They were therefore approved with the rest of the Decree during the final vote, on 4 December 1965. The fundamental questions, however, still awaited a response, and the different tendencies held to their respective positions.

32. Now we shall mention the principal documents which are significant in that they do not speak of concelebration; for, the very nature of the matters which they treat would have either required, or at least would likely have made an allusion to this rite.

a) Among these texts the first place must go to the *Decree on the Oriental Catholic Churches*, which was examined during the third session, in the last two weeks of October,[123] and approved during the same session, on 21 November 1964. The silence in this document is easily explained by the desire to respect the Oriental Catholic Rites,

---

[121] *Ibid.*, pp. 132 ff.: '*Cum ceteris ergo membris huius Presbyterii, unusquisque specialibus apostolicae caritatis, ministerii et fraternitatis nexibus coniungitur: quod iam ab antiquis temporibus liturgice significatur, cum Presbyteri adstantes super novum electrum, simul cum Episcopo ordinante, manus imponere invitentur, et cum Sacram Eucharisticam unanimo corde concelebrant.*'

[122] Cf. *see above*, note 120.

[123] *AS* III–IV.

which do not admit concelebration. Despite the intervention of Msgr Bidawid, it is not impossible that certain Eastern patriarchs would have intervened in order that this question not be treated in this decree.[124]

b) We saw above that, during this session, the schema of the *Decree on the Ministry and Life of Priests* had made no allusion to concelebration, something which is revelatory of the mentality of the Council Fathers. The same goes for the reading of the texts of the other two schemas, later abandoned or integrated into other documents, which had been examined during the same session: a schema entitled *De clericis,* and the other called *De sacerdotibus.* In the former especially, an article was dedicated to the common life of priests (Chapter I, no. 7); and among the means fostering this common life there is no mention of concelebration. And, unless we are mistaken, neither with regards to this text nor the other schema did the Fathers intervene in order to request an exhortation on concelebration.[125]

This silence is even more significant in that the liturgical reform even then remained the object of a sustained activity. Therefore, this silence was not due to forgetfulness, but rather it was a sign that this rite was at the time something foreign to the common mentality, according to which concelebration was not even conceivable except as an occasional happening.

c) Also worth mentioning is the *Decree on the Pastoral Office of Bishops,* where an exhortation on concelebration would not have been out of place; and yet it is never mentioned. This is not surprising after the discussion of the first session, by which we were able to see that the most active centers in favour of the widest possible use of concelebration were monasteries; nevertheless, a declaration on concelebration in line with no. 7 of the Decree on the Ministry and Life of Priests would have been fitting here. However, it would not

---

[124] Msgr Bidawid's intervention itself (*see above*, notes 66 and 88) allows one to think so (cf. *see above*, nos. 19 ff).

[125] *AS* III–IV, p. 825: text of the schema *De clericis*; p. 846: schema *De sacerdotibus*.

have been in the sense of no. 8. The Decree on Bishops had been voted on and approved during the fourth session, 28 October 1965.

d) We spoke about the decisive role of the monastic centers, whose growing influence appeared in the *Acta* of the Council.[126] Yet paradoxically, the *Decree on the Renewal and Adaptation of Religious Life* does not speak of concelebration. How does one explain this silence, which is particularly sensible to no. 15., where 'the common life' is treated?[127] Apropos of this number (which was previously no. 11), 'Some thirteen Fathers asked that the Eucharist be presented as the center of fraternity in the religious institutes.'[128] Such a request could not but obtain the consent of all. What is surprising today is that there was no question of concelebration. This is all the more surprising in that that schema was presented to the vote of the Fathers on 6 October 1965, that is seven months after the vigorous beginning of the liturgical reform; and on the very same day the reform began, 7 March 1965,[129] the Decree *Ecclesiae semper* had draw attention to the rite of concelebration.[130]

Such a silence can be explained in different ways, the most likely being the absence of influential liturgists on the Commission for religious life. However, this explanation does not exclude several others factors which would have had to come into play simultaneously. By way of conclusion we can note that we have here a most certain sign that the idea of concelebration as an habitual form of the

---

[126] Cf. *see above*, notes 64; 67.

[127] *AS* IV–III, p. 526.

[128] *Ibid.*, to which came the response: '*Provisum est.*' By this response the Commission expressed that it believed to have sufficiently satisfied this request without introducing the question of concelebration.

[129] This date had been announced to the Fathers during the third session, 16 October 1964; cf. *AS* III–V, p. 9.

[130] *AAS* 57, 1965, pp. 410–12. This decree, remember, was concerned only with 'the rite of concelebration and Communion under both species.' It established nothing new with regards to the discipline of the new rites, that is regarding when they can be used. See our analysis in Chapter I.

Eucharistic liturgy for religious communities was still at that period, and even until the end of the fourth session, an idea foreign to the Council assembly as well as to the whole of the Church and the religious Orders. Therefore, it remained always as the exclusive deed of a very small minority, even if this latter had somewhat increased among certain circles during the Council. However, outside of these very limited circles the idea did not make progress, as all the silence shows. This fact also belongs to the history of the Council.

33. The contrary fact which imposes itself upon our reflection as we conclude this study, is that of the rapid extension of concelebration during the years following the Council, and even the existence of official documents encouraging this practice. With such an innovation being imposed in the name 'of the Council,' we are faced with two questions, the responses to which will give us our conclusion: 1) Is it truly the Council which prescribed this practice?; 2) Or at the very least, can the post-conciliar evolution legitimately be presented as the homogenous development of the letter and the spirit of Vatican II?

34. What the Council prescribed concerning concelebration can be found in no. 57 of the *Constitution on the Sacred Liturgy*. The text is extremely concise; there is no need for a summary. One can go back and read it (see above, texts C and D). On the other hand, it is important to recall the distinction that was made between the cases for which the Council itself gave the faculty to concelebrate (no. 57, § 1, 1) and those for which it submitted the possibility to the regulation of the bishop and the permission of the Ordinary (§ 1, 2; § 2, 1). It is also the Council that had firmly maintained the right for each priest to celebrate individually (§ 2, 2), which reaffirms the value of private Masses.

As we showed above, the text is clear in itself and in its fundamental orientation. Far from prescribing frequent concelebration, its certain intention is, on the contrary, to limit and regulate it. Although it was a matter of an obvious reading and not of an interpretation in need of a demonstration, nevertheless, faced as we are with a dispute, we shall recall the reasons upon which it is founded or which corroborate it:

a) the first is the immediate sense of Article 57, which no other conciliar text would contradict;

b) the second is that it is in conformity with the thought and practice of the Church before and during the Council, even if concelebration was practiced there (in conformity with Article 57, § 1, 1, *b*);

c) the massive reaction of the bishops in opposition to an arrangement which would have removed the regulation of the new rite from their authority (see above, from number 24 to 28);

d) the official declaration of the Commission in response to the abovementioned reaction, and its responses to the other questions of the Fathers on this subject (see number 27, especially note 106).

To these reasons must be added those which we shall examine in order to respond to our second question, namely: Was the development of concelebration in conformity with the letter and 'spirit' of the Council? However, those reasons are sufficient to be able to affirm that the Council, far from prescribing and even encouraging frequent concelebration, actually desired, on the contrary, its limitation and regulation. Such is its positive contribution, and we are most grateful for it: for both having reintroduced concelebration in these conditions, and at first, having reintroduced it; for it is certain that, practiced judiciously, concelebration, by manifesting the unity of the presbyterate around its bishop, is an act with true ecclesial value.

However, that does not prevent one from noting (and from regretting) that which remains incomplete and imperfect in the conciliar texts, namely the following: the historical errors regarding the Church's liturgical Tradition of the first centuries and the Oriental Rites;[131] the insufficient theological development—one which had been strongly requested during the ante-preparatory and preparatory

---

[131] Despite the very correct development of the Sacred Congregation of Rites during the ante–preparatory phase (cf. see above, note 22).

phases;[132] the lack of preciseness on the disciplinary level;[133] the occasional difficulty of seeing the coherence of the different texts.[134] No doubt an attentive and respectful study will allow one to find that coherence, as we have forced ourselves to do. However, in their lack of precision or clarity, certain texts allow one to see the extreme tendencies which inspired them to the detriment of the general equilibrium. We are thinking in particular of no. 27 of the Constitution on the Sacred Liturgy, and also (but to a lesser degree) no. 8 of the Decree on the Ministry and Life of Priests, with the difference of orientation that is shown in its relation to no. 7.

35. Such is our response to the first question; our response to the second question is practically the same: We see only with difficulty how the postconciliar evolution can be presented as a harmonious development of the Council itself. We see rather a deviation both on the level of the letter as well as the spirit. With respect to the letter, what has already been said seems to suffice; and we do not see how one can object. In fact, it is 'the spirit of the Council' which is invoked above all. However, can the spirit go so far as to contradict the letter?

Yet it must be acknowledged that on this level two 'spirits,' that is, two tendencies, can be seen in the conciliar texts. How could it be otherwise, since these two tendencies existed, and they came face to face both before and during the Council itself? It no doubt would have been possible, and even desirable, that they should come forth from two harmonious texts, where their respective points of view would have been fused together into a happy complement, thanks to a dialogue carried out in charity and truth. However we have seen the reasons which, even on the simply practical level, rendered such a dialogue difficult and limited. These difficulties explain the imperfections of the final text and allow the different tendencies to appear

---

[132] Cf. *see above*, notes 20 and 38.

[133] Cf. *see above*, nos. 26–8 of our work.

[134] Cf. *see above*, nos. 19 *b*); 25 (to the extent that what is said here is applied as well to the final text); 30 *b*).

sometimes in their opposition rather than in what could have been their complementarity. We hasten to add that, nevertheless, it is this very complementarity which dominates at least in number 57 of the Constitution on the Liturgy. Such a fact fills one with admiration for the conciliar institution, especially when one thinks of the difficult conditions in which it had been carried exercised at Vatican II. However, the insufficiencies and internal tensions of the different texts finally approved remain nonetheless. It is on these that the supporters of the widest extension of concelebration base themselves by appealing to the 'spirit of the Council.' It's foolish to present them as supporters of the 'true' spirit of the Council.

What can clearly be seen, on the other hand, are all the reasons which oblige one to recognize there a spirit opposed to the Council and the Church, which by definition are but one (we are speaking here only of the tendencies, by considering in them what is extreme and absolute, and in no way considering the persons who adhere to them and whose sincerity we respect). These reasons are the following. The practiced imposed by this spirit goes against:

a) the letter of the Council;
b) the traditional practice and previous Magisterium;
c) the common good of the Church, to which each new Mass brings the grace of Christ;
d) the immediate good of the faithful: the abundant testimonies of Christians who had been and are frequently deprived of Masses because of the abused extension of concelebration;
e) the true piety of the priest, who can certainly identify more with Christ the High Priest and Sole Mediator in a singular than in a communitarian celebration; for it is in the former that he better represents Christ. One could posit (and as far as we're concerned it seems certain) that the profound 'crisis of priestly identity,' which has affected so many

priests since the end of the Council, is due in no small part
to this abuse of concelebration.

Among the documents of the earlier Magisterium unfortunately
omitted by the preparatory Commission on the liturgy, we can recall
once again that of Pius VI, where he condemns the errors of the Synod
of Pistoia, especially in what concerns concelebration. He condemns
the position that states:

> ... that the mode of life (of religious priests) be not distin-
> guished in any way from that of others, such that one Mass
> alone, two at the most, be celebrated each day, and that it suffice
> for the other priests to concelebrate with the community.[135]

It is not possible to diminish the impact of this condemnation by
trying to see in it only a simple disciplinary measure, having value only
for a time and in determined conditions. We have shown above its
doctrinal foundation, which is principally, if not exclusively, in the
ecclesial value of each Mass. Nor is it possible to limit its impact by
invoking the cases (the very rare cases) of the Catholic Oriental Rites,
for which the Church has allowed daily concelebration;[136] for, we
know very well that, under those special conditions, the Church
consented to give this faculty for a particular good, as for instance,
peace between those Churches and Rome, to the partial detriment of
the general good. It is in this case that one must speak of a disciplinary
norm of limited impact. Moreover, we see too much continuity
between the errors of the Synod of Pistoia and those which triumph
today to underestimate the impact and relevance of the Apostolic
Constitution of Pius VI.

36. Those who try to find in the current and generalized practice of
concelebration the incarnation of the true 'conciliar spirit' can find
only one thing to oppose the aforementioned very weighty reasons:
namely the practice itself and the very large extension it has been

---

[135] Cf. *see above*, note 29.

[136] To our knowledge, before the Council there was only one, which we mentioned in the preceding chapter.

given. This argument acquires a certain strength, which does not allow one to reject it so easily, when one considers on one hand the consensus that seems to be made concerning the new practice, and on the other hand the official texts upon which it is based.

However, the first of these two reasons loses much of its weight if one observes the historical context in which that consensus has been gradually established, as well as its proper limits. It is, in fact, far from rallying the support not only of the faithful and priests, but also of the members of the hierarchy and Roman Curia, just as was stated in our research and in the numerous conversations which we have had on this subject. Moreover, the new practice could easily have passed for a fruit of the Council and of the *sensus fidei*, if it had been developed in a climate other than that which it was. If it had appeared gradually, with numerous episcopal approvals, as the Council had requested, and within the midst of even more numerous manifestations of development in Eucharistic worship, and accompanied by an argument from priestly vocations—then, yes, it would have been necessary to recognize therein the inspiration of the Holy Spirit. But on the contrary, well known is the crisis in which this unlimited extension was instituted and often tyrannically imposed: a growing lack of discipline; an obscuring of the most fundamental truths of Eucharistic dogma; a vertical fall in religious and priestly vocations; a defection of priests in unheard of proportions, etc. Whatever be the fruit or factor of this crisis (and it is no doubt both at the same time), it is a fact that it was in such an environment as this that the new practice had been instituted, in flagrant violation of the conciliar prescriptions.

With respect to the few rare official documents which can be invoked in its favour, it would be interesting to take an inventory of the acts of the bishops allowing it; for, it was these which were first set down by the Council (no. 57, § 2, 1). We do not deny that they existed, but we ourselves do not know them; and we do not see their number and their convergence preceding the encouragements attributed to the upper echelon. In such conditions one must consider the influence of the commissions, and most especially that of the *Consilium,* in order to understand the liturgical reform. With respect to those documents—and we are thinking mostly of one or another instruction from the Sacred Congregation of Rites[137]—it must be noted that their authority cannot be compared to that of the Council's Constitution or that of an Apostolic Constitution such as Pius VI's. These contradictions among the magisterial texts are extremely regrettable, but they cannot trouble the belief of those who are mature in their faith, nor can they pose serious problems of interpretation. There is, in fact, a hierarchy among these different documents. Those which enjoy the greatest authority, and those which in this case are in perfect conformity with them, annul those with lesser authority to the degree that they are opposed. It is according to this hierarchy that they must be interpreted, and not by inverting them.

37. The current practice of concelebration, *insofar as it is general and systematic,* and even at times tyrannical, is not in any way the work of the Council, nor can it find support in its letter or its spirit. This conclusion forces itself upon us with all the more strength, given that our earlier studies have allowed us to see from where this practice came. It is the work of a liturgical movement which developed before WWII, but even more so after the war—sometimes in agreement with authority, but more often in opposition to it. For, here again we must avoid simplistic and destructive dialectics: 'ground work' and freedom of spirit against institution and rigidity of the letter. The reality is more complex. There was some good, even some great good, in the liturgical movement; but that movement also involved itself in some regrettable and dangerous extremes. The Magisterium, for its part, while it did not itself start the movement, was the first to encourage it. However, it did exercise its grace of discernment, approving what was good and trying to correct what was not.

---

[137] Instruction *Eucharisticum mysterium* (*AAS* 59, 1967, p. 66); cf. *LPC,* no. 184, pp. 37 ff; *see above,* Ch. II.

By its constant opposition to the Magisterium, the tendency towards the generalized practice of concelebration followed in the extreme parts of the liturgical movement, as we showed in our earlier works.[138] The Second Vatican Council represented but one episode—an extraordinary important episode, it is true—in the history of this relationship between the liturgical movement and the Magisterium. The latter has simply continued to exercise its work of discernment. It is interesting to note here, as we did above,[139] the continuity and identity that there had been between the reactions to the different manifestations of the liturgical movement's excesses—reactions from the Curia and bishops before the Council, and from the latter in their great majority during the Council. It would be easy to confirm this observation by many other facts.[140] Therefore, at the Council, the Church's Magisterium pursued its work of discernment, approving a certain reestablishment of concelebration, and seeking to take measures for its regulation and limitation.

All that one can say, unfortunately, and what we must have the courage and honesty to recognize is that, embarrassed by the overly pushy behavior of the most ardent supporters from the liturgical movement, but also by the procedures (unceasingly submitting texts for revisions) and the mass and rhythm of too much work, the Council was unable to give the necessary fullness and clarity to its work on this question. Furthermore, some inaccuracies (historical and not doctrinal) have even slipped into the text. These shortcomings and imperfections are what allowed the liturgical movement to bring about the triumph of its theses 'in the name of the Council' after it closed.

---

[138] *La concélébration'Sensus fidei' et 'théologie'* (LPC, no. 185; *see above*, Ch. III); *La concélébration: histoire d'une histoire* (LPC, nos. 186–7; *see above*, Ch. IV).

[139] At the end of no. 23 of this work.

[140] Think, for example, of all the interventions of Pius XII, in 1947, 1954, 1956, or again of the open opposition of the journal *La Maison Dieu*, the organ of the Centre de Pastorale Liturgique, or the directives of the French Episcopate in 1953 (cf. *LPC*, no. 185, p. 35; *see above*, Ch. III).

38. We do not hide the fact that our calling into question of practices and opinions which are today so widespread can appear to some as an attack on the Magisterium of the Council. The weight of habit moves them to identify to such a degree a certain 'spirit of the Council' with the Council itself, that every critique and even simply every questioning of that 'spirit' appears to them to be a grave rejection of the Magisterium itself. And yet, if one considers the matter closely, they are the ones who scorn the Council and who do not respect the authentic Magisterium.

For our part, far from calling into question the conciliar institution in its work at Vatican II, we are showing its greatness, but its limits as well. Both aspects need to be recognized; for, if the Holy Spirit assists the Church gathered in a council, it does so by supporting the activity of men, and not by substituting it. Hence the possibility of resisting His action, not to the point of an error in what concerns the Faith, certainly; but at least enough to create a partial obstacle to the divine work.[141] Regarding concelebration, the greatness of the Council appears in this, that in the midst of circumstances oftentimes difficult,

---

[141] The very timely words of R. Laurentin provide much fruit in this area: 'A council is guaranteed against error; it is not assured of success' (*L'enjeu*, p. 164). 'For while the Spirit is without fault, men are not, and they can limit the Spirit's action ... It is not impossible that a council not be successful regarding a given question, where it would not be able to succeed in a useful manner, and that its decisions be more or less fortunately detailed, more or less adapted to the time. Every form of human activity has its strengths and weaknesses. And as the exercise of personal power must be protected from rigidity, authoritarianism, individualism, so the exercise of collegial power must be protected from disorder, quarrels, confusion and inefficiency. The council therefore is not a panacea. Its decisions are not necessarily better than or as good as those which would have been made by the Pope alone ... Its success is not automatic. It is tied to the implementation of human and supernatural means which can succeed more or less resolutely (p. 94).' These lines had been written on the eve of the Council's opening. To cite them is not to 'put on trial' Vatican II, as some have feared. It is to recall what is a council, and therefore to place it in the conditions of truth necessary for understanding its fullness of grace, but also the limits of Vatican II.

the Magisterium of the Church worked to exercise its ministry of discernment: it recognized the appropriateness of reintroducing in certain cases the practice of concelebration; and it established the fundamental principles that would permit bishops to regulate it. Its limits are those that were mentioned above: neither the doctrinal principles nor the practical norms had been sufficiently clarified, such that after the Council the abuses quickly triumphed.

Thus, far from attacking the conciliar institution, our work, on the contrary, brings to light the work which the Church had realized at Vatican II. Showing that this work of the Church was not finished is to highlight, moreover, an obviousness in complete conformity with the historical condition of the Mystical Body and the People of God. What we are saying is simply that this work seems urgent today. Wherefore, we but refer to the words of John Paul II, cited at the beginning of this chapter: 'the fundamental question' with which we are confronted today is that of 'the correct interpretation, that is the authentic interpretation, of the conciliar Magisterium.'

We do not believe we part from the thought of the Holy Father when we state that, what touches on the liturgy of the Eucharist in a general way certainly represents one of the most urgent aspects of this task, that is to say this 'work' of the Church. What we have said regarding concelebration, contrary to certain ideas currently received by many, is only one aspect of this immense 'work.'

*   *   *

39. We have made the effort to examine closely the Council's *Acta,* in order to be sure that we are leaving out none of the arguments put forth at the Council. However, we see that the ultimate and fundamental reason that pleads in favour of the multiplication of Masses, and therefore the regulated and limited use of concelebration, is found in this essential truth of Catholic dogma: each Mass is the unbloody renewal, the sacramental re-actualization of the very sacrifice of the Cross. It is this which is recalled so well by the liturgical formula of the Roman Missal, cited by the Council at the beginning of its

Constitution on the Sacred Liturgy: 'As often as the commemoration of this Victim is celebrated, the work of our redemption is accomplished.'[142]

It is only on the basis of this truth that we can develop the theology of the Eucharist, its celebration and concelebration, by showing how the unique sacrifice of redemption is re-actualized in this 'commemoration,' that is in this sacramental sign. This is what we shall try to do in later chapters. But first it will be helpful to finish our historical research by showing how the Reform of Luther was opposed to this sacramental renew of the redemptive sacrifice and its multiplication; and how it was opposed at the same time to the movement and development of the liturgy and Eucharist worship in the Church. Such will be the subject of our next two chapters.

---

[142] Secret from the Ninth Sunday after Pentecost (*Constitution on the Sacred Liturgy*, 1).

7 'USELESS AND SUPERFLUOUS MASSES'

DIFFERENT EVENTS HAVE reminded the general public that the year 1980 was the 450th anniversary of the Augsburg Confession. One will remember, in fact, that 20 June 1530, at the command of Charles V, an imperial Diet had been convoked at Augsburg for the purpose, among other things, of 'putting an end to the Lutheran heresy.' The supporters of the new doctrine had been invited to present and to defend 'their opinions in religious matters as well as their grief on the subject of ecclesiastical abuses in need of reform.' Melanchthon was the principal author of the written response to that invitation; and his text, the fruit of numerous revisions, went from being a simple apology to a true confession of faith. This confession, in its original 1530 edition, has always been considered by Protestants themselves 'as having the force of law, as the official expression of the faith of the Lutheran church.'

Thus does Pierre Jundt, the translator of Luther's works, express himself in his introduction to the most recent edition and French translation of that fundamental text.[1] He clarifies as well that if, with respect to his redaction, the 'Confession of Augsburg is the work of Melanchthon,' 'it expresses the complete theological thought of

---

[1] La Confession d'Augsbourg. *Traduction publiée par l'Alliance Nationale des Eglises Luthériennes de France—Introduction et Traduction de Pierre Jundt—Postface de Mgr Armand Le Bourgeois*, Paris–Genève, Le Centurion–Labor et Fides, 1979, p. 42. The earlier French translation of this text goes back to 1949: La Confession d'Augsbourg. 1530 (*Confessio Augustana Triglotta, Gallice–Germanice–Latine*), Editions Luthériennes, Paris–Strasbourg, 1949. Made directly, as was that of Pierre Jundt, from the German text, this 1949 translation gives us a text substantially quite sufficient. It has the great advantage of offering along with the French text the original German, taken from the 1930 critical edition of *Deutscher Evangelischer Kirchenausschuss*, and its original Latin adaptation (more than a translation).—The present chapter appeared in *LPC*, no. 189 (November–December 1980), pp. 38–53.

Luther.'² Read in a solemn session before the Diet, 25 June 1530, it would be refuted by Catholic theologians in the *Liber confutationis,* which appeared on 30 August of the same year. Melanchthon tried to refute this refutation, but this new defense was no more accepted than the Confession itself. After a close examination, the Diet of Augsburg refused it on 19 November 1530. This new *Apology* rallied no less to the cause of Lutheranism a certain number of German princes. Later, having been revised several times, it became 'after the two catechisms of Luther and the Confession of Augsburg ... the fourth credal book of the Lutheran church.'³

This is of some importance. But the principal text remains that of the Confession of Augsburg itself, and its numerous editions show us that it remains even today the fundamental creed of the Lutheran faith.

We pause here for only that which concerns 'the Mass'—this term is used in the very text of the Confession. In the Protestant perspective the reality of the Mass was still possible at that epoch, for, as Pierre Jundt explains, 'in 1530, this word was not really equivocal.' He means that it did not run the risk of signifying the idea of sacrifice.⁴ It is from this point of view, that of a 'Mass' without sacrifice, which Melancthon sought to present a defense in his *Article XXIV: On the Mass.* This article is of extreme importance, the Eucharist being one of the most decisive foundation stones of the Christian Faith. Also, one is not surprised to see that it is around this subject that, after having separated itself from the whole of the Church, the Lutheran Reform internally broke apart. 'On this one point,' writes Jundt, 'on the Lord's Supper, it (the Augsburg Confession) appeared as the fracture point of Protestantism; more than all the others it expresses the faith of all the churches of the Reform.'⁵

---

2   *La Confession d'Augsbourg* (1979), p. 11. All citations refer to this edition unless otherwise indicated.

3   *Ibid.,* p. 39

4   In German: *Von der Messe;* in Latin: *De missa.* cf. p. 84, note 4.

5   *Ibid.,* p. 11

Among all the reflections to which that Article XXIV would give rise, we shall concentrate especially on those that concern the relation which necessarily exists between the *doctrine* of the Mass as sacrifice and the *practice* of the multiplication of Masses. It is here that we shall see the immediate relation—although not apparent at first glance —which also exists between the Confession of Augsburg and the *abused* practice of concelebration. Different though they may be, both result in the suppression of an immense number of private Masses, and therefore in the decrease of the sacramental offering of Christ's sacrifice in the Church. However, as this particular point (the attack against the multiplicity of Masses in the Confession of Augsburg) cannot be known as something abstracted from its context, we shall also note the most typical traits of Melanchthon's profession of the Lutheran faith. As we shall see, they are eminently enlightening for our time.

Article XXIX: On the Mass

1. Melanchthon begins by declaring: 'Falsely are our churches accused of abolishing the Mass.'[6] However, he shows, by what he adds immediately afterwards, that it is, on the contrary, with good reason that this accusation is made. Here are the arguments which he puts forward to refute the accusation (we ourselves have made the sub-divisions):

    a) For it is evident—let it be said without boastfulness—that the Mass is celebrated with more care and seriousness among us than among our adversaries.

    b) Thus the people are instructed with the greatest care and as often as possible about the nature of the Holy Sacrament, the end for which it had been instituted, and the manner in which it is to be used, that is to say for the consolation of anxious consciences.

---

6   *Ibid.*, p. 84. The text of Article XXIV runs from p. 84 to p. 89 of this pocket edition. It is to this that one must refer for all the following citations.

c) No notable modification has been made to the ceremonies
    of the Mass, save that the Latin chants are interspersed here
    and there with German songs for the sake of instructing and
    forming the people.

d) Thus all the ceremonies must have as their principal end
    the teaching of the people, what they need to know of Christ.

The whole of Lutheranism is there. In saying this, we ask the reader
to notice that our critique concerns points of doctrine and mistakes
in reasoning, and not persons and their intentions. We say this
thinking of our contemporaries, confining ourselves to the judgment
of the Church as regards the events of the past, and uniting ourselves
to her prayer for Christian unity. The whole of Lutheranism is there,
we said: the confusion of the objective order and subjective order
(first argument: *a*); reduction of the former to the latter, especially in
the theology of the sacraments (second argument: *b* and *d*); beginning with the maintaining of some ceremonies (third argument: *c*),
of which one could still give an account in 1530, it had been despoiled
of all value.[7] In fact, from the moment that one asserts that the
sacramental mystery is not abolished in the Mass, because first of all,
the latter is celebrated with much fervour, and then because this rite
has for its end only the instructing and *hence only* the provoking of the
interior act of faith—from this moment, one can immediately hold
that in their entirety, *or almost,* the exterior ceremonies are no longer
the celebration of the Mass. They are now but the 'memorial' of
Calvary in Luther's reduced sense of the word—clarified and condemned by the Council of Trent, that is by translating literally 'the

---

[7]   'At the time of the redaction of the Augsburg Confession,' notes Jundt, 'the
      celebration of the Last Supper, apart from the suppression of Communion under
      one species (*communio sub una*), was very similar to the traditional Mass. Hosts
      continued to be used, and the elevation of the Sacrament would not be abolished
      in the parish church of Wittenberg until 1542. In 1538, an ecclesiastic of
      Nuremberg had wished to suppress it; he was chastised as a disciple of Zwingli'
      (*Ibid.*, p. 85, note 1). This proves that liturgical forms necessarily evolve when
      theological principles are changed. We see the same thing today.

commemoration stripped of the sacrifice of the Cross, and not a propitiatory sacrifice' (Session XXII, Canon 3). 'Stripped,' *nudam commemorationem,* that is to say despoiled of all ontological and historical weight, both extensive and recapitulative, which constitutes the very substance of the sacramental mystery. And this latter, as is known, attains its fullness precisely in the celebration of the Eucharist.

The traditional and Catholic Mass, that is the Sacrament of the Eucharist instituted by Christ and transmitted by the Church throughout the ages, was truly abolished. These initial explanations are sufficient for understanding this. The later evolution of Lutheran, Calvinist and other liturgies would be the necessary consequence of this negation of principle, insofar as it is true that the *lex orandi* is always the inseparable reflection and support of the *lex credendi.* This can be seen in our day, and it cannot be otherwise. The least imperfection in the proclamation of doctrine is always and inevitably the point of departure for a ruinous evolution in the practice of the rite. The word, especially at the beginning, ends up invading everything; and in the end it remains alone. For, it is a question principally (and for Melanchthon exclusively) of 'instructing' in order 'to help one understand' intellectually, and thus of provoking the justifying 'act of faith.' The part of the affective sensibility is equally satisfying: the chants, the atmosphere, etc.; for, it is a powerful help to this interior act. But the mystery of the sacramental order and action is abolished, just as all that can be *signified* to the senses, and by them to the soul.

2. Melanchthon continued his Confession by passing over from defense to attack. Forever confusing the different levels, those of piety and sacrament, he tries to justify the innovations of the Lutheran Reform by a doubly calumnious critique of the Church:

> It is not unknown that, before our time the Mass was greatly misused in different ways: a sale was made of it, it was bought and sold; in all the churches Masses had been said, most of the time, for money. Before our time also some learned and just men reprimanded such an abuse time and time again.

Among these men we can note Nicholas de Cusa, Tauler, Chancellor
Gerson, Gabriel Biel. There were abuses, unfortunately all too real,
and this cannot be denied. Listen now as he passes to the level of
principles, complete with an unjust and calumnious generalization:

> Consequently, these venal Masses and these Masses said in a
> corner (*Winkelmess*), which, until now, have been celebrated
> at the incentive of money and stipends, have been abolished
> in our churches.

By 'Masses said in a corner,' explains Jundt, one should understand
'private Masses, celebrated by one sole priest, without the assistance
of the faithful for whom the Sacrament was destined.' These words
call to mind similar statements made by a certain number of experts,
and also, alas, of the Council Fathers who, in ignorance, no longer
accepted the traditional practice of private Masses. At least the
Protestants, in rejecting private Masses, are consistent, since they
deny that the Mass is the sacrament of Christ's sacrifice. But such
critiques on the part of Catholics are less comprehensible; for, they
ought to remember that every Mass, precisely because it is the very
sacrifice of Christ in the mystery of the sacrament, is said and
celebrated for all the faithful, living and deceased, whether or not there
is a congregation present.

However, let us return to the Augsburg Confession. The word
'consequently,' which introduces the sentence just cited, gives one to
understand that the reason for which these Masses had been abolished
is found in the abuses denounced earlier. At first these latter had been
presented as taking place 'most of the time.' They now become a
universal fact, encompassing without exception all Masses said privately 'until now': all being celebrated out of love for money. The
enormity of this judgment on the depths of consciences—not to
mention the fact that it is contrary to the Gospel, good sense and
historical truth—shows well that it is but a pretext for something else.
In fact, if it really was a question of correcting abuses, clearly less
universally spread than the Lutherans maintained, the appropriate

remedy would have been completely different than a pure and simple abolition of all private Masses. One does not cure an evil by suppressing the patient; and the very notion of abuse signifies a bad use of a reality good in itself. Also, the true cause of the abolition of private Masses lay elsewhere, and it is mentioned again in the following:

> Moreover, reprimanded as well was the abominable error according to which it was taught that, by His death, Christ our Savior made satisfaction only for original sin, and that He instituted the Mass as a sacrifice to be offered for the other sins. Thus He would have made of the Mass a sacrifice for the living and for the dead, a means of removing sin and appeasing God.

Here then, this time proclaimed explicitly, is the true reason for the suppression of Masses celebrated in the absence of a congregation. What is denied here is the Catholic truth of the sacrifice of the Mass. But let us take note that this reason is presented to us in a new calumny by which Melanchthon sought to justify the Lutheran Reform. The first one strikes without exception at the consciences of all priests. The second touches on principles. It consists in attributing to the Church a doctrine contrary to the Faith: in making of the Mass another sacrifice, that is to say a sacrifice essentially different from the unique sacrifice of Calvary, the Church would have denied the universal redemptive value of the latter. Yet the Catholic Faith, as the Council of Trent recalled, has always professed, firstly, that the unique sacrifice which saves us is that of Calvary, and secondly, that the Mass is a true sacrifice only because it is not another reality, in its substance, than that unique sacrifice of Calvary, 'perpetuated' on the altar through the ministry of the priest, by means of the sacramental rite (Session XXII, chapters 1 and 2). Mysterious, no doubt, but consistent, admirable in its economy and adorable by the Wisdom and Love which reveals it.

Luther did not understand this; for, what he finally denied, through the sacramental order and over and above it, was the very idea of a created mediation between man and God, between the distressed conscience of the sinner and its Judge. On the other hand, what he did understand perfectly, and Melanchthon after him, was the immediate relation that exists between the *doctrine* of the Mass as sacrifice and the *practice* of the multiplication of Masses. In fact, after having mentioned the theological problems posed on the subject of the fruits of the Mass—and one must remember here that the theology of the 15th century, and still more of the beginning of the 16th century, marked as it was by nominalism, offered an easy target for attacks—after having mentioned the theological problems regarding the fruits of the Mass, Melanchthon continued by connecting what he says here to what preceded, and hence to the doctrine of the sacrifice:

> It is from there that has come the great quantity, the incalculable quantity of Masses.

This is exactly right, even if the explanation which follows is not:

> One intended to obtain from God by such a work all that one needs. At the same time faith in Christ and true worship of God falls into oblivion.

Everything is there: the denial of Christ's action in the sacrament led Luther to reduce the latter to nothing other than a human action. The Mass is therefore conceived as being simply 'a work'—a meritorious work of man—in opposition to 'faith'—only faith, or faith alone, justifying solely by the merits of Christ. Therefore, it is under this double aspect that Luther rejects the Catholic Mass: he accuses the Church of conceiving it as a new sacrifice, one other than Christ's; and he makes the Church see it as a work meritorious of salvation, independently of the merits of Christ, while only the merits of Christ, through the faith that we have in them, justify and save us.

We said already how this presentation was a mere caricature of the Church's true doctrine on the sacraments in general and the Eucharist in particular. We must add a word here in order to show that the Lutheran error is just as big in the notion of meritorious works, and even more so in the notion of justification. In order to do this it seems that we can make use of a completely biblical distinction: one that follows the thought of St Paul, among others—a distinction between justification (*dikaíôsis*) and salvation (*sôtèría*). The first is given to us gratuitously, solely by the merits of Christ; and on our part, solely through an act of faith in those same merits. Here Luther was completely correct, and his faith was Catholic, except for later clarifications regarding the limit of this act of faith. The statements of St Paul on this point are definitive and irrefutable: 'The justice of God through faith in Christ Jesus ... all have sinned and are deprived of the glory of God, and they are *justified* by the favour of His grace in virtue of the redemption (accomplished) in Christ Jesus ... by means of faith' (Rom 3:22–25). 'Man is *justified* by faith apart from the practice of the law' (v. 29; cf. 8, 10; etc.). 'Man is not *justified* by the practice of the law, but only by faith in Christ Jesus' (Gal 2:16), etc. But elsewhere St James warned us, 'Can faith *save*?' (2:14)—Without works, no. 'Thus it is with faith: if it has not works, it is completely dead' (v. 17). More texts could be called up. We must note that those of the first series concerned 'justification,' that is to say the receiving of God's justice, that by which He is faithful to His promise and by which He raises us up, purifying us from sin; to share in His own justice is to participate in the entire mystery of supernatural sanctity. On the other hand, in the second series of texts it is a question of being saved or of 'salvation.' So, while the conversion which 'justifies' comes in time and inaugurates new times, 'salvation' will not be obtained except at the end of time (cf. 1 Thess 5:9; Phil 1:28; cf. 1:19 in opposition to 3:9; etc.). This is why St Paul teaches that 'our *salvation* is the object of hope,' as Fr Lyonnet translates it in the *Jerusalem Bible* (Rom 8:24); but it seems to us that the mind of the Apostle is better rendered thus: 'It is in hope that we are *saved*'—here we give to the preposition 'in' all the force of the Greek *én*: it is in living by and in hope that we come to salvation. What is certain, as the rest of the text shows, is that salvation, the object and fruit of hope, is placed in terms of existence: 'But to hope for that which we do not see, is to wait for it with patience' (v. 25). The Council of Trent defined the Church's teaching on these matters in its Sixth Session (especially in Chapters 7 and 10). It speaks here of justification and the progress or increase (*incrementum*) in justification. Salvation thus appears as the term of the increasing process, which develops from the first moment of justification by faith alone. Salvation is the fullness, as justification is its proper principle.[8]

If Luther did not recognize this distinction and if he denied that man could contribute to his own salvation by his works, it is because he first denied the cooperation that man brings to his own justification in the initial act of faith. For the Reformer, even here there is an unsurpassable abyss separating man from God. It is known how, according to Luther, a justified man remains a sinner intrinsically in his being: *simul justus et peccator*—and not in the Catholic sense, where the elevation by grace to supernatural sanctity leaves behind in the baptized 'concupiscence' in the general sense of an evil inclination to sin, while all that is sin in the strict sense is washed away (Council of Trent, Session VI, Canon 5). Rather, Luther meant this in the sense that man, in no way transformed by baptismal grace,

---

[8]   Rev Lyonnet, SJ, seems to have brought this point out well when he wrote in a note on Romans 4:25 (in his French translation of the Jerusalem Bible): 'Justice is in fact a first participation in the life of the risen Christ, 6:4; 8:10; etc.' These different texts show well how justification by faith alone obtains for us justice, which is sanctity, and how this latter is in us the principle of the new life 'in Christ'. Because Christ Himself lives in us (Gal 2:20) and works in us (Eph 1:11), we do works of justice (2:10) and thus come to the fullness of justification, that is to final salvation, which will be given to us at the end of our life. Whence the exhortation of St Paul: 'Work (*katergazesthe*) out your salvation (*sôteria*) (Phil 2:12)—that is, labor by your works (*erga*) to accomplish your salvation. The Vulgate translates this very accurately: *Operamini vestram salutem*—'work out your salvation' by your works (*opera*). It is difficult to state more clearly the necessity of 'works' for 'salvation'. Regarding justification for salvation by the justice which justification gives us, and the accomplishment of which procures salvation for us, it seems to us that bringing out the distinction and the bond between these two extremes of the process of our salvific justification, namely initial justification and final salvation—bringing this out helps much in clarifying this central problem of Lutheranism.

remains the identical sinner in his being, his 'justice' consisting only in this: that God externally imputes to him the merits of Christ. It is easy to notice here the influence of the nominalism of that time; and yet, if something is at the base of the Pauline experience and doctrine, it is definitely that ontological, radical and decisive transformation of the man: 'Whoever is in Christ is a new creature' (2 Cor 5:17). Why the negation of this transformation apart from the personal drama of Luther? Because what he denied first of all is that in the act of faith man and God truly meet. For Luther, God does not really communicate Himself to man; He does not intimately allow His spiritual creature to participate in His own Trinitarian life; and man does not enter, in the true sense, into communion with that life.

A fortiori Lutheranism would deny that the redemptive sacrifice, by which this grace is given to man, could be 'perpetuated' in a sacrament, and that Christians could receive its effects in virtue of this sacrament and therefore follow Christ more closely into His Passion and Resurrection by all the works of their daily existence. For, it is this very mystery that is denied by the Augsburg Confession in its Twenty-fourth Article, and even more directly in the passage we just analyzed. 3. But what then is a sacrament according to this Confession? This is explained to us after this double introduction—defensive and offensive. In reality, the paragraphs which follow only explain, or better yet only repeat what was already said in the preceding ones. Referring to denounced 'abuses,' true and false ones inseparably mixed together, the text of the Confession continues:

> This is why it was taught, clearly by force of necessity, how to use the Sacrament correctly, namely: First, that for original sin and for the other sins, there is no other sacrifice than the sole death of Christ ... It is an absolutely unheard of novelty in the doctrine of the Church to teach that Christ's death satisfied only for original sin, and not for the other sins.

All this is pure Catholic doctrine; and, consequently, it is pure calumny to accuse the Church of teaching an 'unheard of' novelty. If the Mass were not, in the mystery of the sacrament, the same sacrifice of the Cross, it would not have any value for bringing about the remission of actual sins, Baptism being for each Christian the sacrament which, in virtue of the sacrifice of the Cross, washes away original sin.[9]

> Second, St Paul teaches that we obtain grace before God by faith and not by works. This is clearly in opposition to abusing the Mass in such a way that one imagines that grace is obtained by that work.

The Mass is reduced to being nothing but a 'work' of human liberty: and here we are at the heart of Lutheranism. What one must see, in fact, is that (just as we said above), it is his own false interpretation of justification by faith (which, by the way, was itself conceived in an erroneous manner) that led Luther to deny first the meritorious value of good works, and then the divine efficacy of the sacraments, reducing them as he did to nothing but 'works' of man. In both cases what is rejected is the very mystery of man's communion in divine life, as well as the means by which this communion is realized. Such is the ultimate foundation of Lutheranism; such also is its end. God alone is all; God alone does all. He made all in Christ. However, between Him and ourselves there is an unsurpassable abyss. It is known with what energy, with what force even, Karl Barth recalled this at the beginning of this century. Only faith, 'faith alone,' breaks this abyss. But does it truly break it definitively, as Luther conceived it? No. According to Lutheranism, it can do this only in a nominal manner, juridically, in a purely subjective way; for neither can the grace of Christ transform man to the point of rendering him capable of *works* which would have a truly and divinely meritorious value before God, nor can Christ Himself truly encounter man, touch man, bring man back to Himself by His *sacraments*. Incapable of becoming a 'sharer in the divine nature' (2 Pet 1:4), or 'divinized' as the Greek Fathers say, man cannot then enter into true communion with God. He cannot participate in the communion of the

---

[9]   Cf. Council of Trent, Session V, Canons 4–5.

Trinitarian life, which is his most certain vocation (cf. 1 Cor 1:9; 2 Cor 2:13; 1 Jn 1:3, etc.). Protestantism thus appears as a doctrine of despair. Never can a consistent Lutheran say with St Paul, 'It is no longer I who live, but Christ Who lives in me' (Gal 2:20). Now if Lutherans can often edify us by their faith and charity (and who of us has not experienced this), it is not in virtue of the Augsburg Confession, but rather despite it and in contrary to it.

At the same time as that transformation and communion there is the very reality of created means or mediations which the Protestants deform and ultimately reject. One would object, no doubt, that even in its extreme form, at least one thing is kept, namely the word. However, two things must be noted with regard to this. The first is that this mediation, the written word of the Book, the Bible, is the most disembodied mediation of them all. One can convince them of this by simply comparing it to the living mediations like the ministers of the sacraments and the sacraments themselves. The second is, that the preservation of this mediation, the word of 'Scripture alone,' is in opposition to the first principles emerging from Luther's personal drama: God in His heavenly sanctity is inaccessible to the man of sin and earth that I am. It is the theology of the very Word Incarnate that becomes difficult in these conditions. For, Christ will always be seen either too exclusively as God, such is the tendency of pure Lutheranism; or too exclusively as man, such is the tendency of liberal Protestantism. This latter reduces the word of Scripture to being simply the work of the early community; and from here one can only deduce the final consequences of the principle of the radical disassociation posited at the beginning by Luther himself. Freedom and reason alone remain, falling into rationalism and collapsing finally into atheism. It is so true that the Incarnation reveals God only if one accepts it by faith, in its fullness, with all its historical consequences in the Church. Such is the divine economy of salvation. The act of faith which it requires becomes as a whole both more easy and more difficult. It could even require heroism, especially in the face of the mediation of the 'Church'—think of St Joan of Arc; but it is only in this way that it becomes a source of justification and salvation.

The rejection of these mediations, which are the work of God Who became Incarnate to encounter man, and the rejection of good works which man, justified by faith, accomplishes meritoriously by the grace of Christ in order to encounter God, are intimately tied to each other and go hand in hand. Hence this refusal of the 'Mass'—the celebration of the sacrament of the Eucharist, a mediation and a work, in order to obtain the remission of our debts and the gift of Christ's grace:

> It is known, in fact, that the Mass is used in order to clear away sin and to obtain from God grace and every good, and this not only for the priest himself but also and more so for others, indeed for the whole world, living and deceased.

Such is, in fact, the faith of the Church, considered here as an abuse opposed to the fundamental principle of justification—and salvation—by faith alone: *sola fide*. And such was the object of this 'second point.' This allows us to see at which point the doctrine of justification is the first principle of all of Lutheranism, since it is in its name that the Mass is reduced to being but a human 'work,' and under this aspect, rejected.

But what then is a sacrament? For, those two points restrict themselves to telling us, apropos of the Mass, what a sacrament is not. Nevertheless, with this recognition of the fundamental place of the principle of justification by faith, we are on our way to a response to this question. Here it is:

> Thirdly, the Holy Sacrament was not instituted as a sacrifice to be offered for sin—for that sacrifice had already taken place—but in order to awaken our faith and console our consciences. By this sacrament they understand that grace and the remission of their sins are promised them through Christ. This sacrament therefore requires faith and, without faith, it is received in vain.

That this sacrament, as all the others, requires faith in order to be received is not the object of discussion; for, this is a fundamental principle of Christian dogma which no one contests.[10] Rather, the question here is whether or not the Mass is the sacrifice of Christ 'perpetuated' in His Church. The Catholic Faith has affirmed it from the beginning. Luther and Melanchthon deny it, and their denial has deadly overtones which send chills up the spine: 'the Holy Sacrament was not instituted as a sacrifice to be offered for sin.' If this is correct, the Church has no reason to exist, the Church as an institution being primarily ministerial and sacramental. We are left with only 'the word,' by which we 'are reminded' and 'understand' what Christ did for us 'formerly.' The sacramental 'now' of that 'former time' is rejected. By the word alone man is sent back mentally to the presence of what the Lord did for him formerly and, alone, he makes the superhuman effort of believing, in order that Christ's merits be attributed externally, juridically, to the sinner, who is and will always be such. There is nothing left but the word; and it does not matter who the minister of that word is, all the more so since Luther denied at one and the same time the sacrament of Holy Orders and the infallible Magisterium of Peter. The Church has a religion without sacrifice, and the blood of Christ can no longer flow down upon the members that He wishes to form, to purify 'even unto the end of the world,' to continue to form, purify, vivify, sanctify and lead to salvation. Man remains alone with his sin, the amount of which accumulates—a victim without defense from his 'Adversary,' his 'Accuser' (Rev 12:9–10), who triumphs in this denial of the sacramental sacrifice of Christ and His Church before exulting in its complete suppression, or at least its scarcity. This is an immense gain for the devil, and an equal loss for the Church. For the Mass is the very sacrifice of Christ, the sacrifice of Calvary present

---

[10]   What the Church condemns is the assertion according to which the sacraments had been instituted by Christ *solely* to nourish faith (by provoking it): *'propter solam fidem nutriendam'* (Council of Trent, Session VII, Canons on the Sacraments in General: Canons 5 and 8; etc.)

to the Mystical Body at every moment through the mystery of the sacrament; and it was instituted 'for the remission of sins which we commit daily': *in remissionem, eorum quae a nobis cotidie committuntur peccatorum*, as stated by the Council of Trent (Session XXII, Chapter I). However, the Council only stated what had already been a very traditional doctrine. It was explicitly formulated by St Ambrose, who inspired St Augustine,[11] and through him the entire Middle Ages.

> Christ indeed died once for the sins of the people, but in order to redeem the sins of the people daily.[12]

This is what happens by the Eucharist, as the text proves, showing at the same time that the thought expressed here is deeply rooted in the spirit and teaching of the Bishop of Milan. Addressing himself to consecrated virgins, he tells them:

> Nor would I hesitate to admit you to the altars of God, whose souls I would without hesitation call altars, on which Christ is daily offered for the redemption of the body.[13]

This doctrine would be taken up by St Augustine:

> Christ had been immolated one time in Himself, and nevertheless He is immolated each day in the sacrament;[14]

and by St Thomas Aquinas, who cites this text of Augustine in his *Summa Theologiae*.[15] We shall see in the next chapter what has

---

[11] R. Johanny shows this in his work, *L'eucharistie, centre de l'histoire du salut chez saint Ambroise de Milan* (Coll. 'Théologie historique'—9), Paris, Beauchesne, 1968, p. 152, ...

[12] 'Christus enim semel quidem pro peccatis populi mortuus est, sed quotide peccata populi redempturus' (*Expos. Ev. Sec. Luc.*, 10, 8; *Sources chrétiennes*—52, II, p. 159).

[13] 'Neque enim dubitaverim vobis patere altaria, quarum mentes altaria Dei confitenter dixerim, in quibus quotidie pro redemptione corporis Christus immolatur' (*De Virginibus*, L. II, c. II, 18; *PL* 16, 211). English Translation from *Nicene and Post-Nicene Fathers of the Christian Church*, Second Series (Vol. X).

[14] 'Semel immolatus est in semetipso Christus, et tamen quotidie immolatur in sacramento' (*Epist. 98 ad Bonifac.*; *PL* 33, 363 ff.).

become of this '*quotidie*' with the development of theology and Eucharistic worship. But these few testimonies already allow us to know what the Mass is for the Church.

For the Augsburg Confession, on the other hand, the Mass is not that unique sacrifice, really and mysteriously renewed, or even better, reenacted each day in an unbloody manner. It is only a *nuda commemoratio* made in order to awaken our faith and console our consciences; 'in order to console anxious consciences,' as was said above. One can see that, if it were only this, the strongest consciences would be able to pass it up, contenting themselves with a simple reading of the word from the Book. According to the Confession, the Mass does not give grace, less still does it give Christ Himself to those who receive it with faith; but it is only an occasion and an external means offered to men in order that they might 'understand that grace and the remission of sins are promised to them by Christ.' This is a denial of the faith of the Church, who firmly holds that the Eucharist remits venial sins by the proper effect which it works in us, before doing that which it grants us to accomplish through an act of charity, and not only through faith (Session XIII, chapters 2 and 8).[16]

To these three points explicitly enumerated is added a fourth, which appears at the beginning of the following paragraph:

> Since the Mass is not a sacrifice offered for others, living and deceased, in view of taking away their sins, it must be a communion where the celebrant and others receive the Sacrament, each one for himself.

This means, as what comes next will prove, that when there are no faithful to receive Communion, there cannot be a Mass. We have here a new internal contradiction; for, while on the one hand the Confession recognizes the Mass as only a mere communitarian action, on the other hand it preserves its innate individualism, each one commu-

---

[15] S.T. III, 83, 1.

[16] See the teaching of St Thomas Aquinas on this question: S.T. III, q. 79, article 4–5.

nicating only 'for himself,' each conscience therefore being left in its dreadful solitude before God. Whereas, according to Catholic doctrine, while, insofar as it is the sacrament of the Body of Christ, the Eucharist effectively profits only him who receives it, yet insofar as it is the sacrament of Christ's sacrifice, it profits also those who do not actually participate in it, but for whom it is offered.[17] Whence the possibility and the meaning of sacramental Communion made for someone else: one unites himself sacramentally and associates himself to Christ's sacrifice by asking Him to apply the merits of that act to the person for whom he receives Communion. In Lutheranism, communion is a pure act of faith, since the bread is only a living symbol of the Body of Christ, and not the Body Itself; and the rite, 'a bare commemoration,' of His sacrifice, and not the sacrifice itself. Therefore, one can communicate only for oneself. Radical individualism, which asserts itself again here, will inevitably contradict the communitarian element implied in the need for the congregation's presence at the celebration of the Mass.

These errors have spread far and wide since 1530. And today, as individualism tends to disappear under the effect of the surrounding collectivism, there often remains only communitarianism. Universal socialism does not suppress the evil of individualism except by putting another evil in its place, and one which is even worse: the denial of the person. If we reflect on the abused or even exclusive place often held by the notion of the congregation in the current Eucharistic theory and practice, we would recognize that here also the Augsburg Confession has establised a school—even outside of Lutheranism.

4. The last part of Article XXIV of the Confession justifies the practical conclusions deduced from the Lutheran doctrine. It seeks at the same time to give them an ultimate foundation, this time called for by Tradition. However, let us immediately note, this appeal to the Fathers and to the first centuries of the Church comes too late to be convincing. The true and one foundation of Lutheran Eucharistic

---

[17]   *Ibid.*, art. 7.

theology and practice is in the doctrine of justification by faith, and therefore in the denial of grace's transforming action and the ecclesial mediations by which Christ communicates that grace to us. This then, by means of that body of already formed doctrine, is how Tradition is received, pruned and interpreted. Melancthon's pretentiousness of a pure and simple return to the early Church is unsustainable after the profession of such a doctrine—not to mention the denial of the homogenous development of dogmas and liturgy which it implies,[18] as well as the typically subversive and revolutionary character contained in such an attempt to return directly to the early Church without passing through the whole Tradition, which alone can place us in living contact with that period.

Regarding the liturgy, listen to the practical consequences to which Lutheranism leads:

> Let us then observe among ourselves the following discipline: on feast days, and others as well, when communicants are present, we shall celebrate the Mass and give communion to those who desire it ...

> No other notable change has taken place in the public ceremonies of the Mass. Only the other Masses, the superfluous Masses, for example those celebrated in an abusive manner outside of the parish Mass, have been abolished.

'*Superfluous Masses*'—'superfluous' because they are not necessary, and consequently useless (*unnotigen Messen*): thus the Augsburg Confession calls those Masses celebrated in the absence of a congregation.[19]

---

[18] See our preceding studies: *L'Eglise demande la multiplication des messes* (*LPC*, no. 185, pp. 42–58; *see below*, Chapter VIII) and *Esquisse d'une histoire de la concélébration* (*LPC*, no. 189, pp. 14–30; cf. *see above*, Chapter V: *La concélébration: esquisse d'une histoire*).

[19] 'Superfluous' is an exact translation, *un–notig*, literally meaning 'not necessary'. The *Editions Luthériennes*, in their [French] translation of 1949, nevertheless recognized the need to add force to the German term by doubling the adjectives: 'the Masses are parasitic and abusive'. 'Useless and superfluous Masses' seems to us still more exact.

It is in accord with its own principles that Lutheranism considers these Masses as such, since there are not present at them any 'consciences' whose faith needs to be awakened. One could raise the objection that it would still be praiseworthy for the minister to celebrate the Mass in order to awaken his own faith, by making a commemoration 'for himself' of Christ's Passion. The Protestant response to this objection is well known: the word of Christ suffices for the minister who, besides, does not celebrate the Mass for himself, but for the community. This last statement is correct. But in that 'service' or 'worship' of the community, is not everything ultimately reduced to the preaching of the word? Once again we are faced with the contradiction that was introduced with the denial of the proper characteristics of the sacrament; and we cannot see how Protestantism can escape from it.

*   *   *

Melanchthon began his Confession on 'the Mass' by proclaiming that the Lutherans did not abolish it. Yet what emerges from this Article XXIV is the radical rejection of the Catholic Mass. We wished to underline the most perceptible point of that rejection on the *practical* level, namely the suppression of private Masses, declared 'superfluous and useless'; and we wished to show its immediate relation to the denial of Catholic *doctrine* regarding the sacrifice which each Mass is, in virtue of its sacramental presence and actualization of the one sacrifice of the Cross. However, what we have been moved to state several times over, and what we think was important to bring out as a conclusion, is that that suppression of private Masses, like the denial of the sacrifice of the Mass as such, appears as the ultimate and even necessary consequence of the whole Lutheran doctrine, especially of its fundamental principle, namely justification by faith alone. It seems that one can thus summarize the sequence of this implacable logic: at the beginning we have justification of man by faith alone and the rejection of the Magisterium; this brings about the complete rejection of ecclesial mediations or means; at the end we have the denial of the Mass as a sacrifice, and then (completed after Luther) the denial of the Eucharistic presence of

Christ through the miracle of transubstantiation. And thus, on the level of practice, we end up with the suppression of private Masses, declared *'useless and superfluous.'* The Mass is now only the word, 'the liturgy of the word,' we would say today—a liturgy for a congregation of Christians, who 'make a memorial' of Christ's Passion, and who communicate there, 'each one for himself,' thanks to the awakening of faith which this worship produces in them.

What makes one shudder when clarifying the current problems of the Church by means of this historical data is the extension of these teachings into today's Catholic world. Whether professed explicitly (which is not rare), or adopted by means of the ideas and practices which they inspire, we can see them spreading proportionately and with a disturbing force. It is in this context that we place the problem examined in the preceding studies, that of concelebration, or more exactly, that of the frequency of this rite, along with the suppression of a considerable number of 'private Masses,' which necessarily follows such an excessive frequency of the former. *Useless and superfluous Masses,* says the Augsburg Confession, because there is no congregation immediately present to justify such Masses. Yet is this not precisely the argument used today? We have seen that this argument was made more than once at the Council by supporters of *frequent* concelebration.[20]

Such a connection ought to make one stop and reflect. Is the Church admitting today that Luther was right and that she made a mistake in the 16th century? No, obviously not; this would amount to renouncing herself by betraying the deposit left to her by Christ. The connection which we just made, and which presents itself before us with such force, invites us to reflection. Those who think they are able to elude such a reflection by saying that it does not apply to them (which is true for the most part, no doubt, but only in part) because they profess the Catholic dogma of the sacrifice of the Mass, and

---

[20] See our study: *La concélébration eucharistique dans le Magistère du Concile Vatican II,* in LPC, no. 188, pp. 29; 38; 40; *see above,* Ch. VI. See also Ch. II.

because they hold that in a concelebration there are as many Masses as priest concelebrants—such persons ought to reflect attentively first, on the error which they commit by supporting this opinion, and second, on the fact that concelebration brings about no less, in the life and practice of the Church, the suppression of a great number of private Masses, and therefore of sacramental offerings of Christ's sacrifice by and for His Church.

Yet, we know by history, and especially by the carnal and social nature of man, that practice and doctrine always go together. This is why the decrease in the celebration of private Masses necessarily brings about a decrease in esteem for the Mass insofar as it is the sacrifice of Christ accomplished in time, by the Church and for its salvation. There is but a step from lack of esteem to denial. And this step is quickly made when, with traditional institutions and their intrinsic principles having been called into question, the exterior barriers of the law are no longer present to warn individuals and communities. This can be seen every day.

More serious still, because more immediate and more profound, is the consequence which this decrease in the number of Masses has for the faithful and for the whole world. If, in fact, each Mass is the sacramental immolation and oblation of Christ in, by, with and for the Church—and it is; and if each time a Mass is celebrated in the world, it is the blood of Christ which flows down again, or rather which continues to flow down in the present on sinful humanity—if this is so, who does not see the immense loss which the decrease in the number of Masses brings about for the Church and for the humanity which it has the mission to save? And who does not see the gravity of this loss *today*?

This is why—and we say it again with all our strength—this is why it is urgent that the Magisterium clarify the doctrine of the Church on all the doctrinal and practical questions related to concelebration which the Council did not treat, its work of clarification on this point not having been completed. The post-Conciliar period has not clarified matters, but rather is bringing confusion to the extreme. We believe we have shown this by our analysis: it is the entire liturgical reform which is at stake here, and with it, the whole Christian faith. For, by the dogma of the sacrifice of the Mass which is at the heart of this question, it is the entire Christian mystery which is recalled, celebrated and sacramentally accomplished in the Mass:

> *Quia quoties huius hostiae commemoratio celebratur, opus nostrae redemptionis exercetur.*

> 'For each time the memory (of the immolation) of this Victim is celebrated, the work of our redemption is wrought.'[21]

---

[21] Secret from the Ninth Sunday after Pentecost, moved in the *Novus Ordo* to the Second Sunday of Ordinary Time, and cited in the Council's Constitution on the Sacred Liturgy, nos. 2 and 6. In a sense diametrically opposed, Henri Denis (Episcopal Vicar of Lyon, charged with the permanent formation of priests, and member of CNPL) writes: 'We can better measure today to what degree purely solitary and priestly Eucharists have been able to distort both the meaning of the Eucharist and the community. Not so long ago (just before Vatican II), concelebration would have appeared suspect, because it diminished the number of Masses—a "quantitative" conception of the benefits of Christ's sacrifice' (*La communauté eucharistique aujourd'hui*, in *LMD*, no. 141 (1st Trim. 1980), 53, note 7). What is measured, above all, is the opposition which exists between such a declaration and the traditional doctrine of the Church, as well as the reference to Vatican II as the historical point of departure for this opposition. One will note as well the connection between these 'new' positions and the ancient positions of Protestantism. The only innovation—but it too is now already old—is that of the public adoption and profession of these old errors even within Catholicism.

8 THE CHURCH ASKS FOR THE MULTIPLICATION OF MASSES

EVEN JUST A brief look at the place held by the Eucharist and the manner in which it has been celebrated all throughout the Church's history reveals that, since the time of the Apostles and Apostolic Fathers until our present day, a considerable evolution has taken place. Our intention here is not to retrace that history in its entirety. Others have done so, from different perspectives and in unequally successful ways. What we would like to do is to prove, with the help of some undeniable facts, the manner in which the Church, ever conscience of the essence of the Eucharistic mystery, has become more and more aware throughout time of the treasure which she has in this mystery, and the blessings which she receives when its celebration is multiplied. We shall see how both practice and doctrine brought the decrease in the celebrations of the Eucharist; and whatever the motivations for this may be, it represents not a progress, but on the contrary, a halt, and even a regression in relation to that great movement and development of the Eucharist in the Church.

Tradition, since the end of the 4th century at least, has called and always calls this celebration of the sacrament of the Eucharist, 'the Mass.'[1] Without dismissing other fully legitimate ways of naming the sacrament, we have kept this word because of its traditional, dogmatic, theological and pastoral value. In fact, it places us in direct communication with more than fifteen centuries of the Church's life. It manifests unambiguously what Catholics mean when they speak of 'the Eucharist.' It permits us in our theological reflections to note the distinctions which exist between our celebration and that of Christ at

---

[1]   J. A. Jungmann, *Missarum Solemnia* (Coll. 'Théologie'–19), Paris Aubier, vol. I (1956), p. 219.—The present chapter appeared in *LPC*, no. 185 (March–April 1980), pp. 42–58. To better understand the content, one could approach it from the historical study outlined above in Chapter V.

the Last Supper; and it allows us to see both in their relation to the historical sacrifice of the Cross, 'prefigured' at the Last Supper, 'reproduced' at the Mass, in both cases sacramentally.[2] Finally, it is immediately accessible to the Christian people, and communicates to them the whole of this traditional, dogmatic and theological idea. Such is not necessarily the case with the terms 'Eucharist' and 'celebration,' as beautiful and traditional as these terms are, and even opportune when used in the proper context. In our opinion it is usually more preferable to use the term 'Mass.' In short, neither term should exclude the others.

We add also that we do not pretend that our study will be exhaustive, even within the perspective which we will work. The facts that we will bring forward will sufficiently prove the truth we want to recall, such that anything added will only confirm it, bring out its different and complementary aspects, possibly clarify one or another point regarding it, but not weaken it in substance. We note finally that one of the difficulties that one encounters when studying this question among contemporary liturgists comes from the fact that, even though they might not deny the notion of *sacrifice*, they concentrate their attention principally on the notion of the *congregation*. This often causes them to neglect certain aspects or change certain emphases in their vision of the mystery of the liturgy. Whence the necessity for us to complete, and even at times correct, their presentation of history in order to establish the truth.[3]

---

[2]   We studied this question in: *L'Eucharistie, Sacrement et Sacrifice du Christ et de l'Eglise. Développements des perspectives thomistes* (*Divinitas*, (Rome), 18, 1974 (2), pp. 234–86; (3), pp. 396–436), and in: 'Sacrificium Missae' (*La Pensée Catholique*, no. 153 (November–December, 1974), pp. 7–28); *see below*, Chapter IX.

[3]   One is struck by the fact that, since the beginning of the century, while theologians have striven to develop the notion of sacrifice in the mystery of the Eucharist, liturgists turn more and more towards the aspect of the congregation. With respect to the theologians, we can think of names such as de la Taille, de Lepin and Journet. With respect to the second tendency, which

I. It is very difficult to know what the Eucharistic liturgy was like during the apostolic period as well as during the period that immediately followed it. Certain points, nevertheless, appear with certitude. Ever since the first century the Christian community assembled on Sunday to pray, to offer the sacrifice and to receive Communion. Their prayer was of penance, praise, thanksgiving and supplication. The bishop offered the sacrifice, while the deacons assisted him in his functions. Such is, in a very brief summary, the testimony of the *Didache,* such a precious document which seems to go back to the first century.[4]

The testimony of St Justin, towards the middle of the second century, confirms the existence of this Sunday gathering.[5] While the letters of St Clement of Rome and St Ignatius of Antioch speak of the

---

is found mostly among liturgists, there was a reaction against such an exclusivity by the Dominicans of Saint–Alban–Leysse (Savoie), who were highly encouraged or at least approved by Archbishop de Bazelaire, Archbishop of Chambéry. They dedicated number 7 of their journal *Lumière et Vie* (December 1952)—at that time an excellent journal—to the theme: '*La messe, sacrifice du Christ.*' Notable there, under the signature of P. H. Bouessé, is a review of a book widely diffused, by P. Roguet, *La messe. Approche du Mystère* (Ed. du Cerf). The eminent theologian very delicately remarks to his confrere, already an influential member of C(N)PL, that, in his work, 'the perspective is liturgical ... Under this aspect the first chapter is suggestive: *L'Assemblée* ... The professional theologian will regret that the propitiatory character of the Eucharistic sacrifice is not very much developed' (p. 133). This simple detail says all: beginning with 'the Assembly', one can end up with only 'the Assembly.' The sacrifice is not denied; it simply disappears more and more. It will be denied only at the end; for, eventually one will not be able to see its place or its reason for being in 'the celebration of the congregation.' See below, Chapter XI.

[4]   J. P. Audet, *La Didachè* ... (Paris, Gabalda, 1958, pp. 187–210). See especially Chapters 9–10 and 14 of this work. On could also consult the presentation made in the work of N. M. Denis–Boulet, *Notions générales sur la messe*, in the collected work under the direction of A. G. Martimort, *L'Eglise en prière. Introduction à la Liturgie*, Paris–Tournai, Desclée et Cie, 1961 (pp. 262–4).

[5]   Cf. Martimort, *op. cit.*, pp. 266 ff.

central role played by the bishop and the hierarchically ordered unity of the community gathered around him:

> Special functions are assigned to the high priest; a special place is marked out for the priests, and special tasks for the Levites. The layman is bound by particular precepts for the laity.[6]

II. These principles would be confirmed during the centuries that followed, as attested, for example, by St Hippolytus' *Apostolic Tradition,* from the beginning of the third century. The bishop is the central personage, but he is assisted by a presbyteral body; and through Eucharistic Communion the entire community is gathered together. In reading the text of this prayer one sees that the Eucharistic liturgy is conceived essentially as the accomplishment of Christ's commandment: 'Do this in memory of Me.' It is, therefore, the 'commemoration' of His sacrifice, the prayer of thanksgiving and praise to God for His blessings, the prayer of intercession for the life and unity of the Church—it is this which Communion in the Body and Blood of the Lord will bring about. This is why one hardly conceives of it without the participation of the people.

The two fundamental principles which at that time regulated its frequency and internal direction were on one hand, that which sees in this Sunday liturgy the essential and proper act of the Christian religion's worship, substituting itself for the Sabbath duty of the synagogue; and on the other hand, that which St Ignatius strongly expressed, following St Paul (1 Cor. 10:17), namely, one sole bishop, one sole Eucharist, one sole people, united by the bishop in one sole congregation.

Those same words of institution, having been repeated at every Mass, thus assure us of this: that the liturgy had been understood from the beginning as the immolation and offering of a sacrifice; in it was offered to God 'the Blood of the New Covenant.' St Justin and St Irenaeus, from the second half of the second century, are qualified witnesses of what the Church's thoughts were regarding this mystery.[7]

---

6   *PG* 1, 288–9; cited in Martimort, *op. cit.,* p. 265.

Nevertheless, time would be required for these thoughts to mature, or more correctly, for the Church to develop the theological explanations and deduce all the practical implications. The great work of M. Lepin on *L'idée du sacrifice de la messe d'après les théologiens depuis les origines jusqu'à nos jours*,[8] has shown (this is its only merit) that the first systematic speculative elaborations on this mystery did not take place before the ninth century.[9] As Lepin shows, the Fathers had certainly furnished very valuable testimonies,[10] but without developing this question as they had done, for example, for the Blessed Trinity, the hypostatic union, the Church, grace. In this sense it is true to say that the Church lived, by her faith, the mystery of the Eucharistic sacrifice before seeking to render an in-depth theological explanation of it. It certainly seems that this is the ultimate reason which explains the relative rarity of the Eucharistic liturgy in the beginning[11] and its progressive multiplication throughout the centuries, arriving at what the Church today asks for in this regard. As we shall see, the Council of Trent would mark a decisive stage in this development.

III. Nevertheless, it did not take long before the celebration of the Mass would become more frequent. That knowledge which the Church had of offering the sacrifice of Christ, which we just mentioned, was very

---

7   See: Martimort, *op. cit.*, p. 268. These different texts are also reproduced by several others who studied the question: Jungmann, Cabrol, Journet, etc.

8   'The Notion of the Sacrifice of the Mass According to Theologians from the Beginning to Our Present Day.'

9   We cite this work according to its 3rd edition (Paris, Beauchesne, 1926), see pp. 4 ff.

10   *Ibid.*, pp. 37–97. It is on this point especially that the work of liturgists must be completed by theologians. See also in this regard Charles Journet, *La Messe. Présence du sacrifice de la Croix* (Coll. 'Textes et études théologique'), Paris, DDBr., 1958 (2nd ed), pp. 61 ff.

11   Perhaps there was even at first a certain decrease in the frequency of these celebrations with the progressive disappearance of the *agape* immediately after the apostolic period (cf. Duchesne, *Origines du culte Chrétien*, Paris, De Boccard, 1920, p. 50); however, this hypothesis is weak; *see below*, Chapter XI, I.

influential, even if that knowledge did not reach the degree of clarity that it would acquire over time. On the basis of this primary and fundamental reason, the first causes which would bring about the multiplication of these liturgies were: the cult of the martyrs,[12] the sanctification of certain feast days, or fast days,[13] the Mass being celebrated in Rome at different 'stations,'[14] the desire to pray for the dead, which seems to have been at the origin of the private Masses ...[15]

The frequency of the Mass—the word appeared at the end of the fourth century—remained in much flux according to the various Churches. Quite early on, it seems, the Church in Africa knew the daily Mass, as reported by St Cyprian, St Ambrose and St Augustine.[16] While in the fifth century, at Constantinople, and in general, the practice was to celebrate only on Saturdays and Sundays.[17]

With regards to the fundamental principle of one Mass, an important innovation was the introduction of the practice of celebrating two Masses, and even more if necessary, one after the other, when the Church, the 'basilica,' could not hold all the people at one time. This happened especially on big feast days. Again in the middle of the fifth century, we see Dioscorus, Bishop of Alexandria, consulting Pope St Leo on this matter and receiving a response encouraging him in this practice.[18]

---

[12]   P. Battifol, *Leçons sur la messe*, Paris, Lecoffre–Gabalda, 1941 (reprint of the 1927 edition), pp. 38–42.

[13]   *Ibid.*, pp. 37.

[14]   *Ibid.*, pp. 30–4.

[15]   *Ibid.*, pp. 42–6. In the same vein: 'At the very end of the fifth century, the law that stated that a basilica have but one altar yielded under the pressure of the devotion at the small oratories, where there was a *confessio*, that is an altar in honor of a martyr containing his relics' (p. 42). And if there had been such altars, there were obviously Masses as well. Is it an abused and condemnable 'devotion' or an instinct of the *sensus fidei* which allows the Christian people to understand the benefits that come to them, both for the deceased and for themselves, from these sacrifices and the powerful intercession of the martyrs?

[16]   *Ibid.*, p. 37. For St Ambrose, see R. Johanny, *op. cit.*, pp. 73–83.

[17]   *Ibid.*, pp. 36 ff. Elsewhere Mass was also celebrated on Wednesdays and Fridays.

[18]   St Leo, *Ep. IX, ad Dioscorum alexandrinum*, c. 2 (PL 54, 626–7).

IV. The movement towards the multiplication of Masses would know new developments through monasticism. The private Mass, in the strict sense, that is one celebrated in the absence of the faithful, 'appeared in the sixth and seventh centuries. It became an exercise of piety among monks in the eighth century.'[19] Monasticism was not priestly in its origins. It began to be so when the missions were entrusted to the monks. From this point of view the pontificate of St Gregory the Great (590–604) was decisive.[20] For its part, the increase in the number of monk-priests increased the number of Masses in the monasteries; and thus we end up with a juxtaposition of the *missae privatae* and the *missa conventualis*.[21] Later, still other factors would bring about the multiplication of Masses in the monasteries and convents: the Mass is referred to more and more as a means of salvation;[22] it is during this period that the practice of thirty Gregorian Masses is introduced;[23] there is the institution of votive Masses and foundational Masses,[24] as well as confraternities of prayer;[25] etc. We thus arrive at the multiplication of Masses by one and the same priest, on the same day, for the intention of obtaining the most graces possible. 'On one occasion Gregory of Tours celebrated, in a village near Soissons, three Masses in the same day, on three different altars, in order to purify himself from the accusation of having criminally offended Fredegonda, spouse of Chilberik I.' Morever, it is said of

---

[19] We use principally for this question the fundamental and richly documented work of Otto Nuddbaum, *Kloster, Priestermönch und Privatmesse* (Coll. 'Theophania'–14), Bonn, P. Hansstein Verl., 1961. cf. p. 136.

[20] *Ibid.*, p. 103.

[21] *Ibid.*, see Chapters VI and VII.

[22] *Ibid.*, p. 157.

[23] See, for example, the article '*Trentain grégorien*', in the *Dictionnaire practique de Liturgie Romaine*, published under the direction of Canon R. Lesage, Preface by S.E. Msgr Feltin, Archbishop of Paris (Paris, Bonne Presse, 1952), col. 1047.

[24] O. Nussbaum, *op. cit.*, p. 158.

[25] *Ibid.*, p. 162; cf. p. 167.

Pope Leo III (793–816) that he sometimes celebrated up to seven and even nine Masses a day.[26] Without going to such numbers as these, binating and trinating were not rare; and at times they were even prescribed by bishops or by particular synods.[27]

Contrary to what has sometimes been written and to what often tends to persuade others, the fundamental reason for that multiplication was not the simple 'private devotion' of priests, but, as Nussbaum shows so well (and we can insist still more on this), the profound conviction of the salvific value of the Mass and the benefits which flow from its celebration for the salvation of souls and for the Church. Therefore, in addition to their personal sanctification, it was these pastoral intentions and the Church that multiplied the celebration of Mass.

V. While the fundamental reason for this practice was valid, the practice itself was not without its danger. The abuses were easily foreseeable, and there was no lack in them. The Church set out to correct the abuses with a varied success.[28] With time however, this action would bear fruit; other factors would intervene as well: crises, wars, etc. From the exuberances of the High Middle Ages we pass progressively to the golden age of equilibrium, the 12th and 13th centuries, where the theology of the sacrifice of the Mass would assert its essential foundations in a definitive manner, especially in the work of St Thomas Aquinas.[29] This beautiful equilibrium would not last long. It was followed by the decadence of the next period, which was marked by both the obscurity of 13th century scholastic theology and the emergent decrease in the sacrifice of the Mass. *Lex credendi-lex orandi:* doctrine and worship always go together.

It is difficult to retrace with precision the stages of this decline. However, it is certain that it increased considerably during the great

---

[26] *Ibid.,* p. 175.

[27] *Ibid.*

[28] E. Magnin gathered together a whole series of these disciplinary measures (*ibid,* pp. 487 ff.).

[29] He was preceded by Peter Lombard (cf. M. Lepin, *op. cit.,* pp. 147 ff; pp. 183 ff.).

crises of the Church, beginning in the 15th century. According to E. Magnin: 'In fact, at the beginning of the 17th century, many priests, at least in France, celebrated Mass only very rarely.' It is probable that the same could be said for other countries of Europe. Nevertheless, he adds: 'At the end of the 17th century, Mass was offered more often, even out of simple devotion.'[30] This recovery is due, no doubt, to the Tridentine Reform; however, it had its limits, especially because of Jansenism. Except for pastoral necessity, daily celebration was not recommended; in fact it was even discouraged.[31] It is in the same movement that Eucharistic Communion also became rarer.

VI. The recovery, nevertheless, would end up winning. It was within the logic of the dogma defined at Trent. It would continue through the crisis of the 18th century and be expressed in the Eucharistic renewal of the late 19th century and early 20th century: the first Eucharistic Congress of 1881, a decree by Pope St Pius X on frequent Communion, the Communion of children, the frequent and even daily celebration of Mass for priests, etc. This movement would find a solemn confirmation at the Second Vatican Council, in the decree which, while not obliging, highly recommended priests to celebrate Mass daily. Without trying to retrace all the steps of this movement, we shall simply note some of its principal manifestations in what concerns the frequency of the offering of the Mass; the Council of Trent will serve as our point of departure on the dogmatic level, and we shall continue up until the new point of departure at Vatican II.

Let us note first of all that fortunate vestige of the practices of the High Middle Ages represented by the three Masses of Christmas, as well as those of the Feast of All Souls, 2 November. Granted during the middle of the 18th century to Spain and Portugal by Pope Benedict XIV (Constitution *Quod expensis,* 21–26 August 1748), the privilege was extended to the countries of Latin America by Pope Leo XIII at the end of the 19th century (Letter *Trans oceanum,* 18 April 1897),

---

[30]   *Op. cit.,* p. 484.
[31]   *Ibid.*

and to the entire Church by Pope Benedict XV at the beginning of the 20th century (Constitution *Incruentum altaris,* 10 August 1915). Even as limited as it is in its object, such a development reveals the thought of the Church. Isn't it possible for an analogous movement to take shape in what concerns not simply the lot of the faithfully departed, but the current needs of the Church Militant? The facts seem to indicate that it is.

The dogmatic point of departure for such a movement (in the strict sense of the word dogmatic) is found in the acts of the Council of Trent. On 17 September 1562, in its Session XXII, this Council solemnly taught and defined that:

> Christ ... left to His Church, His beloved spouse, a visible sacrifice, by which the bloody sacrifice, which He would accomplish once [for all] on the Cross, would be represented ... and by which its saving power would be applied for the remission of sins that we commit daily.[32]

On 20 November 1947, after and along with all his predecessors, Pius XII recalled this teaching in his great Encyclical on the liturgy, *Mediator Dei:*

> The Holy Sacrifice of the altar is therefore not a pure and simple commemoration of the sufferings and death of Jesus Christ, but a true sacrifice, in the proper sense, in which, by an unbloody immolation, the High Priest does that which He did on the Cross, in offering Himself to the Eternal Father as a most pleasing Victim.
>
> ... Now the Holy Sacrifice of the altar is the instrument par excellence by which the merits coming from the Cross of the Divine Redeemer are distributed: 'Every time that the memory

---

[32] (Chapter 1). The will of the Council of Trent to define the faith in this chapter has been demonstrated by I. A. de Aldama, *De Sanctissima Eucharistia,* in *Sacrae theologiae Summa* (Madrid, BAC, 1962 (4th ed.)). p. 228. This is why we can speak of a 'dogmatic' point of departure in the strict sense of the word.

of this Sacrifice is celebrated, the work of our Redemption is wrought.'[33]

It can be said that Paul VI and Vatican II only drew, or rather recalled, the practical consequences of this doctrine when, in basing themselves explicitly on it, they invited priests to celebrate Mass daily.

On 3 September 1965, in his Encyclical *Mysterium fidei,* Paul VI stated the following:

> The Mass, even if it is celebrated individually by one priest, is not therefore private, but it is the action of Christ and of the Church. This latter has learned to offer itself, in the sacrifice which it offers, in a universal sacrifice, applying to the salvation of the entire world the redemptive, unique and infinite power of the sacrifice of the Cross. Every Mass is, in fact, offered not only for the salvation of some individuals, but for the salvation of the entire world ... *This is why* We recommend with a paternal insistence that priests, who in a special way are Our joy and crown in the Lord, celebrate the Mass each day, with all dignity and devotion.[34]

On 6 December of that same year, citing in a footnote these words of Paul VI, the Council solemnly continued the exhortation, in its *Decree on the Ministry and Life of Priests:*

> In the mystery of the Eucharistic sacrifice, where priests exercise their special function, it is the work of our Redemtpion which is unceasingly accomplished (cf. *Missale Romanum,* Secret from the Ninth Sunday after Pentecost). *This is why* they are highly recommended to celebrate the Mass every day; even if the Christian faithful cannot be present, it is an act of Christ and of the Church.[35]

---

[33] In *AAS* 39, 1947, pp. 548; 552. On the value of the sacrifice of the Mass, one can read as well, among so many other magisterial texts, the very beautiful Encyclical of Leo XIII, *Mirae caritatis*, of 8 May 1902.

[34] *Ibid.,* 57, 1965, pp. 761–2.

[35] *Presbyterorum Ordinis,* 13. Here, as in the preceding citation, the italics are ours. It is after this last sentence that the Council cites the preceding text of

There are innumerable documents of the recent Magisterium in the same vein which one can cite. We shall limit ourselves to those already quoted, for obvious reasons of brevity and because of their authority. It seems important to note the bond between principle and conse-quence which binds the first two citations to the latter two. The '*this is why*' which is found there, and which we italicized, bears witness to that bond: the first and fundamental reason—and even the only reason in these texts—which moved the supreme Magisterium of the Church to 'recommend' that priests celebrate Mass daily is neither their personal 'devotion' (as important as that it is) nor the particular need of a given individual or community, but the common good and fundamental need of the salvation of the Church and the entire world. From that point of view a remark of extreme importance forces itself upon us: While it is true that priests who concelebrate every day might conform themselves to these lofty recommendations in what concerns their personal devotion (private or communitarian), yet they do not correspond to the intention explicitly formulated. In fact, by concel-ebrating, they certainly do celebrate Mass every day; however, they offer to God, along with the other concelebrants, only one Mass. In such a way they prevent the Church from attaining the goal which it had fixed for them by her exhortations: namely the multiplication of the outpouring of the redemptive fruits upon the world by means of the multiplication of the celebration of the Mass. As one can see, it is this multiplication of Masses that was requested by Vatican II; and the only way to bring it about is not by encouraging the systematic extension of concelebration, but rather the traditional practice of private Masses. This is the way taken by the Church. After having adopted the 'daily' practice of Mass for communities, the Church then encouraged the same frequency on the part of each priest for the common good of the larger Catholic community, which the Church is.

Paul VI.

This rather brief historical study allows one to see how the dogma of the Eucharistic sacrifice, and the practice which flows from it, represent an eminent case of homogenous (and parallel) evolution of both doctrine and liturgy. It also allows us to conclude, once again, that the decrease in Masses which took place after the Second Vatican Council, especially by the multiplication of almost unlimited concelebration, far from being in continuity with the teaching and prescriptions of the Council, is actually contrary to, and a rupture with the Council. This is not surprising. In fact, it often happens in the Church's history that the evils that precede a Council continue and even become worse for a certain amount of time afterwards. One recalls, for example, how Arianism developed all throughout the 4th century, despite the definitions and condemnations of the Council of Nicea in 325. It must also be mentioned that not all the Councils have had the same firmness in their measures to combat error. We can think of the Fifth Lateran Council (1512–1517), convoked for the reform of the Church. The same year in which it ended the great Protestant break publicly manifested itself at Wittenberg, from which the Church still suffers today. It was only with the Council of Trent that the Church was able to provide the means to face the Protestant break. We have seen then that a certain amount of time is always needed, and sometimes even several councils, for the Church to triumph over the errors which oppose her. We have shown in the preceding chapters that it was well before Vatican II that was born the movement which tends not only towards a legitimate return to, but towards an unlimited extension of concelebration and, by this, to a decrease in Masses—this latter being not the sole dreadful consequence, but the principal consequence of that innovation. It is therefore to that movement, and not to the Council itself, that is attached the current practice of concelebration. We are speaking here not of what is traditional and legitimate in the current practice, but what is an innovation in the history of the Church, and even, in our opinion, an abuse.[36]

---

[36] The case of the Oriental Rites cannot be cited here as in opposition. It is true

VII.—This is why we believe that we are simply stating a fact and recalling an undisputable truth when we affirm that the *Church asks for the multiplication of Masses.* She asks for it by way of her Tradition, by way of her hierarchy, by way of her faithful; and the immense needs which she must confront today impose this multiplication with all the more urgency. In order to illustrate this last point, let us recall some examples of what had been done in this regard during the pontificates of Pius XI and Pius XII. Moving backwards in time we shall begin with Pius XII.

1) On 21 April 1957, in his Encyclical *Fidei donum,* he asked, among other things, that Masses be celebrated for the intention of the missions:

> The most excellent of prayers is that which Christ Jesus, the High Priest, addresses each day to God the Father on the altars, when the holy sacrifice of redemption is renewed. Accordingly, let many Masses be offered for the sacred missions, especially in this our time on which the future growth of the Church in many areas is perhaps dependent. This is in accordance with the prayers of our Lord Who loves His Church and wishes her to flourish and to enlarge her borders throughout the whole world.[37]

---

that Benedict XIV, by his Bull *Allatae sunt* (27 July 1755), prescribed Latin missionaries to allow Greek Catholics to concelebrate—not without clarifying that they must pronounce the words of consecration; but one would be wrong to see there evidence of a movement towards an extension of celebrating in such a way. All that can possibly be affirmed, beginning with this intervention and that of 24 December 1743 (Bull *Demandatum*) of the same Pope, is that the Church of Rome intended to respect a practice which it recognized in the Greek liturgical tradition, and not without improving it. And this because, by asking the concelebrants to pronounce the words of consecration, it moved those concelebrations from the status of simply ceremonial to truly sacramental.

[37] *AAS* 49, 1957, pp. 239 ff.

We see that Pius XII bases his request on the very intention of Christ. Commenting on this text in a missionary journal, 'Abbé' Journet (as he was often called even after becoming cardinal) correctly wrote: 'If at each Mass Christ accomplishes the work of our redemption, we see the necessity of multiplying Masses at this crucial time, when entire continents such as Africa are awaking to the conditions of the modern world and are required to opt *en masse* either for or against Christ.'[38]

2) 'On the occasion of the 40th anniversary of the apparitions of Fatima and the episcopal consecration of Pius XII, 13 May 1957, a rosary of Masses (i.e. 40 Masses) was celebrated in the sanctuary of Fatima for the Holy Father's intention.'[39]

3) With a motu proprio, *Norunt profecto* (27 October 1940), the same pontiff recalled the value of the Mass, and he asked that a Mass be celebrated for peace. This was at the beginning of WWII. After the war, in 1952, he continued to say Masses each day at St Peter's in Rome for peace in the world.[40] Are they still celebrated today?

4) It is in this context that is situated the document of the 1953 Assembly of Cardinals and Archbishops of France. Let us mention a few of the more significant passages of this document. Speaking of priests who 'on the occasion of certain meetings easily omit the celebration of their private Mass in order to assist at the Mass of one sole celebrant and to communicate visibly,' (which was called at the time 'the communitarian Mass') the bishops of France recognized that:

> Their intention (was) thus to perform a gesture of unity and to present more clearly before the eyes of all the intimate union

---

[38] *Op. cit.*, p. 334. This commentary was first written for the journal *Les missions catholiques* (Paris, January–March, 1958, pp. 52–5).

[39] T. Videira, OP, *Pio XII e Fatima*, Fatima, Ed. 'Verdade e Vida', 1957, p. 3.

[40] We have for this the particularly qualified witness (because of his duties in Rome) of P. Garrigou–Lagrange, OP, in his report to the International Eucharistic Congress of 1952: *La valeur infinie du sacrifice de la messe et la célébration quotidienne des messes pour la pacification du monde* (in XXXV *Congresso Eucaristico Internacional* — 1952 — *La Eucaristia y la Paz*, Barcelona (s.d.), vol. I, p 38).

between the community offering the Holy Sacrifice and the consecrating priest.

While recognizing also that such a practice cannot be formally condemned, since the priests do not have the strict obligation to celebrate every day, the bishops note the inconveniences and dangers which it causes, especially:

> ... of diminishing among them (i.e. the faithful), and perhaps even among certain priests, the just esteem for the value of private Masses. This consequence will be all the more regrettable as *it appears, on the contrary, opportune* to reinforce the faithful's sentiments of faith in the infinite value of the Holy Sacrifice and *to multiply the number of Masses rather than voluntarily diminish it.* This practice ... is to be *reprimanded* and *reproved* if it is based on *the false idea* that the omission of a Mass is of little importance and that *one collective gesture of unity is better than the offering of several private Masses.*[41]

5) However, it is especially the document entitled *Triduum final du Jubilé de la Rédemption,* from 1953 that we wish to look at. It can be found in numbers 746 and 749 of '*La Documentation Catholique,*' of 20 April and 11 May 1935, special numbers dedicated to that extraordinary event. Ideally some of these texts, official documents or reports of ceremonies, would be cited in their entirety. We shall try at least, by means of some brief citations, to give an idea of what happened at Lourdes that year, from 25 April to 28 April. Here is how Pius XI presented it in his letter dated 10 January 1935, to Msgr Gerlier, then Bishop of Lourdes:

> Indeed, We cannot keep Ourselves from praising unreservedly the plan which you have embraced with such enthusiasm and generosity, at the suggestion of Our dear sons, François,

---

[41]   *La Doc. Cath.,* no. 1147, of 17 May 1953, col. 586. The italics are ours, except for the words 'reprimanded' and 'reproved'. See on this 'note' the remarks we made in our preceding work (*LPC,* no. 185, p. 35, note 70; *see above,* Ch. III, note 75).

Cardinal Bourne (whose recent death we mourn) and Jean, Cardinal Verdier, Archbishop of Paris, namely of celebrating at Lourdes, during this upcoming April, at the miraculous Grotto of the Immaculate Virgin, a Triduum of public prayers, such that, during the three days and three nights which would complete the Jubilee of Human Redemption extended to the entire Catholic world, Eucharistic sacrifices will be offered in that place continually and without interruption.

In fact, could these centenary solemnities come to a more fitting and worthier close than by such a crowning achievement? While so great benefits flow from the most holy work of our Redemption, nevertheless, the divine Eucharist, which is the wonderful center of the Christian life as well as its supreme raison d'être, and by it the sacrifice of Calvary, perpetuated in an unbloody manner—these two constitute not only the greatest treasure that can be conceived by the human imagination, but also that can even seem to throng upon the infinite power of God and to exhaust His infinite mercy.

It is, therefore, towards the august Sacrament of the altar that Christians must direct their thoughts and their piety in this 19th centenary of the reception of such a grace: that they might wash their stains in the torrents of grace which flow from it; that they might expiate their faults; that they might confess and leave behind their trials and difficulties, with which they are oppressed, with Him Who alone can satisfy them, heal them and raise them up to heaven …

Now, today more than ever, there is a need for prayers to solicit that divine aid of which all people, all nations, the entire community of men and countries have such a pressing need. The evils which presently afflict us are of such a weight and such a seriousness, that they seem to leave us no relief; and those which We fear for the future place our hearts in restlessness and anxiety. However, deplorable most of all is the return in many places of pagan practices and doctrines opposed to the heavenly teaching given us by Jesus Christ. Yet ought not punishment to intervene where the stubborn pride of man exists? By rejecting God and His law, by neglecting His help, no remedy is sufficient for the immensity of these evils, on account of which We feel a great suffering in our paternal heart.

Pius XI makes an allusion here to the general de-christianization, but more particularly to the two systems which he would explicitly condemn two years later, on 14 and 19 March 1937, namely Nazism and Communism (by the Encyclicals *Mit brennender Sorge* and *Divini Redemptoris*). He saw already at that time that which would lead to the Second World War. But did he not slow it down? Did he not diminish the cruelty by the remedy he then prescribed, namely the triduum of prayers and Masses at the grotto of Massabielle? He saw there a very specific realization of the prophecy of Malachi, thus giving him a scriptural foundation:

> 'From the East to the West My Name is great among the Gentiles, and in every place a pure oblation is sanctified and offered to the glory of My Name' (Mal. 1:11). While this oracle is now realized daily throughout all the earth, by night and by day, nevertheless We have confidence that, during this period of our blessed days, it will be still more verified, burning with charity.[42]

Commenting on this letter to the priests of his diocese, Msgr Gerlier proclaimed to them in advance:

> ... the uninterrupted celebration of those 140 Masses which, from Thursday, April 25, at 4:00 PM, to Sunday, 28 April, 4:00 PM, will be offered on the altar of the grotto by bishops and priests representing all the nations of the world—a radiant series in which, each day, at three o'clock in the afternoon, a pontifical Mass will mark in a special way the hour of the Savior Jesus' death on the cross—... Lourdes will become, in one solemn moment, perhaps more than one has ever seen, the center of the world's prayer.[43]

---

[42]   Pius XI, Letter *Quod tam alacri*, 10 January 1935, cited in *La Doc. Cath.*, no. 746, 20 April 1935, cols. 965–70.

Two countries would associate themselves to that triduum of Masses in a special way: Italy, in the Diocese of St Ambrose, and Chile, a country consecrated to Our Lady of Mount Carmel. In fact, being the great Archbishop of Milan that Cardinal Schuster was, he obtained from Pius XII the privilege of celebrating the sacrifice of the Mass without interruption during those three days, not in the same place however, but in 72 principal Marian sanctuaries of his diocese.[44] On the other hand, but similar to Lourdes, the bishops of Chile obtained from the Holy Father the authorization to celebrate their Masses without interruption and in the same place. This place was a grotto of Lourdes attached to a sanctuary dedicated to Mary, located near Santiago, Chile's capital.[45]

In addition to these two privileged cases, proved by the *Acts* collected by *La Documentation Catholique,* it is the entire Church which intensely associates herself with this solemn closing, both Marian and Eucharistic, of the Jubilee of Redemption. These acts must be read again in order to get an idea of just what that event then meant. And only by seeing it in the eternity of the divine essence will we be able to measure just how much the whole human race even today owes to that event.

An idea immediately comes to mind while recalling those historical facts and while considering the evils that threaten more than ever before both the Church and the world.[46] And the idea is this: Why

---

[43]   *Bulletin religieux de Tarbes et Lourdes,* 25.1.1935 (cit. *ibid,* col. 972).

[44]   *Ibid.,* cols. 1012–14.

[45]   *Ibid.,* col. 1023.

[46]   We can still recall those dramatic words proclaimed by Pope John Paul II in his Homily of 1 January 1980: 'Between fifty and two hundred million dead, a devastating lack of nutrition, genetic mutations, the change in the ozone, etc.' This homily was given in the Basilica of St Peter, Rome, during the Mass for Peace. According to the writer of *L'Osservatore Romano* (2–3 January, p. col. 4), the Pope even spoke of the 'apocalypse'. No less revealing is his Homily of 31 December of the same year, at the Church of the Gesù, on the theme of 'the last hour' (1 Jn 2:18; cf. *ibid,* p. 2).

not have such an event again? Is that not what the Portuguese did with their 'rosary of Masses' on 13 May 1957? And why shouldn't the International Eucharistic Congress, which is to be held in London in 1981, not do the same?[47] Would such a triduum be any more difficult to bring about now than in 1935? And who would dare say that it is less fitting now than back then?

And where are the Masses for the missions requested by the Encyclical *Fidei donum?* Where is the daily Mass for peace? When we consider how threatened peace is today, we see that it is rather a perpetual Mass for peace that is needed. And if one wishes to get a better idea of that threat, one must recall that the ultimate cause of war is not found in the power of arms pointed at each other, nor in the inequalities of political, military or economic dealings, but in the sin and offense made to God by a humanity which rejects Him.

For, such indeed are the perspectives which give the raison d'être to these present reflections. While awaiting the decisions that our reflections call for, and in our desire to prepare them, we do not believe that we are forcing the conclusions of this study by saying that *the Church, today more than ever, asks for the multiplication of Masses;* and we believe that this request, despite the current errors or gropings, is first of all the request of the Council itself. Looking back in time, one will perhaps judge the current hyper-increase of concelebration as we today judge the unregulated proliferation of private Masses in the Middle Ages. One will see a temporary excess, the fruit of an intoxication produced by the joy of a discovery, or a rediscovery, of an essential aspect of the liturgical mystery of the Eucharist. At the very least, one will see here the fulfillment of Dom Gueranger's prophecies about what he called 'the anti-liturgical sect's efforts to obtain if not the total suppression of, then at least the greatest possible decrease in the number of Masses.[48] The continuity which can be

---

[47]   Note that the original French text of this chapter dates from 1980 [Translator].

[48]   Dom Guéranger, *Institutions liturgiques,* vol. II (Le Mans–Paris, 1841), pp. 607 ff.

observed between the errors of Protestantism, those of the Synod of Pistoia—apropos of which that great pioneer of liturgical renewal of the 19th and 20th centuries made that prophetic observation—and the errors of today, give a particular weight to seeing things in such a way. We saw in the preceding chapter the errors of Protestantism. Here is what Dom Gueranger wrote regarding the Synod of Pistoia:

> However, in order to return to the divine sacrifice, see with what affection one repeats this truth incontestable in itself, but which is so easily abused during this period of disguised Calvinism, that the people offer with the priest, ... However, that is still not enough for the sect. It can insult the Catholic sacrifice, but it cannot abolish it. Henceforth, all its skill would tend to render its celebration more rare ... Later, supported in its audacity by Joseph II and Leopold [Duke of Tuscany, where the town of Pistoia is located], it would be seen forbidding the simultaneous celebration of Masses in the same church; it would even go so far as to reduce the number of altars to one. Enlightened by the prescriptions of Ricci [Bishop of Pistoia], it would find a new means of restraining still more the offering of that sacrifice which is so odious to it: this would be by reestablishing the practice of the early Church, according to which the priests of one church concelebrated at one sole Mass. With regard to the regulars, they would even be forced, tolerating only one or two priests in each monastery ...[49]

---

[49] *Ibid.* In *Mediator Dei*, Pius XII condemned the opinion of those who 'assert that priests cannot offer at the same time the divine Victim on several altars because in such a way they divide the community and put its unity in danger' (*AAS* 39, 1947, p. 556). With respect to concelebration of the first centuries, two things are certain: 1) that the fundamental principle which regulated the celebration of the liturgy in those early years was in no way that of concelebration such as we now understand it, but rather that of the unity of the Eucharist and of the priest celebrant, the mediator between God and men; 2) that the members of the presbyterate who, with time, would gather around the celebrant, the bishop, did not concelebrate in the sacramental and sacrificial sense, since they did not pronounce the words of consecration (cf. DS 3928).

Faced with these errors, it is necessary to recall that the Mass is inseparably both the hierarchical gathering of the Christian people around its Pastor and the sacrifice of Redemption renewed, or re-acted, in the mystery of the sacrament. It is in the simultaneous appeal to both these principles that, in order to respond to the needs of our times, the Church will find the just norm, which regulates in a harmonious manner both the practice of celebration by one priest alone at the altar and that of solemn concelebration. This norm will be fixed, in a more specific way, in view of responding appropriately to the two following objectives: the manifestation of the hierarchical unity of the priesthood (promoted by concelebration), and the giving to the world the greatest fruits of Redemption possible (fostered by the multiplication of Masses). Both objectives are clearly proposed by the Council, but in a hierarchical order of values, permitting one to see which one it insists on more, namely the second.[50] As the cardinals and archbishops of France recalled in 1953, one cannot (except in particular cases) prefer a collective sign of unity to the multiplication of the sacrifice of the Mass. The practical question of regulation has to do with the norm that would determine the particular occasions where such a sign is to be preferred, concelebration being henceforth the mode under which such a sign is given. We saw above that this norm had not been very clearly fixed by the Council. For this reason there arose differences in interpretation which followed it; and the maximalist tendency profited from this confusion by quickly imposing itself.

This being the case, that tendency would end up going against the explicit directives of the Council, especially the directive, established only after a great struggle, which required 'the permission of the Ordinary' for those cases where concelebration was possible, as well as those explicitly contained in the exhortations given to priests by

---

[50] Concelebration 'fittingly manifests the unity of the priesthood' (*Const. On the Liturgy*, 57): it is a question here of a 'hierarchical' unity (*Decree on the Ministry and Life of Priests*, 7). We noted above the Council's insistence on the multiplication of Masses by the priests' daily celebration.

the Decree on their ministry and life. As we saw above, those exhortations to celebrate daily take their true meaning from the motive on which they are immediately founded: in each Mass 'the work of our redemption is accomplished.' Because of these two reasons, which seem to be the principal reasons, and because of their perfect harmony with the progressive development of the Church's Eucharistic doctrine and practice, it cannot be said that the Council left us without any directives regarding the practice of concelebration. If it unfortunately did not give sufficiently precise norms, it did at least indicate in what sense they were to be established.

We are aware of the argument that is used to oppose this interpretation: namely the practice which was introduced after the Council. However, we respond to this argument with our own arguments, which are greater: that that practice cannot pretend to be founded on the same texts of the Council; that it takes up a practice categorically reproved by the Church's supreme Magisterium, which the schismatic Synod of Pistoia imposed and which was solemnly condemned by Pius VI;[51] finally, that it goes against the movement towards the multiplication of Masses, which flows from the entire homogenous development of dogma and the Eucharistic liturgy. On the other hand, the interpretation which we propose is in full conformity with this Tradition as well as the most certain texts of Vatican II. This is why, while maintaining our interpretation, we know we are working most certainly in the way indicated by John Paul II to his cardinals during the 'Plenary Reunion of the Sacred College' of 5 November 1979:

> The Church, insofar as it is a living community of the sons of God united in truth and love, must work today with all its strength *to enter on the right way of bringing to realization the Second Vatican Council* and to separate itself from opposing opinions, by which it seems that each one, in his own manner, deviates from that way.

---

[51] See the texts which support this assertion in *LPC*, no. 184, p. 37; *see above,* Ch. II.

The italics in the text are found in the original, which reveals something of the mind of the Holy Father. Just before this he had denounced those innovations in the Christian life which were 'without foundation in the "integral" doctrine of the Council.' At the same time he gave the criteria to be followed in order to enter into 'the right way' of its realization, by clarifying what is meant by the expression 'integral doctrine of the Council': '"integral doctrine" means, to be understood in the light of the sacred Tradition and with constant reference to the Magisterium of the Church.'[52]

This is exactly the sense of the reflection which we present here, and which we submit to the same Magisterium, to whom it belongs to judge it and to draw the practical conclusions which flow from it, and which urgently appeals to the immense needs of our time. However, in order to establish these practical conclusions on an even more certain foundation, while not excluding new ways to assure multiplication of Masses and even the perpetuity of the Eucharistic sacrifice in certain places or on certain occasions, it would be good to reconsider and try to develop its theology. This is what we shall do now by looking first at the dogmatic data from the Council of Trent, developing it in the light of later theological reflections, these latter being accepted only in the light of the Church's doctrine. We shall then consider again the second request from the Sacred Congregation of Rites on the eve of the Council, namely that before every practical decision be made regarding the use of concelebration, according to historical research, a theological study also be made.[53]

---

[52]   *'Ecclesia proinde—ut viva communitas Dei filiorum in veritate et caritate coniunctorum—magnopere debet his diebus contendere, ut ingrediatur rectam viam exsequendi Concilii Vaticani Secundi et se eodem tempore seiungat ab oppositis sententiis, quarum unaquaeque suo modo exhibetur velut recessio ab illa via recta."'In "integra" videlicet doctrina quatenus, intelligitur sub sanctae Traditionis lumine et quatenus ad constans Ecclesiae ipsius magisterium refertur'* (*Discourse* of 5 November 1979, no. 6; in *AAS* 71, 1979, 1452).

[53]   Ch. VI.

Part Three

Theological Reflection

9 SACRIFICIUM MISSAE

D URING THE ANTE-PREPARATORY phase of the Council, the Sacred Congregation of Rites (since become the Sacred Congregation for Divine Worship) asked, 'that a new and meticulous investigation be made, both liturgical and dogmatic, on the origin, nature and extension of properly sacramental concelebration.'[1] Our preceding studies allowed us to maintain that there has never really been a response to that request. Moreover, it has been noticed that the elements of the historical research that had been gathered were poorly used and that the dogmatic reflection had never been seriously made. Whence the persisting incertitude, not only in those two areas, but also regarding the practical question of the extension given to this new rite—new with respect to its quasi-unlimited use, whereby it has deviated from the traditional discipline of the Latin Church, and even from the Eastern Churches as well, except for a few exceptional cases.

It was for the sake of clarifying those questions that we contributed the preceding studies. After having posited 'the question' of concelebration in general (which we did in the first part—beginning with the specific but central question of the number of Masses), we then

---

[1]   *Acta et Documenta Concilio Oecumenico Vaticano II Apparendo*, I–III, p. 258 (cf. *LPC*, no. 188, p. 23; *see above*, Ch. VI). We reproduce here, with some minor modifications, the text of a conference given in Rome on 2 October 1974 to the International Congress 'Chiesa Viva', '*Orthodoxy and Orthoproxy*'. The French translation appeared in *LPC*, no. 153 (November–December 1974), pp. 7–28. We offer a summary of it, and add certain developments on the Council of Trent, taken from studies published the same year in *Divinitas* (Rome): *L'Eucharistie, Sacrement et Sacrifice du Christ et de l'Eglise. Développements des perspectives thomistes* (18 (1974/2) pp. 234–86; (1974/3) pp. 396–436). See also our work *Note sur le sacrifice de la Messe selon Jacques Maritain et sur 'L'âme du Saint Sacrifice de la Messe' d'après de Père Garrigou–Lagrange* (*Divinitas* 19 (1975/1) pp. 61–78).

looked at the historical research (in our second part), presenting, without avoiding any significant testimony, the documents already collected by researchers and adding what concerns the recent past, namely the history of the Second Vatican Council and the period immediately after it. We also proposed the solution for several theological problems, like that of the number of Masses offered to God in a concelebration, or that of the essential (and not merely accidental) distinction between sacramental and purely ceremonial concelebration. However, there are other aspects which are also to be considered, which can openly appear in view of the whole. In order to complete this work, therefore, we must undertake a theological reflection on the whole of the Eucharistic mystery and liturgy. It is only with this study that we will be able to respond to the request made by the Sacred Congregation of Rites, that is, by saying that 'the nature ... of properly sacramental concelebration' is the only way of clarifying its meaning and value in relation to individual celebration (that is, by one priest at the altar). It is very evident, in fact, that all these questions must first be brought to light, if we wish to establish with certitude practical norms regulating the use of concelebration.

The first thing that theology must do here is to say what exactly is 'the nature' of the Mass; for, the problem of concelebration is but a particular case of the celebration of the Mass in general. And the first voice to be heard in looking for the response to the question is that of the Church, expressed through her Tradition and Magisterium. Now, historically, it is at the Council of Trent that she formulated her faith on this point. Trent is the great Council of justification and of the means by which grace is given to us, namely the sacraments. That response is the following: the Mass is a sacrifice, or more exactly, it is the same sacrifice of the Cross.

The Council did not treat with the same clarity the question of 'how' the Mass is this sacrifice of the Cross. The Tridentine texts nevertheless are not without very clear guidelines for responding to this new question. It is true that the texts did not explicitly treat it, such that, while the defined faith in the dogma makes us hold and profess *that* the Mass *is* a sacrifice, that same faith still remains in search of a definitive explanation on the *how* of that sacrifice; the multiplicity of theories elaborated since the Council of Trent on this topic are proof. It is not that this explanation needs to be invented. It does exist, and it goes back as far as St Augustine at least, according to the tradition in which it has come to us. What is still lacking is the final elaboration which would allow it to be imposed on all in such a way as to become if not a dogma of the faith, then at least a common doctrine among Catholic theologians.

For, for theology, the fact that the dogma is defined is in no way a reason to consider its work complete. Their common object remains the mystery and even, in the case of the Eucharist, the 'Mystery of Faith' par excellence. While the Magisterium, in definitively fixing the faith of the Church in its object and in its expression, responds once and for all to certain questions and at the same time dismisses the corresponding cases (which cannot be but signs of regression, and not the source of true progress in the knowledge of the faith)—while the Magisterium does all this, it does not cease to penetrate the mystery ever more profoundly. On the contrary the Magisterium stimulates the faith, pointing out in an infallible manner the sense in which that faith must be directed.

Such it is in the particular case of the Eucharist, and more especially still in that of the sacrifice of the Mass. This expression, we repeat, is to be retained, since it is the one used by the Council of Trent in its twenty second Session, and since it is a term going back to at least the end of the fourth century[2]: fifteen centuries of Tradition and one solemn dogmatic definition, not to mention the innumerable other magisterial texts, are more than sufficient reason for continuing to speak of 'the Mass' with regards to the celebration of the sacrament of the Eucharist, and for continuing to speak of it as the offering and

---

[2]   A. G. Martimort, *L'Eglise en prière. Introduction à la liturgie*, Paris–Tournai, Desclée, 1961, p. 254.

immolation of the same sacrifice of Christ in and by His Church. It is completely remarkable to see that the definition of the Mass as a sacrifice had been made well before the theological explanation of the *how* of this sacrifice attained a degree of maturity capable of winning over supporters. This ought not surprise us if we remember that the charism of the apostolate, which the Magisterium has inherited, is prior to that of the explanation of the teacher (1 Cor 12:28); it is the mediation of the Church at work in the transmission of the Revelation which is thus given to us for contemplation.

If then the authorized word of the pastors, answerable to the apostolic Magisterium, suffices for pronouncing the faith, this same faith nevertheless does not cease to work, not in order to call into question what the Church believes, but to seek to penetrate it always more in order to enlighten the minds of those who profess the truth of faith, to show the strong foundation of their position, and to avoid as much as possible the intellectual obstacles which can hinder others.

I. The Teaching of the Council of Trent

These preliminary points having placed our reflection in context, we shall now try to show how the Mass is a sacrifice, since the Church supports us here and would have us confess that it in fact is a sacrifice. In order to do this, let us remember the essentials of what the Church teaches us on this matter and what is found in the twenty second Session of the Council of Trent. For, while it is true that, in this key text, the Church defined[3] the fact and not the mode of the sacrifice of the Mass, she nevertheless gave us, regarding that mode, a teaching that goes much further. It is principally in the first chapter of this Session that one finds it, and the essence is contained in the following passage, which we have transcribed by dividing it for the sake of easy analysis (this is the second and third phase of the chapter):

---

[3]   The desire of the Council to define in this chapter is demonstrated by I.A. De Aldama, *De Sanctissima Eucharistia*, in *Sacrae Theologiae Summa*, Madrid, BAC, 1962 (4th edition), p. 228.

1) Christ Who 'was to offer Himself (*oblaturus erat*) to His Father by His Death, once and for all on the altar of the Cross (Heb. 7:24–27)' for our redemption;

2) desiring nevertheless that 'His priesthood [the oblation of which is the essential work] not cease with His own Death';

3) 'left to His Church, His beloved Spouse, *a visible sacrifice*, by which the bloody sacrifice accomplished once [for all] on the Cross would *be represented (visibile ... sacrificium, quo cruentum illud semel in cruce peragendum repraesentaretur)*, by which the *memory* of that same sacrifice would remain until the end of the ages, and by which its salutary power would be applied for the remission of sins which we commit daily';

4) and in order to accomplish this, 'during the Last Supper, the night He was betrayed';

5) 'declaring that He was made a priest forever according to the order of Melchizedek';

6) 'He *offered* to God the Father His Body and Blood under the species of bread and wine';

7) 'and He gave them to the Apostles (whom He then made priests of the New Testament) to be eaten under the symbols of bread and wine';

8) 'and He commanded them, both them and their successors in the priesthood, to *offer* them with these words: 'Do this in memory of Me' (Lk 22:19; 1 Cor 11:24)';

9) 'thus the Catholic Church has always understood it and taught it.'

10) 'For (*Nam*) [Christ] having celebrated the ancient Pasch, which the multitude of the sons of Israel *immolated in memory* of the exodus from Egypt';

11) 'instituted a new Pasch';

12) '[namely] He Himself *would be immolated under visible signs*
by the Church, by the priests (*se ipsum ab Ecclesia per
sacerdotes sub signis visibilibus immolandum*)';

13) 'in memory of His passing from this world to His Father,
when, by the effusion of His Blood, 'He redeemed us, saving
us from the power of darkness and transferring us into His
kingdom' (Col 1:13).'

The second chapter will go on to explain this teaching, affirming that
'in the divine sacrifice which is accomplished at Mass,' the offering
and the Victim are the same as in the sacrifice of the Cross, namely
Christ, 'only the manner of the offering being different' (*sola offerendi
ratione diversa*). The teaching of the Council, which simply takes up
and canonizes the teaching of Tradition (no. 9), is contained in its
essentials in the two phrases which we just related, the second (nos.
10 to 13) being the complement of the first (nos. 1 to 9). This is
indicated by the conjunction '*Nam*,' which connects the two. This is
important for understanding the weight of the terms used, especially
in what concerns the offering and immolation. We shall try then to
analyze them in order to bring out in a more particular manner what
concerns the *how* of the sacrifice of the Mass.

The first thing to be brought out, if not the first to be noticed, is the
historical character of these two phrases, as of the whole chapter. They
are presented as an account of what our Lord did at the Last Supper.
The double relation of the Last Supper to the Cross on one hand, and
to the Mass on the other hand, is thus clearly marked out; and it is this
which allows us to understand how the Mass, like the Last Supper, is a
sacrifice. For, if the Mass is 'a visible sacrifice,' which is explicitly
affirmed (no. 3), it is necessary that the Last Supper be one as well,
since the Mass reproduces the rite instituted at the Last Supper.

It is its relation to the Cross that shows how the Last Supper was
a sacrifice. Now this relationship is clearly indicated by the historical
unfolding of events: Christ, at the moment of its institution, was on
the point of offering Himself to His Father on the Cross (no. 1); it

was 'the night He was betrayed' (no. 4); and this offering which He would accomplish on the Cross (no. 3), He did in the rite which He instituted, since under the signs of bread and wine it was already His Body and Blood which He offered to His Father (no. 6). The connection between these two parts of the phrase (nos. 1 and 6) shows that the term 'offering' designates here also the totality of the redemptive sacrifice. Whence we must conclude that the Last Supper was a sacrifice by its ordination to the Cross: it was already, in the sign, the same offering which would be made to the Father on Calvary.

With respect to the mode of this sacrificial offering in the sacramental sign, it is also indicated that the sign *represents* the bloody sacrifice to be accomplished; *the Last Supper is that sacrifice by representing it in view of its accomplishment.*

The second phrase confirms that the offering made at the Last Supper had been a sacrifice. It presents the Last Supper, in fact, as an immolation by recalling that it had been made in to order to substitute the New Pasch for the old. Now the Pasch takes place through the immolation of the victim, a fact that is explicitly recalled (no. 10). Therefore, it is a true immolation that takes place, ritually, in the action of Christ accomplished at the Last Supper 'under visible signs' (no. 12)—in view of the renewal of this act by the Church, no doubt, but also in immediate view of the effective and bloody immolation, which would take place immediately afterwards on the Cross. This is what had been said at the beginning of the first phrase (no. 1), this latter being its complement. Such is the immediate relation between the Last Supper and the Cross: insofar as it was a sacramental sign, it truly accomplished by way of representation what would be effectively realized on Calvary; and it accomplishes it 'symbolically' in view of this effective accomplishment. This effective orientation to the realization in the life, death and resurrection is the essence of sacramental symbolism.

The ordination of the Last Supper to the Mass is even more strongly brought out. It is even declared explicitly: at the Last Supper Christ instituted a rite in view of its renewal by the Church (nos. 3 to

6). Thus it is that, after Himself having been immolated 'on the altar of the Cross' (no. 1) 'by the pouring out of His Blood' (no. 13), He continues to be immolated 'by the Church, by the priests, under the visible signs of bread and wine,' in the rite instituted by Him, and accomplished 'in memory' of His passing to the Father (no. 13).

If therefore the rite of the Mass reproduces that of the Last Supper, one sees that, like the latter, it is only by its reference to the sacrifice of the Cross that it is itself a sacrifice, both an offering and an immolation. By this we see again that the Mass is not the simple repetition of what happened at the Last Supper. On one hand, Christ no longer acts alone, but rather 'by the Church, by the priests' (no. 12); and most of all, between these two events the bloody sacrifice of the Cross had taken place, to which both the Last Supper and the Mass, insofar as they are sacramental signs, have an essential reference. This is why, while the reference to the Cross is always essential, at the Last Supper the representation was a prefiguration, and at the Mass it is a true commemoration. And just as the Last Supper was ordered to the Mass insofar as it was the institution of the sign, so it can be said that it was a sacramental representation in anticipation of the sacrifice of the Cross. And the very purpose of the Last Supper was to leave to the Church the sacrament of this sacrifice, but also to take up the Church unto itself—assuming into the Pascal sacrifice of Calvary the totality of the Mystical Body. This last statement, however, goes beyond what can be drawn from this chapter of the Council of Trent.

These explanations allow us to understand how the double relation of the Last Supper to the Cross and the Last Supper to the Mass implies no contradiction. Moreover, it also allows us to understand the corresponding double relation according to which the Mass is related to the Last Supper and to the Cross, and to see how both, the Last Supper and the Mass, are essentially related to the Cross. Insofar as they are sacramental signs effectively produced in reality, they are immediately ordered to the Cross by representing it. But on the level of the institution of the rite, they are related to each other: the Last

Supper represents the Cross in view of the Mass which is, on the level
of the sign to be reproduced, its proper final cause; and the Mass
represents the Cross thanks to the Last Supper, which is, on the level
of the sign reproduced, its primary exemplar cause. What takes place
at the Mass as at the Last Supper is therefore essentially, by representation, 'the offering to the Father of the Body and Blood of Christ
under the species of bread and wine' (no. 6), that is 'the immolation
of Christ Himself under sensible signs' (no. 12); for, what Christ
instituted at the Last Supper was 'the New Pasch' (no. 11). This last
expression designates most especially here 'the visible sacrifice' which
Christ left to His Church (no. 3) and 'Himself' Who is the victim
'under the visible signs' of bread and wine (no. 12). It is this 'Pasch'
which Christ leaves to His Church in order that she might offer it and
immolate it continuously 'in memory' of His 'Passing' to His Father
(no. 13) and for the sake of applying it to His members (no. 3).

Such, it seems to us, are the principal teachings that one can and ought
to draw from that fundamental text of the Church's Magisterium. And
we can see that such teachings go quite far in the explanation of the mode
of the sacrifice of the Mass. Essentially, the text says the following:

1) the Mass is a sacrifice: 'a visible sacrifice' 'a true and authentic sacrifice' (*verum et proprium sacrificium: can. 1*);
2) namely, the very same sacrifice of Christ, offered and
   immolated on the Cross;
3) it is that sacrifice *by representing it* under visible signs;
4) according to a rite instituted for that end by Christ at the
   Last Supper.
5) The immediate finality of the sacrifice of the Mass is the
   application of the sacrifice of the Cross to the members of
   the Church.
6) We add a final essential element, which we have not yet
   mentioned, but which touches upon the first lecture: the
   institution of the priesthood is tied to that of the Mass, and

the celebration of this sacrifice 'by the Church' is made exclusively 'by the priests' (no. 7).

We would like to mention even more particularly, in relation to the first point, that the unicity of the sacrifice of the Cross is solemnly proclaimed (*chap. 1; 2; can. 4*); in relation to the second and fifth points, that the sacrifice appears as being at once an offering and an immolation, and that it is ordered to Communion (the terms 'oblation' and 'immolation' are taken most often in a global sense, designating the totality of the sacrifice); and finally, in relation to the third point, that it is expressly defined that the Mass—and therefore the representation which it makes—is not a 'pure and simple commemoration' (*nudam commemorationem: can. 3*), but rather, as we have seen, a sacrifice in the true and proper sense of the word.

The two principal questions, which are posed in the face of these affirmations, are the following: 1) How does the multiplicity of the sacrifices, which the multiplicity of Masses brings about, not touch on the unicity of the sacrifice of the Cross?[4] 2) How, in the sacrifice of the Mass, is there an oblation and an immolation at the same time?[5] Since the Mass, like the Last Supper, is a sacrifice by being a representation of the sacrifice of the Cross, it is the nature of this representation which we must define in order to respond to these two questions, and to all the others. Yet it is this crucial point which the Council of Trent left undefined. Moreover, in a certain sense, it tends to conceal it.

---

[4]   This here, theologically speaking, is Luther's fundamental objection; for him, Christ the one Mediator is also the one Redeemer in this sense that, no act outside of His own has salvific value. The Catholic explanation of the unicity of Christ's mediation and redemption is made not by excluding the other mediations and other acts which have salvific value, but by the recapitulation of every mediation and every salvific act in Christ. He is the only Mediator, the other mediations being participations in His. He is the one Priest and one Victim of the one redemptive sacrifice; every priesthood is a participation in His own, and every immolation and offering of a sacrifice takes its value from His. With respect to the Mass, it is, by the sacramental sign, the same sacrifice of the Cross.

[5]   It is under this form that St Thomas poses the question of the sacrifice of the Mass: *S.T.* III, q. 83, a. 1.

The same Council adopts and seems to consecrate by its authority the distinction made by theologians between the sacrament and the sacrifice in the Eucharist. The first is treated in the thirteenth Session, which bears almost exclusively on the Body and Blood of Christ; the second is the object of the twenty second Session, which we just analyzed. Without a doubt this distinction is neither absolute nor still less explicitly taught by the Council. Everything in the twenty second Session speaks of the sacrament; and the second chapter of the thirteenth Session, in speaking of the institution, allows one to see the connection that exists between the sacrament and the sacrifice. The fact is, nevertheless, that that connection had been practically forgotten, and that it is the hardening of the distinction between sacrament and sacrifice which ended up rendering unintelligible the true nature of the sacrifice of the Mass. The sacrifice, in fact, is accomplished by the representation of the sacrifice of the Cross, and this representation is essentially a sacramental act. If one is ignorant of this truth, which is found everywhere beneath the Council texts, then the internal coherence of the Catholic dogma becomes difficult to perceive. On the other hand, with this truth all is made wonderfully clear. Let us try then to shed some light on it. And for this we shall refer to the principal theologian who inspired the Fathers of the Council of Trent, St Thomas Aquinas. Citing St Augustine, he affirms: *Semel immolatus est in semetipso Christus, et tamen quotidie immolatur in sacramento.*[6] It is the whole force of that immolation *in sacramento* which we must grasp.

II. The Doctrine of St Thomas Aquinas

Let us recall first of all that, for St Thomas, a sacrifice, which is the act par excellence of religion, requires an immolation. For, he says, 'every sacrifice is an oblation, but the opposite is not true.'[7] What is needed for an oblation to become a sacrifice is precisely that it be made in

---

6   St Augustine, *Epist. 98; PL* 33, 363–4; cited by St Thomas in *S.T.* III, q. 83, a. 1.
7   *Ibid.*, II–II, 85, 3, ad 3.

view of a sacrifice, which by its very nature includes an immolation, as the examples which he gives show;[8] and this is in complete conformity with Sacred Scripture: 'Without the outpouring of blood there is no remission (of sins)' (Heb 9:22).

These few references are sufficient to make us understand that the Mass cannot be presented as the simple offering of the sacrifice formerly immolated, and less still as a simple prayer to God that He might accept the sacrifice of Christ accomplished on the Cross—a Calvinist explanation adopted in our day by Max Thurian.[9] With respect to the fundamental reasons for which a sacrifice requires an immolation, it is the theology of the Redemption which must seek them. Ultimately it is sin which makes death a necessity (Rom 5:12): man, by shedding his own blood, needs to render to God the good that he wanted to steal from Him, namely life, and even the source of life. It is sin, therefore, which requires an immolation, that is, the sending of a victim to death. This reparation is a requirement of strict justice with regards to the one who committed the sin, even if he who had been offended is able to not require it. In acting thus, he goes beyond justice alone; yet he will not go against it.[10] St Thomas, who

---

[8]   *Ibid.*, 86, 1c.

[9]   'It can be said that, at the Holy Meal, we offer Jesus Christ to God insofar as we pray to God that He will receive for us the sacrifice of His death' (Du Moulin, *Bouclier de la foi*, 1635, CLVII). This text is placed by Max Thurian in the epigraph of his book *L'Eucharistie Mémorial du Seigneur Sacrifice d'action de grace et d'intercession* (Neuchâtel, Delachaux et Niestlé, 1963). He effectively calls this the 'theology' of the sacrifice of the Mass. See in particular the chapter titled 'Le sacrifice eucharistique' (pp. 223–57). The author himself explicitly declares: 'Our plan was to study the sacrificial character of the Eucharist in the light of the biblical memorial' (p. 259). Therefore, it is a question only of 'a memorial.' This is the heresy explicitly condemned by the Council of Trent; and one can see the huge ambiguity which burdens the expression 'Eucharistic sacrifice' in this context. It is under the cloak of ambiguity that it had been accepted by the Protestant members of the 'Concilium', charged with the liturgical Reform in the second edition of Article 7 of 'Institutio generalis' of the 'Novus Ordo Missae'.

[10] St Thomas, *S.T.* III, q. 46, a. 2.

shines much light on this subject, remarks that it is out of a gift of the greatest love and mercy that God wished to respect the exigencies of His own justice. Furthermore, is it not by the offering of love and obedience accomplished by Christ at the heart of His bloody immolation that this same immolation becomes a sacrifice, that is, an act done both for the glory of God and the salvation and sanctification of man? This is why, St Thomas explains, in voluntarily offering Himself in His Passion by love, Christ offered a sacrifice acceptable to God. While those who killed Him, who immolated Him, far from offering a sacrifice, actually committed the gravest of all crimes.[11] Whence it happens that, if it is the immolation that makes the oblation, that is to say that which is offered, the victim of a sacrifice—for there to be a sacrifice (of an animal) there must be the pouring out of blood, and this is the immolation—it is even more true that the oblation alone, that is to say the voluntary offering to God, makes the immolation a sacrifice. We must make a distinction, in this explanation inspired by the sacrifices of the Old Covenant, between the oblation which precedes the sacrifice—although in itself it is already a sacrifice insofar as it is made in view of it—and that which accompanies the sacrifice in the strict sense and is one with it, that is to say the immolation. The former is made by the faithful laying their offering in the hands of the priest; the latter is made only by the priest, the mediator between God and men. This is what takes place at Mass, the sacramental representation of the sacrifice of the Cross.

But before we show this, let us recall again that third essential element of every sacrifice: communion. Insofar as it is an act of religion, the sacrifice has for its aim the ordering of man to God—man recognizing in God his beginning and his end, and rendering to God under this aspect the worship due to Him.[12] Insofar as he is a creature,

---

[11]   Ibid., III, q. 47, a. 4.

[12]   S.T. II–II, q. 81, a. 3; cf. q. 84, a. 1: 'Sed aliquid est quod soli Deo exhibetur, scilicet sacrificium'; cf. q. 85, a. 1: the sacrifice is offered to God 'in signum debitae subiectionis et honoris'.

man stands before God as a servant before his master: he must order himself to God by subordinating himself to Him. All his activity is regulated by obedience. There is here both a service and worship rendered to God.[13] But man is a free creature created to love, and 'God is love' (1 Jn 4:8), inviting man to enter into a relation with Him, similar to that of a Bride and Bridegroom, or a child and his father. The relation of obedience and service is not denied for all that, but it is transfigured by love. And the radical ontological movement, by which man tends toward God and is ordered to Him, becomes an aspiration to a communion of love. It is in Christ's Incarnation and by His Pascal sacrifice that this communion, doubly impossible for man, is realized. We say doubly impossible, first of all because of the infinite distance which separates the created from the Uncreated, and secondly because of the revolt of created freedom against God: sin.

Oblation, immolation, communion: such then are the three fundamental elements of every sacrifice. The first two are constitutive parts; the third, the essential finality. All of these are found in the Mass. And as the Mass is a sacrifice by its sacramental representation of the sacrifice of the Cross, so it is by deepening our knowledge of the notion of sacrament that we can see how it realizes the sacrifice by representing it 'in the sacrament,' *in sacramento.*

Two notions enlighten all of Thomistic sacramental theology: that of sign and that of instrument.[14] Their order is to be respected; for, if it is as an instrument in the hands of God that the sacrament causes or produces its effect, which is grace, it is no less a sign before all else. This is why it has a causality only in dependence of its signification: it produces only what it signifies and only by signifying it (*significando causant; causando significant*).

---

[13]   On this compenetration of worship and service, see II–II, q. 81, a. 3; a. 1; a. 2; a. 8. This double sense is found in the Hebrew root 'BD (he who gives obed: servant), especially in Ex 3:12; Deut. 3:13; etc.

[14]   Sign: *S.T.* III, q. 60, a 1; Instrument: q. 62, a. 1.

One can add to this that the sacrament is a manifold sign,[15] referring back to the action of Christ which it makes present by signifying it, and by this, permitting it to produce its effect; and therefore the sacrament refers back to that effect itself only by means of the representative signification of the cause that produces it, namely the first action of Christ. This is what St Thomas teaches when he defines the sacrament as 'the sign of a sacred reality which sanctifies man.'[16] The traditional theory which distinguishes in the sacrament the *sacramentum tantum,* the *res et sacramentum,* and the *res tantum,* and appropriately applies this distinction to the Eucharist, expresses well this double fundamental signification of the sacrament. However, in order to understand this, it is necessary to know exactly the signification of each of those terms.

The *sacramentum tantum* is the sacramental sign itself in its sensible and perceptible reality, and in its value of signification: matter, action and word. The *res et sacramentum* is the reality first signified which will work the sanctification of man for the glory of God: fundamentally, this is the Pascal sacrifice of Christ, 'the Passion of Christ,' as St Thomas constantly says. The *res tantum* is the reality ultimately signified, produced by the preceding element, namely the grace which signifies man and builds the Church. Translated such into immediately accessible terms, and no less precise for all that, this theory reveals the soundness of its profound intuition, and it allows us to notice what happens in every sacrament, but most especially in the Eucharist. (The application by which one wishes to see in the *res et sacramentum* the 'character,' cannot take place except by analogy; and it deviates from the first sense of the three terms, which is the one that we give here.)

With respect to the question of how it can be possible that a sensible action communicates life, and divine life at that, one which is purely spiritual, it is necessary to recall first of all that man, to whom this life is communicated, is a being of flesh; and therefore, it is in the

---

15 *Ibid.,* III, q. 60, a. 3.
16 *Ibid.,* III, q. 60, a.2; a. 3.

order of reality for him to receive life, even the most spiritual life, by means of a material and sensible element and action. Secondly, one must remember that it was precisely to respond to this order of reality that the Word had become Incarnate, and that He instituted the sacraments to continue to touch through His Church all His members by a physical contact with His own Flesh. There is nothing magic in a sacrament; or rather, magic does in a deranged way and for the purpose of evil that which the Church does in the sacraments for the purpose of our salvation. For, one must not forget that the Author of the sacraments, Christ, is the Author of life. Moreover, He is life itself, and He has the omnipotence of God. Therefore, He has the power of instituting an action to be reproduced upon matter for the sake of applying life to man, charging that action and matter as He does with the life that He wants to communicate by means of them. The sacramental matter, water, oil, bread and wine, acts only in an action and by means of a word. Therefore, it does not act except insofar as it is used and animated, as it were, by a will which, through the minister and his intention, is that of the Church and of Christ Himself. Now Christ has the power to act upon souls by His Church, by His ministers, as by words, actions, and sensible material elements, which He places in their hands. By the power which He conferred on them for this end, and by the intention through which they bind themselves to Him, by means of the Church, He endows their words, their actions and the matter which they use, with this power.

That is what takes place in a sacrament,[17] the being of which, St

---

[17] This is what is expressed so well by E. Masure, when he emphasizes the unity of Christ and the Church more than the sacramentality of the action in question: 'In restoring unity to the mystery of Christ and His Church, one must try to see how an action of flesh bears in itself the life which animates it; and if there is a problem in this compenetration of flesh and spirit, it is no different than the problem of a composed human, which is our very definition and what we live out all the time. The problem is even double for the mystery of the Incarnation which we already believe in. When the manuals ask how a material element of water or oil can produce in us the grace and life of God, they forget that this

Thomas teaches, is entirely related to that of the Principal Agent Who acts through them.[18]

What one must remember is that the sacramental sign does not signify, and therefore does not effectively produce, the ultimate effect of grace except by first signifying the one act which is the source of this grace, namely the Pascal sacrifice of Christ; by signifying this latter, the sacramental sign really re-presents it for the sake of producing grace. This movement from the sacramental act to the giving of divine life is essential for the sacrament: it really signifies by the sign the action of Christ (that is, it really accomplishes the action of Christ) only in view of its consummation in the life of that person to whom it is applied in that same sign.

It is in the framework of this theological explanation that we must understand the key notion of 'representation,' which we found in the heart of the Council of Trent's teaching on the sacrifice of the Mass. However, in addition to the Eucharist, it is the whole of the sacramental order that is at stake here; for, the sign which constitutes the sacrament does not *effectively produce* grace except in the measure that it *really represents* the one source of that grace, which is the Pascal mystery of Christ, in view of that production of grace. The reality of the representation is therefore required for the efficacy. Together they stand or fall; and as they are both bound to the signification, so it is to this latter that we must continually return in order to see what happens in each sacrament.

---

element is acted upon by an action, and that this action is that of a body, itself traversed by a will, and that this will is that of a minister acting in the name of the Church of whom he is a member, and that this Church, the Bride of Christ, is, in the strongest sense of the word, animated by Him, her Head.' (*Le sacrifice du Christ mystique*, Paris, DDBr., 1950, p. 46). St Thomas insists as well on the fact that the minister of the sacrament is the minister of Christ only by being the minister of the Church: *Sum. Theol.*, III, q. 64, a. 1; a. 6; a. 8; a. 9; etc.

18   *Ibid.*, III, q. 62, a. 4; q. 63, a. 2.

III. The Sacrifice in the Sacrament

In order to see what takes place in the Mass, the celebration of the sacrament of the Eucharist, let us examine now *the sacramental sign* (*sacramentum tantum*) in which it is accomplished.

This study, with respect to St Thomas, moves us immediately to an initial observation, namely that while he analyzes well the sacramental rite of the Eucharist, he does this only as the very last question of his treatise.[19] For, it is resolutely in view of the sacrament that he begins the study of the Eucharist; and for St Thomas, this sacrament is first and foremost the bread and wine transubstantiated into the Body and Blood of Christ. It is this theology, adopted by St Thomas from a tradition which preceded him, which is at the origin of the division made by the Council of Trent between the sacrament and the sacrifice. In itself, nevertheless, that distinction not only does not tend towards opposition, but on the contrary moves toward a harmonization, as this text, among a hundred others, proves: *Hoc sacramentum prae aliis habet quod est sacrificium.*[20] It is interesting to note that it is in studying the 'effects' of the Eucharist that St Thomas discovers this intercompenetration of the sacrament and sacrifice: it is the sacrament itself, taken in its totality, which is the sacrifice. This implies reciprocally that the sacrifice is completely in the sacrament.

If he studies first and foremost the sacrament under its limited aspect, namely that according to which it designates the Body and Blood of Christ really and substantially present under the species of bread and wine, it is primarily because this was in fact the first speculative question which he needed to resolve; and secondly, because this article of faith had already during his day been subjected to attacks against which he needed to defend it—attacks especially of Berenger of Tours; and finally, it is because the sacrifice was at that time so unanimously recognized that he did not feel the need to justify

---

[19]   *Ibid.*, III, q. 83.
[20]   *Ibid.*, III, q. 79; a. 7. ad. 1.

it. It is no less remarkable to see the richness of the teaching that St Thomas gives us on the sacrifice itself, according to and in the perspective of the sacrament. And it is no doubt to the presence of the sacrifice in the sacrament and the sacrament in the sacrifice that one must return in order to understand the teaching of the Council of Trent on the sacrifice of the Mass.

1. What, then, is 'the sacramental sign' (the *sacramentum tantum*) in the Eucharist and in its celebration? In a restricted sense, and the one used most frequently by St Thomas on account of the perspective he adopts, the sacramental sign is the bread and wine: 'the bread and wine offered,' he clarifies.[21] We must, nevertheless, widen this perspective since he himself calls 'sacrament' the totality of the celebration of the Eucharist.[22] It is interesting to note that in the study which he makes, he distinguishes that which happens (*quae aguntur*), the actions and ceremonies, and that which is said (*quae dicuntur*), the words. The sacramental sign in the Eucharist is therefore not only the matter of the bread and wine, but along with them, the collection of actions and words by which the Eucharist is celebrated: from the sign of the cross to the final *Ite missa est*, but most especially from the offertory to the Communion inclusive. Therefore, it is this whole which must be analyzed in order to see what takes place in the Eucharist, that is to say, in order to see how it is a sacrifice, including an oblation, an immolation, and ending with a communion.

Even if it is the ceremonies from the offertory to communion that ought to be especially studied, it is nevertheless necessary to recall that the two parts of the Mass, the prayers, chants and readings up to the Creed, and then those from the offertory to the end of Mass, form a single whole.[23] St Thomas explains that the function of the first part

---

[21] *In IV Sent.*, d. 8, *Expos. Textus* (Ed. Moos: n. 286).

[22] As can be seen in q. 83 of his *Summa Theologiae*, especially in its title, '*De ritu huius sacramenti*', and in other articles, like 4 and 5.

[23] Contrary to what one reads in Martimort cited above: 'It is very important to understand and to teach that the principal aim of the liturgy of the book is not the preparation of the celebrants and the faithful for the liturgy of the

is to prepare the people 'for the celebration of the mystery.'[24] However, the most profound reason for this unity, without denying what was indicated by St Thomas, but rather re-enforcing it, is that the sacrifice of the Mass belongs to the New and Eternal Covenant, and that this Covenant between God and His people has for its basis the Law which God gives to His people, and in which He makes known to them both His will: His promises for those who do it, and His chastisements for those who do not. This had been shown very strongly in the Old Covenant.[25] And if it is true that the Holy Spirit took the place of the 'letter' (II Cor 3:6), it is no less true that the aim and the fruit of the New Covenant are to give to man the power of accomplishing the will of God manifested in the Law (Rom 8:4). The immolation of the sacrifice which, in the poured out blood, seals the pact of the Convenant, always requires the knowledge of God's will and His promises. It is here, in our opinion, that one finds the profound reason why the first part of the Mass, with the prayers and readings, precedes the part with the sacrifice, and the reason for the unity of the whole which they form.

2. 'The reality which takes place in the sign,' the *res et sacramentum* (or better perhaps, the *res sacramentalis*) is what takes place through the sign, and therefore through a mode of signification, for the

---

Eucharist. Certainly it does fill that role admirably, but this is an extra, and not the essential reason for its existence. The two synaxes, that of the Word of God and that of the Sacrament, are independent in their origin and their end, however complementary they might be.' These assertions are made without proof; and the example that is brought forward immediately afterwards is insufficient for justifying such general propositions (*op. cit.*, p. 345—let us note that this work is a collaboration, and that this passage belongs to Denis–Boulet). One will note also the expression 'the liturgy of the book', which has no function in tradition, and which is at the same time trendy and insufficient for signifying the first part of the Mass.

[24]   '*Sic igitur populo, praeparato et instructo, acceditur ad celebrationem mysterii*' (III, 83, 4c).

[25]   Especially by Von Rad, Mendenhall, etc. See R. De Vaux, *Les Institutions de l'Ancien Testament*, Paris Cerf, 2 vol., 1958–1960.

purpose of its fulfillment in life. In order to understand this reality the signification of the sign must be clarified. And in order to do this it is necessary to study the nature of the material element used, the action which is made over it or by it, and the words that accompany the action in order to complete the clarification of the sense.

a) The first thing to be looked at is the institution. Christ does what He signifies by the matter which He uses, by the action which He accomplishes, and by the words which He pronounces, namely, two things:

He sacrifices Himself in offering Himself to the Father for His disciples;

He gives Himself to be eaten by them.

Both things presuppose that the bread is His Flesh and the wine is His Blood. The sacramental truth of the signs, the matter of the bread and wine, is therefore the condition of the sacramental truth of the action that is made with them. It is attested to by the words of *institution:* 'This is My Body; This is the cup of My Blood'; and by the words of *the promise:* 'I *am* the bread of life' (Jn 6:48, 51).

The most apparent action is that by which Christ gives Himself to be eaten: the meal. Nevertheless, it takes place only after that by which Christ offers Himself and immolates Himself in sacrifice. How does Christ make His sacrifice at the Last Supper? And what amounts to the same question: How does He signify it? By action and words:

The action: what gives it its meaning is first of all the context of the Pascal sacrifice (Lk 22:15: 'this Pasch'; and the date); but it is also the fact that the drama of the Passion is already begun—it is 'the night He was betrayed,' and He had already been betrayed, at least in the heart of Judas (1 Cor 11:23; Lk 22:3);

The immediate action: the double separated consecration, *signifying and thus bringing about* the separation of His Body and His Blood, in which death consists; this signification, to be sure, is not immediately evident, but Tradition has shed light upon it, and it holds a central place in the theology of St Thomas.[26] By this action, then, Christ immolates Himself for His disciples;

The words: the blessing or the thankgiving (Mt 26:26; Lk 22:19) is the offering to the Father; the words pronounced over the wine which, by the explicit mentioning of the Covenant, positively signify the pouring out of blood and the sacrifice; the Covenent, in fact, is not concluded except in the sacrifice and the pouring out of blood.

The conclusion: without words the action made over the matter would not be sufficient for signifying, that is to say, for bringing about, the sacrifice. However, with the words by virtue of the omnipotence of Christ, it signifies and therefore brings about the sacrifice:

- in order to be accomplished and consummated by Christ Himself on the Cross;
- in order to be reproduced by the Church in the Mass;
  Let us clarify:
- in order to be consummated on the Cross; for, every sacramental action is ordered to the accomplishment in life of that which it brings about in the sign;
- in order to be reproduced at the Mass; for, the action of Christ was the institution. It, therefore, was done explicitly in order that this renewal might take place by His Church.

b) The sacramental sign of the Mass reproduces that of the Last Supper. It redoes that which happened there, but with the twofold difference that we have already mentioned above: the first, is that between the two the blood immolation and Christ's Resurrection took place; the second, is that henceforth Christ would no longer act by Himself, but by the Church and her ministers: *ab Ecclesia, per ministros,* as the Council of Trent says.

i) Because in the meantime Christ's Pasch had been immolated in the reality of life and death, whereas the rite of the Last Supper was, in sign, both its commencement and prefiguration[27] That of the Mass

---

[26]   *S.T.* III, q. 76, a. 2; q. 78, a. 3; etc.

[27]   *Ibid.,* III, q. 83, a. 5; see also the St Thomas' *Commentary on the Gospel of St*

is the renewal, in the same sign, of the totality of the mystery, begun at the Last Supper and consummated on the Cross, in view of the accomplishment by and in the Church.

For, as we said, every sacrament is ordered to the accomplishment in the reality of life of that which it accomplishes in the reality of the sign. Therefore, it is necessary that the Mass be ordered to a real immolation in life. Such in fact is the case: in the continuation of the Pascal mystery, the Mass is to the sacrifice of the Church and her members what the Last Supper was to the sacrifice of Christ. In the Mass, the members of Christ are immolated in the sign, sacramentally. They are united to the sacrifice of Christ, which that same sacramental sign brings about; and they are thus efficaciously ordered to the completion of their own sacrifice in life. The sacramental sign instituted at the Last Supper and reproduced at the Mass received in the meantime from the sacrifice of the Cross and from Christ's Resurrection the power of life, which renders it capable of drawing the Church and all her members into the same sacrifice of the Cross, and thus capable of leading them to the glory of the final resurrection.

ii) This first difference moves us to an understanding of the second. At the Last Supper Christ did all; His Apostles did nothing but receive. At the Mass, on the other hand, they become active. They are, along with Christ, the mediators between the people and God; but first they are the mediators between the people and Christ Himself. They are those who receive the offerings of bread and wine from the people in order to place them in the hands of Christ. They are like the hands and voice of Christ.

At the Last Supper Christ Himself takes the bread and wine; at Mass it is the people, the assembly of the faithful, who bring forward the offerings in order to place them in His hands through the ministry

---

John, Chapter 13, lect. 1. One must undersand that in each of these three moments, the Last Supper, the Cross and the Mass, the totality of the Mystery is accomplished, in order to be perfected finally in glory. This is why we say that the Last Supper is the beginning but also the prefigurative, sacramental and real representation of Christ's Pascal sacrifice.

of the priest. From here we have a new meaning given to the bread and wine: in them, at offertory, are the things that the faithful offer to Christ for the sacrifice which will be accomplished. This latter meaning is in no way in opposition to the first, that by which 'the sacrament,' that is the sacramental sign constituted by bread and wine, designates Christ's Body and Blood: aren't the faithful the Mystical Body of Christ? And isn't the fundmental purpose of the sacrament of the Eucharist to make them pass into and remain in Christ and Christ in them (Jn 6:56)? We shall discover that at the Last Supper, by 'taking' the bread and wine 'in the sacrament'—in the sign—it was His Mystical Body that Christ already held, in order to make it pass with Himself, in His sacrifice, from this world to the Father.

What He did alone at the Last Supper He does with His Church and through her at the Mass; and it is there that we discover the true meaning of the offertory and its properly sacrificial nature. The admirable prayers which form it in no way form a doublet with those of the canon, contrary to what is all too often said;[28] and it will be most necessary to correct such errors as well as the practical consequences that follow them. In order to understand the meaning of the offertory one must remember the double oblation which takes place in every sacrifice: the oblation of the victim to be immolated, which the faithful bring forward to the priest, the mediator between God

---

[28]   This misunderstanding about the offertory already appeared in Martimort's book: 'One will notice in all those offertory prayers textual echoes, as it were, of the canon' (*op. cit.*, p. 374). It would be a case of echoes preceding the sound itself. Regarding the prayer '*Suscipe sancta Pater*', one reads earlier in this same text: 'it is the least good of those that had been chosen for the offertory; it is expressed in the singular, it uses the term 'spotless victim' to designate the bread which is not yet consecrated' (p. 373) (These lines are also from Denis–Boulet). As such, the historical erudition is not sufficient to give the liturgical sense. This is because the knowledge of the liturgy belongs first to faith and theology; and for a historian of the liturgy this is proof that a theological meaning, which is very much obscured, places all the traditions on the same level without taking into consideration the preeminence which Providence has willed to give to the tradition of Rome.

and themselves; and the effective oblation of the victim to God, which takes place in its immolation, and which is the duty of the priest alone. Therefore, the oblation of the offertory is not, and has never pretended to be, the immolation of the sacrifice, which is accomplished at Mass in the double consecration; rather, it is the oblation of the matter of the sacrifice, which is something completely different.

And yet, as such, that oblation already has the value of a sacrifice: first, because it happens only in view of the sacrifice to be accomplished in the matter thus offered, which here is the sacramental sign of the victim to be immolated, and because an oblation made in view of the immolation of the sacrifice is already in itself a sacrifice—by its ordination to the sacrifice to be accomplished in it: *et oblatio est et sacrificium,* says St Thomas.[29] The second reason why the oblation has sacrificial value is because, seeing that that sacrifice is to be accomplished in Christ's sacrifice, it is allowed and even necessary to speak of it already as the sacrifice of Christ. Thus one can justify the expression '*immaculatam hostiam*' in the first prayer, '*Suscipe sancte Pater.*' This is also the reason why the offertory prayers are said by the priest and not by the people.

The offertory is presented therefore under a twofold aspect: from the Church's part (namely the faithful and the priest himself insofar as he is also one of the faithful), the offering, in the sign, of the matter of the sacrifice, that is to say of their own selves and their own lives represented and signified by these gifts, the oblations; and from the part of the priest insofar as he is Christ's minister, the prayer of offering the matter of his own proper sacrifice, whereby he prepares and, to a certain extent, anticipates the oblation which he will make of this sacrifice in the consecration. The traditional Roman offertory prayers expressed admirably this double aspect of what could rightly be called the mystery of the offertory: it is the mystery of the '*admirabile commercium,*' which is the entire work of the redemptive Incarnation.

---

[29]   *S.T.* II–II, q. 86, a. 1.

The sacrifice in the strict sense, at its offering and its immolation, during both the Mass and the Last Supper, is accomplished sacramentally by the separate action and double consecration of bread and wine, the words of which (especially those said over the wine) speak of the sacrificial signification by their explicit reference to the Covenant: this double consecration, by 'representing' it in sign, really accomplishes the immolation of the Body of Christ and the pouring out of His Blood. St Thomas, who is here more than ever a faithful echo of Tradition, teaches this with the most perfect clarity.[30] Therefore, it is here that the reality of the sacrifice is to be found, and nowhere else; and one cannot help but be confused in seeing how these truths, so obvious when looked at in the light of Scripture and Tradition, have been able to be so completely forgotten for such long periods of time. The cause of this is to be sought in—among others—the rationalism of the modern age, which greatly diminished the meaning of the symbol, and consequently the mystery of sacramentality.

It is, therefore, all these truths which must be called to mind in order to understand the wonderful formula of St Augustine, upon which St Thomas basis himself in order to affirm that Christ is truly immolated at Mass: '*Semel immolatus in semetipso Christus, et tamen quotidie immolatur in sacramento.*' 'Immolated once for all in Himself, Christ is nevertheless immolated each day in the sacrament.' This means sacramentally, that is under the mode and by means of sacramental representation, but also and most especially in 'the sacramental sign' of bread and wine, and in the reality, at once single and double, which it signifies and which it is, namely the individual Body of Christ Himself and the members of His Mystical Body. To understand this is to understand how the Mass, the celebration of the sacrament of the Eucharist, is both the sacrifice of Christ and of His Church. It is the perfect sacrament of Christ's sacrifice accomplished in the sacrament of His Body the Church, the bread and wine offered;

---

[30]   Cf. *see above*, note 566.

and it is the sacrifice of the Body His Church, the faithful, offered and immolated sacramentally in its own sacrifice.

3) Beginning there, the fruits of the Mass, the *res tantum*,[31] appear to be in internal coherence with the mystery.

They are first of all declared by Christ Himself, after the miracle of the multiplication of the loaves, in the discourse of the promise, at the synagogue of Capharnaum. The bread: this is the sign. It is what nourishes life—the firstfruit of the Eucharist is life. Whence the name traditionally given to this passage of St John's Gospel, 'the discourse on the bread of life.' This life is given not only by material eating of the Body, but also through it, by union with Christ Himself (Jn 6:56); and it is in us as the principle of eternal life (Jn 6:58). These fruits are produced because they are signified by the nature of the sign and the action that accompanies it. It is a question here of a food and its consumption. This is in fact the way human life is maintained. However, this consumption takes place in a sacred action, namely in a meal of communion.

It is in the priestly prayer that Christ tells us what is the fruit that He ultimately desires from His sacrifice: the communion of all His members in Himself and with the Father: 'That they all may be one, as thou, Father, in me, and I in thee; that they also may be one in us.' (Jn 17:21). We can see here the continuity that exists between the discourse of the promise and the request of the priestly prayer. In the former, Christ said, 'He who eats My Flesh and drinks My Blood remains in Me and I in him' (Jn 6:58.). At the Last Supper, He said, 'Since I am in them, may they be one with Me and with each other, *as* I am one with the Father, that is, the Father being in Me and I in the Father' (cf. Jn 10:30; 38). This fruit is produced because it is signified by the nature of the sign used and by its symbolism: numerous grains united in one bread and grapes in one wine. Thus it is brought out in a sort of holy rivalry by the Fathers and frequently

---

[31] This is the third point to be examined in order to complete the study of the sacrament of the Eucharist.

recalled by St Thomas. But it is signified even more by the action of Christ, 'taking' the bread and the wine, uniting Himself by this action to His Mystical Body, and then giving Himself to be eaten by His disciples, and thus showing the profound level at which this union must be realized.

Finally, *the* new *life* given by Christ to those who *communicate* in His offered Body and Blood, and therefore in his sacrifice, will triumph in the personal sacrifice of the Christian, and therefore in his death. Such is the personal fruit of the Eucharist: charity which will traverse death as its conqueror; for, by charity, man's immolation will become *the continuation of Christ's sacrifice.* This personal and ultimate fruit of the Eucharist, the conforming of the Christan to Christ in His Pasch, is therefore produced by this sacrament insofar as it is the sign of the pascal sacrifice. And this crossing of death in order to come to glory certainly seems to concern not only each member of the Mystical Body insofar as he is an individual, but also the totality of that same Body as such.

This conforming to the suffering Christ realized by the Eucharist is not habitually brought out enough. Yet it is demanded by the signification of the sacramental sign; and St Thomas has the merit of strongly underlining it by noting that it is not simply the Body of Christ that we receive, but the Body of Christ immolated and suffering.[32] This is why, as he says, the Eucharist brings about the perfection of man by uniting him to Christ's Passion.[33]

In this way the Eucharist brings man to glory, the former being a sort of anticipation of the latter: such are the two final fruits of the Eucharist. While the Eucharist does not give glory immediately, it does give 'the power to come to it';[34] and as that which the Eucharist

---

[32]   *S.T.* III, q. 79, a. 1.

[33]   *Ibid.,* q. 73, a. 3.

[34]   *Ibid.,* q. 79, a. 2.

gives is the glorious Blody of Christ,[35] it is as a pledge and, we could add, as an anticipation of glory.[36]

These explanations allow one to situate the relation between the sacrifice and the meal in the Eucharist, or more accurately between the eating, the meal and the sacrifice. The distinction between the first two terms seems to us very clear. While the celebration of this sacrament ends in the eating, which gives the *life* of Christ by assimilation, and while this eating happens at a meal, which brings about the *communion* of Christ's members in their Head, the Eucharist remains first of all a *sacrifice*, the one redemptive sacrifice. For, it is by this sacrifice alone that the life is given to us and that our communion is realized with and in God. The sacrifice is without a doubt immediately ordered to the eating and to the meal, where the sacramental communion is consummated. However, the meal and the eating take their true sense only from the sacrifice by which they become a communion 'in the sacrament' for the purpose of allowing us to participate in it, and then in the life and death of Christ, in order that we might finally come to the Pascal resurrection and eternal life promised to us by Christ (Jn 6:58). The sacrifice and the meal-eating are therefore inseparable, neither one understood without the other, just like the sacrament and the sacrifice. This is what we said at the beginning of our work: in the Eucharist all is the sacrament, and all is the sacrifice; for, the sacrament is completely in the sacrifice, and the sacrifice is completely sacramental. And if our communion of love in Jesus with the Father is the ultimate aim of every work, this communion is itself essentially sacrificial: here below in blood and for all eternity in glory.

*   *   *

Such is the broad outline of a theology of the sacrifice of the Mass founded on that of the sacrament. Without a doubt this theology of the sacrament had not been explicitly proposed by the Magisterium

---

[35] *Ibid.*, q. 81, a. 3.

[36] *Ibid.*, q. 73, a. 4; cf. q. 60, a. 3.

apropos of the sacrifice of the Mass; and yet, the whole theology of the Mass adopted by that same Magisterium is full of such theology. This is why it is not surprising to see the perfect harmony that exists between this theology and that dogmatic teaching: when the Council of Trent speaks of 'representation' of the sacrifice of the Cross at the Mass, it is the expression constantly employed by St Thomas which the Council adopts. And when St Thomas uses it, it is in the sense which we said, and which comes to him from St Augustine and the entire Tradition, namely that of sacrament. This is why there is nothing surprising in this theology of the sacrament, which seems to be the true key for entering into the knowledge and continuous development of the dogma defined at Trent.

This theology allows us, more particularly, to respond as clearly as possible to the two major difficulties opposed to the sacrificial character of the Mass. For the immolation and for those who deny that the Mass can be an immolation, the matter is immediately manifest: the sacramental sign brings about, under its own proper mode, the act which was formerly accomplished by Christ on Calvary and which will always be accomplished in the life of the Church; and it brings it about precisely in view of this accomplishment. This is why, in what concerns the sacrifice of the Church—a participation in, a complement to and completion of Christ's sacrifice—it is this sacrament which gives the Church the power to accomplish it.

Regarding the unicity of Christ's sacrifice, this theology shows how the Mass not only does not undermine it, but, on the contrary, assures it and allows it to be accomplished. For, while Christ's redemptive sacrifice is one and unique, the sacrifices of men are numerous. The real question, then, is of knowing how they are but one with Christ's, taking their value from His alone (it is precisely this value which Luther denied). The response clearly appears in this theory of the sacramental sacrifice of the Mass. The sacrifice accomplished at Mass cannot be fully equated with the sacrifice of the Cross for the fundamental reason that it is not of the same kind, and the same is true for the sacrifice of the Last Supper. It is the same sacrifice which is accomplished in both cases, but under two different modes: at the Last Supper and at Mass, under the mode of the sacramental sign and rite; on the Cross, in the reality of life and history. The first of these two modes is ordered to the second, where it is completed by finding there its signification and its full realization. And the second, that of the sacrifice of Christ on the Cross, is destined to extend itself to all men. Now it is precisely the sacramental act of the Last Supper renewed at the Mass, at all Masses, just like it had been prefigured in the ritual sacrifices of the Old Covenant and the natural law,[37] which allows Christ to extend the sacrifice of His own life to all the members of His Mystical Body, and thereby take up and recapitulate all their sacrifices in order to offer them in His own to the Father. By the movement of love from the Holy Spirit He makes the pleroma, the fullness of His one sacrifice of propitiation and adoration, of praise and thanksgiving: the one Eucharist of Redemption 'to the praise of glory of His grace' (Eph 1:6).

Such then, in three tracts, is a summary of a fundamental dogmatic theology of *Sacrificium missae*. As we see, it is nothing other than bringing to light the truths contained in dogma, that is to say, in revelation, as the Church, to whom they had been confided, teaches us. To develop and demonstrate its value one could either show its internal coherence or all its foundations in Scripture and Tradition. But it is above all its practical consequences about which one must think; and the most urgent of these is the revision—at least on certain points—of the current liturgical 'reform.' Its inspiration had not always been in line with that Tradition. To prove this it suffices to reread the *Institutio generalis* which gave us the *Novus Ordo Missae*, and which was difficult to reconcile with dogma. If one adds to this a look, even a brief look, at the fruits of this 'reform,' one cannot but be convinced more still of the urgent need to revise it; for, a great number of these fruits, whatever be their real benefits, which are either very limited or could

---

[37]   *Ibid.*, III, q. 73, a. 6; cf. Council of Trent, Session XXII, Chapter 1.

have been required in another way—these 'fruits' are the increasing desacralization of the Mass, its evolution into forms further and further from the faith, and the division of Catholics over this central article of their *Credo and their life of prayer: Lex orandi, lex credendi.*

The work of revision and return to Tradition is urgent therefore; for, the Mass—which we just showed—is the heart of the entire life of the Church, the source of all her divine energy, the end of all her efforts. It is, says the Second Vatican Council, 'the source and summit of all evangelization.'[38] The same return to Tradition, or more accurately the same effort for a development of the liturgy going in the sense of Tradition, imposes itself in the area of concelebration. The development of that theology of the sacrifice of the Mass will convince one still more.

---

[38] *Presbyterorum Ordinis,* no. 5: *'Quapropter Eucharistia fons et culmen totius evangelizationis apparet.'*

10 THE LITURGY: MYSTERY, SYMBOL AND SACRAMENT

WHILE DOGMA TEACHES us that the Mass is a sacrifice, and while the theology of the sacrament—developed from a dogmatic perspective—allows us to 'comprehend' it as one, that is so say how it is the same sacrifice as that of the Cross, the accepted vision is nevertheless capable of being further developed. This is necessary in order to respond to the question which concerns us: namely, the sense and value of a singular Eucharistic celebration (by one priest only at the altar) and of a Eucharistic concelebration by several priests; also, and ultimately, the sense and value of the multiplication (not multiplying) of the redemptive Sacrifice through sacramental celebration in and for the Church.

If one considers that it is in the liturgical action that the sacramental sign is placed, then one sees that the development of which we are in need must take place essentially on the foundation and in the framework of a reflection on the mystery of the Sacred Liturgy, which is to say the Sacred Liturgy of the Mystery. The liturgy, in fact, is the Mystery, in the New Testament meaning of the word, celebrated, made present and working here and now in the Church by means of the sacramental sign. Mystery and sacrament therefore are the two great realities that need to be studied in order to come to an understanding of the liturgy. To a certain degree one can say that they overlap each other. This is why the Latin word *sacramentum* is often used by the Fathers to translate the Greek word *mysterion*. But this can be said only to a certain degree, at least for the present moment; and in any case both of these words each have their own nuances. The Mystery, in the New Testament and especially in St Paul, is the salvific work of the Lord considered both insofar as it had been hidden 'from eternity' in God (Rom 16:25) and in its 'economy,' that is in the 'dispensation' of its manifestation in time (Eph 3:8). Beginning with the Father, it is realized by the redemptive Incarnation of the Son (2 Cor 5:17; Eph 5:25; etc.). In the end it gathers together everything and everyone, that is, all the elect, in order to restore all in Christ to the Father (Eph 1:9; Col 1:13 ff). Therefore, it is that Mystery, considered in its totality, which is pursued in the sacraments in order to be accomplished by them in the Church, and most especially by that which is the keystone and the fullness of the entire sacramental order, the Eucharist. In this way the Mystery and the sacrament mutually shed light on each other: the Mystery is that which is accomplished in the sacrament; the sacrament is that by which the Mystery is accomplished or comes to its perfection in time. By the sacrament, the Mystery becomes the Liturgy; by the Mystery, the sacrament and therefore the liturgy are the work of men's salvation for the glory of God. This is why all of the theology of the liturgy is both the theology of the Mystery and the theology of the sacrament. Or more precisely: the theology of the Mystery is accomplished in the sacrament, and by it in the Church, and by the Church in the world.

However, we must clarify further; for, in this perspective all is Mystery, all is sacrament, all is liturgy. This is why, when first considering the Mystery in order to find therein the primary foundation of the theology of the sacraments and the liturgy, we shall search especially for that which will by its nature give us this foundation. We shall find it both in its essence and in its economy; then we shall continue on into the constitutive elements that internally structure it and into the modes of its accomplishment in time. This will be the object of our first part. Then, with the Mystery being carried out and accomplished in the Church, this reflection on its structure and its economy will continue with a theology of the sacrament, the proper means for this accomplishment. At the heart of the sacramental order is found the Eucharist, sacrament and sacrifice, where the Mystery is reproduced in its entirety. We showed in the preceding study, beginning with the Council of Trent and with the help of St Thomas

Aquinas, how the celebration of the Eucharist is a sacrifice because it is a sacrament, 'the sacrament of Christ's Passion.' We based our position on what we then explained. We shall try to develop this theology of the sacramental rite by showing how 'the Mystery' is consummated, by going from what Christ accomplished during His earthly life to what He does now in His Church, and from that ecclesial and sacramental action to its eschatological consummation. In other words, by going from the Mystery, or more precisely from the mysteries, of the life of Christ to the sacraments of the Church, and from this latter to the eschatological and glorious consummation of the whole Mystery.

At this point of our reflection we are faced with a new inquiry. The current revival of studies on symbolism and their notable impact on theology and on liturgical practices is well known. We must, therefore, develop our reflection on the sacramental order with the help of those studies on symbolism. This will be the object of the third part of our study. It is an important and delicate task, but one which is urgent and which will prove to be highly beneficial.[1]

That multiple illumination, 'mysterious' and 'economic,' sacramental and symbolic, will allow us to return in our next studies to 'the liturgy,' taking this word in the sense that it so often had among the Eastern Fathers, that is, referring to the Eucharist and the Mass; we shall also be able to see more profoundly how its essence is in that 'sacramental' realization of the 'Mystery of faith,' *Mysterium fidei*.

I. The 'Mystery' and Its Economy

While the notion of the Mystery is most especially Pauline, it is not unknown in the synoptics, who identify it with what is for them the central reality of the Gospel, the Kingdom: 'the Mystery of the Kingdom of God' (Mk 4:11; Matt 13:11; Lk 8:10). St John also uses it, signifying by the term the salvific plan of God as it is accomplished

---

[1]   This chapter appeared in *LPC*, no. 191 (March–April 1981), pp. 10–57.

in time (Rev 10:7). This is the fundamental sense that it has in St Paul as well: 'That He might make known unto us the Mystery of His will, according to His good pleasure, which He hath purposed in Him, in the dispensation of the fullness of times, to re-establish all things in Christ, that are in heaven and on earth, in Him' (Eph 1:9–10).

This text, especially if light is shed on it by other passages where the same notion of Mystery is found—this text shows us both the central place that it occupies in Pauline theology as well as its aptitude for expressing the heart of the gospel message, which is the object of our faith. A certain number of binomials and parallelisms—some antithetical, others complementary and explanatory—shed light on it and allow one to see how the Mystery prolongs itself and is consummated by the sacraments.

The Mystery is both *hidden* and *manifested*: hidden, because conceived in God, 'developed in silence from all eternity,' and manifested now to men through Jesus Christ (Rom 16:25). Announced by the Scriptures (Rom 16:26), it is now proclaimed with a new fullness by the Apostles and the Prophets 'in the Spirit' (Eph 3:5). And yet it still awaits its realization and its definitive manifestation, which will take place only at the parousia (2 Thess 2:1–8); this is why in the present time, which is now the time of the Church, the Mystery remains both hidden and manifested. Faith alone can know it: it is 'the Mystery of faith' (1 Tim 3:9); and this latter, consequently, is always both a certitude in what it holds in obscurity and an aspiration for the fullness of that possession *in the light.*

From the fact that the Mystery is both hidden and manifested, and that it is *manifested* to the extent that it is *realized* (third parallelism), there flows a second paradox (and a fourth parallelism) essential to its economy: it is *already realized* while remaining at the same time *still to be realized.* Thus it is that St Paul could affirm both, and without contradiction, that Christ has already destroyed death (2 Tim 1:10) and that this latter will be the last enemy destroyed by Him (1 Cor 15:26; the same word, *katargeô*, is used in both passages). Already realized, the Mystery is in its principle Christ Himself, in Whom it is completed by His Resurrection and Ascension; still to be realized, it is in its pleroma, its fullness, the Church, the Body of Christ, in which it continues in order to be completed. Furthermore, it is 'the whole creation' recapitulated in Christ which aspires towards its eschatological accomplishment (Rom 8:19).

This is why the Mystery is 'economy' (Eph 3:9); for, this progressive dispensation in time is needed in order first of all to prepare, as by a divine pedagogue, the coming of Christ 'in the fullness of time' (Gal 3:24; 4:4). And, this latter having come and the Mystery having been realized in its center, a new 'time' is needed, that of the Church, in order that Christ might perfect and 'complete' by her (Col 1:24) His work of salvation and recapitulation. In itself Christ's Resurrection and Ascension perfect all. But this new time enters in after them as a delay and expansion of time for the accomplishment of the Mystery in and through the Church. If the Incarnation, Passion, and Resurrection-Ascension are three foundational times of the realization of the Mystery through and in Christ during His earthly life, at the center of history, then these three times will to some extent be found again in the life of the Church, the Passion of the Church, established in her condition of Body and Bride of Christ, and her glorious Resurrection, during the Parousia (Rev 21:2). Only then will the end of history, begun with Christ's Resurrection, and even with His conception, be consummated. And this is because the Church, in the time that will be allotted to her for this, will have fulfilled her mission, which is precisely that of consummating the Mystery of Christ. This takes place by the power of the Holy Spirit, in Whom the Church had been conceived and by Whom she was born, on the day of Pentecost. This takes place by her witness, her preaching and her liturgy, that is to say, by her celebration of the sacraments of the Mystery, the permanent source of that outpouring of Christ's Spirit risen in His Mystical Body. It takes place by her whole life.

Going from Christ to the Church and from the Church to Christ, the Mystery is both *one* and *multiple*. One, for the work of God is essentially the gathering together of men into unity, with all the divisions of sin having been overcome (Gal 3:28), and in the end 'there will no longer be but Christ, Who is all in all' (Col 3:11). Multiple, for that unity does not suppress persons, but accomplishes them. We are now at heart of the 'Mystery of God,' as it is called by St Paul (Col 2:2), which is essentially a mystery of communion and of Trinitarian communion. Two Pauline formulas, in which is included the ensemble that forms the Epistles to the Corinthians, firmly express it: by God the Father, 'you had been called to the communion of the Son, Jesus Christ, our Lord' (1 Cor 1:9); 'the grace of our Lord Jesus Christ, the love of God and the communion of the Holy Spirit be with you always' (2 Cor 13:13). Here then is the Mystery in its most intimate and most essential aspect: it is the communication of the communion of Trinitarian Persons with the spiritual creatures, angels and men; and it is the entrance of the latter into the participation in that communion. It is there, in that communion of the Three Persons Who alone are God, that is founded and will be perfected the double aspect of unity and multiplicity which characterizes the Mystery, and which will also mark the sacraments. We must find again, in them, as in the Mystery, the presence and the action, one in its Trinity, of the Father, Son and Holy Spirit. Let us note this now: it is only in this Trinitarian perspective that the theology of the Mystery, that is, of the Incarnation and of the Redemption, can take place in the Holy Spirit. The same goes for sacramental theology, since the sacraments are the great means and signs by which the Mystery is consummated in time.

This unity in multiplicity appears also in the extension of the Mystery across space and time; for it is men of every place and time whom Christ wishes to gather together in Himself by the Holy Spirit. It is here especially that the sacramental order will reveal its necessity; for, it is necessary that the risen Christ touch men with His glorious flesh in order to communicate to them His Spirit and to insert them into His Body, the Church (1 Cor 12:12). This contact is necessary by reason of the nature of man, which is both spiritual and carnal, which the Redemption takes up completely, 'spirit, soul and body' (1 Thess 5:23). To make this possible the Word became flesh and, having become flesh, instituted the sacraments. A few long developments will be necessary here. Let us say in a word that the action of Christ, accomplished 'once for all' in time (ephapax; Heb 7:27), can touch all men of all times because all are connected to Him, whether as Creator or as Redeemer, and because the different times of history find in Him the principle of their unity.

We shall consider those problems later, when we study the foundations of the symbolic and sacramental order; but we must say something about it now in order to clarify this aspect of the Mystery. It is that unity of time in the multiplicity of successive instances which compose it which we would like to develop further. This unity is of a totality, which must be present to each of the multiple instances that compose it in order to give it meaning. Reciprocally, each instant is the bearer of the totality, from its beginning to its end; and it is only in the instant that the totality is realized. We see this in human existence. Each instant engages it. The past expresses itself there; the future is there in seed. But man aspires to an instant, that is to say, to an act which, by its fullness, will be the accomplishment of its existence and, by that fact, the suppression of its unfolding in that succession of instances. He aspires to this, but he cannot give himself to it. For such an act will be both the fullness of time and its eternity; the fullness of the duration and the suppression of its realization by the succession of instances. What we say of the existence of persons is equally applied to the life of societies, that is, to history. Yet Christ has—at least initially—realized this action, both the fullness and end of time, by His Mystery, the sum total of all mysteries, the '*acta et passa*' of His temporal life in history.

This is one of the most important aspects of that '*pleroma,*' that fullness, which God is pleased to have dwell in Christ (Col 1:19).

Christ accomplishes time by His Mystery. By His Incarnation He unites Himself to all men of all times; and He even unites them to Himself. Consequently, in the course of His mortal life, He took upon Himself all their actions, their good actions, of which He is the principle, in order to accomplish them; He took up their evil actions in order to destroy them in His flesh on the Cross. By His Death and Resurrection He finished destroying that source of death, which is sin, and He acquired the power of giving us the principle of His own life, the Holy Spirit. His Resurrection is especially, in its principle, the accomplishment of history; for, although situated in a precise time and place of that history, it represents the entrance of renewed humanity into a place and duration where, as St John says, 'time is no longer' (Rev 10:6); then, 'the Mystery of God shall be accomplished' (Rev 10:7). This is why 'Christ's past is not completed like that of a creature who belongs only to earthly time; Christ's time is continued in a current present, which is concerned with a new time inaugurated by the Resurrection ... Christ's act engages on one hand a part in the future of human history, on the other hand its past, because it puts an end to the ancient era of that history and establishes a new era,'[2] the eschatological era, the 'last times' (1 Tim 4:1). The truth is that only Christ and the Virgin Mary are fully *established* in this new situation, but Christians are *introduced* into it thanks to their contact with Christ by means of the sacraments. Here is why and how Christ can touch men of all times. Why: because by means of His flesh which is formed and united to Himself, He carries them all in Himself, drawing them along with Himself into His Passion and glory, and because, having risen in this glory, He introduced history into His final accomplishment, projecting into it all His energy in order to bring it to this completion. This is why the fullness of the Mystery is 'Christ all in all'

---

[2]   Fr Benoit, OP, *Les récits de l'institution et leur portée*, in *Lumière et Vie*, no. 31 (February 1957) 62. J. Dupont OSB, mentions in the same sense the 'eschatological note' of the Eucharist: '*Ceci est mon Corps, Ceci est mon Sang*', in *Nouv. Rev. Théol.*, 80, 1958, pp. 1040–1.

(Col 3:11) and more especially Christ living in each of His members (Gal 2:20). How: essentially by the sacraments, which assure this contact of Christ's flesh with all the places and times of history. The sacraments of the New Covenant do this with the fullness that Christ has given them by instituting them; the sacraments of the Old Covenant did this only imperfectly, to the extent that they were connected to, by prefiguring, the mysteries of Christ's earthly life.[3] It is the entire action of the Church which one must consider here, considering it as sacramental insofar as it is the action of Christ Himself by means of these ecclesial mediations. However, one must especially consider the sacramental liturgical action in the strict sense; for it is here above all that Christ acts. And at the center of the liturgy is found the Eucharist.

For the sake of showing the central place of the Eucharist in the life of the Church, it is of no little interest to note that it is most especially in Christ's own life that we observe that temporal ecomomy, and that in that economy the Passion is the center. It is here first and foremost, in the earthly life of Christ, that each movement carries by its very nature and accomplishes for its part, the totality of the Mystery. The Incarnation is already the kenosis of the Cross, since there the Word veils His glory in order to make Himself one of us (Phil 2:6–7). Moreoever, the Cross is the accomplishment of the Incarnation, at least if one considers it under this aspect of kenosis, since Christ, although without sin and because He is without sin, carries to the extreme the condition of the sinner which is ours and which He makes His own through His Incarnation (Phil 2:8). It is, however, in the Resurrection itself, where He completes His Mystery, that Christ remains the Word Incarnate and immolated 'for us and for our salvation.' This then is why and how He appears before the Father in interceding for us: He presents to the Father His wounds and His blood (Heb 9:12, 24), that is to say the love which goes 'to extremes' in His Passion (Jn 13:1). It is the slain Lamb Whom the

---

[3]   St Thomas Aquinas, *S.T.* III, q. 62, a. 6.

blessed adore in the eternal heavenly liturgy (Rev 5:9). There, in that immolation of love, there is the fullness of His glory.

Two things are to be considered here. The first is the central place of the Passion in the mysteries of Christ's life; the second is the presence of all the moments of His Mystery to the resurrected and glorified Christ. They are both important for the Eucharist, for this latter is directly the sacrament of the Passion; but it is necessary to see that, through that particular moment, it is the totality of Christ's Mystery that is present and complete in this sacrament. The Incarnation is continued—analogically speaking of course—in that Christ nourishes with His own flesh the members of His Body; the Passion, because He unites them to His sacrifice and allows them to participate in it; the Resurrection, because He allows them to enter into the glory where He Himself is already established. It is from that glory, where all the moments are equally present to Him, that He continues this work, especially in the sacrament of the Eucharist. We already explained above, from the point of view of time and history, how all these moments of the Mystery are present in the eschaton as complete. We wish to add here, from the point of view of the efficacy of the sacraments, that it is thanks to this eschatological and glorious completion that these signs of the Mystery can produce their effect of grace. They do this, in fact, by the operation of the Holy Spirit, Who is the great reality of the New Covenant (2 Cor 3:6; Acts 2:17, 32–36). During His earthly life Christ instituted the ministerial priesthood and the sacraments; however, it was only after His Resurrection, by the gift of His Spirit, that these institutions became for us living sources of His life in us. Thus we see how this reference to the eschatological end of the Mystery, the glorified Christ, is no less important than that of its principle, situated in history's past, namely the Incarnation and the Passion, for understanding the liturgy and the sacraments, and especially for knowing their historical and eternal immensity, their salvific efficacy, and their eminently sacred character.

A final aspect of this economy of the Mystery still to be mentioned, and a final parallelism antithetical to it, is that this 'Mystery of piety,' as St Paul calls it (1 Tim 3:16) is completed only in a daily struggle against 'the mystery of iniquity.' This latter, in fact, 'is always at work' (*energetai*; 2 Thess 2:7) against the Mystery of Christ, as the Mystery of Christ is against it. Therefore the Mystery in its totality is this struggle which keeps increasing (2 Thess 2:3, 8, ff), not only between the action of Christ's Spirit and the sin which is in us (Rom 8:1, ff; 2 Cor 3:16, ff; 4:4; Eph 6:12, 17), but also between Christ Himself and the Adversary (Mt 12:25–29; Jn 12:31). The power of the Adversary is such that our only recourse against him is the power of Christ. We do this through faith, hope and charity working (Eph 6:13–17) by tireless prayer (Eph 6:18), and therefore also, by that supereminent form of the Church's prayer, 'the divine Liturgy.'

While this last assertion has its foundation in the texts of the New Testament, it is based especially on the life of the Church and on her Tradition. We were able to see how, the more the centuries rolled on, the more the Church recognized the treasure that she had in this sacrament of sacraments, the Eucharist.[4] It is not surprising, therefore, that this sacrament became the central issue, or at least one of the principal issues, of the great battles of the Church in the modern times. For, it is by the Eucharist first and foremost that the Mystery of Christ is accomplished in time. Vatican II, following Pius XII, made some very valuable statements regarding this topic, especially when it declared that, 'the Eucharist is the source and summit of the entire evangelization.'[5] Therefore, it is, on the other hand, principally by its attacks against the Eucharist as well as the priesthood and revealed truth that 'the mystery of iniquity is at work' today and moves toward

---

[4]   See our work: *L'Eglise demande la multiplication des messes*, in *LPC*, no. 185; *see above*, Ch. VII.

[5]   '*Quapropter Eucharistia ut fons et culmen totius evangelizationis apparet*' (Vatican II, *Decree on the Ministry and Life of Priests*, no. 5). Cf. Pius XII, Enc. *Mediator Dei*, AAS 39, 1947, pp. 550 ff.

that temporary victory which the New Testament announces to us (2 Thes 2:3; Rev 13:7). The more the Eucharist, the 'Mystery of Faith,' the sacrament par excellence—the more it recoils, the more 'the mystery of iniquity' progresses. One cannot escape from this antithesis, which reveals itself as one of the most essential elements of the theology of the Mystery and the sacraments, and which tells us something about the meaning and seriousness of the current crisis.

II. From the 'Mystery' to the Sacraments and From the Sacraments to the 'Mystery'

In the preceding reflections we developed the different aspects of the temporal economy of the Mystery. Each of them was an occasion for us to see how that Mystery requires and truly includes the sacraments in order to be accomplished in its totality. It can be seen even better by looking back to what we called the internal structure of the Mystery, and which is also the intrinsic principle of its entire economy. It is here that we can also see and theologically justify the sacraments' internal structure and manner of operation.

'The Mystery of God,' St Paul teaches us, is that loving plan that He conceived in Himself from all eternity to allow us to enter into a communion of knowledge and of love, which is His own life. And it is by the Incarnation of His Word that He accomplishes this. The Incarnation therefore is, in a certain sense, the alpha and omega of that plan of love. Consequently, it is to this that we must turn our gaze if we wish to better know the Mystery in its essential structure as in the principle of its operation; and what is said of the Incarnation can be said of the sacraments as well. And if it is true that this Mystery, which begins with the Incarnation, is continued by the sacraments, it must also be admitted that Christ's humanity constitutes the primordial sacrament of this entire economy.[6]

---

6   It is important to take note here of the precision in the words. We do not say, as often happens today, that 'Christ' is 'the sacrament of God', but that His

We shall consider then first of all the Incarnation itself. When the Angel announced the word of God to Mary and when she accepted it by handing herself over to it, it was the Father Himself Who 'sent'—*misit*—His Word and, with the Word, His Spirit. Let us recall that notion of the temporal 'mission' of the Divine Persons; for, it is this notion, rooted in the Trinitarian 'processions,' which allows us to know the continuity between the event that then took place, the point of departure for the whole 'Mystery of Christ' or 'Mystery of God,' and the eternal life of the Trinitarian communion.[7] The Father 'sends' His Son by conceiving Him according to the flesh in the womb of the Immaculate Virgin. And the Word comes, conceiving Himself in her according to that flesh which He created in her womb in order to unite Himself to it hypostatically, that is to say by subsisting in that flesh, making it subsist and exist in Him. However, this work is 'accomplished' only by the 'mission' of the Holy Spirit, Who, sent by the Father and the Son, comes to bring about this unique union of the Virgin with the Word. It is by His action in her that Mary believes and that she welcomes the Word of the Father, not only in her mind, but even in her flesh. This is why it is said that what had been conceived in her was the work of the Holy Spirit (Matt 1:20). This work is properly one of union and therefore of fecundation: one of communion and of life.

---

humanity is the sacrament of the Word and of the Trinity—which is something totally different. Christ cannot Himself be the sacrament of God insofar as He is Himself God in His Person. This is why to call Christ, without any further clarification, 'the sacrament of God', which He is in His humanity, is to run the risk of reducing Him to this alone; and therefore one would be tempted to consider Him simply as man and deny His divinity.

[7] Let us recall that definition of 'mission' '*ad extra*' of the Divine Persons as formulated by St Thomas, but which, unfortunately, was not used sufficiently in his theology of grace: 'The mission of a Divine Person is a fitting thing, as meaning in one way the procession of origin from the sender, and as meaning a new way of existing in another.' (*S.T. I, q. 43, a. 1*).

It is thus that Christ's humanity is constituted by the operation of the entire Trinity; and that we contemplate in that humanity both the principle of the whole Mystery as well as the prototype of all the sacraments. For, His humanity, by its union with the Word, is in itself the first of the sacraments by which God saves us: a 'conjoined' instrument of the Godhead, while the sacraments of the Church are only 'separated' instruments.[8] From that perspective the very event of the Annunciation, as related to us by St Luke, appears to us as a solemn liturgy, grandiose in its simplicity. This is the first of all the Christian liturgies, and the first moment of the great Liturgy of the 'Mystery of God.'

Two distinctions will help us penetrate that economy, which goes from the Mystery to the sacraments and from the sacraments to the Mystery: the first, between the time of Christ's earthly life and that of the Church, which begins with Pentecost; the second, between being and acting. These will allow us to bring out the two principles that we need in order to understand the sacraments, starting with the Mystery of God: namely, *continuity,* which appeared in the passing from Christ's life to the history of the Church, and *analogy,* upon which the distinction between being and acting sheds some light. When we speak of the liturgy, it is first of all the time of the Church that we are considering and the Church's action in the celebration of the sacraments. Yet the sacraments are signs of the Mystery. In defining them as such we make reference to the liturgy of the Mystery, which leads us to consider it as a liturgy, that is to say as an action by which man renders glory to God and receives holiness from Him. For, it is in this that the liturgy consists. Therefore, in the Church it is this *usus sacramentorum* by which man renders to God the worship due to Him and receives from Him the grace of salvation, which He gives to us—both things being accomplished only in and through Christ.[9] This is why the liturgy of the

---

8   St Thomas, *S.T.* III, q. 62, a. 5.

9   'In the use of the sacraments (*'in usu sacramentorum'*), two things are to be considered, namely divine worship and the sanctification of man; the first

present time cannot be celebrated except by reproducing (in a manner which still needs to be clarified) and by *continuing* by the signs, which the sacraments are, the *acta et passa* of Christ's earthly life. The liturgy of the earthly Church in her present condition is therefore essentially this ecclesial accomplishment of the actions of Christ by which God is glorified and man saved. This is why we say that, just as the humanity of the Word Incarnate is the primordial sacrament of His work of salvation, so the mysteries of His earthly life are the first foundation of the whole liturgy, and the fundamental liturgy of His entire Mystery. This Mystery is extended and continued in the present time through the liturgy of the earthly Church, in union with that of the heavenly Church, by means of the sacraments, in order to come at the end of history to the glorification in which the heavenly liturgy alone will remain. St John allows us to get a glimpse of its splendor in the Book of Revelation, especially chapter five.

And here again, as in the earthly life of Christ—but this time in its fullness, since His whole heavenly Body will be there—the Liturgy and the Mystery will be but one; while in the present time the Liturgy is but a part of the Mystery, although it is the first and principal means of the latter's accomplishment. It is therefore between this principle, Christ's earthly life, and this end, the Resurrection with its completion in the Parousia, that the present liturgy of the Church is placed; and it draws its efficacy from this double relation, as we noted above. What we wish to mention here is the mysterious character that flows from that double relation into our liturgy and the liturgical character of the Mystery itself. We would also like to note the totally relative nature of the sacraments, and consequently the necessity (in order to understand them) of considering them only in this relation of conti-

---

concerns man in his relation to God, the second regards God in His relation to man' (*S.T.* III, q. 60, a. 5.). It is an implicit definition of the liturgy that St Thomas gives us here, consisting essentially in the '*usus*'—the celebration and administration, or reception—of the sacraments.

nuity, and even of tension, which exists between Christ's earthly life and His Resurrection: their principle and end.

But in order to recognize the continuity, the analogy which exists between the mysteries of Christ's life and the sacraments of the Church must be shown. This is easily done by distinguishing the 'being' point of view from the 'acting' point of view. This is a chief element in sacramental theology; for, only this analogy allows one to justify the continuity of which we speak: the continuity reveals the analogy, but it is the analogy that establishes the continuity.

To speak more accurately, it does not need to be establishd, but rather developed. The Augustinian definition of the sacraments immediately brings this to light: '*Accedit verbum ad elementum, et fit sacramentum.*'[10] This can be rendered only by one sentence: the word (pronounced by the priest) draws near to the material element, makes contact with it, unites itself with it, and the sacrament is made. We see this especially in the two major sacraments of Baptism and the Eucharist. This very dense phrase shows well both the distinction between being and action, and the analogy between sacrament and Incarnation, that is, between the sacraments and the Mystery. What belongs to acting is signified by the two words '*accedit*' and '*fit*.' What concerns being, in the more general sense of the constitution of a thing, is signified by the two elements which compose and constitute the sacrament: the '*verbum*' and the '*elementum*' (material). The Liturgy of the Church consists then in this acting, that is to say, in the act or in the collection of acts, by which the word is united to the matter for the glory of God and the salvation of men. This is why, we repeat, the theology of the sacraments cannot be done except in the framework of a theology of liturgy—for it is in the liturgy that the act which establishes the sacraments takes place—and therefore in a theology of Mystery, for that act is the continuation of the act of the redemptive Incarnation. This is also the reason that the High Priest

---

[10]   St Augustine, *In Joan. Tract.* 80, 3; *PL* 35, 1840; cf. St Thomas, *S.T.* III, q. 60, a. 6.

of the Liturgy, as of the Mystery itself, is always Christ: acting in the latter by Himself, and acting in the former through His ordained minister. One can see the analogy that assures this continuity. It is an analogy of structure, first and foremost at the level of being; for, in the Incarnation we see this union of the Word and the element, the sacraments. Or better: in the sacraments, as in the Incarnation, we see this union of the Word and the material element—a union of the uncreated Word and human flesh. Next, there is the analogy of operation at its most profound level, that of the Trinitarian opera-tions; for, we are going to find again in the sacraments that which we said of the Incarnation: namely that act of the Father, the Principle without a principle, Who sends His Son; the act of the Son, the Word Incarnate and High Priest of the Mystery and the Liturgy, Who with the Father sends the Spirit; and finally, the act of this Spirit, Who 'perfects' the work of the Father and Son by bringing about the desired union and thus making the sacraments fertile, whereby He allows us to communicate in the life of the Son and in His relation to the Father.

To better show this, let us consider Baptism, which is the first of the sacraments, and let us approach from the Incarnation, the princi-ple of the Mystery. We saw above how the Incarnation was the work of the whole Trinity, the 'mission' of the Second and Third Persons continuing in time their eternal 'processions.' The same goes for Baptism, as the formula for the sacrament indicates: 'I baptize you in the name of the Father and of the Son and of the Holy Spirit.' The action of the Son appears first; for when Peter or Paul baptize, it is Christ Himself Who baptizes.[11] But if the Son does it, so too does the Father; for, as Christ declared to us: 'The Son cannot do anything of Himself' (Jn 5:19); 'As the living Father has sent Me, and I live by the Father' (Jn 6:58); 'the Father Who dwells in Me accomplishes the works' (Jn 14:10). This is because the Father and the Son are one (Jn 10:30). And if They act together in their creature, it is necessarily in

---

[11] St Augustine, *In Joan. Tract.* 6; *PL* 35, 1428; cf. Vatican II, *Sacrosanctum concilium*, no. 7.

order to send Their Spirit into it. This is what they do in Baptism, in order to engender in us Their own life: it is 'by the Spirit that one must be born' (Jn 3:8), by a 'new' birth, which is the birth 'from on high' and which happens 'through water and the Spirit' (Jn 3:5). The mentioning of the water in this last passage proclaims the economy that binds that gift of the Spirit to the material element of the sacrament, and through the material element to the flesh of Christ. The Spirit Who is given to us is therefore Christ's Spirit, that is to say from the Son marked with the unction of the Spirit in His humanity (Jn 1:32 ff; 3:34; cf. Lk 1:35). He unites us to Himself in order to make us in Himself sons of the Father (Rom 8:14–16; 1 Cor 6:11).

What takes place in Baptism therefore is essentially a generation, and even a regeneration: man being purified from sin and snatched from death in order to be introduced into the condition and life of the sons of God. It is here that we see the analogy and the continuity with the Incarnation, and through it, with the eternal generation of the Word. As in the Incarnation, the Father sends the Son, but henceforth it will be through the mediation of Christ's flesh. He conceives Him in the soul of the one He baptizes and conceives the baptized in His Son made man. The Son, Who is the Word, conceives Himself in that soul, which He Himself created, by uniting Himself to it, conceiving it and giving it birth through participation in His own life. Yet this happens only by sending with and by the Father the Holy Spirit (Jn 14:26; 15:26), Who marks it with His 'seal' (2 Cor 1:22; Eph 1:13) and His 'unction' (1 Jn 2:20, 27), that is to say, He makes the soul 'Christian' (anointed) and transforms it into Christ (2 Cor 3:18), allowing it to live His life (Gal 5:25; 2:20). Such is the new being, 'the new creation' (2 Cor 5:17), the baptized: he is the son of the Father in His only beloved Son. And such is his life: a participation in the life of that Son, and therefore, in Him, in the life of the eternal Word, that is to say in that eternal generation by which the Word is spoken by His Father, and being spoken, also glorified in that unique and common 'spiration' of the Spirit of love. Thus it is that, by the

Father, in the Son and Holy Spirit, man enters by participation into the communion of the life of the Trinity. The whole meaning of his present life is to bring to its perfection this generation, this engendering. This is what the Church unceasingly works for by her preaching, her sufferings (Gal 4:19) and especially by the sacrament of the Eucharist: 'As the living Father hath sent Me, and I live by the Father; so he that eateth Me, the same also shall live by Me' (Jn 6:58). The two great truths that we wish to illustrate here are clearly proclaimed in this word of Christ: the analogy and continuity which exist between the mystery of the Incarnation and the sacrament of the Eucharist in particular, but also the sacraments in general; and therefore, it exists first of all with respect to Baptism, and then, between the life of Christ and that of the Christian. We see at the same time the necessity of passing through the flesh of Christ, and therefore through the sacraments, in order for this Mystery of communion and life to be accomplished: 'Unless a man be born again of water and the Holy Spirit, he cannot enter into the kingdom of God' (Jn 3:5).

We must insist on this last point; for a certain poorly understood spiritualization, even sometimes a unilateral insistence, on the role of the word, has led in our day to what could be called a docetism, or better yet a sacramental occasionalism: God does not truly act through the signs that are the sacraments, but simply on their occasion; and this action remains secondary in every way.[12] This is demonstrated so well by the current term 'sacramentalization' and the subordinate place given to it in relation to the term 'evangelization,' which centers completely on the preaching of the word. It says that what matters is the proclamation of the evangelical word and the

---

[12] St Thomas, *S.T.* III, q. 62, a. 1. We shall frequently return to this text, where St Thomas refutes that opinion; for he notes here the difference that exists between the simple action by way of sign, and the sacramental action, which, while using the sign, goes beyond it. What the sacrament adds is the properly instrumental aspect of the 'efficacious' sign, the word, matter and action, in which it consists and by which the flesh of Christ is extended in order to touch us (cf. *ibid*, q. 62, a. 4.).

adherence to the faith which it brings. There will always be time later for bestowing the sacraments, which almost appear as a mere formality and not as something necessary for the work of salvation. It is true that, on the other hand, there was for some years a tendency toward a certain reduction in the value of the sacraments, but this was under the sign of a 'symbolism,' which rendered the rediscovery extremely ambiguous. We shall return to this later.

No doubt it is necessary for the adult to believe if he wishes to receive Baptism, but it is only by the sacrament that he will be reborn in Christ and receive the life of faith. That is why, in the solemn sending of His Apostles, Christ places the sacrament of Baptism before instruction in the Christian life (Matt 28:19–20). For, while it is the Holy Spirit Who gives us the life of Christ, it is given to us only through His humanity. A contact that is both carnal and spiritual is therefore necessary. The fact of the primacy of the spiritual element explains why man can be saved by a simple desire—even only implicit—for Baptism, as the Church teaches.[13] However, even in this case, the desire is not efficacious except by its reference to Christ's flesh, and more directly to the water that flowed from His side in order to save us from sin, and which touches us through the sacrament.[14] Moreover, the word of Christ is categorical: 'Unless a man be born again of water and the Holy Spirit, he cannot enter into the kingdom of God' (Jn 3:5). It is every aspect of the Incarnation that is at stake here. The Word is made flesh through the work of the Spirit in Mary, and He pours forth His Spirit into the Mystical Body—which is the aim of all His work (Jn 7:37–39)—only by means of that same flesh, extended and continued in the sacraments which He Himself instituted for that end. For this reason everyone has need of Baptism and the Eucharist. It is known that this latter is not strictly required for eternal life; but it is practically needed in order to avoid sin and to

---

[13]   *Ibid.*, III, q. 66, a. 11; cf. Council of Trent, Session VI, Chapter IV.

[14]   *Ibid.*, III, q. 66, a. 3.

come to the perfection of charity.[15] This is why we think it can be said that it is strictly necessary for the life of the Church in its totality.

One can see this need for the mediation of the sacraments even better when one understands how they act, namely as *signs* and *instruments*. These two notions also belong to traditional sacramental theology,[16] and they will allow us to develop the analogy and continuity that exist between the Mystery and the Liturgy. This obliges us to return once again to the first of the mysteries, the Incarnation. In order to be the primordial sacrament of the work of salvation, the humanity of Christ must be not only the *instrument* of the divinity, but also and first of all its *sign*. His humanity is the 'conjoined instrument' of the Word, as opposed to the sacraments, which are only 'separated instruments.'[17] But in what, and more accurately, of what, does His humanity come to be the sign? It is a sign of God and His love because, 'the glory of God' (2 Cor 4:6) shines on the face of Christ before our eyes, and because all of His work shows us His love and mercy (Jn 3:16; 1 Jn 4:9). However, more must be said; for in Christ the sign reaches the level of an image. A Son by His eternal generation, Christ is the very image of the Father.[18] As man, He is, like all men, 'in the image' of God (Gen 1:27); but by the fact that it is the same Person of the Son Who subsists in His humanity, He is both[19]: of the whole Trinity, the uncreated communion of Whom is reflected by all of Christ's being and acting; and, more directly, of the Person of the Son, Whose humanity reproduces its characteristics more directly from the fact that it is united hypostatically to Him. In the same way His humanity will be both the sign and the instrument of the Trinity; for, the Three Persons operate

---

[15]   *Ibid.*, III, q. 73, a. 3; cf. Council of Trent, Session XXI, Chapter IV.

[16]   This can be seen in the preceding chapter. One will remember in particular the priority of the notion of sign: the sacraments 'cause' only because they 'signify' and through signifying.

[17]   *S.T.* III, q. 62, a. 5. cf. *see below*, p. Ch.XI.

[18]   *Ibid.*, I, q. 35, a. 2.

[19]   This will be found later in the baptized in an analogous manner.

together in it, and more particularly, the instrument of the Word, Who subsists in it, soul and body.

We must add a clarification to what we said above regarding the analogy of the union of the 'word' and the 'element' in the sacraments and in the Incarnation. For, the eternal Word unites Himself to material flesh only by means of the soul that He created in order to inform it. There is no doubt that the Word subsists immediately in both, soul and body; but the body, 'the *elementa*' is fitted by that hypostatic union to the Word of God only through the created soul that informs it.[20] This takes place in such a way that His soul appears somewhat as the created word, which the uncreated Word pronounces over carnal matter in order to make it His Body, to unite Himself substantially in it, and to accomplish by it His redemptive work, 'the Mystery of God.' We thus see more clearly still at what point Christ's humanity, soul and body, 'word' and 'element,' is truly the primordial sacrament, the first sign and instrument of the Redeemer Word and of the entire Trinity.

This is why—we understand better now—everything in the being and acting of Christ *reveals* and *realizes* for us the Mystery of the Trinitarian communion. In His being: just as God is the Trinity, that is a communion of God and the Son in Love, so the Word in His Incarnation is also a communion—a communion of the Word, the soul which He created and the body which He made His own, and of the Father with all humanity by means of that singular humanity, which the Word makes His own in order to gather all to His Father in the Breadth of Their Spirit of love. This could be developed further by showing the analogy and continuity that exist between the Person of the Word and the 'created grace' of the Hypostatic Union, and between this latter and the baptismal character.[21] However, this will

---

[20]   *S.T.* III, q. 6, a. 1.

[21]   We are borrowing here an idea very dear to Fr Philippe de la Trinité, OCD (see his article: *Théologie trinitaire de la grâce et des vertus théologales. Pour une évolution homogène de la pensée thomiste*, in *Divinitas* 17, 1973, 159–79, where

be another discourse, still difficult to hold, due to a lack among theologians of an adequate metaphysic of the substance and a lack of agreement on the place of the Christian 'character' in the person.[22] It is nevertheless into these perspectives that a reflection on the revelation of the Trinitarian communion in Christ's being opens up. It is revealed also in His acting, that is to say, in the mysteries of His earthly life; for, it is in these, from the Incarnation to the Parousia, that Christ realizes His plan of communion inscribed in His very own being. Consequently, in each of His works one finds signs of the Trinitarian communion: in the Incarnation—we already showed it—because it is its principle; in the Passion, because it is the sacrifice of love that seals the covenant between God and humanity; in the Resurrection

---

there are references to all his preceding studies on this question since 1936). In the same vein one could read the developed research of Fr Robertus a Sancta Teresia a Jesu Infante (Roberto Moretti), OCD: *De inhabitatione SS. Trinitatis, Doctrina S. Thomae in scripto super Sententiis*, Rome, Fac. Theol. OCD, 1961 (with an important preface by Msgr A. Combes). Fr L. Bouyer also moves in this direction when he deplores the absence of the Trinitarian perspective of the *Sentences* in the theology of grace in the *Summa* (*Le Consolateur. Esprit et Saint et Vie de grâce*, Paris, Cerf. 1980, pp. 259–72). But this allows us to make a remark about him, namely, that Dom Lucien Chambat (*Présence et union*, Paris, 1959; cit. pp. 271 ff) is not 'the only modern Thomist' to have shown the reduction made by St Thomas from the *Sentences* to the *Summa Theologiae*. The three names that we just cited are proof of this. That being said, we agree with him with regards to the lack of Thomists and other theologians who have gone in that direction, the only one which would allow one to recognize fully the supernatural.

22   It is known that St Thomas places the character in a 'power of the soul', not in the soul's essence, specifically in its 'cognitive power' (III, q. 63, a. 4.). For many reasons this doctrine does not satisfy us. This insufficiency comes both from the lack of development of Trinitarian perspectives, which we noted in the above footnote, as well as the incomplete character of the thomistic metaphysic of the substance. For, it is in this latter, insofar as it is the principle of ontological subsistence in us, in which the character must be placed. We would like, God willing, to return some day to this question, which seems to us of the highest importance for Christian anthropology, both natural and supernatural.

and Ascension, because they are the fruit and consummation of that covenant, that is, of that finally reestablished communion. Therefore, it is because the mysteries of Christ's life are the signs and instruments of the communion that is God, and one which He wants to extend to us—it is because of this that the sacraments of the Church, a continuance of those mysteries, are also signs and instruments of that same Mystery, that is to say, the signs and instruments of the plan of love of the Trinity.

While the Incarnation is the first of these mysteries, and Baptism is a sacrament of this, the Passion is the second mystery, and its sacrament is the Eucharist. No doubt all the sacraments represent, to a certain degree, the Passion that saves us; for, it is from the Passion that they take their efficacy, and because, as we said above, each one of the mysteries of Christ's life contains all the others in itself. But if we consider the sacraments in their signification, and therefore in their own efficacy, it must be said that Baptism is not the sacrament of Christ's Passion except insofar as it plunges us into both His Death and His Resurrection (Rom 6:2–6), while the Eucharist signifies and represents immediately the sacrifice by which Christ redeemed us. This then is, in the strongest sense of the word, 'the sacrament of Christ's Passion'; and its proper effect, insofar as it is a sacrament, is 'to make us perfect in our union with the suffering Christ' and the Christ Who immolates Himself for us.[23] Furthermore, with the immolated and risen Christ now being in glory, the Eucharist communicates to us His glorious life. This is why the Eucharist is the sacrament of communion par excellence: communion with Christ in the sacrifice of the Covenant, and later, on the way, 'viaticum,' towards communion with Him in glory (Jn 6:54); and that will be the work of the Holy Spirit in us (Rom 8:11). For, it is always by being in us, giving us His Spirit, that Christ gives us life. In the same movement the Eucharist nourishes and tightens the Church's communion: 'For we, being many, are one bread, one body, all that partake of one bread'

---

[23]   St Thomas, *S.T.* III, q. 73, a. 3.

(1 Cor 10:17). To which we must add—and which is no less important—that the Eucharist, being not only a sacrament but also a
sacrifice, the very sacrifice of Christ, communicates its fruits of life
not only to those who participate in it and receive it as a sacrament,
but also to all those for whom it is offered as a sacrifice.[24] This is why
it is truly 'the Mystery of faith' in its totality, and why it is the most
fitting and most powerful means by which that Mystery, 'the Mystery
of Christ,' continues to be at work (*energetai*) in the Church, and
through the Church in the world. It is by the Eucharist before all else
that the energies of the immolated and glorified Lamb pour themselves into His Body in order to allow it to triumph over the 'Mystery
of iniquity' and to arrive with the entire ecclesial Body at the fullness
of His glory.

It is this which we would like to demonstrate now. In order to do
this we must take up again and develop that reality of the sacrifice by
seeing how it is at the center of the historical vision of the Mystery,
according to which all is in all, each stage bearing in itself whatever
preceded it in order to complete them, and those which follow it in
order to prepare them. Furthermore, this is why no stage is a pure and
simple repetition of the preceding one; for, as one stage takes up the
other only in order to project it towards that which will follow, one
step more is taken towards the final completion of the Mystery. The
immense fresco of this history can be understood with the help of this
very simple schema, which indicates the principle of its economy's
foundation: *preparation, realization, completion*; but also according to
that elementary dialectic, which goes from the reality to the sign and
from the sign to the reality, from the history to the rite and from the
rite to the history. In a word: from the Mystery to the Liturgy and
from the Liturgy to the Mystery, in order to be completed, beyond
time and history, in the glory of the eschaton.[25] For, while all begins

---

[24] *Ibid.*, III, q. 79, a. 7; cf. Council of Trent, Session, XXII, can. 3.

[25] We prefer this word to 'eschatology', whose ambiguity was shown by J. Carmignac (*Le mirage de l'eschatologie. Royauté, Règne et Royaume de Dieu ... sans*

with a primary reality, the plan of love conceived and 'hidden in God for all eternity,' that plan will be realized and come to eternal completion only in matter and through a temporal unfolding. For which reason there is the need for signs for its revelation to other beings of flesh like us, but also for its realization; and this especially for the central act of every religion: the sacrifice. St Augustine noted this, and the history of religions clearly confirms it: 'Whether they be true or false, religions cannot gather men together except by reuniting them by means of visible signs or sacraments.'[26] And it is known how he saw in each of the visible sacrifices of those religions 'the sacrament, that is to say, the sacred sign of the invisible sacrifice,'[27] that is, that interior act by which man offers himself to God in order to enter into communion with Him.[28] But seeing that man is opposed to God through sin, the first thing that the sacrifice must do is to repair or expiate that sin. Expiation and communion are therefore the two poles of every sacrifice; and they cannot be completed except by the immolation and oblation of the entire victim to God, as happens in the sacrifice of the holocaust.

What will be this victim? Man himself. However, since human sacrifices had been forbidden by God, man was replaced by an animal, which had value only by being a sign of man. This is the first meaning of Abraham's sacrifice (Ex 22); the second was as a prefiguration of the sacrifice of Christ. For, in the final analysis, it is man himself who would have to immolate and offer himself to God. But only Christ would be able to do this, since He was God and man. As God, He

----

eschatologie, Paris, Letouzey et Ané, 1979). The *eschaton* is the end of history; it had been realized by the mysteries of the Incarnation, the Passion and the Glorification of Christ, and it will be consummated by His Parousia, at the end of the 'last times', which He opened when He restored His Kingdom among us.

26 *Contra Faustum*, XI; *PL* 42, 355. In order to verify the foundation of this statement, one could consult the monumental *Histoire des croyances et des idées religieuses*, by M. Eliade (3 volumes), Paris, Payot, 1976.

27 *De Civitate Dei*, L. X., ch. V; *PL* 41, 282. cf. See below, note 607.

28 St Thomas, *S.T.* III, q. 22, a. 2; cf. q. 48, a. 3.

would have power over His own life; as man, He would have a body in which He could immolate Himself. All that preceded this moment had only been the *preparation*, in the reality of history and in signs, of that which Christ would have to be and do. All that would follow this moment would only be the *completion* of what He would do and realize by His Incarnation and His Paschal sacrifice. In Christ, in the mysteries of His earthly life, all the signs become history and history is accomplished. And yet every sign still remains, whether because His flesh always remains and even becomes in its fullness the epiphany of the spiritual, or because Christ's Ascension and Pentecost open up a new time, that of the Church, for the *final* completion of the Mystery. It is for this new time and this completion that Christ instituted those new signs, which are the sacraments. However, different from those of the time of preparation, the sacraments do not prefigure Christ's Mystery and His Paschal sacrifice: they represent these mysteries already accomplished, and they prefigure only their eschatological and glorious completion. This is why the sacrifice of Christ, at the center of history, abolishes all other sacrifices by completing them in Him; and this is why His sacrifice will henceforth be the only sacrifice, unceasingly perpetuated by His sacrament, the Eucharist, and always working towards completion in the life of the Church and of Christians, the Body and members of the whole Christ.

It would be good for us to pause and reflect awhile on these truths. They tell us of the immensity of what takes place at each Mass, each one of those 'Liturgies' being, like the historical and trans-historical reality which it represents and accomplishes 'in the sign,' the recapitulation and the fullness of the entire Mystery. It will be necessary in particular to recall what had been the preparation of the Incarnation itself, in history and in the signs, how it began with creation, that first modeling of the flesh, which the Word needed to make His own. We need to recall how it was carried out, after sin, by the numerous promises of a salvific lineage, since the proto-evangelium (Gen 3:15), and the series of particular 'elections' by which that flesh and that lineage had been immediately prepared, from Abraham to David, and from David to Joseph and Mary (Matt 1:1–16). On the level of the sign all these were preparations according to various degrees, inasmuch as they were prefigurations of the Elect par excellence, Christ. And all this was the work of the Holy Spirit, from His action over the waters in creation (Gen 1:2), to that which He accomplished in the womb of the Immaculate Virgin for the Conception of Christ's flesh. It is this flesh which is rendered present and which is given to the Church in the Eucharist: the completion of that immense preparation—immense, more still because of that of which it is the germ, namely the Church and the renewed creation; and by the gift which will spring out from it for the accomplishment of this work, the Holy Spirit. For, it is always from the flesh of the glorified Christ, that is to say, both crucified and risen (Jn 17:1), that the Holy Spirit springs forth to build the Church. This is essentially what the Holy Sacrifice of the Mass brings about.

With respect to the preparation of this sacrifice, the one redemptive sacrifice, that of Christ at the center of history—with respect to this preparation, it is not only in all the sacrifices of Israel that one finds it, but also in all those religions previous (more theologically speaking than chronologically) to that of the Chosen People, to the extent that they had a true worship of God and not the worship of demons of pagan idolatry (1 Cor 10:20–21). In fact, just as the Incarnation is the assumption by the Word of all creation by means of the individual humanity in which He came to subsist, so His sacrifice takes up again in itself, in order to sanctify and render them pleasing to God, all that the religious sacrifices of humanity had in them that was good, and which, moreover, resulted from that one redemptive sacrifice. It is here especially that the dialectic of the sign and history comes into play; for, human sacrifices excluded, any good that those religions offer can only be but the remotely prefigurative sign of the sacrifice that God demands, and which is the total gift of Himself. God alone could offer this real sacrifice to Himself, a sacrifice that would become the center of history: He would do this by His Incarnation and by the immolation of His 'flesh' on the cross, a flesh which He would assume for this purpose. It is from this sacrifice, *historical* as all the others, that these others would take their meaning and power, these latter being but *signs* of the former. It is under this aspect that they can be given to man to be accomplished in their own life and *history*.

From this assumption of all the sacrifices from the time of preparation into His own redemptive sacrifice, Christ gives us a proof in the sign that He instituted both for the sake of perpetuating His sacrifice, but also for the sake of assuming the preparations that preceded it. For, it is by this sign, the Last Supper of Holy Thursday, that He takes them up and makes them His own. Various testimonies, as well as the explicit words of Christ, prove that the Last Supper had been a sacrifice, and that it brought about this assumption of all the past sacrifices. By His words, in fact, Christ places the action that He works in relation with the sacrifice that He was going to offer the day after on Calvary—somewhat in the way that the ancient prophets formerly worked symbolic actions, or more precisely, prophetic actions, realizing in a sign the event that they would announce.[29] In

---

[29] J. Dupont showed this well: 'It is the symbolic aspect that appears first, and the nuance of the institution narrative concerns this aspect. In saying of the bread that He broke, "This is My Body," and of the wine in the cup, "This is My Blood," Jesus proclaims by a prophetic action the sacrifice that He is about to accomplish on Calvary. It is nevertheless an efficacious sign; for, by eating of that bread and drinking of that cup the Apostles really enter into the Covenant that the sacrifice on Calvary will seal' (*Art. cit.*, p. 1035; see on the preceding page the examples of those 'prophetic actions' in the Old Testament: Jer. 27–8; 1 Kings 22:11; 2 Kings 13:17). Msgr A Descamps borrowed this idea (*Les origines de l'eucharistie*, in *L'Eucharistie, symbole et réalité* (Coll. 'Réponses chrétiennes') Gembloux–paris, Duculot–Lethielleux, 1970, pp. 57–125; cf. p. 94). However, it is Fr Benoit who best shows how, namely by the power of Christ and by the opening of the eschatological era which He brings about—how the action of Chirst, the institution of the sacrament of the Eucharist, how it surpasses in impact, in realism and in efficacy the

fact, more than symbolic, even more than prophetic, Christ's action was 'sacramental.' Here is its exact nature, the meaning and impact of which we are trying to develop here. And there is a second fact, which shows us the sacrificial character: the framework in which it is celebrated; for it is a liturgy and a liturgy of the Jewish Passover, in other words, the immolation of the Paschal lamb.[30] In our opinion it is extremely significant that the Last Supper, with its Paschal context, looks back to the sacrifice of the Egyptian exodus (Ex 12:3–14), and not to that of the Old Covenant (Ex 24:4–8). And yet, in presenting itself explicitly by the words of Christ as the sacrifice 'of the New Covenant' (Matt 26:28; cf. Heb 8:6 ff), it also looks back to the sacrifice of the Mosaic Covenant. But it does this for the sake of suppressing it; first, by replacing it, for that first sacrifice is revealed as powerless (Heb 10:1); and second, by accomplishing 'in truth' the promise of liberation that it contained, but which was first of all the liberation from Egypt.

In addition to these two sacrifices, there are all the sacrifices of Israel's history that are found assumed and accomplished in the sacrifice of Christ, whose inherent unity has been correctly emphasized.[31] And ever since the time of the Fathers, Christian reflection has

---

symbolic and prophetic actions of the Old Testament Prophets (*Art. cit.*, pp. 62–71). What J. Dupont says of the Last Supper, Fr De Vaux correctly says of every sacrifice: 'The sacrifice is the essential act of external worship. It is a prayer in action; it is a symbolic action that renders efficacious the interior sentiments of the one offering it and the response that God makes to it. It is somewhat similar to the symbolic actions of the prophets' (*Les Institutions de l'Ancien Testament*, Paris, Cerf, 1960, vol. II, p. 340).

30 On the Passover, its origin and signification, cf. R. De Vaux, *op. cit.*, pp. 382–94. Called into question by some, the Paschal character of the Last Supper cannot be doubted. It is supported by the most rigorous exegetes. J. Betz cites in support of it (*Eucharistie in der Schrift und Patristik* (Handbuch der Dogmengeschichte Bd. IV, Fzkl. 4a) Fribourg, Herder, 1979, pp. 8–9): J. Jeremias, *Die Abendmahslworte Jesus alttestamentlichen Motive in der urchristlichen Abendsmahlüberlieferung* (in *Evangelische Theologie*, 1967); A. Jaubert, *La date de la Cène* (1957).

shown how the multiplicity of those sacrifices had been necessary in order to prefigure and prepare the riches of the one sacrifice of Christ,[32] which was a 'holocaust,' a 'sacrifice of communion' and an 'expiatory sacrifice.'[33] It was not, however, a 'benediction' (*berakah*), the typical form of worship in the Jewish synagogue, which can only be said to be found there assumed and accomplished by being radically transfigured and surpassed.[34] In addition, the matter used by Christ, bread and wine, and the title of 'the great High Priest according to the order of Melchizedek,' which was given to Him, show, by means of the sacrifice of that mysterious personage (Gen 14:18–20), that all the sacrifices of the pagan world before Israel and before the Incarnation are present and assumed at the Last Supper: and through the Last Supper, at Calvary; and through Calvary, at the Mass.

Thus it is that Christ's Paschal sacrifice appears to us at the center of history and time: between its preparation, in history and in signs, and its completion, in signs and in history. Christ in His Mysteries is Himself history and sign, assuming all that was sign into the sign, which He Himself is, accomplishing all that is history in the fullness of history, which He Himself realizes, establishing the new era of history, that is the eschatological era of the last days, in order that that may be accomplished what He realized in Himself, instituting signs

---

[31] R. De Vaux, *op. cit.*, p. 313.

[32] St Augustine, *De Civitate Dei*, L. X, ch. XX (*PL* 41, 298); *Contra adv. Leg et prophet.*, L. I, ch. XVIII (*PL* 42, 624); etc. cf. St Thomas, *S.T.* I–II, q. 103, a. 3; a. 8; q. 107, a. 2.

[33] R. De Vaux, *op. cit.*, pp. 290–9: cf. pp. 302 ff; pp. 340–4.

[34] L. Bouyer, *op. cit.*, p. 346; cf. Neh 9. Fr Bouyer presents 'the Eucharistic prayer' as being 'the final development of the Jewish, or rather Hebrew, *berakoth* ... ' (p. 344). But this is a development that carries with it an essential overstepping (cf. J. Betz, *op. cit.*, p. 11, bases himself on the works of J. P. Audet). Fr J. Lecuyer, basing his position on the Epistle to the Hebrews, Chapters 9 and 10, insists on the connection between the sacrifice of Jesus and 'the solemn liturgy of Kippour' (*Le sacerdoce dans le Mystère du Christ* (Lex Orandi, 24), Paris, Cerf, 1957, p. 22). More points of view and citations could be brought forward. See below, Chapter XI, I.

by which, before anything else, that accomplishment will take place: the sacraments which He bequeathed to His Church.

However, in order to see fully at what point the sacrament of the Eucharist is central in that accomplishment of the Mystery, we must recall again that the economy of preparation, of realization and of completion, which associates the earthly life of Christ with that which precedes it and with that which follows it, is found again in the very depths of the Mysteries of that life. Its three principal moments, we said, are the Incarnation, the Paschal Sacrifice, and the Resurrection. We also saw how the first *prepares* and already contains the second; how the second is the fuller *realization* of the first; and how the third, the Resurrection, along with the Ascension and entrance into glory, is the *completion* of both. Because He was God in His Person, Christ could not not rise; and because He was made man for sinners, 'it was necessary that He suffer in order to enter into His glory' (Lk 24:26). The Resurrection is therefore the final end of the Incarnation and the fruit of the redemptive Sacrifice, itself the fullness of the Incarnation. That Sacrifice thus appears to us as the center of the Mystery of Christ's earthly life, *a center which is both the fullness and the totality of that which it gathers together*. Yet the Mass is the sacramental sign of this center. Therefore, one sees, or rather one cannot but get a glimpse of, the universal dimensions of the Mystery, which is accomplished there and which will be accomplished in the Church. For, all that she will do will be but the completion of that which Christ already realized for her. He has done for her all that she must do for Him; therefore, it is from Him that she receives all that she must do for Him through Him. And this 'wonderful exchange' is the primary thing that takes place in the Eucharist.

We can summarize these reflections on the economy of the Mystery and on the relation between the Passion, or the Passover of Christ, and the Eucharist, by the following three propositions:

   a) the Mystery of Christ's earthly life is the realization, the center and the fullness of the history of salvation;

b) Christ's Passover is the realization, center and fullness of the Mystery of Christ's earthly life;

c) the Eucharist is the sacrament, that is to say the realization, in and by the sign, of this fullness of history, which is the one Passover of Christ; and by that fact, the Eucharist is the means par excellence of the accomplishment of His Mystery in the eschatological time, which He opened up for that purpose.

This is why, while Baptism cannot be repeated—since it is the sacrament of our birth in the life of Christ, and once born or reborn one cannot be born or reborn again—on the other hand, it is essential to the Eucharist to be constantly renewed; for, each day we must succeed in dying to the life of sin and being born in the life of Christ. Such is the meaning, for us as individuals, of the Mass and daily Communion,[35] 'the superstantial bread' that Christ teaches us to ask for (Lk 11:3), meaning, according to a most certain traditional interpretation, His Eucharistic Body.[36] However, to that fruit of life, which the Eucharist gives to each of the faithful who receives it as a sacrament, is added that which it brings to the entire Church, for whom it is offered as a sacrifice;[37] whence the necessity of its daily immolation for all the members of the Mystical Body. Whence also the immense good which the Church receives from the multiplication of that immolation; thus she has more and more clearly understood it, the more she herself has entered into the knowledge and accomplishment of the Mystery.[38]

How can this happen? We shall explain how with a bit more detail at the end of the third part of this work, after having developed the notions of sign and instrument with the help of symbolism. But in

---

[35] St Thomas, *S.T.* III, q. 80, a. 10.

[36] See the texts collected by J. Carmignac (*Recherches sur le 'Notre Père'*, Paris, Letouzey et Ané, 1969): Tertullian, Origen, St Cyprian, St Cyril of Jerusalem, St Ephrem, St Ambrose, St Jerome, St Augustine, etc.

[37] Cf. *see above*, note 24.

[38] Cf. *see above*, note 4.

order to conclude these reflections in line with what we have said here, we shall show now how the entire Trinity is at work in the Liturgy of the Eucharist, and how the Eucharist is, each time, the means *of a new 'mission' of the* sanctifying *Spirit* in the Church. While Baptism is the continuation of the Incarnation, as the sacrament by which we are born into the life of the sons of God in Christ, the Eucharist is the sacrament by which we arrive at the fullness of that life; for it allows us to communicate in the paschal mystery of His Death and Resurrection. In the Eucharist as in Baptism, the principal function of which is to introduce us into that Mystery, the entire Trinity is at work. This work, which appears to be especially the work of the Son, is accomplished only by the will of the Father, and 'is perfected' only by the operation of the Holy Spirit. It is by the Holy Spirit that are realized the conception of Christ in the womb of the Immaculate Virgin, and the conception of Christians, through Baptism, in the Mystical Body of Christ, and therefore in the womb of the Church. The Holy Spirit does not operate alone, but insofar as He is 'sent' by the Father and the Son, and therefore with Them.

The same can be said of Calvary and the Eucharist, not only in a general manner because the Spirit is the inspiration of all of Christ's life (Lk 4:1, 14, 18; 10:21; 11:23) and the life of the Church (Act 1:8; 2:23), but more precisely because He is the Spirit of love and of life. He is the Love which urged Christ to give His life (Jn 15:13), and the life, that is the breath, the spirit of life (*ruah; pneuma; spiritus*: Gen 2:7) is in the blood (Lev 17:11, 14). This is why, while pouring out His Blood, it is His vital spirit that Christ exhales and offers to the Father. Such is the meaning of His last word from the Cross: 'Father, into Your hands I commend My spirit' (Lk 23:46). However, as this breadth of life is infused by the Holy Spirit, it is that same Spirit Who leaves Christ's Body with and in His spilt Blood, with and in His last word and breath. Christ's Spirit is therefore inseparable from this created, vital spirit; and the uncreated, Holy Spirit springs forth and is poured out into the Church through the created spirit. It is for this reason that, ever since the Incarnation, the sacraments have been necessary for communicating the Holy Spirit to Christians. By the sacrifice of Calvary the Holy Spirit returns to the Father, having inspired the offering of love, reparation, praise and thanksgiving. In the power acquired by Christ in His Resurrection, the Spirit comes down again on the disciples in order to form them into the Church and to move them to a profound participation in the Paschal Mystery, where He will unceasingly flow down upon them.

This is also signified by the symbolism of water, developed in a special way by St John. Water is both the life and the Spirit (Jn 7:37–39). It flows with the blood, which gives the former its efficacy, from the side of Christ crucified (Jn 7:19–34); and it is poured out upon the Church from the throne, where the Lamb is now seated in glory, at the right hand of the Father (Rev 22:1). It is through water that Christ works in Baptism, while in the Eucharist He acts immediately through His own Blood.

This is what takes place at each Mass, whether the priest is alone or together with the faithful. Alone, the priest better represents Christ in His Passion; for, the Savior was dramatically alone at that moment. Together with the faithful, he better represents Christ in glory, where all will be united around Him. In both these cases what takes place in the liturgy of this sacrament is what took place at Calvary. This is why the Mass has a purifying and animating power for the whole Church. At Mass Christ Himself pours out His Blood and offers it to the Father for His Church. The Father receives this sacrifice, and in it the sacrifice of the Church. The Spirit springs forth, mounting up towards the Father in the Blood of Christ, and, by that same Blood, flows down into the Body of the whole Church; for, it is for the whole Church that Christ's Blood is poured out and offered in sacrifice. Thus each Mass is like another redemptive beat of the Heart of Christ. He draws in the blood of His Church—for it is in her and through her that He offers Himself—in order to communicate His own Blood to her; and He does this in His own Spirit, through Whom He will unite Himself to the Church, having been completely purified and sanctified. One can thus understand the words of the Church herself, when she presents the Eucharist as 'the source and summit of evangelization,' and more profoundly still, as 'the (very) work of our Redemption.' One can understand as well the exhortations that she addresses to her priests to celebrate this sacrifice every day;[39] for, it is only by the priest that, when all stains are blotted out and all divisions suppressed, the Mystery of the divine communion will be consummated in the Church. The Bride, united by the Spirit to the Bridegroom, will then enter through Him, with Him and in Him, by all His fullness, into all the fullness of the eternal communion of the Father.

III. From the Symbolic Order to the Sacramental Order

What we presented up to this point represents an initial development of sacramental and liturgical theology in a mysterious perspective, at once Trinitarian and historico-salvific, taking for its point of departure the Incarnation and concluding in a keen awareness of the action of the Holy Spirit. We saw the analogy of structure that exists between the Mysteries of the redemptive Incarnation and the sacraments of the Church, as well as the continuity of the economy where they are accomplished. This economy, considered in its totality, includes the time of preparation, which is also that of prefiguration. Also, its inner law is to go from the sign to the reality in order to go from the latter to the former, in view of a final and definitive realization: the prefigurative sign of the time of preparation, the historical realization by the Mystery of Christ to the center of time, new and re-presentative signs of this Mystery: the sacraments of the New Covenant, in view of the realization, or better, of the eschatological completion in the

---

39   Paul VI, Enc. *Mysterium fidei, AAS* 57, 1965, pp. 761–2; Vatican II, *Decree on the Ministry and Life of Priests*, no. 13. Noting that many priests do not celebrate when they are not in a community, the Sacred Congregation for Catholic Education recently recalled this exhortation of the Church ('Instruction' of 3 June 1979 (published in *L'Osservatore Romano* of 12 April 1980), no. 26).

glory of that same unique Mystery. Thus we contemplate the Incarnation and its Mysteries at the center of the whole history of salvation; we contemplate Christ's Passion at the center of the Mysteries of the Incarnation; and at the center of the accomplishment of these Mysteries (and through them) we contemplate the accomplishment of the Mystery in its totality, that is, the accomplishment of the entire history of salvation, namely the Eucharist. Such is that economy, and such are its fundamental laws. At the same time that they allow us to see the supereminent place that the Eucharist occupies, they show us that nothing is accomplished which had not been prepared by being signified, and that nothing is signified unless realized in view of a final and more perfect accomplishment and, in the end, one which is definitive and glorious.

One will note that such a theology of the Liturgy as a theology of the Mysteries has no need to fear the inaccuracies of certain theories on the 'mysterious' in general. Rich with profound insights though they might be, such theories do not always sufficiently recognize the specificity and proper action of the Christian Mysteries. In the reflection that we present, on the other hand, while the Liturgy is understood fundamentally by beginning with the first reality of the Mystery, which is manifested, celebrated and accomplished in it, that reality is enlightened first by the economy of the history of salvation, and second, by the theology of the sacramental sign. It is by this latter in fact that the Mystery becomes the Liturgy; and it is by this Liturgy, an essential element in the general economy of the Mystery, that the Mystery will be accomplished in time. As can be seen, all passes through the signs, which should not be surprising in the regime of the Incarnation. And thus one can understand all the interest that there is in comparing these reflections with the data of current research on the symbol and symbolism. This is a profitable way of examining and developing that fundamental sacramental theology, that is, this reflection on the sacramental order as such. A knowledge of its ontological status and its historical condition will allow us moreover to understand better the mode according to which the sacraments work in the present time, and thus to see the whole meaning and value of the Eucharist.

While for some time now theology has appealed once again to symbolism in its effort to understand the sacraments better, a certain distrust has, for quite awhile, kept theologians from following this path—at least in modern times, for such a method was familiar to the Church Fathers. There seem to be two reasons that explain such distrust; both are immediately connected on the historical level. The first reason is the fact that, in what concerns the Eucharist, ever since the errors of Berengar of Tours in the 11th century, and more still since the Protestants in the 16th century, the dogma of the real presence, 'according to the property of nature and the truth of the substance,'[40] seems to be placed in peril the moment that one insists even a little on the value of the sign or the symbolic aspect of the reality that constitutes this sacrament. Symbolic presence became at that time synonymous with allegorical presence, which carries with it the negation of the real presence. In fact—we immediately add this in order to avoid all misunderstanding—the expression 'symbolic presence' is not sufficient; it is a 'sacramental presence' of which we must speak, which means much more. However, the symbolic aspect of the sacramental mode of presence is not to be denied. The second reason for the distrust is that western thought, after having called into question the value of conceptual knowledge, was launched into an inquiry that led it to the exaltation of reason over understanding, which ended up making science, both experimental and mathematical, the type par excellence, and then the end-all of human knowledge. The positivism and scientism of the last century was the flowering of this historical process, which denied to imaginary or symbolic representation all value of knowledge.[41] A third reason for the mistrust, at

---

40 This formula, imposed by the Council of Rome (11 February 1079) on Berenger of Tours (DS 700), was to be a determining factor in the rest of the theological reflection and formulation of the Catholic dogma.

least among those theologians most concerned with fidelity to revealed truth, is found in the oftentimes equivocal—when they are not downright unacceptable—results, which come today from a certain number of studies which have recourse to symbolism in their development of sacramental and liturgical theology.

Yet this aspect of the sign and symbol of sacramental reality cannot be neglected, for the very simple reason that the sacraments are first of all signs[42] and because these signs are eminently symbolic, as the commentaries of the Fathers and the better contemporary studies allow us to affirm. Regarding the Council of Trent, we simply mention it here. What it dismisses is the Protestant error, which wants to make the sacraments 'purely external signs of grace or justice received through faith (alone)' (Session VII, can. 6). All of their efficacy would then consist in simply stirring up an interior act of faith, which would be a purely symbolic mode of acting. On the other hand, the Council of Trent teaches that the sacraments themselves confer grace, and that they do this by 'signifying' it: 'they contain the grace that they signify' (*ibid*). This implies the reciprocal idea: that they signify the grace that they 'contain,' and that they give this through the action of the Church, who celebrates them and administers them. Efficacy and signification are therefore inseparable; and it must even be said that, while the latter is ordered to the former, the former is subordinate to the latter: while the sacrament is the sign for giving Christ's grace, it gives that grace only by signifying it, and therefore in the measure that it signifies it. For this reason there is a need to develop this aspect of sign and signification, and of doing so by having recourse to symbolism. It is not a question here of following the latest trends without any consideration whatsoever, but rather, for theology, of taking up a good

---

[41] G. Durand outlined well the main points of this history in the first chapter of his little work, *L'imagination symbolique* (Coll. SUP), Paris, P. U. F., 1964. We are using the third edtion (1976). Aside from its a priori anti–catholic dogmatism, this work offers a good introduction to the problems that it treats.

[42] This statement is based on Tradition and the Tridentine dogma.

which is its own in order to explore it and to prevent or redress incorrect uses of it. For, in these delicate matters a simple nuance sometimes separates truth from error; and the difference that it makes is huge.[43]

The first difficulty to be resolved by whoever treats the question of the symbol comes not only from the multiplicity of works on the topic, but also from the multiplicity of the disciplines in which it had been studied since the beginning of the century. Thus it is that the International Society of Symbolism (Brussels) is made up of logicians-mathematicians, linguists, ethnologists, psychiatrists and experts in aesthetics.[44] Gilbert Durand, who since 1968 directed the *Centre de Recherche pluridisciplinaire et interuniversitaire sur l'Imaginaire et le Symbole* (CRI), accurately recalls that ethnology and psychoanalysis are two sectors where western thought has rediscovered the symbol and its importance in the individual and social life.[45] However, there is a third sector, which, although it appeared later, compensated for its late arrival by the importance it assumed ever since, namely linguistics,[46] with its structuralist and semiological extensions.[47] How does one choose among so many disciplines? It is rather toward a synthesis of the different disciplines that one must tend, by adding to

---

[43]   See Complementary Note # 1 at the end of this chapter.

[44]   Cf. J. Paulus, *La fonction symbolique et le langage*, Bruxelles, cf. Dessart, 1972 (2nd edition, review), p. 8.

[45]   G. Durand, *op. cit.*, pp. 42; 129.

[46]   *Ibid.*, pp. 51 ff.

[47]   In a very thorough study, *Élements des sémiologie* (in *Communications* (Ecole Pratique des Hautes Etudes–Centre for the study of mass communication) 4, 1964/2, 91–135), Roland Barthes tries to 'deduce from the linguistic of analytical concepts, of which one thinks *a priori*, that they are sufficiently fertile for allowing one to begin semiologic research,' semiology itself being defined as 'the science of all the systems of signs' (p. 92). See especially the second section, '*Signifié et signifiant*' (pp. 103–14), with the comparative table of the different types of signs from p. 104: '*Signal, indice, icône, symbol, signe, allégorie*'—where one can see the two senses, general (p. 92) and particular (p. 104), of the word 'sign'.

them the metaphysical foundations that they often lack, in order to develop the needed philosophy of the symbol.

In this task we must turn to the first two disciplines, namely psychology and ethnology; and we do this without rejecting the contributions of the third category of disciplines, linguistics. In fact, the definition of the sign, beginning with which linguistics study the symbol, has its origin in phenomenology. Yet, in this reflection we shall not try to distinguish what comes from phenomenology and what was found before it. Experience is not only its point of departure; it pauses there and makes it its proper object. It represents 'the last horizon' in which the world is grasped. Consequently, the world is reduced to the condition of phenomena. It is ever and always only that which appears to a conscience. The mind never goes so far as to affirm it as a being. And it refrains from finding a meaning beyond that which it places there itself. If, in fact, the world is nothing but phenomena, nothing but manifestation, then it is nothing—and even, it is not—beyond the knowledge that I have of it. It cannot therefore have any meaning in itself; and the mind can do nothing but analyze the formal processes, that is, the relations of the forms of its manifestation. Such in fact is the task that is assigned to structuralism, which is—after existentialism, but in a diametrically opposed way, and along with all the other analytical logics and philosophies by passing through linguistics—which is, we say, the inevitable term of the phenomenological enterprise. And this is because phenomenology is not truly concerned with 'the things,' that is, with beings, contrary to what it pretends ('*zuruck zu den Sachen*'), but only with the experience of things; and therefore it never leaves idealist subjectivism—the mind continues to hold itself as the first and last object of its own reflection. In such a vision, where the world is nothing but phenomena, that is to say nothing but manifestation, nothing but the relation of a thing represented and a representation—in such a vision as this, the sign, under its diverse forms, will never be but *the relation of the signifying to the signified*. In itself there is not some thing that signifies, but it is directly defined as that relation of signification; and that to which it places its relation is not a thing, but only a 'signified,' a product of the process of 'signification.' Such a discipline can give, and give effectively, some extremely interesting results in its own proper order—although one could denounce its often highly sophisticated character. However, it cannot pretend to establish itself as a philosophy. It always remains in search of a meaning, which can only be given by a metaphysics of being and a theology of history.

It is not surprising, therefore, to see psychologists and ethnologists, as well as those whom one would call 'traditionalist' thinkers (in the esoteric sense of the word[48]), or their historians[49]—it is not surprising to see such persons go beyond the researches of these analytical (but not logical) philosophies—or even these grammars of signification—and place themselves in agreement on a certain number of definitions for the sake of developing their own researches. Moreoever, the agreements to which they have come are remarkable. It is obviously in that same line, while remaining attentive to the work of linguists and semiologists, that the theologian in search of a philoso-

---

[48]   Some authors come to mind here such as R. Guénon, whose work *Symboles fondamentaux de la Science sacrée* could be consulted. Posthumus collection put together and published by Michael Valsan, Paris, Gallimard–NRF, 1962. In the subtitle one can read (only on the cover) the word 'Tradition', under a symbolic medallion evoking the figures of tarots. It shows a royal figure with two faces, surmounted by the epigram 'HIS'. All throughout the book Guénon appeals to 'The primordial Revelation, the work of the Word as the Creation' (p. 37), and to its Tradition. See also the classic work of R. Alleau, *La science des symbols. Contribution à l'étude des principes et des méthodes de la symbolique générale* (Coll. 'Bibliothèque scientifique'), Paris, Payot, 1977.

[49]   We note as an example the very remarkable work of H. Corbin, *L'imagination créatrice dans le soufisme d'Ibn'Arabi* (Paris, Flammarion, 1958; 2nd edition, 1975). This work greatly influenced G. Durand (cf. *op. cit.*, p. 129). The symbol is here placed above dogma (p. 178; pp. 206 ff) and the 'theophany' which the symbol permits is opposed to the Incarnation (p. 8; pp. 28 ff; p. 178). Ibn'Arabî is one of the principal representatives of the Islamic Shiite esoterism.

phy of the symbol must work, in order to create for himself the instrument that he needs in his reflection on the sacraments.

Let us clarify first of all the meaning of the words that we must use. Sign is used in two ways: first, the more general, as a representative substitute for a thing; and second, more particular, as a determined type of those different modes of representation. In the first case—it includes everything—these latter are as so many particular species of the genus 'sign': signal, indication, symptom, image, allegory, symbol, etc. In the second case, the sign is opposed to those other forms in a manner that is explained differently by different authors and different disciplines. More particularly, the sign is opposed to the image and to the symbol.

The *image* or the portrait represents the thing or the person by reproducing its characteristics. It proceeds by way of resemblance and imitation.[50] The symbol, on the other hand, by the fact that it relates to a reality non-representable by way of imitative reproduction, rests not on simple resemblance, but on a more profound community. More than to the image, the symbol is opposed to the *allegory*; for, this latter[51] relates to a reality that can also be represented in another way, while the symbol, as such, relates to a non-representable reality. In its loftiest form the symbol is the epiphany of the Transcendence of the 'Totally Other.'[52]

---

[50] Cf. J. Paulus, *op. cit.,* p. 11.

[51] Allegories often 'depict' death, justice, progress, etc.

[52] Cf. H. Corbin (*see above,* note 46); G. Durand: 'the symbol constitutes, in its restorative dynamism in the quest for meaning, the very model of mediation of the Eternal in the temporal. Thus, this little book of introduction, beginning with Freudian psycoanalysis, leads to the theophany' (*op. cit.,* p. 129); G. Van der Leeuw: 'The symbol is a participation of the sacred in its present configuration. Between the sacred and its figure exists a communion of essence' (*La religion dans son essence et dans ses manifestation. Phénoménologie de la religion* (Paris, Payot, 1948, p. 439)). Despite the lack of precision in the concepts, one can know the intended idea.

The proper characteristic of the symbol, therefore, is this relation by means of a sensible reality with a purely spiritual reality, which cannot be adequately manifested to the mind in simple signs or in concepts; and this explains its other characteristics. The first is the multiplicity of meaning, and of meaning belonging to the different levels of being and conscience; the sign, on the other hand, has only one meaning, and one that relates to a reality placed on the same level of being: the clouds that accumulate are a sign that it is going to rain, but the same clouds can be a symbol of the darkness wherein God hides Himself, while water is the sign of life which it gives to the body and the soul. But at the same time, while the sign relates simply to some thing other than itself, the symbol 'has the function of introducing us into an order of which it must itself be a part, and which presupposes itself in its radical otherness ... '[53] This function the symbol can fulfill thanks to its polyvalence, the multitude of significations that it includes, relating to the different levels of being in which it participates and allows one to participate. It mobilizes therefore man's whole being: spiritual, intellectual, affective and sensible; and it puts that being in act in order to attain the goal that it indicates. It is essentially dynamic, therefore, operative or efficacious, if you will. It does not limit itself to representing or expressing; it sets in motion a process of operation. But this does not take place except by the images that it produces and by the affective movements that it triggers. The symbol gives a sense to that which is apprehended by it, and that meaning sets man in motion. Grasping the real in its totality, spiritual and material, it addresses itself to man completely, and not only to his conceptual intellect. It thus involves a process, which is both a spiritualization of the world and an incarnation of the spiritual.

We must mention here the essentially social character of the symbol. Without a doubt pathological psychology discerns individuals from the processes of symbolization; but we know that it is

---

[53]   E. Oortiques, *Le discours et le symbole* (Coll. 'Philosophie de l'Esprit'), Paris, Aubier, 1962, p. 65.

necessary, in one way or another, to attach them to social processes. The archetypes of Jung are not the only means for doing this. Ethnology, for its part, shows us directly how symbols are the means par excellence which allow a social group to establish itself and to recognize itself. The symbol, in its constitution and its utilization, is a pact, a convention. That does not mean that it is purely arbitrary with respect to the choices of its sensible support, for which, on the contrary, it always has a natural foundation. What it does mean is that, in its use, it is the great means that constitutes and unifies the social group, each one recognizing itself by recognizing it and admitting it as a member of that group.

However, this happens fully only when developed in the myth and in rites. A myth is a symbolic narrative, which speaks to man about the origin of the world and his own origin, and along with this origin, the end of the world and man. A rite is an action, or a collection of actions, allowing one to relive the founding events related by the myth in order to participate therein, to enter into contact with the supra-human energies that are found there, and thus to arrive at immortality, the full realization of human destiny. It is interesting to observe that these different functions of the symbol and the rite: reestablish the original unity, exorcise the fatality of destruction, assure the immutable permanence in the being, by being refound on the level of pathological psychology, the difference being in the fact that the founding element to be revived, or the menace of death to be exorcised, is found here in the relations—principally familial—of childhood, that is to say, in the period of the personality's establishment.

While psychologists note the primitive character of the symbol and the symbolizing activity of the conscience[54], ethnologists focus on its

---

[54]   See the works of Janet, Wallon, Piaget (*La formation du symbole chez l'enfant*, 1945), and of so many others (cf. J. Paulus, *op. cit.*, pp. 9–24). 'Jung, Fromm, S. Langer and Piaget have noted the emulation (not withstanding the very different points of view), the generality and spontaneity of the "language of symbols", which, while it differs from the rational language of signs, does not for all that contain the irrational. *Pre–logic form rather than anti–logic form of*

primordial and universal character. These facts are easily compre-
hended when one goes back to the *foundations of symbolism*. They
come down ultimately to one sole foundation, which could be called
the principle of totality: reality forms one whole; but in immediately
distinguishing the two complementary principles in which this first
principle is verified: the one precedes the many, which forms that
totality only by beginning with the one; and, the mind precedes
matter, in which the former is expressed when it expresses itself, and
it is by the mind that matter finds both its unity and its meaning.
Therefore, matter forms one whole with the mind; and matter will be
for the mind both a sign and an instrument, that is, a signifying reality
and a means of efficacious action.

Such a vision of the world implies the notions of analogy and
participation, which are in fact the foundations of symbolism. They
are also found in the primitive mentality as well as in the most
developed metaphysics, that of Greece and the Christian West. The
progress that there is from both is that which frees analogy from
participation and which allows the former to shed light on the latter.
For the primitive mentality there is, in fact, hardly anything but
participation, in virtue of which the symbolic sign is, by a quasi-
identification, the very thing that it represents.[55] In reality, it will be
only in a more developed vision of the real, and thanks to a more
extensive meaning of analogy, that the symbol will become that which
it is—the distance between it and that which is made present by it

---

thought ... ' (ibid, p. 24).

[55] G. Van Der Leeuw: 'Only the communion of essence makes the symbol.' ' ...
There is a communion of essence (participation, Lévy–Bruhl). The image *is*
the thing that it represents; the signifier is but one with the signified' (*op. cit.*,
p. 439). But the author does not sufficiently clarify his 'phenomenological'
description, and when he pretends, as he does here, to explain the Eucharist
and the real presence by this general theory of the symbol, he confuses the
planes of primitive subjectivity and ontological reality. See also from the same
author: *L'homme primitif et la religion*, Paris, Puf, 1940, pp. 31, 41, 45, 55; etc.
The notion of 'participation' is always at the basis of symbolism.

being more clearly perceived. There is here another essential trait of the symbol, namely that simultaneity in it of presence and absence, of proximity and distance.

This trait is found also in the temporal and historical dimension, where there is verified as well the principle of totality, the foundation of the symbol. This latter allows man, by means of the rite, to come into contact with his origins. But where are they situated? '*In illo tempore*'; but what is 'that time'? The dilemma here is the following: if it is a question of purely mythical time, what relation can it have with the history in which we are? If, on the other hand, it is situated in history, how can it transcend history, which is necessary in order to give it a meaning and pluck us out of it? The symbol, myth and rite, does not confront this problem 'logically.' It practically asserts—which has been recognized by the hybrid concept of 'mythisto-ry'—both the existence and the difference of those two dimensions, intra and supra-historical, of the duration in which we are, and of its origins; and it presents itself as the means par excellence of the passing from one to the other. Here one can see the necessity of the repetition of rites—at least of some of them—until that passing is completed.

Psychology, in its use of symbolism, often ignores these metaphys-ical and religious perspectives; and the time that it considers is that of human existence, not that of the history of humanity. In fact, the problem which must be confronted is that of the constitution, or the reconstitution of the personality of the individual. But if this is sought in the foundations of its symbolism, one will find, analogically, the principle of totality, which we will state later, with its different applications. The same goes for psycho-sociology, which is estab-lished and developed by having recourse to psychology, ethnology, social phenomenology and history.

Having sketched out the symbol and recalled its foundations, we must still say a word about its function; for it is, we said, essentially dynamic or operative. How? In order to answer this question we must distinguish two levels, that of human, individual, social and even cosmic processes, and that of not only supra-human forces, but those which surpass all that belongs to nature and the world. These forces, when they intervene, do not exclude the processes of the first level; rather, they assume and utilize them. On the human and intra-mundane level, the symbol operates in the following manner: it provokes images and, through these, it triggers affective movements. It ties together the elements belonging to the different spheres and facts in order that they might meet. It is, moreover, that which the word sym-bol signifies according to its etymology: to throw together (*sun ballein*). Thus it is in psychology, in literature, in social life, etc. And *it is in this that consists symbolic action in the strict sense.*

However, as man is plunged into a world that surrounds him from all sides and in which there is unceasingly at work supernatural and preternatural forces and beings, symbolic action will be the privileged means of entering into contact with them. At this stage it doubles as an *action* which, according to the situation, will be *religious* or *magical*: religious, when the rite in which the symbol is used serves to render to God due worship and to obtain His grace; magical, when the action taken has for its purpose the capturing of the forces of preternatural powers in order to place them at its service. In this case, the symbol acts after the manner of a sign, or a code—here its character of a pact reappears—triggering the action of the transcending power, with this latter joining itself to the symbolic action in the strict sense, such as it enjoys on the human and mundane level. These two modalities of action are found in the rites of natural religions, where it is at times difficult to distinguish the magic from the religions; and it can also prove problematic in another way, namely, in separating that which is the magical rite from that which is simply the utilization of unknown forces of pyschism or the cosmos. In any case, what we said in our second part about the relation of analogy and continuity between the Incarnation of the Word and the sacraments allows us to affirm now that the action of the sacraments, while assuming the symbolic and religious elements, infinitely surpasses them; for, the sacraments are the signs and instruments of Christ Who acts in them.[56]

One can see here the complexity of these questions. At least the broad lines allow themselves to be discerned, as well as the two poles around which they are ordered, that of the intra-mundane action of the symbol, and that of its opening onto a world beyond. These are, in fact, the two directions in which the current renewal of symbolic studies turns.[57] In the first, all is brought back to the human and mundane dimension alone. It is, above all, of a psychological inspiration, but it has recourse as well to the data of history and phenomenology of religion, interpreted in a psycho-sociological reducing perspective. In the second, which is based especially on the data of those historical and phenomenological sciences, but without neglecting an appeal to psychology, one launches upon Gnostic perspectives, esoteric or not, but in fact often 'traditional' (always in the sense of the word that it has among the authors cited above: Guénon, Alleau, Corbin; G. Durand himself, in the final analysis, seems to go in this direction.).[58]

*   *   *

Such then, in three tracts, is the current situation of studies on the symbol, which the theologian must confront, and which calls for an urgent reflection on the symbolism implied in the sacramental order.[59] Right away we are able say why neither of those two directions in which contemporary studies on the symbol move are acceptable to us: neither that of the psycho-sociological reduction, since its negation of the Christian supernatural is immediate; nor that which seeks to insert Christianity into the multiform current issuing from

---

[56]   Cf. above, note 12. This prevents one from adopting a magical attitude when using a religious and even sacramental rite.

[57]   They appear clearly in chapters two and three of G. Durand's work, *L'imagination symbolique.*

[58]   Cf. *see above*, note 52.

[59]   See the *Complementary Note II* at the end of this chapter.

the 'primordial Tradition,' for the destruction of Christianity in that which it has of the irreducible is no less certain. Certainly, it is welcome and even included in a certain relation with the divinity, but in the manner in which the Roman Empire welcomed Christ and offered Him a place in the pantheon: this inclusion and this welcome being the most subtle of its negations. The fact of analogies between Christian rites and non-Christians rites remains no less undeniable. But the question which is posed is, Which 'includes' which? Is traditionalism correct when it 'includes' Christianity by inserting it into its collective vision and reducing it to nothing but one of its manifestations among others? Or is Christianity correct when it 'includes' the other religions by seeing them in its recapitulative and historico-salvific vision as so many preparations—or oppositions—to the Son of God's coming to save us? We know the response of the faith. But this response, which the comparative study of religions already imposes with astonishing force, is later shown to us by the revealed truth of the Incarnation in the Christian assumption of all that those other religions contain that is good and true in their symbols, myths, rites and most especially in their sacrifices; this assumption takes place through the human flesh of Christ, through Israel, which immediately preceded it, and through the Church, who continues it. It is through Christ and His sacrifice that they had a salvific value. It is through Christ that they find their historical meaning; but He assumes them only by purifying them of all that they possess which is imperfect (highlighted by the history of Israel's religious institutions), and by making them submit to a radical transfiguration, which happens only with the establishment of the religion of the New Covenant.

While he refuses these psychological or 'traditional' reductions or recoveries of the Christian fact, and of the sacraments most especially, the theologian does not recognize any less both the symbolism of these sacraments as well as the analogies that it presents with that which can be found elsewhere and which are studied by the diverse aforementioned disciplines. Therefore, it is necessary for the theologian to consider and judge the results of their research. This is what we began to do above, when we showed the notions in which such studies had resulted, the foundations of symbolism and its mode of action and efficacy. However, we must now take up our analysis again and proceed in it. Regarding the notions, we can make them our own, as well as that which concerns the symbolic, religious and magical acts: it is the aspect of resemblance of the analogy that exists between all these domains, where symbolism enters into play. On the other hand, we also noted what was insufficient in the foundations that were given it: the primitives in a non-reflective manner; the modern authors in a reflective manner. What is lacking to those foundations, that is, to that philosophy (implicit or explicit) of the one and the many, of participation and analogy, of spirit and matter, but also to those conceptions of time and history—what is lacking is, on one hand, a metaphysic of being and, on the other hand, a satisfying reflection, both philosophical and theological, on the future and on history. We shall try to show this.

Only a metaphysics of being, we said, allows one to construct this philosophy of the one and the many, of participation and analogy, capable of founding a Christian symbolism. By it, in fact, each being receives its proper ontological status and its place in the ensemble of beings. Each one is, notwithstanding its different modalities, a substance participating in being, which is found in all. This is what allows one to establish the relations of participation and analogy that exist on one hand, between each of the beings and the absolute and infinite Being from which they proceed, and on the other hand, between the beings themselves. This is the only way to avoid the confusion of an indefinite monism, which is either (pan)theistic or materialistic, and which, in effacing the ontological differences between beings, dissolves the substance, and therefore, in the final analysis, the human person itself as well. All is in all, certainly; but in the absence of an adequate metaphysics of being, as is the case especially in the esoteric and primitive symbolism, there no longer remains anything but the All, where all ends up merging and disappearing. The unity of that totality is one of confusion, and not one of harmony and communion. In order for this latter to take place there is a need for persons encountering each other in consideration of their otherness: what allows one to see how this is possible, is that metaphysic of being, along with the philosophy of participation and analogy that flows from it, assuring the substance of beings (*entia*) in the being (*esse*). This is why, in a monistic vision of the real, the symbol is not truly a symbol, as we noted above, but a presence of that which it represents, through a quasi-intentional identification. Here again, therefore, in order to conceive correctly the relations, especially those of presence and absence, of participation and otherness, implied in symbolism, one must have that vision of the real where each being finds its proper ontological status.

If the different modern philosophies do not have in general this sense of being, on the other hand, one does find among them every trend that has a very developed sense of history. And yet here again, some adjustments are necessary, for one easily confuses natural evolution and human history. That is the whole drama of evolutionism raised to an absolute explanatory system; or again, among theologians, one identifies profane history and history of salvation, which leads to Christian progressivism in the political sense of the word.[60] From the first to the second, from evolution to history, there is the passing from the pure natural finality inscribed in beings to a destiny proposed to a free will. From the second to the first, from human history to the history of salvation, this passing is brought about through the assumption of that free will by the Son of God made man, in order to save and 'divinize' all men and the cosmos themselves.

Time is the extent of duration that measures and gives rhythm to the action of beings in the world; this is why there are as many modes

---

[60] Fr G. Fessard, SJ, remains one of those who has best denounced this evil. On the distinction between these three levels of historicity, see: *De l'Actualité historique*, Paris, DDBr., 1960 (vol. I, pp. 77–93 and *passim*).

of temporality as there are levels of being: some are cosmic action and time, others human action and time, and still others history of salvation action and time. But everywhere the being tends toward unity. This is why, just as the multiplicity of beings situated in space aspires to unity and forms a whole, a *cosmos*, a '*natural history*' or an evolution, so the multiplicity of moments of social action forms a whole, a *history*, and the multiplicity of the time of Christ's redemptive work forms a whole, the *history of salvation*: the Mystery, as St Paul tells us to call it. And that unity of the different moments of time in the history that it forms happens only through the participation of each and everyone in the principle of their duration, eternity, and according to the laws of analogy. It is this unity of totality that is at the heart of all symbolism.

While the duration of the material world and the movement of cosmic evolution sufficiently reproduce on their own level the one immutable stability of eternity through the regularity of their cycles and repetitions, the properly human duration aspires to more. With regards to the individual, this was seen above by means of the single analysis of the present instant, which engages both the entire past and the entire future of man in a desire which moves the soul toward an instant—an instant which will be the fullness of duration without repetitive succession. The intense action realizes this desire up to a certain point, but it passes, and man falls back into the succession of instances and into the dramatic sentiment of decrepitude that is attached to it. All drifts away and rushes towards death, which is for each one the end of existence and time.

How does one escape this? Such is the great question, the only one really, of human existence; and it is in order to respond to it that man, at all times, has had recourse to rites and symbols, which necessarily presuppose, consciously or not, a vision of time, of history and of eternity. How does one escape time? This is the same as asking: 'How is one established in eternity?' We know the response of natural religions. Not conceiving human time except after the type of natural or cosmic time, these religions see it either according to an image of human life, or as an indefinite succession of cycles unceasingly repeated. All effort then consists in rejoining, individually or collectively, the unchanging world, which must follow the present life, which will happen only by quitting it or by exiting the unceasing movement of those cycles. It is, under thousands of different forms, to this end that tend all the rites of the religious history of humanity. The symbolic action reproduces the event that is at the origin of history, or the state of that which is at the center of the wheel of cycles, in order to allow men to participate therein. By returning to the origin or center, men assure their destiny: they receive the energies that allow them to escape the destruction that awaits them at the end of their existence. And the action is repeated as often as necessary.[61]

---

[61]   G. Van Der Leeuw noted this character: 'the repetition proper to worship' (*La religion dans son essence* ... , p. 351). Just as G. Durand, who highlights 'that power of restorative repetition of the symbolic object' (*op. cit.*, p. 16, note 2). He cites H. Corbin: 'The symbol ... is never *explained* once for all, but always to be deciphered anew, just as a musical score is never sight–read once for all, but always demands a new performance' (*op. cit.*, p. 13). R. Didier: 'The sacrament shares in the features that we recognized in religious rites and ... these latter furnish the sacrament with the basis upon which this latter takes its original meaning. I would hold above all that the sacrament, like the rite, is the re–accomplishment of the founding Word, a re–accomplishment that constitutes the Christian subject and the Church' (*Mythe et rite, révélation et sacrament*, in *L'eucharistie, le sens des sacraments. Un dossier théologique*. A multi–disciplinary research under the direction of Raymond Didier. Faculty of Theology of Lyon, 1971, p. 180). The remark is correct for the condition of a rectified being: rites and sacraments do not refer only to a 'founding Word', but to a 'founding Action'. There again we see the reducing tendency, not only of the sacrament to the word, but also of the Christian sacrament to the religious rites. The same tendency is found in a study otherwise completely remarkable, but which is only all the more dangerous by the reducing tendency that it reveals, by A. Vergotte: *Dimensions anthropologiques de l'eucharistie*, in the collaborative work already cited: *L'eucharistie, symbole et réalité* (pp. 7–56). The flaw of this study is in a conception of the symbol that reduces all of its efficacy to the intentional order, without seeing how the word of Christ

Such then is, in general, the conception of time that serves as the foundation for the symbolism of natural religions. The principle of totality, which is at the foundation of everything, is found there, but under a circular and dynamic form. The whole is established—or reestablished—through a return to the beginning or center; the symbol is what allows one to put each instant of existence in contact with both this beginning and with the end. The beginning and the end, which are considered as the center (especially in certain forms of Hinduism), make up the sole immovable point around which all the rest turns ... according to indefinite cycles. One is freed from time, the place of matter and of suffering, only through a return to the center, the place of pure spirit and beatitude. It will be easy to show how the same principles are found again in psychology, at the level of individual existence, and this even in a non-religious perspective. At each moment of his existence, man, in order to find the meaning of that existence, needs to know it as a whole, which can happen only by being conscience of both its beginning and its end. The psychopathologist shows how the symbol helps the mentally ill to do this. In the history of peoples there are important historical or mythological figures that allow societies to satisfy this need; the symbolic function that they thus exercise takes nothing away from their historical reality when they have one. For, the symbol does not need to be mythical—in the sense of non-historical—in order to exercise this function. What is important, is that it puts one in contact with one's origins, thus allowing the individual or the community both to have contact with their end and to move towards it.

* * *

We are now ready to place one in relation with the other: the order of symbolism with the order of sacramentality. It would be enough

---

empowers the sacraments to surpass that order. Without a doubt the author speaks as a psychologist, but his explanation in fact goes beyond psychology, and is considered to be sufficient, theologically speaking, in the current climate.

for us to compare what we just said with that which the two preceding sections revealed to us. The determining factor which intervenes between these two orders is the Incarnation; and the relation that the Incarnation establishes between them, on the basis of an analogy that goes very far, is both a relation of continuity and of going beyond. It is the entire economy of the Mystery that is at stake here; and our present reflection on the two orders, symbolic and sacramental, is going to allow us to develop it still more. We mentioned above the directing principles: that dialectic that goes from preparation to realization, and from realization to accomplishment; and that which goes from the sign to history, and from history to the sign. Regarding the first, let us note that one could also (and perhaps more fittingly) speak of preparation, accomplishment, and consummation or perfection. For, in reality, Christ *accomplishes* that towards which the actions and signs that *prepared* Him tend; nevertheless, His work is still to be *consummated* and completed through the Church. It is thus that His earthly life appeared to us as the center of this history of salvation, His Paschal sacrifice being the center of His own life. This explains the analogy and continuity between His Incarnation and the mysteries of His earthly life on the one hand, and on the other, between those same mysteries and the sacraments by which He consummates the former in His Church. From Christ to the Church: this is the continuity that dominates.

On the other hand, there is an analogy among the time of preparation, where the natural symbolic order is located (from the point of view of the theological chronology of salvation history), and consequently an analogy between that same order and that of the sacraments instituted by Christ. This implies both a resemblance, a continuity; as well as a dissemblance, a rupture and surpassing. Therefore, by the fact of the Incarnation which intervenes between the two, there is between the symbolic order and the sacramental order both continuity and surpassing: continuity, because the Word in becoming Incarnate assumes the entire symbolic order inherent in the world, the spiritual and carnal nature of man; surpassing, because by the fact of that assumption by the Word, the natural symbolic order is purified, transfigured and elevated to a status and possibility of action of which it had not been capable by itself.

For which reason there is this difference: while from pre-Christian symbolism to the Incarnation there was, on the basis of a profound analogy, both continuity and surpassing, with this latter winning out; from the Incarnation to the sacraments, there is simply continuity. The economy of the Mystery tells us the reason. Whereas the redemptive Incarnation realizes and accomplishes that which preceded it by raising it from the human level to the divine by participation—whence the surpassing which is produced and which is a passing from a natural ontological status to a supernatural; on the other hand, that which follows the Incarnation and continues the Mystery only consummates and perfects that which had already been realized in it. Here we have simple continuity. And yet, this itself is in view of an ultimate surpassing, which will take place through the eschatological consummation and transfiguration in glory. However, it will be not so much a passing from one ontological state to another as from an historical condition to a trans-historical condition.

In order to place the order of sacramentality in relation to that of symbolism it is necessary to recall again what we said above, namely that symbolism is never encountered in a pure state. This is why, when it is employed in a religious act, symbolism is always placed between two poles: the side of the worship of God, which will find its completion in the Incarnation; and the side of magic and the worship of demons. It is not possible to escape this alternative; the conflict which it carries with it is inherent in the history of salvation. Therefore, insofar as they were already assumed by the Divine Mercy, there was a certain action of Redemption in the 'natural' symbolism of rites and religious symbols before Christ; which explains why they were able to have a certain 'supernatural' efficacy. This is true especially of the rites of the Mosaic

Covenant, which immediately prepared the coming of Christ;[62] nevertheless, the same goes for those religions which preceded, to the extent that they were a remote preparation for the Incarnation. However, this assumption of natural symbolism by that first connection to Christ will only be fully complete by His coming; and the passing beyond which follows from it will also only be complete by and in the sacraments that Christ would institute in order to continue His work—whence their incomparably superior efficacy. In an opposite sense, all demoniacal and magical symbolism also continues, and even intensifies its action in opposition to Christ's. This is 'the mystery of iniquity' always working against 'the Mystery of piety.'

Having made that important clarification regarding the assumption of symbolism by the Christian sacramental order, and regarding the permanent opposition to it assumed by the demoniacal forces, we must now continue our comparative study by looking at the metaphysic of being and the conception of time and history, which are at the foundation of this sacramental order. This will allow us to see how the sacrament of the Eucharist can be frequently repeated in time without multiplying the Mystery of the one historical action that it 'represents.' In truth there is no need to mention again here what we already explained above. The metaphysics that establishes the sacramental order and its symbolism is that metaphysic of being, of analogy and participation, which alone allows one to assure each being its own ontological subsistence and its relation to the Being from Whom it proceeds, as well as its relation with the other beings. Present in various degress of purity and elaboration among the Fathers of the Church, this metaphysic has its foundation in the Bible; it is that which the Second Vatican Council meant when it claimed for the Church that 'ever-valuable philosophic patrimony,' and shown in St Thomas Aquinas, the 'master' par excellence of speculative theology (*Decree on the Formation of Priests*, nos. 15 and 16).

---

[62]   St Thomas, *S.T.* I–II, q. 103, a. 2; III, q. 62, a. 6.

With respect to the vision of history, it belongs to the 'Mystery' we presented in our first part and developed in the second part. Its great novelty is to give to historical time an absolute principle, namely creation, and not a mythical principle; it also gives an equally absolute end, the Parousia, which will be the consummation of history and not its suppression or an escape from it. It is only in this ontologico-historical framework that the Christian sacraments can be somewhat understood, and that one can see what separates them from symbolism (a symbolism which is nevertheless assumed by them); in other words, one can see to what extent they pass beyond symbolism. While this is no place to revisit as a whole the explanation of our metaphysic and our vision of history, nevertheless it will be useful to note some individual aspects as well as the ontological and historical orders.

From the ontological point of view, we must mention along with St Thomas the 'incomplete,' 'fluid,' 'transitive'—and thus essentially relational—character[63] of the sacramental order. As signs and instruments, the sacraments exist only through their relation with Him Who uses them, namely Christ; and they exist only for the work that He represents and continues by them, the work of His Mystery. They exist only by the action which establishes them in this relation, that of the liturgy. They exist then only in this action.

That being said, one can see the sacraments' historical condition. This condition is determined by the paradoxical fact that Christ virtually put an end to history by *accomplishing* it in Himself, and that at the same time He opened up that new temporal space for the sake of its *consummation*, the time of the Church. By the fact that the Mystery is already accomplished through Christ in the time of His coming, the '*kairos*' of salvation, the time of the Church is but the extension, the delay 'until He comes' (1 Cor 11:26), of that one '*kairos*' (2 Cor 6:2). Because this latter is located in the time of human history, each liturgical celebration of the sacraments is an act that is also located

---

[63]   '*Esse transiens et incompletum*' (*ibid*, III, q. 62, a. 4); '*esse fluens et incompletum*' (*ibid*, a. 3).

in this time, and which can therefore be repeated and multiplied. But because what it realizes is the Mystery of Christ formerly accomplished, 'once' for all (*ephapax*: Heb 7:27; 9:12; etc), and thus placing an end to that history, the same celebration is neither the repetition nor the multiplication of that Mystery: it is its *sacramental continuation* in that historical extension and delay of the one '*kairos*' that is the present time, for the sake of its accomplishment in the Church.

Here also, that is to say in this relation to time, the sacramental order accomplishes the symbolic order by going beyond it; the former assumes the latter by making it submit to a complete reversal. With the coming of Christ, in fact, time no longer seeks to make itself eternity; rather it is eternity which irrupts into time in order to raise it up to itself. This is why, while man, before and after Christ, seeks through religious rites and symbols to come into contact with the founding event of his history in order to escape the decrepitude of his temporal condition (i.e. death), this condition henceforth is no longer found at the origin, but rather at the center of time: at the theological center of an historical time—and not at a mythological and trans-historical center, around whose beginning and end would turn the imaginary wheel of infinite cycles. The origin of time is no less recaptured, for it is the world created by Him and fallen into original sin that the Word makes His own by becoming Incarnate in order to save it by His sacrifice. But this takes place only by that central act of the Lord, Who, by recapturing that origin, redeems it and leads it to its end. Therefore, it is recaptured only through that irruption of eternity into time, an irruption that does not abolish the present time, but rather saves it and accomplishes it by making it enter into its end, in both senses of that word. The completion of time will take place only at the Parousia, when that *accomplishment* will have been *consummated* through the Church. This is why Christian salvation does not consist in fleeing time, seeking to exit it; rather, on the contrary, it consists in 'redeeming' time, as St Paul says (Col 4:5; Eph 5:16), in allowing time to be penetrated by the salvific action of Christ and to enter into the eschatological '*kairos*' of salvation.

The sacraments of the Church—those direct actions of Christ in the present time, established now in eternity and the source of every ecclesial and Christian action in that time—the sacraments, we say, contribute to the aforementioned 'redemption' of time. This is why the Church sees in the sacraments the beginning and end of her whole mission, mysterious beings that they are. They are the presence in time, that is, in the moment that they are accomplished, of the eternity-made-history, in order that history might be made eternity. The sacraments are totally relative and essentially dynamic and operative beings; for they, especially the Eucharist, actualize now a Mystery that was accomplished historically in the past; but their proper task is to put an end to history by ushering the eschaton into it, and by ushering history into this eschaton. This is the unique task that they continue, and this is why they can and must be renewed unceasingly without the Mystery of Christ being multiplied. They are able to do this without contradicting the *fact of their entirely relational being and their historical and eschatological condition*: the sacrament is the present actualization, in a real and efficacious sign, of an act both past and eschatological (in the sense of something which brings history to its consummation), namely the Mystery of Christ. One could say that the act is historically past and mysteriously present, provided this is correctly understood. The Mystery assumes history: its acts are placed there. Yet in assuming it, the Mystery accomplishes history: the acts of Christ complete history by opening up that eschatological era for its consummation. The sacraments are these eschatological acts of Christ; and they must be multiplied, because that Mystery is not consummated except in time, from which it needs to recapture all of its moments. It does this by a battle against 'the mystery of iniquity,' which is always 'at work' for men's destruction (2 Thess 2:7).

With regards to the way in which they act, we find again a relationship with symbolism, a relationship of continuity and of going beyond.

Symbolism, taking hold of the Mystery in all its dimensions, establishes the natural substratum for it; for, it is found there fully assumed. But this assumption, having been founded first of all in the Incarnation of the Word, brings about a going beyond, which it is of the highest importance to emphasize vis-à-vis docetism and sacramental occasionalism (as we did above), as well as the aberrations of which we shall speak in a moment. In fact, the sacraments instituted by Christ are not simply external signs or 'cryptograms' of His Mystery 'on the occasion' of which God acts directly on man; they are truly, by Christ's institution of them, symbolic signs and efficacious instruments of His flesh and His salvific action. Therefore, it is truly through the sacraments (granting to their mediation the fullest sense of the word) that Christ continues and consummates His Mystery in the Church, 'by the will of the Father and with the cooperation of the Holy Spirit.'[64]

It seems possible, on these foundations, to see how we should judge the different attempts, past and present, at having recourse to symbolism in sacramental theology (see our *Complementary Notes* at the end of this chapter). The decisive criteria, which will allow us to discern the true from the false, is the fundamental fact that makes all the difference between the symbolic and sacramental orders, namely the Incarnation of the Word. Therefore, when one is confronted with an explanation or elaboration of the liturgy that has recourse to symbolism, the question to be asked will be, whether that symbolism is used with not simply a reference to the Incarnation but with a true subordination to it, or whether it is detached from the Incarnation, despite its purely nominal reference to it. The entire Catholic Tradition has used symbolism in the first way, and oftentimes with an incredible exuberance of detail. After the period of rationalism and secularization that obliterated the meaning of the symbol, and with that the meaning of the liturgy as well (at least in the Latin Church), the return to symbolism

---

[64] *'Domine Jesu Christe, Fili Dei vivi, qui ex voluntate Patris, cooperante Spiritu Sancto, per mortem tuam mundum vivificasti ... '* (*Roman Missal*, Prayer before Communion).

that we have seen for some years now has frequently become—certainly not without any reference to Christ—a liturgy that no longer has any Christian appearance, but without which that reference would not be determining of any true subordination. Here, as elsewhere, the name of Christ is but a label to cover up a project that results only in gutting Him out of His Mystery. The proof of this is that the reality celebrated is no longer the Mystery or mysteries of Christ, the Word made man in order to save men, but rather man himself in the different phases of his life and history. Without a doubt, as a result of the Incarnation Christ dwells in those who have received Him and they themselves live in Him, such that it is truly their being and their existence that are assumed, redeemed and transformed in His mysteries, and therefore in the liturgy. However, what is celebrated there, immediately and in the strict sense, are those mysteries that save us; and therefore, the worship that is offered goes to God 'in Christ,' not to man himself and his existence. Yet it is this celebration of man to which the trend of the new liturgy tends—as some of its theoreticians openly declare—through a symbolism that, despite a superficial and provisory reference to Christ, ultimately directs itself toward the cosmic symbols of 'the universal alliance.' In such conditions as these the rediscovery of symbolism does not represent progress, but rather a striking regress. Or if there is progress there, it does not belong to the 'Mystery of piety.'

Such are the broad outlines of a theology of 'the sacramental order,' and therefore of the liturgy, elaborated from the biblical notion of mystery, and developed with the help of symbolism. It is on these foundations that we will be able to return now to the celebration of the sacrament of the Eucharist, the center of this 'order' and heart of the entire liturgy. Here again it will be necessary to examine critically the principal explanations that are currently given. We shall do this in the light of traditional principles and the developments that they seem to call for, as we have just demonstrated. From there we shall be able to propose a theological explanation of the Mass most fitting for knowing the mystery. And finally, we shall speak of the respective meaning and value, in and for the Church, of the individual celebration and the concelebration of the sacrament and sacrifice of the Eucharist.

At the end of history, the Mystery and the Liturgy will be but one, all the sacraments having been abolished, abolished because accomplished and consummated in the fully glorified Body of the Lamb and His Bride. In fact, in glory, the fully consummated Mystery will itself be the Liturgy of the Church. Regarding the sign: there will no longer be any others but those of that humanity assumed by the Word, all ecclesial mediations being both recapitulated and transfigured in that humanity, and all renewed creation becoming before the eyes of the elect that great open book that sings of the glory of God (Ps 19:1).

Complementary Notes

I. (Cf. see above, note 43). An example will illustrate the urgency of this work of clarification: namely, a report prepared for a gathering of the French bishops at Lourdes in 1971. It had for its object and title: *The Church, A Sign of Salvation In the Midst of Men;*[65] therefore, it was the notion of sacrament that was at the center of its reflection. In order to develop this, instead of beginning with Christ and the Church, as must be done in good theology, the authors of the report started with the world. They were conscious of the radical reversal they were thus undertaking; for, they themselves presented this change as a clearly decisive 'reversal of attitude' (p. 11). Consequently, the sacraments are no longer essentially signs instituted by Christ that work by His power; they become but 'the mundane reality that is unveiled to the eyes of faith signified as an action of God, an action for salvation,' such that 'there is efficacy in and by signification' (p. 32)—and only there. The notion of efficacy *ex opere operato*, though it is dogmatic (Council of Trent, Session VII, can. 8), is nevertheless rejected as 'pre-conciliar'

---

[65] *Eglise, signe de salut au milieu des homes, Eglise–Sacrement. Rapports présentés à l'Assemblée plénière de l'Episcopat français. Lourdes 1971,* by Robert Coffy and Roger Varro, Paris, le Centurion, 1972.

(p. 12). Yet, it is one thing to recall the link that exists in the sacraments between efficacy and signification; and it is another thing to reduce the former to the psychological process triggered by the latter. This is to fall back into the errors of Luther. And one goes even further than him, when, bluntly detaching oneself from the institution of Christ, one considers as a sacrament 'every visible thing insofar as it is a manifestation of salvation' (p. 33).

One could possibly admit, though not without prudence, that in a very wide sense and in certain contexts, such a notion of sacrament could be used. However, to take it as the basis for a reflection on the Church-sacrament, as this report does—and therefore as a point of departure for a theology of action, and a theology of the liturgy and the Church's sacraments as well—it is not possible to do this without deducing the 'reversal' proclaimed by the authors to its final consequences. The liturgy in particular will no longer be the celebration of the great salvific acts of Christ the Redeemer in the signs instituted by Him for that purpose, but the celebration of the events of human existence and the world; for, the history of salvation and profane history have been confused here. The liturgy, then, will no longer be first and foremost the action of Christ working through and in His Church in order to sanctify her and glorify His Father, but rather the action of men, inventing their own signs and rites in order to give meaning to their life; for, according to the report, this is the fundamental question that is put to men today (p. 27–8). Where western tradition and culture are found, they cause such signs and rites to express this meaning in Christian concepts; but the moment that they begin with the world and not with Christ and His Church, nothing prevents them on other continents from turning to other traditions and languages. Such a reflection opens up the liturgy to all kinds of possible evolutions; one can now see the importance of this remark for mission countries. Moreover, when one reflects on the influence wielded by this report, cited continuously and everywhere ever since, one sees the urgency of our reflection on the relation between (symbolic) signification and (sacramental) efficacy in the sacraments. II. (Cf. see above, note 59). This reflection on symbolism did not just lack, but clearly lacked hindsight and a critical sense. It had been especially the work of liturgists, and was developed according to a wide range, which though in the end was straight enough, went from the reductive psycho-sociological interpretation to a symbolism, adding more or less 'traditionalism.' Some examples will allow us to observe it, and to see at the same time that the directions of the 1971 Report had been widely followed. In a work entitled, *Du symbolique au symbole* ('From the Symbolic to the Symbol'), known also by its subtitle, *Essai sur les sacrements* ('An Essay on the Sacraments'), Louis-Marie Chauvet, professor of sacramental theology at the Institut Catholique of Paris, offers as an object of reflection the *human 'reality'*, and he begins 'by way of language, going "from the symbolic to the symbol"' (pp. 9–10). Yet it is the sacraments which are to be discussed. We find therefore the 'reversal' advocated by the 1971 Report: it begins with the human reality, and not with what Christ instituted; and the study continues by means of the human sciences, and not primarily in the light of revealed truths. The point of departure is everything here; for it is obvious that both need illumination. In giving priority to the human reality and the science of languages, and in subordinating his interpretation of the gospel message to that science, the author necessarily ends up reducing the efficacy of the Christian sacraments to the totally human symbols that constitute them: 'The operativity of the sacraments is not physical, nor metaphysical, but *symbolic*' (p. 215). On the basis of the principles posed at the beginning and developed throughout the work, this assertion amounts to a negation of the sacramental efficacy in the strict sense. Not to mention the vagueness of the expressions used: what is a metaphysical 'operativity'? The book does contain a number of interesting reflections, but they require a fundamental correction in order to be used without equivocation.

Heading in the same direction, F. Isambert goes even further still in the conclusion of his work, *Rite et efficacité symbolique* ('Rite and Symbolic Efficacy').[66] He openly envisages, at the end 'of a pastoral letter that emphasizes the understanding of the symbol and the symbolic participation more than the action of grace' (p. 212), the possibility of an evolution, which would lead us, not 'towards a simple cultural adaptation of religious expression,' but 'towards a mutation of religion itself' (p. 213). He only poses the question there; this sentence is the last in the book. But by the principle proclaimed on the preceding page (p. 212), which hides under the shelter of the 'pastoral letter' and represents a declared negation of the Christian sacraments, he clearly indicates his response.

Henri Denis, the Episcopal Vicar of Lyon and Assistant Director of the CNPL, made this response his own through another way. In his small work, *Des sacrements et des hommes*,[67] he explains that it is a question now of 'celebrating life' (p. 113). 'The sacred,' he says, has undergone 'a shift,' and with it, 'religion itself.' Both are found in 'the contingent existence' of man, 'the dignity of the person,' 'the human communion'… 'the relationship with the world' (p. 107). He will have to divide the seven sacraments over these different realities, always in the line of the 'reversal' proclaimed at Lourdes in 1971: Baptism will be the 'sacrament of the redeemed contingent existence' (and not the action of Christ redeeming man and his existence); confirmation will be the 'sacrament of growth and its risks' (and not the action of Christ marking the Christian with His Spirit of strength); etc. (*ibid* ff.) The author is perfectly conscious that there is a 'mutation' here (p. 121 and *passim*); and he does not hide from us the end to which, according to him, it must lead us, namely, to 'reunions to be celebrated with elementary cosmic symbolisms' (p. 103). One

---

[66] F. Isambert, *Rite et efficacité symbolique* (Published in the same 'Collection de recherche du CNPL'.), Paris, Cerf, 1979.

[67] H. Denis, *Des sacrements et des hommes. Dix ans après Vatican II*, Lyon, Chalet, 1976.

would truly error if one believed that these principles of 'reversal' and 'mutation' would remain without effect. Moreover, the authority and real power with which they are invested who profess such principles cannot even be imagined. In addition, the theoreticians are often themselves the practitioners. If, in a former time, these latter moved us toward a liturgy, which, under pretext of restrengthening the human and natural symbolism of the sacraments, celebrated human existence in place of the mysteries of Christ,[68] in a latter time it leads the faithful—or at least those who have deserted the Church by observing these mutations—toward a 'covenant' identified purely and simply as 'the symbolic order,' and of which we are told that it 'reunites us in the name of the absent.'[69] Either this language does not have any meaning and thus only destroys the faith through brainwashing, or it does having meaning and what it proclaims, in disturbing terms, is the construction of another faith and another Church. Yet the mass of texts that can be cited here,[70] the coherence that exists

---

[68] See the journal *Notes de Pastorale Liturgique*, no. 129 (August 1977): *Dossier: Signes et Symboles*. Beginning with 'the symbolic experience' (p. 7), the CNPL (under whose direction the journal is published) leads us to conceive 'the celebration as a symbolic act' (p. 15), the sacrament being thus reduced to the symbol; and it explains that the liturgy consists in 'celebrating life' (p. 17). Its point of departure is the event of my human life. It (i.e. the liturgy, which will be a 'feast') 'will reveal to me and build up my being man' (p. 16). At this level the inversion of the Christian *cultus* is complete.

[69] This is what is taught by the Abbé A. Delzant, professor at the Institut Catholique of Paris, in his work, *Croire dans un monde scientifique* (Documents du Centre Jean–Bart, Coll. 'Dossiers Libres'), Paris, Cerf, 1975, p. 49. See the excellent analysis of this book in the brochure, *Du progressisme à l'Ordre symbolique. La religion des temps nouveaux?* (published by 'Action Familiale et Scolaire', 31, rue Rennequin, 75017 Paris, 1975).

[70] There would be a thick dossier put together here. To the example given in the preceding note we add a few more. The journal *Initiales*, published by the CNER (Centre National de l'Enseignment Religieux, 6, av. Vavin, 75006 Paris), explains (in its December 1979 issue) how 'to celebrate' (the word is often taken in an absolute sense) 'with a star or with a fairytale' (p. 33), for example with one of Andersen's fairytales or a Scottish legend (pp. 13–14).

between them and the principles set forth oblige us to recognize that this language has a meaning, and that the direction that it takes is what we said.

The task of the theologian is to show this. The task of the pastor is to take the appropriate measures to confront it. This latter is the more urgent, for it is a question of the salvation of souls.

'Both of them,' it says, 'relate the rites of initiation.' The March 1980 issue shows how to animate 'a penitential celebration' with the help of the symbol, which is a stone: 'Each *'penitent'* presents his stone bearing his name and agrees to say, '[insert one's own name], I forgive you your sins in the Name of the Father, and of the Son, and of the Holy Spirit. Go and sin no more' (p. 28). Without the confession of sins or penance: the symbolic action suffices. This is because, explains the journal *Points de repère*, also directed by the CNER, in a 'Dossier' titled *Initier à la messe* (no. 45, December 1980): 'The initiation ... allows one to enter into a group ... To be initiated is to have been placed in the presence of persons, object or words, which give the meaning of the individual and collective life' (p. 6). The Mass is an 'initiation' of this genre (it is superfluous to note the abuse in such a context, represented by the reference to the traditional term of Christian initiation). The real presence and the sacrifice disappear. All that is left is the Congregation and the Word, with the symbolic actions that accompany it, for the celebration of 'the mystery of the presence of God to man', in an openness to a 'possible, always new and unexpected', to which the Spirit gives birth (pp. 10–13). Everything is creativity in order to give a meaning to life, a meaning that one discovers through these symbolic initiations, sacramental or not, which reveal the presence of 'God' in the world and in the life of men. The reference to 'the love of Christ' loses all its value because of its vagueness, and the Church is no longer but a community directed by its animator, himself directed by the 'Centers' of initation inspired by the CNER, the CNPL, and other national organs of the episcopate. (We sincerely thank the devoted person who furnished us with this documentation, to which, once again, a hundred others could be added. We emphasize this for those that we produce are not exceptions, representing some 'errors of development', but rather simple samples of a collection whose general direction they reveal.).

11 THE MASS: MEAL, 'BLESSING', CONGREGATION OR SACRIFICE?

ALTHOUGH IT MOVES directly toward the deepest understanding of the liturgy, the path that we have followed in our preceding studies is of a dogmatic type.[1] Beginning with revelation, the traditional data of theology and the Magisterium, we recalled what the Mystery of Christ is, in its totality as in its economy. Three essential truths thus presented themselves to us, beginning with the New Testament notion of 'mystery': first, the fact of the accomplishment of this Mystery, that is to say of the history of salvation in Christ and in His redemptive work; second, the opening up of new times, eschatological times, for the final realization of redemption, that is, the 'new creation,' with the paradox that flows from it and that characterizes the present period of history—namely, the relation to an 'eschaton'[2] (undetermined with respect to its date) of a history's consummation already realized in its new principle, Christ; and third, the foundation of the Church and the institution in it of the sacramental order, the privileged instrument of the ultimate consummation of the entire Mystery.

It is, then, in the framework and at the heart of this economy that the liturgy is placed—the proper act, the first and ultimate act, of the Church. Among the sacraments that she celebrates, or more correctly, in which she celebrates and works to consummate the Mystery of Christ, we note the eminent place occupied by Baptism, and still more by the Eucharist, with their respective references to the Incarnation and the redemptive Pasch of the Lord.

---

[1] The text of the present chapter had been published in *LPC*, no. 193 (July–August 1981), pp. 11–41, under the title: *Le Saint Sacrifice de la Messe et sa célébration.*

[2] That is, an 'end' or a 'finish'.

An analysis of the symbol has allowed us finally to develop this central reality of the sacrament and to clarify the status of the sacramental order in general. Three principles have surfaced: 1) the symbol is that which reunites the realities that are diverse and yet correspond to each other; 2) it is the fact of the Incarnation that makes the difference between the symbolic and sacramental orders; 3) for, it is by the flesh of Christ and by its continuation in the sacraments that the Mystery is accomplished, that is to say that the Holy Spirit is given to us, in order to unite us to Christ and lead us in Christ to the Father. These three principles, as can be seen, are of extreme importance for explaining the causality, the efficiency, of the sacraments.

These considerations will need to be developed in detail; and we will revisit some of them here. But for the moment we have to move on to something else, but always for the sake of responding to the one question which occupies us: How is the Mystery of Christ realized in the liturgy? This is, in effect, what we need to understand in order to clarify the vital questions that make up the object of all our studies, those of the meaning and value of the different ways of celebrating the sacrament of the Eucharist. Therefore, our task here will be more immediately focused on the liturgy, in the sense that it will be more by the study of its history and its rites that we will try to see how the Mystery is accomplished there. The two approaches, moreover, are complementary. For, if the dogmatic data, developed through our two-fold reflection on the Mystery and the symbol, necessarily sheds light on the properly liturgical reflection, this latter in turn enlightens, confirms and develops in a powerful way the results of the first approach. Once again the truth of Prosper of Aquitaine's maxim is verified: … *ut legem credendi lex statuat supplicandi.*[3] We must not harden the distinction between these two methods. They are not only complementary, but implied in each other. This is expressed in the abridged form of the above maxim: *Lex orandi, lex credendi.* It is also

---

[3]   *De vocatione omnium gentium,* I, 12 (*PL* 51, 664 ff.), and borrowed by the Holy
      See as its own teaching (DS 246). cf. *see below,* Conclusion.

shown by the 'mystagogies' of the Eastern tradition—those introductions to the mystery of the liturgy where dogma and the explanation of the rites are inseparably united.[4] It is in this line—which is also that of the great Western commentaries on the liturgy—that we would like to place this last part of our research.

Let us note also that our reflection ought to progress on a two-fold level, that of a properly liturgical reflection, with its own theological foundation, and that of an examination of the contemporary liturgical movement. In itself these two plans are directly connected, the first serving as the basis for the second and being developed within it. Nevertheless, insofar as it represents a 'movement,' the second level is established and operates according to its own proper mode and very often where theological arguments are no longer but instruments, modified and used in view of an end pursued for itself. For this reason there is a distance that exists between the theological reflection and the activity of that liturgical movement. This distance will inevitably be felt in our analysis, sometimes giving the impression that we are leaving the level of theological reflection—which interests us—when we deal with the study of the liturgical movement and its representa-

---

[4]   Cf. R. Bornet, OSB, *L'intelligence spirituelle de la liturgie selon la Mystagogie de saint Maxime le Confesseur* (Pont. Athaen. Anselmianum)—*Extrait de la these de doctorat, 'Les commentaries byzantins de la divine liturgie du VII au XV siècle'*, in *Archives de l'Orient Chrétien* (no. 9), Paris, Institut des Etudes Byzantines, 1966. The word 'mystagogy' has two senses: that of an introductory sacred action in the mystery, especially through the liturgy; and an 'oral or written explanation of the mystery hidden in Scripture and celebrated in the liturgy' (p. 21). It is this second sense that is used here. 'The mystagogy' borrows its method from spiritual exegesis, adapting it for its own ends' (p. 28). 'The 'Mystagogy' of St Maximus the Confessor opens the series of commentaries on the Byzantine liturgy. It is this, then, which will mark the beginning of our research. Simeon of Thessalonica, whose activity and work was at the end of the Byzantine Empire, will naturally make up the end of this research' (p. 29). With the work of St Maximus, 'The Explanation of the Eastern Mystagogies' of Nicholas Cabasilas (ca. 1354) is the most known of the Eastern mystagogies; we shall make use of it in the next chapter.

tives. And yet this study is still necessary, for it is in the framework of that liturgical movement, or at least in relation to it, that the contemporary liturgical reflection is developed. Therefore, one will not want to forget that, in addition to our analysis, and to the facts or authors of the liturgical movement, it is always the profound knowledge of the liturgy's mystery that concerns us; all the discussions having for their end the establishment of the theoretical 'mystagogy' of which we are speaking, and from there, the practical 'mystagogy' that is the liturgy itself with its practices.

In this sense, along with Cardinal Ratzinger[5] and then Romano Guardini and Joseph Pascher,[6] we believe that it is a good idea to begin with the following question: What is the fundamental structure of the Mass? And first of all: What is the primary principle that will allow us to see how the different parts of the Mass are structured or organized? As Heinz Schürmann correctly noted in 1955, the question does not belong only to the liturgy or even only to exegesis and history, but all the more so to dogmatic theology.[7] One cannot insist too much on the importance of this preliminary question, especially in our day. In fact, from the manner in which one responds to it will

---

5   *De la Cène de Jésus au sacrament de l'Eglise,* in *L'Eucharistie, pain nouveau pour un monde rompu* (in collaboration) (Coll. 'Communion'), Paris, Fayard, 1981, pp. 35–51; cf. p. 34. Hereafter we shall cite this collective work with the abbreviation *PNMR*.

6   Cited by Ratzinger (*ibid.,* pp. 35, 36). See also H. Schürmann, *Die Gestalt der urchristlichen Eucharistiefeier,* in *Münchener Theologie Zeitschrift,* 6, 1955, pp. 107–31. According to this work, it is R. Guardini who seems to have launched the notion of *fundamental structure* (*Grundstruktur*) apropos of the Mass. He proposes it in a startling manner, when he asserts in 1939 that: 'The fundamental and supporting structure of the Mass is the meal. The sacrifice does not enter in or appear here as the structure; but rather it is behind the whole … not as the structure, but as the reality, as the source, as something presupposed' (*Besinnung vor der Feier der heiligen Messe* (Mainz, 1939), II, pp. 76 ff; *cit. ibid.,* p. 107). This is the thesis refuted by Schürmann and by Cardinal Ratzinger after him.

7   H. Schürmann, *loc. cit.,* pp. 130 ff.

follow one's whole knowledge of the liturgy. It is often from a lack of clarifying this that the dialogue between one trend of liturgical theology and another is today so difficult, if not downright impossible. This is why, we know, all our work will be in vain, if we do not take pains to examine the principal responses that are currently given to the question, and if we do not justify what we think ought to be the response. The somewhat thankless trouble that we shall undergo for this purpose will not be lost, for the soundness of our conclusions will appear with all the more force.

I. Meal, 'Blessing' or Congregation?

1. For some, then, 'the fundamental structure (of the Eucharist) is that of a meal.' This thesis, launched within the French liturgical milieu after WWII, had been supported by liturgists such as those we already cited, Joseph Pascher,[8] by theologians such as P. G. de Broglie,[9] and before them, by writers such as Romano Guardini. The thesis is based on the fact that the very first celebration of the Eucharist develops in the framework of a meal, the Last Supper, and on the fact that the rite concludes with the eating of the Victim. Without denying that the meal is an essential aspect of the Mass, one can ask whether the meal truly represents by itself the ultimate element that allows one to understand the Mass and to discern its internal structure.

---

[8] See the reference in Ratzinger, *loc. cit.*, p. 36, and for more details, in H Schürmann, *loc. cit.*, p. 107. The no. 18 issue of *LMD* (1949/2), titles '*Le repas, le pain et le vin*', bears witness to the launching of this idea after the Second World War.

[9] *Pour une théologie du festin eucharistique.* Extracts of a conference at the Eucharistic Congress of Nantes, 1947, Institut Catholique of Paris. According to Dom. J Juglar (*Le sacrifice de louange* ('Lex Orandi'—15), Paris, Cerf, 1953, p. 20), Fr De Broglietries to form a synthesis of the Eucharistic doctrine around the fundamental notion of the meal. The text of this study can be found in *Doctor Communis* (2), 1949, pp. 3–36; (3), 1950, 16–42, 'but with some considerable modifications and additions' (p. 3). See Chapter XII.

From an historical point of view, in fact—and we are speaking here of the history of the liturgy—while it can be disputed whether the institution of the Eucharist is developed in the framework of the Pascal meal, on the contrary, that which characterizes its very first evolution is precisely the progressive and rapid detachment from that framework, as well as from the Jewish meal, sanctified by the *Berakah,* the blessing, and the 'Agape.' We shall return to this later (in our second part). Let us note here that the history of these origins remains obscure; whence the gropings of historians. Fr Battifol would even deny the very existence of the Agape, in which some (Renan, following liberal Protestants) see the early form of the Eucharist.[10] H. Leclerq, for his part, recognizes the existence of this practice, but he sees it as a separate reality. There was, he says, '*two distinct acts,* a meal in common and a Eucharistic Communion.'[11] Hanssens holds for the same; but his long research confirms above all the difficulty of the question.[12] This latter was entirely revived, if not surpassed, when there was recognized in the ritual of Christ's Last Supper the Jewish 'blessing' of the meal. The attentive analysis of the treatise of 'blessings,' *Berakoth,* contained in the Talmud is at the origin of this connection.[13] In any case, whether it's a question of this Jewish meal or the Agape (of pagan origin), the fact is that the liturgy of the Eucharist is constituted by making use of both.

In reflecting on these facts and on the difficulty that the authors encountered in harmonizing them, a hypothesis comes to mind. The existence of the Agape is certain during the second century, more still during the third century, and doubtful for any time before the second.

---

[10]   *Etudes d'histoire et de théologie positive,* Paris, 1902, pp. 310 ff.

[11]   Article, '*Agape*', in DACL I (1924), 785. Leclerc notes the definitive decline of the agape beginning in the fourth century. The Third Council of Carthage (397) forbids all meals in the churches (col. 820).

[12]   *L'Agape et l'Eucharistie,* in *Eph. Lit.* (Roma), 41, 1927, pp. 525–48; p. 42, 1928, pp. 545–71; p. 43, 1929, pp. 520–9.

[13]   Cf. H. Chirat, *L'eucharistie et l'agape; de leur union à leur disjunction,* in *LMD,* no. 18 (1949/2), pp. 48–60. Cf. pp. 50 ff.

On the one hand, the existence of the Jewish meal preceding the Eucharist in the strict sense is certain in its origins. The New Testament attests to it often.[14] It is equally certain that the tendency to separate them appeared quite rapidly, even if it was slow to catch on everywhere. From then on one can ask whether on one hand, the appearance and development of the rite of the Agape cannot be explained by the need to return to a meal in order to seal the fraternal encounter, especially in small groups; and on the other hand, whether before the Jewish meal and its 'benediction' had been rediscovered, historians would have wanted to see an Agape there, the existence of which does not appear with certitude until later. What is certain is that the Christian Eucharist is established in its own liturgy by making use successively of both the Jewish meal and the pagan Agape (pagan with respect to its origin); therefore, it is mixed up with a meal other than that which is proper to it—its own meal being essentially sacramental and spiritual.

In addition, both liturgical practice as well as sacramental theology, remind us that, except for the priest, sacramental communion is not strictly required for the celebration of the Eucharist. This fact alone ought to make reflect those who wish to find in the meal *the* fundamental structuring principle of the Eucharistic liturgy. Another fact, of the pastoral and dogmatic orders, shows again the insufficiency of that thesis: it is that, in making the meal the first principle of the Mass, one inevitably ends up diminishing and finally denying altogether its sacrificial character, or at the very least, identifying the sacrifice with the meal.[15] But this position reveals either a theologically unsupportable thesis,[16] or an equally indefensible biblical archaism.[17] For

---

[14] *I Cor* 11: 20–22; *Acts* 2: 42–6; 6:1 ff; 20:7, 11; 27:35; *Lk* 24:30–5. On all these texts see the commentaries of Schürmann, *loc. cit.*, p. 116 ff.

[15] Cf. L. Bouyer, art. '*Sacrifice*', in his '*Dictionnaire théologique*', Tournai, Desclée, 1963, p. 588.

[16] We are alluding to all those theories that, since the beginning of the 16th century, try to prove that the Mass is a true sacrifice because there is in it a true destruction of the Victim, which takes place, according to some, at

Luther, this negation of the sacrifice in the Eucharist takes place in the beginning; and it is in order to bring this out that he replaces the word 'Mass,' with all its traditional Catholic content, with the word 'supper.' However, as we saw, this manner of using the term 'supper' for the Eucharistic rite represents an unheard of novelty, without any foundation in Tradition.[18] Let us recall that 'supper' in German is 'Abend*mahl*,' that is 'evening *meal*'; therefore, the word evokes more directly than the French the idea of a meal. Whether one wishes or not, by making the meal the essential and structuring element of the

Communion. The authority of Bellarmine, less fortunate on this point than on others, of De Lugo and of Vasquez does much to lend credit to this idea. See M. Lepin, *L'idée du sacrifice de la messe d'après les théologiens depuis l'origine jusqu'à nos jours*, Paris, Beauchesne, 1926 (3rd edition), pp. 429 ff. It is from there that develops the thesis of 'the real immolation' necessary for the sacrifice, this immutation having to be destructive. Cf. *see below*, note 712.

[17]   A. Loisy, in his *Essai historique sur le sacrifice* (1920), also holds that the major element of the sacrifice is the immolation insofar as it is a destruction of the victim, the essential sacrifice thus consisting in the eating of the victim following its immolation (cf. H. Cazelles, who sums it up in these terms, in *Eucharistie, benediction et sacrifice dans l'Ancien Testament*, in *LMD*, no. 123 (1975/3), pp. 7 ff). Loisy follows here Robertson Smith (*Lectures on the Religion of the Semites*, 1899), who sees in the meal a way of sealing a covenant. A. Gelin showed that the rite celebrated by Melchizedek, the priest–king of Jerusalem, was that of a meal of a covenant between him and Abraham (*Jérusalem dans le dessein de Dieu*, in *Vie. Spir.*, 86, 1952 (no. 372, April) pp. 353–6, cf. p. 355: Gen 14:18; cf. 31:46, Jos 9:14). P. Lagrange admits the existence of a 'peace sacrifice' prior to the holocaust (*Etudes sur les Religions sémitiques*, Paris, 1905, 2nd edition, p. 273). But for him, the essential act of the sacrifice remains the immolation (pp. 271 ff; cited by Cazelles, *loc. cit.*, pp. 8 ff). We have here only some simple points of reference. Whatever be the most ancient form of the sacrifice, this much is certain, that one cannot reduce it to the reality of the sacred meal that is but one among others, and nothing more. In Israel, the most complete form of the sacrifice is the holocaust, in which the victim is entirely offered to the Lord.

[18]   J. A. Jungmann, *Abendmahl als Name der Eucharistie*, in *Zeitschrift für Katholische Theologie* 93, 1971, pp. 91–3: 'a novelty without precedent', cited in Ratzinger, in *PNMR*, pp. 38 ff.

Mass, one will always end up with the sacrifice being overshadowed. The history of the liturgical movement since the end of the Second World War has proven this all too well, despite the knowledge and good intentions of its founders, and even if the notion of meal seems today to give way to that of congregation. These two are moreover immediately linked from the very beginning, as can be seen in the work by Fr Broglie on the 'Eucharistic feast.'[19]

2. We recalled above the discovery among liturgists of the Talmudic tract on the *Berakoth* ('blessings'). Exegetes and historians have been familiar with it for a long time now. They even showed the relationship of these texts and rites with not only the Last Supper, but also the Eucharistic liturgy, especially in the early Church.[20] However, it is only after the war

---

[19]   '*Festin eucharistique*'. We will see this again in our conclusion (cf. *infaa*, Ch. XII). This notion of meal or supper, in order to explain the sacrifice, has not disappeared however. The no. 123 issue of *LMD* (3rd trim. 1975), titled, '*Eucharistie, repas du Seigneur ou sacrifice?*' uses it. No precise response is given to the question thus posed, but the sense in which the reader is directed is clear. He is told, on one hand, about the shift that takes place in late Judaism from the sacrifice to the worship meal in the Temple (Perrot, p. 44). And if another article takes up the notion of sacrifice, it is for the sake of interpreting it in an overwhelmingly anthropological manner, by openly avoiding the Tridentine dogma and reducing the sacrifice to a 'memorial', understood in a purely psychological sense (L. M. Chauvet, pp. 60–3; 76–8). One will note the reduction of the sacramental to the symbolic (pp. 62, 78).—Closer to us still, despite falling into those extremes, J. Roche takes up this theme: *Table du Seigneur, source de vie*, in *Esprit et Vie* 91, 1981 (no. 14; 9 April), pp. 214–24. 'Mystery and sacrifice,' he writes, 'the Mass is a meal.' (p. 220). Etc.

[20]   Cf. V. D. Glotz, *Tischgbete und Abendmahlsgebete in der altchristlichen und in der griechischen Kirche* ('Text und Untersuchungen' hgb, v. Gebhardt u. Harnack, XXIX, 2b, 1905); A. Baumstark, *Das eucharistiche Hochgebet und die Literatur des nachexilischen Judentums* (*Theologie und Glaube*, II (1901), 353–370); *Messe in Morgenland* (1906). Other references can be found, and especially the Latin translation of the principal Jewish texts in the valuable work of A. Hängi and I. Pahl, *Prex eucharistica. Textus e variis Liturgiis antiquioribus selecti* (Spicilegium Friburgense), Fribourg, Ed. Universitaires, 1968, pp. 2–57 (section drafted by Fr L. Ligier, SJ). We shall cite this work under the appreviation *PE*.

that these facts find an echo among liturgists and that the latter recognize their importance. We saw the conclusions that they draw from them for the historical problem of the Agape. But the fundamental thesis that a certain number of them make use of was, under its most radical form, that the Christian *eucharistia was only* the continuation of the Jewish *berakah*. This then, according to some authors, is where one will find the fundamental structure of the Mass: the Mass is essentially a prayer of 'blessing,' giving to this word all the richness revealed by the Biblical and Talmudic tradition. This manner of seeing things, with different variations and nuances, wins in our day a certain number of votes, its most fervent defender being Fr Louis Bouyer.

However, others preceded him, like Gregory Dix, who was its first inspirer;[21] and others were his contemporaries, like Fr Audet, OP, whose firsthand works on the *Didache* and the *Berakah* had considerable influence.[22] Fr Louis Ligier, SJ, profressor at the Gregorianum, also made a contribution, and he published in a Latin translation the principle Talmudic texts on the question.[23] For his part, Dom Odon Casel, OSB, borrowed the same idea from the works of Baumstark, but without drawing the same consequences.[24] Most recently an

---

[21] G. Dix, *The Shape of the Liturgy*, Westminster, Dacre Press, 1945. L. Bouyer wrote a long and very laudatory review of this important work in *LMD*, no. 18 (1949/2), 146–150; and its profound inspiration on him can be seen in his article in the same issue: *La première eucharistie dans la Cène* (pp. 34–47). It can be said that it was with the work of Dix that began the systematic studies on the origins of the Eucharist. The history of these studies is outlined by L. Ligier, *Les origines de la prière eucharistique: de la Cène du Seigneur à l'Eucharistie*, in *Questions Liturgiques* 53, 1972, pp. 181–201.

[22] *La Didaché Instructions des Apôtres* ('Etudes Bibliques'—29), Paris, Gabalda, 1958; *Esquisse historique du genre littéraire de la 'Bénédiction' juive et de l' 'Eucharistic' chrétienne*, in *Rev. Bibl.*, 65, 1958, pp. 371–99.

[23] See *PE*. From the same author: *De la Cène de Jésus à l'anaphore de l'Eglise*, in *LMD*, no. 87 (1966/3), pp. 7–51; and numerous other studies.

[24] *Le memorial du Seigneur dans la liturgie de l'antiquité chrétienne. Les pensées fondamentales du Canon de la Messe* ('Lex Orandi'—2), Paris, Cerf, 1945 (translated from the German 5th edition), pp. 18 ff.

important thesis revisited the entire question, but it considers the Eucharist solely insofar as it is a prayer.[25] Its author, Cesare Giraudo, shows the existence of a 'literary structure,' which is continually found again, although under extremely varied historical contexts and forms—from the 'prayers of the Covenant' of the Old Testament, to the Christian Eucharist. Critiquing the excessive simplifications of Auget's thesis, he has the origin of the Eucharistic prayer going back not only to the Judaic and Talmudic *berakoth,* whether those from the synagogue or from the home, but in addition, back to the *tôdah* of the post-exilic period (Ne 9), and even to the prayers of the first pact of the Covenant, or at least to those of its renewal by Joshua (Jos 24:2–15). This work, although it suffers from several serious defects, bears on the problem of the origins of the Eucharistic prayer with extremely valuable insights; we shall have the occasion of seeing this. We could not even dream of considering in detail the analyses proposed by all these scholars. The studies done in this area are far too numerous, and considering every little detail would prevent us from making more general conclusions. This is, however, what many have desired to do, and not without injury to both the history and knowledge of the liturgy. We shall limit ourselves therefore to presenting the thesis of the 'blessing' in its essentials and its literary foundations, in order then to propose a critical evaluation and to show the complements that it calls forth.

Among all the *Berakoth* of Judaism, there is one that shows a striking resemblance to the Eucharistic liturgy: it is the *Birkat-ha-Mazon,* or the 'after dinner blessing-thanksgiving.'[26] The flexibility of its form and the possibility of adapting it to the different circumstances and religious feasts explains that it was able to be used, at least as a general exterior framework or structure, by Christ, during the

---

[25]   C. Giraudo, *La struttura letteraria della preghiera eucaristica. Saggio sulla genesi letteraria di una forma. Toda veterotestamentaria. Beraka giudaica. Anafora Cristiana* ('Analecta Biblica'—92), Rome, Biblical Institute Press, 1981.

[26]   Cf. *PE,* pp. 8–12.

Last Supper. Having established these facts, with the details and references to which we could only refer the reader, Fr Ligier concludes: 'It is sufficient to propose that the initial schema of the anaphora had been inspired by the *Birkat-ha-mazon* under its Paschal form.'[27] The interesting thing about this hypothesis is the renewal that it allows one to make—beginning with the Jewish prayer of 'blessing'—of the concept of 'the thanksgiving,' in which the practice ended by reducing the word 'Eucharist.'

Audet, perhaps, is the one who best developed this point. He shows how the 'blessing' 'is before all else a cry of admiration before the 'wonders' of the sign accomplished. Foundation and form, the essentials of the blessing are there.'[28] Whence the two elements that form it early on: the expression of that adoring admiration and the evocation of the motif that it provokes (it is the anamnesis prematurely). Fr Audet gives as an example the prayer of Abraham's servant, when he recognized in Rebecca the future bride of Isaac: 'Blessed be the Lord God of my master Abraham, who hath not taken away His mercy and truth from my master' (Gen 24:27).

Occasional and spontaneous as it was in the beginning (see again Ex 18:10–11), the 'blessing' became cultic little by little—a third element being added to the two previous ones, namely, after the anamnesis, a return to the initial exclamation (a true invitation to praise) under the form of a more developed doxology (p. 379 ff). A further evolution introduced the 'supplicating blessing,' that is, the prayer of asking and of intercession (p. 381; cf. 1 Kngs 8:56–61). However, what always dominates is the initial movement, where, in a gesture of adoration, the proclamation of the divine Name has the value of a confession of faith (p. 378; cf. Gen 14:19). In the momen-

---

[27] Art. cit., p. 33. Just as Th. J. Talley, *De la 'berakah' à l'eucharistie, une question à réexaminer*, in *LMD*, no. 125 (1976/1) 11–39 (a critique of Audet's thesis): 'The *Birkat–ha–Mazon* was the source of inspiration that gives the model of the first Eucharistic prayer: praise—thanksgiving—supplication ... ' (p. 35).

[28] Art. cit., p. 377. For the rest of this chapter, the numbers of the pages indicated in parentheses refer to this article.

tum of that first movement, admiration, joy, gratitude, proclamation of the Name of God and confession of faith are the sentiments and acts that animate the Jewish prayer of 'blessing,' and, after it, that of the Christian 'Eucharist.' This latter, therefore, is both an *exomologesis* (confession) and a *eulogia* (blessing). It is a fact that these terms are found again in the narrations of the institution of the Eucharist (p. 385 ff). Together they explain the meaning of this last word. And it is no small advantage to find this whole early force in the New Testament concept of *eucharistia*.

Another merit of Audet's work is that he insisted on the fact that 'the distinctive element of the entire *eucharistia* is its motif, or its anamnesis' (pp. 390; 387). The very structure of the prayer and rite show this: the prayer of 'blessing' is entirely relative and subordinated to the event that it awakens and of which it makes a 'memorial'—in Hebrew the word is *zikkaron*. However, the principle thus posited will work against the general impact of the conclusions that the author believes to be able to deduce from his research, not without hiding what they provoke, on the liturgical level, namely, 'conscious choices whose impact is immense' (p. 396). For, it obliges one to consider with the greatest attention the precise element that will determine the radical novelty and irreducible transcendence of the rite instituted by Christ at the Last Supper, namely, His own Passover. It is a memorial of this that He invites His disciples to celebrate. And by reason of its sacramental nature, that memorial is no longer a simple prayer of evocation, but a renewing act, and like an eschatological act accompanied by a prayer. And it is this act that would henceforth become the center and essence of the Christian 'eucharistia.'

For this reason, but also because of the too restrictive limits of his historical research (accurately noted by H. Cazelles), the work of Audet, as remarkable and as valuable as it is in what it presents, cannot be approved without reservations in its final conclusions. It is not possible to identify, as the author practically does, the Eucharist of the Church with the *Berakah* of Judaism (p. 372). Nor is it possible, on the purely philological level, to support the equivalence of the word *eulogein* and *eucharistein*. The sacrifice of expiation, in particular, even if it is recalled (p. 391), has no place here. Only the 'sacrifice of praise' remains.

The insufficiency of Audet's historical research, we said, has been shown by H. Cazelles. After having recalled the broad outlines of the history of sacrifice in Israel, the eminent exegete concludes that, now 'one can'—and therefore one ought—'to avoid the impasses where the assimilation of the Eucharist moves us to the *berakah* of the synogogal non-sacrificial type.'[29] He nevertheless maintains with Audet that, 'the Eucharist signifies more than a thanksgiving in the sense of thanks' (p. 26). However, he observes that, 'the more that the sacrificial theology of the Eucharist in the New Testament is established, the more one distances himself from the vocabulary of the blessing of the meals of Jewish sects' (*ibid*). Discretely but surely, it is towards the sacrifice that Fr Cazelles' thought turns. And yet he leaves behind the notion of meal. The passage where this transition appears is worth citing in its entirety:

> The Eucharist, both in the Gospel narratives of the Institution as in the ecclesial practice that renews the Last Supper, is a sacred meal accompanied by signifying words. Yet the sacred meal exists before the Bible, in the Bible and outside of the Bible; but in the last centuries of our history, the end of sacrifice calls to mind most especially the sacrifice-expiation. Some texts of St Paul (Rom 3:25; 4:25; 8:4; Tit 2:14), from Luke (1:68; 2:38; 24:21; Acts 7:35) and other texts from the New Testament (Matt 20:28; Mk 10:45; Heb 9:12) interpret the death of Christ as a ransom. Christ's sacrifice, therefore, was considered rather as a holocaust, and the result from this is a theology of the sacrifice of a very juridic and very bloody redemption. 'Without the shedding of blood there is no

---

[29] Art. cit., p. 27. We shall look back directly at the pages of this article later in our chapter. Giraudo, who also refuses this assimilation, also recognized in Audet the merit of having widened the notion of thanksgiving (op. cit., p. 264).

remission (*aphesis*)' (Heb 9:22). The problem was one of knowing how to see a sacrifice in the Eucharist (p. 7).

Let us pass over the 'juridic aspect' and recall nevertheless that the 'interpretation' of Christ's death by the authors of the New Testament is that of Revelation itself. The interest of this text is to show how, beginning with a definition of the Eucharist founded on the meal —how the exegete is moved by the study of the texts to see there a sacrifice before anything else. Whence his question: How is that meal a sacrifice? He gives us no response under this form; but his whole work leads one to go beyond both this notion of a meal and that of a 'blessing' in order to see in the Eucharist essentially a sacrifice. He insists particularly on the *todah* and the *schelâmîn*, both forms of sacrifice having a long history. We saw in our preceding work that Christ's sacrifice takes up and 'accomplishes' the totality of sacrifices from the time of preparation. While the study of history and the vocabulary allows the presence of one or another type of Jewish sacrifice to appear in the Last Supper, a complete study of biblical theology, and not simply literary or philological, would cause one to see all these there. This is what is pointed out in the initial observation of Fr Cazelles' article, which we mentioned above.

But let us return to the work of Fr Ligier. While beginning with the Jewish liturgy of the meal, he also, like Audet, puts his finger on that central element that is the 'memorial'; and unlike Audet, he understands that this element obliges one to inquire about the true nature of the Last Supper. 'In this context of a meal,' he writes, 'the acts of Jesus—taking the bread or the cup, breaking, distributing—the acts of Jesus are self-explanatory. But one of them, the blessing pronounced over each of the two elements, is left to His mystery.'[30] Unfortunately, he does not develop this 'mystery.' Even if, apropos of those acts, he emphasizes that 'they alone ... are what constitutes the memorial of the Lord Jesus' (p. 22), the principal reference of his reflection, as we saw, remains the *Berakah,* or more precisely the *Birkat-ha-mazon* (p. 33).

---

[30]   Art. cit., p. 17.

In addition, what he brings out in his conclusion is the continuity that there is 'from the Last Supper of Jesus to the Church's anaphora,' namely 'the continuity of a liturgical structure of prayer, that of thanksgiving for the meal, in a Paschal context' (p. 49). This conclusion is undisputable. However, it becomes false if it pretends to define the whole of the Christian Eucharist; for, it does not bring out the going beyond that takes place in the very heart of that continuity. It passes over in silence the fact that, in the Eucharist, that prayer accompanies a 'memorial' whose 'mystery' is that of an action: the sacramental action of the sacrifice of Christ and of the Church. Certainly, it does not deny it; it simply does not speak of it at all.

Fr Bouyer goes even further still in the sense of this reduction of the Christian Eucharist to the prayer of a Jewish blessing. According to him, the Eucharistic liturgy is nothing but the development of the Jewish liturgy of the *Berakah*. Correctly understood, this assertion can no doubt receive an acceptable and very profound meaning, but under one condition, that it show the transcendence of that development in relation to its preparation and the break by which a passage is made from one to the other. To recall this is not ipso facto to fall into a dark anti-Semitism! Yet Fr Bouyer affirms only the continuity. He even goes so far as to say that the Catholic Church is 'but the Jewish Church thus highly developed,' that is to say 'modified in the more or less secondary elements, but constant in the essentials.'[31] These assertions—surprisingly enough, it must be said—show where an error of method can lead, and error which consists in extrapolating unjustifiably the conclusions drawn from an element of truth not stored in the totality of which it is a part. This first error brings about many others, even on the level of historical interpretation of texts, and more still when one comes to their theological explanation. This is why (to limit ourselves to the chief points) that manner of favouring to the extreme the element of 'blessing' of the Eucharist inevitably causes one to reduce the Eucharist to nothing but a prayer of benediction pronounced

---

[31]   *De la liturgie juive à la liturgie chrétienne,* in *PNMR,* pp. 17–34. cf. p. 31.

within the course of a meal.[32] The logic of the words have their own strength, or if you prefer, the dynamic of the words have their own internal logic, which necessarily prevails in the long run over the initial intentions of those who make use of them. The 'action' disappears behind the 'blessing'; and with that only the word remains. One then finds himself in 'the religion of the book.' Yet Christianity is not a religion of the book, but the religion of Christ the Lord, 'the Living One,' as St John calls Him in the Apocalypse (1:17). Forgetting this and following the path of that minimizing return to the *Berakah* alone does not result in a neo-judeo-Christianity, but in something entirely new: a Christiano-Judaism, so much are the problems of the Church and those of the liturgy immediately connected.[33]

Despite all the valuable things that it brings us and that are to be held onto, the Jewish notion of *Berakah* cannot therefore be considered as representing the first principle leading to a knowledge of the liturgical and theological structure of the Mass. It does not allow us to make a synthesis of the elements that compose it, and it results, if one holds exclusively to it, in concealing some more important elements, such as that of the sacrifice.

3. Before showing how the sacrifice is effectively the first internal principle that allows one to know the structure of the Mass, we must still examine a third attempted explanation, one that is perhaps less scholarly than the last, but no less widespread. One word can sum it

---

[32] Significant in this sense was the subtitle of the book, *Eucharistie*, published by Fr Bouyer in 1966: '*Théologie et spiritualité de la prière eucharistique*' (Tournai, Desclée). The fruit of many years of work and an immense erudition, from disputable points of view, this work contains absolutely remarkable pages on the liturgy, and it remains a mine of historical information. However, its subtitle proclaims that that which one sees in the Eucharist is before all else a prayer. It is for him only that, while in fact the Eucharist is first and foremost an action. This is the position of H. Cazelles, mentioned in a work that we shall return to later.

[33] On this link between the passing from the Jewish liturgy to the Christian liturgy, and that of Israel to the Church, see J. Ratzinger, Art. cit., in *PNMR* pp. 42; 50.

up, *congregation.* And one sole fact will show the favour that it enjoys: it is this word that has served as a foundation for the official liturgists in trying to impose on the Church their erroneous conception of the Mass. We allude to the first version of the famous Article 7 of the *Institutio generalis* of 1969, which presented the *Novus Ordo Missae:*

> The Last Supper of the Lord or the Mass is the sacred synax or congregation of the people of God reunited, under the presidency of the priest, in order to celebrate the memorial of the Lord. This is why the promise of Christ is applied eminently to the local assembly of the Holy Church: 'Where two or three are gathered in My Name, I am in their midst' (Matt 18:20).

As can be seen, at the beginning and the end of these two phrases, joined to each other by the phrase, 'this is why,' it is the notion of the congregation that one encounters. Therefore, it is definitely on this that the rest depends, namely, the real presence and the memorial itself. Clearly, something did not go right in the workings of the Curia. The Congregation for the Doctrine of the Faith would never have been able to approve such a definition of the Mass. And in fact it modified it as soon as it was given the opportunity, which took place after the Holy See received numerous protestations.

It is neither out of pleasure nor is it gratuitously that we recall this episode—as revealing as it is painful—of the current liturgical Reform, as will be seen in a moment. It is a milestone in the course of a history began well before it, and which seems today to be reaching its final developments. In fact, it is since WWII that this notion of congregation has developed. It is known how Pius XII, in 1943, needed to condemn the 'false mysticism,' which wished 'to unite in one sole physical person the Divine Redeemer and the members of the Church.'[34] After the war, in order to indicate only some points of reference that were still but a tendency, it was the small book of Fr Roguet, *La Messe, approche du*

---

[34]   Encylcical *Mystici Corporis*, AAS 35, 1943, pp. 217; 231; 234; where Pius XII denounces the 'false mysticism' that wants to make of Christ and His members one sole physical person. Cf. DS 3806; 3814; 3816.

Mystère, that began with a chapter dedicated to 'The Congregation.' Beginning with 'that which is more immediately visible,' he proposed the following definition: 'the Mass is a gathering.'[35] There seems to be nothing wrong with it, although one can say the same about many of the other meetings of Christians; and yet the impulse had been given. The Mass would become, without any distinction, the action of the Christian community coming together and for the purpose of coming together.[36]

---

[35] *La Messe. Approches du Mystère* (L'Esprit liturgique—3), Paris, Cerf, 1951, p. 9. To be just, we mention that Fr Roguet clarifies that he is speaking about an hierarchical gathering of which Christ is the Head: 'He contains it and recapitulates it in Himself'—just like the priest, who represents Christ (p. 14). However, the order adopted would prevail over these doctrinal clarifications. By beginning with the congregation, one ends up presenting the Mass as 'the action of the community, of the Church' (p. 54). This is true; but the reference to Christ tends to disappear. This is what would take place afterwards, as is clearly shows by G. Colombo: *'La dimension christologique de l'eucharistie'*, in *PNMR*, pp. 82–99. We note especially pages 92 to 97 of this remarkable contribution. Fr Roguet's book saw numerous editions. The last of which belonged to a collaboration, 'Livre de Vie' (Paris, Seuil, 1971).

[36] A. M. Roguet, op. cit., p. 54. cf. I. H. Dalmais, *La liturgie, acte de l'Eglise*, in *LMD*, no. 19 (1950/1), pp. 7–25; etc. On what point the underlying theology of Roguet's abovementioned book was false, one can see in the manner in which he expresses himself in the limited framework of a *'Session of Liturgical Preachers'*, organized by the CPL, at Vanves, in September 1946. Under the title: *'Les slogans du prédicateur liturgique'*, we see some of the active and efficacious force of ideas that he recommends to preachers to inculcate into the hearts of their audience: *'On the nature of liturgical prayer.* The liturgy is the action of the people. It is *your* affair ... You come to the Church as beggars, always in order to ask. While it is, above all, done with thanksgiving, with adoration; this is why it is joyful, brightening. However, in coming to Mass for the sake of asking, you row against the current: allow yourself to be taken by that force of admiration, of thanksgiving, of forgetfulness of self. *The altar.* The altar is primarily a table (look at it). The Mass is, therefore, primarily a meal. *The Mass.* The Mass is not the business of the priest alone. It is yours. Without you he could not celebrate Mass. He is your delegate ... One does not *assist* at Mass; one *participates at Mass*. Better still, one *celebrates* Mass. By Baptism you have become *capable* of celebrating; it *ordains* you 'priests'—into a subordinate and collective priesthood' (*LMD*, no. 10 (1947/2),

A reversal was there potentially, which would need to come to realization later.

Fr De Lubac, in his book, *Meditation sur l'Eglise,* goes in the same direction. There are several wonderful reflections in this book, among which, that so well-known formula: 'It is the Church that makes the Eucharist, but it is also the Eucharist that makes the Church.'[37] This was not lacking in equivocation however; for, he places the Church at the beginning and end of the Eucharist. This was inscribed there in the general current; and it is this that was retained, and not the scholarly and very accurate explanations by which the author explains the true meaning of his formula. There is the logic of language. Fr De Lubac even has a very beautiful passage where, following K. Barth, he stigmatizes a certain ecclesiocentrism. 'If the Church,' writes the reknown Lutheran theologian, 'has no goal except its own service, then it carries in itself the stigmas of death.'[38] In this we cannot but agree with him. Developing this thought Fr De Lubac shows how, in the immanent trend of the time, the Church that thus withdraws into itself tends to become 'the sacrament of Humanity.' Citing A. Comte, he shows how, in the movement thus launched, 'finally the religion of the God made

---

pp. 172–3).   Such then was the theology of the author of *La Messe. Approches du Mystère.* Some of those slogans are manifestly false. In others, error is mixed in with truth, but the error ends up being recovered and, in the end it alone remains. What the audience retains—what he wished to inculcate by these slogans—is that the Mass is a meal, *not* a sacrifice; that it is indistinctly the action of the entire congregation, *not* that of Christ acting through His ordained minister, the priest, gathering His Church (and therefore the congregation) around Himself in order to offer the sacrifice to God; that all the baptized are equally priests, and that he who officiates (or presides) is but the delegate of the congregation. All things considered, the congregation alone remains, the one subject of the celebration, which is actually the concelebration of all without distinction. One can see the continuity from 1946 to 1969 (Article 7—and *passim*—of the '*Institution generalis*') and from 1969 to 1981.

[37]   H. De Lubac, *Méditations sur l'Eglise* ('Théologie'—27), Paris, Aubier, 1953, p. 113.

[38]   K. Barth, *Esquisse d'une dogmatique,* p. 144: cited by De Lubac, op. cit., p. 194.

man results...through an inevitable dialectic, in an anthropology,'[39] that is to say, the religion of man who makes himself God.

The perspicacity of the philosophy is admirable; but we ask whether theologians then took adequate steps to oppose the revolution that it proclaimed. In a work published just after the Council, Fr Congar returned to the question of "The Church' or Christian Community, the Integral Subject of the Liturgical Action.'[40] He clearly posed a problem, and his text abounds in very pertinent reflections. He recalls the principles, but his conclusion is confusing. He hardens the nuances in opposition; and what finally wins out is the necessity of diminishing the hierarchical aspect, the 'scholastic,' 'tridentine' aspect of the *Ecclesia* in order to exalt its communitarian aspect, in line 'with the Council' (i.e. Vatican II). This conclusion, which should be reflected upon, was announced in the title of the article. The hierarchical nature of the Christian community is recalled, but in the end it fades away, and with it the liturgy's divine orientation.

Closer to our day, Henri Denis considers the question in an important work titled, 'La communauté chrétienne aujourd'hui.'[41] He asks whether 'the Eucharist has not ... become sometimes the mirror where the group sees itself and contemplates itself, with the security of Jesus the Liberator or a Spirit of fusing Love.'[42] The response for him has to

---

[39]   A. Comte, *Système de politique positive*, vol. II, p. 108; vol. III, p. 455; *cit. ibid*

[40]   *'L'Eglise' ou communauté chrétienne, sujet integral de l'action liturgique*, in *La Liturgie après Vatican II. Bilans, Etudes, Prospectives*. Under the direction of J. P. Joussa and Y. Congar ('Unam Sanctam'—66), Paris, Cerf, 1967, pp. 241–82. Such a work, under such a pen, in such a collection, shows well in what direction the liturgical movement after the Council turned, in continuity with its direction before the Council. See especially the conclusions of Fr Congar (pp. 276–82). It can be said that, on the level of the exposé, the principles are maintained (p. 269: The Church, the hierarchy and community: 'It is in the arrangement of these two values that some nuances can be shown'); but the thought clearly appears pointed in the direction of the community to the detriment of the hierarchy.

[41]   In *LMD*, no 141 (1980/1), 37–67.

[42]   *Ibid.*, p. 47.

be in the affirmative; and we do not know how better to describe what has become of the Mass today, at least in many cases. However, the only evil that Denis sees there is not this withdrawing of man in on himself, but rather the break with other communities that celebrate themselves the same way: 'The communion with the universal will then be lacking again.' We read: is lacking. It is against this pulverization of the Church into small groups that he is trying to react. However, one doubts whether he was successful; for, his vision and his effort remain entirely marked by the minimizing immanentism.

Then, most recently, another member of the CNPL, Louis-Marie Chauvet, professor of sacramental theology at the Institut Catholique of Paris, published a little brochure, untitled, which had been kept as a doctrinal guide for the preparation of the International Eucharistic Congress in Lourdes (1981).[43] These references suffice to show the importance of this little work. It goes well beyond what the modesty of its size and presentation would lead one to think. Moreover, as one quickly realizes, this is the work of a master whose system is well designed—insofar as the error cannot be coherent, for an attentive analysis does not allow one to detect its internal contradictions. For all these reasons, the *Thèmes de réflexion* merits a special examination.

The author announces his intention right from the start. He does this with a gesture that is fully laden with meaning, and which very

---

[43] Here is the description of that brochure, published without any other reference except for what we give here, in the order that one reads it on the cover: '*Congrès Eucharistique International*, 16/23 juillet 1981. Louis–Marie Chauvet: *Thèmes de réflexion sur l'Eucharistie—Deuxième série, Théologie*' (a list of the four parts of the work follows). The '*Thèmes*' is part of a series published under the care of the Congress' Preparatory Commission. Its preface is written by Msgr Jean François Motte, OFM, *Responsable de la Commission pastorale du Congrès* (pp. 4–5), and Auxiliary Bishop of Cambrai. The preface sums up the work well: 'An active and efficacious aspect of ideas runs through the whole of these reflections: The ecclesial body is the truth of the Eucharistic Body' (p. 4). Taken literally—and it must be taken this way—such an assertion goes far. Next in our work we shall see again the pages of this brochure. On L. M. Chauvet, cf. see above, note 667.

much emphasizes the continuity of the movement that we are analyzing: namely, by taking for his point of departure the famous Article 7
of the presentation of the Novus Ordo Missae, and by citing it in its
early version, something which Paul VI, he says, needed to correct.
This return to the first edition is for him only a statement of his
intention. After having declared that it was a question there of a
'definition ... of the Mass as beautiful as it is brief,' he notes its two
constitutive elements: the gathering and the memorial, and he shows
the connection between the two. The gathering, he says, exists for the
memorial; but the memorial, and along with it the presence of Christ,
does not exist except by the gathering. One cannot conclude then—as
with the prayer of 'blessing'—to a primacy of the memorial. Here it
is the congregation that is first and last; for, it is by the congregation
and for the congregation that everything is done. The Church,
identified with this congregation, is 'the fundamental sacrament' (p.
6). It is presented again at the beginning as the fundamental sacrament 'of the encounter with Christ' (ibid). But at the end it appears
as that which is truly in the framework of this thought, namely, as the
''sacrament' of the new humanity' (p. 35): 'Of the new humanity
inaugurated in Christ's Resurrection,' it is said. But who is this Christ
who fades away before 'that new collective Adam' that represents the
new humanity? The questions are posed in a series, for, in fact, all
adhere to each other. What can be deceiving is the fact that the
language of the author moves into a permanent equivocation. But
once one knows the keys of his discourse, the equivocation falls and
the deeply revolutionary sense of the thought shines through. Moreover, it manifests itself openly as an 'anti-sacral return, and as an
'anti-sacrificial worship' (p. 47).

How have we come to this? We have come to this no doubt by a
rejection of the Magisterium and an erroneous interpretation of
Scripture and the Fathers; but with regards to the *pars construens* (if
one may speak that way), it was by an intensive use of symbolism and
a radical inversion of the order of revelation. We showed in our

preceding study how the sacramental order had been established by Christ on the basis of the natural symbolic order, by taking it up and elevating it to possibilities that surpass it. We witness here an opposite movement; and this first 'return' is, on the level of realization, at the foundation of all the others.

Thus it is for the relations of Christ and the Church. 'The Eucharist,' writes Chauvet, 'is precisely the great sacramental figure of that symbolic interweaving of Christ and the Church' (p. 11). The function of the symbol, then, is to realize that 'interweaving of the two rigorously differentiated terms (Christ and Church)' (p. 14). Unfortunately, the following shows that this differentiation is far from being as rigorous as the author says. It ends up even becoming quite problematic by the fact of the reduction of the sacramental instrumentality to a simple symbolic function. Thus, when one reads, regarding Christ, that 'His sacramental presence in the bread and wine is ... to be understood as the crystallization of His presence in the congregation' (p. 20), what one understands is, above all, that Christ is present primarily in the congregation, whose primacy is reaffirmed, and that this presence 'is crystallized' later in the bread and wine. The sacrament is therefore the 'crystallization' of the congregation, where Christ is already present, in the signs of the bread and wine. Its function is to allow that congregation to become conscious of this presence of Christ in it and even, by widening its perspective, in the entire universe: 'the Eucharistic presence is to be thought of as the crystallization of Christ's presence through the Spirit in humanity and the universe' (p. 20 ff; the italics are in the text). In these propositions the negation of the Christian sacraments is obvious; however, the question that they pose on the identity of Christ is no less grave.

If at the end of the first part or the first theme of the reflection, dedicated to the congregation, one believes to be able to define the thought of the author by saying, '*In principio erat Ecclesia, id est congregatio,*'[44] then after having read these pages of the second theme,

---

[44] 'In the beginning was the Church, that is, the congregation.'

dedicated to the presence of Christ, one sees that it is necessary to go even further and say, '*In principio erat humanitas, erat mundus* ...'[45] The fourth part confirms this interpretation. Titled, 'The Sacrifice of Christ and the Church,' it is completed by referring the 'Christian' back to the construction of the world. Anti-cultic, anti-sacrificial, it is said explicitly that the Eucharist is but a gathering where, by a purely symbolic action, the congregation sees itself entrusted with the essentially immanent task of taking charge of history, with all the 'socio-political implications' that this includes. It is in this direction that the third part already turns, dedicated as it is to the 'memorial' (cf. p. 39). This latter, it says, ought not plunge us 'into the lethargy of a faded dream.' It is a 'project of liberation,' rooted in a tradition (p. 29). To which one can respond: And who says that this project, this 'memory of the future' (p. 33), is not plunged into the utopia of a future dream?

However, the most interesting thing about this third theme of reflection is the handing over to us of another key to the dense thought of L. M. Chauvet, that of becoming. It is here, in fact—at the same time as the reduction of the sacramental to the symbolic—that he comes to realize that identification of Christ with the congregation, first and finally with humanity and the world. The name of Teilhard de Chardin was not mentioned, but this is definitely his world here. Fr Chauvet pretends to reject metaphysics, but this is only in order to reject the dogma of transubstantiation, and with it that of the real and substantial presence of Christ (p. 24). For, what he rejects is solely the metaphysics of being, the philosophical basis of that dogma; and he does this for the sake of adopting a metaphysic of becoming, the foundation of his entire system; so true is it that there is no theology without philosophy. 'Humanity,' he writes, 'and in solidarity with it, the universe, have their identity in their future. This future is also that of Christ Himself' (p. 36). This is, as can be seen, the refusal of being; and it is the adherence to a philosophy of becoming. For, if it is true

---

[45] 'In the beginning was humanity, it was the world ... '

that an action is defined by its end, a being is defined by its nature, despite the words and categories used to express this. And a being inserted in an historical action continues to be defined by its nature insofar as it is a being; while its free and historical action receives its meaning from its end. This latter, for the whole of humanity, is unknown to natural reason; this is why a philosophy of history, parallel to the philosophy of being, is always impossible. All the attempts made in this sense have never been but crypto-theologies. Thus, to define Christ by His future is to reduce Him to the world, itself thought of exclusively in terms of becoming. This is the very negation of Christianity. Christ is the Word Incarnate. And from the point of view of history, henceforth he does not have a future (insofar as He never had one): He is the future of the world, or rather, its 'eschaton.' He accomplished His work, 'perfected' His Mystery, which is 'completed' now in His Body, which is the Church, and through it, in the world. With these reflections on eschatology one sees the universal impact of the 'reversals' that are asked of us here with regards to the Eucharist. The world is an evolving process where humanity, and in it 'the Christ,' 'becomes' the Church is the primordial sacrament of this humanity in becoming, and of its 'encounter with the Christ.' And it is in the Eucharist first of all, thanks to the symbolism of its rites, that this becoming is manifested before being realized in its 'socio-political' engagements (p. 48; 54). But who then is that 'Christ' who has stability only in this completely intra-mundane becoming? One will end up posing this question, and posing it with an increasing restlessness.

In limiting ourselves to what concerns us here, we shall conclude this all too brief analysis with some reflections that seem to us to be of the greatest importance. First of all, regarding the work itself. Let us say it again: it represents a very wide trend, and it belongs to a major author of the subject. We mentioned the passages where he openly manifests his thought and shows the principles that allow one to unveil it where it is not expressed as clearly. Most of the time, in fact, his thought is presented as being concerned with adhering to Tradition, even with routing error. This, moreover, is why one can find there more than one very accurate reflection. But it is in this precisely that the author appears as a master: in that consummate skill that he has of using the traditional data, seemingly in order to follow it, but in reality only to 'reverse' it. It is there, at the same time, that he is so dangerous.[46] Regarding his theses, without returning to what was already said, we simply note the two following points: first, the reappearance, in spite of everything, of the memorial's decisive role; and second, the importance of taking the idea of the congregation as the Eucharist's fundamental principle.

The decisive role, in spite of everything, of the memorial: for, it is the proper act in which the congregation is realized; at such a point one could be tempted to present this thesis as that of the memorial as much as that of the congregation. Given the purely subjective and symbolic manner in which the memorial is conceived, one thus returns to Protestantism. But while this pattern departs from individual liberty in order to make a memory of Christ's redemptive act located in the past, it is a question here of a memorial of the future, which is the work of a collective humanity (p. 35). This position represents no less authentically the outcome of Protestantism, such as it has evolved through its Hegelian transformation. At the begin-

---

[46] In the hope of making ourselves understood, we voluntarily maintained the neutral tone of an objective analysis required by the theologian. But before the clear negation of the faith, the theologian would fail in his duty if he did not point out the offense made to God and the scandal given to the Church. For, theology remains first of all an activity of faith. It has always been the case that the truth is not loved; it brings fear (Jn 3:20). But the violence is not on the side of him who recalls it; it is the work of those who falsify it and who deprive the people of God of it, priests and faithful together. And this is the worst of all evils, under its seemingly painless forms; for it is something done to minds and souls. Let this much at least be said here, in order to prevent the danger of indifference or acclimatization, to which one will inevitably be exposed when staying perpetually on the level of analysis alone and in the deceitful climate of academic or 'scientific' serenity, which is obligatory here.

ning and the end—subject to later developments—what one finds, therefore, is the congregation, which celebrates itself by symbolically celebrating its life and its becoming.

One sees at the same time the impossibility of taking this reality of the congregation as a first principle of Eucharistic theology. For, to do so, one turns on their head, right from the beginning, the relations of the different elements that are present there face to face—and first and foremost that of Christ and the Church, but also that of the priest and the congregation (p. 9, where the author seems to defend the dogma; p. 10 and 45, where he destroys it by wishing to retain only Christ's priesthood), that of the Church and the world, etc. It is not surprising then to find at the end, with all their subversive implications, the consequences of this initial 'reversal,' which consists in beginning with the congregation and not with Christ.

Brief and elementary as they might be, these observations ought to make one ask oneself whether the author is aware of the two following facts. The first, is that the tendency analyzed here (making the congregation the whole of the Eucharist) is without a doubt very widespread in the Church today, albeit to different degrees. The second is that repetition, in its initial version, of the 1969 Article 7. This choice, in 1981, on the occasion of the International Eucharistic Congress in Lourdes, could not have been due to chance. In the defiance that it represents it manifests a certain continuity.

Most recently, on the eve of the International Eucharistic Congress in Lourdes, J. M. Chauvet returned to the presentation of his theses.[47]

---

[47] Agapé, *L'Eucharistie de Jésus aux chrétiens d'aujourd'hui*, Paris, Droguet et Ardant, 1981. Preface by J. F. Motte, Auxiliary Bishop of Cambrai. This important volume (548 pp.) is practically contemporary with the CEI. It manifests a very clear desire to pursue beyond that Congress the effort undertaken on the occasion of its preparation in view of imposing what Msgr Motte calls 'the new vision of the Eucharist as it has emanated from the Second Vatican Council' (p. 6). What we saw in Chauvet, whose contribution is the key to this collaborative work, suffices to show how that 'vision' is opposed to both Vatican II and Catholic dogma; but it is the vision of the collegial bodies

The interest for us in this new presentation comes from the fact that it brings to light the link that unites the reduction of the Eucharist to the meal, the sacrifice to the memorial, itself reduced to a pure 'confession of faith' (pp. 177–87), and the absorption of the ministerial priesthood into the community, whose action is presented as being immediately Christ's (pp. 288–301). It is not the faithful who are linked to Christ and made into the Church through the mediation of the ministerial priesthood, but rather the priest who sees himself connected to Christ through the mediation of the community. This latter is immediately, this is to say without mediation, the 'Body of Christ,' and the priest is but 'the sacramental figure of the congregation—it is the Church of Christ—and of that which it makes—it acts as a body ('priestly' we shall say later) of Christ by the Spirit' (p. 293). The thought is shifty, inevitably; but the orientations are clear, as well as certain negations, like that of the ministerial priesthood (pp. 297; 300; etc.).

We find again the three themes that we just examined: meal, 'blessing' (which is at the same time a 'confession of faith') and congregation. And we see at the same time that which unites them (in themselves and in the present liturgical movement), and at what point they are destructive of the Eucharistic mystery as soon as they are no longer attached to the central reality of the sacrifice.

II. The Holy Sacrifice of the Mass

The first principle that allows one to understand the structure of the Mass is the sacrifice. It may also be said that it is the Eucharist; but that only postpones the question, for the Mass is in itself the celebration of the Eucharist. The two words signify then a reality fundamentally identical, which we must define. To do this, that is, to enter into the knowledge of His mystery, it is necessary to begin not with a common notion of sacrifice, but with the unique reality of the one

in charge in France of the Pastorale liturgique. 'Agapé' is the name that was given to the group of the five authors who contributed to this volume. Cf. see above, note 691.

redemptive sacrifice of Christ.[48] This assertion is imposed first of all for reasons of the Biblical, traditional and dogmatic order, which we recalled in our preceding studies. But it is imposed no less in for strictly liturgical reasons, insofar as one can still distinguish those different domains. On the level of these last questions, in fact, the borderlines fade away, the liturgy being the realization of the Mystery, and therefore of the incarnation of dogma. However, in trying to hold to that level of the study of the rites and their history, we shall try to mention the reasons that support our assertion.

The first, negatively, is the incapacity of the different theories examined earlier for synthesizing the elements that compose the 'divine liturgy,' but also for showing the continuity throughout history. The first places at the center that which was but the initial historical framework and what remains a final rite: the meal. The second ends up favouring the prayer, and with it, the word, to the detriment of the central and essential action, which that prayer is supposed to accompany and not replace. By showing the subordination of the 'blessing' to the 'memorial,' this theory, however, begins to recognize the central place of the sacrifice. It does not arrive there because it fails to bring out the true nature of that 'memorial' of the Christian Eucharist. It does not take into account, at least not enough, the sacramental nature, which makes it the mysterious act by which the one redemptive sacrifice is actualized in, with and for the Church. The third trend examined obscures even more this sacramental nature of the memorial, and ends up making the congregation, and it alone, not only the end, but also the beginning, subject and object, in short the substance and all of the Eucharist. This distorts them all at the same time.

---

[48]   This is what Cardinal Ratzinger finally does (Art. cit., in *PNMR*, p. 51). In the same volume, and in the same sense, see the article, which we already cited, from G. Colombo (especially pp. 92–7) and no less remarkably in these key pages of A. Chapelle (pp. 143–52).

Positively, our principal argument is that everything in the liturgy begins with the sacrifice, preparing for it or flowing from it. The examined theories themselves say whether they have been developed. A meal? But what meal? That of the sacrifice of communion. A *Berakah*? But in honor of what 'wonderful' intervention of God? The redemptive sacrifice, which the 'memorial' instituted by Christ actualizes in the sacrament. A congregation that establishes itself? But how? And what congregation? That which forms the ecclesial body of Christ and which gathers together, builds up and unites in the praise of God the Spirit Whom Christ, through His Paschal sacrifice, merited to send with the Father—and Whom He sends effectively through the sacramental sacrifice of the Eucharist. The reality of the sacrifice, one can see, integrates all that the preceding theses contain of the truth. It is the sacrifice, and the sacrifice alone, that allows one to make a synthesis. This will be seen more by analyzing the different parts of the Mass.

1. It will not be useless to begin by showing how the sacrifice is also that which allows one to understand *the history of the liturgy,* especially in its origins, and to know its continuity since the Last Supper. It is also the sacrifice which, at the same time, allows one to resolve the crucial problem in question here, as Cardinal Ratzinger showed, namely that of the passing from Israel, and more immediately from post-exilic Judaism, to the Church. Like Fr Ligier, in his article on this passing, *De la Cène de Jésus à l'anaphore de l'Eglise,*[49] the Archbishop of Munich (i.e. Ratzinger) begins with the works of the exegete Heinz Schürmann on the question;[50] however, he brings out the consequences better, while separating them on certain points.[51] In the

---

[49] Cf. see above, notes 671; 675; 678. Ligier begins the article of Schürmann mentioned in note 654 above.

[50] *PNMR,* p. 5, where the author returns to a more recent work of H. Schürmann: 'Die Gestalt der urchristlichen Eucharistiefeier', in *Ursprung und Gestalt, Erörterungen und Besinnungen zum Neuen Testament,* Düsseldorf, 1970, pp. 77–99. But it seems that this contribution only uses the theses which, for the most part, were already found in the 1955 work.

[51] Cf. *PNMR,* pp. 44 ff.

evolution that goes from the Last Supper to the liturgy of the Church, Schürmann distinguishes three phases:

1) the Eucharist at the Last Supper ('Abend*mahl*': the evening *meal*) in the act of the institution by Christ;

2) the Eucharist linked to the communitarian meals during the apostolic period;

3) the Eucharist separated from the meal after the apostolic period, or perhaps, from the apostolic period itself.[52]

The important point for us in this demonstration, completely convincing for the most part, is the following: although during the Last Supper it was celebrated within the context of a meal, the Eucharist in the strict sense had, vis-à-vis the meal, 'a relative independence and its own significance.'[53] How could it have been otherwise? The novelty is found here at the heart of the former; but it was not yet brought out: 'The Christian fact did not yet exist as an independent reality,' observes Ratzinger. And he poses this 'fundamental thesis': 'The Last Supper of Jesus is indeed the foundation of the entire Christian liturgy, but it is not yet [at that moment] a Christian liturgy.'[54] This is to be understood, as the next passage proves, insofar as the structure of the ritual goes: 'The fundamental act of Christianity is accomplished within Judaism, but it had not yet found its own proper structure of the Christian liturgy.' It would find it only when, because of the fact of the Crucifixion and what followed it, Christianity would be obliged to leave Judaism in order to assert itself. It would leave, then, in both senses of the word: it would go forth from it; but also, it would detach itself from it.

One can see here the beginnings of the historical error committed by all those who, from Renan to Hans Küng,[55] accuse the Church of

---

[52] See again, in the same vein, H. Chirat, who locates this separation 'during the years 60–80' (Art. cit., p. 59).

[53] H. Schürmann, op. cit. (1970), p. 193; and in his 1955 article, pp. 113–15.

[54] J. Ratzinger, Art. cit., p. 42.

[55] Küng was explicitly cited by Ratzinger, p. 42, note 11.

having been unfaithful to Jesus, of having created an abyss between Him and herself, because, they say, she did not reproduce all the actions down to the smallest details dictated by the Jewish context. On the other hand, the facts of history, and most precisely those that establish the necessity according to which the Church is found separating herself from an Israel that refused its Christ, that is, its Messiah—these facts of history 'show that there *could not have been* direct formal continuity between Jesus and the Church. One must search for the unity with Jesus, then, in a necessary discontinuity of form.'[56] This continuity in discontinuity appears in a very particular way in the preaching of 'the good news of salvation': this is the passing from the proclamation of the 'Kingdom of God' made by Jesus to the Jews, to the proclamation of Christ Himself made by His Apostles to the pagans, to whom the notion of 'Kingdom' did not speak as to the Jews. With regards to the Eucharist, there would be the passing from the Last Supper, that is to say, from the meal of the last Passover to the Eucharist, which Christ had instituted for His Church. This is what takes place in the next two passages. 'The communitarian meal of the early Christians,' continues Schürmann, 'was not the repetition of Jesus' Last Supper (which Jesus did not command to be repeated), but the continuation of the community of the daily table of Jesus with His disciples.'[57] The supper at Emmaus, after the Resurrection, is a typical example of this continuity; and one commits a fatal error in seeing it as a celebration of the Eucharist. After that meal, 'the Eucharistic gestures, henceforth united to each other, follow as an autonomous action, the prayer of thanksgiving—the *eucharistia*—situated in a separate and more elevated place. *I Corinthians* 11:17–34 shows clearly that this is how it took place.'[58] Such then is the first phase of the establishment of the Christian liturgy of the Eucharist. It is entirely founded on the actions and words of Christ: 'Do this in

---

[56]   *Ibid.*, p. 43.

[57]   H. Schürmann, op. cit. (1970), p. 85; *cit. ibid.* p. 44. In the 1955 article, p. 116.

[58]   Ratzinger, Art. cit., p. 44. cf. *see above*, note 52.

memory of Me.' But the liturgy is thus established, that is to say as a ritual structure, by using the framework in which Jesus still needed to act, namely the ritual of the Jewish Paschal meal. Led by the Holy Spirit, the early Church retained the essence of that which Jesus did and ordered to be done after Him, '*touto poiete,*' namely the double consecration of bread and wine. It is 'this' which constitutes the Eucharistic memorial. We shall see later how the Church adapted accordingly the prayers that accompany this central action.

The third phase, which is the second of the Christian liturgy's process of elaboration, would achieve the evolution that we observe in completely separating the Eucharist from the meal. Schürmann himself sees the proclamation of this in the words of St Paul: 'Do you not have homes in which to eat and drink?'[59] This separation is both a result and a point of departure. It is by beginning with that, in fact, from the point of view of the form or ritual structure that the liturgy will take on a body and develop in the Church. And always, within all these developments, what will be rediscovered and what will assure continuity, will be the reproduction of the central actions accomplished by Christ within the Last Supper; and this will give order to the redoing 'in memory' of Him that which, since apostolic times, is used in order so that 'the memorial of the Lord' might appear as belonging to it alone: namely the double consecration of bread and wine.

Yet this act is a sacrifice; more precisely, it is, by virtue of the sacrament, the very sacrifice of redemption. 'This is My Blood of the covenant' (Mk 14:25; Matt 26:28); 'This cup is the new covenant in My Blood' (1 Cor 11:25; Lk 22:20): these words alone, placed in their immediate and general context, suffice for proof. The immediate context is that of the Passion. These words announce it, accomplishing it in advance in a prophetic and sacramental action. In return, it is from the Passion, afterwards, that they will take all their meaning in the minds of the disciples. The general context is the economy of

---

[59] H. Schürmann, op. cit. (1970), p. 92; *cit. ibid.,* p. 47. 1955 article, p. 123, note 77. cf. 1 Cor 11:22.

redemption, this latter being accomplished completely by the sacrifice (Heb 9:15–28; cf. v. 22). In speaking of the 'blood of the covenant,' Christ Himself refers back to the sacrifice by which Moses had sealed the first covenant between God and His people (Heb 9:20; cf. Ex 24:8). In saying, 'the new covenant,' he referred to the exilic and post-exilic proclamation of the substitution of that first covenant—founded on the law and broken by Israel's infidelity—by a new covenant, founded on the gratuitous gift of the Spirit (Heb 8:8–13; cf. Jer 31:31–33; Ex 36:25–28).

The recalling of these texts allows us to understand and assert two things. The first is that the Christian Eucharist is essentially not simply *one* sacrifice among many, but *the* sacrifice of the new and eternal Covenant. The second is that this central reality of the sacrifice is what allows one to know, in the dialectic of its economy, the profound continuity of the economy of salvation and, in it, that of the history of the sacrifice.

2. Schürmann's analysis, taken up by Fr Ligier and by Cardinal Ratzinger, bears directly on the historical process, which allowed the Eucharist to make use of the framework of the meal in which it had been born, in order to establish it as the Christian liturgy. It did not lose its character of a meal. On the contrary, it discovered it in that which it has of its own, that is, in its subordination to the central act of the sacrifice. We ought to note here that Schürmann's work bears on the gestures, on the acts, whereby it is different from the majority of contemporary studies on the Eucharist. Today the Eucharist is studied principally, and often even exclusively, only insofar as it is a prayer. Typically representative of this mode are the works of Ligier, Audet, Bouyer, Chauvet, Giraudo, which we used or mentioned above. Their way is, in itself, excellent; but the complaint that we can make about these authors is that they cling to their way practically as if it were sufficient. Not seeing in the Eucharist any more than a prayer of 'blessing,' of praise, of 'confession' or something else, they fail to

see what is central and most important in it: the action which is its heart, the sacrifice.

H. Cazelles was able to avoid this danger. In a very dense and suggestive work on '*L'anaphore et l'Ancien Testament,*'[60] he recalls that, in the beginning 'one finds essentially some prayers of thanksgiving, of intercession and the epiclesis,' even if 'the place of these can vary, before or after the institution narrative.' And he adds, 'We are therefore at the heart of the sacrificial action' (p. 11). Right away, therefore, he distinguishes prayer, made of words, and sacrifice, which is an action; and he subordinates the former to the latter. While admitting that the prayers have their origin in the Jewish ritual (which henceforth is indisputable), he observes that this ritual, in its synogogal form, 'cannot have the anaphora, for the anaphora is linked to the consecration and immolation of the victim'—rites which disappeared with the Temple (*ibid*). If then, in its literary form and even for a large part of its theological sources, the anaphora or Eucharistic prayer is inspired by the Jewish prayer, that which makes it distinct, the central act of consecration, has another origin. It is by the analysis of the word *Eucharist* that Cazelles researches it, and finds it, in addition to the four narrative of institution, in the sacrifices, and more precisely in a well determined sacrifice of the Old Testament, the *zebah tôdah.*

While in Luke (22:17) and St Paul (1 Cor 11:24) it is a question only of the Eucharist: *eucharistein eipèn* (*gratias agens dixit*), Matthew (26:26) and Mark (14:22) speak of the Eucharist for the wine and the eulogy for the bread: *eulogésas églasen kai ... eipèn* (*benedicens fregit et ... dixit*). For which reason the question arises: 'Is it necessary to assimilate the eulogy and the Eucharist?' (p. 12). With regards to the first word, one responds that it is frequent in the Septuagint, where it is practically equivalent with *brk*, the Hebrew and Jewish blessing (Old Testament). Yet what about the second word, the Eucharist?

---

[60] H. Cazelles, *L'anaphore et l'Ancien Testament*, in the collaborative work, *Eucharisties d'Orient et d'Occident* (Coll. 'Lex orandi'—46–47), Paris, Cerf, 1970, I, pp. 11–21.

While it is rare in the Septuagint, this vocabulary is frequent in Hellenistic Judaism (p. 13). The analysis of a certain number of texts from this period as well as from others, as those of Qumran or the 'Document of Damas,' cause the exegete to recognize first, that *eucharistein* signifies 'singing hymns in honor of God' (p. 15); second, it signifies that the songs are presented as a celebration and a 'confession' (hitpahel from the word *ydh*) of the Lord's lofty deeds, that is to say, as a *hôdah*: 'We are thus,' he concludes, 'directed no longer towards *brk* but towards *ydh*' (p. 16); third, that 'this terminology is precisely that of the Old Testament. However, from the part of these words, we have a very interesting sacrifice: the sacrifice *tôdah*, not mentioned by Qumran, it seems to me' (*ibid.*). To this is added the fact that Aquila, translating the Bible from Hebrew into Greek in the second century, always renders *tôdah* by *eucharistia*.

These observations legitimately lead the author to rediscover the study of the sacrifices of the Old Testament, which he does by beginning with the priestly code of Leviticus (Lev 6–7). He reveals there, among the principal forms, the *holocaust,* where the victim is entirely burned up for God; and the *shelâmîm,* or the sacrifice of communion, of which the *zebah tôdah* (Lev 7:12–15) is but a particular form (p. 17). One part of the victim was burned on the altar, being thus offered to God, while the other was restored to him who offered it, in order for him to eat it and thus enter into communion with his God. Yet why the term *tôdah* for a certain type of these sacrifices of communion? Because they 'included a hymn, a confession of the grandeur of the God of Israel, it is the *tôdah*' (p. 18). After having proven the antiquity of this type of sacrifice (especially beginning with Amos 4–5), Cazelles shows that, beginning with Jeremiah (17, 26; etc.), it appears as 'characteristic of the return and the restoration.' 'In fact, it is since the return from exile and the rebuilding of the Temple that the *tôdah* blossomed in Israel' (p. 19). 'It is the sacrifice of the return and of the redemption' (p. 20).

Nevertheless (but upon reflection the fact is not surprising) Pharisaism would give it a restricted part—Esseneism as well—while it would multiply the sacrifices of expiation (just as the other work of the same author shows, which we used above). If the *tôdah* tends to disappear in later Judaism, 'on the other hand, it had its place in the Christian community for whom the Temple was the Body of Christ' (p. 20 ff), and for whom, above all, the true sacrifice of redemption had been accomplished.

Such then is, according to this analysis, the origin of the word *Eucharist*; and such is the reason for which it prevailed over other terms, not allowing itself to be identified with any of them. Its connection with the different terms that surround it, 'to celebrate,' 'to praise,' 'to bless,' etc., is obvious, and the 'thanksgiving' ('Eucharist'), in a sense, includes them all. But the reality that this word immediately signifies is different; it is the sacrifice accompanied by that 'thanksgiving,' in the widest sense of the word. The Eucharist, therefore, is a sacrificial reality first of all; but it is also and inseparably an act of thanksgiving, of blessing, of praise, of confession, of intercession or supplication, and of communion. In other words, the term *Eucharist* signifies the very act of Christ, that of the Last Supper 'accomplished' at Calvary, that is to say, the sacrifice of redemption—that which seals in the blood of the Word Incarnate, the new and eternal Covenant of God with men. This is why the central reality that constitutes it is the consecration; but it is surrounded by prayers, praises, etc., and it is completed by communion.

Brief as it is, this work of Cazelles is, we believe, extremely suggestive. Moreover, it is convincing for the orientation that it indicates and with respect to the substance of its conclusions: the Eucharist is not simply prayer, but prayer accompanied by a sacrifice; or better, it is a sacrifice accompanied by prayer. This explanation also seems admissible when it indicates in the Old Testament *tôdah* the origin of the word *eucharistia* to signify the action of the Church taking up that of Christ at the Last Supper, and to signify it primarily as a sacrifice. One arrives at this same conclusion, despite the intentions of the author, when one reads the thesis of C. Giraudo, whom we mentioned above. This very thorough research has for its end the rediscovering of the origin of the Eucharistic anaphora, by keeping itself on the strictly literary plain. For this the author researches, and in fact establishes, the existence of a form, or more exactly a 'literary structure,'[61] which is found again, beginning with the Eucharistic prayer, in those of Judaism and, in addition, those of the Old Testament. With regards to Judaism, he finds it sufficient to borrow the results already acquired when analyzing the different forms of the *berakôth*—both those from the family and those from the synagogue—that are found there. But he does this in a new and threefold manner: first, by the very exhaustive analysis; then, by bringing to light that constant 'literary structure,' and not simply of a certain number of common themes and terms; finally and most importantly, by the illumination that those *berakôth* themselves receive from the prayers of the Old Testament, which preceded them and from which they came.

The great merit of this thesis is the fact that it goes back, beyond Judaism, to the prayers of the Old Testament, that is, to the forms of prayers which, despite the date of their composition, have been formed from the first reality of Israel's history, the Mosaic Covenant. Here are some of these Old Testament prayers; the author distinguishes five types, the analysis of which are the object of his first part: those that accompany the injunction of the Covenant (Jos 24:2–15); and those of the adherence to the Covenant (Jos 24:17–18); those[62] of the sovereign's complaint against his people (Deut 32:4025), and the complaint of the people against their sovereign (Ps 44); and finally, the *tôdah* (Nem 9:6–37), in which the people 'confess'[63] their sin before

---

61 Op. cit., pp. 8, 176, 225, etc. This research had been inspired, with respect to its immediate object, by a work of Fr Beauchamp, *Propositions sur l'alliance de l'Ancien Testament comme structure centrale*, in Rech. Sc. Rel., 58, 1970, pp. 161–93 (cit. pp. 14, 19, etc.), and, through this latter work, by structuralism.

62 But it is the literary form, more than the prayer itself that is analyzed here.

63 This is the sense of the word *ydh*, whence comes the substantive *tôdah*.

God, having recourse to His fidelity, His promise, His mercy; whereby the people 'confess' also His greatness in these attributes. The aim of the *tôdah* is obviously the renewal of the Covenant, the people's recovery of their relations with their God in order to receive His protection and blessing. A look at a certain number of *tôdôth* follows; the word is taken here insofar as it signifies uniquely that type of prayer and 'confession,' in both senses of the word.

The number of texts studied and the detail of the analysis imposes in an indisputable manner the conclusions of this first part (pp. 160–77): there exists a literary structure common to all these prayers; a very ancient structure, since its point of departure is in the pact of the Covenant; a fundamental structure, since it will reach its summit in the renew of that Covenant, after the Exile, thanks to the 'confession' by Israel of its sin. This is the *tôdah* of Nehemia. This is the reason why the author retains this word in order to signify the collection of these texts, which, with Beauchamp, one could perhaps more correctly call the 'prayers according to the covenant' (pp. 164, 177). Giraudo himself contantly brings out the fact that they are not understood, and even their structure is not explained, except by the relation that they have with that founding event of Israel's history. The sole reality involved is always the relation of God with His people and the chosen people with their God.

It is this relation that the *tôdah,* as a form type of the 'prayer according to the Covenant' on the part of a guilty Israel, seeks to renew. From this it has its twofold structure, taken from the forms of prayer found before and afterwards in the *berakah* and in the *anaphora* (p. 173). The first part is 'anamnetic': it 'recalls' and 'confesses' at the same time the fidelity of God and the infidelity of Israel. The second is 'epicletic': basing itself on the fidelity of God, it 'appeals' for His mercy upon Israel. The first part will present therefore an historical character, and it will be developed in 'confession,' in praise and in 'blessing.' Thus it is that, with this last element coming to dominate, Judaism will pass from the *tôdah* to the *berakah,* from the confession—with all that this word contains here—to the blessing. The second part will be the place of the prayer of request or intercession; but oftentimes the motive of this request comes to be inserted, and ends up by terminating, in a return to the praise of the initial confession: this will be the final doxology.

The motive upon which the prayer of request is based is taken up from the historico-anamnetic part; for, it cannot be found except in the fidelity and mercy of God recalled by that first part. It thus constitutes an 'embolism' (a parenthesis), being inserted as it is in the second part, which of itself is epicletic. But this embolism, by reason of its crucial importance, will end up becoming the anamnesis par excellence: it will be the 'memorial,' the *zikkarôn* (*zkr* means 'to recall,' 'to remember' or 'to remind one'), that is, the recalling or the remembering of the supreme act (or particular event) in which God showed His fidelity and mercy, and on which the person praying bases himself in order to address God. It is thus that, from the simple 'parenthesis' that it was in the beginning, this 'memorial' will constitute the summit not only of the epicletic section, but of the entire prayer. In the Eucharistic anaphora the memorial will be the narrative of the institution.

While we are now going back in time, it seems necessary to go beyond Chapter 24 of the Book of Joshua, all the way back to the deuteronmic narrative of the pact of the Covenant by Moses on Mount Sinai. It is from this first historical (if not redactional) period that one rediscovers the bipartite structure of the prayer or discourse, which accompanies the fundamental act establishing the relations between the Lord and His people (Ex 19:3–6). In the first part, God 'recalls' for His people what He did for them: He delivered them through their exile from Egypt—this is the historico-anamnetic section (v. 4); in the second part, He offers to His people His Covenant, showing them His demands and promising them His protection—this is the part which is not epicletic, since it is God Who addresses Himself to His creature, but an injunction of the Covenant

(vv. 5–6). It is this second part that will return and be transformed into an 'epiclesis,' that is to say an invocation and a request, when the people will turn towards their God and renew the Covenant with Him. We have the very first and fundamental model of such a bipartite structure, the Covenant itself, which will continue to return later. The author makes an allusion to it (pp. 17–21, especially in footnotes 5 and 7), but without developing that point insofar as it merits it according to his own declaration: 'It is only in considering the Covenant as a fundamental structure around which the different forms (of discourse and prayer) crystallize,' that one can become aware of both their variety and the permanence in them of one and the same structure (p. 38; cf. pp. 47, 106, 173, etc.). For indeed, this structure is always radically that of the Covenant, with its bipartite economy: that which the Lord did for Israel; that which Israel must do for the Lord. As a result of Israel's sin, but also as a result of its trust in the Lord's fidelity to His Covenant and His promises, this initial structure would develop according to the following schema-type: that which the Lord did *for* Israel, *and* that which Israel did *against* the Lord; that which Israel asks the Lord to do again *for* it, *and* that which it undertakes to do in the future *for* the Lord. The one goal pursued in both is the assurance of the relationship between God and His people. In the end only praise remains—adoration, thanksgiving, blessing, glorifying—as the supreme form of service to God (*'abodah*).

The numerous texts analyzed effectively show the existence and permanence of that fundamental structure under a great variety of particular forms, and especially through the different periods of Israel's history: before the exile, that is, at the moment of the return and restoration, where the *tôdah* dominates, typically represented by Nehemiah (this prayer will be the archetype of the synogogal prayer); in later and Talmudic Judaism, where the *berakah* becomes the form par excellence of prayer; and finally, after the accomplishment-sur-passing of the promises through Christ, in the *anaphora* of the Christian Eucharist.

Having thus retraced the outline of this thesis, whose multiple observations offer an extremely rich source of reflection, we must mention its limitations, but also its consequences, or even the rectifications that it calls for. We shall do this by limiting ourselves to the point of view at hand, that of the sacrifice—a point of view that is equally essential to the subject if not to the author's preoccupations. His declared intent is to rediscover in Judaism and in the Old Testament the origin of the Eucharistic prayer. He does this by limiting himself to a strict point of view on the literary structure. It is his right, and it is a good method. Nevertheless the fact remains that, inevitably, and even explicitly in his conclusions, he often goes beyond that point of view in order to mention both thematic aspects as well as theological problems. With regards to the literary research, we already spoke of the interest he had in bringing out the discourse of the Mosaic pact of the Covenant, since it is in this that one finds in its primary place the fundamental structure that would later be developed. What he ought to have done then, was to show that, in that pact, the *discourse* accompanies the *act* of sacrifice, in which alone the Covenant was sealed, and that consequently, the presence or absence of the sacrifice influenced in a decisive manner the prayer of Israel—if not its structure, at least in its content and orientation, aspects mentioned frequently by the author.

Finally, the author needed to show, or at least mention, the transformation undergone by the *zikkarôn* ('memorial') into the Christian anaphora. In fact, through the mystery of the sacrament instituted by the Word Incarnate, the supreme act of fidelity and divine mercy, the sacrifice of redemption and of the new and eternal Covenant, would be not only 'recalled,' 'confessed' and 'proclaimed,' but it would be 're-acted.' This the author does not say—which can be justified all the less, seeing that in some openings that he gives by way of conclusion, he mentions some theological perspectives to which his research could lead. This research should have been mentioned in the first place, especially where he rebukes scholastic theology and those inspired by it for having unjustifiably increased the importance of the consecration, and therefore the 'memorial,' detaching it from the rest of the Eucharistic prayer (p. 363). One must recognize and deplore the fact that this last critique is not without foundation. But with regards to the importance of the consecration, one could say to the author, that it is the entire history of the structure retraced by his analyses that leads one to show the importance of that moment of the 'memorial' in that literary structure, that is, in the prayer of the people of God, whether it be the *tôdah,* or the *berakah,* or the *anaphora* (cf. p. 176 and *passim*). Furthermore, his analysis of the classical formulas of sacramental theology, '*in persona Christi,*' '*in persona Ecclesiae,*' reveal a conception of the sacramental ministry clearly deficient, and it leads to assertions that are hard to accept (pp. 363–5). The priest of the New Testament, in his double relation to Christ and the Church, no longer clearly appears in his specificity and with his proper and exclusive power. This vagueness, it must be noted, goes hand in hand with that of the sacrifice, which we noted. In fact, although mentioned several times, this essential aspect finds no place in this study on the Eucharist (which is ultimately the object of the study). However, there is here an evil into which one almost inevitably falls whenever one reflects on the Eucharist by considering it exclusively as a prayer.

Therefore we can say that—despite the intentions of the author—this thesis, if one grants it the supplements that it calls for, establishes that the Mass, the celebration of the Eucharist, is before all else a sacrifice. These supplements are two in number, and they bear on the two points that perhaps C. Giraudo brought out better. We return to them by way of conclusion: 1) the author shows admirably that the literary structure of the prayer, whose existence and permanence he establishes, has for its foundation the fundamental, and even founding, fact of the Covenant: the supplement called for by this fact is that that Covenant was not sealed except in a sacrifice; 2) he shows with no less force that the summit of this prayer, in both the request and in the praise that it addresses to God, is the 'memorial,' that is, the recall of the 'lofty divine deed' on which the sinner bases his request for mercy: the supplement needed here, with regards to the Eucharistic anaphora, is that, by the power of the sacrament instituted by God Himself, this 'memorial'—the narrative of the institution—is henceforth an action and not simply an evocation; it is the re-actuation of the sacrifice of redemption, the sacrifice of the new and eternal Covenant accomplished by Christ in the reality of the sacramental sign at the Last Supper, and in the reality of the history of salvation on the Cross.

We now catch up with H. Cazelle's work, where the word *tôdah* is taken for *zebah tôdah* and signifies the sacrifice of communion accompanied by a prayer to the glory of God. It is true that Christ's sacrifice is not simply the taking up of this particular type of sacrifice; for, His sacrifice accomplishes them by surpassing all sacrifices of the Old Covenant. Likewise, the prayer that accompanies it is not simply one of praise, but also of supplication and intercession. However, it suffices for our subject that the word *tôdah* signifies a sacrifice, and that it is that which caused the adoption of the Greek word *eucharist* in order to signify it with all that it includes.

These conclusions confirm what we were able to deduce from the fundamental work of Schürmann, taken up by Ratzinger. Starting with its origins, we established that the Mass is essentially a sacrifice, and even how it is one. Given that, it is now possible for us to enter into a more in-depth knowledge of the mystery of its liturgy. This will be the object of our next chapter.

III. The Theology of the Sacrifice and the Eucharist

Before coming to the subject of this section it would be useful, especially in view of the theology of the sacrifice of the Mass, to show again how Christ's sacrifice, with its sacramental sign instituted at the Last Supper and renewed at each Mass—how it is not only the central act from which and around which the Christian liturgy of the Eucharist is constituted insofar as it is in continuity with, and even surpasses, that of Israel, but also and more profoundly, how it is the central act where the entire economy of salvation history is established. We recalled the major phases of this economy in our preceding study: preparation, accomplishment, consummation. What must be brought out is the fact that each of these phases does not recapture and accomplish the preceding phase except by surpassing it. We just saw this for the Church and Judaism apropos of their respective prayers and liturgies. The sacrifices of the time of preparation are therefore both taken up again and abolished by the sacrifice of Christ. It is in such a way that He 'accomplishes' them: He brings them to their end by elevating them to a perfection that infinitely surpasses them. And although Christ's sacrifice, which is therefore both the last and the fullness of all sacrifices—although it is carried out during the entire time of its consummation in the Church by means of the sacrament instituted for this, it will nevertheless disappear at the time of its eschatological accomplishment: it will disappear with respect to its sacramental form, which it has for the present time, in order to give way to the heavenly liturgy of glory, which alone will remain. The form of this latter is still unknown to us, even if the Apocalypse allows us a glimpse (5:6–14). However, what we can say, on the basis of the economy of salvation history, is that it will take up again all that it will have prepared in order to bring it to completion in a superior way.

There is absolutely no need for, and it is even better to avoid, recourse to the Hegelian concept of '*Aufhebung*' (which sets apart, suppresses and conserves at the same time), in order to notice that economy. The concept of '*completion*' suffices, in the sense of an act which leads a process to its end. 'Completion' seems to render adequately the typically New Testament concept of '*teleiôsis*' (Heb 7:11) or '*teleiôtes*' (Col 3:14), with all the other derivatives of the verb '*teleioô*' (=to lead to its end/*telos*), and this in the two senses of the word 'end': to lead to one's term, that is, to bring to one's perfection, but also to one's disappearance. To complete is to perfect, but it is also to destroy. It is not by chance that, of the twenty-three times where it is used in the New Testament, the verb '*teleioô*' appears nine times in the Epistle to the Hebrews, which is the important text of the theology of salvation history considered from the central point of view, that of its consummation in the priesthood and sacrifice of Christ.

A double consequence flows from these reflections: first, that humanity and all the things of this world do not come to their final perfection except by passing through destruction; and second, with regards to the sacrifice, that it must not be understood as reaching completion in this destruction, but as a passage through it, towards this final completion. Scheeben had seen this in the last century. He showed with insistence that the 'transformation' required by theologians as essential to the sacrifice must not be understood simply as 'destructive,' but ultimately as 'perfective'[64] and, we could say, 'accomplishing.' The ultimate Agent of this ultimate accomplishment is the Holy Spirit, the eschatological and Messianic Gift par excellence. We shall show this later.

These conclusions, which obviously require infinite developments, allow one better to see that the sacrifice is at the heart of religious history, that is to say, of the entire history of humanity, and that the Passover of Christ is itself the center of that history. The Passion is the work that takes history up again and 'completes' it, because by taking it up it 'completes' in a transcending, divine-human manner, all the sacrifices. However, two questions at least need to be examined more closely in order to understand these conclusions. They will help

---

[64]   M. J. Scheeben, *Dogmatik*, L. V (*Gesammelte Schriften* (Fribourg, Herder, 1958) Bd. VI/2, no. 1247). Unfortunately we cannot elaborate on Scheeben's teaching, the relevance and fruitfulness of which are still astonishing. We refer to the excellent study by B. Fraigneau–Julien, PSS, *Le sacrifice du Christ et le sacrifice de l'humanité selon Scheeben*, in *Rech. Sc. Rel.*, 1957, pp. 321–337, as well as to his book, *L'Eglise et le caractère sacramental selon M.–J. Scheeben*, Paris, DDBr., 1958, where one will find in an appendix a particularly explicit text of Scheeben on the Eucharist (pp. 160–3). cf. *see above*, notes 16 and 17.

us enter more deeply into the knowledge of the sacrifice and, consequently, to understand why the oblation must be multiplied in the present phase of the economy of salvation, that is, in the time of its consummation. These two questions are the following: 1) Why is this destruction of man and creation required in order for them to reach their completion? By applying a twofold sense of the word, one could say: Why must they be completed, that is to say, destroyed, in order to be ultimately completed, that is, divinely perfect? 2) Moreover, how can a destruction end up in a reconstruction? For, it is most evident that the two 'completions' are not located on the same level, and that the second, if it must be realized, can take place only on a superior level and in a superior way.

1. Divine Revelation has a clear response to the first question. If there is no redemption without the spilling of blood (Heb 9:22), it is because, having his principle in God, man cannot have an end except in Him; and also because, being separated from God by sin, man cannot return to Him without repairing his fault. Yet since this latter consisted in an attempt to possess life without God (Gen 2:9), its reparation, in justice, cannot be made except through loss of that life (Gen 3:3–22). The sacrifice is the act which transforms this simple loss, a punishment of justice, into a reparative offering tending towards the reestablishment of communion. Man's final goal is, therefore, to find life again, which is what he seeks to do by reentering into communion with God, by recognizing Him as his Creator, by repairing his revolt against Him and by uniting himself to God as his ultimate end. Moreover, since God is sanctity itself, or sacrality—the same Hebrew word, '*QDSh*,' means both holy and sacred—the sacri-fice is that which 'makes sacred'—that is, holy and living by this sanctity—him who offers it. Yet 'God alone is holy,' and no one is holy except through a participation in His sanctity. God alone is 'living,' and no one can live except by a gift from God. Such a gift, of life, of holiness, remains always eminently gratuitous on the part of God; for, He owes it to no one and least of all to the sinner who revolted against Him. In order to attain its goal, the sacrifice requires divine acceptance.

In order for this to happen the sacrifice itself must be perfect, 'complete,' so as to be acceptable to God and accepted by God.

The time of preparation had been simultaneously that of the progressive ascent of human sacrifice towards this perfect sacrifice—the progressive refinement of Israel's cult shows this—and that of the equally progressive discovery of man's radical impossibility to realize this perfection. The prophets proclaimed this more and more loudly to Israel (Amos 5:21 ff; Os 6:6; 8:11–13), while the increased consciousness of sin lead the people, or at least a part of the people, to multiply the sacrifices of expiation.[65] The Epistle to the Hebrews would raise the definitive acknowledgement of this powerlessness of the sacrifices of the old covenant in order to arrive at perfection (Heb 10:1: '*oudepote dunatai ... teleiôsai*'; etc.). The preparation consisted in this twofold but inseparable movement: the refinement of the cult and the consciousness by Israel of its radical powerlessness. When this preparation was accomplished, 'in the fullness of time' (Gal 4:4), Mercy could intervene in order to accomplish the word of Justice: the Word became flesh in order to realize the perfect sacrifice. He alone could do this, for He alone was holy: He was 'the Holy One of God' (Mk 1:24); and He alone was able to do it in the name of all of humanity, for by becoming Incarnate He became its Head. He became 'the New Adam' (1 Cor 15:45: 'the eschatological Adam'). By reason of this link which He established between Himself and all men, what He accomplished in His redemptive work was destined to be communicated to all: 'God desires that all men be saved and come to the knowledge of the truth' (1 Tim 2:3; cf. Rom 5:18; 8:29; etc.). After this, therefore, the only task possible for men will be to realize, that is to say to accomplish, what will have been realized. The words of St Paul, 'I complete in my flesh what is lacking in the sufferings of Christ for His Body the Church' (Col 1:24), is the classic place that

---

[65]   This is what also appears in the fact mentioned by H. Cazelles: 'In the last centuries of our history (that of the Old Covenent), the term sacrifice meant before all else the expiation sacrifice' (Art. cit. (*see above*, note 17), p. 7).

indicates this task of the Church. However, the passage also shows its relation with the work definitively accomplished by Christ. An attentive analysis of the vocabulary allows one to clarify this.

Christ, we said, has 'finished' the work of reconciling men with God by His perfect sacrifice (Col 1:20). The verb '*teleioô*' expresses this completion, especially in the Letter to the Hebrews. But if Christ has 'finished' everything, what remains to be done after Him? There still remains the 'accomplishment' or the 'completion,' that is, the bringing of this completion to its 'fullness.' This is what is expressed by the verb '*antalaplerô*,' used by St Paul in the passage above. It is formed not from the root '*télos*,' which means end, but from the word '*plérôma*,' which signifies fullness, totality, whose importance in Pauline theology is well known. Such then is the task of the Church: not to lead Christ's sacrifice to a greater *perfection*, which is impossible, but to begin with its perfection (qualitative, intensive) and to work to expand it towards the *fullness* (quantitative, extensive), that is, towards the totality of humanity and the cosmos, in order to assume them into it Christ and lead them back in Christ to God. One could also say: begin with the fullness of Christ in order to realize the fullness of the Church. St John and St Paul invite us there (Jn 1:16; Col 1:19; 2:9–10). It's a question, then, of extending the fullness, which is perfect in the Head, to 'the Church which is His Body,' and which is thus, St Paul adds, 'the fullness of Him Who has in Himself the totality of fullness' (this seems to be the way to translate Eph 1:23). The Church is the pleroma, the fullness of Him Who is in Himself the fullness. The Church is the fullness of the fullness. She simply realizes that which is already realized in Him: she accomplishes it. It is for this end that Christ established the Twelve, that is, the apostolic and priestly ministry, and that He confided to them, along with the task of announcing the Gospel to all men, the Eucharist, the sacrament of His sacrifice. He commanded them to celebrate it, that is, to immolate and offer sacramentally His own unique sacrifice, 'until He comes again' (1 Cor 11:27), in order *to prepare* and *to anticipate* its eschatological completion in glory.

In order to summarize the theology of the sacrifice taken from this quick outline, we would say that it is:[66]

1) an act of reparation for the offense made to God;
2) in view of obtaining His grace (His gratuitous kindness) and of reestablishing communion of life with Him;
3) it is also, if it is received, an act by which man renders thanks to God for His goodness;
4) a proclamation of God's goodness and His dominion over all things, and a song of praise to God's glory (cf. Eph 1:6, 12, 14).

More schematically still, one could say that man and God are the two persons who encounter each other in the sacrifice, and that this sacrifice, consequently, has for its end both (and inseparably) the obtainment of God's grace for man and the offering of man's reparation, supplication, thanksgiving and praise to God. The imperfect sacrifices of the time of preparation insisted in their multiplicity on one or another aspect of the total and perfect sacrifice. This latter, as Christ alone can accomplish it, contains all the others together. This is why it is at the same time a sacrifice of the Covenant, a sacrifice of reparation, of thanksgiving, of communion and praise.[67] Before it, because this perfection was not yet realized, the multiplication of the

---

[66]   We shall abstain from multiplying references here; but one will recognize in our summary the fundamental characteristics of the theology of the sacrifice from St Augustine (*De civitate Dei*, L. X, cap. 5–6) and St Thomas Aquinas (*S.T.* I–II, q. 102, a. 3; II–II, q. 85–86; III, q. 22, a. 2; q. 58, a. 3; q. 79, a. 5; q. 82, a. 4; *Contra entiles*, III, q. 119–120; etc.).

[67]   The reflections of St Thomas on the different sacrifices of the Old Covenant (an echo of Tradition,) are still quite interesting (*S.T.* I–II, q. 102, a. 3). One can find a brief, very up–to–date synthesis of these sacrifices and their history in an article by H. Cazelles, cited above (note 665), and especially in the works of Fr De Vaux, *Les Institutions de l'Ancien Testament*, Paris, Cerf, 1960 (cf. vol. II, pp. 291–347); *Les sacrifices de l'Ancient Testament*, Paris, 1964 (See other reference in Cazelles, Art. cit., p. 9, note 2).

different types of sacrifices was necessary, and as powerless as it was necessary. Nevertheless, they were not devoid of all efficacy, thanks to the connection that they had with Christ's sacrifice, which they prefigured and prepared. After Christ there can no longer be any other sacrifice other than His, which is at the same time impossible to renew on account of its perfection, its 'completion,' and yet perpetually renewable on account of that same perfection, its 'fullness'; and thanks to the mystery of eschatological time, which the Resurrection opens up, and the mystery of the sacramental order, which Christ instituted precisely in view of that renewal and this ultimate consummation. This is what we showed in the previous chapter.

2. Yet *how can this happen?* How can the sacrifice, which appears for the time being as a work of destruction, bring about this final reconstruction? To this second question one sole response is possible, that found in Sacred Scripture: *by the work of the Holy Spirit* (cf. Lk 1:34 ff). The soul of the sacrifice, that is, the soul of the work that God wishes to realize by the Spirit, is love. The immolation is nothing without the offering, which alone makes it a sacrifice. And this latter, in turn, cannot be fully pleasing to God except that its deepest inspiration be love. Yet love, the supernatural and divine love of which we are speaking and which alone can please God, is the Holy Spirit, Who inspires love in the heart of man (Rom 5:5). It is, indeed, by the Holy Spirit that man's sacrifice is pleasing to God; and it is also by the Spirit that, the sacrifice being pleasing to God, He showers down upon man graces of redemption, sanctification and communion. The sacrifice thus appears from now on under its most profound aspect, namely the completion of that 'wonderful exchange'—*admirabile commercium*—between God and humanity.

We must, however, clarify these points. Two things: first, the differences and the relation between the sacrifice of the Redeemer, Who is holy, and man, who is a sinner; second, the economy that rules the relationship between the ritual and sacramental sacrifices and the personal sacrifice. These two questions shed light on each other, and together they allow us to better understand the efficacy of the sacrifice. We call a 'ritual sacrifice' that where the victim is a different reality than the offerer, an inanimate thing or a living being; and a 'personal sacrifice' is that where the immolated victim is the offerer himself. The time of preparation was the time of ritual sacrifices par excellence. One must understand that these sacrifices were ordered to the personal sacrifices of those who offered them, having value only by these latter. The sentiments of the sinful men who immolated them were, first of all, fear, humility, contrition, rising up little by little to love of God, to thanksgiving and praise. Christ, in offering Himself, accomplished and 'completed' all the ritual sacrifices. His sacrifice, essentially personal, was thus the fullness of the ritual sacrifices. His sentiments could not be of contrition, since He was without sin (1 Pet 2:22). They were completely of love of the Father—to Whom He wished to offer an adequate reparation for our sins, and of mercy towards sinners—whom He wished to save from the consequences of their sins.

After Christ, therefore, there were no longer ritual sacrifices. There was only *the* 'sacramental sacrifice,' that is, the immolation and offering '*in sacramento*' of the one redemptive sacrifice. In offering it to God, men are filled at the same time with the sentiments that are fitting to them insofar as they are sinners: humility, contrition, etc.; they are also filled with the brightness that is theirs insofar as they are members of Christ. They share in His love for the Father and for other men; and this supernatural love transfigures without suppressing all the other sentiments that they feel as sinners. The participation in Christ's sacrifice has for its end precisely the increase in them of the power of that love, in order that they might 'complete in their flesh—that is, in their temporal existence—that which is lacking in the sufferings of Christ for His body which is the Church': in order that they might complete the capital and ecclesial sacrifice of Christ through the personal sacrifice, which they make of themselves in their life and death.

This, we say, is the work of the Holy Spirit. Let us not forget that huge theological questions are implied here. However, in order to clarify them and to respond briefly to what we posit, it will suffice to recall schematically the Holy Spirit's role in salvation history, by considering first of all what it had been in the historical accomplishment of Christ's Mystery. This can be summed up in a few statements. Conceived (Lk 1:35) and consecrated (Jn 6:27; 10:36) by the action of the Holy Spirit, Christ had been immeasurably filled with that same Spirit (Jn 3:34). Having lived under the Spirit's guidance and impulse His whole moral life (Lk 4:1; etc.), it is by the Spirit especially that He was offered as a Victim for sinners. Having risen by the Spirit's action (Rom 1:4; 8:11), He received the power to pour out the Spirit on the men who receive Him—which He did at Pentecost (Acts 2:33)—in order to conceive them (Jn 1:12–13), consecrate them (Eph 1:13), sanctify them (1 Cor 6:11), and therefore sacrifice them, but also in order to raise them up on the last day (Rom 8:11) and gather them together in the unity of His ecclesial Body (1 Cor 12:13; Eph 2:16; 4:4). The entire theology of the Holy Spirit would have to be considered here in order to develop each of these points.[68]

By developing these points more we can see, beginning with Christ, how the entire history of salvation is this anticipation, this coming of the Holy Spirit, and this accomplishment of the word of God by His action in creation, and then in redemption. From the beginning we see Him 'hovering over the waters,' desiring, as it were, to enter into them and take possession of them (Gen 1:2). This desire could not be accomplished except with the '*Fiat*' of the Immaculate Virgin Mary (Lk 1:28), 'the beginning of the new creation.' At the end, in glory, it is the stream flowing 'from the throne of God and of the Lamb' that vivifies the heavenly Jerusalem (Rev 22:1 ff). For, at the center of salvation history, it is already this stream of living water flowing from the side of the 'glorified' Lamb, Who is slain and risen,

---

[68]   The literature on the subject is multiplying (Mühlen, Bouyer, Congar, etc.).
       We simply note the excellent point of departure that is found, from the point
       of view of biblical theology, in number 4 of the Constitution on the Church,
       Lumen Gentium.

but also from the side of His Church and of those who believe in Him: for, 'from His side shall flow streams of living water.' The ambivalence, and not ambiguity, of the designation of that 'side' is willed: from Christ the Holy Spirit is poured forth into those who believe in Him; and from those believers He is poured forth into the world in order to lift it up to the Father. However, the same Spirit is first poured forth from the Church into believers through the sacraments.

Thus the economy of the gift of the Spirit is the same in all cases. In fact, we have here only one sole economy, which is that of the very history of salvation. It is realized at different moments from Christ and according to the principles that we were able to see at work in Him: because He had been holy, He was able to sanctify. Conceived by the Holy Spirit, it is by the Spirit that He accomplished the work of sanctification, the summit of which is the sacrifice of the new Covenant; and He accomplished it with the intention of pouring out the Spirit, the basis of this Covenant (2 Cor 3:6). Not only His action, but His flesh itself thus becomes the source and instrument of the Spirit's outpouring. The Fathers of the Church developed these ideas very early, especially that of the humanity of Christ, the instrument—'*organon*'—of the divinity for the work of salvation.[69]

The same goes for the Church, Christ's Body and Bride, the extension and fullness of His flesh. Because, like Him, the Church had been conceived by the Holy Spirit on the day of Pentecost, she became holy and the source of sanctification, which she is by pouring forth the sanctifying Spirit. There is no other source. It is the same unique source, which is the flesh of Christ, but extended to us through the visible mediation of the Church, her priesthood, her sacraments and her saints.

---

[69] This concept of the instrument goes back to the beginnings of patristic theology, as it is first found in St Iranaeus. cf. W. Metzger, *Der Organgedanke in der Christologie der griechischen Kirchenväter* (Pont. Ath. Anselmianum), Münsterschwarzach, 1968, cf. St Irenaeus, *Adv. Haer.*, II, 33, 3.4. cf. see above, Ch. X.

What we are saying here about the Church is said first of all about the Blessed Virgin. Before having conceived the Word in her flesh through the working of the Holy Spirit, she herself had been 'immaculately conceived'—she *is* the 'Immaculate Conception'—through the working of the same Spirit. This is why she is associated in a unique way with the work of redemption in order that she might now, with Christ, pour out the Holy Spirit into the Church.

The Church exercises her proper mediation through prayer, where she appears more as Bride. This can be called her ascending mediation. Insofar as she is Mother, she is united to Christ in order to pour out His Spirit with Him. This is her descending mediation. Insofar as she is His Body, she is Christ Himself, and she continues His activity; she does this through her ministers, by their preaching and especially by the celebration and administering of the sacraments. While Christ's flesh is 'the conjoined instrument of the Divinity,' His sacraments are Its 'separated instruments'; and yet these are always immediately united to that Divinity, since it is always Christ Himself Who acts through them.[70] The Body of Christ, the Church, has another meaning also, namely insofar as it is not the subject but the object of Christ's sanctifying action: all the men who are to be saved and gathered together 'in Him.'

Among the sacraments the Eucharist dominates. Like Christ and like the Church, which together form a whole, the Eucharist gives the Spirit, because it is primarily by it that the Church is sanctified. In addition to sacramental theology, it is the entire theology of grace that one would have to consider and develop here in a pneumatic and Trinitarian perspective. Let us say this much with regards to grace, that the two aspects of the mystery to be taken as a whole are: first, that the Three Persons of the Trinity far always inseparably at work

---

[70]   St Thomas Aquinas, *S.T.*III, q. 62, a. 5. It is directly from St John Damascene, the collector of the entire Greek patristic tradition, that St Thomas borrows this notion of 'instrument' (cf. *ibid*, 8, 1, 1m., citing the *De fide orthodoxa*, L. III, cap. 15).

when they operate outside of themselves; second, that each One of the Persons, by the very fact that He acts in communion with the Other Two, operates only according to that which is proper to Him.[71] It is not simply a question of a vague 'appropriation,' but of a 'proper' action of Persons. Far from placing in danger the *unity* of the Trinitarian action, this bringing to light of the *'proper'* action of the Persons is, on the contrary, that which allows one to recognize it *in the mystery of its trinity.* It is thus that the Father acts only through the Word and the Spirit. He works and comes only by 'sending' Them, this action being the temporal continuation of His eternal generation and spiration. The Word acts only as one 'sent' and 'sending' the Spirit with the Father, this action being the temporal continuation of His eternal ('passive') generation and spiration. Finally, the Spirit acts only as one 'sent,' this act being the continuation in time of His eternal ('passive') spiration. This means that, infused into the creature by the Father and the Word, the Holy Spirit has for His 'proper' action the communication to that creature of the Breadth that He Himself is, in order to elevate it, in its dynamism, to the principle from which He proceeds: the Father and the Word. It is thus that the Spirit completes and 'perfects' the unique and inseparable work of the Trinity in creation and in redemption. Having done this first in the Immaculate Virgin Mary and in Christ, it is from these two, from their holy flesh and action, and from their extension, that the Church, from her flesh

---

71   *Ibid.,* I q. 45, a. 6; where, regarding creation, St Thomas writes: 'Creation is not proper to any one of the Persons, but to the whole Trinity. Nevertheless, it is not according to Their procession that the Divine Persons exercise their causality in creation.' The extremely important principle posited here has not been sufficiently considered. It is this principle that establishes the doctrine, Augustinian in its origin, of the 'vestiges' of the Trinity in things (cf. *ibid.,* art. 7; q. 93). The same goes for man all the more, created as he is in 'the image of God' (93, 1.5–6), and for redemption, that 'new creation' (2 Cor 5:17), where God comes to dwell in man by grace (*S.T.*I, q. 43, a. 3). It is the entire theology of grace that needs to be remade in this perspective (cf. see above, note 599).

and her action, especially from her sacramental and Eucharistic action, does the same in the rest of humanity and in all of creation.

The Eucharist, the flesh and action of Christ and the Church, is therefore the sacrament par excellence of the accomplishment of that Mystery. When we say that it is by the Spirit that the Eucharist works, we now understand better that it is always first of all Christ Himself, in union with the Father, Who is at work. The Eucharist is His instrument, the '*organon*,' in which He renews the totality of His Mystery, from the Incarnation to Pentecost, and by which His flesh enters into contact with each of His members in order to nourish them by communicating His Spirit to them (cf. Jn 6:55–63), in order to lead them into His glory.

How does this happen on the level of celebration and rites? This is what we must try to see now, at least in a rough outline.

12 THE CELEBRATION AND MULTIPLI-CATION OF THE SACRIFICE

H AVING RECOGNIZED IN the sacrifice the central reality of the Eucharist and the first principle that explains the structure, we must now show how, in fact, everything in the Mass is centered around the sacrifice. In order to do this we can borrow the words we began with in order to affirm that the Mass is essentially the sacrifice of the new and eternal Covenant: 'This cup is the New Covenant in My Blood' (Lk 22:20). These words are at the center of theology, but also at the center of the liturgical celebration of the Eucharist. What we shall focus on here is that, while the Eucharistic sacrifice, because it is the very sacrifice of Christ, realizes the synthesis of all the sacrifices of the time of preparation (expiation, thanksgiving, praise, etc.), what is most essential to it and around which all the other elements are organized, is the fact that it is the sacrifice of the Covenant.

I. The Principle and Fundamental Structure of the Mass

1. This observation will allow us to bring to light the liturgical structure of the Mass. In fact, the schema according to which the sacrifice of the Old Covenant had been celebrated during the time of preparation is known to us;[1] and it is from there that we must begin, if one admits at

---

[1] It is true that the works of exegetes have been concerned primarily with the 'literary genre' of the Covenant: S. Mowinckel, *Le Décalogue* (Paris, 1927); G. Von Rad, *Das formgeschichtliche Problem des Hexateuch* (Stuttgart, 1938); G. E. Mendenhall, *Law and Covenant In Israel and the Ancient Near East* (in *The Biblical Archaelogist*, 1954); W. Noran, *De Foederis Mosaici Traditione* (in *Verbum Domini* 40, 1962, 5–36); etc. But the rite in which this Covenant is sealed between God and His people includes a sacrifice, and it unfolds according to a structure whose essential characteristics can hardly be called into question. It is these which we are interested in here. The study presented in this chapter first appeared in *LPC* no. 194 (September–October 1981), pp.

least that, in addition to the surpassing, a real continuity exists between the Old and New Covenants. We shall see, in fact, how the structure of the liturgy (for it is one), in which the Old was sealed, is found again after some changes, in the New. Referring the reader to the works of specialists for a more detailed analysis, we shall note here the essential composing elements of this sacrifice such as it is found in the '*elohist*' narrative of the Sinaitic Covenant.[2]

The ceremony unfolds in two parts: 1) the offering of the Covenant made by the Lord and the acceptance of the people (Ex 19); 2) the sacrifice that seals the Covenant in the blood (Ex 24). By developing this more, one notes in the first part, that the initiative comes from God, Who presents His claims on obedience: His kindness towards Israel (Ex 19:4), and His dominion over the whole earth (verse 5). He also presents His desires (verse 5, developed in chapter 20:1–7)—this is 'the law' and the 'torah,' the Decalogue—and His promises (verse 6). The people respond by committing themselves to observe the law (verse 8), and Moses transmits this response to the Lord (*ibid.*). One will recognize in the two sections that compose this first part the two-part structure, which characterizes the discourse of the Lord proposing and enjoining the Covenant on his people. This structure, analyzed in our last chapter, would become the proto-type of all the 'prayers according to the Covenant,' composed later by Israel.

In the second part, after the people accepted the law and the Lord's offer (Ex 24:4), Moses sealed the Covenant in blood: he offers a

---

28–56.

[2]   We follow here the division of Fr Courroyer (*Bible de Jérusalem*): Ex 19:3–9 (where the two traditions, 'yahwist' and 'elohist' are mixed); Ex 24:3–8. In that latter chapter, the 'yahwist' tradition seems to be used in verses 1–2 and 9–12. One can see now what distinguishes our analysis from that of Fr Giraudo, a summary of which is found in our preceding chapter, and others as well. While these authors limit themselves to examining the prayer which accompanies the sacrifice, or which is refered to there, it is the inseparable whole formed by the prayer (or the words) and the sacrifice (the action) that we are considering.

sacrifice of communion. After the immolation of victims, 'of calves,' half of the blood was poured on the altar (verse 6), which represented the Divinity; with the other half the people were sprinkled by Moses, saying, 'This is the blood of the Covenant, which the Lord made with you concerning all these words' (verse 8). The 'words'— *'Debarim'*—of the Lord are His commandments. According to the 'yahwist' version, the Covenant finally concludes with a meal of the leaders of the people with God at the summit of the mountain (verses 9–11). One can see here a very first proclamation of the Messianic eschatological meal. What is most important to note, however, is that throughout the entire narrative, while the two parties of the Covenant appear to be the Lord and the Chosen People (chosen, that is, by Him, in Ex 19:5), at the same time, the figure of the mediator, Moses, plays a decisive role; for, it is only through him that God speaks to His people and the people respond.

Such was the first Covenant, essentially conditional; for, it was tied to the people's observance of the Lord's 'words,' and the blood of calves was unable to give the people the Spirit of the Lord, Who alone could make them capable of keeping His commands. On the other hand, the New Covenant is both unconditional and definitive; for, sealed in the blood of Christ, it gives the Spirit to those who enter by faith into Him, the one Mediator (1 Tim 2:5), and it thereby makes them capable of keeping His word. The analogy of structure, however, which exists between the two Covenants, is no less real. The profound reason for this is that, in both cases, there is first of all a proclamation of God's word, which man must receive by faith; and then there is the immolation of a sacrifice, which seals this reciprocal commitment. The difference is in the content of the word: a simple religious and moral commandment in the first case; an offer of mercy and salvation in the second. It is also in the nature of the mediator: he is but a man chosen by God in the first case; in the second case it is the Son of God made man. Finally, the difference of the sacrifice: the identification of the perfect Priest and perfect Victim is realized only in the New

Covenant. These differences, which are no doubt essential, do not prevent, once again, the identity of the structure, which we showed to exist in both the Covenant itself and in its liturgical celebration. This structure is found again, or is already found, in a certain manner, in the very life of Christ, the perfect Mediator of the perfect sacrifice: after having announced His 'law,' 'the good news of salvation,' He ratified the Covenant that He offered in His own blood and poured forth the Spirit that is its foundation (2 Cor 3:6).

That structure is found again especially in the Eucharistic liturgy, where the first part is dedicated to the reading of the Law, Old and New; the reading is followed by the people's acceptance of it, proclaimed in the 'Credo'; after this, in the second part, the sacrifice is offered by the priest, the sacramental minister of the one Mediator; and the sacrifice ends with communion. Thus we find the classical division of the Mass into two parts: the 'Mass of the Catechumens,' in which the proclamation of the Gospel takes place; and the 'Mass of the Faithful,' which contains the sacrifice and communion.[3] In reality there is but one sole Mass, one sole sacrifice. The first part prepares the faithful. The second, essentially in the consecration,

---

[3]   Fr Lebrun, *Explication de la Messe* ('Lex–Orandi'—9), Paris, Cerf, 1949, p. 8. Second edition of the first volume of the monumental and classical work of the great Oratorian. Published between 1716 and 1726 (in 4 volumes), the first part frequently republished since, this work remains one of the greatest 'litteral, historical and dogmatic' commentaries of the Mass that we possess. One ought, nevertheless, to bring up–to–date his historical information by having recourse to, among others, that other classic text, the '*Missarum solemnia*' of J. A. Jungmann (*Missarum solemnia, Eine genetische Erklärung der römischen messe*, Wien, Herder, 1952 (3rd edition; vol. 2)); J. M. Hanssens, *Institutiones Liturgicae de ritibus orientalibus*, Rome, Pont. Univ. Gregorianum, 1930–1932 (vols. 2–3 and *Appendix*); A. Raes, *Introductio in liturgiam orientalem*, Rome, Pont. Ist. Orientale, 1947; H. A. Schmidt, SJ, *Introductio in liturgiam occidentalem*, Rome–Fribourg, Herder, 1960, which contains a large bibliography; etc. See also the collaborative work, directed by A. G. Martimort, *L'Eglise en prière. Introduction à la liturgie*, Tournai–Paris, Desclée, 1961, and the *Manuale di Storia liturgica* of M. Righetti, Milano, 1966.

brings to realization the Lord's sacramental 'memorial.' By communion the priest and faithful finish by uniting themselves to the sacrifice in order to receive its fruits and to consecrate themselves to the service of God. If we add the rites of the beginning and the end, we end up with the following schema, which shows how all is organized and structured around the central act of the sacrifice (we are inspired here and in what follows by the Roman liturgical tradition):

The faithful come together. The priest enters.

I—THE WORD:	Prayers
	Readings (Word)
	Credo
II—THE SACRIFICE:	Offertory
	SACRIFICE (Canon. Consecration)
	Communion
	Dismissal. Priest exits. Faithful depart.

Everything that precedes the act of the sacrifice is preparation: the faithful (readings; prayers), the matter for the sacrifice (offertory). All that follows the sacrifice is consummation: communion (with its thanksgiving) and dismissal. The detail of the second part clarifies this still more:

1) OFFERTORY:	Preparation and presentation of gifts (procession);
	OFFERING (offertory actions and prayers);
	Prayer over the gifts and introduction to the sacrifice.
2) SACRIFICE:	Praise (Preface, 'Sanctus');
	Offering (prayer for acceptance: 'Te igitur');
	Intercession ('Memento');
	SACRIFICE (intrinsic immolation and oblation)
	Anamnesis (new prayer of offering);
	Intercession ('Memento');
	Praise (final doxology).
3) COMMUNION:	Preparatory prayer ('Pater');
	COMMUNION;
	Prayers of thanksgiving.

Along with the centrality of the sacrifice this table allows one to see the necessity for us, located in time, of developing through successive moments that which makes but one thing in the central act of consecration, that is, in the very oblation of the one sacrifice of Christ. This is why, with that progressive development, repetition is one of the great laws of the liturgy. It is important that each moment has its proper significance. This is what is verified in the numerous prayers or 'orations' of the Mass, and especially in those by which the oblation of the sacrifice is made: there are those that belong to the offertory; those that precede the consecration and by which the Church, after having praised God for His gifts (Preface, '*Sanctus*'), asks that her sacrifice be acceptable ('*Te igitur,*' '*Hanc igitur*'); those that follow the consecration (anamnesis: '*Unde et memores… offerimus*'), where the Church offers henceforth not her own sacrifice in Christ's still to be accomplished, but Christ's sacrifice, which was just accomplished, by entering into it. Finally, there is the offering with prayer—without a special prayer on the part of the Church—realized by the central act of the consecration, that is to say, by Christ Himself offering and immolating sacramentally, '*hic et nunc*' in the Church, His one redemptive sacrifice. Anticipating a bit the analysis we are about to make, we can say that these remarks on the multiplication of prayers of offering that are found throughout the Mass, show once again how its act of sacrifice is truly its center and structuring principle.

2. One can also see this by considering the outline of the 'Eucharistic Prayer—anaphora and Canon—whose structure we already looked at. This 'Prayer' coincides exactly with the central section of the table that we just presented, the *sacrifice.* We saw how, in the extension of and dependence on the Old Testament *tôdah* and *berakah* of Judaism, this 'Prayer' is composed of two parts. The first, initially historico-anamnetical, and then principally one of praise, recalls the '*mirabilia Dei,*' the lofty deeds of God's fidelity and mercy towards His people: this is the Preface and the '*Sanctus.*' The second is epicletic, the appeal

to God that He might act again and save His people: this begins with the '*Te igitur*' and ends with the Canon's final doxology.

The conjunction '*igitur*' ('therefore,' or 'consequently') is also of Judaic and Old Testament origin, designating the link that unites the two parts;[4] it is because God has done for His people all that the first part just 'recalled,' that it is possible for that people to turn again to Him, despite their sin, in order to 'appeal' and ask for a new intervention of His mercy. This structure of the whole, 'recall'–'appeal, 'anamnesis-epiclesis, '*memores*'–'*memento*'—this structure did not prevent a new appeal for God's salvific action from being inserted into the second part. Present first of all by mode of embolism, that is, by a later addition and a parenthesis, this new anamnesis saw its importance increase with time, and developed into the summit not only of the second part, but of the entire 'prayer': this is the 'memorial'(*zikkarôn*), which is effectively, especially in the anaphora, the center around which the whole of the movement towards God is organized and realizes its economy. We also note how, by virtue of the sacramental institution of Christ, this 'memorial' in the Eucharist is not a simple evocation of a memory; it is the realization of an action. The institution narrative, in which it consists, through the power given to its words by Christ, actualizes its sacrifice. This is why the 'memorial' is, '*in sacramento*,' the consecration, the immolation and offering *hic et nunc* in the Church.

By thus becoming the central act of the prayer and of the entire Eucharistic liturgy, it loses, along with its initial trait of embolism, that of the anamnesis as well, or more precisely, it sees it transformed. The consecration is the recalling and proclamation of the redemptive sacrifice, because it is first of all and essentially its sacramental actualization. This is why the liturgy felt the need for a new prayer to follow, '*Unde et memores*.' It is called the 'anamnesis' because it is founded on the action that was just realized, actuated and therefore 'recalled'; but it is in itself of an epicletic nature, for it has for its object the 'appealing'

---

4   Cf. C. Giraudo, op. cit., pp. 348–53.

for Divine Mercy in order that that Mercy might accept the offering made to It. (One will note the great flexibility in the words 'anamnesis,' 'embolism,' etc., according to the different points of view adopted; their meaning needs to be determined in each case by their immediate context.). Then come the following prayers of intercession: '*Memento,*' '*Nobis quoque.*' The Canon is completed by the final doxology, which takes up again, '*in Christo,*' the trisagion, the triple '*Sanctus,*' which concluded the first part, such that the entire Eucharistic prayer is contained between these two exclamations to the glory of God.

II. Theological Analysis of the Structure of the Mass

Such then is the structure of the Canon. It confirms and testifies even more that which the structure of the whole of the Mass already brought to light, namely, that the sacrifice is both the center, the summit, and even in one sense, the whole of the Eucharistic liturgy. That being established, we can now try to develop the theology of this 'Holy and Divine Liturgy,' the Mass. We shall do this by responding to four particular questions, which will allow us at the same time to see better how this sacrifice bears its fruits of redemption, and under which form its celebration is the most fruitful for the Church. These questions are the following: 1) Who offers the sacrifice; 2) Who is offered, and what?; 3) How does the offering take place?; 4) How does one participate in its fruits? Each of these can be the object of a long treatise; we shall try to bring out the essential points.

1. *Who offers the Holy Sacrifice of the Mass?* Christ, the priest, the Church: Christ as High Priest, whose ordained minister simply takes His place in the central act of the consecration; the Church, for it is the entire Church that He associates with the offering of His sacrifice, as is signified in particular in the rites of offertory and the prayer of the anamnesis (we shall return to this later); the priest, the minister of the sacrifice of Christ and the Church, by whom Christ gives Himself to His Body to make it His own, and by whom the members

are united to their Head in order to become one with Him. Like Moses, the priest is the mediator between God and His people. He is a mediator, however, in a very superior manner, namely, not insofar as he is a prefiguration of, but rather the sacramental minister of the one Mediator. The role of Moses did not shine any less light on his own, to a certain point. What appears then is both the eminent hierarchical nature of the ecclesial assembly, beginning with Christ, as well as its trait of totality and the irreplaceable role which the ministerial priest plays there.

But more precisely, because he is the mediator by his ministerial and vicarious office, the priest participates in the double office coming from the double nature of Christ. By His divinity Jesus is God present among men, Emmanuel. By His humanity He represents men before God; He is their Head and High Priest. Likewise, analogically, by the priestly character which unites and conforms him to Christ the High Priest, the ministerial priest is Christ Himself, present and acting in His Church; but he is also the representative and voice of the Church, giving herself to her Lord. According to the different moments of the Mass and the different prayers that he says or acts that he accomplishes, the priest will speak or act sometimes 'in the name and person of Christ,' sometimes 'in the name and person of the Church.'[5] There

---

[5] See the article of Y. Congar cited above (*LPC*, no. 193, p. 23, note 39; cf. *see above*, Chapter XI, note 40). In the same volume, see the article by B. D. Marliangeas, OP, '*In persona Christi*', '*In persona Ecclesiae*.' *Note sur les origines et le développement de l'usage de ces expressions dans la théologie latine* (pp. 282–8). The author summarizes there a thesis since published: *Clés pour la théologie du ministère. In Persona Christi, in persona Ecclesiae*. Preface by Y. M. Congar ('Théologie historique', 51), Paris, Beauchesne, 1978. Very thoroughly documented, this work is a mine of information on the genesis and meaning of those expressions. We cite, as an example, this beautiful formula of Suarez: '*Licet sacerdos non sit realiter Christus, tamen mystice est Christus, in cujus persona loquitur, et vere profert eadem verba, quae Christus protulit; ergo et oblatio, quatenus ab illo est, sub hac ratione est aeque digna, et ejusdem valoris*' (*Disp.* 79, XI, 4. Vivès 21, 756; cit. p. 202). In his conclusion, Fr Marliangeas clearly emphasizes that, regarding the 'qualification to express publicly the

is no contradiction here, but simply the consequence of his office of mediator between the two parties, which must encounter each other. The supreme exaltation and supreme effacement of the priest! What a tragedy for him if he retains only one of these two aspects of his mission—for, then he would equally falsify the other.

St Robert Bellarmine sums up well the theological tradition regarding this point when he writes:

> Christ offers insofar as He is the priest (*primarius Sacerdos*), and He offers through the man priest (*per sacerdotem hominem*) as through His own minister. The Church does not offer as the Priest [Christ] through His minister, but as the people through the Priest. Thus Christ offers through an inferior, the Church through a superior.[6]

Citing this passage in *Mediator Dei,* Pius XII draws from it a twofold teaching: 'The priest represents the people because he represents the person of Our Lord insofar as He is the Head of all the members,' and not because he is a delegate of the congregation; he alone, therefore, enjoys the priestly power that makes him fit for offering the sacrifice.[7] This doctrine is what establishes the possibility of Masses said privately, the people being present in the person of the priest.

The faithful, however, by their Baptism, also participate in Christ's priesthood, albeit in another manner.[8] They participate also, therefore, in the offering of the sacrifice; and we shall see later how they do this. It is very important to keep together these two truths in order to avoid the two opposite extremes, namely the 'clericalization' and 'laicization' of the liturgy. The notion of the hierarchy, taken in its

---

prayer of the Church': In the case of the priest, it is founded on the priestly 'character', on the sacrament of Holy Orders as a participation in the office of Jesus Christ's mediation' (p. 243).

6   *Disputationes de Controversiis christianae fidei* (1575–1588), vols. III, III. Controv., L. VI: (*De Missa*, II), cap. 4.

7   *AAS* 35, 1947, pp. 553 ff.

8   *Ibid.*, 555. Cf. St Thomas, *S.T.* III, q. 63, a. 3.

widest extension beginning with Christ, is what allows us to do this. More than any other ecclesial action, the liturgy is one hierarchical action, precisely because it is an eminently priestly action. For, it is a question here of the hierarchy of the priesthood, which leaves completely open the question of sanctity and charity. In himself, the priest is the Christian called to be the most immediately united and configured to Christ in love, that is to say, to Christ, Priest and Victim of His own sacrifice. The Holy Spirit, however, is free. Man also is free in the response he gives to the Spirit. This is why the hierarchy of sanctity is not necessarily parallel to that of the priesthood. But this latter, by reason of its office, is essentially and completely visible; the hierarchy of sanctity is only partially so, according as it summons the mission of the Church or one or another Christian in the Church.

To return now to the active participation of the faithful in the offering of the sacrifice—the object of the Magisterium's continual concern since the beginning of the liturgical movement in the 18th century—it is manifested exteriorly by all that the liturgical action provides for: attitudes, responses, chants, and especially sacramental communion. Among the actions there is one of particular value, which the recent liturgical reform has not handled well, the offertory procession. We mention this now, since it shows in a very strong way the point that we are bringing out here, namely the hierarchical and communitarian character of the ecclesial action that is the liturgy of the Mass. In fact, by delivering the offerings into the hands of the priest, the congregation of the faithful manifests the gift it makes of itself to Christ in view of the sacrifice. The respective roles of the priesthood and the laity are thus clearly signified; and the hierarchy of action that is accomplished is, at the same time, made perceptible to all. 'Clericalization' and 'laicization' are both driven away in order to give place to the organic and hierarchical unity of the ecclesial Body of Christ.

2. *Who is offered?* To this question the response is the same, and according to the same hierarchical order: Christ, the priest and the

Church, but also all of humanity and even the cosmos, by reason of their connections to Christ's humanity, 'Who is before all, and by Him all things consist' (Col 1:17 ff). The hierarchical order is best manifested here. The people offer themselves with the priest as through their mediator; and the priest accomplishes the sacrifice only as the minister of Christ, 'the one Mediator' (1 Tim 2:5), Who acts directly through him at that greatest moment of the immolation.

This identity of the priest who offers and the victim who is offered must be affirmed, with regards to Christ, because of the sacramental identity of the sacrifice of the altar with that of Calvary.[9] From there one can see how the ministerial priest and the congregation are also immolated, always in virtue of the sacrament and in conformity with the economy of the ritual, sacramental and personal sacrifices, which we mentioned above (at the end of the preceding chapter). Christ Himself is the Priest and Victim of His own sacrifice; it is also in Him that this identity is realized in its fullness. This was prefigured long before in *the ritual* sacrifices of the Old Covenant; for, the victim there was always a substitute for the person who offered it, or for him who was offered. In *the sacramental* sacrifice of the Church, the victim is offered to God under the form of the oblations or offerings: bread and wine. They will represent Christ. Indeed, they will be Christ Himself after the consecration in virtue of transubstantiation. They will first represent the Church however; for, it is the Church who offers herself to Christ in them, in order to be united to Him and consecrated in Him to the Father in the Holy Spirit: 'Through Him, with Him and in Him'—*'per ipsum, cum ipso et in ipso'* (final doxology of the Roman Canon).

There are numerous texts that can be used in support of these totally traditional explanations. We shall cite here only one from St Athanasius. He poses first the following principle: 'All that Scripture says that the Son received, it is by reason of His Body that He received,

---

9   Council of Trent, *Session XXII, Cap.* 2: *'Una enim eademque est hostia, idem nunc offerens ... qui se ipsum tunc in cruce obtulit.'*

which are the first fruits (or beginnings—*aparchè*) of the Church.'
This is why: because Christ is in His Body the initial principle of the
Church: 'When He commends His Spirit into the hands of God, it is
insofar as He is man, and it is in order to commend *all men* into the
hands of God.'[10] Citing this text, Pius XII adds that the same thing is
reproduced in the Eucharistic sacrifice, which is the unbloody renewal
of the sacrifice of the Cross: 'Since [Christ] Himself, Priest and
Victim, acts there as Head of the Church, what He offers and immolates is not simply Himself, but all Christians and also, in a certain
way, *all men.*'[11]

With respect to the priest, he is called, more so than the rest of the
faithful, to immolate himself with and in Christ. He alone, in fact, has
the privilege of saying, 'in My Name,' 'by being the medium of the
very person of Christ' ('*gerens personam Christi*'), the words of
consecration; that is, he alone can be that by whom Christ Himself
says the words over the offerings, in which the entire Church and even
all of humanity and the entire cosmos are symbolically represented:
'This is My Body. This is My Blood.' The priest is, at that one
moment, by the power of the sacrament of Orders, which he then
exercizes in his supreme act and by a 'specific sacramental identification' (to use the words of John Paul II), Christ Himself, immolating
Himself in and for His Church.[12] His whole life, therefore, must
become the accomplishment of that immolation.[13]

---

10 St Athanasius, *De Incarnatione*, PG 26, 1004.
11 Exhortation '*Menti nostrae*', 23 September 1950: ' ... *non modo semetipsum,
    sed christianos universos et quodam modo omnes etiam homines offert et immolat'*
    (*AAS* 42, 1950, p. 666).
12 Epist. '*Dominicae Cenae*', 8 (24 February 1980): '*Sanctissimum Sacrificium
    offertur 'in persona Christi' ... Offertur nempe 'in persona': cum celebrans ratione
    peculiari et sacramentali idem prorsus sit ac 'summus aeternusque Sacerdos''* (*AAS*
    62, 1980, p. 128). See in the same vein the text of Suarez cited above (see
    above, note 724).
13 The Second Vatican Council insisted on this 'vocation of priests to holiness',
    precisely insofar as they are priests (*Decree on the Ministry and Life of Priests,*

We thus see the outline of what will later appear more clearly, in the analysis of the rite, as the great truth of the sacrifice: it is, through the work of the one Mediator, the 'wonderful exchange,' the *admirabile commercium,* that takes place between God and man.

3. *How does the sacrifice take place?* Even more than the last question, this one is huge, even if we limit ourselves to its liturgical dimension. For, with regards to its dogmatic aspect, we can refer back to those explanations where we showed, according to St Augustine and St Thomas, Dom Vonier, Cardinal Journet, etc., that the sacrifice is accomplished essentially *'in sacramento,'* that is, in the sacramental act and according to the sacramental mode.[14] On the basis of this doctrine we shall strive to show here how, in the celebration of the Mysteries, the sacrifice is accomplished at three times, according to an economy that goes from the *offertory* to the *consecration* in order to be completed in the *communion.*

a) *The Offertory.* We mentioned above, in responding to the question 'Who offers?' the very simple and very clear meaning of this rite; and yet it is often the object of a certain incomprehension, even an aggressiveness which cannot be concealed. These reactions leave one a bit perplexed when one considers, on one hand, the antiquity of those actions and the prayers that accompany them; and on the other hand, the manner in which Luther, who understood perfectly the traditional value, both liturgical and theological, of the rite, erupted against it. Fr H. B. Meyer, SJ, who dedicated a thesis to the study of the Mass in the 'Reformer,' was able to write that, while the sacrificial aspect of the Eucharist and the celebration of private Masses was the object of Luther's harshest attacks, the offertory was that part of the Mass that he most violently combated.[15] Its significance was

---

3).

[14] We developed this point of doctrine in our work: *L'Eucharistie, Sacrement et Sacrifice du Christ et de l'Eglise. Développements des perspectives thomistes,* in *Divinitas* (Pont. Acad. Theologiae Romanae), 18, 1974, pp. 234–86; pp. 396–436. See above, Chapter IX.

[15] H. B. Meyer, SJ, *Luther and die Messe. Eine liturgiewissentschaftliche Untersu-*

understood very well by Luther, as the following text shows. It is taken from the work entitled, '*Formula missae et communionis*' (1523): 'Eighthly, then comes that abomination, to which is fixed all that preceded; this is why it is called the offertory. It is here that almost everything rings out and manifests the effects of the oblation'—that is to say the sacrifice, '*oblation,*' the Latin word used here translates into the German '*Opfer,*' which means sacrifice. 'This is why,' continues the "Reformer," 'rejecting all that manifests the oblation [sacrifice] and the whole of the Canon with it, we retain that which is pure and holy, and thus we began our mass.' A description of the 'preparation' of the bread and wine follow: 'for the blessing,' etc.[16]

Here then is the precise reason why Luther rejects the offertory: because with its gestures and prayers it signifies that the 'action' that follows is a sacrifice. Such indeed is the sense that it has had since, that is, since its appearance in the second or third century.[17] Here again we can cite Bellarmine as a witness of this liturgical and theological tradition. Regarding the prayer '*Veni Sanctificator*' and the words '*sacrificium ... praeparatum,*' which are found there, he writes that this manner of speaking is exact, for it refers to the prayers of *oblation* that preceded. Thus, he explains:

> That first oblation [that of the offertory] was a preparation for the second [that of the consecration], in which, in the strict sense, the sacrifice consists. This is why we are right in speaking of the 'prepared sacrifice,' when the matter that has to be

---

chung über das Verhältnis Luthers zum Messwesen des spatter Mittelalters, Paderborn, Verl. Bonifacius, 1965, p. 156.

[16] Luther, *WA* (*Werke*. Ed. De Weimar), XII, p. 211.

[17] Jungmann brings forward the testimonies of Tertullian, Hippolytus, St Irenaeus, who speak about this presentation of the gifts, the '*oblation*', the 'offering'; he also cites St Augustine in order to conclude that, from the 6th century on, this rite of the oblation of the faithful existed in practically all of the liturgies (*Missarum solemnia*, II, pp. 271 ff). One sees, however, that the rite that was imposed universally at that time had been practically already widespread for two or three centuries.

consecrated to God (*Deo sacranda*), is dedicated (*dedicata*)
to Him by a certain oblation.[18]

There are not two sacrifices: one at the offertory, of bread and wine; the
other at the consecration, of Christ's Body. There is one sole sacrifice,
that of the whole Christ, Head and members. The members offer
themselves to the Head by the offertory; the Head assumes and makes
the members His own by the consecration of the matter, in which they
were 'offered.' For, the sacrifice is accomplished in this matter, which
represents first of all the members and what these latter themselves offer
to the Head, in order that He might make them His own Body and
immolate and offer that Body to God in His own sacrifice.[19]

Closer to our day, Dom Juglar, to cite yet one more example, also
understood and expressed very well this meaning of the offertory. He
shows the historical development according to which, 'from a simple
material preparation of the elements of the sacrifice, the Offertory, as
its name indicates, takes on a sense of an offering: a prerequisite offering
of bread and wine, which will be consecrated.' This is why, he adds:

The Offertory is totally related to the Eucharistic sacrifice; so
related that we make use of it in order to ask, by way of anticipation,
that that latter sacrifice be accepted and that we might experience its
fruits. This appears in many of the secrets, and in almost all of the
prayers introduced during the Middle Ages in order to accompany
the acts of preparation.[20]

The fact that those prayers are more recent than the actions that
they accompany in no way diminishes their value. The eight or ten
centuries of existence that they can count already give them a certain
weight of tradition[21]—this cannot be denied. To see here simple

---

[18]   Op. cit. L. VI, cap. 17.

[19]   Cf. *ibid*, L. V, cap. 27: '*Non enim sunt duo sacrificia, sed unun ... quod est panis
in corpus Domini transmutatum, sive corpus Domini in specie panis Deo oblatum.
Atque hinc est quod in missa non offertur panis ut sacrificium perfectum, sed ut
sacrificium inchoatum et perficiendum.*' This text shows well the inseparable
link which unites the offertory to the consecration.

[20]   J. Juglar, op. cit. (*see above*, Ch. XI, note 9), pp. 187 ff.

'prayers of devotion' for the intention of the priest, is a free interpretation, which moreover would not take away that traditional value, which they had acquired throughout the centuries.[22] The historical truth, however, is that their intention corresponds to a liturgical development that made felt the need to accompany each action with a word. Yet nothing is more in conformity with the sacramental order, where it is the proper characteristic of the word to express the meaning of the action that it accomplishes.[23] This need is so great that it reappears today; but it is to 'the animator' that is entrusted the job of giving those explanations—something that does not happen without destroying the sacramental unity of the rite, nor without a 'laicization' of the liturgy. We also note the historical and ecumenical misinterpretation committed in seeking to diminish what the sacrifice in the Eucharistic liturgy signifies at a time when the best of Protestant thought seems to rediscover, through the study of the Church's early Tradition, that the Mass is truly a sacrifice.[24]

---

[21] P. Salmon, OSB, *Les prières et les rites de l'offertoire dans la liturgie romaine au XIII et XIV siècle* (*Eph. Lit.*, 43, 1929, pp. 508–19), showed the Gallican origin of these prayers. They are found in France in the 11th century; and they were imposed definitively in Rome in the 13th century under the Franciscan influence.

[22] Karl Lehmann rehabilitated this notion of the priest's personal prayer in the celebration of the Mass: *Le prêtre en sa messe. A propos d'une prière privée*, in *L'eucharistie, Pain rompu pour un monde nouveau* (Paris, Fayard, 1981), pp. 153–60.

[23] Cf. St Thomas, *S.T.* III, q. 60, a. 7, where he shows that determined words are required in the sacraments in order to clarify the meaning of the 'sensible things'. Such is the function of the offertory prayers, as Dom Salmon shows: 'We are present here at an evolution of a rite ... The paten and the host must be presented and elevated during the recitation of the offering formula ... The prayer that accompanies this action is fixed. The '*Suscipe Sancte Pater*' explains the rite that is unfolding, and it keeps the attention of him who is acting' (Art. cit., pp. 514 ff).

[24] Jean De Watteville, *Le sacrifice dans les textes eucharistiques des premiers siècles* ('Bibliothèque théologique'), Neuchâtel, Delachaux et Niestlé, 1966. The author, a Protestant pastor at La Haye, shows 'that, from the apostolic period

b) *The Canon*, whose complete traditional title is '*Canon actionis*,' that is, the 'rule of action,'[25] is called by the Greeks '*anaphora*,' a word which literally signifies 'elevation,' and which signifies in the Eastern tradition the offering of the sacrifice. The two expressions meet therefore: 'the action,' which takes place in this central part of the Eucharistic liturgy is 'the offering of the sacrifice.' It is accompanied by a prayer, the '*Prex eucharistica*,' but is not reduced to it, this latter being, on the contrary, entirely related to the immolation of the sacrifice.

The schema that we proposed above shows how, after the offertory, this 'action' opens up and ends with a praise of adoration. Here we must take up again—in order to profit from it—all the truth that there is in the works of Frs. Audet, Giraudo and others on the '*Berakah-eucharistia*.' The ultimate end of the sacrifice, in fact, is always the praise of the glory of God; but in the present time, which is the '*Kairos*' of redemption, the sacrifice also exists in order to repair men's sins and to obtain for them God's grace.[26] This happens by the pouring out of Christ's blood and the prayer of supplication. This explains the importance of these prayers in the Canon itself. With respect to the immolation of the victim, it has a real place, albeit in an unbloody manner, '*in sacramento*,' through the double and unique

---

until the threshold of the 4th century, there is no break in Eucharistic conception between the New Testament and the Fathers of the Church,' and this is especially the case with regards 'to its sacrificial significance'. Presenting the well–documented work of Watteville in these terms, the Pastor Marc Boegner notes that this could only delight Catholic theologians. He does ask, however, whether the same could be said about the Protestant theologians (p. XII; XV). He always presents this with sympathy; and the fact that it had been received by a collection such as the 'Bibliothèque théologique' of the Delachaux editions, is not without significance.

[25] J. A. Jungmann, *Missarum Solemnia*, III, pp. 7 ff; I, p. 217.

[26] These are the two ideas to which St Thomas Aquinas constantly returns (*S.T.* III, q. 48, a. 3: where he borrows from St Augustine), extending them from the sacrifice to the sacraments, and then to the whole of theology (q. 60, a. 4; q. 63, a. 1), and even to the entire Christian life (q. 63, a. 3), which is thus centered on the sacrifice.

consecration which realizes the sacrament. This act—we are not too weary of saying it, for the whole mystery is there—this act, this sacramental and eschatological act is not a new immolation of Christ. It is the present actualization of His unique immolation, performed in order that His blood be poured out now upon His people.[27] And with the drama of Calvary, it is the entire 'Mystery of Christ' that is found again, re-actuated in the 'mystery of faith.' There is an equivalence between the two, for Christ has entered into His glory, having accomplished His work. It is this which the prayer of the anamnesis, the '*Unde et memores,*' evokes, immediately after the act of the sacrifice, where the other moments of the redemptive Mystery are recalled: 'His blessed Passion, but also His resurrection from the dead and His glorious ascension into heaven.' And it is only by remembering the totality of the Mystery that the Church, in whose name the priest speaks again here, offers to God's 'majesty,' by taking it 'from (her) gifts, the pure Victim, the holy Victim, the Victim without stain,' that is, Christ Himself, having become for the Church 'the holy bread of eternal life and the cup of eternal salvation.' We shall see later the

---

[27]   For this question we can refer to the remarks we made in our article '*Note sur le sacrifice de la Messe selon Jacques Maritain ...*' (*Divinitas* 19, 1975, 61–78). We see there (p. 67) that the presence of the sacrifice of the cross is not that of a thing, but of an act: 'which cannot happen except by the accomplishment of that act itself'. And we add: 'The sacrifice of the Mass is not the same as that of the Cross accomplished formerly, but the same sacrifice of the Cross accomplished now,' namely under the sacramental mode, thanks to which there is not simply an identity of nature between the two numerically different sacrifices, but a substantial identity of a unique sacrifice realized under two different modes. Cardinal Journet, who defined the Mass as a 'presence of the sacrifice of the Cross', shows also by the following this idea of an actualization of that sacrifice for the sake of realizing its presence: '*That act*, by which the Savior Jesus two thousand years ago saved all times and space, is pushed into divine eternity, where it is imperishably present and *reactualized each time there is a consecration*' ('*Adorable eucharistie*', a conference given to contemplative religious, 1971, in *Le mystère de l'Eucharistie*, Paris, Téqui, 1981, p. 66. Italics are ours).

very particular rite by which certain Eastern liturgies express symbolically the actuation of the mystery of Pentecost in the Mass.

In this perspective, that of the actuation of the totality of Christ's Mystery, the actions of the elevation of the victim merits a special mention, whether it concerns that which takes place in the consecration or that which accompanies the final doxology. Whatever be the details of their historical origin, their profound significance is the following. By thus elevating the immolated and glorified Christ, in order more to present Him to His Father than for the adoration of the faithful, the priest identifies himself with Christ the High Priest, and he and the whole Church join Christ in the act by which the latter eternally presents Himself before the Father, with the power of His poured out blood, in order to intercede in our favour (Heb 7:25; 9:12–24; 12:24). Thus, the two intentions, adoration and intercession, become but one; for, in adoring Christ, the faithful associate themselves with His offering and present their own 'eucharist' to God.

It is here, then, primarily and essentially, that the 'admirable exchange' of the sacrifice is accomplished: Christ takes the Church's sacrifice in order to place it and accomplish it in His own; the Church's sacrifice and the Church herself, by Christ's acceptance, enter into the sacrifice of her Lord. Just as it does not matter in what manner the Word becomes Incarnate, but rather the fact that He took flesh from and in the womb of her who represents both the ultimate 'small remnant' of Israel and the immaculate first fruits of the Church, so it does not matter in what manner He offers His sacrifice in the Mass, nor what matter He makes the substance of His Body, but rather the fact that it is from and in that bread and wine which His people offer to Him for that purpose during the offertory, and in which the people give themselves symbolically to Him. Such that while at Calvary, where she had already been represented by the Virgin Mary, the Church had been offered and immolated in Christ as in her Head, on the altar she consciously and freely ratifies that offering of herself in and through her Head. This happens through her action of offertory, before the action of sacrifice that Christ accomplishes at the consecration. The Church does this again, after the sacrifice, by her prayer of anamnesis, which the priest pronounces in her name,[28] and by her final 'Amen,' an acclamation of the people of God the importance of which cannot be emphasized and solemnized enough.[29]

In order to make known the exchange of the divine and the human that takes place in the sacrifice, we returned to the parallelism that exists between the consecration, where Christ takes possession of His Church in order to give Himself to her, and the Incarnation, where the Word took possession of the Immaculate Virgin, the first fruits and 'Mother of the Church,' in order to give Himself to her. We also recalled that, while the Church had been present and immolated on Calvary in the flesh of Christ, insofar as the whole Body is present in its Head, the Church had also been represented there through the person of Mary, who then received from Christ the title 'Woman' (Jn 19:26), and thus appeared as 'the New Eve' from the side of the 'New Adam,' that is, as the type of the Church-Bride. From this twofold link it happens that the Virgin Mary is equally present at the sacrifice of the Altar and that she continues to exercise there her co-mediation in the radiance of Christ's one mediation. It seemed opportune to mention in passing this aspect (still too little known) of the Eucharistic Mystery. We really need, however, to look to the studies especially dedicated to this question in order to develop it appropriately.[30]

---

28 St Robert Bellarmine, *loc. cit.*: '*Sacrificium autem in persona Christi principaliter offertur. Itaque ista oblatio consecrationem subsequens est quaedam testificatio quod tota Ecclesia consentiat in oblationem a Christo factam et simul cum illo offerat.*' Cited by Pius XII, in *Mediator Dei, AAS* 35, 1947, p. 554. Bellarmine speaks of the oblation, while with the liturgists we call it the 'anamnesis'. We showed above, however, that, while it begins with the words of the anamnesis, the prayer '*Unde et memores*' is epicletic, asking God to accept the Church's *offering*. One thus discovers that it is indeed the oblation which is the heart here.

29 Pius XII, *ibid*, p. 560.

30 In 1980, the Days of the 'Société Française d'Etudes Mariales' were dedicated to this theme. See '*Etudes Mariales*', '*Bulletin de la SFEM*', pp. 36–7, 1979–

c) *The communion.* The exchange, which began at the offertory by the offering of the Church and was realized in the consecration by the action of Christ, remains in expectation for its consummation. It will take place in the communion, where Christ's flesh will become the Church's nourishment. By the consecration Christ made His own that which the Church offered in her preparatory offering. Here, it is the Church who makes her own that which Christ offered in sacrifice to His Father for her in the consecration: His immolated flesh and poured out blood. The exchange is thus consummated. The Church is given to Christ, Who makes her His own. Then Christ was united to His Church in order to offer her in Himself to His Father. Now He gives Himself to her in order that she might make Him her own, certainly, but this is ultimately in order to finish making her His own. For, in the communion it is not Christ Who is transformed into man, but man into Christ.[31] And this whole movement of exchange must go back to God, Who is its beginning, 'for the praise of the glory of His grace, in which He graced us in His beloved Son' (Eph 1:6).

It is in this way that 'the Eucharist makes the Church,' that is to say that Christ Himself forms for Himself His Mystical Body, each Christian uniting himself by the Eucharist to Christ, and in Christ to the Father, and all Christians thus entering into the great communion of the 'Mystical Body.' The fact that this expression first signified the sacramental Body of Christ, and then later came to designate the Church, is highly significant. If it risks the danger of cutting off the Eucharist from the Church,[32] in itself it marks out well the continuity that exists between

---

1980, titled: '*Marie et l'Eucharistie.*' We mention in particular the works of H. Crouzel on the Ante–Nicene Fathers; of Fr Yousif, on St Ephrem, as well as the doctrinal synthesis if P. M. J. Nicolas, and our own contribution: *Présence de Marie à l'Eglise dans l'Eucharistie.*

[31] According to the famous text of St Augustine: '*Nec tu me in te mutabis sicut cibum carnis tuae, sed tu mutaberis in me*' (*Confessions*, L. VII, cap. 10, 16).

[32] This danger was noted by Fr De Lubac, in his book *Corpus Mysticum. L'Eucharistie et l'Eglise au Moyen Age* ('Théologie'—3), Paris, Aubier, 1949 (2nd edition).

the two. It is this which is expressed by St Thomas, a privileged witness of Tradition, when he writes and repeats that the Eucharist is 'the sacrament of the Church's unity.'[33] What we have here is nothing other than the accomplishment of Christ's promises: 'He who eats My flesh and drinks My blood lives in Me and I in him' (Jn 6:56).

The Lord immediately adds: 'As the living Father has sent Me, and I live by the Father, so he that eats Me shall live by Me' (verse 57). And St Augustine comments: 'Let the faithful become the Body of Christ if they wish to live by the Spirit of Christ. Nothing lives by the Spirit of Christ except the Body of Christ.'[34] It is because He communicates to us the Holy Spirit that Christ, through His Body, allows us to live His own life. We explained why and how at the end of our second part, and we shall return to it in a moment. We would like simply to recall here how this action of the Spirit in communion is signified liturgically. For the Roman tradition, in its fixed parts, one scarcely finds anything except the prayer '*Supplices,*' situated after the consecration, and in which was seen the true 'epiclesis of the Roman Mass,' which corresponds, moreover, to the most ancient form of the epiclesis.[35] It invokes 'the heavenly blessing and grace' upon those who will communicate. The Byzantine liturgy symbolizes this action of the Holy Spirit in the communion by the rite of '*Zeon.*' Water and fire being the symbols of the Spirit, a drop of hot water (warmed by fire), is poured into the chalice at the moment of communion in order

---

[33] S.T. III, q. 73, a. 2 Sed contra: citing 1 Cor 10:17; '*Ex quo patet quod Eucharistia sit sacramentum ecclesiasticae unitatis*'; cf. *ibid* a. 1; a. 3; a. 4; etc.

[34] *In Ioan. Ev. Tract.* 26, 13: '*Fiant corpus Christi, si volunt vivere de spiritu Christi. De spiritu Christi non vivit nisi corpus Christi*' (PL 35, 1612).

[35] Cf. L. Bouyer, *Eucharistie*, pp. 300–304. B. Botte, *L'ange du sacrifice et l'épiclèse de la messe romaine au moyen age*, in *Rech. De Théol. Anc. et Mediev.*, 1, 1929, 285–308; F. Carol, art. '*Anamnèse*', in *DACL* 1, 1892. cf. J. A. Jungmann, *Missarum solemnia*, III, p. 108. Others, on the other hand, want to see the epiclesis of the Roman Canon in the prayer '*Quam oblationem*', which immediately precedes the consecration (cf. C. Giraudo, op. cit., pp. 353 ff). Moreover, one must recognize that, despite the absence of the mention of the Holy Spirit, its epicletic character is undeniable.

to signify that the blood of Christ will give the Holy Spirit to those who receive it. In his 'Mystagogy,' Nicholas Cabasilas explains the symbolism of this rite, unknown in the West, but completely doctrinally founded.

> It signifies the descent of the Holy Spirit on the Church. This descent took place for the first time after Christ had been immolated, after He rose and accomplished the whole economy. Since then this descent *has always taken place after the sacrifice is accomplished:* the Paraclete comes, in fact, to those who communicate worthily in this sacrifice.[36]

After communion, its prayer and its thanksgiving, the liturgical celebration of the Mystery is complete. Its realization in life will begin, or rather will be pursued; for it is in the liturgical action that the life of the Christian begins. It is there also that that life will be completed. In this perspective, although this interpretation seems lacking in historical foundation in the texts,[37] one can understand the final *'Ite missa est'* not only as a dismissal, but as a sending on a mission as well. This is not a simple, pious and free interpretation, but an intrinsic requirement of the liturgical act. For, it is in order that we might accomplish in our life His sacrifice, in which we communicate, that Christ, by His flesh and blood, fills us with His Spirit.

Thus the liturgical celebration of the Holy Sacrifice of the Mass is completed. The entire Mystery of Christ, its whole 'economy,' according to the expression of Nicholas Cabasilas and the Greek Fathers, is actualized there. It is normal then to find there, at the center, the divine-human reality of the *'admirable commercium,'* and at the end, the sending on a mission. St Augustine praised both. 'By a mutual participation,' he said, 'He realized with us a wonderful exchange (*'mirum commercium'*): ours was that by which He is dead, and to Him belongs

---

[36] N. Cabasilas, *Explanation of the Rites of the Divine Liturgy*, nos. 11 and 12.

[37] According to B. Botte and Ch. Mohrmann, *L'Ordinaire de la messe, Texte critique, traduction et etudes* (Paris–Louvain, Cerf–Abb. Du Mont César, 1953), pp. 145 ff.

that by which we live.'[38] And again: 'If you are the Body of Christ and His members, it is your Mystery that is placed on the table of the Lord: it is your Mystery that you received.'[39] In the same sermon and in the same style, extremely dense and concise (St Augustine is occasionally capable of this), he proposes the idea of the mission when he adds immediately after: 'It is to this that you respond 'Amen' ... Be the member of Christ in order that your 'Amen' be true'; that is, be truly, by your whole life, a living and faithful member of Him Whom you received. And do this 'until He comes again'; for, the Mystery, accomplished sacramentally in the liturgy and by the works of truth in life, waits in expectation for its eschatological completion. The entire meaning and value of the Eucharist is being the source of strength of which the Christian is in need in order to hold out and await this.

4. *How are its fruits communicated to us?*—By the Holy Spirit, we said, insofar as He is the One Who 'completes' the work of the Trinity in His creation, and more still in redemption. He does this by His 'proper' effect, which is to draw us into His 'Breath,' and in this, into the movement of love that goes from the Father to the Son (Jn 6:44) and above all, for us, from the Son to the Father (Jn 14:5; Rom 8:14 ff). Here again Nicholas Cabasilas sums up well the thought of the Fathers, such as we ourselves tried to synthesize it (at the end of our second part):

> ... because the Holy Spirit at first filled up the flesh of the Lord, the bearer of the divinity, ... from that flesh as from a source, and with it, He is poured into the Church, and continues to be poured into her. This is what John, divinely inspired as he was, expressed in these words: 'From His fullness we have all received' (Jn 1:16).[40]

---

[38] *Sermo guelferbytanus 3 (PLS 2, 545–6)*: 'Mirum proinde nobiscum egit mutua participatione commercium: nostrum erat, unde mortuus est; illius erit unde vivamus.'

[39] *Sermo CCLXXII (PL 38 1247)*: 'Si ergo vos estis corpus Christi et membra, mysterium vestrum in mensa Domini positum est: mysterium vestrum accipitis.'

[40] N. Cabasilas, *Explanation of the Rites of the Divine Liturgy*.

Two questions are to be examined here: 1) How does the Holy Spirit intervene in the Eucharist in order to sanctify it, to consecrate it, to fill it with Himself? 2) How, from there, does He communicate Himself to the faithful? We already treated these in our preceding reflections, but we must now gather together all that we said in order to synthesise it and bring it to completion.

*   *   *

With regards to the first question, one can practically reduce it to the *epiclesis,* that prayer invoking the Holy Spirit in order that He might descend upon the offerings and upon the Church in order to sanctify them. This prayer has an important place in the liturgies as well as in the Eastern sacramental theology (albeit later); while the West has not attributed to it the same importance. One can see the outline of this in the offertory prayer '*Veni Sanctificator,*' which is clearly addressed to the Holy Spirit. Is the prayer '*Quam oblationem,*' which immediately precedes the consecration, an epiclesis? It seems difficult to affirm this.[41] We saw above how it is necessary to see the proper epiclesis of the Roman liturgy in the prayer '*Supplices,*' which follows the consecration. It must be noted, however, that it is not pronounced over the matter to be consecrated, but only over the people who will communicate. Most importantly, it must be stated that the words of the epiclesis are those of a prayer, and that they are not sacramental in the strict sense: they do not contribute to the 'confecting' of the sacrament. Very timely as they are, insofar as they recall the action of

---

[41] J. A. Jungmann, *Missarum solemnia*, III, p. 110. Some, nevertheless, have done so (cf. see above, note 755). The Reform of the Roman Missal returned the epiclesis to a place of honor. The 'Prex II' asks after the consecration that those who communicate be 'gathered together by the Spirit into one body.' The 'Prex III' invokes the action of the Holy Spirit before the consecration: 'Sanctify them (the offerings) by Your Spirit,' and after, in order to ask that 'the Spirit make of them (the faithful) one eternal offering to Your glory'. Just as the 'Prex IV' has an epiclesis before and after the consecration. This insistence on the epiclesis is one of the characteristic marks of the recent liturgical reform.

the Holy Spirit, they are not necessary either for the consecration of the matter or for the communion of the faithful.

We have a clear proof of this with regards to the consecration in the fact that this invoking of the Holy Spirit is found very often after it. Thus in the anaphora of St James:

> Send Thy Holy Spirit upon us and upon these gift that we offer Thee ... in order that they might make of the bread this holy Body of Christ, and of this cup this precious Blood of Christ, in order that they might serve for all who receive them as a remission of sins and eternal life ... and the strengthening of Thy holy Church.[42]

Similarly in the anaphora of St John Chrysostom:

> And we beseech Thee, our God ... : send Thy Holy Spirit upon us and upon these gifts presented; and grant that this bread become the precious Body of Your Christ ... and that in this chalice there be the precious Blood of Your Christ ... in order that they serve for those who receive them ... as a remission of sins.[43]

More examples could be cited.[44] In all these cases one notes the twofold movement of the epiclesis, corresponding as it does to the twofold movement that realizes the '*admirabile commercium*' of the Eucharist: the Holy Spirit is invoked in order that He might make of the bread the Body of Christ and that that Body might sanctify those who receive it, and that it might build them up in the Church, that is, in order that it might make of them the Mystical Body of the same Christ. Especially noteworthy is that this invocation of the Holy Spirit takes place after the consecration, which makes sense with regards to the second intention, but not to the first. For, it is a dogmatic truth that transubstantiation, and the immolation and oblation of the sacrifice along with it, takes place, in virtue of the sacramental words of Christ, in the

---

[42] A. Hänggi–I. Pahl, *Prex eucharistica* (Fribourg, Ed. Univ., 1968), pp. 244–61.
[43] *Ibid.*, pp. 224–8.
[44] Anaphora of St Basil (*ibid*, pp. 348–56), of St Mark (*ibid*, pp. 102–14), etc.

consecration.[45] The epiclesis of the Roman Canon is therefore much truer when it restricts itself, after the consecration, to invoking the Holy Spirit upon the faithful, in order that their communion in the sacramental Body of Christ might sanctify them. It is interesting to note that such was already the case in the Canon of Hippolytus:

> And we ask Thee to send Thy Holy Spirit upon the oblation of the holy Church. In gathering them together, allow Thy holy ones who receive it, to be filled with the Holy Spirit, that they might be truly strengthened in faith, that we might praise Thee and glorify Thee by Thy Son (or servant: *'puerum'*) Jesus Christ ... [46]

In these conditions, what meaning, one will ask, is to be given to those epicleses of the Eastern liturgies, which invoke the Holy Spirit in order that He might bring about transubstantiation after it has already taken place? The only meaning possible is that of an anamnesis: this invocation explains what just took place, and it 'recalls' that it is by the working of the Holy Spirit that the consecration is made. It remains that, while it presents the great advantage of expressing that action of the Holy Spirit in the central act of the Mass, this prayer, by the place that it occupies in these liturgies, constitutes an anomaly. It represents a still imperfect stage, at least on this point, in the development of sacramental theology.

---

[45] This truth had been proclaimed at the Council of Florence (DS 1321; 1352) and at the Council of Trent (*ibid*, 1633–7). It is this that obliges priests to pronounce the words of consecration in order to concelebrate sacramentally (*Decree of the Holy Office*, 8 March 1957: *ibid*, 3928; cf. see above, Ch. IV and Ch. V). Touching the very essence of the sacrament, and founded on its institution by Christ, these truths are valuable for all times, independently of the idea that one was able to make of the consecration at different epochs and in different regions of the Church. That the epiclesis does not contribute sacramentally and that it is not necessary for the consecration is also taught by the Church's Magisterium: by Pope Benedict XII in 1341 (*ibid*, 1017), by Pius VII in 1822 (*ibid*, 2718), by St Pius X in 1910 (*ibid*, 3556), etc.

[46] Ed. Dom Botte ('Sources chrétiennes'–11), Paris, Cerf, 1946, p. 33.

Furthermore, there is a proof in an anaphora that, even in the Eastern tradition, this invocation of the Holy Spirit is not considered as an absolute necessity for the consecration. The anaphora, not one of the smallest, is of Serapion. Here it is the Word Who is invoked, always after the consecration, in order to bring about the transformation of the offerings:

> God of truth, let Thy Holy Word come upon this bread in order that it may become the Body of the Word, and upon this cup that it may become the cup of the Blood of the Truth; and grant that all who will communicate will received the remedy of life, etc.[47]

By this epiclesis of the Word, that is, the uncreated Word, this formula is, in one sense, nearer to the truth of the sacraments, since it is by the created word of Christ, which He Himself pronounces through His minister, that the mystery is accomplished. It is by this Word, Himself sent by the Father, that the Holy Spirit is sent in order to 'make' the sacrament along with all that it includes. For, the Spirit does not act except by 'completing' the work of the Three Persons of the Trinity in the Eucharistic liturgy: the consecration of the matter offered by the faithful and the sanctification of the faithful thanks to the consecrated matter, and consecrated by Christ by means of His priestly minister and the sacramental words in which the entire Trinity is at work.

With regards to the consecration, what is at stake here is the priestly power of the priest, as Fr Congar saw so well.[48] We would add

---

[47] *Prex eucharistica*, pp. 128–32.

[48] Y. M. Congar, *Pneumatologie ou Christomonisme dans la tradition latine*; in 'Ecclesia a Spiritu Sancto edocta' (*see above*, note 36), p. 50: 'To insist on the causality of the words of institution, is to begin to consider the functional person of the priest.' Several references follow on that 'sacramental value of the functional person of the priest,' among others St John Damascene, *De proditione Iudae*, hom. I, 6 (*PG* 49, 380) and the Western tradition. These reflections allow one to see the necessity of developing the question of the epiclesis through an historical, liturgical and theological study. We note the suggestive study, although without a true conclusion, of C. Lepelley: *Le Saint Esprit et l'Eucharistie: la signification de l'Epiclèse*, in *Les quatres fleuves*, no. 9

that, even more so it is the 'form' of the sacrament, although these two aspects are inseparably connected. This is why, while in itself the prayer of the epiclesis before the consecration is an excellent thing insofar as it signifies the essential aspect of the Mystery, namely, the action of the Holy Spirit in the consecration, a certain insistence, nevertheless, on its importance cannot be without equivocation; for, through the minimization of the words of consecration the proper function of the priest is affected. Yet there is here a twofold misinterpretation, theological and liturgical. If it is absolutely certain, in fact, that the Holy Spirit brings about the consecration, this happens only according to His own proper mode, which is that of the 'completion' of the Trinitarian action, an action that is always indivisible. And this happens most especially starting with the word of the Word Incarnate. This is why His action is not linked to a previous prayer of invocation, but to the word that Christ pronounces through His minister over the matter to be consecrated. Christ's humanity is the *'organon,'* the 'conjoined instrument' by which the uncreated Word acts in order to send the Spirit together with the Father. In virtue of the priestly character, which unites and conforms him to Christ the High Priest, the person of the priestly minister is the 'separated instrument' through which the Word Incarnate acts in the sacrament. Therefore, in virtue of this character, it is by that word of the priest (but a word that really is always Christ's) that the Spirit acts in order to consecrate the gifts in an action that is common with the Father and the Word.

In the consecration, therefore, the person of the priest disappears to some extent behind that of Christ, Who pronounces the words Himself. In that supreme disappearance, however, that same person of the priest is exalted; for, Christ does not use His priest as an instrument without a soul. He takes him up in his whole human reality and He does not act through him except by identifying him, in some

---

(Paris, Beauchesne, 1979), pp. 79–94; and especially: *Le Saint Esprit dans la liturgie* (Bibliotheca 'Ephemerides Liturgicae'–8), Rome, Ed. Liturgiche, 1977 (Acts of the 16th Week of Liturgical Studies of the Holy See).

way (namely sacramentally) with His own person. The supreme effacement: the supreme exaltation of the priest.

*   *   *

In the communion, which is the proper means by which the Eucharist completes the production of its fruits, it is still by His minister that Christ gives Himself as nourishment to His members. He gives them His sacramental Body in order to make of them His Mystical Body. And it is by His immolated and glorified Body that the Spirit is given to those who communicate. Here especially a previous prayer of invocation to the Holy Spirit is fitting: both, in order to obtain from God the abundance of His grace, that is the gift of the Holy Spirit Who operates, and in order to dispose the hearts of the faithful to receive that grace. We saw above the rite of the '*Zeon*,' by which the Byzantine liturgy symbolizes this action of the Holy Spirit in those who communicate in the Body of Christ. Furthermore, it is known that, where 'sacramental communion' is not possible, a certain participation in the fruit of the Eucharist can be obtained by what is called a 'spiritual communion,' that is, by that act which makes one united to the sacramental Body of Christ by faith, charity, and desire.[49] Where the desire is great, the fruits of such a communion can be as well. This fecundity is the secret of God. And it is equally necessary to recall that without that spiritual communion, the sacramental is but a sterile reception, even culpable reception, of a Substance the divine majesty of which one does not perceive.[50]

One will ask, 'And what about those who do not directly participate at the Mass, what fruits can they draw from it?' This question is of the greatest importance for us; for the ecclesial value of private Masses and, consequently, of the multiplication of Masses will depend on the response that will be given. Yet the liturgy, the theology of the sacrifice and intercession, as well as the traditional practice and teaching of the Church, are formal and unanimous here. The Mass: each Mass is a

---

[49]   Council of Trent, *Session* XIII, *cap.* 8: St Thomas, *S.T.* III, q. 80, a. 1.
[50]   Council of Trent, *ibid*; St Thomas, *ibid*

source of graces because it is the source of a new outpouring of the Holy
Spirit for the entire Church and even, in a certain manner, for all of
humanity. The liturgy: these are all the prayers of the Roman Canon—without speaking of the other prayers of this rite or of the other
liturgical traditions—which proclaim that universal intention. The
sacrifice: the prayers mention that it is offered first of all ('*In primis*') 'for
the holy Catholic Church,' for the living and the dead (twofold
'*Memento*'), etc. The theology of the sacrifice: the entire Old Testament
would have to be reread here. We simply cite the case of holy Job, offering
holocausts for his children (Job 1:5), and that of Judas Maccabeus, who
made an offering of sacrifices in the Temple for the deceased (2 Macc.
12:43). And the one sacrifice of the New Testament, that of the one
Mediator, had been offered in ransom for the sins of the whole world (1
Jn 2:2). Yet it is this one sacrifice that is immolated and offered at Mass.
The traditional practice of the Church, while it has not returned to the
ritual sacrifices that had been abolished by Christ's sacrifice, has been
that of multiplying always more the sacramental offering of Christ's
sacrifice. We have already shown this.[51] With respect to the teaching of
the Church, it would suffice to recall the dogma formulated at Trent: the
sacrifice of the Mass does not profit only those who communicate
(*sumenti*), but 'it must be offered for all the living and deceased, in
satisfaction for sins and penalties, and for other necessities.'[52]

St Thomas gives us the theological explanation of the doctrine
upon which rests all the testimonies, in saying that, the Eucharist
profits those who receive it 'by mode of sacrament and mode of
sacrifice,' while for the others, those for whom it is offered, it profits
only 'by mode of sacrifice.'[53] What does that mean, 'by mode of

---

[51]   Cf. see above, Chapter VIII.

[52]   Council of Trent, *Session XXII, can.* 3.

[53]   This distinction is explicitly made by St Thomas Aquinas (*S.T.*III, q. 79, a. 7).
       It was already virtually present in his predecessors, especially his teacher, St
       Albert the Great (see the references in A. Piolanti, *Il Corpo mistico di Cristo e
       le sue relazioni con l'eucaristia* ('Studi di Teologia medievale'–1), Rome, Pont.
       Univ. Lateran., 1969 (publication of a most remarkable thesis from 1930), pp.

sacrifice'? And furthermore, how does one explain that efficacy of union with the Body of Christ 'by mode of sacrament'? The response to both these questions, as we have seen, is based on the following truths: Christ in the Eucharist renews the totality of His Mystery; He does this as Head, Who contains in Himself the totality of the Body; He does this in His own Body, which, crucified and glorified, is used as an 'instrument' in order to communicate the Holy Spirit by Whom He Himself lives.

Because Christ renews, that is, because Christ actualizes here and now the totality of His Mystery around His Passion, one must say of this sacramental act that which is said of the acts of the historical accomplishment of that Mystery, especially of the Paschal sacrifice. By it He merits and makes satisfaction (no longer by Himself, since He is now in glory, but by and in His members), He prays and intercedes for us;[54] by His death He draws us along into the death to sin, and by His resurrection He draws us into glory.[55]

188–90). Without formally adopting this distinction, the Council of Trent uses it practically for defending the value of private Masses (*Sess.* XXII, *cap.* 6). On the modern discussions raised by this question, see Piolanti (op. cit., p. 189): Does the Eucharist produce the grace of union with Christ as a sacrifice or as a sacrament? (M. de la Taille, *Mysterium Fidei*, 3ʳᵈ ed., 1931, p. 541). However, these discussion are outdated if one considers that it is by the gift of the Holy Spirit that the Eucharist unites us to Christ both as a sacrifice and as a sacrament; and especially if one ceases to oppose these two insepara-ble dimensions of the Eucharist, namely the sacrifice and sacrament. It is by both that the Eucharist is made and brings forth its fruit.

[54] Cf. St Thomas, *S.T.* III, q. 48, a. 1 (merit), a. 2 (satisfaction); *Suppl.*, q. 71, a. 1; a. 9 (Christ presents His prayers and suffrages to the Father). St Albert the Great emphasizes the aspect of suffrage and merit (*In IV Sent.*, d. 45, a. 1, sol.; cf. A. Piolanti, op. cit., p. 136). Just as St Robert Bellarmine, who insists more on the power of this intercession of Christ's sacrifice: it obtains (*impetrat*) what it asks for: 'Sacrificium missae vim habet per modum impetrationis: et ejus propria efficientia est impetrare' (*De Missa*, II, cap. 4). Etc.

[55] This can be affirmed on the basis of the truth recalled above: the celebration of the Eucharist reproduces the totality of Christ's Mystery. cf. *S.T.* III, q. 56, a. 1–2; q. 79, a. 2. See also q. 73, a. 4 and q. 60, a. 3 (the sacraments are a sign

Christ can do all this because we are united to Him as members to a Head, forming with Him 'almost one sole mystical person,' says St Thomas. As such, the reparation that He offers to His Father and the merit that He acquires has value for us.[56] More profoundly, it is thanks to that union that He communicates His Spirit to us, Who makes that union ever more intimate and alive.

And it is by His Body, as by an instrument or a source, that He communicates His Spirit to us. Fr Mersch justly remarked that the notion of causality or efficiency, without disappearing, tends to fade away here behind the notion of influence or influx.[57] More exactly, one is explained by the other. To the notion of instrument and the image of a source we must add another comparison, that of the relation between the head of the body and the members. We thus refer back to the study on the capital grace of Christ. This must be developed on one hand, by the doctrine of the union of the soul and body, and on the other hand, by the Trinitarian doctrine of divine processions and missions. We mentioned above the broad outlines

---

of the 'glory', for which they give us grace). One can compare to this doctrine the hymn from the Office of the Blessed Sacrament: '*O Sacrum convivium ... et futurae gloriae nobis pignus datur.*'

[56] It is the whole truth of the Mystical Body that is at stake here: '*Christo data est gratia non solum sicut singulari personae, sed inquantum est caput Ecclesiae, ut scilicet ab ipso redundaret ad membra*' (St Thomas, *Sum. Theol.*, III, q. 48, a. 1). '*Caput et membra sunt quasi una persona mystica. Et ideo satisfactio Christi ad omnes fideles pertinet sicut ad sua membra. Inquantum etiam duo homines sunt unum in caritate, unus pro alio satisfacere potest*' (ibid, 2, ad. 1).

[57] E. Mersch, *Le Corps Mystique du Christ. Etudes de théologie historique*, Bruxelles–Paris, l'Ed. Univ.–DDBr., 1951 (3rd ed.), vol. II, pp. 183 ff. See p. 195, note 2: 'The traditional doctrine is that this influx is twofold: internal and external, or the infusion of grace and the external government. The first is the most essential and proper to Christ; the second is exercised also by ecclesiastical superiors in Christ's name. S. T. III, q. 8, a. 6; *De Veritate*, 29, 4, ad.2.' It must be added, however, that especially through the sacraments, the 'instruments separated from the divinity', the ministerial priesthood contributes to spreading the interior influx. And this can be extended to all the members of the Mystical Body by reason of the communion of life that exists among them.

of this latter doctrine. Now we see the light that the first can shine on our understanding of this efficacy, or influx, of the Eucharistic sacrifice insofar as it is a sacrifice offered for the Church.

The soul, St Thomas teaches, following Aristotle,[58] is united to the body as its form and its 'motor.' As the form, it is immediately united to the body, by definition.[59] As 'motor,' it moves the body through the 'spirit,' which it influences.[60] This physiological notion of the spirit ('*spiritus,*' breath) has given place to others with the progress of science. We hear about a nervous influx, or even of the electromagnetic currents that travel between cells, etc. But the profound reality is always the same, and it is always as mysterious and indefinable, for the very reason that it is the reality of life. The persistence of these notions of influence, of influx and of others in trying to define its operations, is significant. Thus, explains St Thomas, just as the 'spirit' flows from the soul of the body and makes the members move, so the Holy Spirit flows forth from Christ in order to move His members. We see that St Thomas practically identifies the notions of head and soul here,[61] but this point is of secondary importance. Christ therefore is the Head of the Church, or its soul, not in the sense of its substantial form,[62] but because He is the one Who moves the members of His

---

[58] And in complete conformity with biblical anthropology, despite the fact that it is in another language.

[59] St Thomas, *S.T.* I, q. 76, a. 1.

[60] *Ibid.*, a. 7; a. 4.; etc. The importance of this notion in thomistic anthropology, which is here that of its time, has not been noted enough.

[61] *Ibid.*, III, q. 8, a. 2. This question 8 of the *Tertia Pars*, dedicated to the 'capital grace' of Christ, contains the substance of a treatise on the Church as the Mystical Body of Christ. St Thomas uses the expression: '*Tota Ecclesia dicitur unum corpus mysticum per similitudinem ad naturale corpus hominis*' (a. 1). It is in article 2 that he practically identifies the head with the soul, in order to explain its comparison (which is that of St Paul): that belongs to the soul what is said of the head, namely, 'to influence' (the word used) the members. cf. *In Ep. ad Eph.*, 1, *lect.* 8 (61); etc. (The numbers in parentheses are from the Marietti edition.). On the *capital grace* of Christ, cf. *De Ver.*, 29, 4–5.

[62] To assert this would be to fall into the error condemned by Pius XII, and which

Body by sending them the Holy Spirit: 'He gives grace or the Holy Spirit by a certain efficiency';[63] because He is 'the Head [Who] ... bestows grace on the Church's members';[64] etc. Thus we find again here the communication of the Holy Spirit from the humanity of the Word Incarnate in the continuation of His intra-Trinitarian procession from the uncreated Word:[65] 'Christ works through His Holy Spirit.'[66] This doctrine had practically been taken up again by Pius XII in his Encyclical on the Church, the 'Mystical Body' of Christ.[67] He develops it most especially with regards to the Eucharist, which, he teaches, 'communicates to us the very Author of the heavenly grace in order that we might draw out that Spirit in Him.'[68] If therefore the

---

is easily explained by the historical context in which the Encyclical *Mystici corporis* is written.

[63]   St Thomas, *S.T.* III, q. 8, a. 1. By reason of His hidden role, St Thomas compares the Holy Spirit to the heart, without insisting on this comparison (*ibid*, 3 m). cf. Card. L. M. Ciappi, *Gesù Cristo: Capo o Cuore del Corpo Mistico*, in *Il Cuore di Cristo Centro del Mistero della Salvezza*, Roma, Il Cuore di Cristo Editrice, 1981, pp. 162–8.

[64]   *Ibid.*, 6, 2 a.

[65]   One must say about this communication, emission or mission of the Holy Spirit what one says about grace (the production of which is brought to 'completion' in man by the Holy Spirit), namely that only the Word, with the Father, is His *author* ('*auctor*') because He is God, and therefore He alone sends Him with authority ('*auctoritas*'); but that His humanity concurs in this mission instrumentally ('*instrumentaliter*'), by reason of His hypostatic union with the Word. cf. *ibid.*, q. 8, a. 1. This mediation of Christ's humanity is at the basis of the entire theology of the Church, of the priesthood (ministerial and baptismal), and the sacraments, which are extensions of this humanity. Therefore, it is only by this 'capital' mediation and its hierarchical and ecclesial extensions that the Holy Spirit is poured forth into the Church. It is here also that one can find the place and mission of our Lady. We cannot overemphasize today the importance of this doctrine, as well as the urgent need to develop it. For, this created participation in the mission (uncreated in its origin) of the Holy Spirit is a profound mystery. One must note, however, that it is first of all apropos of Christ's created humanity that one encounters it.

[66]   St Thomas, *In Ep. ad Eph.*, II, lect. 5 (121).

[67]   Cf. *AAS* 35, 1943, pp. 215 ff.

Holy Spirit is the source of grace,[69] we say, then let us say that His immediate or ultimate source is Christ, Who, being the source of the Spirit, is in Himself the cause or source of grace.[70] He is the source of the source. And this is why He is, in the Eucharist, 'the common good of the Church.'[71]

We see from then on what the sacrament of the Eucharist gives to those *to whom* it is given: the very source of the Holy Spirit and His grace, Christ, Who thus unites us to His sacrifice and allows us to unite

---

[68]   *Ibid.*, p. 233.

[69]   St Thomas, *In Ev. Joann.*, VII, *lect.* 5 (1090). Commenting on the words of Christ: 'If anyone is thirsty, let him come to Me and drink' (Jn 7:37 ff), St Thomas writes the following: *'Qui bibit credendo in Christum, haurit fontem aquae, quo hausto, vivescit conscientia, quae est venter interior hominis, et etiam ipsa fons erit. Unde dicitur* see above (4:13), *'Qui biberit ex hac aqua, fluet in eo fons aquae salientis.' Hic autem fons, qui hauritur, est Spiritus Sanctus.'* We could compare these words to the doctrine mentioned above (note 64), namely, by believing in Christ and uniting oneself to Him, which happens only by the power of the Holy Spirit, man receives this Spirit into himself, and he lives and becomes capable of communicating Him to others. Possessing in himself the Source, he becomes himself a source by participation. This is realized to the greatest degree when, conformed to Christ the High Priest through the priestly character, the priest accomplishes the very acts of Christ, the sacraments, especially the Eucharist. At this moment, more than any other, it is Christ Himself Who lives and acts in him (cf. Gal 2:20); and there is a difference of nature, and not simply of degree, between these acts and the other acts of the Christian life.

[70]   *Ibid.*; cf. VI, *lect.* 6 (963 ff); III, *lect.* 6 (544); etc. The notions of source, cause and principle are taken here interchangeably; one understands why in the twofold perspective of the mission of the Holy Spirit and the production of grace. It is not a question of choosing between the two, but of shedding light on the second by means of the first, and adding the third, and reciprocally.

[71]   *S.T.* III, q. 65, a. 3: *'Bonum commune spirituale totius Ecclesiae continetur substantialiter in ipso eucharistiae sacramento.'* We find the explanation of this assertion in the *Commnentary on the Gospel of John* (VI, *lect.* 6 (954)): *'Cujus ratio est, quia continetur in ipso causa universalis omnium sacramentorum, scilicet Christus.'* See the thesis of J. Travers, *Valeur sociale de la Liturgie d'après saint Thomas d'Aquin* ('Lex orandi'–5), Paris, Cerf, 1946.

ourselves to it, in order that we might be able then to follow Him into His glory. We see also what the sacrifice alone gives to those *for whom* it is offered, even if they do not communicate in it sacramentally, even if they do not directly participate in its offering, and even if they do not know, at that moment, that it is offered for them: it merits for them this grace; it asks for it on their behalf; and first and foremost, it offers to the Father this superabundant satisfaction for their sins, Christ's satisfaction—'completed' by all that His accomplishment, realized in and by His Church, brings for the consummation of the redemptive work (cf. Col 1:24). For, it is the entire Church who, at each Mass, is offered and offers herself to the Father in Christ and through His priestly minister. Through the power of this reparation, these merits and this prayer, each Mass already obtains a certain effusion of the Spirit, a certain gift of grace for those for whom it is offered. They receive Him to a greater or lesser degree according to the gratuitous and merciful will of God, by reasons of the mysterious link, more or less immediate, which they have with Christ and the Church, but also according to the measure of their own interior dispositions. And this grace moves them to conversion, to come back to God and live always more for Him—which they will do by coming one day to receive the sacrament of the Eucharist.

This is what Nicholas Cabasilas said in the passage cited above: 'Since Pentecost, that descent of the Holy Spirit has always taken place when, in the Eucharist, the sacrifice is accomplished.' This is also what is expressed in the well-known prayer over the offering, cited by the Second Vatican Council at the beginning of its Constitution on the Liturgy: each time a Mass is celebrated, 'the work of our redemption is wrought' (*opus nostrae redemptionis exercetur*). Whence the conclusion that St Thomas logically draws: 'With the number of Masses the oblation of the sacrifice is multiplied. And therefore, it is also the effect of the sacrifice and the sacrament that is multiplied.'[72] This conclusion is also the Church's, who, the more she

---

[72] *S.T.* III, q. 79, a. 7: '*In pluribus vero missis multiplicatur sacrificii oblatio. Et ideo*

considers these truths, the more she encourages the practice of the private Mass in view of that multiplication of fruits from the one redemptive sacrifice.[73]

This is also what Luther relentlessly attacked, first by denying that the Mass is a sacrifice, then by using all his efforts to abolish what he called 'the horror of private Masses.'[74] Here the 'Reformer' was logically progressing within his own position. His doctrine and his attitude were diametrically opposed to that of the Church; but he was right in this, that there is a necessary connection between the dogma of the Mass as a sacrifice, the practice of private Masses, and the practice of the multiplication of Masses as offerings of that sacrifice for the salvation of the world.

This connection, it can be said, appears again today; for, from the disappearance of the consideration of the Mass as the 'Holy Sacrifice' comes both the loss of the sense of private Masses and the loss of the ecclesial value of the multiplication of Masses. This sense and this value, on the other hand, reappear when the doctrine of the Mass as a sacrifice is rediscovered. This is why, after having denounced (in the first part of the preceding chapter) the imprecision and inexactness, or even flagrant errors of the different teachings that try to explain the Eucharist, and that tend, to various degrees, to efface that central truth of the sacrifice of the Mass—after having denounced these, we showed (in the second part of that same chapter) how this truth is what furnishes the first principle that allows one to know the fundamental structure of the Eucharist. And after having analyzed (in

---

multiplicatur effectus sacrificii et sacramenti.'

[73] Cf. see above, note 771 and Ch. VIII.

[74] The title of one of his works: '*Von dem Greuel der Stillmesse*' (1525; WA 18, 8–36). Luther multiplied the attacks against private Masses. See also: '*Von der Winkelmess und Pfaffenweihe*' (1523; WA 38. See especially pp. 179–185; pp. 190–1, where one finds his famous discussion with the devil on the question); '*Disputatio contra missam privatam*' (1536; WA 39, pp. 134–73). His position on this point had been fully borrowed by all of Protestantism, as shown by Article 24 of the Augsburg Confession (See above, Chapter VII).

the present chapter) that structure of the liturgy of the Mass and the manner in which the divine action is exercised, we now deduce the consequences—as immediately practical as they are eminently salvific. For, the effusion of Christ's grace and the Holy Spirit's action in the Church principally depend on the unceasingly renewed offering (Mal 1:11) of the sacramental sacrifice of Christ and the Church. We would even be tempted to say, in considering the essentially sacramental character of the economy of redemption, that they depend completely on it (at least usually).

III. The Holy Sacrifice of the Mass and its Celebration and Multiplication

Having showed in the sacrifice the central reality around which the liturgy of the Eucharist is organized and structured, we must now see how it is also the fundamental principle upon which is constructed the theology of this liturgy. Concretely, we must develop the mystery of the *sacrifice* of the Mass, and show how it is around this that the other elements are integrated: the meal, the blessing and the congregation. We shall do this by way of synthesis. The truth is, the manner in which this integration takes place already appeared to us in the preceding analyses; but it will be useful to reconsider those various notes made in passing, and present an integral view. We shall then be prepared to understand—which is the goal of our work—the sense and the value of the different modes of celebrating the Mass, and consequently, to say (at least with respect to the principles) how they are to be harmonized for the greater good of the Church and glory of God.

The most perfect and most complete form of the celebration will definitely be that which shows best, from the sacrifice and the priesthood, the hierarchical and communitarian nature of the Eucharist. For, the act that is realized is not only a sacrifice, an act proper to the priesthood, but also the sacrifice of the Covenant, an act of the entire community encountering its Lord through the person of the mediator. To speak with precision, it is not simply the common notion of sacrifice, but that historically unique notion of the sacrifice of the 'New and eternal Covenant,' which allows one to know the structure of the Eucharist, both in its Mystery and its liturgy. It is meal, congregation and 'blessing' all at once; but it is in the framework of this unique sacrifice that the synthesis of the whole liturgy and the history of salvation is made.

1. The error of Fr De Broglie in his work, *Pour une théologie du festin eucharistique*, typical of the movement which in the years immediately after the war, launched or re-launched the idea of the Mass as both a meal and assembly[75]—his error, beside some very accurate and profound reflections, was not that he asked what, 'according to the Lord's intentions,' was '*essential*' in the action that He bequeathed to the Church.[76] In this he was perfectly correct. Where he erred was when he sought the essence first and foremost in the exterior rites of the Last Supper. This is how the aspect of the meal or the 'feast' came to him as a principal reality, especially for restoring the communitarian aspect of the Eucharist, and how he sought to understand the reality of the sacrifice by beginning with the meal. He did not see, as Schürmann did, the singularity and relative autonomy of the 'memorial' that Christ instituted during that meal; nor did he see that it was this action of Christ that the essence of Christ's intention and commandment was about. The meal was included therein, certainly—'Take, eat and drink'—but in subordination to the sacrifice—'This is My Body, which is given up for you; this cup is the New Covenant in My Blood.' This subordination does not appear in the exposition of Fr De Broglie: 'God ... can,' he writes, '*find Himself associated with us, or associate us with Himself, across from the same meals,* in such a way that those same meals are then presented *to God and to men,* in order that each one might benefit in his own way—God, under the form of the sacrifice; men, under the form of nutrition.'[77]

---

[75] Cf. see above, Chapter XI.

[76] Art. cit., pp. 7–10.

This manner of expression is not exact. In fact, it reduces the Eucharist for men to nothing but a meal: nutrition and a feast; and it does not say that it is beneficial and salvific for them insofar as it is a sacrifice, the very sacrifice of their redemption. Consequently, it does not see that the nutrition that is eaten in this meal is the immolated Victim. The eminent theologian rediscovers these truths, which he would not even dream of denying; and we follow him unreservedly when he adds a bit further: 'This manner of conceiving the sacrifice as associating us to God in one and the same feast is moreover classical and traditional.' Here, in fact, he correctly says that what associates us to God is first of all the sacrifice; for, it is in the sacrifice that the Covenant takes place, and the feast or meal appears as the complement to that primary and fundamental act.

Perhaps it would be possible to object to this by saying that this manner of presenting the matter goes against one's own intention. The meal appears here to be the end of the sacrifice and the latter, consequently, as a means in view of that end. Yet the end is more important than the means, which is subordinated to it and has its reason of being in relation to it. It is, therefore, the notion of the meal that dominates and explains definitively what the Eucharist is. To this we can easily respond by calling attention to the fact that this meal is itself for the sake of a communion, and that this communion that is to be fully realized is a communion of the Christian in the sacrifice of Christ. Therefore, it is this reality of the sacrifice which is at the end, as it is at the beginning and center of the whole Eucharistic mystery. The meal itself receives its proper character from the sacrifice and returns to it.

It would be fitting, furthermore, to distinguish in the meal the two complementary aspects: the eating and the feast that is to say, the eating in common. The first is the individual eating; it assures nourishment and realizes, in the Eucharist, the communion of each member with the Head. The second is communitarian; it corresponds to the fact of eating the same nourishment together, a sign and

---

[77]   *Ibid.*, p. 20.

profound means of human communion, and it assures, in the Eucharist, the building-up of the Mystical Body, that is, the communion of all the members with each other thanks to the communion of each one with the one Head of that Body. In such a way Christ's Mystical Body is built up through His sacramental Body.

We thus meet up with the thesis of those who see in the congregation—which is the Church—the fundamental principle that explains the liturgy and the Eucharistic mystery. One can see the element of truth upon which this thesis is founded; but an error can also be discerned here, which the thesis commits when it makes the reality of the congregation into an absolute principle, and especially when it ceases to see it in its relation to the sacrifice. For, just like the meal, it is to the sacrifice that the building-up of the congregation returns. It is by beginning with the sacrifice that the building-up of the congregation is realized; and it is from the sacrifice, therefore, that it takes its proper nature. It is by beginning with the sacrifice that it is realized, because it is the sacrifice that seals the Covenant, and because it is in the Covenant that the Church is built up, the 'people of God,' the assembly of all Christians. It is from the sacrifice that the congregation takes its proper nature, because the people thus established is the 'priestly and holy people' of the Covenant (Ex 19:6), whose vocation is to be united to their God in order to 'serve' Him, that is, in order 'to render worship' to Him (Ex 3:12) 'in spirit and in truth' (Jn 4:24), in justice and in love. The Church is a Paschal community.

This leads us to the theme of the 'blessing,' which the Paschal mystery assures and makes rise up to God, by giving to this word 'blessing' the profound and very vast meaning that it has here, a meaning in which is included thanksgiving, honor, praise, adoration and glorification of God. Certainly, everything in the Eucharist is a 'blessing,' for everything there is for the glory of the Lord and His grace. But it is by the sacrifice of Christ that God is supremely glorified, and it is the glory of this sacrifice that is rendered to Him in the Eucharist. Like the realities of the meal and the congregation, the 'blessing' does not find its proper nature and its Eucharistic meaning except in the central reality of the sacrifice. The prayer of 'blessing,' which accompanies the immolation and the oblation of this sacrifice, has for its end only the expressing of that which takes place essentially in the sacrifice itself.

We see this in Christ's 'priestly prayer' in St John: 'Father, glorify Thy Son in order that Thy Son might glorify Thee' (Jn 17:1). This prayer can be considered as the Eucharistic prayer par excellence; for, it is the one that accompanies the one sacrifice of redemption, which is accomplished in every celebration of the Eucharist. The Father glorifies and 'blesses' the Son, first, by allowing Him to accomplish by His Passion 'the work' of His love, the redemption of men (verses 2–4); then, by raising Him and establishing Him in His glory (verse 5). The Son glorifies the Father by revealing through that same Passion the love with which He has loved men: He thus reveals to them the Father's 'Name' and the fact that He is the Father of Mercies (verse 6; cf. Jn 3:16); and the Son will glorify the Father again when, exalted at His right hand, He will finish making Him known to men (verse 26), which He will do by sending them the Holy Spirit (Jn 16:13). This mutual glorification of the Father and the Son is accomplished by the whole mystery of the redemptive Incarnation; but it is in Easter that it is completed and reaches its summit, for it is there that love, which is its substance, is revealed and is given to the extreme, through the pouring out of Christ's blood and the offering of His life; and because this triumph of love in the gift of self to the point of death is necessarily completed by the Resurrection, which is not a simple return to the former life, which was marked by sin, but an entrance into the new life of glory, a holy and eternal life in the knowledge and love of God (Jn 17:3, 26).

These reflections on the Eucharist as a meal, a congregation and a 'blessing,' and on the manner in which these three essential aspects are integrated in the central reality of the sacrifice, help us to see better in what exactly the sacrifice consists; this, in its turn, allows us to understand better how that sacrifice is the alpha and omega of the Eucharistic celebration and Eucharistic theology. Here again, in order to show this in a final synthesis, it is sufficient to gather together a few principal reflections made during the previous chapters.

The Holy Sacrifice of the Mass is the sacrifice of Christ's Passover. This means that it is not simply death and destruction, but also and ultimately resurrection and new 'creation' (2 Cor 5:17). Not one without the other, nor even simply one beside the other, nor one after the other, but one *by* the other: death in view of life, entrance into life by that passage through death of temporal life. The 'transformation' that is accomplished is not simply 'destructive' but 'perfective.'[78]

The Passover being the summit of Christ's life, it takes up that life in its totality in order to accomplish it. The sacrifice that is its heart and proper work contains therefore in itself the totality of the 'Mystery' of redemption in order to 'complete' it. To speak of the sacrifice in this perspective is to name the part for the whole, *'pars pro toto,'* or better the whole through the part. It is, then, the whole 'Mystery of Christ' that is realized *'in sacramento'* in the celebration of the Eucharist; and it is to this totality that, he who assists and participates at Mass, unites himself and communicates.

He thus enters into communion with God Himself; for, the sacrifice is the act that realizes the Covenant between God and men. The sacrifice, the outpouring of blood and the immolation of the victim that it includes is the form that this Covenant, willed from the beginning by the Creator, had to take after sin. A Covenant of redemption, the sacrifice is an entrance into the communion in God's love. Through the outpouring of blood and death, it is love that goes to extremes, *'usque in finem'* (Jn 13:1); it is love giving itself to the furthest possible limit. It is in view of this gift that God allowed sin. And it is by this gift that He is supremely glorified: glorified before the eyes of men, to whom He gives such a manifestation of His love for them, and glorified by men in the measure that, believing in this love, they receive him and

---

[78] Cf. see above, Chapter XI.

themselves enter, by their union with Christ, into that immolation, in order to give themselves to God 'in an extreme way.' This is why, always after Christ, their Head and High Priest, by uniting themselves to His sacrifice, men pass to the life of glory, where that eternal Covenant is complete. This is what takes place through Eucharistic communion, in which there is given to us 'a pledge of eternal life' (' ... *et futurae gloriae nobis pignus datur*'); 'not that it leads us immediately into glory, but it gives us the strength to go there.'[79] For, such is the eschatological and transcendent end of the Covenant.

It is in this way that the Covenant reveals both its divine origin and its nature: the Covenant is an entrance into the uncreated communion of the Three Persons of the Most Blessed Trinity. Sealed by the one sacrifice of the one Mediator, the Word Incarnate, it realizes the '*admirabile commercium*,' the wonderful exchange, which is its one end, and which reproduces in the spiritual creature the *périchoresis* of the Divine Persons. God became man in order that man might become God—by participation (2 Pet 1:4): as the Father gives Himself to the Son and the Son to the Father, so the Son of God made man gives Himself to men that they might give themselves to Him, and in Him to the Father. This is the whole object of Christ's 'priestly prayer,' at the moment that He is about to accomplish His sacrifice and seal the Covenant (Jn 17:21–26). And we have here the work of the Spirit, 'Who proceeds from the Father and the Son,' and Who is sent into our hearts in order to inflame them with that love (Rom 5:5), the substance of the Trinity (1 Jn 4:8), 'to the praise of the glory of His grace' (Eph 1:6, 12, 14). The sacrifice, the path by which the Covenant is realized, and that communion along with it, thus appear, we could say, as the created communion with the uncreated communion, which is the Trinity. Everything there is love and glory: love, because each person and each participant has no other desire and no other activity than the giving of himself to the other; glory, because it is in that reciprocal gift and without limit that the glory of God consists, and because man,

---

[79]   St Thomas, *S.T.* III, q. 79, a. 2.

glorified by that received gift, enters by it, under the action of the Holy Spirit, into communion with the Son, Whose eternal act and Whose every work in time is to glorify the Father.

Here then is what the Mass is; and here is how the theology of its celebration is organized. It is the sacrifice of the 'New and eternal Covenant,' where Christ is immolated and offers Himself to the Father, as a Victim of reparation for sins and of redemption for sinners; and He offers Himself to men as food in order to bring them back in Himself to the Father in His sacrifice. The supreme act of justice, love and mercy; the Mass is the 'blessing,' that is to say, the redemption and grace for men. It is also, at the same time, a thanksgiving and infinite praise to God's glory. It is a sacrificial and therefore eminently priestly act; it is a pact of the Covenant, and therefore essentially theological and communitarian. It is priestly and communitarian, and therefore essentially ecclesial and hierarchical. The Mass is the sacrifice of the Covenant, which gives us eternal life through the Blood of Christ, the Breath of the Spirit, in the gift of the Father, and therefore an essentially eschatological feast, where the Church is built up, fortified and already tastes the joys of glory in the participation of the eternal communion of the Most Holy Trinity.

One also understands, in these perspectives, the historical development of the celebration of the Eucharist in the Church. In the first phase, that of the apostolic and immediately post-apostolic period, where the first Christian community enjoyed the fruits of redemption just accomplished, it is the aspect of the eschatological feast that dominates. Then, very soon afterwards, the Church would begin to emphasize more and more the act of the sacrifice. She felt the need to strengthen her march in this world, to be purified, to be fortified, and to defend herself in the ever new and ever more intense battles that she would encounter. Faced with the Lutheran negation, on the threshold of the great conflicts of modern times, the Council of Trent solemnly affirmed this central reality of the sacrifice. That the Church returns today to the aspect of the eschatological feast, the ecclesial and communitarian action, as well as the 'blessing' for the glory of God, is a sign of the times. However, it is another, no less important sign of the times that the insistence on these truths is done to the detriment of that which is their keystone, the sacrifice. The meaning of these two opposed signs is clear. They both indicate the eschatological intensification of the times in which the Church now lives. The first marks out the aspect of anticipation of glory; the second, that of the intensification of the struggle of falsehood against truth. The tragedy of this falsehood, which always presents itself as a rediscovery of the pure evangelical truth, brings to the Church a loss as serious as the Church's need is great for the Blood of Christ in order to be purified and strengthened in these present conflicts.

2. This is why it is very important to clarify the sense and value of the different forms of celebrating the Eucharist, in order to see how to regulate its usage in view of the world's redemption and God's glory. The preceding reflections allow us to do this. In showing us what the Mass is, they recalled for us what the two essential and inseparable ends are for which the Church celebrates the Mass. These two ends are precisely those we just mentioned: the salvation of men and the praise of God, the building-up of the Church and the glorification of the Trinity—two ends which ultimately make but one, namely the salvation of the world for the glory of God. By starting with this twofold and unique principle, it will be possible to determine the modes of celebration that bear the most fruit for the Church and the most glory to the love of God.

Concretely, the difficulty we are concerned with resolving today is that of harmonizing the two major forms of celebration, that is, fixing the norms that would regulate their use: 1) celebration by one sole priest at the altar; 2) and the sacramental concelebration by several priests together. For, these norms do not always exist. The Second Vatican Council limited itself to giving only general indications; and its thought, though clear in its orientation, is still difficult to discern on certain points. One must also not forget the usefulness that this could have in bringing back that eminently traditional and rich form, namely ceremonial concelebration.

The normal form of the Mass is that where the priest at the altar gathers in prayer the people entrusted to him. And as the fullness of the priesthood is given to the bishop, who is assisted in his ministry by his clergy, priests, deacons and other ministers, *the normal solemn form* of the Mass is that in which the pontiff officiates, surrounded by his clergy, in the midst of his people. Such, in fact, was the traditional form during the first centuries of the Church, always present in the East, and preserved in the West under the form of the 'Pontifical Masses,' but also, to a certain extent, in the 'High Masses' with deacon and sub-deacon. It is under this form that the Church better appears as 'that multitude gathered in the unity of the Father, Son and Holy Spirit'—an expression of St Cyprian, used by the Second Vatican Council.[80] For, in such a way the priest better represents 'Him Who is offered for us in sacrifice,' as Symeon of Thessalonica said. Symeon is speaking here of the 'first pontiff,' his reflection being concerned with what we call today the 'ceremonial' concelebration of the Byzantine Church. He insists on the preeminent and mediating function of this 'first ponfiff,' the only one to consecrate and to offer the sacrifice, by affirming that 'the others participate and profit through the mediation of this medi-ator,' the only one here 'to represent' the one Mediator. Then, the bishops, priests and assisting ministers come into the sanctuary, but not as the first pontiff.'[81] As one can see, it's a question here of a very solemn celebration, at which even the bishops participate. But by reserving to him who is called 'the first pontiff'[82] 'the offering in sacrifice of the mystical host,' this liturgy shows at the same time both the unique role of the minister and representative of the one Mediator

---

[80] Const. 'Lumen Gentium', 4.

[81] Symeon of Thessalonica, *De sacra liturgia*, cap. 99 (*PG* 155, 296).

[82] Whatever be the titles that designate him for receiving this place and this function.

that comes back to the priest, and the essentially priestly and hierarchical nature of the Eucharistic congregation.

In comparison to this solemn pontifical celebration (a true ecclesial concelebration, although only 'ceremonial'), what is better, this or the 'sacramental' concelebration, ('concelebration' simply, in the modern sense of the word), where several priests consecrate and offer together one sole sacrifice in one sole action? This latter manifests, it is said, 'the unity of the priesthood,' and therefore the subordination of the priests' priesthood to Christ's priesthood, Who remains the one High Priest and Principal Celebrant of every Eucharistic liturgy. This is correct. The question, however, which is posed here, is about the appropriateness and frequency of such a manifestation. In order to respond correctly, it is necessary to consider that this manifestation of the unity of the priesthood (*'unitas sacerdotii'*) necessarily brings about a certain overshadowing of the unicity of the 'priest' (*unicitas sacerdotis*), that is, the unicity of our sole Mediator and High Priest, Christ. Signified in an extremely expressive manner by the presence of the priest alone at the altar, this unicity inevitably disappears somewhat when several priests are gathered together and on equal footing around the same altar.

This drawback does not exist in ceremonial concelebration, which, on the other hand, manifests at the same time the *'unicitas sacerdotalis,'* the unicity of the High Priest Mediator, by reserving to Him alone the sacramental celebration of the Mystery, and the *'unitas sacerdotii,'* the unity of the priesthood and all the priests in Christ, by liturgically associating in a particular way the priests present at the celebration of the sacrifice. This latter is normally offered by 'the pontiff,' that is by the bishop, or by a religious superior. This is why we mentioned above the possibility of resorting to that form of celebration and concelebration.

We say this thinking in particular of the cases of gatherings of priests, more or less numerous, where a sacramental concelebration is not justified, or not daily, when the gatherings are prolonged several days, like retreats, congresses, etc.; or again, when it is not justified for all, as for when the number of priests present is too great. These concelebrations of great number, in fact, are not without drawbacks, especially for the priests themselves, who often find themselves in conditions hardly favourable and in little conformity with the sacred majesty of the act in which they are participating. It would, perhaps, be preferable in such cases, even on very solemn occasions, to limit the number of 'sacramental' concelebrants. The other priests could be associated in a special way to the liturgy and thus concelebrate ceremonially. The dignity of the ceremony would increase, and with it, the sense of the priesthood in its essence and its hierarchy.

Perhaps there could also be here a solution to the problem of the conventual Mass, whether habitual or occasional, whether through the ceremonial association of all religious priests in the celebration of the liturgy (which would be possible especially in the case of smaller communities) or through the association of some of them, acting as representatives of the whole, which would be more fitting for larger communities.[83]

These are only simple suggestions; our intention here is not to enter into the details of practical questions, but simply to pose them. We also wish to show that there are other ways to resolve such questions than the solutions imposed in the last several years, solutions widely imposed and poorly established. Their foundation is even so weak, that the aforementioned solution, the systematic and quasi-obligatory use of concelebration, represents in reality an unprecedented rupture with Tradition. These words of Pascal provide one with a fruitful meditation:

It is horrible that they should set before us the discipline of the Church today as being so good that to try to change it is criminal. Formerly, it was infallibly good, and it was apparently no sin to change it; and now, being what it is, we may not wish to have it changed! [84]

---

[83] On the subject of the conventual Mass, cf, see above, Chapter IV.

[84] B. Pascal, *Pensées*. [English Translation by H. F. Stewart, Pantheon Books, 1965]. Pascal expresses himself thus apropos of the ordination of priests. He

What Pascal calls 'the discipline,' and hence laws, is valid *a fortiori* when, as is the case here, it is a question only of a practice, and one which is recent and entirely new.

This drawback of sacramental concelebration, that of overshadowing the '*unicitas sacerdotis,*' is limited and contained within reasonable boundaries when concelebration is only occasional, as the Council desired, and very solemn, as it always was when it first began (the second half of the 8th century), that is, around the Pope, in Rome. The drawback will even disappear when the so-called 'principal celebrant' is the bishop or religious superior. In these conditions, concelebration presents the advantages claimed for it: the manifestation before the Church of the *hierarchical* unity of the priesthood, and the priests' consciousness of their attachment to the bishop and of their communion with their brothers in the priesthood at the service of the Church. On the other hand, its drawbacks take on dangerous proportions when concelebration becomes *habitus*, and the religious superior, the monastic abbot, and even the bishop take a place among the concelebrants, as something perfectly natural. This last case, of which one could cite plenty of examples, is a misinterpretation that affects both the priesthood and the liturgy of the Eucharist, as these two realities are closely connected. In small communities or in certain huge gatherings, whose pagan character Fr Bouyer justly denounced, the boundaries between the priests and the faithful disappear.[85]

---

continues: 'We have certainly been allowed to change the custom of not making priests without exercising such care that hardly any were found worthy; yet we are not allowed to regret the custom of making priests of so many who are unworthy!' Formerly, one would say, we had such a sense of the salvific efficacy of the sacrifice of the Mass, that we multiplied their number, sometimes to the extreme. Think of the medieval exhuberances. Today, on the other hand, this sense has so disappeared that we excessively reduce the number to the greater harm of the Church.

[85]   Fr Bouyer shows well the ambiguity in the current rediscovery of the communitarian sense of the liturgy. If one is delighted at this, he adds that: 'it is indeed a very bad sign that the values of adoration and contemplation, yesterday concentrated on a Eucharistic devotion in fact foreign to the Eucharist (a),

One can see, then, the other drawbacks of frequent and systematic concelebration. The sense of the priesthood being deeply affected, and with it, that of the Mass as a sacrifice, it is consequently the recognition of the value of the private Mass and the multiplication of Masses that tends to disappear. Only the congregation remains, raised to the highest level in its auto-celebration. The majority of cases, no doubt, do not go to such excesses; but it remains that it is the logical termination of the movement triggered and favoured by the abusive and uncontrolled use of concelebration. In this context, the favour enjoyed by the theory of the Mass as a gathering of a congregation is not something brought about by chance, but the fact of an immediate correspondence. The most serious damages caused by the abuse of concelebration, however, are on the one hand, that it brings about in very many cases the privation of Masses for the faithful, and on the other hand, that it results in an immense loss of graces for the Church and the world on account of the decrease in the number of Masses. We refer here to that which we said at the end of our first part.[86]

---

scarcely appeared to have flowed back onto our celebration of the same, but rather have disappeared purely and simply with the progressive disappearance of the practices, where they had been housed: 'benediction of the Blessed Sacrament', 'thanksgiving after Communion', etc. In these conditions, the collective celebration which animates neither the contemplation and less still the adoration of Christ present in His mystery, greatly risks being degraded into one of those 'huge gatherings' dear to contemporary paganism, superficially haloed in an aura of Christian sentiments' (*Eucharistie*, p. 16). This citation illustrates well the merits and demerits of Fr Bouyer. We cannot but agree with him regarding the subject that he stigmatizes so well. We regret, however, that his very accurate views are so often accompanied by inacceptable errors and excesses: here, that condemnation of devotions that he claims are foreign to the Eucharist (a), 'Benediction of the Blessed Sacrament', etc. and which moreover belong to the development of the Church's purest Eucharist tradition. 'The Council', Paul VI and John Paul II have never ceased to encourage such devotions. In fact, they belong by full right to the Eucharistic 'cult'.

[86] Cf. see above, Ch. III, II, § 2: 'The Value of Concelebrated Masses'.

On the other hand, by rediscovering the Eucharist as a sacrifice and an eminently priestly act, one discovers at the same time the possibility and value of the 'private' Mass, even the solitary Mass: it gives back to the priest a truer and more complete sense of his priesthood; it assures a more frequent celebration of the Mass for the faithful; and it brings with it the multiplication of that sacramental offering of the redemptive sacrifice for the salvation of the world and the glory of God. This is the reason why the Church, to the extent that she has become more conscious of the Mass' efficacy as a sacrifice, has not ceased to encourage its private celebration and multiplication. We must also recall that, in this form of celebration, the Mass is not called 'private' except by reason of its exterior modality. Because the priest, a mediator by his ministry, represents Christ and the entire Church—because of this, the 'private' Mass in itself and in its profound reality is still an act of the whole Christian community. Therefore, it is the whole Church who prays and 'blesses' God, who is immolated and offered to His majesty 'in the sacrament.' And it is also for the whole Church, indeed, for all of humanity, that in each of these Masses Christ, and His ministerial priest in Him, offers Himself to His Father as the Victim of redemption for the sins of the world. By each Mass, therefore, the one Mediator pours out upon this world of sinners His purifying Blood, and by this Blood, His 'Holy and Life-Giving Spirit.'

What blessings could be preferred or even compared to these?

*   *   *

There is still much more that can be said, we know. We hope at least to have come to know and to have made known the essentials. Our reflection began with that simple question, purely theoretical in appearance: How many Masses are offered to God in a concelebration?[87] However, the more we progressed in our study, the more we discovered the immensity of the doctrinal, historical and pastoral perspectives, which were hidden within that 'simple question.'

[87]   Cf. see above, Ch. I.

Indeed, the entire theology of the Eucharist, as well as the theology of the priesthood, is involved here; included as well is the theology of the Church and redemption, insofar as this latter passes through the priesthood, the Church and the Eucharist for its accomplishment. This concerns, therefore, the very mission and life of the Church, both priests and lay faithful together; it concerns the salvation of the world.

For, if it is true that the priest exists for the sacrifice, then he inevitably loses his identity, that is, the sense of his dignity and his vocation, when he stops making the sacrifice the center of his life.[88] And if it is true that Christ's Blood, by giving the Holy Spirit, is the life of the Church, and that it is by the Holy Sacrifice of the Mass that this Blood and this Spirit are poured out on the Church, then it is necessary that the Eucharistic offering of that sacrifice be multiplied, in order that its effects be multiplied for the Church's salvation and life.

This implies a 'moderation' in the use of concelebration.

---

[88] This ordination of the priest towards the altar and the sacrifice is strongly contested today; and yet it is one of the points most consistently affirmed by Tradition. The Second Vatican Council echoed this when it taught that: 'In the mystery of the Eucharistic sacrifice ... the priests exercise their principal office.' In this sacrifice, in fact, 'the work of our redemption is accomplished' (The Council's text mentions in a footnote here that these words are from the Secret of the Ninth Sunday after Pentecost.). 'This is why,' the same text continues, 'the daily celebration of their Mass is strongly recommended, for it is always an act of Christ and the Church, even if no faithful can assist' (Decree '*Presbyterorum Ordinis*', 13). With regards to the connection between the priest and the altar, that is, with the sacrifice, this has its roots in the very beginnings of the history of the priesthood and religion, such that the reduction of the priest to a simple teacher of the word is always a sign of religious decadence. Citing 1 Samuel 2:28 and 2 Chronicles 26:16–18, Fr De Vaux writes: 'The priest is therefore most properly 'the minister of the altar', and this Christian expression finds in the Old Testament its authentic letters of nobility' (*Les institutions de l'Ancien Testament*, vol. II (Paris, Cerf, 1960), p. 210). With the destruction of the Temple, he continues, 'the religion of the Torah supplanted the ritual of the Temple and the priests were supplanted by the rabbis' (*ibid*). Today, the priests are supplanted by the 'liturgical animators' and 'theologians'. The process continues.

These two requests make but one on the practical level; for, limiting concelebration will normally, if not necessarily, bring with it a return to the private Mass and the multiplication of Masses. To hope for such a return, for the good of priests themselves, the good of the faithful who wish to participate at Mass, the good of the Church and the entire world, there is nothing else to do but to return to the teaching of the Second Vatican Council and the traditional practice of the Church. From this teaching and this practice we will find a very current echo in the recent exhortation from the Sacred Congregation for Catholic Education. Denouncing 'certain practices that have infiltrated here and there in our day,' it asks, 'that future priests be warned that the Church *strongly recommends to priests the daily celebration of the holy Mass, inasmuch as it is an act offered by Christ and the Church for the salvation of the whole world, even if they are not bound by any pastoral obligations or if none of the faithful are able to participate.*'[89]

It is evident that the 'practices' deplored by that Congregation come from the idea that sees the Mass essentially as a gathering. We showed above the development that it has undergone today, sometimes even on the level of certain local hierarchies. What meaning does the private Mass have in such circumstances? It seems equally obvious that the systematic practice of concelebration greatly favours this conception of the Mass. This is why we do not see how it is possible to encourage and to recall at the same time the importance of the value of each Mass for the Church. For, the more concelebration develops, the fewer celebrations of Mass there are in and for the Church. Yet, as we saw (and we could add more references), each Mass is a new sacramental outpouring of Christ's Blood, and by that Blood, of the Holy Spirit, on the Church and humanity.

---

[89]   *Instruction On the Liturgical Formation In the Seminaries*, 3 June 1979 (published in the *L'Osservatore Romano* on April 12, 1980), no. 26.

CONCLUSION

AFRIENDLY CONVERSATION WAS at the origin of this book. A no less cordial correspondence indicates to us what must be its conclusion. The conversation dealt with the question of whether in concelebration one sole Mass is offered to God, or if there are as many Masses as concelebrating priests. Many other problems relative to concelebration—like its frequency—depend on the response that we gave to the first question. In fact, if, as is the case, one sole Mass, one sole sacrifice is offered to God when several priests concelebrate the Eucharist, the frequency of concelebration brings with it a decrease in the number of Masses in the Church; this, of its very nature, will result in a decrease in the Eucharistic sacrifice's fruits of salvation. It is this problem, the frequency of concelebration, which was the object of our cordial correspondence, recently held with a monk. To one letter, in which we told him we regretted being in disagreement with him, his monastery and him to whom it belongs, regarding the too frequent and even systematic use of concelebration—to this he responded the following:

> Regarding the subject of concelebration, you tell me you are sorry that you do not agree with … us. You ought to say, "with the universal practice of the Church such as it is currently lived out." For, we are simply conforming to N … and to N … , knowing that it has a supreme normative value that is imposed on all theologians.

Such a proposition is obviously unacceptable. In fact, it ends up making the practice its own rule, indeed, the rule of the faith itself. Nevertheless, it ought to be reproduced; for, it expresses the current opinion perfectly, before which shatter all the historical and theological arguments that can be advanced, even the most evident. It is, to paraphrase the above letter, the '[quasi] universal opinion of the Church's priests and faithful today'; especially in religious communities.

This is why it seems useful, at the end of this book, first, to show how such an opinion is false, and second, to sum up our position, at least with respect to the essentials, in a certain number of propositions that clarify what we said, and even more so, what we did not say. They will indicate at the same time the points relative to concelebration, which seem to need to be reviewed or developed; and they will state the reasons for and meaning of our request for the multiplication of Masses. (One can compare these propositions with the conclusions of our first part; see the end of Chapter III).

*   *   *

1. Although the problem at hand is the consideration of a liturgical practice as such, that is, in its liturgical and pastoral aspect, by speaking of 'the supreme normative value that is imposed on all theologians,' our correspondent raises again the debate over the rule of the faith. In fact, it is good to consider this one last time. From there we can return to the properly liturgical aspect. Yet, on that level of the faith, the principle stated is manifestly false: first, because a practice has never been as such a sole supreme norm for theological and dogmatic reflection; and second, because still less can it pretend to have such a role, if one considers it only 'as it is currently lived out,' that is, independently of its antiquity and its roots in tradition. This canonization of relevance, that is, of the present time without reference to the past, is a common attitude today. It is not superfluous to note the gravity of not recalling how much this goes against the very meaning of Tradition, the homogenous development of which is the law of the Church.

2. One might object that the universality of the current practice carries the weight of a norm insofar as it is the sign of that rootedness in Tradition. In this case one must not attribute to it that weight (or value) by considering it principally in its relevance, as one is invited to do by presenting it 'as it is currently lived out.' One must, on the other hand, add to the two criteria of universality (spatial) and unanimous consent, that of antiquity. Such is the teaching of Vincent of Lerins, a teaching long used by the Church: '*Curandum est, ut id*

teneamus quod ubique, quod semper, quod ab omnibus creditum est' —
'One must take care to hold to that which has been believed everywhere, always and by everyone.' And Vincent adds: '*Hoc est enim vere
proprieque catholicum*' —'This is what is truly and properly Catholic.'[1]
Thus the universality of a practice and the unanimous consent which
it enjoys will be of no value without being rooted in Tradition, and,
from there, in apostolic revelation, a rootedness that cannot be
asserted without the criteria of antiquity.

It is obvious that such a criteria cannot—under pain of an impossible fixism—be taken in too literal and too material a sense. We
know, however, that just as he was a defender of the immutability of
dogma, Vincent of Lerins was also a defender of its homogenous
development. He fixed the fundamental law in a formula as well
known as it is authoritative: it is necessary, he says, that everything
that touches the faith be maintained '*in eodem dogmate, eodem sensu,
eademque sententia*' —'within the dogma itself, within the same sense,
within the same thought.'[2] This widely used formula had been
canonized by the authority of the Church at the First Vatican Council.[3] The immutability of the faith has for a condition this substantial
continuity in the development of its different articles. Likewise a
liturgical practice would not have the value of a witness of the faith
except to the extent that it could establish its own continuity with the
ancient forms of Tradition.

Thus, without that antiquity and without that deep-rootedness in
Tradition which it assures, a current opinion or practice, even one
which is universal and enjoys unanimous consent, is without normative value for the faith. Of such a situation Vincent of Lerins gives the
example of Arianism, a heresy that was universally widespread in its

---

[1]   The work of Vincent of Lerins is found in *PL*, vol. 50, cols. 637–86. The maxim
       cited is taken from his *Tractatus pro catholicae fidei antiquitate et universitate
       adversus omnium haereticorum novitates*, commonly called '*Commonitorium*',
       chap. 2. *PL* 50, 640.
[2]   *Ibid.*, chap. 23, *PL* 50, 668.
[3]   *Const. de fide catholica*, chap. 4 (DS 3020).

day and that received the unanimous acceptance of bishops and theologians. Only a few, the best, like Athanasius of Alexandria and Hilary of Poitiers, were opposed to it. Their testimony shows us that the universality and unanimity of the heresy were not absolute; and since one is able to maintain that they were quasi-absolute, inasmuch as the error was widespread, it proves that those criteria cannot suffice, the number not being able in itself to establish the truth in those matters where quality necessarily wins over quantity.

On the basis of these principles and the examples that they illustrate, we see the abuse that one commits in making a liturgical practice 'the supreme norm that is imposed on every theologian,' even if we suppose that it was universally adopted, and especially if we consider it only or principally 'as it is being lived out today.'

3. It is still true, one might say, that it is the liturgy that fixes the rule of the faith, according to the adage of Prosper of Aquitaine, also adopted by the Magisterium: '*ut legem credendi lex statuat supplicandi*'—that the law of prayer (the liturgy) establishes the law of the faith (dogma).'[4]

In reality, the meaning of Prosper of Aquitaine's formula, taken up again in the '*Indiculus*,' under the authority of the Pope Celestine I, in the first half of the fifth century, is much more limited. A remarkable study has shown, on the basis of decisive historical proofs, that in his initial intention it was only aimed at Pelagianism. To those who rallied around it and who maintained the possibility for a man to observe God's commandments without grace, Prosper responds by basing himself on that text of St Paul where he tells Timothy to pray for all men (1 Tim 2:1–2). Yet, he continues, this prayer is made in all the Churches: everywhere, in all the liturgies—which establishes the '*lex supplicationis*,' the rule of prayer—one prays for all men and for all their needs. Thus it is recognized and practically professed that all men have need of God's grace—obtained by prayer—in order to do good. Such then, in conclusion, is the rule of faith, the '*lex credendi*,'

---

4   This text had been reproduced in the '*Capitula pseudo–Caelestina*', also called '*Indiculus*', around 431 (DS 246).

that must be held against the Pelagians. And one sees how it is possible to affirm this from the liturgy. This reasoning is summed up in the formula cited above: ' ... that the law of prayer—which must be addressed to God in order to obtain grace—dictates *the law of the faith*—which is, that grace is necessary for human freedom in order to obey God.'[5]

From this particular sense one passes on to one more general, that which makes the liturgy a witness of the Church's faith. This sense is particularly legitimate, but it would be an abuse to make the liturgy the supreme criteria of the faith, and especially one sole liturgical practice. The liturgy is simply placed in the collection of witnesses of Tradition, as we noted above. From then on the question that is posed is that of knowing under what conditions a particular liturgy—in time and space—can be considered an authentic witness of the Tradition and faith of the Church. To this question we also had a response, that is, the criteria that Tradition itself gives us, and after it the Magisterium and theology: more than its universality, this liturgy needs to prove its antiquity, its deep-rootedness in Tradition and its conformity with faith and dogma.

In the final analysis then, it is the '*lex credendi*' that judges, after having inspired it, the '*lex orandi*,' the dogma of the liturgy, and not the other way around. Because the former inspires the liturgy, the faith finds in it its expression and witness; but the value of that expression and witness always remains, in the last instance, submitted to its judgment.

This is what St Cyprian asserted when he declared, apropos of the baptism of heretics who converted and against the argument that some wanted to draw from custom (*consuetudo*): '*Non est de consuetudine praescribendum, sed ratione vincendum*'—'It is not a question of

---

5   Cf. B. Capelle, OSB., *Autorité de la liturgie chez les Pères*, in *Rech. Théol. Anc. Méd.*, 21, 1954, pp. 5–23. See pp. 5–6, where the author sums up the results of the research by K. Federer, *Liturgie und Glaube. Eine theologiegeschichtliche Untersuchung* (*Paradosis*, 4), Fribourg (Suisse), 1950.

prescribing by custom, but of conquering by reason.'[6] Clearly distinguishing not only custom and truth, but also custom and tradition, he strongly affirms that 'without truth, custom is nothing but error grown old': '*Consuetudo sine veritate vetustas erroris est.*'[7]

Consequently, every liturgical practice must be examined and judged in light of not only Tradition, but also dogmatic truth. This was recognized in our day by a liturgist as well-informed as Fr C. Vagaggini, to name but one. After the philological and historical analysis of a liturgical tradition, he says, 'one must give a higher judgment in the light of the doctrine of the faith.'[8] This is because it is in the cultic reflection and expression that the liturgy looks back to the dogma as its source and the final court that will judge it.[9] However, it can also reflect particular theological opinions. History shows that this has often happened, and it cannot be otherwise.[10] Furthermore, the matter is fully legitimate when those opinions are orthodox and Catholic.

4. While it is judged by dogma insofar as it is an expression and witness of the faith, a liturgical practice ought to be judged also and *a fortiori* insofar as it is a properly liturgical practice. In either case and in either way it will not be able to be the supreme norm that is imposed on every theologian.

5. Nevertheless, one would still say, if it is correct that a liturgical practice, even one that is 'universal' during a given period—if it is

---

[6]   Text cited by B. Capelle, Art. cit., p. 14.

[7]   That Cyprian fell into thinking, after Tertullian, that converted heretics must be rebaptized, changes nothing with respect to the strength of his reasoning here.

[8]   Op. cit., p. 405.

[9]   This is the teaching of Pius XII in the Encyclical '*Mediator Dei*': 'Thus the sacred liturgy neither designs nor establishes the Catholic faith absolutely and by its own authority, but rather, being a profession of the heavenly truths submitted to the Church's supreme Magisterium, it can provide arguments and testimonies of great value in order to decide on a particular point of Christian doctrine' (1st Part; *AAS* 39, 1947, p. 541).

[10]   Cf. C. Vagaggini, op. cit., pp. 411 ff; B. Capelle, Art. cit., p. 19.

correct that it cannot be in itself the rule of faith and cannot be a rule at all without antiquity and deep-rootedness in Tradition, it still can become so insofar as it is the manifestation of the mind of the living Magisterium of the Church. This is most likely the implicit reasoning that inspired the comment of our correspondent; for, it is here that the thought of many begins today. This opinion, we hasten to say, is not devoid of a certain value; for, it is true that the Magisterium, to which the truly or allegedly universal practice would refer, is indeed the 'proximate norm' of the faith. The error here is making it, without any clarification, the 'ultimate norm.'

This reasoning and this attitude are not without recalling those of the patristic period, or even those from the time of the Apostles, where the apostolic origin of tradition, justly held as the supreme norm, was, one would think, sufficiently proven by the universality and antiquity of that tradition (doctrinal or practical). These traits serve then as immediate criteria referring back to the supreme criteria of apostolicity, as Dom Capelle showed with regards to the liturgy. The classical formulas of Vincent of Lerins, which we quoted above, simply express this conviction; it is this which give them value from the historical and traditional point of view. Nevertheless, the brightest of the Fathers had seen well how excessive it is to have recourse to only universality and antiquity—more often presumed than proven—for asserting the apostolicity of a tradition. St Irenaeus stated that higher criteria were necessary. Those that he mentions, the tradition of the Churches of apostolic origin, especially that of Rome, show that the quality of testimonies is more important for him than the number.[11] They reveal at the same time an orientation from where shall come the practically decisive criteria, in modern times, for a very large part of the Catholic opinion and of theologians themselves: the authority of the Church's Magisterium. Thus a universal practice, or an allegedly universal practice, will be an immediate criteria that draws its normative value

---

[11]   Cf. B. Capelle, Art. cit., p. 15.

from the fact that it will be the sign and proof of the Magisterium's mind, the ultimate norm of the faith.

Paradoxically, in our present period of disputes and subversion, such an attitude is still more widespread than one might think. In a certain way, it is even more developed in comparison to the preceding period, which is explained by the need in the current confusion for an immediate and incontestable criteria. Yet, adopted without discernment, this attitude constitutes an abuse; for, the Magisterium is but 'the proximate norm of the faith,' a norm itself in need of a norm (*norma normata*), that is, regulated by divine revelation, which alone is 'the ultimate norm of the faith.' The Magisterium draws all of its weight from its conformity to the supreme norm, and it is imposed in the measure that it uses its authority in order to affirm that conformity. This is its proper grace: that capacity of discerning the authentic sense of divine revelation. For which reason it has the power to tell the faithful what they must believe and do. The Second Vatican Council very clearly reaffirmed this grace of the Magisterium and its subordination, or more exactly, this proper grace of the Magisterium in its subordination to 'the Word of God, written or transmitted.'[12]

It is only in the case of dogmatic definitions that there is a total and absolutely certain identity between the two norms, 'proximate' and 'ultimate,' because in this case the Magisterium engages the fullness of its grace and authority in order to say in a 'definitive' manner what is the revelation, and therefore the faith, of the Church. In the other cases there is a gradation, the differences of which it is of the greatest importance to respect, for both the faith and the life of the Church. They go from the degree where the Church's authority is engaged in such a manner that it is in fact imposed on all, to that degree where the Magisterium simply expresses a preference, even to respecting possible opinions and practices. One sees then the necessity of learning to discern in the Church's teachings and directives the degree of authority with which they are presented.

---

[12]   Constitution, *Dei Verbum*, no. 10.

On the level of opinion and its formation, one observes furthermore, that according to the various needs and circumstances, some appeal today to the authority of the Roman Magisterium, invoked in an often imprecise and abusive manner, or to the authority of exegetes and theologians, direct and competent interpreters of revelation, or to the authority of local Churches, the only ones, some claim, to which priests and faithful must submit: recourse to these different magisteriums taking place each time as to a final judge. This split of authority, the lack of coordination, not to mention the contradictions that exist among those different tribunals and the absolute weight that some want to confer on them in order to impose their decisions on the faithful, are so many signs of the current crises of the Church. The freedom and truth of theological work does not gain from this.

6. Let us return, however, to the connection, suggested by Dom Capelle's work's, between the attitude of the Fathers, settling too hastily on the (presumed) universality of a custom in its apostolic origin, and that of our contemporaries arguing from the universality—also often presumed more than it is proven—of a practice in order to assert its conformity with the Magisterium. Such an attitude asked, or asks, in the first case, that the apostolic origin alone be able to establish that universality; and in the second case, that magisterial origin be able to establish it. In both cases there is a flagrant begging of the question. On one hand, one asserts that it is necessary to be conformed to the current practice—which is declared universal—because it will be the expression of, in one case, an apostolic tradition, in the other, the mind of the Church. And on the other hand, in order to prove that this practice is truly the manifestation of either an apostolic tradition or the mind of the Church, one puts forward no other argument than its universality, true or supposed. We end up in a vicious circle; for, we end up finally and concretely making the practice its own rule. We also end up placing the criteria of the number, that is, of quantity, above that of quality—not to mention the difficulty that there is in verifying even today those quantitative proportions. One

forgets all the other factors that can intervene, in particular, the pressure of temporal power or opinion, to impose on all an opinion or practice to the point of making it almost universal. We can never meditate enough on the history of Arianism, or, in the other direction, the precautions taken by the Magisterium, when it wished to assure itself of the universality of a dogma. We are thinking, for an example, of the investigations made by Popes before defining the dogmas of the Immaculate Conception (1854) and the Assumption (1950).

7. For it is true, as the Second Vatican Council correctly restated, that, 'the universality of the faithful, having the unction that comes from the Spirit (1 Jn 2:20–27), cannot fail in the faith,' and that, 'by that supernatural sense of the faith, when 'from the bishops to the last of the lay faithful' (St Augustine), it brings to truths concerning faith and morals a universal consensus, it manifests this particular property, which is that of the entire people.'[13] But we saw, on one hand, how the application of such a principle is a delicate task, especially during a time of massification and universal leveling, where the means and techniques of opinion forming have reached a degree of efficiency never known before; and on the other hand, that the criteria of number cannot have in itself the absolute value attributed to it, for example, by the modern democratic principle, according to which the sole fact of the majority, even taken on one vote, suffices to impose on all 'the will of the people.'

8. Yet, with regards *not* to the principle of sacramental concelebration, nor that of a certain widening of its practice, as the Council desired, *but* with regards to its systematic and practically obligatory use, it is certain that this use, while obviously huge, is far from being 'universal,' for very many priests and higher authorities (even in Rome) in no way support it, neither on the practical level nor in its doctrinal principles. The testimonies that we gathered prove this, and we could present others, if needed. We also saw that, even if it later received official encouragement, this practice cannot present itself as the mind

---

[13]   Constitution, *Lumen Gentium*, no. 12.

of the Council. We showed, on the contrary, that the Council Fathers wished that the new practice be limited, and that it be under the control of their authority, outside of some very rare cases foreseen by the general law. The normal form of Eucharistic celebration would remain that where the priest alone is at the altar as Christ, the 'one Mediator,' Himself alone when He offered up the sacrifice that saves us. We were also able to mention the conflicts at the price of which that will of the bishops had succeeded in imposing itself and became concretized in the finally approved texts. We likewise had to recognize another truth: when concelebration was finally introduced into the monasteries and parishes, it was done without respecting the rules fixed by the Council; the authorization of the bishops was practically not even asked. With their authorization it was the authority of the Council itself that was thus circumvented. Finally, must we recall that the new practice adopted that which the schismatic Synod of Pistoia wished to impose, and which was condemned by Pius VI?

In considering these facts, it is difficult for the theologian, especially for the historian, to consider the practice that we question here as the expression of the mind of the Council and the Church. It would seem more accurate to see here one case among so many others where, in the name 'of the Council,' a practice had been imposed, which in fact opposed the Council. Paul VI himself, and after him John Paul I and John Paul II, frequently denounced this process, even if they did not wish to list the concrete abuses that it brought with it. Would they have considered the systematic use of concelebration as we have examined it as one of these abuses? 'Obviously not,' would say those who adopted it and who are of the great majority, though not of the 'universality.' And yet these reasons and facts that we mentioned are there, proving the opposition that exists between the Council, the liturgical tradition, the needs of the faithful and the theology of the fruits of the Eucharist on the one hand, and on the other hand, the new practice that has been introduced in the Church.

9. And one would like to make this practice, from the sole fact of its very wide diffusion (a bit hastily called 'universality'), the supreme norm resolving the debate ... Such a claim, widespread though it be, is not only not sustainable, but it reveals an error that goes very far. It would be good to show this. We mentioned above that which explains, psychologically, the need, in the current splitting of the Church's structures, for a certain and easily accessible criteria in order to resolve the multiple questions that are posed to the faithful. That criteria is indeed the authority of the Church; for, such in fact is its function, being for all the 'proximate norm' of the faith. Moreover, the Church does in fact provide the norm, but in the conditions that we recalled, namely, according to a whole series of degrees and forms, which already makes the practice not as simple and as obvious as some would like it. Where the error appears in an obvious manner, is when one wants to make the Magisterium as such, and according to no matter what form it manifests itself, the 'ultimate norm' of the faith. It thus becomes for the average Catholic opinion that which the authority of apostolic origin was for the first Christians. The fundamental difference between the two attitudes is that, formerly it was in fact the 'ultimate norm' of the faith to which one directly appealed, that is, divine revelation transmitted to the Church by the Apostles; while now, it is to the authority entrusted with teaching and interpreting that revelation to which one refers—and to it alone. One thus transfers to a secondary and relative (or dependent) authority the absolute value that belongs by definition to its proper source alone.

Such an error is extremely serious. It agrees with that canonization of the present time, which we denounced above; and together they contribute both to the eradication that strikes consciences and the society of the sources of truth, and to the absolutization of the relative, an approach that is at the beginning of all types of totalitarianism. We can guess what will take place in such conditions, and we can see what in fact happens all too often, the extolled return to the origins to boot. The phenomena of auto-satisfaction, and almost auto-idolatry, which is thus produced, makes the Church considered in her human element alone her own proper source and end. It is because of this that she is definitely led to be the prey and victim of all the demons of this time.

10. We say it again in conclusion: with regards to concelebration, or better, with regard to *the aspect of its current practice, which we consider here,* to wish to justify this practice—beginning with its alleged 'universality'—on the authority of the Church's Magisterium, is a doubly abusive approach. First, because that 'universality' does not exist. Far from it. This can be seen if one wishes to pay attention to all those who evade it and who end up making much of the world. Then, because the massive use that can be observed, and which cannot be denied, cannot prove by itself alone its foundation in the Magisterium, nor can it weaken the facts that prove the absence of such a foundation. The practice of systematic concelebration, being in no way prescribed by the decrees of the Second Vatican Council, and having no basis for itself except for some later minor documents, moreover, going in a direction opposed to that of the conciliar Constitution—this practice is opposed not only to the orientations of Vatican II, but also to the entire most ancient and most constant tradition of the Church.

Therefore, more just is the attitude of that professor of liturgy, who frankly declared: 'One must admit it, it is an innovation.' And he added: 'The question is, 'What does it signify and what value does it have?'' It is to this question that, on the eve of the Council, the Sacred Congregation of Rites wisely asked that one respond, before any decision be made with regards to the practice of concelebration. Seeing that that response was never given, both before, during or after the Council, our entire work has had no other end than to gather together the historical, doctrinal and liturgical elements which will allow one to discern in what direction the response needs to go. Such was the sole end of the studies that make up this book.

* * *

We think we can sum up those different studies, at least with regards to the fundamental points, in the following propositions. Out of concern for clarity, we shall present them under three different headings: doctrinal, historical, and liturgico-pastoral. It is evident, however, that these three perspectives are not separable. One will not be surprised, then, to see the propositions of a latter heading taking up again, to place them in a better light, the elements already presented under an earlier heading.

The Doctrinal Level

1. *Concelebration of the Eucharist, both sacramental and ceremonial.* *Sacramental concelebration* is that where all the concelebrating priests recite the canon out loud, or when they at least pronounce the words of consecration contained in the institution narrative.

   Ceremonial concelebration is that where this act is reserved to him who today is called the principal celebrant, and who is traditionally the bishop. The hierarchical priestly head of the Church, he represents Christ the High Priest and one Mediator; and he offers the sacrifice, assisted by his presbytery and surrounded by the community of the faithful.

2. *Sacramental concelebration,* the very principle of which had been contested throughout history (12th-13th centuries) and still is today (in certain non-Catholic Oriental Rites), *is based on theology* (St Thomas established it once for all—Chapter I), *on the practice of the Church* (since the 8th century—Chapters IV and V), *and on the Magisterium* (which spoke on this subject especially at Vatican II—Chapter I and *passim*).

3. *In both sacramental and ceremonial concelebration, one sole Mass is offered to God.* This assertion, dictated by good sense and by language ('concelebrate' means to celebrate together one act of worship), is established by theological reason (First Part). It is also based on the declarations of the Magisterium, especially the *Decree* of the Sacred

Congregation of the Rites, '*Ecclesiae semper*' (7 March 1965) and the *Decree* of the Second Vatican Council, 'On the Ministry and Life of the Priests' (*Presbyterorum ordinis,* no. 8).

4. Between sacramental concelebration, which the Latin Church and a part of the Oriental Catholic Rites currently use, *and ceremonial concelebration,* the only one known in antiquity and the High Middle Ages—whose tradition is strongly maintained today in a part (the most important part, it seems) of the Oriental Rites—between these two types of concelebration *there is an essential difference in what concerns the priests and the exercise of their priesthood.* In the first type only the concelebrants co-consecrate the sacrament with the principal celebrant. They do not do so in the second type of concelebration; instead, they keep silent during the canon—it is not possible to celebrate priestly, that is, to 'confect' a sacrament (*conficere sacramentum*) without pronouncing the sacramental words essential to it. This is why this difference holds not only for our modern period, where sacramental theology is fully formulated, but also for the previous periods.

5. *Each Mass,* being the very sacrifice of Christ, the one redemptive sacrifice of Calvary, *has an infinite value.* Each Mass is an act of the entire Church; for, she is present there both in Christ, Who offers Himself for her as her Head, and in the priest, who represents her, and prays for her and in her name (See *Presbyterorum ordinis,* no. 13, and numerous other magisterial documents). It is this which establishes the *value of Masses said 'privately,'* that is, those celebrated by a priest in the absence of any assistants: *each Mass pours the redemptive Blood of Christ upon the Church and the whole world.*

6. While each Mass has in itself an infinite value, the dispositions of men for receiving its fruits are always imperfect and in this sense limited. For this reason the number of *celebrations of the Mass is so important for multiplying the fruits of salvation.* Established by this elementary, but sufficient, theological reasoning, this salvific fecundity of the multiplication of Masses is also proven by the liturgical practice of the Church and the attitude of the Magisterium. As history shows,

throughout the ages the Church has become progressively aware of this fecundity; she has done so first by practicing, and then by officially encouraging always more, the multiplication of Masses.

The Historical Level

7. *The traditional form of concelebration is that which we today call 'ceremonial'*: here the bishop alone consecrates the sacrament, but he does so surrounded by his presbytery, and with the participation of the faithful. This form of concelebration is the only one that the Church recognized during the first eight centuries. Its practice was universal at that time; it was maintained up until our day in a great number of Oriental Rites, which do not want to allow the other type.

8. *Sacramental 'concelebration' did not appear until the 8th century*, in Rome, where it was reserved to the Pope and his cardinal priests. It underwent a certain limited development, especially in Rome and other cities where the Pontiff resided. It always preserved its original exceptional character and its great solemnity. *Sacramental concelebration practically disappeared in the 12th century, and reappeared in the 15th/16th centuries*, the period when *one would see it pass from the Latin West to some Eastern Rites.*

9. *It is the practice of this sacramental concelebration that the Second Vatican Council wished to take up again and expand.* It wished, nevertheless, to keep it *within certain limits*, which needed to be defined concretely, but whose way it had already paved. The Council kept for the future the composition of 'a new rite of concelebration, which would be inserted into the Roman Pontifical and Roman Missal' (*Sacrosanctum concilium*, no. 58).

This form of concelebration *is not, therefore, that ancient, universal, and traditional ceremonial concelebration.* This sacramental concelebration always appeared as an innovation, and was often considered as a rupture with Tradition, and its practice always had an exceptional character.

10. The more the centuries past, the more the Church became aware of the riches of the Eucharist. This is revealed not only by *the history* of theology and the Magisterium, but also and primarily by *liturgical practice*. We observe, in fact, *the progressive multiplication of celebrations of the Mass by reason of its value*: 1) *as a sacrifice offered* for a part or *for the whole of the Church*; 2) *as a proper and central act of the priest's life* (a development of the monastic priest and the 'private Masses' in abbeys; cf. *Presbyterorum ordinis*, no. 13); 3) *as a daily nourishment for the faithful* (Decree of Pope St Pius X).

The Liturgical and Pastoral Level

11. *The meaning and value of Eucharistic concelebration are* essentially *to manifest the unity of the priesthood* (*Sacrosanctum concilium*, no. 57, § 1), in the participation of the priests in the one priesthood of Christ and in *their hierarchical communion with the bishop* (*Presbyterorum ordinis*, no. 7), and also in the *fraternal communion that exists between themselves* (*ibid*, no. 8). One will note the order of values: the fraternal communion among the priests is subordinate to their hierarchical communion with the bishop, this latter being the condition for the former. Moreover, it is *the unity of the whole Church*, 'gathered together and ordered under the authority of the bishops' which concelebration manifests (*SC*, no. 26). Its value, as one sees, is in this *manifestation of ecclesial unity*; and this unity is that of *a communion*, which is, starting from Christ and the priestly Order instituted by Him, essentially *hierarchical*.

These principles are what must regulate the liturgy of concelebration.

12. *The meaning and value of private Masses* are those mentioned above (no. 4). The Mass is the sacrifice of Christ and the Church: *each Mass allows the redemptive sacrifice of Christ to pass into the body and life of the Church, and the Church herself into the sacrifice and pascal mystery of Christ*. Because men receive the gift of God only gradually, there is a need for 'private' Masses, both for priests and for lay faithful, and

for the multiplication of Masses for the life of the whole Church and the salvation of the world (see above nos. 5 and 9).

13. *An authorized declaration will be necessary* on the doctrinal and practical levels in order to shed light on the questions raised here, not only those that remain without a response, but also those that, despite the responses already given, are still not clear in the minds of a great number of priests and faithful.

On the practical and disciplinary level, there is the problem of harmonizing the consequences that flow from the principles mentioned in the two preceding numbers. It is a question of determining when, in what circumstances and under what conditions is it fitting to concelebrate the Eucharist, and how, at the same time, to maintain the principle of celebration by one sole priest as the normal form of Eucharistic celebration, how to effectively make possible this form of celebration, and how to encourage in a concrete way the multiplication of Masses in order to multiply the fruits of grace. In other words, the liturgical discipline ought to be inspired at the same time by the principle that shows the meaning of concelebration as a manifestation of the unity of the hierarchical priesthood and the ecclesial community, and by that which affirms the infinite value of each Mass, both for the priest (who must see and live in it the supreme and central act of his priesthood), for the faithful (for whom it is also life), for the entire Church, and furthermore, for all of humanity, whose salvation the Mass is, for the glory of God, the ultimate end of the liturgy.

Such are the criteria, eminently liturgical and pastoral as they are, which must determine the response to be given to that problem of harmonizing Eucharistic celebration and concelebration.

* * *

That problem is the current situation of the liturgy in the Church. We are not the one who is posing the problem; we simply manifested its existence by explaining it. Because the fruits of Redemption are poured out upon the world and principally through the sacramental re-actuation of the Sacrifice of the Cross, which is the Mass, and because this aspect of the economy of salvation is all too often forgotten today, it is this most of all that we wished to recall. We did so by insisting on the most immediate and most important practical consequence: that necessity of multiplying Masses for the salvation of souls—and therefore for the very unity of the Church. For, while concelebration manifests this unity and develops a sentiment for it, the multiplication of Masses contributes still more to building up that unity by multiplying the effusion of Christ's grace.

The Holy Sacrifice of the Mass is of infinite value: such is the fundamental truth to which one must constantly return in order to examine on the doctrinal level all the problems related to the celebration of the Eucharist, and to find the solution to those problems posed later on the practical level. The current situation in the Church and the international circumstances are sufficient to proclaim (if one looks at them closely) the urgent need for these solutions, for the salvation of the world and the greater glory of the Most Holy Trinity.

CPSIA information can be obtained at www.ICGtesting.com
Printed in the USA
BVOW05s0550170715

408927BV00002B/83/P

9 780852 443101